Mergers and Acquisitions

A Practitioner's Guide to Successful Deals

Mergers and Acquisitions

A Practitioner's Guide to Successful Deals

Editor

Harvey A. Poniachek

Rutgers University, USA

NEW JERSEY • LONDON • SINGAPORE • BEIJING • SHANGHAI • HONG KONG • TAIPEI • CHENNAI • TOKYO

Published by

World Scientific Publishing Co. Pte. Ltd.
5 Toh Tuck Link, Singapore 596224
USA office: 27 Warren Street, Suite 401-402, Hackensack, NJ 07601
UK office: 57 Shelton Street, Covent Garden, London WC2H 9HE

Library of Congress Cataloging-in-Publication Data
Names: Poniachek, Harvey A., editor.
Title: Mergers & acquisitions / [edited by] Harvey A. Poniachek (Rutgers University, USA).
Other titles: Mergers and acquisitions
Description: New Jersey : World Scientific, [2018] | Includes bibliographical references and index.
Identifiers: LCCN 2018041492 | ISBN 9789813277410 (alk. paper)
Subjects: LCSH: Consolidation and merger of corporations.
Classification: LCC HG4028.M4 M4526 2018 | DDC 658.1/62--dc23
LC record available at https://lccn.loc.gov/2018041492

British Library Cataloguing-in-Publication Data
A catalogue record for this book is available from the British Library.

For any available supplementary material, please visit
https://www.worldscientific.com/worldscibooks/10.1142/11188#t=suppl

Desk Editor: Shreya Gopi

Typeset by Stallion Press
Email: enquiries@stallionpress.com

Printed in Singapore

Contents

Preface

The survival and prosperity of any corporation over the long term depend on its ability to grow and develop through a process of investment, restructuring, and redeployment. Corporate restructuring could be accomplished internally by shifting resources from mature and declining business activities to new ones with more attractive growth potential. Alternatively, restructuring could occur externally through mergers and acquisitions (M&As), which have become an essential vehicle for corporate change since the late 19th century.

Broadly defined M&A forms include expansion through M&As; joint ventures; contraction through divestitures or sell-offs; various changes in corporate control and ownership, including going private and leverage buy-outs; and rearrangements through recapitalization and bankruptcy reorganization. Several types of synergies could arise from M&A restructuring, including expansion of sales and earnings, reduction in cost, and lower taxes and cost of capital.

The M&A evolution in the past quarter century has been driven primarily by corporations' rush to implement strategic plans deigned to seize or enhance competitive advantage; achieve strategic diversification; participate in emerging technologies with attractive growth prospects; take advantage of favorable economic and business conditions and changes in the regulatory environment; and address political changes and globalization opportunities and threats. This book integrates business strategies and experience with formal analysis relating to M&A deal making; it provides a coherent statement on

M&A by utilizing scholarly work with best practices by industry. The material presented reflects the main stream of corporate finance and M&A practices as reflected in deal-making process. The book recognizes that M&A activities involve a broad spectrum of concerns and specialists. Hands on experience and learning are obtained by addressing real-world merger issues, analytical concepts, and procedures, such as valuation and pricing of deals. The book addresses the M&A process in the context of investment analysis and strategies, including the various market complexities.

M&A transactions are complex and risky and are affected by the state business cycle, financial conditions, regulations, and technology. Approximately two-thirds of all M&A deals fail, and this book seeks to provide an effective framework for achieving greater success. M&A transactions involve a host of participants with different specialization and responsibilities (including corporate executives and board members, investment bankers, accountants, tax specialists, attorneys, and financial institutions). The M&A process commonly involves the identification of the target, due diligence, valuation, entering into an agreement, protecting against various risks, addressing funding and taxation implications, determining the transaction structure, addressing antitrust, assuring shareholders' approval, and postmerger integration.

The book provides extensive analytical review and applications of critical M&A issues, including valuation, leverage buyouts (LBOs), payment methods and their implications, tax issues, corporate governance, and the regulatory environment, including antitrust in M&A. The book globalizes the M&A model by extending it to cross-border business, reviews of risk and select hedging methods, and addresses postmerger integration. It is authored by academics and practitioners and provides an authoritative treatment of the subject.

This book is written for practitioners and students and it addresses the entire process of M&As in a comprehensive framework that is predominantly embedded in corporate finance. This book is intended as a reading text for a course in M&A for undergraduates and MBA programs and for practitioners as a handbook.

This book has its genesis with my teaching Restructuring Firms & Industries and Mergers & Acquisition courses at NYU, Stern School of Business, The City University of New York at Baruch College, and Pace University since 1995 at both the graduate and undergraduate levels, and teaching finance and economics at the Rutgers Business School since 2011. The interest in M&A expensed exponentially with the merger boom in the 1990s to date and courses offered have proliferated.

The chapters in this book are standardized, contain information on the state of the art of the subjects covered, and constitute a cross-over between a textbook and reading book. The chapter outline/format is as follows: introduction, the main issues, analytical approaches, models, practices, and a summary of key points.

Harvey Poniachek

About the Editor

Harvey A. Poniachek is a Ph.D. economist, University at Albany of the State University of New York, with corporate experience in consulting, banking and financial markets, professor of corporate finance and economics and is author of books and professional articles. He is currently an Assistant Professor of Professional Practice of Finance & Economics at Rutgers Business School. Previously, he was the Director of Valuation Services at RSM McGladrey, Inc. New York, involved in valuation of financial derivatives, private equity, and intercompany pricing. He has worked for the U.S. Treasury Department as Lead Economist in the area of transfer pricing, and was engaged in valuation of intellectual property and tangible assets; was Senior Manager and Economist at E&Y; and VP & Economist at Bank of America, where he gained extensive experience in the banking industry and capital markets, and advised multinational companies and senior management on currency and money market trends, trading strategies, foreign country risk and opportunities.

Professor Poniachek has taught corporate finance, financial management, international finance and economics at New York University's Stern School of Business, the City University of New York's Baruch College, and at Pace University, Lubin School of Business.

He has published books, including *International Corporate Finance* (Routledge, London); *Cases in International Finance* (John Wiley); *Direct Foreign Investment in the United States* (Simon & Schuster); *Monetary Independence Under Flexible Exchange Rates*

(Lexington Books); chapters in books, including "Foreign Exchange Rate Determination" in *International Finance Handbook* (John Wiley); "The International Financial Markets" in *Handbook of International Business* (John Wiley); and articles, including "Medtronic Revisited: Outcome Under OECD's BEPS Recommendations", Bloomberg BNA, Tax Management Transfer Pricing Report; "The New Role of Intangibles in International Intercompany Transactions", Bloomberg BNA, Tax Management Transfer Pricing Report; "A New Paradigm for Intellectual Property Ownership and the Implication on MNEs' Intercompany Transactions", International Transfer Pricing Journal, BNA; "Coping with Expanding State Transfer Pricing Rules", The CPA Journal; "Transfer Pricing of Global Financial Dealing", BNA, International Transfer Pricing Journal; "Cost Sharing Agreements: Main Features and Implication", The International Transfer Pricing Journal; "Veritas Software Implications for the U.S. Temporary Rules", BNA, Transfer Pricing Report; "Valuation of Distressed Companies and Securities", Valuation Strategies; "Valuation of Hedge Funds", The CPA Journal; "Valuation of Financial Companies", RSM McGladrey; "Intellectual Property Issues facing MNCs", Metropolitan Corporate Counsel; and "Alternative Definitions of Money in an Open Economy", Kredit und Kapital.

He has also reviewed books and articles, including the following: Daniel Stillit, *Event-driven Investing and Corporate Finance: Where Investment Banking Meets the Market, A "Whole Deal" Approach* (The MIT Press); Roger D. Blair and Mark Rush, *The Economics of Managerial Decisions* (Pearson); Thomas J. O'Brien, *International Financial Economics: Corporate Decisions in Global Markets* (Oxford University Press); J. Ashok Robin, *International Corporate Finance* (McGraw-Hill Irwin); Donald DePamphilis, *Mergers, Acquisitions, and Other Restructuring Activities, 3rd Ed.* (Academic Press). He has also edited the following: Ingo Walter, *Mergers and Acquisitions in Banking and Finance: What Works, What Fails and Why?* (Oxford University Press); Thomas A. Pugel, *International Economics, 14 Ed* (McGraw-Hill Irwin); Stephen L. Curtis, "Transfer Pricing for Corporate

Treasury in the Multinational Enterprise", *Journal of Applied Corporate Finance*; Thomas A. Pugel, *International Economics, 13 Ed* (McGraw-Hill Irwin); Thomas A. Pugel, *International Economics, 12th Ed.* (McGraw-Hill Irwin); and Richard M. Levich, *International Financial Markets: Prices and Policies, 2nd Ed* (McGraw-Hill Irwin).

About the Contributors

Alina Niculita

Alina Niculita is Director of Valuation Services at Morones Analytics, LLC, Portland, Oregon. She specializes in business valuation and was president of Shannon Pratt Valuations, and has appraised numerous companies from many industries and of all sizes up to several billion in revenues. Ms. Niculita has conducted business valuations for a variety of purposes including transactions, buy-sell agreements, gift and estate tax, marital dissolution, bankruptcy, reorganizations, ESOP, financing, and matters involving intangible assets and personal versus enterprise goodwill. Ms. Niculita has consulted on large and complex litigation cases with complex disputed valuation issues such as cost of capital, discounts and premiums, valuation methods and approaches, adjustments to financial statements, management forecasts, and other issues. Ms. Niculita has served as an author, co-author, and contributing author of several business valuation articles, book chapters, and books, including several with Dr. Shannon Pratt. She has spoken on business valuation topics to various audiences.

Andrew J. Sherman

In addition to being a published author of nearly 30 books and serving as an adjunct professor in the MBA programs at the University of Maryland and Georgetown University Law Center, Andrew Sherman is a Partner and Chair of the Washington, D.C. Corporate Department of Seyfarth Shaw LLP. His practice focuses on issues affecting business growth for companies at all stages, including developing strategies for licensing and leveraging intellectual property and technology assets, intellectual asset management and harvesting, as well as international corporate transactional and franchising matters.

Chris Droussiotis

Chris Droussiotis' training and expertise is in the area of Investment Banking. He possesses over 30 years of experience by working for major money center banks in various executive management positions including Bank of America Merill Lynch, CIBC Oppenheimer, Mizuho Financial Group, Bank of Tokyo-Mitsubishi Trust UFJ, Sumitomo Mitsui Banking Corporation and Mitsui Nevitt Banking Corporation. Chris Droussiotis is currently a Managing Director, General Manager and the Head of the Leveraged Buyout Financing Group, Private Equity Sponsor Group & Structured Finance Department at Sumitomo Mitsui Banking Corporation, managing a loan portfolio of over $8 billion of large cap and middle market leveraged loans, as well as investments in SPV funds, CLOs and BDCs that are backed by leveraged loans and high yield bonds.

Chris Droussiotis earned an MBA from Fairleigh Dickinson University, and has been an adjunct professor at several universities, including Fordham University's School of Business, Fairleigh Dickinson University, and Baruch College. Courses he has taught include Quantitative Analysis in Business, Investment Analysis, Managerial Finance, Fixed Income Markets, and Derivatives.

Christophe Van Gampelaere

Christophe Van Gampelaere is a partner at Global PMI Partners, an international advisory firm focused solely on integrations and carve-outs. He is a Finance and Culture oriented M&A professional with deep experience in a range of industries. He is a trainer, certified coach, a Lego Serious Play facilitator, Family Constellations practitioner and an academic at the Brussels Diplomatic Academy of the VUB University. Christophe is co-author of *Cross-border Mergers and Acquisitions* (Wiley, 2016).

Dovrat Bashan

Dovrat Bashan, Esq, is a Senior Counsel for M&A at Siemens Corporation with over 15 years of M&A practice, representing Siemens in buy-side and sell-side, public and private M&A transactions across industries. Prior to joining Siemens, Dovrat worked as an M&A attorney in the Mergers and Acquisitions practice group of White & Case LLP, representing publicly traded companies in a broad range of industries including the hospitality, pharmaceutical and retail sectors, in connection with domestic and cross-border buy-side and sell-side mergers, share purchase agreements, "going private" transactions and other business combinations. Over the years Dovrat has represented private equity firms in the sale and acquisition of portfolio companies through mergers, sales of stock, asset purchases and joint venture transactions. Dovrat is an LLM graduate of NYU School of Law and a bachelor of laws (LLB) and business administration, with strong focus on corporate finance.

Frank A. Oswald

Frank A. Oswald is a partner at Togut, Segal & Segal LLP in New York. He has more than 30 years of restructuring experience and has represented the interests of chapter 11 debtors, creditors' committees, trustees, distressed investors, plan administrators and other parties in the fields of health care, automotive, real estate, retail, transportation, professional services, energy and the environment. Mr. Oswald's representative cases include Toisa Limited, SunEdison, Avaya, Aeropostale, Chrysler, General Motors, Enron, American Airlines, Eastman Kodak, Tower Automotive, Saint Vincents Catholic Medical Centers, Cabrini Medical Center, Our Lady of Mercy

Medical Center, Forum Health, Sound Shore Medical Center, N.Y. Westchester Square Medical Center, Grubb & Ellis and Loehmann's Department Stores. Mr. Oswald is a member of: the U.S. Bankruptcy Court EDNY Chapter 11 Lawyers Advisory Committee; New York City Bar Association Bankruptcy Committee; Board of Turnaround Management Association (New York Chapter); a member of the Healthcare Committee of ABI; and several other restructuring and insolvency law-related organizations.

Heike Luecke

Heike Luecke is a Lecturer in Law at Kingston University Business School, London, Department of Accounting, Finance & Informatics, and Lecturer in Law, Postgraduate Course Director of Real Estate, Head of the Kingston Law Clinic. Heike was visiting Scholar, St John's University, New York, in the academic year of 2016/17, and is starting an MSc program in Taxation at Oxford University in September 2018. Heike earned a Ph.D. from Kingston University, specialized in Insolvency Law; LL.M., Kingston University, studied Business Law and graduated with distinction, and also holds a law degree from Ruhr-Universität Bochum.

Jerome Schwartzman

Jerome Schwartzman is Director, Head of M&A Tax Services at Houlihan Lokey, New York, a global investment bank. His expertise is in mergers & acquisitions, financial restructuring, valuation, and capital markets. He is a transactional attorney with a broad range of domestic, foreign and cross-border tax due diligence and tax structuring experience for both private equity and corporate clients. He works closely with corporate and tax counsel to resolve acquisition structure and deal issues and has also served as an expert witness in litigation and arbitration matters. Mr. Schwartzman started his career as an attorney in the Office of the Chief Counsel of the IRS.

Mr. Schwartzman has been a frequent speaker on tax topics and has authored/co-authored numerous pieces on tax issues, including a chapter on bankruptcy/restructuring tax issues in a restructuring treatise, and notable articles such as "The Renewed Importance of Purchase Price Allocations," CFO Magazine (May 10, 2018) (with Oscar Aarts and Winston T. Shows III), "To Incorporate or Not To Incorporate — Post-Tax Reform, That is the Question: How Tax Reform's New 21% Corporate Tax Rate Has Changed the Math," Houlihan Lokey (February 25, 2018) (with Winston T. Shows III), "How Tax Reform Will Drive Deal Making," Private Equity International (February 15, 2018) (with David Lee and Winston T. Shows III) and "What You Need to Know about Inversions," CFO Magazine (February 19, 2016) (with Steven Tishman).

Katherine A. Crispi

Katherine A. Crispi, JD, is a restructuring associate at Allen & Overy, New York, which together with Washington, D.C., has more than 175 lawyers that handle sophisticated and complex domestic and cross-border transactions and cases. She was previously an associate at Togut, Segal & Segal LLP, a nationally-recognized corporate restructuring and bankruptcy boutique representing sophisticated clients in complex Chapter 11 cases in the Southern District of New York and other jurisdictions around the country. Katherine was law clerk at several courts, including U.S. Bankruptcy Court, District of Delaware, U.S. District Court for the District of Massachusetts, and at Gallet Dreyer & Berkey, LLP. Publications include *State Regulators' Dodd-Frank Enforcement Authority: Initial Suits and Their Implications; New Requirements for New York Non-Profit Organizations* (with Jay L. Hack, Esq.); and *Not Just The Luck Of The Irish: A Contractual Solution To The Problems Of Sovereign Debt Restructuring*. Katherine earned a JD from Fordham University School of Law and BA from Wellesley College.

Kyle J. Ortiz

Kyle J. Ortiz has represented debtors in some of the largest and most complex chapter 11 cases of the past decade, including: Westinghouse, SunEdison, Aeropostale, American Airlines, and Lehman Brothers Holdings, Inc. Mr. Ortiz has also represented creditors and lenders in the financial services and real estate sectors. Mr. Ortiz's pro bono work has been recognized by both the Legal Aid Society and the New York State Bar Association. Prior to beginning his legal career, Mr. Ortiz founded Operation ASHA in Cambodia, an arm of the worldwide tuberculosis treatment organization, Operation ASHA. Operation ASHA in Cambodia has grown to over 50 tuberculosis treatment centers serving over a million people in 1,283 villages in and around Cambodia's capital, Phnom Penh. Mr. Ortiz currently sits on the U.S. Board of Directors for Operation ASHA Worldwide. Mr. Ortiz received his B.S. degree from Northern Michigan University, where he graduated as Outstanding Graduating Male, served as student body president, and was the student commencement speaker at his graduation. Mr. Ortiz earned his M.P.P. degree in 2006 from the Harris School of Public Policy at the University of Chicago, and his J.D. degree in 2009 from the University of Chicago Law School where he was an Edmund Spencer Scholar.

Nick Rosenberg

Nicholas Rosenberg is an associate in the Corporate Department of Seyfarth Shaw LLP's Washington, D.C. office. His practice focuses on counseling clients on various issues related to the formation, financing, and growth of their businesses and advises both established and emerging companies in a range of business and corporate law matters. He has represented a wide range of clients including individuals and companies in connection with various transactions such as mergers, acquisitions, joint ventures, leveraged buy-outs, venture financings, and other commercial transactions. He frequently advises clients on business strategy and guides them as they consider and execute significant transactions.

Peter F. De Nicola

Peter F. De Nicola is Director of Taxes, FUJIFILM Holdings America Corporation, heading the tax function for FUJIFILM's Americas region. He has over 40 years of diverse tax experience, including 28 years at FUJIFILM. In his role as Director of Taxes, Peter oversees the company's transfer pricing policies, domestic and international tax compliance for North and South America and is heavily involved in mergers, acquisitions and restructurings. Prior to joining FUJIFILM, he held various tax management positions with General Signal, Emery Worldwide and Siemens. A Certified Public Accountant, Peter earned a BS in Accounting and an MBA in Taxation from New York University. He currently serves on the Board of Directors of the Tax Executives Institute and is President of the Stamford Tax Association. In addition to authoring numerous articles on taxes and investments, he has been interviewed in the *Wall Street Journal* and on Bloomberg Television.

Robert M. Gordon

Robert M. Gordon is Managing Director, True Partners Consulting LLC, Chicago. He specializes in the taxation of complex domestic and international transactions, including M&A, joint ventures, and general federal and international tax planning. Before joining True Partners, he was Assistant General Tax Counsel and Head of Tax for BP America's U.S.-based manufacturing and retail division. Bob speaks regularly at professional venues and is a leader in the American Bar Association's Tax Section, where he is an officer of its Corporate Tax Committee. He was an adjunct professor at Loyola University's graduate school of business in Chicago. He received his bachelor's degree with honors from the University of Illinois at Chicago and his J.D. from Northwestern University School of Law, where he served on the editorial board of the Northwestern University Law Review.

Stefan Hofmeyer

As a partner with Global PMI Partners, Stefan Hofmeyer develops and implements repeatable solutions for private equity firms and companies looking to build in-house M&A integration expertise. In addition to his domestic client integration efforts, Stefan holds interest in cross-border delivery and has worked on strategic corporate development and integrations between the Americas, China and Europe. Stefan is a co-author of *Cross-border Mergers and Acquisitions* (Wiley, 2016), holds degrees from the University of Iowa and Pepperdine University, and is an alumnus of Harvard Business School and Stanford University executive education programs. A native of Iowa, Stefan moved to California in the mid-1990s where he can be found sailing on San Francisco Bay with his wife Ada and daughter Anika.

Chapter 1

Introduction to Mergers and Acquisitions

Harvey Poniachek
Rutgers Business School

Introduction

Mergers and acquisitions (M&As) are quite popular in the business world and are often the principle strategy for corporate growth and restructuring. Most major companies have conducted numerous M&As throughout their history. M&As include a variety of activities and types, and could be horizontal transactions between companies with similar products or services, vertical, involving companies with different value-added activities, or conglomerate, involving companies in completely different industries. See Exhibit 1 for the definition of broadly defined M&As.

The parties to a merger are the buyer, usually referred to as the acquirer or bidder, and the seller or target. In a narrowly defined merger or acquisition, one company acquires another and the acquirer is the surviving party and remains in business, whereas the target company ceases to exist. Mergers are motivated by various objectives, including expectations for synergy that could be generated from expansion of sales and revenues, reduced cost, and lower cost of capital. The premise of synergy is that the sum of the parts is more valuable than the parts, or 2 + 2 = 5.

Exhibit 1: M&As: Broadly Defined Activities

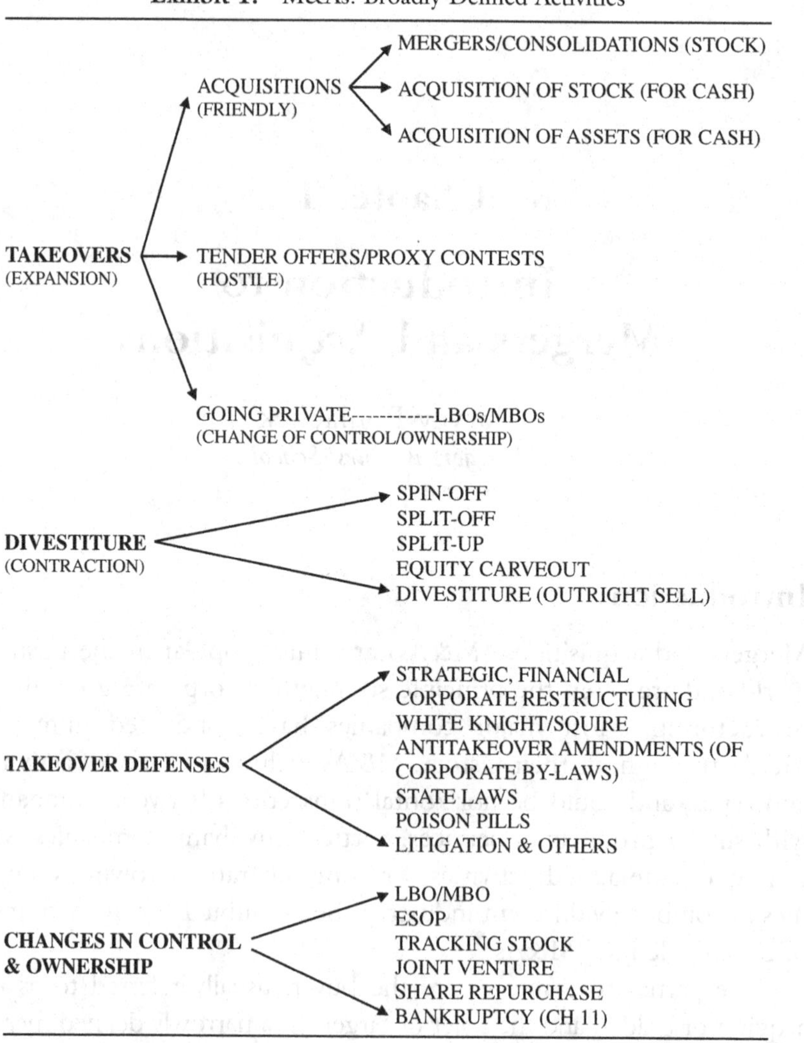

M&As change the ownership and control of a public corporation, with senior management of the target firm usually departing after the merger and a new management team takes over. Target's shares or assets are purchased for various consideration, including cash, stock or a combination of both.

M&A transactions are more complicated and much larger than ordinary capital expenditures. In light of their complexities and magnitude, M&As constitute a most significant corporate financial decision that commonly involves various specialists. M&As are legally intensive and subject to various laws and regulations and subject to various taxation laws and accounting requirements.

In mergers, sellers generally do better than buyers and following an announcement of a bid target shareholders receive an average gain of 25–30%; whereas acquirer's shares usually decline, but in aggregate the value of the shares increases by some 5%.[1]

This chapter reviews M&As data, growth through M&A, merger trends and influences, M&A models, performance, and risk.

Growth Through Mergers

The survival and prosperity of corporations over the long term depend on their ability to grow and develop through a process of restructuring and redeployment of resources. Corporate restructuring could be accomplished internally, or organically, by shifting resources from mature and declining business activities to new activities with more attractive growth potential. Alternatively, restructuring could occur externally, or inorganically, through M&As, which have become an essential vehicle for corporate change and a dominant feature of the American economy since the late 19th century.

GE experience in the 1980s and 1990s reflects the significance of pursuing growth strategy via M&As. Under the leadership of Jack Welch, the President and Chairman of GE during 1981–2001, the company made 993 acquisitions at an estimated cost of approximately $165 billion and divested of over 400 businesses valued at an estimated $28 billion. During this period, the company's revenue has grown to $130 billion in 2000 from $21 billion when Mr. Welch became chairman in 1981. GE experienced 9.9% compounded annual

---

[1] Richard A. Brealey and Stewart C. Myers, *Principles of Corporate Finance, 6th Ed.*, Irwin McGraw Hill, 2000.

growth rate (CAGR) during 1985–2000, of which 4 percentage points came from acquisitions.[2]

There are limits to growth through M&As due to a limited pool of available targets, antitrust concerns (GE failed to takeover Honeywell due to EU antitrust concerns), risk, and disadvantages of becoming too big. Jeffrey R. Immelt, Mr. Welch successor as CEO & Chairman of GE, adopted a new policy that has divested of many of the acquisitions made under the prior administration, and embarked on a new strategy.[3] It seems that Mr. Immelt implicitly repudiated Mr. Welch's growth model by moving to dismantle parts of the sprawling GE empire by divesting of NBC Universal and GE Capital, and acquiring some prize companies.

The issue is whether the conglomerate growth model through M&As that Mr. Welch promoted at GE is still viable? Data shows that during the 18-year tenure of Mr. Jeffrey R. Immelt as GE's chief executive,[4] the company's stock underperformed against the S&P 500 index of the overall stock market performance. For instance, GE shares dropped 25% over the past 10 years, in contrast with a 59% rise for the S&P 500, rival industrial conglomerate Honeywell's stock has more than doubled, and United Technologies gained 67%. Yet, Mr. Immelt pointed to the increased strength of the company's industrial businesses, their competitiveness, and large market shares.

Merger Trends and Main Influences

We observe a variety of mergers waves in the past century and a quarter, see Exhibit 2. The mergers since the late 1800s were driven primarily by favorable economic and financial conditions, deregulations, technological innovations, shifts in the competitiveness of companies, globalization, and reasonable valuations, see Exhibit 3. The financial crisis and recession during 12/2007–6/2009 caused a sharp decline

[2] WSJ, "Some Wonder How Long GE Can Rely on Deals for Growth", July 31, 2001.

[3] https://www.ge.com/investor-relations/sites/default/files/ge_webcast_presentation_04212017.pdf.

[4] James B. Stewart, Did the Jack Welch Model Sow Seeds of G.E.'s Decline? *New York Times,* June 15, 2017, B1, pp. 1 & 4.

Exhibit 2: Historic Merger Waves

- 1897–1904: Horizontal mergers, 1st wave
- 1916–1929: Vertical mergers, 2nd wave
- 1960s: Conglomerate mergers, 3rd wave
- 1981–1989: Big deals decade & LBOs, hostile takeovers, 4th wave
- 1992–2007: Strategic mergers, 5th wave
- 2009 to date: Emergence of the hedge funds and private equity, 6th wave[5]

Source: Patrick A. Caughan, *Mergers, Acquisitions, and Corporate Restructuring, 5th Ed.*, Wiley, 2011, Ch 2; Weston, J. Fred *et al.*, *Takeovers, Restructuring and Corporate Governance, 4th Ed.*, Prentice Hall, 2004, p. 7 and Ch 7.

Exhibit 3: Merger Waves' Main Influences

- Favorable economic conditions
- Technological innovation
- Conducive financial environment
- Favorable regulatory changes
- Favorable infrastructure changes
- Globalization
- Industry organization
- Economies of scale and scope

Source: Harvey Poniachek.

in M&As activities, but a solid rebound has occurred thereafter. Going forward, the 2016's M&A trend is expected to continue as companies seek innovative and transformative transactions to complement organic growth to enhanced scale and synergistic strategic fits.

M&As encompass a wide spectrum of transaction types that afford firms the ability to adjust relatively fast to new challenges and opportunities and maintain or achieve competitive advantage. Broadly defined M&A activities include expansion through M&As; joint ventures; contraction through divestitures or sell-offs; various changes in corporate control and ownership, including going private and leverage buy-outs; and rearrangements through recapitalization and bankruptcy reorganization. Exhibit 3 defines the scope of M&A activities.

[5] Defined as the 6th wave by Harvey Poniachek.

M&A Data

The year 2015 marked the busiest ever for mergers and acquisitions, whereby US companies announced more than $2.1 trillion in transactions, and global M&A volume topped $4.7 trillion in aggregate.[6] A Deloitte survey of nearly 2,300 executives and managers from US corporations and private equity firms showed that 87% of the respondents expected their M&A deal activity to sustain or exceed the 2015's record. Similar results were also reported by Dealogic[7] and EY. See Exhibits 4 and 5 for global and North American M&As.

Exhibit 4: M&As Worldwide

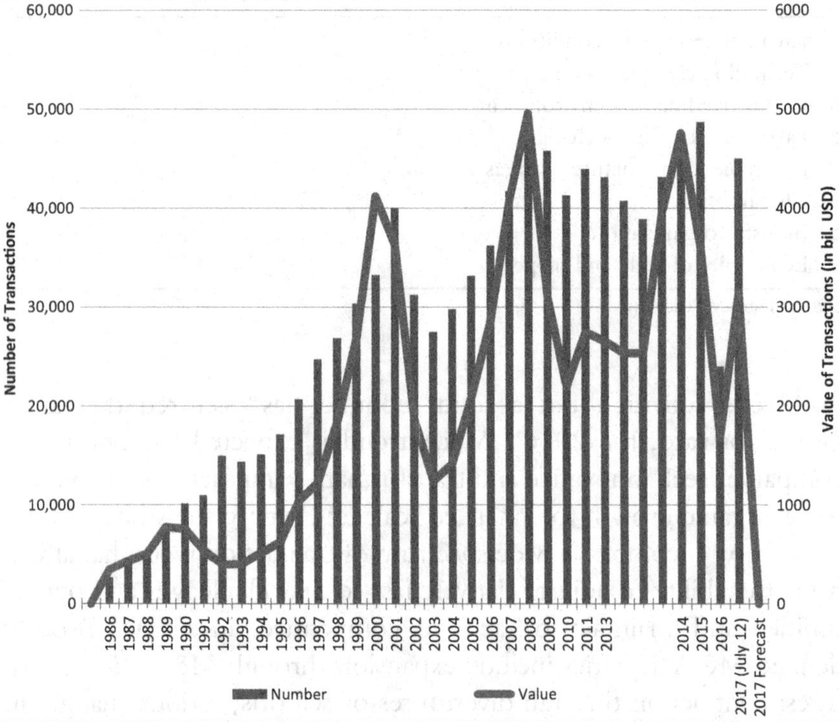

Source: https://imaa-institute.org/mergers-and-acquisitions-statistics/.

[6] Deloitte, M&A Trends Report 2016. From February 19 to March 15, 2016, a Deloitte survey conducted by On Research polled 2,292 executives at US companies and private equity firms to gauge their expectations, experiences, and plans for M&As in the coming years.

[7] http://www.foxbusiness.com/markets/2016/10/17/m-outlook-for-2017-rosy.html.

Exhibit 5: M&As North America

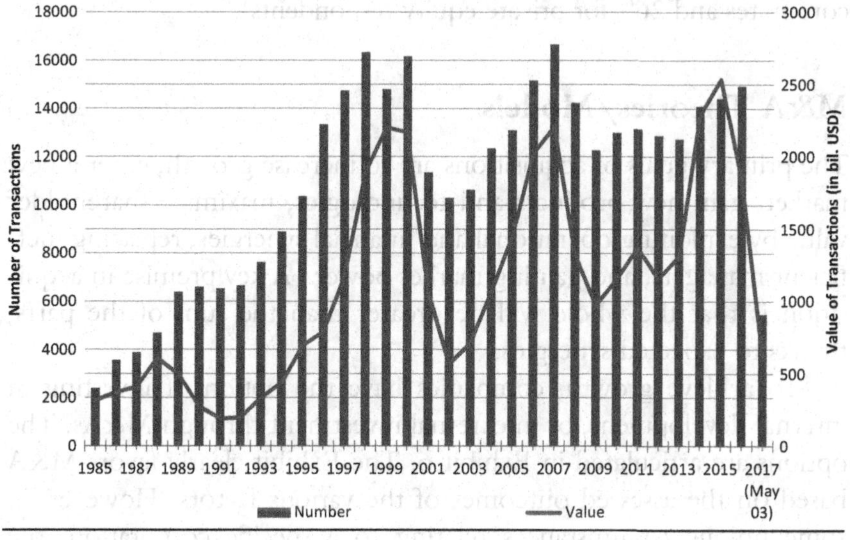

Source: https://imaa-institute.org/mergers-and-acquisitions-statistics/.

Several factors are driving the optimism, including excess cash, high stock prices, and interest rates at historically low levels. While low interest rates and easy access to funds have allowed many acquirers to orchestrate deals, continued economic uncertainty, particularly in Europe and in several markets across Asia, are expected to be a key concern. Despite global economic concerns, 75% of corporate respondents are still searching for a slightly larger share of cross-border deals, while 84% of private equity are seeking acquisitions in foreign markets.

Going forward, more divestitures are planned, with 52% of the corporate respondents stating that their company plans to pursue divestitures to shed noncore assets in the year ahead to help focus their business, and in some sectors to raise capital. The industries that are expected to generate the most M&A activity in the years to come are technology, oil and gas, financial services, and healthcare.

Private equity respondents expressed concern about deals that did not meet expectations over the last 2 years, with 56% of those surveyed saying more than half of deals had not returned expected value, up from 54% in 2015. Gaps in execution and integration of deals comprised the key reason why deals did not generate the expected value (23% for corporates and 26% for private equity respondents).

M&A Theories/Models

The primary goals of acquisitions are to increase growth, enter a new market, gain new products and technologies, maximize shareholder value by exploiting operational and financial synergies, replacing inefficient managers, and gaining market power.[8] A key premise in acquisition is that the whole will be greater than the sum of the parts, thanks to expected synergies.

To achieve growth, companies have the option of investing in internal development, or in external investment through M&As. The options are articulated in Exhibit 6. The Exhibit clearly favors M&A based on the assessed outcomes of the various factors. However, in some unique circumstances relating to a specific corporation, the assessed effects of the various variables cited above could be quite different than displayed in Exhibit 6 and instead favor internal development. That is, the analysis of the internal versus the external investment feasibility hinges on the implications of the various factors cited here.

Exhibit 6: M&A Versus Internal Development

	M&A	Internal Development
Lower Cost	+	
Acquire Know-How	+	
Quicker	+	
Higher Risk		+
Acquire New Market	+	
Acquire New Products	+	
Synergy	+	

Source: Harvey Poniachek.

[8] S&P Global Market Intelligence, Quantamental Research, August 2016.

There are various theories of M&As,[9] but practitioners formulated models in terms of several variables. For instance, Bain & Company[10] formulates an M&A model that consists of five stages as follows:

- o M&A strategy — make your M&A an extension of your growth strategy, identify the target and formulate how M&A will create value,
- o Deal thesis — examine how each deal creates value, apply existing capabilities to enhance value to the target,
- o Due diligence and valuation — test the deal rational, set a walk away price, determine where you can add value,
- o Merger integration planning — plan your postmerger integration (PMI) and determine what's needed to integrate, and integrate where it makes sense, and
- o Merger integration execution.

---

[9] Theories of M&As by Weston, J. Fred, *et al.*, *Takeover, Restructuring & Corporate Governance, 4th Ed.*, Prentice-Hall, 2004, Ch. 6:

Value Increase
Efficiency Theories
Operating Synergy
Diversification
Financial Synergy
Strategic Realignment
The q-ratio (Tobin's q was developed by Prof James Tobin in 1969 as the ratio between the market value and replacement value of the same physical asset)
Information Signaling
Hubris — acquirer overpays for target
Agency Problems
Distribution: taxes, market power, redistribution from bondholders & labor,
Others — the industry life cycle.
Excellence in Financial Management, Course 7: Mergers & Acquisitions (Part 1), Prepared by: Matt H. Evans, CPA, CMA, CFM, Published March 2000.

[10] Bain & Company, The renaissance in mergers & acquisitions, 2014. See for instance Sudarsanam, *Creating Value from M&A*, FT Prentice Hall, 2003, who identifies a five-stage model of M&A which views M&A as a multistage process rather than a transaction, consisting of the following functions: Corporate strategy, Organizing for acquisitions, Deal structuring and negotiation, Postacquisition integration, and Postacquisition audit and organizational learning.

McKinsey & Company[11] identifies the strategic rationale for an acquisition that creates value as follows:

- o Improving the performance of the target company,
- o Removing excess capacity from an industry,
- o Creating market access products,
- o Acquiring kills or market technology more quickly or at a lower cost than they could build in-house, and
- o Picking winners early and help them develop their businesses.

Process, Performance

The M&A process commonly involves the preacquisition assessment to establish if a merger strategy would be beneficial, identification of the target, due diligence, valuation, entering into an agreement, protecting against various risks, addressing funding and taxation implications, determining the transaction structure, addressing antitrust, and assuring shareholders' approval and PMI. M&A transactions require an effective process that involves a host of participants with different specialization and responsibilities (including corporate executives and board members, investment bankers, accountants, tax specialists, and attorneys).

Merger performance could be addressed from three different perspectives.

- o Macro benefits of mergers — for the entire economy/sectors, improved efficiency and operational performance;
- o Micro effects — companies/sectors engaged in mergers benefit from enhanced efficiency or redistribution effect; and
- o Is a shareholder's value increased by an M&A? Is it maintained over time?

M&A transactions are complex and risky, yet they remain a significant corporate business growth strategy. Approximately two-thirds of

[11] Marc Goedhart, Tim Koller and David Wessels, The Five Types of Successful Acquisitions, Web, 2010.

all deals fail, and the vast majority of corporate executives acknowledge that their companies have not achieved the financial outcomes and operational synergies that were projected at the time of deal consummation.[12] A Deloitte survey of 1,000 US executives in late 2016 provides further insights into factors contributing to success and impediments to successful mergers, as shown in Exhibits 7 and 8.

Several types of synergies could arise from M&As. M&As are often induced by expected synergy that could be generated from operating and/or financial sources and provide additional value to the combined firms that are unavailable to these firms operating

Exhibit 7: Factors Contributing to Successful M&As

	% of Respondents
Effective Integration	22
Economic Certainty	19
Accurately Valued Target	19
Proper Target Identification	17
Sound Due Diligence Process	12
Stable Regulatory and Legislative Government	11

Source: Deloitte, M&A Trends, Year-end report 2016, survey of 1,000 US executives, September 2016.

Exhibit 8: Impediments to Achieving Successful M&As

	% of Respondents
Insufficient Due Diligence process	88
Improper Target Identification	83
Not Valuing the Target Accurately	81
Changing Regulatory and Legislative Environment	81
Failure to Effectively Integrate	78

Source: Deloitte, M&A Trends, Year-end report 2016, survey of 1,000 US executives, September 2016.

[12] Crowe Horwath, "Critical Pillars for M&A Success" Survey While Corporate Deal-Makers Are Optimistic, Recent M&A Results Are Disappointing, 2013.

independently.[13] Synergy is commonly allocated between the transacting parties, predominantly in favor of the target company. Operating synergies affect the combined firm economies of scale, pricing power and growth potential, and show up as higher expected cash flows. Financial synergies include tax benefits, diversification, a higher debt capacity, and more attractive uses of excess cash and show up as higher cash flows and/or lower cost of capital.[14]

M&A can analytically be addressed in the context of corporate finance as changes in the deployment of assets (through expansion and contraction), funding (and its effect on capital structure, cost, and risk), and ownership and control, and assessed in the general context of capital budgeting. M&As are strategic decisions that should fit into the buyer's overall strategic plan, should be consistent with the company's goal of maximization of shareholder wealth, and be justified in terms of the capital budgeting analysis. Determining the financial feasibility of a prospective M&A transaction requires the application of a capital budgeting analysis. The analysis applies the net present value (NPV) and considers the investment cost, the expected future benefits in present value terms and deems the investment

---

[13] Aswath Damodaran, The Value of Synergy, Stern School of Business, October 2005.

[14] Ibid., Damodaran defines *operating and financial synergies* as follows. *Operating synergy* allows firms to increase their operating income from existing assets and higher growth or both and could be of four types.

1. *Economies of scale*,
2. *Greater pricing power*,
3. *Enhanced functional strengths*, and
4. *Higher growth in new or existing markets.*

Financial synergy benefits can take induce higher cash flows and/or a lower cost of capital as follows:

1. A combination of a firm with excess cash and a firm with attractive projects, could yield new investments,
2. *Debt capacity* can increase because merged firms' earnings expand and their cash flows may become more stable and predictable, thus affording greater borrowing,
3. *Larger tax benefits*, and
4. *Diversification* could lower cost of capital and raise profit.

feasible when NPV > 0. In evaluating a proposed M&A, several issues need to be addressed,[15] including: Is the merger and acquisitions generating economic gain or synergy? Would the merging and acquisition parties be worth more together than separately? And would the shareholders of the M&As parties be better off post merger than before?

The Book's Scope

This book integrates business strategies and experience with formal analysis relating to M&A deal making. It provides a coherent statement on M&A by integrating scholarly work with industry's best practices. The material presented is anchored in the mainstream of corporate finance and M&A practices as reflected in deal making process. The book recognizes that M&A activities involve a broad spectrum of concerns and specialists.

This book surveys the main theories/literature on the various forms of M&As and addresses the institutional setting and provides principles and analytical methods for addressing financial management issues and decision making in the area of M&A. We discuss the legal framework, including issues relating to antitrust in M&A, corporate governance, and antitakeover defenses. The book provides extensive analytical review and applications on valuation methodologies for publicly traded and privately held companies, address accounting and taxation for M&A, leverage buyouts (LBOs), and payment methods and their implications of risk and benefit and hedging of risk. We globalize the M&A model by extending it to international markets, review restructuring methods and PMI.

As the joint product of contributing authors from academia and practitioners, **the book** *provides a comprehensive framework (model) of the M&A process.* The book addresses M&A in the context of

[15] Richard A. Brealey, Stewart C. Myers and Alan J. Marcus, *Fundamentals of Corporate Finance*, McGraw Hill Irwin, 2004, Ch. 22, Sec. 22.4, pp. 596–600; Stephen A. Ross, Randolph W. Westerfield, and Jeffrey Jaffe, *Corporate Finance, 9th Ed.*, McGraw Hill Irwin, 2010, Ch. 29, Sec. 29.6.

investment analysis and strategies, including the various market complexities. M&As encompass a wide spectrum of transaction types, of which the most significant transactions/deals are addressed by the book.

This book was written for practitioners and students and it addresses the entire process of M&As in a comprehensive framework that is predominantly embedded in corporate finance. M&A transactions require a host of participants with different specialization and responsibilities (including corporate executives and board members, investment bankers, accountants, tax specialists, attorneys, and financial institutions). It addresses a broad scope of issues involving the merger process, and it's intended to provide the market participants with a comprehensive state of the art statement on various subject matters, including valuation of privately held firms. This book provides a complete process for doing deals that addresses both the macro issues as well as the nuts and bolts needed to do deals. This book recognizes that M&A activities involve a broad spectrum of concerns and specialists. Hands on experience and learning is obtained by addressing real world mergers, analytical concepts and procedures, such as valuation and pricing of deals. The chapters in this book are standardized, contain the most recent literature relevant for the subject covered, and constitute a crossover between a textbook and reading book.

The material presented is anchored in the main stream of corporate finance and M&A practices as reflected in deal making process. The book is designed for professional staff (including bankers, attorneys, accountants, analysts) and students. It's expected that valuation providers are likely to avail themselves of the full literature on the subject, but the staff in a transaction would probably be perfectly satisfied with a concise statement on the subject. This book provides a summary of the merger process in one succinct text.

The chapter format is as follows:

- Introduction. The main issues, highlight of the literature, the take away from this chapter & learning objective
- The Main Issues: Discussion, market example(s), theory, data, charts

- o Market Implications
- o Analytical Approaches: Models, practices
- o Summary of key points: The main points addressed in this chapter and the implications for market participants and readers

This book has its genesis with my teaching Restructuring Firms & Industries and Mergers & Acquisition courses at NYU, Stern School of Business, The City University of New York at Baruch College, and at Pace University since 1995 at both the graduate and undergraduate levels, and teaching finance and economics at Rutgers Business School since 2011. The interest in M&A expended exponentially with the merger boom in the 1990s to date and courses offered have proliferated.

- o Chapter 2 addresses the framework and process for deal structuring and the various complexities involved;
- o Chapter 3 addresses the due diligence process in assessing the M&A target;
- o Chapter 4 reviews and examines the legal and regulatory framework and its implications on M&A;
- o Chapter 5 addresses corporate governance and control involved in M&A transactions and management;
- o Chapter 6 examines takeover defenses;
- o Chapters 7 and 8 deal with valuation methods and practices relating to public and private companies;
- o Chapters 9 and 10 address accounting and tax implications of M&As;
- o Chapter 11 analyzes the financial engineering of leverage buyouts;
- o Chapter 12 reviews restructuring and divestitures through various methodologies;
- o Chapter 13 discusses cross-border M&As;
- o Chapters 14 and 15 deal with bankruptcy and reorganization in the US and EU; and
- o Chapter 15 addresses post-merger integration (PMI).

- Market Implications
- Analytical Approach [illegible] Models, practices
- Summary of key points: The main points of each [illegible] chapter and the implications for market participants and readers.

This book has its genesis [illegible] with my teaching [illegible] Divestiture, and Mergers and Acquisitions courses at NYU Stern School of Business, [illegible] University of New York [illegible] College, and at Pace University since 1995 at both the graduate and undergraduate levels, and teaching finance and economics at [illegible] Business School since 2011. The [illegible] MBA [illegible] experienced [illegible] the merger [illegible] in the 1990s [illegible] and [illegible] have [illegible].

- Chapter 2 addresses the framework and process for restructuring and the [illegible] involved.
- Chapter 3 addresses the due diligence process in assessing [illegible] M&A targets.
- Chapter 4 reviews and examines the legal and regulatory [illegible] and their implications on M&As.
- Chapter 5 addresses corporate governance and [illegible] M&A [illegible] and management.
- Chapter 6 examines [illegible] takeover defenses.
- Chapters 7 and 8 deal with valuation [illegible] and [illegible] public and private companies.
- Chapters 9 and 10 offer a [illegible] of [illegible] M&As.
- Chapter 11 [illegible]
- Chapter 12 reviews [illegible] methodologies.
- Chapter 13 discusses cross-border M&As.
- Chapters 14 and [illegible] both [illegible] and emerging markets in the US and [illegible].
- Chapters 15 and [illegible] (ECB).

Chapter 2

Doing the Deal: The Framework

Harvey Poniachek
Rutgers Business School

This chapter reviews mergers and acquisitions (M&As) data and trends, merger models and performance, addresses mergers versus internal development, reviews the merger process and decision making, discusses M&A transactional forms, deals protection provisions, consideration and exchange ratios and pricing collars.

M&A Data & Trends

The year 2015 marked the busiest ever for M&As, whereby US companies announced more than $2.1 trillion in transactions, and global M&A volume topped $4.7 trillion in aggregate.[1] A survey by Deloitte of nearly 2,300 executives and managers from US corporations and private equity firms shows that 87% of the respondents stated that

[1] Deloitte, M&A Trends Report 2016. From February 19 to March 15, 2016, a Deloitte survey conducted by On Research polled 2,292 executives at US companies and private equity firms to gauge their expectations, experiences, and plans for M&As in the coming years.

they expect their deal activity to sustain or exceed the better 2015's record. Similar results were also reported by Dealogic[2] and EY. A number of factors are driving the optimism, including excess cash, high stock prices, and interest rates at historically low levels. The respondents cited global economic uncertainty as a key concern, surpassing strategy, planning, valuation, and pricing as the top factor impacting deal success.

More divestitures are planned going forward, with 52% of corporate respondents saying that their company plans to pursue divestitures to shed non-core assets in the year ahead to help focus their business, and in some sectors to raise capital. The industries that are expected to generate the most M&A activity in the years to come are technology, oil and gas, financial services, and healthcare.

While low interest rates and easy access to debt have allowed many acquirers to orchestrate deals, continued economic uncertainty, particularly in Europe and in several markets across Asia, is expected to be a key concern as they hunt for deals. Despite global economic concerns, 75% of corporate respondents are still searching for a slightly larger share of cross-border deals, while 84% of private equity are seeking acquisitions in foreign markets. Private equity respondents expressed concern about deals that had not met expectations over the last 2 years, with 56% of those surveyed saying more than half of deals had not returned expected value, up from 54% in 2015. For both segments of respondents, gaps in execution and integration of deals comprised the key reason why deals did not generate the expected value (23% for corporates and 26% for PEI respondents).

See Exhibits 1 and 2 for M&A data issued by the UNCTAD.

[2] http://www.foxbusiness.com/markets/2016/10/17/m-outlook-for-2017-rosy.html.

Exhibit 1: Annex Table 10. Value of Cross-Border M&As by Region/Economy of Purchaser, 1990–2015 (millions of dollars)

Region/economy	2010	2011	2012	2013	2014	2015	% of 2015
World	347,094	553,442	328,224	262,517	432,480	721,455	100.00
Developed economies	224,759	431,899	183,858	120,683	256,853	585,860	81.21
European Union	23,108	142,022	18,998	33,725	37,821	270,096	37.44
North America	120,717	173,653	110,097	90,306	136,534	207,851	28.81
Canada	35,614	35,922	37,569	30,672	47,561	87,826	12.17
United States	85,104	137,731	72,528	59,633	88,973	120,024	16.64
Other developed economies	59,779	85,056	31,920	59,740	63,631	59,963	
Japan	31,271	62,263	37,795	58,275	45,645	50,381	6.98
Africa	3,792	4,393	629	3,212	5,449	3,358	
Asia	79,865	80,499	92,819	108,511	140,880	110,342	
China	29,828	36,364	37,908	51,526	40,779	43,653	6.05
Latin America and the Caribbean	16,725	16,385	30,735	16,021	8,490	5,340	

Source: ©UNCTAD cross-border M&A database (www.unctad.org/fdistatistics).

Exhibit 2: Annex Table 9. Value of Cross-Border M&As by Region/Economy of Seller, 1990–2015 (millions of dollars)

Region/economy	2010	2011	2012	2013	2014	2015	% of 2015
World	347,094	553,442	328,224	262,517	432,480	721,455	100.00
Developed economies	259,926	436,926	266,773	230,122	301,171	630,853	87.44
European Union	118,187	184,582	128,270	126,585	179,679	260,467	36.10
North America	97,616	179,459	94,203	67,043	51,919	313,368	43.44
Canada	13,272	33,315	29,450	23,618	34,399	14,629	2.03
United States	84,344	146,144	64,752	43,424	17,520	298,739	41.41
Japan	7,114	4,671	1,791	4,423	6,637	3,203	0.44
Africa	7,493	8,634	(1,254)	3,818	5,152	20,414	
Asia	37,723	55,967	33,360	47,829	96,188	46,398	
China	6,758	11,501	9,524	31,066	54,913	9,660	1.34
Latin America and the Caribbean	29,013	18,927	22,586	35,587	25,565	12,134	

Source: ©UNCTAD cross-border M&A database (www.unctad.org/fdistatistics).

M&A Models & Performance

There are various theories of mergers and acquisitions,[3] but practitioners formulated models in terms of several variables. For instance, Bain & Company[4] formulates an M&A model that consists of five stages as follows:

1. M&A strategy — make your M&A an extension of your growth strategy, identify the target and formulate how M&A will create value,
2. Deal thesis — examine how each deal creates value, apply existing capabilities to enhance value to the target,
3. Due diligence and valuation — test the deal rational, set a walk away price, determine where you can add value,

---

[3] Theories of M&As by Weston, J. Fred, *et al.*, *Takeover, Restructuring & Corporate Governance, 4th Ed.*, Prentice-Hall, 2004, Ch. 6.

Value Increase
Efficiency Theories
Operating Synergy
Diversification
Financial Synergy
Strategic Realignment
The q-Ratio (Tobin's q was developed by Prof *James Tobin* in 1969 as the ratio between the market value and replacement value of the same physical asset)
Information Signaling
Hubris — Acquirer Overpays for Target
Agency Problems
Distribution: Taxes, Market Power, Redistribution From Bhs & Labor
Others — The Industry Life Cycle.

Excellence in Financial Management, Course 7: Mergers & Acquisitions (Part 1), Prepared by: Matt H. Evans, CPA, CMA, CFM, Published March 2000.

[4] Bain & Company, The renaissance in mergers & acquisitions, 2014. See for instance Sudarsanam, *Creating Value from Mergers and Acquisitions: The Challenges*, FT Prentice Hall, 2003, who identifies a five-stage model of M&A which views M&A as a multistage process rather than a transaction, consisting of the following functions: Corporate strategy, Organizing for acquisitions, Deal structuring and negotiation, Postacquisition integration, and Postacquisition audit and organizational learning.

4. Merger integration planning — plan your postmerger integration (PMI) and determine what's needed to integrate, and integrate where it makes sense, and
5. Merger integration execution.

McKinsey & Company[5] identifies the strategic rationale for an acquisition that creates value as follows:

1. Improving the performance of the target company,
2. Removing excess capacity from an industry,
3. Creating market access products,
4. Acquiring kills or market technology more quickly or at a lower cost than they could build in-house, and
5. Picking winners early and helping them develop their businesses.

Merger performance could be addressed from three different perspectives:

- Macro benefits of mergers — for the entire economy/sectors, improved efficiency and operational performance;
- Micro effects — are companies/sectors engaged in mergers benefit from enhanced efficiency or redistribution effect; and
- Are SHs value increased by M&As? Is it maintained over time?

Success and Failure of M&As

- Success was defined in terms of *the economic profit model* whether (% econ profit / invested capital in the acquisition) > WACC;
- Econ profit = noplat – invested capital × WACC; or econ profit = ebit(1 – t) – invested capital × WACC[6];
- McKinsey & Company's study of 116 mergers between 1972 and 1982 shows that 61% were failures, 23% were successful and 16% were not accounted for[7];

---

[5] Marc Goedhart, Tim Koller and David Wessels, The Five Types of Successful Acquisitions, Web, 2010.

[6] Copeland, *Valuation, 3rd Ed.*, 2000, Ch. 8.

[7] Ibid, p. 114.

- A recent survey by McKinsey of 160 acquisitions in 1995–1996 shows that only 12% of the acquirers managed to accelerate their growth over the next 3 years, and 42% lost ground[8];
- Bain's worldwide research project of more than 1,600 publicly traded companies and more than 18,000 deals from 2000 through 2010 shows that M&A was an essential part of successful strategies for profitable growth. During this period, total shareholders return (TSR) averaged 4.5% per year, compared with 3.3% for companies that were inactive in M&A.

Reasons for Failure

- Acquirers were over optimistic in their assumptions
- Acquirers overestimated expected synergies
- Acquirers overbid in the heat of the bidding process
- Poor postacquisition integration

Why Mergers and the Merger Process

To achieve growth, companies have the option of investing in internal development and generating organic growth or generating growth by investing in M&As. The choice of the appropriate strategy is articulated in Exhibit 2. The exhibit clearly favors M&A based on the assessment of the various factors. However, circumstances could be quite different and in favor of internal development. That is, the analysis hinges on empirical facts and information about the various factors affecting cited here that could be unique for different cases.

The merger process and decision making are fully state in Exhibit 6.

M&A Transactional Forms

Many acquisitions in the US commence with preliminary negotiations and/or discussions between the acquirer and the target company.[9]

---

[8] McKinsey Quarterly, Why Mergers Fail? 2001, #4.

[9] Richard Hall, *United States of America Takeover Guide*, Cravath, Swaine & Moore LLP, 2014.

Exhibit 3: M&A Versus Internal Development

	M&A	**Internal Development**
Lower Cost	+	
Acquire Know-How	+	
Quicker	+	
Higher Risk		+
Acquire New Market	+	
Acquire New Products	+	

Exhibit 4: Sources of Synergy

- Synergy is the additional value created by either reducing the amount of resources employed for the same level of output, or expanding output and revenue, or by expanding the product offerings and R&D capabilities as follows.
- *Cost synergies are obtained from a reduction of cost thanks to avoidance of duplications, and/or* economies of scale, such as administrative costs and overhead costs;
- *Revenue synergies relate to* increasing the revenues, often related to economies of scope, thanks to expansion of the customer and cross selling;
- *Financial synergies* related to decreased costs of capital through lowered risks, better cash flows and increased financial margins;
- *Market synergies* related to higher margins achieved through increased negotiation capabilities towards suppliers and customers.

Subsequently, the acquirer and the target company enter into an agreement that sets the terms and conditions of the acquisition and the structure of the transaction. Companies involved in M&A negotiate confidentiality agreements or letters of intent that are referred to as a "Non-Disclosure Agreement" (NDA). The letter of intent, sometimes referred to as a "memorandum of understanding" (MOU) is more common in private transactions than in public company deals. The M&A transaction structure has important consequences for the deal, the tax treatment of the transaction, and the speed at which the transaction will be completed. There are several acquisition methods

Exhibit 5: The Merger Process: An Input–Output Model

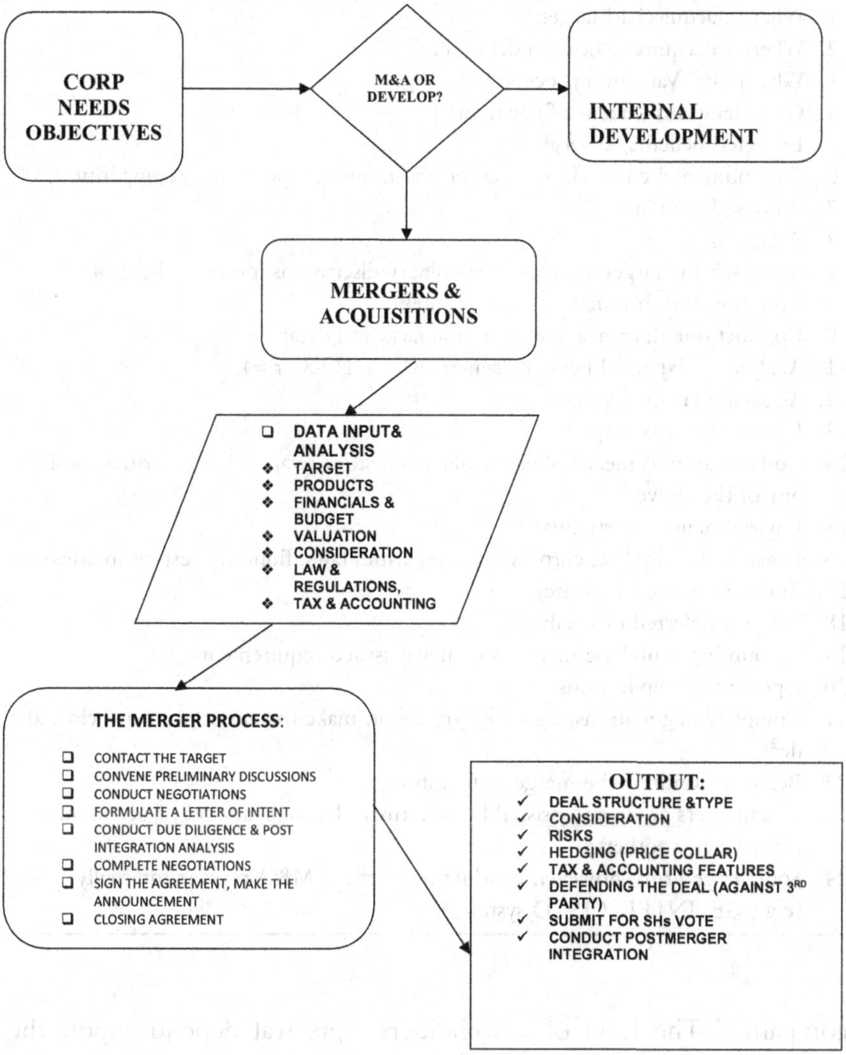

for acquiring a US public company: The acquirer can utilize the state merger statutes and apply a single-step merger. The acquirer and the target company must enter into a merger agreement that requires the approval of the board of directors and the shareholders of the target

Exhibit 6: The Merger Process and Decisions Making

1. What to acquire? Id target;
2. Where to acquire? Location decision;
3. What price? Valuation process;
4. Considerations (means of payments);
5. Expected benefits/synergies?
6. Environmental constraints: legal, tax, accounting, operational/competition;
7. Proposed structure;
8. PMI;
9. Approach the target, convene preliminary discussions, propose the deal structure, and formulate a letter of intent;
10. Conduct due diligence and verify the facts and data;
11. Analysis — expected benefits/synergies? 1 + 1 = 3 or =4;
12. Assessed benefit & price;
13. Is it an attractive target?
14. Consideration (=means of payment): cash, stock swap, other securities, or a mix of the above;
15. Environmental constraints;
16. Legal (state corp law, corp by-laws, securities laws, fiduciary responsibilities);
17. Antitrust (justice dept, ftc);
18. Tax (tax deferred or taxable?);
19. Accounting (purchase methods — newly issued requirements);
20. Operational implications;
21. Complete negotiations, sign the agreement, make the announcement, close the deal;
22. Begin or continue the merger integration;
23. The mergers process is assisted by investment bankers, attorneys, accountants, tax specialists, others;
24. Some large firms, however, conduct most of the M&A process internally (e.g., GE, INTEL, CISCO systems).

company.[10] The level of shareholders' approval depends upon the state of incorporation of the target company, but Delaware requires an approval by a majority of the outstanding shares. In addition, a single-step merger is subject to federal securities laws.

[10] Richard Hall, *United States of America Takeover Guide*, Cravath, Swaine & Moore LLP, 2014.

The main transactional forms of mergers and acquisitions are as follows:

Merger or Consolidation;

- Asset Purchase;
- Stock Purchase;
- Joint Venture.

Statutory Merger or Consolidation

In a merger, two or more corporations are merged into one of the entities, which is the surviving entity of the merger. In a consolidation, the entities are consolidated to form a new entity. The stock of the non-surviving entity or entities is exchanged into stock of the surviving or resulting entity, cash or some other form of consideration. Upon completion of the merger or consolidation, the surviving entity will operate the combined business and file a certificate in the jurisdiction(s) of incorporation.

There are several versions of statutory mergers as follows:

1. *Direct Statutory Merger*: The target company is merged into a newly formed subsidiary of the acquirer.

2. *Forward Triangular Merger*: The target is merged into a subsidiary of the acquirer, that is, the target's business (both assets and liabilities) is transferred to a wholly owned subsidiary of acquirer, and the target's stockholders receive stock, cash, debt, property, or a combination thereof of acquirer (subsidiary's parent).

3. *Reverse Triangular Merger*: A new subsidiary is formed by the acquirer (generally newly formed) and it is merged into the target, the target's stockholders receive stock, cash, debt, property, or a combination thereof, of acquirer (subsidiary's parent), and shares of acquisition subsidiary are converted into shares of target. The target becomes wholly owned subsidiary of acquirer and its corporate identity is preserved. In the above three forms of merger and consolidation, no minority stockholders remain after the merger. However, the acquirer

must assume all liabilities of target (fixed and contingent, disclosed and undisclosed), but direct exposure of the acquirer is limited in a triangular merger because such liabilities are of its subsidiaries. Stockholders of nonsurviving corporations may have dissenters' appraisal rights permitting them to receive cash for their stock in an amount equal to an appraised market value set by a court.

4. *Asset Purchase*: An acquirer may purchase either substantially all or part of the assets of a corporate target in return various consideration, including stock, cash, debt, property or a combination thereof. In addition to the tax advantages, there are several advantages to a purchase and sale of assets, including the following: the buyer can acquire all or only selected assets and all or only selected liabilities; he can avoid dealing with minority stockholders in many circumstances; unless all of the assets are purchased substantially, no stockholder vote of the target is required; and typically there are no appraisal rights for dissenting stockholders.

There are several disadvantages to a purchase and sale of assets: Corporate identity of target is not preserved for the acquirer; numerous consents to assignment of contractual rights may be required, potentially causing delay and giving rise to additional costs; acceleration of certain obligations may get triggered and require prepayment of the target's indebtedness; if significant amount of real estate is involved, transfer taxes, recording fees, etc. may be substantial; if intellectual property is registered in many jurisdictions, many assignments need to be filed; sales tax and bulk sales problems are possible; and if assets purchased and sold constitute substantially all of the assets of target, a stockholder vote of target is usually required.

5. *Stock Purchase*: An acquirer may gain control over a target by purchasing stock from the target's stockholders, rather than merging with the target or purchasing its assets. The acquiring corporation may negotiate with individual stockholders or if the target is a public company, it may make a tender offer. The acquirer can make a tender offer directly to the target common shareholders to purchase their shares and then follow a second-step merger to

eliminate minority shareholders.[11] A tender offer is regulated by the federal securities laws. Regardless of whether the transaction is done through a tender offer or a single-step merger, the federal and state regulations focus on disclosure to ensure that target shareholders are given sufficient time and the information to make a fully informed decision.

A stock purchase provides several advantages: The target's corporate identity is preserved together with special franchises, licenses, permits, and local qualifications to do business (other than those that may be affected by a change in control); the target's contract rights will not be impaired (unless specific contractual provisions require consent for changes in control); transaction is relatively simple when the target is closely held; it can be implemented through an exchange offer if management opposes the transaction.

Stock purchases have several disadvantages: They may result in less than total acquisition with resulting minority stockholders, giving rise to possible future questions of fiduciary obligations to such stockholders; and the target is acquired subject to all its liabilities, including any undisclosed liabilities.

6. *Joint Venture*: Joint ventures are a common approach for combining businesses at a relatively low-cost means by which coventurers can share benefits from particular assets or advantages, such as technology, expertise, name recognition, governmental contacts or financial clout. Joint ventures can be mere contractual arrangements or can be structured as jointly owned entities such as corporations, partnerships (either general or limited) or limited liability companies. Coventurers will generally want their arrangement to be clear with respect to their respective rights as to allocation and distribution of the economic benefits of the joint venture, under what circumstances the joint venture may be terminated and the consequences of termination to each coventurer.

---

[11] Richard Hall, *United States of America Takeover Guide*, Cravath, Swaine & Moore LLP, 2014.

7. *Spin-offs Combined with M&A Transactions*: A tax-free spin-off or split-off that satisfies the requirements of Section 355 of the Internal Revenue Code can be used in combination with a concurrent M&A transaction. For example, "Morris Trusts" and "Reverse Morris Trusts" transactions effectively allow a parent corporation to separate a business and combine it with a third party in a transaction that is tax-free to parent and its shareholders if certain requirements are met.

8. *Tender Offers*: In a tender offer, the acquirer makes a direct offer to the target's shareholders to acquire their shares, conditioned on the acquirer holding at least a majority of each class of target stock upon the close of the tender offer. Following the tender offer, the acquirer and the target merge pursuant to their merger agreement. Upon consummation of the offer, if the acquirer holds at least the statutorily prescribed percentage usually 90% pursuant to Section 251(h) of the DGCL, the acquirer can complete the acquisition by a short-form merger, thereby avoiding the need to solicit proxies or hold a shareholders' meeting.

Amendments to the tender offer rules in 2000 reduced the timing disparity between cash tender offers and exchange offers by allowing the 20-business-day time period for certain exchange offers to begin as early as upon filing of a registration statement, rather than upon effectiveness of the registration statement. Delaware corporate law Section 251(h) eliminated the need for a stockholder vote to approve a second-step merger following a tender offer where the buyer owns 90% stock to approve the merger pursuant to the DGCL and the target's charter.

9. *Mergers of Equals*: Combinations between large companies of similar sizes are often referred to as "mergers of equals" (MOEs). MOEs provide an alternative to an outright sale of a company, and are typically structured as tax-free, stock-for-stock transactions, with a fixed exchange ratio without collars or walk-aways, and with a balanced contract often containing matching representations, warranties and interim covenants from both parties. MOEs often provide little or no premium above market price for either company. Instead, an exchange ratio is set to reflect relative assets, earnings and capital

contributions, and market capitalizations of the two merging parties. A proper exchange ratio can provide a fair and efficient means for the shareholders of both companies to benefit from merger synergies.

10. Major types and characteristics are addressed below.
    - **Horizontal Mergers** involve two firms operating and/or competing in the same kind of business activity, could provide economies of scale & scope, regulated by antitrust legislation;
    - **Vertical Mergers** occur between firms in different stages of operation. Designed to internalize transactions and benefits. Internalization of advantages brought by lower transaction cost through more efficient contracting, reduced/eliminated bargaining cost, harmonization of corporate objectives, reduced risk, thanks to greater information availability, institutional adaptations to cope with regulations;
    - **Conglomerate Mergers** involve firms in unrelated types of business activity and distinguish between three types
        - — Product Extension where mergers broaden the product lines of firms. Mergers between firms in related business;
        - — Geographic Market Extension through mergers of firms in nonoverlapped markets;
        - — Pure Conglomerate via merger-involved unrelated business activities.

Approaches to M&A

The main approaches to acquiring control of a US public company are through cash tender offers or exchange offers that are commonly followed by a statutory merger[12] as follows.

---

[12] David Offenberg and Christo Pirinsky, How do Acquirers Choose between Mergers and Tender Offers? *Journal of Financial Economics*, volume 116, issue 2, May 2015, pp. 331–348. The authors state that bidders have a preference for speedy execution in order to minimize competition for the target. Due to existing

The acquirer can utilize the state merger statutes and apply a single-step merger. The acquirer and the target company enter into a merger agreement approved by the board of directors and the target shareholders of the target company.[13] The level of shareholders' approval varies among states, but Delaware requires an approval by a majority of the outstanding shares. A single-step merger is subject to federal securities laws, known as the proxy rules, that require that the target company files with the SEC a proxy statement for approval.

The acquirer can make a tender offer (of cash for stock, or stock for stock, or cash and stock for stock) directly to the target common shareholders followed by a second-step merger to eliminate minority shareholders. The second step merger, or a "back-end" merger, squeezes out the remaining shareholders without the approval of the target's stockholders if the acquirer and target enter a merger agreement giving the acquirer authorization to complete the merger after obtaining a majority of the target's stock. The acquirer must pay the minority stockholders the price and type of consideration that the acquirer pays to stockholders who tender shares into the tender offer. Target stockholders in a second step merger have appraisal rights.

In a cash tender offer, Schedule TO must be filed with the SEC, but the tender offer could proceed before receiving comments from the SEC. A tender offer requires filing with the SEC a registration statement (which includes the bidder's prospectus) on Form S-4 along with the exchange offer document on Schedule TO and must be declared effective by the SEC before the bidder can acquire any shares in the target. The offer document may be disseminated prior to the completion of the SEC's review, but cannot be used until the registration statement of the securities to be issued is declared

---

regulations, tender offers provide substantially lower completion times than mergers and, as a result, are the acquisition method of choice. However, a tender offer signals to the target good market opportunities at a higher share price. In equilibrium, bidders trade off speed and costs, recognizing that tenders are faster but have higher premiums. Deals in more competitive environments and deals with lesser external impediments on execution are more likely to be structured as tender offers.

[13] Richard Hall, *United States of America Takeover Guide*, Cravath, Swaine & Moore LLP, 2014.

effective. An exchange offer may also require approval by the bidder's shareholders, if the securities to be issued as consideration constitute more than 20% of a class of securities listed on the NYSE or Nasdaq, and shareholders must approve it.

Friendly or Hostile Bids

Market practice is that friendly transactions that use shares as consideration will be structured as single-step mergers; and hostile transactions are structured as tender offers. In a friendly transaction, the tender offer or exchange offer will be made pursuant to a negotiated merger agreement with the target company and its board of directors. A hostile bid is usually structured as a tender or exchange offer. The legal requirements relating to M&A differ whether the deal is friendly or hostile, and whether the considerations are cash or stock.[14]

A friendly merger that is funded by cash requires the acquirer to file a proxy statement with the SEC that describes the deal. Upon review and clearance of the statement, the statement is issued to shareholders along with a proxy card that needs to be filled out and returned. The deal has to be approved at a shareholders meeting and closed.

A friendly merger funded with stock requires the issuing of a proxy statement as in the case of a cash transaction, but the securities offered in exchange for the target shares need to be registered with the SEC. Upon completion of the proxy statement and share registration both documents are the registration statement and proxy statements are mailed to shareholder along with a proxy card to be filled out by the shareholders. The deal is voted on the shareholders meeting.

Hostile deal funded with cash. The acquirer issues a tender offer to buy forwarding tender offer material to the target shareholders consistent with the William Act requirement. Due to the short time table, the SEC does not have the opportunity to review and comment on the materials, but it might do so subsequently.

---

[14] Patrick A. Gaughan, *Mergers, Acquisitions, and Corporate Restructuring, 5th Ed.*, Wiley, 2011.

Hostile deal funded with stock for stock requires filing a registration statement with the SEC by the bidder prior to launching the tender offer. The statement needs to be cleared by the SEC prior to its dissemination to shareholders.

Deal Protection and Deal Certainty[15]

Merger agreements include various provisions to afford deal protection to ensuring that the other party remains obligated to consummate the transaction. The key provisions are

1. "deal protection" devices intended to regulate interloper risk,
2. closing conditions giving a party a right to walk away from a transaction without liability if a "material adverse effect" (MAE) or "material adverse change", and
3. remedies available in connection with a party's failure to comply with the agreement or otherwise close, including failure to obtain the requisite financing or governmental approvals. These provisions can significantly influence whether an M&A transaction will be completed, renegotiated or abandoned in the face of postsigning changes in circumstances.

Deal Protection Devices

Mergers agreement commonly include various provisions to provide the transacting parties with flexibility to address futures events. "Deal protection" devices include break-up fees, no-shop clauses, force-the-vote provisions and shareholder voting agreements. These devices permit bidders "to protect themselves against being used as a stalking horse and [provide] consideration for making target-specific investments of time and resources in particular acquisitions.[16]

[15] This section follows Wachtell, Lipton, Rosen & Katz, Takeover Law and Practices, March 2016, http://www.wlrk.com/files/2016/TakeoverLawandPracticeGuide.pdf.

[16] Delaware courts have recognized that deal protection devices are permissible means of protecting a merger from third-party interference, where such provisions (viewed holistically) are reasonable under the circumstances.

Break-Up Fees

A break-up fee is payable by the target in the event that the target terminates the merger agreement to accept a superior proposal. Termination fees may deter other potential acquirers from making an acquisition proposal after an agreement has been reached.[17]

Break-up fees can be triggered if target's shareholders fail to approve the merger. The size of a break-up fee is typically lower than a break-up fee triggered in connection with an alternative offer. A break-up fee can also be triggered when a party terminates due to the board changing its recommendation in favor of the deal, or if a party enters into an alternative transaction during a "tail" period following termination for failure to obtain shareholder approval where an alternative acquisition proposal was made public prior to the shareholder vote.

"No-Shops," "No Talks" and "Don't Ask, Don't Waive" Standstills

A "no-shop" provision in a merger agreement provides that a selling company will not encourage, seek, solicit, provide information to or negotiate with third-party bidders, but generally allows the seller to respond to unsolicited offers by supplying confidential information and to consider and negotiate with respect to certain competing bids.

"Go-shop" provisions that allow the target company to actively solicit competing offers are a variation on the typical no-shop clause. Go-shops provide a period after the merger agreement signing — usually 30–50 days — in which the target is permitted to affirmatively solicit competing bids. The Court of Chancery has stated that the absence of a go-shop provision is not *per se* unreasonable.

---

[17] According to the Delaware Court of Chancery, there is no accepted "customary" level of break-up fees, but such fees of 4.4% of equity value is "near the upper end of a "conventionally accepted" range. In some cases, purchasers are entitled to expense reimbursement instead of a fee in the event of a no-vote.

Board Recommendations, Fiduciary Outs and "Force-the-Vote" Provisions

Public company merger agreements generally include provisions requiring the board of directors of the target to recommend that shareholders vote in favor of the merger agreement, except in specified circumstances. Merger agreements often include provisions that permit a party to terminate the agreement to accept a superior proposal, subject to payment of a termination fee and other conditions — commonly known as a "fiduciary out." A Delaware corporation may submit the merger agreement to shareholders even if the board, having deemed the merger agreement advisable at the time of execution, subsequently changes its recommendation. This is referred to as a "force-the-vote" provision.

Crown Jewels

The "crown-jewel" lock-up is a device in which the target company grants the acquirer an option to purchase, or obtain the benefit of key target assets in the event that the proposed merger does not close. This lock-up gives the acquirer assurance that even outside of a successful merger, it will nevertheless get key pieces of the target's business. The device may serve to deter competing bidders, since even with a superior topping bid, the competing bidders may not get the deal they are seeking (i.e., at best they may get a deal without the crown jewels).

MAE Clauses

Virtually all domestic public company merger agreements allow the buyer to refuse to close if there has been an MAE or a "material adverse Event" in the target company's business. This MAE is one of the principal mechanisms available to the parties to a transaction to allocate the risk of adverse events transpiring between signing and closing.[18] Because

[18] The Court placed the burden of proving a material adverse effect on the buyer and clarified that an MAE must be a long-term effect rather than a short-term failure to

the MAE provision allows an acquirer to refuse to close if there has been an MAE on the target company's business, it can also serve as a lever for renegotiating a transaction.

Committed Deal Structures, Optionality and Remedies for Failure to Close

Traditionally, strategic buyers, with significant balance sheets, were expected to fully commit to the completion of a cash acquisition whereas financial sponsors, who often depended on borrowing a portion of the purchase price, negotiated for financing conditions that allowed the sponsor to exit the deal in the event that it was unable to obtain financing on the terms contemplated by the financing commitment papers executed at signing.

The reverse termination fee required the buyer to pay a fee in the event the buyer failed to close due to an inability to obtain financing (later expanded to a failure to close for any reason). The reverse termination fee often was the seller's sole remedy in the event of a failure to close.

The consideration used in a particular transaction depends on the characteristics of the deal and the relative bargaining strength of the parties. In all-stock and/or part-stock mergers, the value of the consideration may be dramatically altered by stock market changes. Stock prices volatility could affect the accretion/dilution perspective for the parties.

All-cash transactions have the benefit of being of certain but require cash on hand or ability to borrow, and they have a tax effect on the seller.

All-stock transactions are subject to price risks between signing and closing. Such risks can be hedged by using an exchange ratio pricing with a collar. Let's first address a fixed exchange ratio and then consider an exchange ratio plus a price collar.

---

meet earnings targets. In addition to the difficulty in establishing that an MAE has occurred, parties seeking to invoke MAE clauses have also had difficulty overcoming the long list of exceptions that a typical MAE clause contains.

Fixed and Floating Exchange Ratios

The simplest pricing structure in a stock-for-stock transaction is to set a fixed exchange ratio at the time a merger agreement is signed. It affords equal maximum risk-sharing between the parties. A floating exchange ratio with a collar provides a fixed number of shares but at different values. The exchange ratio is set based on an average market price for the acquirer's stock during some period, normally 10–30 trading days, prior to closing. Thus, the acquirer would agree to deliver a fixed value (e.g., $30) in stock for each of the target's shares, with the number of acquirer's shares to be delivered based on the market price during the specified period. An acquirer bears the market risk of a decline in the price of its stock since, in such event, it will have to issue more shares to deliver the agreed value. Because a dramatic drop in the acquirer's stock may require the acquirer to buy its target for far more shares than had been intended at the time the transaction was announced, thereby causing a dilution of ownership. A target's shareholders bear little market risk in this scenario and correspondingly will not benefit from an increase in stock prices since the per-share value is fixed.

In order to mitigate the risk posed by market fluctuations, parties may desire a longer measuring period for valuing the acquirer's stock. Longer measuring periods minimize the effects of market volatility on how many acquirer shares will be issued as merger consideration. Additionally, acquirers favor longer measuring periods because, as the transaction becomes more likely and approaches fruition, the acquirer's stock may fall to reflect any anticipated earnings dilution. By contrast, a target may argue that the market price over some period immediately prior to consummation provides a better measure of consideration received.

Acquirers must be cognizant of the fact that the price of their stock may decline precipitously based on events or circumstances having little or nothing to do with the value of the acquirer. To protect against having to issue a very high number of shares, agreements with floating exchange ratios frequently include a "collar" that places a cap on the number of shares to be issued and, at the same time, a floor on the number of shares that may be issued. Effectively, such agreements provide upper and lower market price limits within which the number of shares to be delivered will be adjusted. The size of the

Exhibit 7: The Exchange Ratio Model & the Implications on EPS

1. P offer × S target = P buyer × ΔS buyer.
   The left hand side of the above equation states the value of the target; the right hand side that states the value of stocks that the buyer needs to issue is exchanged for the target's stocks.
2. (P offer/P buyer) = (ΔS buyer/S target) = R, the exchange ratio.
   Note that the exchange ratio could be defined in two manners, that is, either as the price ratio on the left hand side, which is the convention in the marketplace, or by the ratio of the shares to be exchanged.
3. (P offer/P buyer) = R, the exchange ratio.
4. P offer = P buyer × R, the exchange ratio.
5. EPS of buyer pre merger = (NI/S) of buyer.
6. EPS of buyer post merger = (NI buyer + NI target + synergy)/(S buyer + ΔS buyer).
7. EPS post merger > EPS pre merger. The outcome is accretive and positive.
8. EPS post merger < EPS pre merger. The outcome is dilutive and negative.
   If dilution is unacceptable, the buyer could either reduce the offer price and the number of new shares to be issued in the exchange; or propose to modify the consideration to include both stocks and cash. Inclusion of cash in the consideration might require grossing up for the the tax implications, and therefore raise the target price and acquisition cost of the target company.

The variables:
P = price per share,
S = number of shares,
EPS = earnings per share,
NI = net income.

range determines the degree of protection afforded to the acquirer, and correspondingly, the amount of the market risk borne by the target's shareholders.

Merger Models

Excellence in Financial Management, Course 7: Mergers & Acquisitions (Part 1), Prepared by: Matt H. Evans, CPA, CMA, CFM, Published March 2000

Mergers and acquisitions are now a normal way of life within the business world. In today's global, competitive environment, mergers

Exhibit 8: The Price Collar Bcorp & Tcorp

		Tcorp Price per Share	Bcorp Price per Share		
Modify Ex Ratio	43.3818	0.4338	$100		
Ceiling	43.3818	0.5634	$77		Bcorp purchased call options on Tcorp & Tcorp sold call options on itdelf
Average	39.438	0.5634	$70	Avg Price	
Floor	35.4942	0.5634	$63		Bcorp sold put options on Tcorp & Tcorp purchased put options on itself
Stock	16.9020	0.5634	$30		
Cash	18.5922				

Notes: Ex Ratio = Exchange Ratio; Bcorp = Buying Corporation; Tcorp = Target Corporation; Ceiling = Avg price × (1 + 0.10); Floor = Avg price × (1 – 0.10).

are sometimes the only means for long-term survival. Virtually every major company in the US today has experienced a major acquisition at some point in history. And at any given time, thousands of these companies are adjusting to postmerger reality.

M&A Defined

When we use the term "merger", we are referring to the merging of two companies where one new company will continue to exist. The term "acquisition" refers to the acquisition of assets by one company from another company. In an acquisition, both companies may continue to exist. However, throughout this course, we will loosely refer to M&As as a business transaction where one company acquires another company. The acquiring company will remain in business and the acquired company (which we will sometimes call the Target Company) will be integrated into the acquiring company and thus, the acquired company ceases to exist after the merger. Mergers can be categorized as follows:

- *Horizontal*: Two firms are merged across similar products or services. Horizontal mergers are often used as a way for a company to increase its market share by merging with a competing company.
- *Conglomerate*: Two firms in completely different industries merge, such as a gas pipeline company merging with a high technology company. Conglomerates are usually used as a way to smooth out wide fluctuations in earnings and provide more consistency in long-term growth. Typically, companies in mature industries with poor prospects for growth will seek to diversify their businesses through mergers and acquisitions. For example, General Electric (GE) has diversified its businesses through M&As, allowing GE to get into new areas like financial services and television broadcasting.

Reasons for M&A

Every merger has its own unique reasons why the combining of two companies is a good business decision. Synergy value can take three forms: (1) higher revenues: By combining the two companies, we will realize higher revenues than if the two companies operate separately. (2) lower expenses: By combining the two companies, we could realize lower expenses than if the two companies operate separately. (3) lower cost of capital: By combining the two companies, the overall cost of capital could be lowered.

The underlying principle behind M&As is often synergy, which is described as 2 + 2 = 5; Company A is valued at $2 billion and the value of Company B is $2 billion, but when the two companies merge together, their total value is $5 billion, which is thanks to the additional value which we call "synergy".

Mergers can also be driven by opportunities of bargain buying, diversification, and growth motivation such as: (1) Bargain purchase of an underpriced target company; (2) Diversification in terms of industry or geographically that could smooth out earnings and provide more consistent long-term growth and profitability; (3) Short-Term Growth — Management may be under pressure to turn around sluggish growth and profitability by an M&A.

The Overall Process

The M&A process can be broken down into eight phases.

Phase 1 — Preacquisition Review: The first step is to determine if an M&A strategy is necessary. A plan should be developed on how growth will occur through M&A.

Phase 2 — Search & Screen Targets: The second phase within the M&A process is to search for possible takeover candidates. Reliance on outside investment firms is common.

Phase 3 — Investigate & Value the Target: The third phase is called "due diligence". The main objective is to identify adverse issues and various synergy values that can be realized through a merger. External experts and investment bankers assist with this phase.

Phase 4 — Acquire through Negotiation: The process of negotiating an M&A could vary in time and difficulty. This negotiation is sometimes called a "bear hug." In cases where opposition is expected from the target, the acquiring firm will acquire a partial interest in the target; sometimes referred to as a "toehold position." This toehold position puts pressure on the target to negotiate without sending the target into panic mode. In cases where the target is expected to strongly fight against a takeover attempt, the acquiring company could make a tender offer directly to the shareholders of the target, bypassing the target's management. Generally, tender offers are more expensive than negotiated M&As due to the resistance of target management and the fact that the target is now "in play" and may attract other bidders.

Phase 5 — Merger Agreement: If all goes well, the two companies will announce a formal M&A agreement.

Phase 6 — Regulatory Approvals: The acquirer would have to seek approval of the antitrust authorities, the securities exchange regulators, and others, depending on the specific market.

Phase 7 — Tender Offer: Once the regulatory authorities approve the transaction, the buyer submits a tender offer to the target shareholders for their approval of the transaction. Sometimes, the shareholders of the acquiring company need to approve the deal as well.

Phase 8 — Post-Merger Integration: The two companies are integrated, with the buyer being the surviving company, and the target becoming a subsidiary.

Chapter 3

The Due Diligence Process in M&A Transactions

Jerry Schwartzman
M&A Advisory Services, Houlihan Lokey

Introduction

The due diligence process is an integral part of merger and acquisition (M&A) transactions. It enables the buyer to confirm basic information about the target, identify any adjustments to Earnings Before Interest, Depreciation & Amortization (EBITDA), consider any structuring alternatives, and to confirm the understanding about the business.[1] Different buyers have different approaches to the timing of the various diligence processes. For sophisticated strategic acquirers that have large internal teams, they may have spent substantial time with target management and executed a Letter of Intent (LOI). Once they execute an LOI, they request that the various diligence teams commence their processes and expect them to move quickly to speed

[1] See Peter Howson, *Due Diligence: The Critical Stage in Mergers and Acquisitions*, Gower Publishing Limited, 2003; "M&A: The Intersection of due diligence and governance," Deloitte On the Board's Agenda (May 2016); "Post-Deal Success Starts at Due Diligence Stage," *BNA Corporate Counsel Weekly*, November 25, 2015, volume 45, p. 357; Trent Dykes and Mimi Hunter, "M&A Due Diligence Overview and Objectives, (Part 1)," The Venture Alley (November 14, 2011) ("Dykes and Hunter").

the process along to contract signing and closing. These types of buyers may have specific timelines, may require weekly reports on the status of the diligence process and any material issues, and may even require weekly conference calls with all diligence team members.[2]

At the other end of the spectrum, there is the small private equity shop that is buying a target with an unsophisticated financial environment ("receipts in a shoebox"). In that case, the private equity shop, because of its limited staff, may need substantial assistance from diligence teams in such basic matters as confirming the revenue and expenses of the target. In this situation, the financial due diligence team may commence its work on behalf of the buyer in advance of other teams, such as the legal diligence team. These are two ends of the spectrum and, of course, there is everything in between. Below, we explore various facets of the due diligence process. It is worth noting that every deal is unique.

The Purpose of the Due Diligence Process

The first purpose of due diligence process is to identify any "red flags" (deal stoppers or material issues) and to confirm critical facts regarding a business prior to its acquisition.[3] This may include legal due diligence to confirm ownership, business good standing, and qualification. It also includes financial due diligence to confirm the cash earnings EBITDA of a business. This is particularly relevant in determining the purchase price (which is often EBITDA times a multiple) and to provide relevant information for negotiating the purchase price and the proper amount of working capital. Though EBITDA is often used as

---

[2] See, e.g., Adolph, Gillies, and Krings, "Strategic Due Diligence: A Foundation for M&A Success," *Strategy + Business*, September 28, 2006.

[3] See, e.g., Jean Murray, "The Importance of Due Diligence When Buying a Business," *The Balance*, November 6, 2016 ("If you are buying a business and you don't want any nasty surprises, you must do your due diligence"); Josh Patrick, "The True Purpose of Due Diligence," *Stage2 Planning Partners* ("Due diligence is about finding problems").

the metric for pricing deals, ultimately the buyers are typically looking at the business in terms of free cash flow.

Red flags and deal stoppers are items that would stop the M&A process and that should be immediately communicated to the potential buyer.[4] The efficiency of a due diligence team may be gauged to some extent by the speed with which it can identify and communicate a deal stopper. One example is where a deal process was stopped within the first few hours of financial due diligence. In that example, in a business carveout from a larger company, the financial due diligence team reviewed the financial statement audit workpapers and identified an item that materially reduced the carveout business's EBITDA, but which was not identified in the seller's audited financial statements because it was not material to the larger business, though it was material to the target carveout business. With the EBITDA adjustment, the earnings were not sufficient to reach the purchase price that was agreed to in the LOI. The financial due diligence team called the buyer as soon as the adjustment was identified — after reviewing the audit workpapers for approximately 2 hrs. The buyer halted the due diligence process for several weeks until it could negotiate a much lower purchase price with the seller.

Another example of a red flag is where management does not want the due diligence teams to talk directly to the controller or the local country CPA in a foreign jurisdiction. That may be a warning sign that there are material issues. In a recent transaction, the CFO refused to allow the diligence team to speak to the local country tax advisor in a non-US jurisdiction. After more than a month of back and forth on access to the local country advisor, it was discovered that the target was materially noncompliant in that jurisdiction, which resulted in material tax exposures.

---

[4] See, e.g., Philip von Mehren, "4 Stages of Conducting a Compliance Due Diligence," *Latin American Private Equity & Venture Capital Association*, September 23, 2014 ("The first stage in the compliance due diligence process is to carry out an informal preliminary risk assessment. The focus is to assess the extent to which the target is vulnerable to compliance risk and to identify any immediate potential "red flag" issues which need to be investigated further").

While the due diligence process may be said to begin when a buyer starts reviewing a potential target's publicly available information or, more likely, once it has started talking directly to the target's management, the due diligence process commences in earnest once the buyer and target have executed an LOI or Indication of Interest (IOI). The LOI typically provides an exclusivity period during which the buyer will complete its due diligence and sign a contract. Once the LOI and the Nondisclosure Agreement (NDA) are signed, the diligence teams start the process of reviewing the pertinent documents and holding discussions with management and the target's external advisors to confirm basic facts and to identify any issues.

While identifying red flags is not a discrete phase of the diligence process and the search for red flags or deal stoppers continues throughout the process, identifying red flags earlier rather than later in the process is beneficial, especially to the potential buyers.

Though this may sound cliché, an ounce of prevention is worth a pound of cure, and that proves true in due diligence.[5] One example is where a client decided to perform tax due diligence without outside assistance. Because the target was an "S" corporation, the client structured the transaction to achieve a tax basis step-up, which provided substantial value for the approximately $100 million deal (approximately $25 million net present value benefit). Unfortunately, the client missed the fact that the target inadvertently terminated its "S" corporation status and therefore the client would not obtain the benefit of the tax basis step-up. This issue was discovered the evening before the contract was scheduled to be signed. Fortunately, the target was able to preserve the "S" status after obtaining clearance from the IRS, but, needless to say, had this not been discovered at the last minute, the buyer may have lost the $25 million benefit.

Overall, most buyers would much rather identify any material issues regarding the target business before signing a contract than pursue the sellers for any damages after the business has been

[5] See Michael Schaefer, "Financial Due Diligence, An Ounce of Prevention is Worth a Pound of Cure," *Boulay*, January 4, 2016.

acquired. This is particularly true where the sellers remain to operate the business, in which case the buyer may have to divert sellers/management from running the business to deal with a request for indemnification.

The Different Types of Buyers and Targets

Buyers typically fall into two main classes. Financial buyers, which are private equity funds and hedge funds, which typically buy businesses with a view to selling them at a profit in 3–5 years. The other class of buyer is the strategic buyer, which is a corporate/business acquirer, which intends to buy the target business as part of its business strategy (e.g., expansion of existing business lines, new business line or as a competitive advantage). These acquirers buy with an intention of holding the acquired business and not with a view to exit the acquired business in the near term.[6]

Target businesses come in all shapes and sizes, and understanding the legal form of the target is critical to the diligence process. A target could be a multinational publicly traded company, such as when Vivendi acquired Seagrams, or a small mom-and-pop business operated as a sole proprietorship. Target businesses also come in different legal entities, including corporations, partnerships, Limited Liability Companies (LLCs), sole proprietorships, groups of assets, and divisions. Different countries may also have special entity classifications, such as the US "S" corporation, which is a tax advantaged combination of the corporation and the partnership. Divisions can be a group of assets, a corporate subsidiary, or a combination of subsidiaries and assets.

Target businesses can be located in one jurisdiction or can be located in two or more jurisdictions. If a target has operations in more than one jurisdiction, specialized diligence teams may be required for each jurisdiction, particularly if the target's jurisdictional information is in different languages.

---

[6] See Martos-Vila, Rhodes, and Harford, "Financial vs. Strategic Buyers," *Harvard Business School Working Paper*, April 9, 2014.

Types of Due Diligence

The due diligence may include a number of areas, such as legal, general business, Human Resources (HR), financial, tax, Information Technology (IT), treasury, insurance, and compliance/regulatory. The scope of due diligence and the types of diligence required will depend on the target and, to some extent, on the size of the transaction.[7] The scope of each diligence is agreed upon by the potential buyer and the diligence teams. While the discussion below is generally stated in the context of buy-side diligence where the diligence teams represent prospective buyers, the process is similar for sell-side diligence, where diligence teams assist the owners of a business prepare the business for the sale process (sell-side diligence is discussed separately below).

General Business Diligence

General business diligence focuses on the operations of the business and the business model. In many instances, the potential buyer has performed substantial diligence on this aspect of the target business prior to engaging diligence teams. Depending on the nature of the business, this may include understanding the target's customer base, the target's sales force, customer satisfaction, warranty issues, working capital requirements and seasonality. Strategic buyers will want to confirm the target's strategic fit with the buyer, understand the revenue enhancement to the buyer, and identify/confirm any potential cost savings or integration issues. Buyers will also use this process to evaluate the target's management.

Legal Due Diligence

Legal due diligence focuses on such matters as the legal standing of the target/selling entity and authority to execute the proposed

[7] See, e.g., Richard Harroch, "20 Key Due Diligence Activities in A Merger and Acquisition Transaction," *Forbes All Business*, December 19, 2014 ("Harroch").

transaction, and a review of outstanding or threatened litigation by or against the target. It may include a review of the corporate records (e.g., articles of incorporation, the corporate charter and by-laws, the stock ledger, and board minutes, financings, general governmental regulatory matters, ownership of property, including real, personal and intellectual, a review of material agreements (e.g., supplier, vendor, and customer agreements), employee and consultant agreements, and attorney letters to auditors). If the target owns any critical IP, legal diligence will likely focus on ensuring the target owns the IP and that it has properly protected the IP in each material jurisdiction. If the target has bought or sold any subsidiaries or divisions, legal diligence may identify any contingent liabilities that the target may have. Either the legal diligence team or a separate insurance team will review the target's insurance policies and requirements.

For certain transactions, more specific legal regulatory diligence may be required if, for example, the target is in a regulated industry such as banking or utilities. For certain transactions, a Hart-Scott-Rodino filing may be required (notification to the Federal Trade Commission and Department of Justice for antitrust review).

Financial Due Diligence

Financial due diligence is primarily focused on confirming that the target's historical financial performance is consistent with the financial statements and any management adjustments.[8] That is, the focus of the financial due diligence is ultimately the target's EBITDA, which is typically the critical element in determining the purchase price (as noted above, buyers are ultimately interested in a business's free cash flow, though EBITDA is used as a substitute metric). Most of the financial team's work is performed analyzing information received from management (or through the data room or banker), reviewing the audit workpapers prepared by the CPA which performed the audit of the target's financial statements, and from discussions with

[8] Lamb and Smith, "Understanding the Differences Between an Audit and Financial Due Diligence," Maxwell Locke & Ritter, www.mlrpc.com/articles, January 31, 2017.

management about the in-house financial team and the financial processes (e.g., closing of the books).

The starting point for the financial diligence is the governing principles for the target and the buyer. For example, if a US-based buyer is acquiring a US company, the buyer will want to confirm that the target's historical financial data is consistent with US Generally Accepted Accounting Principles (GAAP). An EU-based buyer would want to confirm or conform a target's business to International Financial Reporting Standards (IFRS) or perhaps local country GAAP.

The financial diligence will identify any adjustments that may be required to properly report earnings, consistent with the applicable accounting principles, as well as to identify any debt-like items. It may also include a review of margin increase/decrease, fluctuations in costs, and any projected material capital investments. Also included is a review of the Accounts Receivable and Accounts Payable ageing. The financial due diligence findings are usually communicated in a Quality of Earnings (QoE) report.

A typical QoE report contains Key Findings, which indicate the most important findings of the financial diligence process which varies depending on the target's industry, followed by a detailed review of the QoE (and in some cases a Free Cash Flow Analysis), Sales/Gross Margin Analysis, Net Debt and Debt-Like Items Analysis, and a working capital analysis. The QoE analysis includes reported (financial statement) earnings, any adjustments to earnings proposed by management and additional adjustments proposed by the diligence team. A typical QoE issue is whether revenue is recognized into earnings at the proper time under the applicable GAAP.

For closely held businesses, a typical adjustment to earnings would be for personal expenses that are charged through the company, but are not real business expenses. Personal expenses often include payroll costs of family members who perform no services for the company, personal use of cars, payments of personal credit cards, and sports tickets or other entertainment functions enjoyed by the owners and not incurred for business purposes.

A QoE report may also include an "EBITDA Bridge" that tracks changes to EBITDA over a specific period, a Customer Analysis, a Balance Sheet Analysis, and often includes the tax due diligence findings.

The QoE generally includes a calculation of the target's working capital needs that should be included with the target on the acquisition Closing date of the transaction. The importance of understanding the target's working capital needs and the mechanics of calculating the working capital adjustment in the acquisition agreement cannot be overstated. Finally, the financial diligence may include a review of the reasonableness of management's financial performance projections. Buyers often rely on the financial due diligence team to evaluate financial management and the target's financial environment, particularly whether there are appropriate procedures to ensure proper reporting and to prevent fraud.

Tax Due Diligence

Tax due diligence includes a review of the legal entities to be acquired, the jurisdictions in which they have tax reporting requirements, and whether taxes have been timely and accurately paid.[9] The taxes include federal, state/local, sales/use, property and payroll taxes in the US. Other jurisdictions may involve other taxes, such as VAT. Though not technically a tax, tax due diligence teams typically review a target company's unclaimed property (escheat) compliance.

Tax diligence generally also includes identification of any structuring opportunities to provide tax benefits to the buyer. This may include whether the transaction can be structured to provide the buyer with a step-up to the tax basis of the assets. A tax basis step-up increases free cash flow through increased tax depreciation and amortization. The availability of a tax basis step-up generally depends on the legal structure of the target company, and may also include more complex

---

[9] See Matthew Teadore "Tax Due Diligence: Because What You Don't Know Can Hurt You," Cohn Reznick, www.cohnreznick.com/insights/newsletters, June 4, 2015.

structuring techniques, such as allocating a portion of the purchase price to the sellers' personal goodwill, or an LLC drop-down.

The tax due diligence, perhaps in connection with the HR diligence, may identify any issues with nondeductibility of change of control payments under Internal Revenue Code (IRC) Section 280G (golden parachute payments), identify the target's compliance with any IRC Section 409A nonqualified compensatory agreements, and identify any independent contractors who are at risk for reclassification as employees.

HR Due Diligence

HR diligence involves reviewing the internal HR function, reviewing employee manuals and policies, employee data (demographics, location), material employee agreements and severance arrangements (including change of control agreements that may require substantial cash payments), employee compensation structure, union agreements and relationship, any labor disputes, general benefits, retirement benefits including benefit plans, labor relations, recruiting/training/development and other matters. A key focus may be non-US employee considerations, especially for jurisdictions in which it is difficult or costly to terminate personnel.

IT Due Diligence

IT diligence reviews the target's IT infrastructure, the sufficiency of the IT for the business and any planned or required upgrades, compatibility of the target's IT with the buyer's IT infrastructure and integration (for strategic deals), key risk areas and plans to address any risks. IT due diligence has become more important as IT plays a growing central role in business operations and financial reporting.

Compliance and Regulatory Due Diligence

Compliance and regulatory diligence may be necessary if the target's business is regulated and the diligence would focus on regulatory requirements, the target's compliance with required regulatory requirements, review of the in-house compliance team and the target's compliance history. If the target is located in more than one jurisdiction, diligence may need to be done in all (material) jurisdictions.

Roles

The client (i.e., the buyer) is typically the quarterback for the diligence process and manages each of the diligence teams and coordinates diligence findings, which are reported to the management committee or the person who decides whether to proceed with the transaction. Depending on the nature of the client, it may be a midlevel person at a private equity firm or may be the primary business development person at a large multinational buyer, with assistance from the buyer's internal legal, finance, tax, HR, and IT teams.

The quarterback elevates any red flags or material concerns to the decision makers as early as possible in the process. If there are no red flags or deal stoppers, the quarterback's job is to ensure that the deal price is properly vetted and to ensure that the purchase agreement properly reflects the agreed-upon structure of the transaction and addresses all material concerns. This often requires the quarterback to arrange conversations between the drafting attorneys and the respective diligence teams (e.g., for tax and HR). It may also require a review of the any working capital adjustment mechanism and language.

The client's internal team may also participate in onsite discussions with management, at the same time or separately from the various diligence teams. Typically, each team has a primary liaison with the client that is responsible for communicating with the client and completing the diligence in a timely fashion. In many due diligence processes, it is helpful to have a working group list to facilitate contact between the relevant parties and teams.

The Timing of the Due Diligence Process

General Timing

As noted above, large sophisticated strategic buyers often have clear timelines for the diligence process, whereas other buyers may have a sense of timing, but without the formalities. Private equity buyers always want diligence finished "yesterday". In some cases, this is driven by the "exclusivity period" during which the target grants the buyer the exclusive right to buy the business. Once that period ends, the target is able to court other buyers.

For "auction" processes where a target is being marketed broadly through a highly orchestrated process, the bankers may have a timeline to quickly identify the most likely buyers and then close the deal as quickly as possible. During the auction process, a number of buyers may have separate due diligence teams reviewing the business. Sellers may use the auction process to limit the amount of information provided to potential buyers, or limit the amount of time that potential buyers have to carry out diligence on the target and to create a competitive bidding environment.

However, there are occasions where buyers will use due diligence to slow down the process. This may be the case where current earnings performance is trending lower than expected and the buyer slows the diligence process to determine whether performance improves or whether a lower purchase price needs to be negotiated.

Of course, there are many situations where the due diligence process is "hot and cold," that is, the process may go quickly at times, while proceeding slowly at others. As noted above, each deal process is unique.

The NDA

A critical part of the due diligence process is execution of the NDA or confidentiality agreement.[10] This protects the target from having its nonpublic information disseminated to others, including competitors, customers or suppliers. Typically, the potential buyers execute an NDA with the target and the buyer's advisors sign a joinder to the NDA. While confidentiality is always a very serious matter, this is particularly so when a potential buyer or buyers are

---

[10] See Trent Dykes, "M&A Due Diligence: The Diligence Process (Part 2)," *The Venture Alley*, December 12, 2011 ("Dykes Part 2").

strategic and could gain a competitive advantage by accessing the target's information. As a result, in addition to requiring that the potential buyers execute strict NDAs, the target may limit access to certain information until the buyer pool is narrowed to the most likely buyers.

Obtaining Information

Once the diligence process commences, typically after an LOI or IOI is signed, the next step is to provide a request list to target management.[11] The list or lists will cover all of the diligence categories and are drafted by the respective diligence teams and tailored specifically to the target business. Some buyers have their own generic lists which they may provide to target management earlier in the process.

One of the most important factors in the timing of the due diligence process is the flow of information. If target management can provide most or all of the requested information fairly quickly, the process will also likely move quickly. The process may be impeded where the information is not well organized, not in accessible format (excel) or cannot be located. This problem may be exacerbated where the target has subsidiaries or branches outside of the parent company's jurisdiction and local documentation is not in the parent company's primary language.

Information is typically provided to potential buyers through a "data room".[12] A data room is an electronic database controlled by the target's bankers or advisors, which organizes the target's information into categories, such as general corporate documents, financial, tax, legal, regulatory, property, HR, and IT. Data rooms range from the sophisticated, such as Intralinks and Merrill Data Site, which have broad functionality, to much less sophisticated sites that are more or less shared file sites with little functionality and little or no organization. These online data sites have almost entirely replaced the data rooms of old, which were actual rooms with boxes of documents.

[11] See Dykes Part 2.
[12] See Harroch.

Other Considerations

The extent of a buyer's involvement in the due diligence process may depend on the buyer. For private equity buyers, the private equity deal team will be intimately involved in the due diligence process and may often be onsite for meetings with management and for any facilities tours. Often, the private equity team has already spent substantial time with management and may act as the gatekeeper for information requests from the various diligence teams.

Sophisticated strategic buyers may rely on their advisors to interface directly with target management and their advisors. One issue presented by the diligence process is whether the target's employees know about the process. For businesses of all sizes, knowing that the business is being sold can be disruptive. Consequently, often only senior people are aware of the transaction, and they need to have a story that explains the requests for information and the presence of the diligence teams. Often, the diligence teams are explained as outside advisors assisting management in a review.

The results of the due diligence process may be discussed among the various diligence teams, particularly with respect to review of the purchase agreement, including the impact on the structure of the transaction and the representations and warranties, along with any carveouts from the Representations and Warranties (R&W). It may also involve a discussion of the working capital adjustment and any escrow terms.

Lenders often perform their own review and may request a discussion with the diligence teams to discuss their findings. To gain access to the diligence reports prepared for the buyer, lenders will typically be required to sign nonreliance letters indicating that they made their decision to lend based on their own diligence and would not be relying on the results of the diligence report. These letters generally protect the diligence teams from any liability to the lenders.

The Contract Drafting Process

As the diligence teams finalize their findings and the buyer and seller have decided to proceed with the transaction, the buyer's and seller's legal team will start drafting the acquisition agreement. As part of this process, the buyer's legal team may discuss material findings with the various diligence teams to ensure that the buyer is adequately protected from any known or potential exposures identified during the diligence process.[13]

Part of the drafting process may involve a "working capital" adjustment to the purchase price. This ensures that the business has adequate working capital once the buyer takes over the company. This can be a particularly delicate part of the drafting process and the lawyers often discuss with the financial due diligence team which items belong and do not belong in the working capital adjustment.

R&W Insurance

R&W insurance for M&A transactions has been available for decades. However, due to costs, it has been typically reserved for extremely material issues in large transactions, for example, the tax-free status of a spin-off.

More recently, R&W insurance has been used more often in middle market transactions to cover basic issues. In the private equity world, it has become fairly commonplace, though perhaps less so in the strategic market.[14] As part of the process, the insurer may request a discussion to review the due diligence findings with the various teams (e.g., legal, financial, tax). As a result of the findings and discussions, the insurer may seek to exclude certain potential risks from the R&W insurance. One recent example is where there was a material unclaimed property issue and the insurer excluded the potential unclaimed property liability from the R&W insurance.

Completion of the R&W insurance process typically clarifies certain issues and the parties can then finalize the purchase agreement. As with lenders, the R&W insurer typically executes a nonreliance letter before obtaining the diligence reports prepared for the buyer.

---

[13] Dykes Part 2, and Dykes and Hunter.

[14] See "Due Diligence," www.referenceforbusiness.com/small/di-eq/due-diligence.

Due Diligence from the Investment Bankers' Perspective

From the sell-side banker's perspective, the diligence process allows the seller to control the process and to create a highly competitive process that will elicit the highest price for the target.[15] For example, the bankers may prepare a data room that holds only high level information. The first step may be to provide data room access to a number of potential buyers and request nonbinding bids by a specific date. During this part of the process, the bidders may or may not have access to management and/or external advisors. If access is allowed, it is typically limited.

From this first round of bids, the bankers will choose the best bidders that will be given access to additional information and perhaps additional access to management and their external advisors. In this process, the bankers use the data room as a tool to provide just enough information to whet the bidders' appetites, but not too much. There are also examples of this process being used to withhold material information so that the ultimate buyer will have to rely on the R&W in the purchase agreement to protect itself against any potential exposures that could not be identified by the information provided.

Due Diligence from the Target's Perspective

Shock. Then panic. That may be the description by the owners and management of closely held businesses when besieged by the onslaught of due diligence teams. The diligence teams request documentation and internal analyses, such as the articles of incorporation, the stock ledger, financial statements (audited, reviewed, compiled or whatever the target has), monthly trial balances, the detailed general ledger accounts, federal and state income tax returns, employee records, and seemingly endless amounts of documents. The diligence teams may also ask for information in a format that the target does not have available.

---

[15] See Kaufman and Owsley, *The Role of the Investment Banker*, LexMed Publishing, 1998.

The diligence teams also ask seemingly endless questions. And the diligence teams will likely require a minimum of documentation and information to formulate their basic understanding of the business, which will be used as the basis for further document requests and further questions. This minimum information is usually required before the diligence teams meet with management.

The diligence teams will meet with management to discuss the documents. For example, the financial due diligence team may spend 1 or 2 days meeting with management to discuss the target's accounting systems, the financial audit process, any material issues such as revenue recognition. Through this process, the financial diligence team assesses the quality of the target's internal financial controls, the quality of the financial numbers, and the quality of the management team. These findings are used to identify any adjustments to the EBITDA of the target, which is typically used as the basis for the purchase price. The findings are also reported to the client, including the quality of management.

This process is extremely intrusive and demanding. As a result, management is tasked with satisfying the diligence requests while continuing to run the business, which is quite daunting.[16]

A Word on Sell-Side and Vendor Due Diligence

Vendor due diligence (VDD) was primarily a European concept in which the target hires due diligence teams to perform financial and tax due diligence and to provide the diligence results to the potential buyers in a VDD report. The buyer typically steps into the shoes of the buyer and therefore can rely on the facts and analysis in the VDD report. Of course, the bidders will also have the opportunity to discuss the VDD findings with the professionals to confirm the results and ask for additional information and additional questions that were not addressed in the vendor report.

---

[16] "Selling Your Company: Working Through Due Diligence," *Allied Business Group*, September 2011 ("To survive due diligence, remain calm, honest and cooperative").

Sell-side due diligence is not a new phenomenon in the US, though it has become more common over the past few years. The US sell-side diligence is performed on behalf of the target but, unlike European VDD, it is not legally inherited by the buyer. Instead, it provides the owners with insight into the selling points for the business and provides the owners an opportunity to understand and perhaps address any potential issues. This is sometimes known as putting lipstick on the pig. The bidders' due diligence teams still typically perform robust due diligence even where there is a sell-side diligence report.

In certain circumstances, sell-side due diligence reports may be provided to bidders in the data room, while other times, the results of sell-side diligence is provided to target management, which picks and chooses what information to provide to the bidders.

The primary benefit of sell-side due diligence is to manage the sellers' expectations of the value of the company by identifying any adjustments to EBITDA, which may be significant in the closely held context where the owners often treat the company as their personal piggy bank, including having family members on payroll where they provide limited or no services to the company. Sell-side diligence may also identify positive adjustments to EBITDA, something which buyers' due diligence teams will rarely disclose to sellers. In addition, sell-side diligence can identify any potential issues so that management can address them prior to the M&A process. This may include resolving any issues with legal title to the equity or assets.[17]

The Role of Due Diligence Post Acquisition

Sometimes items identified during the diligence process cannot be resolved prior to closing the deal. For example, if the company is in the middle of litigation that will continue post Close, the buyer's legal team may choose to oversee the litigation and provide input as requested by the buyer.

---

[17] See Schwartzman, Deren, and Shows, "The Art of the Graceful Exit," *The Deal*, May 27, 2015.

Where the transaction involves a carveout of a business from a larger business, the buyer and seller may agree to a Transition Service Agreement (TSA) that provides for the continuation of certain services by the seller to the buyer/target business for a specific period (e.g., 12 months) after the closing of the transaction. This provides the buyer time to obtain critical services that cannot be obtained immediately and may include accounting, tax, HR and IT. The terms of the TSA are often based on the work and analysis of the diligence teams.

Any number of issues can arise post Close and the buyer may rely on the experience and knowledge of the diligence teams to assist them as these matters arise.

The Forest for the Trees

Given the multitude of investigations as part of the due diligence process, it's easy to understand why buyers get caught up in the process.

Though difficult, it makes sense to take a step back before and/or during the process to ensure the buyer's ultimate objectives are part of the plan. A few things to consider are integration of the acquired business with the buyer's business (for strategic acquisitions and private equity add-on acquisitions) and the exit timeline and strategy for financial buyers.

Another consideration is business incentives.[18] Many state and local governments provide businesses with incentives in the forms of grants and tax abatements. While some of these incentives are statutory, the most favorable incentives are negotiated. Because buyers have the most leverage before a deal is closed and preferably before it is announced, buyers should consider identifying any incentives opportunities as early in the process as possible. Understanding the

[18] See Norton Francis, "State Tax Incentives for Economic Development," Urban Institute, February 29, 2016. See also Press, Schwartzman, *et al.*, "Economic Development Incentives in a Down Economy," *The Journal of Multistate Taxation and Incentives*, June 2008.

availability and value of incentives may also give a buyer an advantage in an auction process and may provide an increased Internal Rate of Return (IRR) for a buyer.

Once a deal has been announced or closed, buyers lose a lot of leverage for negotiating incentives. That being said, all is not lost, and buyers should always consider the availability of incentives, even after Close. For those target companies that already have incentives, some incentives have claw back or other punitive measures upon a change of control. Even where there is no change of control provision in an incentives agreement, the buyer should discuss the change of control with the granting authority to ensure that the incentives will continue post Close. If the buyer plans to expand the target business, particularly headcount and capex, this may be an opportunity to seek an increase to the incentives package.

Summary

Due diligence is a daunting and dynamic process that is critical to M&A transactions. It requires orchestration of numerous professionals in various areas of expertise that often need to be completed in a fairly short time frame. The success of a deal may depend on the ability of the various diligence professionals to identify any material issues, provide the buyer with the appropriate information on how to value the business and protect the buyer from any potential exposures.

Chapter 4

The Legal and Regulatory Framework of the M&A Market

Harvey Poniachek
Rutgers Business School

Introduction

This chapter reviews the principal laws and regulations dealing with mergers and acquisitions (M&As) in the US. The US has a dual legal system of state and federal governments, and M&A activities are regulated at both the state and federal levels. Merges are governed by corporation laws of the states in which the target companies are incorporated, but the federal government regulates transactions involving securities, antitrust policies, and acquisitions in several regulated industries.

The US federal securities law includes the Exchange Act of 1933, the Securities Exchange Act of 1934, and the regulations promulgated under the Securities Exchange Commission[1] (SEC) and enforced by it. Tender offers are subject to the federal rules and regulations of the Securities Exchange Act. Solicitation of votes to approve a merger by the target company shareholders needs to

[1] http://www.sec.gov/about/laws/sa33.pdf.

comply with federal rules and regulations on proxy statements under the Exchange Act. In a merger involving securities as consideration, the securities are subject to registration requirements of the Securities Act, unless an exemption from the registration requirements is available.

The Securities Act governs the offer and sale of securities in the US, and requires that companies offering securities for sale disclose important financial information through the registration of securities, including information of their business, management and certified financial statements.[2] Registration statements are subject to SEC examination for compliance with disclosure requirements in order to enable investors to make informed judgments about whether to purchase a company's securities.

Antitrust issues are administered by the Federal Trade Commission[3] (FTC) and the Department of Justice (DOJ) and, to a lesser extent, by states. The Hart–Scott–Rodino (HSR) Act[4] requires premergers and acquisitions notification to the FTC and the DOJ by merging companies to enable the government to analyze the effects of proposed transactions on competition before the acquisitions are approved and consummated.

Foreign acquisitions of US businesses are fee of exchange controls, and government regulation,[5] with several few exceptions. The Committee on Foreign Investment in the United States (CFIUS) is an interagency committee authorized to review transactions that could result in control of a US business by a foreign person, to determine the effect of such transactions on the national security of the

---

[2] However, some securities are exempt from the registration requirement, including private offerings to a limited number of persons or institutions; offerings of limited size; intrastate offerings; and securities of municipal, state, and federal governments.

[3] https://www.ftc.gov/news-events/media-resources/mergers-and-competition/merger-review.

[4] Hart-Scott-Rodino Annual Report Fiscal Year 2015.

[5] Baker & McKenzie, A Legal Guide to Acquisitions and Doing Business in the United States, January 1, 2007.

US.[6] CFIUS operates pursuant to the Defense Production Act of 1950, as amended by the Foreign Investment and National Security Act (FINSA) of 2007.

Various other federal agencies, such as the Federal Communications Commission[7] (FCC) and the Federal Reserve Board[8] (FRB) and several other government agencies apply additional regulatory requirements over acquisitions in media and communications, banking, utilities, insurance, and airlines.

The Sarbanes–Oxley Act[9] was signed into law in 2002 and mandated several reforms to enhance corporate responsibility, enhance financial disclosures and combat corporate and accounting fraud. It also created the Public Company Accounting Oversight Board (PCAOB) to oversee the activities of the auditing profession.

The Dodd–Frank Wall Street Reform and Consumer Protection Act[10] was adopted in 2010. The legislation is designed to reshape the US regulatory system in several areas including consumer protection, trading restrictions, credit ratings, regulation of financial products, corporate governance and disclosure, and transparency.

Exhibits 1 and 2 highlight the US regulatory environment.

---

[6] https://www.treasury.gov/resource-center/international/Pages/Committee-on-Foreign-Investment-in-US.aspx; Final Regulations Issued on November 14, 2008, The US Treasury Department, on behalf of the Committee on Foreign Investment in the United States (CFIUS), issued final regulations governing CFIUS on November 14, 2008; Committee on Foreign Investment in the United States, Annual Report to Congress, CY 2014, Public Unclassified Version, Issued 2016.

[7] https://www.fcc.gov/about-fcc/what-we-do.

[8] http://www.federalreserve.gov/aboutthefed/default.htm.

[9] http://www.soxlaw.com/.

https://www.sec.gov/about/laws.shtml.

[10] https://www.whitehouse.gov/economy/middle-class/dodd-frank-wall-street-reform; https://www.sec.gov/spotlight/dodd-frank.shtml; https://www.sec.gov/about/laws.shtml.

Exhibit 1: Summary of the US Regulatory Environment

Mergers and acquisitions in the US are governed by state corporation laws, federal and state securities laws, antitrust laws; the Sarbanes–Oxley Act and the Dodd–Frank Act.

- **State Corporation Laws**
  US corporations are incorporated in states and are governed by state corporation laws, rather than by the Federal Government. States corporation laws regulate corporate governance, finance, securities, and antitrust, as well as other legal issues of doing business. Although states have their own laws, approximately 60% of the Fortune 500 companies are incorporated in Delaware and follow the Delaware General Corporation Law; Nevada follows Delaware in providing special incentives to attract corporations; and 24 states follow the Model Business Corporation Act, while New York and California are important due to their sheer economic significance. Some states have adopted legislation to impede hostile tender offers to companies registered in the states, and corporations have adopted antitakeover defenses in their articles of incorporation.

- **Securities Laws**
  Several laws govern M&As in the US, including the Securities Act of 1933, the Securities Exchange Act of 1934 and the regulation promulgated by the SEC, the Williams Act of 1968 relating to tender offers, and antitrust laws; the Sarbanes–Oxley Act of 2002 addresses financial disclosure, corporate governance, auditing, and reporting; the Dodd–Frank Act of 2010 addresses the financial services industry.

- **Antitrust Laws**
  Federal and state antitrust laws were legislated through the Sherman Act of 1890, the Clayton Act of 1914, the Federal Trade Commission Act of 1914, and the Hart–Scott–Rodino Antitrust Improvement Act of 1976. States have antitrust laws but rely predominantly on the Federal Government for the administration of antitrust laws for M&As: US antitrust law prohibits M&As that could reduce competition or create a monopoly. Proposed M&As in the US must file HSR premerger notification with the US DOJ or the FTC. Parties to proposed transactions wait 30 days after the filing to complete the acquisition, and the DOJ or FTC may request additional information during the waiting period thereby prolonging the waiting period. Parties to deals are not permitted to proceed their proposed deal before the government's approval.

- **Foreign Direct Investment Laws**
  Foreign acquisitions of US businesses are free of exchange controls, government regulation.[11] That is, a foreign-owned enterprise is free to invest capital and to

(*Continued*)

[11] Baker & McKenzie, A Legal Guide to Acquisitions and Doing Business in the United States, January 1, 2007.

Exhibit 1: (*Continued*)

remit profits, repatriate capital and pay interest and royalties to a non-US parent without any restriction. Foreign-owned enterprises enjoy equal access to federal and state incentives and benefits programs, with few exceptions, and some states offer tax and other incentives to attract foreign manufacturers to their states. However, certain acquisitions of US companies by foreign-owned enterprises are subject to some regulations and reporting requirements.

- The Exon-Florio provision authorizes the President of the US to review certain M&As of US companies or businesses by non-US entities. The US President is empowered to suspend or prohibit any such acquisition, or order divestment of the acquired company if the acquisition has been completed, if such transactions might threaten US national security. The US President has delegated the authority to CFIUS.

- **Industry Specific Laws**
Ownership by non-US persons of certain restricted industries is limited or regulated by the federal government or some state governments. Restricted industries include the defense, banking, insurance, domestic air or water transportation, fishing, and radio and television broadcasting industries and in some states, the railroad industry and agricultural and other real estate.[12]
Various other federal agencies, such as the Federal Communications Commission[13] (FCC) and the Federal Reserve Board[14] (FRB) and several other government agencies apply additional regulatory requirements over acquisitions in media and communications, banking, utilities, insurance, and airlines.

- Sarbanes–Oxley Act[15] was signed into law in 2002 and mandated several reforms to enhance corporate responsibility, enhance financial disclosures and combat corporate and accounting fraud. It also created the Public Company Accounting Oversight Board (PCAOB) to oversee the activities of the auditing profession.

- The Dodd–Frank Wall Street Reform and Consumer Protection Act[16] was adopted in 2010. The legislation is designed to reshape the US regulatory system in several areas including consumer protection, trading restrictions, credit ratings, regulation of financial products, corporate governance and disclosure, and transparency.

---

[12] Baker & McKenzie, A Legal Guide to Acquisitions and Doing Business in the United States, January 1, 2007.
[13] https://www.fcc.gov/about-fcc/what-we-do.
[14] http://www.federalreserve.gov/aboutthefed/default.htm.
[15] http://www.soxlaw.com/.
https://www.sec.gov/about/laws.shtml.
[16] https://www.whitehouse.gov/economy/middle-class/dodd-frank-wall-street-reform; https://www.sec.gov/spotlight/dodd-frank.shtml; https://www.sec.gov/about/laws.shtml.

Exhibit 2: The Regulatory Framework for M&As

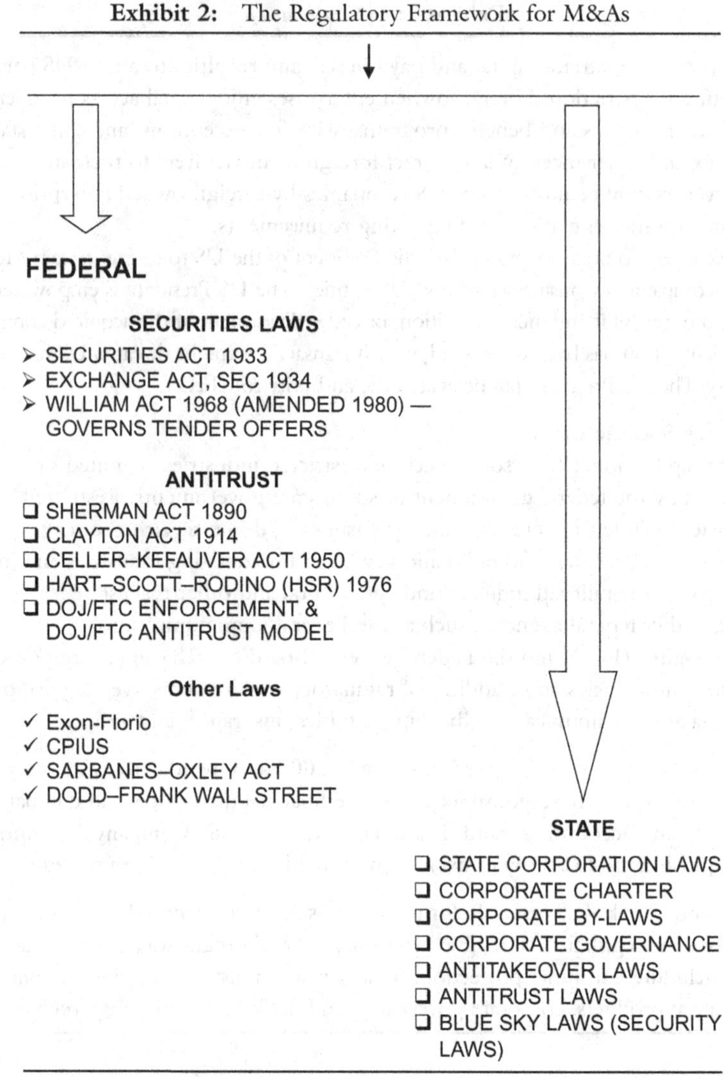

FEDERAL
SECURITIES LAWS
SECURITIES ACT 1933
EXCHANGE ACT, SEC 1934
WILLIAM ACT 1968 (AMENDED 1980) — GOVERNS TENDER OFFERS
ANTITRUST
SHERMAN ACT 1890
CLAYTON ACT 1914
CELLER–KEFAUVER ACT 1950
HART–SCOTT–RODINO (HSR) 1976
DOJ/FTC ENFORCEMENT & DOJ/FTC ANTITRUST MODEL
Other Laws
Exon-Florio
CPIUS
SARBANES–OXLEY ACT
DODD–FRANK WALL STREET
STATE
STATE CORPORATION LAWS
CORPORATE CHARTER
CORPORATE BY-LAWS
CORPORATE GOVERNANCE
ANTITAKEOVER LAWS
ANTITRUST LAWS
BLUE SKY LAWS (SECURITY LAWS)

Source: Harvey Poniachek.

State Laws and Regulations

US corporations are incorporated in states and are governed by state corporation laws, which regulate corporate governance, finance, securities, antitrust, as well as other legal issues of doing business. States have their own laws, and approximately 60% of the Fortune 500 companies are incorporated in Delaware and follow the Delaware General Corporation Law; Nevada follows Delaware in providing special incentives to attract corporations; 24 states follow the Model Business Corporation Act[17]; and New York and California are significant players due to their sheer economic size.

Each of the 50 states regulate securities transactions pursuant to blue sky laws unless pre-empted by Section 18 of the 1933 Act. Almost every state requires that securities, other than covered securities, sold in the state be registered.[18] However, under the National Securities Markets Improvement Act (NSMIA) of 1996, offers and sales of "covered securities" need not be registered under state blue sky laws.[19]

---

[17] Model Business Corporation Act (2010), American Bar Association.

[18] *Outline of Legal Aspects of Mergers & Acquisitions in the U.S., 15th Ed.*, 2013, Overview of State Securities Laws.

[19] SEC, Report on the Uniformity of State Regulatory Requirements for Offerings of Securities That Are Not "Covered Securities", *Pursuant to Section 102(b) of the National Securities Markets Improvement Act of 1996, October 11, 1997*, https://www.sec.gov/news/studies/uniformy.htm.

An offering of securities must be registered under both the federal Securities Act of 1933 ("Securities Act") and applicable state securities laws, unless an exemption from registration is available. This dual system of federal-state regulation has extsted since the Securities Act was adopted. However, the National Securities Markets Improvement Act of 1996 (NSMIA) significantly realigns the regulatory partnership between federal and state regulators. Securities Act Section 18(a) pre-empts state "blue-sky" registration and review of specified securities and offerings. NSMIA refers to the securities in these pre-empted offerings as "covered securities." That is, covered securities include securities listed or authorized for listing on a national securities exchange.

Offerings of "covered securities" are for the most part subject only to federal regulation. Offerings of securities that are not "covered securities" continue to be subject to a dual system of federal-state regulation, including registration and review. However, NSMIA recognized the vital role played by the states in the regulation of offerings of securities that are not "covered securities." Securities that are not "covered securities" remain subject to state registration and review, and include, among others:

- securities traded on the Nasdaq Small Cap system or quoted on the NASD OTC Bulletin Board system;
- securities listed on securities markets other than the NYSE, AMEX or the National Market System of the Nasdaq Stock Market ("Nasdaq NMS");

State Antitakeover Laws

The corporation law applicable to an M&A transaction is determined by the state in which the target company is incorporated.[20] State corporation law restrictions on takeovers vary and in some cases reflect a policy of seeking to protect the interests of the state or other constituencies, in addition to the interests of the target's stockholders.[21] States apply various antitakeover controls,[22] as follows.

Business Combination Statutes

Business combination statutes prohibit an acquirer from consummating a business combination for a period after becoming a stockholder. The effect of such statutes is to reduce the attractiveness of pursuing a takeover target in the face of opposition from the target's board by limiting the acquirer's ability to consolidate the acquisition through a second step squeeze-out transaction.

For instance, Delaware General Corporation Law (DGCL) prohibits an acquirer of 15% or more of a company's outstanding stock

---

- various debt securities of nonlisted issuers, including asset-backed and mortgage-backed securities;
- securities issued in private placements under Section 4(2) of the Securities Act that do not meet the requirements of Rule 506 under Regulation D;
- securities issued in Rule 504 and 505 offerings under Regulation D; and
- securities issued under Regulation A.

[20] Michal Barzuza, The State of State Antitakeover Law, *Virginia Law Review, vol. 95, 2009, pp. 1973–2052.* The author examines state antitakeover law outside Delaware, and finds substantial variations from Delaware's law. Unlike Delaware, most of the states with relatively strong constituency and pill endorsement statutes do not impose enhanced fiduciary duties on managers in change-of-control situations. Instead, they apply only the ordinary business judgment rule to management's use of antitakeover tactics. This Article provides support for adopting Delaware's enhanced fiduciary duties — Unocal, Revlon, and Blasius — as federally imposed minimum standards.

[21] Emiliano Catan and Marcel Kahan, The Law and Finance of Anti-Takeover Statutes, New York University School of Law, Law & Economics Research Paper Series, Working Paper No. 14–30, 2016.

[22] Joseph V. Cuomo, State Regulation of Hostile Takeovers: The Constitutionality of Third Generation Business Combination Statutes and the Role of the Courts, *St. John's Law Review*, volume 64, issue 1, 1989, p. 1.

from engaging for a 3-year period following the acquisition, in any business combination with the company.[23] More specifically, under DGCL § 203 Business Combinations with Interested Stockholders,[24] merging companies are subject to the following regulation: A corporation shall not engage in any business combination with any interested stockholder for a period of 3 years following the time that such stockholder became an interested stockholder, unless:

(1) the board of directors of the corporation approved either the business combination or the transaction which resulted in the stockholder becoming an interested stockholder;
(2) upon consummation of the transaction which resulted in the stockholder becoming an interested stockholder, the interested stockholder owned at least 85% of the voting stock of the corporation outstanding at the time the transaction commenced, excluding for purposes of determining the voting stock outstanding (but not the outstanding voting stock owned by the interested stockholder) those shares owned (i) by persons who are directors and also officers and (ii) employee stock plans in which employee participants do not have the right to determine confidentially whether shares held subject to the plan will be tendered in a tender or exchange offer; or
(3) the business combination is approved by the board of directors and authorized at an annual or special meeting of stockholders ... by the affirmative vote of at least 66⅔% of the outstanding voting stock which is not owned by the interested stockholder.

Control Share Statutes

Control share statutes restrict the ability of acquirers to vote shares that they acquire without board or unaffiliated shareholder approval

---

[23] State of Delaware, Title 8, Corporations, Chapter 1. General Corporation Law, Subchapter IX. Merger, Consolidation or Conversion. See http://delcode.delaware.gov/title8/c001/sc09/index.shtml.

[24] State of Delaware, Title 8, Corporations, Chapter 1. General Corporation Law, Subchapter VI. Stock Transfers, http://delcode.delaware.gov/title8/c001/sc06/.

beyond certain thresholds. The effect is to prevent an unsolicited acquirer from voting shares obtained in a transaction without the approval of the target's board. Delaware does not have a control share statute.

Fair Price Statutes

The fair price in the second-step merger should at least equal to the highest price paid by a bidder for shares it previously acquired. Over a fourth of the states have fair price statutes but Delaware does not.

Director Discretion Statutes

A board of director does not need to focus only on maximizing stockholder value when considering a potential business combination, but should consider the impact of the decision on all other stakeholders as well. Over a fourth of the states have such statutes.

Authorized Defenses

Over a third of the states authorize defensive action, either by statute or case law, by a target's board to defend against a hostile bid, including adopting a shareholders' rights plan (a poison pill) without shareholder approval.

Federal Securities Laws

The Securities Act of 1933[25]

The Securities Act of 1933 has two basic objectives: (1) Require that investors receive financial and other significant information concerning securities being offered for public sale; and prohibit deceit, misrepresentations, and other fraud in the sale of securities. The primary means of accomplishing these goals is the disclosure of important and

[25] https://www.sec.gov/about/laws.shtml;http://www.sec.gov/about/laws/sa33.pdf.

accurate financial information through the registration of securities. This information enables investors to make informed judgments about whether to purchase a company's securities. (2) Securities sold in the US must be registered. The registration provides:

- o a description of the company's properties and business;
- o a description of the security to be offered for sale;
- o information about the management of the company; and
- o financial statements certified by independent accountants.

Registration statements and prospectuses become public shortly after filing with the SEC. Registration statements are subject to examination for compliance with disclosure requirements. Some securities that are exempt from the registration requirement include:

- o private offerings to a limited number of persons or institutions;
- o offerings of limited size;
- o intrastate offerings; and
- o securities of municipal, state, and federal governments.

The Securities Exchange Act of 1934[26]

With this Act, Congress created the Securities and Exchange Commission (SEC) with broad authority over all aspects of the securities industry. This includes the power to register, regulate, and oversee brokerage firms, transfer agents, and clearing agencies as well as the nation's securities self-regulatory organizations (SROs). The various securities exchanges, such as the New York Stock Exchange, the NASDAQ Stock Market, and the Chicago Board of Options are SROs. The Financial Industry Regulatory Authority (FINRA) is also an SRO.

The Act also identifies and prohibits certain types of conduct in the markets and provides the Commission with disciplinary powers over regulated entities and persons associated with them. The Act empowers the SEC to require periodic reporting of information by

[26] http://www.sec.gov/about/laws/sea34.pdf.

companies with publicly traded securities. Companies with more than $10 million in assets whose securities are held by more than 500 owners must file with the SEC annual and other periodic reports that are available to the public.

Proxy Solicitations

The SEC requires that shareholders of a company whose securities are registered under Section 12 of the Securities Exchange Act of 1934 receive a proxy statement prior to a shareholder meeting.[27] The information must be filed with the SEC before soliciting a shareholder vote on the election of directors and the approval of other corporate action. Solicitations, whether by management or shareholders, must disclose all important facts about the issues on which shareholders are asked to vote. Solicitations, whether by management or shareholder groups, must disclose all important facts concerning the issues on which holders are asked to vote. Regulations 14A and 14C of the Exchange Act govern solicitations of shareholders in proxy contests and consent solicitations for the control of a public company's board of directors.

Under the Exchange Act, parties who will own more than 5% of a class of the company's securities after making a tender offer for securities registered under the Exchange Act must file a Schedule TO with the SEC. The SEC also requires any person acquiring more than 5% of a voting class of a company's Section 12 registered equity securities directly or by tender offer to file a Schedule 13D. Depending upon the facts and circumstances, the person or group of persons may be eligible to file the more abbreviated Schedule 13G *in lieu* of Schedule 13D.

All executive officers and directors and 10% or more shareholders of a company with securities registered under the Exchange Act (i.e., through the filing of a Form 10 or Form 8-A) are subject to the Exchange Act Reporting Requirements related to the reporting of certain transactions. The initial filing is on Form 3 and is due no later than 10 days of becoming an officer, director, or beneficial owner.

---

[27] http://www.sec.gov/answers/proxy.htm.

Changes in ownership are reported on Form 4 and must be reported to the SEC within two business days. Insiders must file a Form 5 to report any transactions that should have been reported earlier on a Form 4 or were eligible for deferred reporting. If a form must be filed, it is due 45 days after the end of the company's fiscal year.

Tender Offer

A tender offer is a broad solicitation by a company or a third party to purchase a substantial percentage of a company's registered equity shares for a limited period.[28] The offer is at a fixed price, usually at a premium over the current market price, and is customarily contingent on shareholders tendering a fixed number of their shares or units. Such an offer often is extended in an effort to gain control of the company.

The Williams Act[29] of 1968 was enacted as amendment to the Securities Exchange Act of 1934 and addresses tender offers. The Act requires any person who makes a tender offer for a corporation to disclose to the SEC the source of the funds used in the offer, the purpose of the offer, the plans if successful, and any contracts with the target corporation. The Securities Exchange Act requires disclosure of important information by anyone seeking to acquire more than 5% of a company's securities by direct purchase or tender offer. As with the proxy rules, this allows shareholders to make informed decisions on these critical corporate events.

Section 13(d) of the Exchange Act requires the disclosure of an acquisition of 5% of equity in a public company by filing Schedule 13D and Schedule TO with the SEC within 10 days of the acquisition. Required information disclosure includes the identity of each person deemed to be a beneficial owner, the nature and size of such person's interest in the securities, the source of funds used, such person's purpose in acquiring the securities (including future plans with respect to any transactions involving the issuer) and any contracts or other arrangements with respect to any securities of the issuer.

---

[28] https://www.sec.gov/answers/tender.htm.
[29] https://www.sec.gov/about/laws.shtml.

Sections 14(d) and (e) of the Exchange Act govern tender and exchange offers. The filings required by Section 14(d) of the Exchange Act and Regulation 14D provide information to the public about persons other than the company who make a tender offer.[30] A bidder must make its offer available to all holders of securities of the same class, and the price paid to each holder must be the best price offered to any holder of the same class of securities.

The Williams Act and the SEC's promulgated regulations control tender offers and affect the manner and length of time in which transactions are conducted. Tender offer rules apply when a company offers securities and/or cash in payment for a target's outstanding securities, and the regulations vary with the type of payment offered.[31] In an exchange offer transaction of stock for stock, the tender offer rules apply in addition to the requirement that the issuer registers the offered stock or meets the conditions for an exemption.

The Williams Act does not define what constitutes a "tender offer."[32] However, in *Wellman v. Dickinson*,[33] the court approved the use of eight factors suggested by the SEC to determine whether a series of purchases constitutes a tender offer and triggers the US tender offer rules. Not all the eight factors need to be present for a transaction to be deemed a tender offer, and the weight given to each factor element varies with facts and circumstances of the transaction.[34] The eight factors are as follows:

1. Active and widespread solicitation of public shareholders;
2. Solicitation made for a substantial percentage of the target's stock;
3. Offer is at a premium to the prevailing market price;

---

[30] https://www.sec.gov/answers/tender.htm.

[31] Lynn, David M., Tender Offer Considerations for Cash Repurchases and Exchange Offers, Morrison Forester, News Bulletin, July 1, 2009.

[32] Amy Bowerman Freed and Alexander B. Johnson, Overview of Tender Offers, LextsNexts, June 2007.

[33] See 475 F. Supp. 783, 823–24 (S.D.N.Y. 1979), *aff'd on other grounds,* 682 F.2d 355 (2d Cir. 1982), *cert. denied,* 460 US 1069 (1983).

[34] Thomas Lee Hazen, *Federal Securities Law*, 2nd *Ed.,* Federal Judicial Center, 2003.

4. Terms are fixed rather than negotiable;
5. Offer contingent on the tender of a fixed minimum number of shares to be purchased;
6. Offer is only open for a limited period of time;
7. Offerees are subjected to pressure to sell their stock; and
8. Public announcements of a purchase program for the target's securities precede or accompany rapid accumulation of large amounts of the target's securities.

The acquirer commences a tender offer by publishing a summary offer in a daily newspaper with national circulation and the tender offer commences at noon on that day.

Tender offers are governed by federal securities laws and the SEC regulations, as well as by the state corporation laws.[35] Under the Securities Exchange Act of 1934, parties who will own more than 5% of a company's securities following a tender offer must file a Schedule TO with the SEC. The SEC also requires any person acquiring more than 5% of a voting class of a company's registered equity securities directly or by tender offer to file a Schedule 13D.

The SEC's tender offer rules generally do not apply to tender offers that result in ownership of 5% or less of the outstanding shares, also known as "mini-tender offers." "Mini-tender" offers are tender offers that, when consummated, will result in the person who makes the tender offer owning less than 5% of a company's stock.[36]

The acquirer sets the terms and conditions of its offer to purchase shares, including the price it will pay and the number of shares it is seeking to buy. The minimum number of shares is set to obtain a majority of the target's shares. The offer is made to all stockholders and they each pay the same price. The tender offer must be open for at least 20 business days, a tender offer statement on Schedule TO

---

[35] B. Jeffrey Bell, ESQ, Morrison Foerster, The Acquisition of Control of a United States Public Company, 2016; https://media2.mofo.com/documents/1302-the-acquisition-of-control-of-a-united-states-public-company.pdf.

[36] https://www.sec.gov/answers/miniten.htm.

must be filed with the SEC with a significant amount of disclosure,[37] and the offer must be kept open for at least 10 US business days following any change in price or a change in the percentage of the class of target securities sought. If the offer is oversubscribed, the acquirer is required to purchase a pro rata portion of the shares tendered by each stockholder. In addition, each shareholder has the right to withdraw any shares tendered at any time during the period that the tender offer remains open. SEC rules and merger agreements permit the acquirer to use one or more "subsequent offering periods" to keep the offer open in order to purchase the minimum required number of shares. If the issuer increases the consideration offered after the tender offer has commenced, then the issuer must pay the same to all security holders whose tendered securities are accepted for payment.

Within 10 business days of commencement of a tender offer, the target must file a Solicitation/Recommendation Statement on Schedule 14D-9 with the SEC and deliver it to its stockholders, which contains the target board's position on the tender offer. The target's board must disclose its views on the tender offer by recommending the acceptance or rejection of the offer, expressing no opinion, or explaining that it cannot take a position at that time. The target must also disclose whether its financial advisor believes the acquirer's offer is fair and whether the executive officers and directors intend to tender their shares.

---

[37] The information required by Schedule TO includes:

- A summary term sheet;
- Information about the issuer;
    - The identity and background of filing persons;
    - The terms of the transaction;
    - Any past contacts, transactions and negotiations;
    - The purposes of the transactions and plans or proposals;
    - The source and amount of funds or other consideration for the tender offer;
    - Interests in subject securities;
    - Persons/assets retained, employed, compensated or used;
    - Financial statements;
    - Additional information;
    - Exhibits; and
    - To the extent applicable, information required by Schedule 13E-3.

If the acquirer completes the tender offer and obtains 90% of the target common shares (in some states, this percentage is as low as 85%), the acquirer can implement a squeeze out of the minority shareholders through a short-form merger, without the approval of any other shareholder of the target company, and acquire all remaining target common shares. Minority shareholders have the right to seek appraisal through a court proceeding, but it should not delay the implementation of the short-form merger. If the acquirer does not receive several target common shares sufficient to permit a short-form merger, the acquirer and the target company will then proceed to implement a long-form merger.

Under Section 251(h) of the Delaware General Corporation Law, if a target company is incorporated in Delaware and the acquirer makes a tender offer for all its shares pursuant to an agreement with the target board of directors and obtains enough shares of the target company, the acquisition could be implemented. The acquirer could acquire the remaining target common shares for the same consideration as the acquirer paid in the tender offer. Target shareholders that are acquired in a 251(h) merger will have the right to seek appraisal. Other than Rule 13e-3 (if applicable), there are no disclosure requirements imposed by the federal securities laws with respect to the 251(h) merger.

Antitrust Laws

US antitrust laws were first legislated in 1890 with the passage of the Sherman Act and then in 1914 with the enactment of the Clayton Act and various refinements through amendment over time.[38] The HSR Antitrust Improvements Act (or HSR Act) of 1976[39] requires companies to file premerger notifications with the FTC and the Antitrust Division of the DOJ. The HSR, together with Section 13(b) of the

---

[38] Alden F. Abbott, A Brief Overview of American Antitrust Law, The University of Oxford Centre for Competition Law and Policy, The Competition Law & Policy Guest Lecture Programme Paper (L) 01/05.

[39] http://uscode.house.gov/view.xhtml?req=granuleid%3AUSC-prelim-title15-section18a.

FTC Act and Section 15 of the Clayton Act, enables the FTC and the Antitrust Division of the DOJ to prevent anticompetitive mergers.[40]

The premerger notification program provides the government agencies with information about large mergers and acquisitions before they occur.[41] HSR preacquisition notification regulations require companies to refrain from consummating merger transactions before the expiration of specified waiting periods, thereby enabling the government to analyze the effects of the proposed acquisition on competition before the acquisition is consummated.[42] For instance, in fiscal year 2015, the premerger notification program was instrumental in alerting the FTS and DOJ to transactions that became the subjects of numerous enforcement actions against anticompetitive mergers.

The FTC has revised the monetary thresholds that determine whether companies are required to notify federal antitrust authorities about a transaction under Section 7A of the Clayton Act.[43] The HSR Antitrust Improvements Act, Section 7A of the Clayton Act, requires companies proposing a merger or acquisition to notify federal authorities if the size of the parties involved and the value of a transaction exceed certain monetary thresholds, in the absence of an applicable exemption. The FTC revises the thresholds set forth in the HSR Act annually, based on the change in the gross national product. As a result of this revision, the size-of-transaction threshold for reporting proposed M&As subject to antitrust enforcement increases from $76.3 million for 2015 to $78.2 million for 2016.

The parties to certain proposed transactions must submit premerger notification to the FTC and DOJ. Premerger notification

---

[40] Hart–Scott–Rodino Annual Report Fiscal Year 2015, https://www.ftc.gov/system/files/documents/reports/federal-trade-commission-bureau-competition-department-justice-antitrust-division-hart-scott-rodino/160801hsrreport.pdf.

[41] https://www.ftc.gov/enforcement/premerger-notification-program.

[42] Randolph Tritell and Elizabeth Kraus, The Federal Trade Commission's International Antitrust Program, FTC, April 2016. The FTC's international antitrust program aims to (i) support the FTC's competition enforcement program by assisting with international aspects of investigations and litigation, (ii) promote cooperation with competition agencies in other jurisdictions, and (iii) promote convergence of international antitrust policies toward best practice.

[43] FTC Announces New Clayton Act Monetary Thresholds for 2016, January 21, 2016.

involves completing an HSR Form, also called a "Notification and Report Form for Certain Mergers and Acquisitions." The notification requires information concerning the proposed transaction, financial information of the transacting parties, lists of subsidiaries, and the identities of holders of 5% or more of its stock. The regulations require the submission, together with the notification form, of any documents prepared in connection with the transaction "for the purpose of evaluating or analyzing the acquisition with respect to market shares, competition, competitors, markets, potential for sales growth or expansion into product or geographic markets."

After filing the HSR form, the parties cannot close the acquisition unless a 30-day waiting period has expired so that the reviewing agency (either the FTC or the DOJ) has an opportunity to determine whether the proposed transaction raises substantive antitrust issues. This waiting period is reduced to 15 days in an all-cash tender offer. If the initial waiting period expires with neither the FTC nor DOJ making a second request, the parties can proceed with the transaction.

However, the reviewing agency may seek additional information about the transaction during the waiting period by making an informal request or by issuing a second request, which can include a lengthy set of document requests and interrogatories. A second request extends the waiting period by 30 days from the date that the required additional information is submitted. Compliance with a second request can take several months. At the conclusion of the HSR notification process, the reviewing agency can approve the transaction as proposed, seek to block it in court, or reach a settlement with the parties to the transaction. Settlements can involve restructuring the proposed transaction so that fewer assets are acquired or may involve an agreement by the acquirer to restrict the manner in which it conducts business following the closing.

In many merger investigations, the potential for competitive harm is not a result of the transaction as a whole, but rather occurs only in certain lines of business. The parties may resolve the concerns about the merger by agreeing to sell off the particular overlapping business unit or assets of one of the merging parties, but then complete the remainder of the merger as proposed. This allows the procompetitive benefits of the merger to be realized without creating the potential for anticompetitive harm. Many merger challenges are resolved with a consent agreement between the agency and the merging parties.

The government (or another plaintiff) may challenge a merger before it is consummated and seek an injunction blocking the merger. If an antitrust agency concludes that consummation of the transaction would constitute a violation, it may institute litigation based upon alleged violations of the Federal antitrust laws. The government (including state attorneys general (AGs)) may also challenge a merger after it is consummated, seeking divestiture. However, most merger challenges are resolved through consent decrees. Merger consent decrees generally require that overlapping businesses or smaller sets of assets be sold to competitively suitable acquirers approved by the antitrust agency.

The FTC administrative proceedings may result in a cease and desist order (including divestiture of acquisitions). Violation of an FTC order may lead to a civil penalty action in Federal court. The FTC may also seek disgorgement. of anticompetitive profits in actions in Federal court.

All 50 states have antitrust statutes, which are similar to the federal antitrust laws, and may be enforced by the state AGs and by private parties. State AGs may also bring actions under the federal antitrust laws. Both federal and state antitrust statutes allow for private antitrust enforcement.

The Horizontal Merger Guidelines

The Antitrust Division of the DOJ and the FTC have jointly issued guidelines setting forth the methodology they will use in determining whether proposed mergers or other combinations are likely to be challenged as violating the Federal antitrust laws. The Horizontal Merger Guidelines[44] (Guidelines) outline the principal analytical techniques, practices, and the enforcement policy of the DOJ and the FTC with respect to M&As involving actual or potential competitors under the federal antitrust laws. The principal federal statutory

[44] US DOJ and the FTC, Horizontal Merger Guidelines, August 19, 2010, https://www.justice.gov/atr/horizontal-merger-guidelines-08192010.

provisions governing mergers include Section 7 of the Clayton Act, 15 U.S.C. § 18, Sections 1 and 2 of the Sherman Act, 15 U.S.C. § 1, 2, and Section 5 of the FTC Act, 15 U.S.C. § 45.[45] Most particularly, Section 7 of the Clayton Act prohibits mergers if "in any line of commerce or in any activity affecting commerce in any section of the country, the effect of such acquisition may be substantially to lessen competition, or to tend to create a monopoly."

Merger enforcement policy is complex and it evolved over time, and since 1982, it is articulated by the Horizontal Merger Guidelines that contain five key sections that constitute an integrated framework for assessment of the competitive effects of a merger. The Guidelines constitute a model that affords the FTC and DOJ to assess the competitive effect of a merger, but its application is still subject to a considerable amount of judgmental inputs. Therefore, different analysts are likely to come up with different conclusions.

The government seeks to identify and challenge competitively harmful mergers. Most merger analysis is necessarily predictive, requiring an assessment of what will likely happen if a merger proceeds or if it does not. These Guidelines are intended to assist the business community and antitrust practitioners by increasing the transparency of the analytical process underlying the Agencies' enforcement decisions. They may also assist the courts in developing an appropriate framework for interpreting and applying the antitrust laws in the horizontal merger context.

Merger analysis does not consist of uniform application of a single methodology, but is rather a fact-specific process through which the government, guided by their extensive experience, applies a range of analytical tools to the available and reliable evidence to evaluate competitive concerns in a limited period of time.

The unifying theme of these Guidelines is that mergers should not be permitted to create, enhance, or entrench market power or to facilitate its exercise. A merger enhances market power if it is likely to encourage one or more firms to raise price, reduce output, diminish

---

[45] Guidelines; William Blumenthal, King & Spalding, Washington, D.C, Mergers Analysis Under the U.S. Antitrust Laws, 2016, http://www.kslaw.com/library/pdf/wb_merger_outline.pdf.

innovation, or otherwise harm customers as a result of diminished competitive constraints or incentives. A merger can enhance market power simply by eliminating competition between the merging parties. This effect can arise even if the merger causes no changes in the way other firms behave. A merger also can enhance market power by increasing the risk of coordinated, accommodating, or interdependent behavior among rivals.

These Guidelines describe how the government analyze mergers between rival suppliers that may enhance their market power as sellers. Enhancement of market power by sellers often elevates the prices charged to customers. Enhanced market power can be manifested in nonprice terms and conditions that adversely affect customers, including reduced product quality, reduced product variety, reduced service, or diminished innovation. Enhanced market power may also make it more likely that the merged entity can profitably and effectively engage in exclusionary conduct. Regardless of how enhanced market power would be manifested, the Agencies normally evaluate mergers based on their impact on customers. The Agencies examine effects on either or both of the direct customers and the final consumers.

Enhancement of market power by buyers, sometimes called "monopsony power," has adverse effects comparable to enhancement of market power by sellers. The first step in the merger analysis is to identify the relevant product and geographic markets and assess whether the merger would significantly increase concentration in any of those relevant markets. The measure of concentration takes into account the pre- and postmerger size.

Market Definition and Concentration

When the Agencies identify a potential competitive concern with a horizontal merger, the market definition allows them to measure market shares and market concentration of the merging parties.[46] The

[46] US Department of Justice and the Federal Trade Commission, Horizontal Merger Guidelines, Issued: August 19, 2010.

measurements are useful to illuminate the merger's competitive effects. A reduction in the number of competitors could reduce competition and cause product prices to rise, which may predict the competitive effects of a merger. Market concentration and market share data are normally based on historical evidence, but the Agencies may project historical market shares into the foreseeable future when this can be done reliably. Each firm's market share is based on revenues in the relevant market.

Market concentration is often a useful indicator of likely competitive effects of a merger, and the Agencies consider both the postmerger level of market concentration and the change in concentration resulting from a merger. The Agencies give more weight to market concentration when market shares have been stable over time. The Agencies may consider the combined market share of the merging firms as an indicator of the extent to which others in the market may not be able readily to replace competition between the merging firms that is lost through the merger.

The Agencies calculate the Herfindahl–Hirschman Index (HHI) of market concentration, by summing the squares of the individual firms' market shares, and thus gives proportionately greater weight to the larger market shares. The Agencies consider both the postmerger level of the HHI and the increase in the HHI resulting from the merger. See Exhibit 3 for details.

Entry

As part of their assessment of competitive effects, the Agencies consider whether the prospect of entry into the relevant market could alleviate adverse competitive effects if such entry could expand output and keep low prices so the merger will not harm customers. A merger is not likely to enhance market power if entry into the market is very easy and merged firms probably could not raise price or otherwise reduce competition compared to the level that would prevail in the absence of the merger.

Exhibit 3: Post-Merger Market Concentration Types

The Agencies employ three standards for markets concentration:

- Unconcentrated Markets: HHI below 1,500
  Mergers resulting in unconcentrated markets are unlikely to have adverse competitive effects and ordinarily require no further analysis. Mergers involving *small change in concentration* by an increase in the HHI of less than 100 points are unlikely to have adverse competitive effects and ordinarily require no further analysis.
- Moderately Concentrated Markets: HHI between 1,500 and 2,500
  Mergers resulting in moderately concentrated markets that involve an increase in the HHI of more than 100 points potentially raise significant competitive concerns and often warrant scrutiny.
- Highly Concentrated Markets: HHI above 2,500
  Mergers resulting in highly concentrated markets that involve an increase in the HHI of between 100 points and 200 points potentially raise significant competitive concerns and often warrant scrutiny. Mergers resulting in highly concentrated markets are likely to enhance market power. The presumption may be rebutted by evidence showing that the merger is unlikely to enhance market power.

Efficiencies

A primary benefit of mergers to the economy is their potential to generate significant efficiencies and thus enhance the merged firm's ability and incentive to compete, which may result in lower prices, improved quality, enhanced service, or new products. Efficiencies also may lead to new or improved products, even if they do not immediately and directly affect price.

The Agencies credit those efficiencies that are likely to be accomplished with the proposed merger. However, efficiencies are difficult to verify and quantify, in part because much of the information relating to efficiencies is uniquely in the possession of the merging firms.

Failure and Exiting Assets

A merger is not likely to enhance market power if imminent failure of one of the merging firms would cause it to exit the relevant market. By exiting the market, customers will be worse off than they would be with the merger.

Regulation of Acquisitions by Foreign Persons (Exon-Florio)

Foreign acquisitions of US businesses are free of exchange controls, and government regulation,[47] with several few exceptions. That is, a foreign-owned enterprise is free to invest capital and to remit profits, repatriate capital and pay interest and royalties to a non-US parent without any restriction. Foreign-owned enterprises enjoy equal access to federal and state incentives and benefits programs, with few exceptions, and some states offer tax and other incentives to attract foreign manufacturers to their states. However, certain acquisitions of US companies by foreign-owned enterprises are subject to some regulations and reporting requirements.

The CFIUS is an interagency committee authorized to review transactions that could result in control of a US business by a foreign person, to determine the effect of such transactions on the national security of the US.[48] CFIUS operates pursuant to Section 721 of the Defense Production Act of 1950, as amended by the Foreign Investment and National Security Act of 2007 (FINSA). FINSA codifies aspects of the structure, role, process, and responsibilities of the CFIUS (or "the Committee") and the role of executive branch departments, agencies, and offices in CFIUS's review of transactions for national security concerns.

The CFIUS process generally begins formally when parties to a proposed or pending transaction jointly file a voluntary notice with CFIUS containing information required by § 800.402 of the regulations, commencing a review period of up to 30 days. During the review period, CFIUS members,[49] through the Department of the

---

[47] Baker & McKenzie, A Legal Guide to Acquisitions and Doing Business in the United States, January 1, 2007.

[48] https://www.treasury.gov/resource-center/international/Pages/Committee-on-Foreign-Investment-in-US.aspx; Final Regulations Issued on November 14, 2008, The US Treasury Department, on behalf of the CFIUS, issued final regulations governing CFIUS on November 14, 2008; CFIUS, Annual Report to Congress, CY 2014, Public Unclassified Version, Issued 2016.

[49] The Secretary of the Treasury is the Chairperson of CFIUS, and notices to CFIUS are received, processed, and coordinated at the staff level by the Staff Chairperson of

Treasury as Committee Chair, may request additional information from the parties. CFIUS concludes action on the majority of transactions during or at the end of the initial 30-day review period. In certain circumstances, CFIUS may initiate a subsequent investigation, which must be completed within 45 days. In some circumstances, CFIUS may also refer a transaction to the President for decision within 15 days of CFIUS's completion of the investigation. Parties to a transaction may request withdrawal of their notice at any time during the review or investigation stages.

If CFIUS finds that the covered transaction does not present any national security risks or that other provisions of law provide adequate and appropriate authority to address the risks, it will then advise the parties that CFIUS has concluded all action under section 721 with respect to such transaction. If CFIUS finds that a covered transaction presents national security risks and that other provisions of law do not provide adequate authority to address the risks, then CFIUS may enter into an agreement with, or impose conditions on, parties to mitigate such risks or may refer the case to the President for action.

CFIUS, who is the Director of the Office of Investment Security in the Department of the Treasury. The members of CFIUS include the heads of the following departments and offices:

1. Department of the Treasury (chair)
2. Department of Justice
3. Department of Homeland Security
4. Department of Commerce
5. Department of Defense
6. Department of State
7. Department of Energy
8. Office of the US Trade Representative
9. Office of Science & Technology Policy

The following offices also observe and, as appropriate, participate in CFIUS's activities:

1. Office of Management & Budget
2. Council of Economic Advisors
3. National Security Council
4. National Economic Council
5. Homeland Security Council

The US Department of the Treasury issued final regulations on November 14, 2008 which clarify the procedures governing the national security reviews of certain cross-border transactions conducted by the CFIUS under the Exon–Florio Amendment to the Defense Production Act of 1950 (Exon–Florio). Exon–Florio grants the President the authority to block or suspend any merger, acquisition or takeover of a US entity by a foreign entity where there is "credible evidence" that a "foreign interest exercising control might take action that threatens to impair [US] national security." The President has delegated this authority to CFIUS. The revised regulations retain many features of the prior regulations, but several changes have been made to implement Section 721, increase clarity, reflect developments in business practices over the past several years, and make additional improvements based on experiences with the prior regulations.

Industry-Specific Regulations

Ownership by non-US persons of certain restricted industries is regulated by the federal government or state governments. Restricted industries include the defense, banking, insurance, domestic air or water transportation, fishing, and radio and television broadcasting industries and in some states the railroad industry and agricultural and other real estate.[50] Regulators in these fields can scrutinize acquisitions to determine whether an acquisition is consistent with the public interest and with industry-specific policy goals.

Sarbanes–Oxley Act of 2002

On July 30, 2002, President Bush signed into law the Sarbanes–Oxley Act of 2002, which he characterized as "the most far reaching reforms of American business practices since the time of Franklin Delano Roosevelt." The Act mandated a number of reforms to enhance corporate responsibility, enhance financial disclosures and combat

[50] Baker & McKenzie, A Legal Guide to Acquisitions and Doing Business in the United States, January 1, 2007.

corporate and accounting fraud, and created the "Public Company Accounting Oversight Board," also known as the PCAOB, to oversee the activities of the auditing profession.[51]

Dodd–Frank Wall Street Reform and Consumer Protection Act of 2010

The Dodd–Frank Wall Street Reform and Consumer Protection Act was signed into law on July 21, 2010 by President Barack Obama. The legislation set out to reshape the US regulatory system in several areas including but not limited to consumer protection, trading restrictions, credit ratings, regulation of financial products, corporate governance and disclosure, and transparency.[52]

Summary

This chapter addressed the principal laws and regulations relating to M&As in the US. The US legal system is complex and is composed of a dual structure that contains states and federal governments, with M&A activities being regulated at both levels. Merges are governed by corporation laws of the states in which the target companies are incorporated, but the federal government regulates transactions involving securities, antitrust, and acquisitions in several regulated industries.

It's very beneficial to be knowledgeable of the legal environment that is applicable to mergers, but this chapter is not a substitute for seeking legal advice in doing deals. There are essential legal services that law firms that specialize in M&A could offer to acquirers and targets, and each side party commonly hires their own law firm, in addition to an investment bank.

---

[51] http://www.sec.gov/about/laws/soa2002.pdf. All Commission rulemaking and reports issued under the Sarbanes–Oxley Act at http://www.sec.gov/spotlight/sarbanes-oxley.htm.

[52] http://www.sec.gov/about/laws/wallstreetreform-cpa.pdf. You can find links to all Commission rulemaking and reports issued under the Dodd–Frank Act at http://www.sec.gov/spotlight/dodd-frank.shtml.

Chapter 5

Corporate Governance and Control: The Board's Role in M&A

Andrew J. Sherman and Nick Rosenberg
M&A, Seyfarth Shaw

2015 was the biggest year ever for global mergers and acquisitions (M&As) transactions with over $4 trillion of mergers being signed — which may not include the tens of thousands of middle-market and smaller deals that are not reported. So far, it seems like 2016 will be a bit slower than 2015, but for 2017 and beyond, it looks like M&A activity will continue at a fast pace. 84% of industry experts surveyed by KPMG expect to initiate an M&A transaction in 2017, and almost 75% anticipate doing multiple deals. In this type of fast-paced M&A environment, boards need to be up to speed on current trends and best practices. The fuel behind the acceleration of M&A activity breaks down into several subcomponents:

(a) the low-cost and virtually unlimited access to capital for transactions and investment;
(b) globalization and the acceleration of growth in emerging markets have led to an increase in both outbound and inbound cross-border transactions;
(c) technology and the velocity of change and intensity of competition have forced companies to diversity, integrate supply chains and gobble up market share; and

(d) the graying of the world's population means that the baby boomer generation is preparing to sell or transfer the ownership control of the enterprises they launched 20 or 30 years ago — Mass Mutual estimates that over $40 trillion in intergenerational wealth will be transferred from 2014 to 2025 across the globe.

Boards must embrace key principles of due diligence, buy versus build analysis, financial analysis, and risk assessment as primary factors in their decision-making and evaluation process, both for M&A as well as other capital investment proposals. Transactions should help drive shareholder value and be aligned with both short-term and long-term strategic objectives and be accretive not dilutive to the market price of the company's shares as well as the brand, reputation, and consumer perception of its core products and services. Transactions must be structured and implemented in a manner where they will be able to withstand the second-guessing and searching of an increasing pool of shareholder activists and by courts who seem increasingly more willing to play "Monday morning quarterback" in their analysis of transactions. Screens and filters need to be in place to ensure that risk is avoided and strategic objectives are met. Analysis must be conducted to predict and mitigate any postclosing litigation risk or costly postclosing integration challenges. The new corporate governance paradigm and state of the law is that boards can and will be held accountable and responsible for misguided strategies and/or transactions which are not carefully assessed and evaluated.

Boards and company leaders must embrace the notion that there is no more complicated transaction than an M&A. The issues raised are broad and complex, from valuation and deal structure to tax and securities laws. It seems that virtually every board member executive in every major industry faces a buy-or-sell decision at some point during his or her tenure as leader of the company. In fact, it is estimated that some executives spend as much as one-third of their time considering M&A opportunities and other structural business decisions. The strategic reasons for considering such transactions are also numerous, from achieving economies of scale to mitigating cash-flow risk via diversification to satisfying shareholder hunger for steady growth and dividends. The federal government's degree of intervention in M&A transactions varies from administration to administration, depending on the issues and concerns of the day.

Recent years have witnessed a significant increase in M&A activity within a wide variety of industries that are growing rapidly and evolving overall, such as healthcare, information technology, education, infrastructure, and software development, as well as traditional industries such as manufacturing, infrastructure, consumer products, and food services. Many developments reflect an increase in strategic buyers and a decrease in the amount of leverage, implying that these deals were being done because they made sense for both parties. That was far from the case with the highly leveraged, financially driven deals of the late 1980s.

Boards of companies in small to middle-market segments need to understand the key drivers of valuation since they are often able to focus their operating goals to maximize the potential valuation range. Therefore, it is important to know that the multiple a company achieves for its business directly correlates with the following characteristics:

1. Strong revenue growth
2. Significant market share or strong niche positions
3. A market with barriers to entry by competitors
4. A strong management team
5. Strong, stable cash flow
6. No significant concentration in customers, products, suppliers or geographic markets
7. Low risk of technological obsolescence or product substitution

Successful mergers and acquisitions are neither an art nor a science but a *process*. In fact, regression analysis demonstrates that the number-one determinant of deal multiples is the growth rate of the business. The higher the growth rate, the higher the multiple of cash flow the business is worth.

For example, boards need to understand that when a deal is improperly valued, one side wins big while the other loses big. By definition, a transaction is a failure if it does not create value for shareholders. The easiest way to fail, therefore, is to pay too high a price. To be successful, a transaction must be fair and balanced, reflecting the economic needs of both buyer and seller, and must convey real and durable value to the shareholders of both companies. Achieving this involves a review and analysis of financial statements, a genuine understanding of how the proposed transaction meets the economic objectives of each party, and a recognition of the tax, accounting and legal implications of the deal.

A transaction as complex as an M&A is fraught with potential problems and pitfalls. Many of these problems arise either in the preliminary stages, such as when the parties force a deal that shouldn't really be done (i.e., some couples were just never meant to be married). Other times, inadequate, rushed or misleading due diligence results in mistakes, errors or omissions; risks are not properly allocated during the negotiation of definitive documents; or it becomes a nightmare to integrate the companies after closing. These pitfalls can lead to expensive and protracted litigation unless an alternative method of dispute resolution is negotiated and included in the definitive documents.

The board can and should play a key role in overseeing the M&A deal team and C-level executives in making sure that valuations are accurate and being assessed properly, that due diligence is complete and that the integration which follows a deal does not in the end undermine the company's very reason for doing the deal to begin with. When boards fail to play an active role in the deal process, a company can wind up entering into a transaction that it later regrets. Classic mistakes include a lack of adequate planning, an overly aggressive timetable to closing, a failure to really look at possible postclosing integration problems, or, worst of all, that projected synergies turn out to be illusory. By engaging in the M&A process early and often, developing a strategy and process, and carefully overseeing the role of the executive team, a board can make sure that a company does not make any of these classic mistakes.

Specific Board Responsibilities

Generally, proposing, planning and implementation of M&A transactions are the responsibility of a company's executive team. With the board's oversight, it is the executive team that will develop the acquisition plan which leads to M&A transactions. But that does not mean that the board won't play an integral role in the M&A process. An engaged board will develop the company's overall strategic direction and might determine that growth should be driven through acquisition. In the alternative, it might determine that the best way for a company to maximize value to shareholders is to sell itself or certain of its key assets. The board must understand that its decision-making process, the depth and breadth of the information it considered to make its decision, and the reasonableness of the board's actions will all be under the microscope as viewed by shareholders, stakeholders, regulations, activists, and possibly even the courts.

It is in this environment, that the a company's executive team will develop a specific acquisition strategy which might lead to the identification of M&A targets, perhaps with the help with an investment bank or other advisors. The board will also identify and assess key risks, supervise and test the premises of a proposed transaction and ensure that the M&A transaction being proposed by the company's executive team will be in the best interests of the company and ultimately drive shareholder value. If the company wishes to sell, the board will give its input into that approach as well as evaluate various offers and determine whether a deal being offered is fair and maximizes value for shareholders

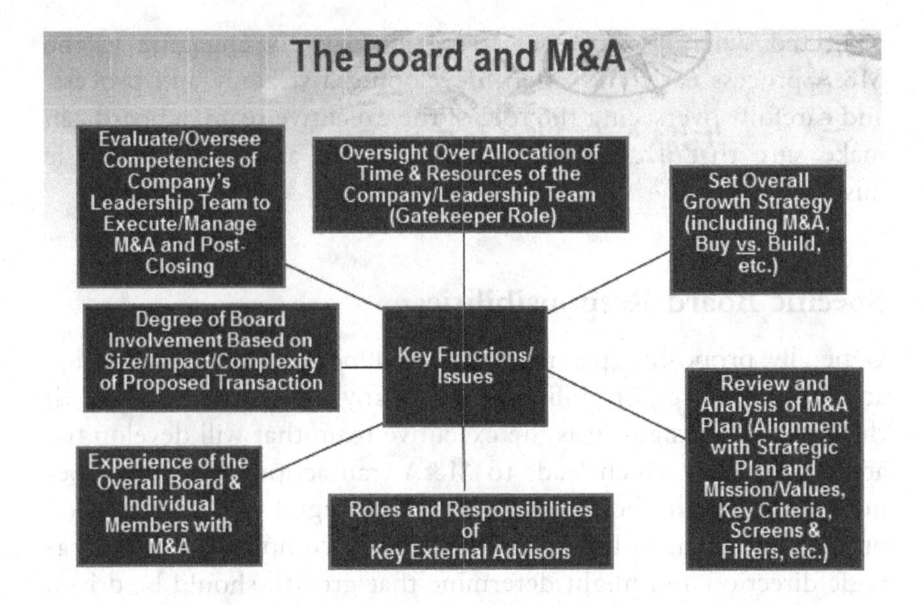

The board's role in the context of M&A can be broken into its macro roles and micro roles. In the macro, the board should:

- Embrace and meet its various fiduciary obligations. This will be addressed further in the next section;
- Oversee the company's management as it negotiates the contours of a particular deal;
- Test and confirm the economic premise of the proposed transaction — namely, perform its own analysis of the management's justification for doing the deal to see if it reaches the same conclusion;
- Confirm the value proposition that the deal offers to the company's shareholders;
- Confirm that management has taken necessary steps to mitigate the risk of the transaction and reduce the chances of conflict and litigation later on;
- Assist management in addressing the fear, uncertainties and doubts of employees and company teams; and
- Confirm that management is planning the postclosing integration adequately.

In the micro, the board should:

- Confirm compliance regarding timing and scope of disclosure of the transaction to various constituencies particularly with an eye towards prevention of any insider trading;
- Consult with the executive team regarding the due diligence process to make sure that all necessary steps have been taken to mitigate postclosing risk;
- Confirm that the company has obtained key third-party approvals, whether regulatory or contractual. In some instances, the board may actually assist the company in this respect; and
- Review the allocation of purchase price to confirm that allocation of the risks and rewards of the transaction is fair and reasonable relative to upside.

Legal Responsibilities

The board's responsibilities with respect to M&A go well beyond providing strategic advice and oversight. The board's obligation to drive shareholder value results from its fiduciary duties to the company. Fiduciary duties are legal obligations which fall into two broad general categories: the duty of care and the duty of loyalty. When directors violate these duties, courts may impose monetary liability upon them or invalidate or enjoin their actions. The key starting point for understanding the nature and scope of these duties and how they dictate the board's role in M&A is considering what actions and decisions a court will not disturb.

Under the business judgment rule, directors are presumed to have made a business decision on an informed basis, in good faith, and in honest belief that their actions were taken in the best interest of the company. And when they do in fact act in this manner, directors will not have their decisions second-guessed by a court, even if the decision turns out to be a bad one. That is, directors' fiduciary duties do not bar them from taking business risks, and courts generally are not in the business of substituting their business judgment for that of directors, or otherwise engaging in substantive evaluations of business decisions or outcomes with the benefit of 20/20 hindsight.

So when will a court disturb a business decision made by a board of directors or impose liability on such decision makers? It is when the directors act in a manner contrary to the presumptions of the business judgment rule, i.e., when they fail to act on an informed basis, in good faith, or in honest belief that their actions are in the best interest of the company. These are issues that judges and lawyers are in a position to scrutinize; business expertise is not necessary. The focus of the judicial review, therefore, is on the *process* undertaken by the board, particularly whether that decision-making process was materially flawed or inadequate, or whether it was tainted or driven by personal interests instead of the company's interests. These concepts are embodied in the directors' duties of care and loyalty.

Duty of Care

When making a decision, directors must actively gather material information regarding the company's affairs and then act upon that information with the diligence, care, and skill necessary to make a rational business decision. Board members are entitled to rely primarily on the data provided by officers and professional advisers, provided that they have no knowledge of any irregularity or inaccuracy in the information. But they cannot act in a grossly negligent manner. That is, they risk breaching their duty of care when they remain willfully ignorant of material information or, even in possession of such information, rush a decision so they cannot reasonably and responsibly evaluate the options. I've even seen cases in which board members were held personally responsible for misinformed decisions if their duty of care was not taken seriously.

In the context of selling the company, the duty of care means that the board must "undertake reasonable efforts to secure the highest price realistically achievable given the market for the company."[1] This standard is actually tougher than the one the court employs when applying the business judgment rule to ordinary board decision, which as noted above only requires that the board act in an informed

[1] *In re Netsmart Technologies, Inc. Shareholder Litigation, 2007* WL 1576151 (Del. Ch.).

manner, in good faith and with the assumption that their actions are in the best interests of the company. Because in the context of M&A the board has "Revlon duties", when looking at a board's actions in a sale, the court will take a substantive look at what a board did to get the highest reasonable price.

Because the board has these Revlon duties, it should develop a process whereby it will maximize shareholder value, which drills down into fair pricing, fair dealing, and a strong plan for postclosing integration and value maximization. While not a requirement under Revlon, the board may engage in an auction process to fetch the highest price for the company. It also might mean that once the company receives an offer, it should actively seek additional offers to make sure that the company is getting the best deal possible. In any event, the board should be well educated on various devices it can employ to make sure the company is getting the best deal. Furthermore, the board should carefully document its role in the M&A process and the various steps it took to maximize the sale price so that it can demonstrate that it undertook such reasonable efforts.

Consider how the Delaware Chancery Court viewed the possible sale of Netsmart Technologies, Inc. Its decision in *In re Netsmart Technologies, Inc., Shareholders Lit.* criticized Netsmart's board's decision to only consider private equity firms as potential buyers to the exclusion of strategic buyers. The court also criticized the board's failure to keep minutes of an important meeting where this decision was made. This emphasizes the point that process and record keeping are important if a board is not going to breach its fiduciary duties during the M&A process.

Recent Delaware cases have established that in a limited set of circumstances, the business judgment standard may apply in the context of M&A. In *In re MFW Shareholders Litigation* (Del. Ch. May 29, 2013) (referred to as MFW), which was decided in 2013, the Delaware Chancery Court held that when reviewing a going-private transaction with a controlling stockholder, the merger receives the approval of either (i) a special committee of directors independent of the controlling stockholder that is fully empowered to decline the transaction and such committee relies on its own advisors and satisfies the duty of care in negotiating the sale price or (ii) a majority of the stockholders not affiliated with the majority stockholder, provided that such stockholders are uncoerced in their vote and fully informed.

Another recent Delaware Chancery Court case, *In re Volcano Corporation Stockholder Litigation*, demonstrates that the MFW logic can apply to other situations as well. In Volcano, the court determined that the tendering of shares by a majority of fully informed, uncoerced, disinterested stockholders, essentially has the same effect as a majority vote of unaffiliated stockholders, effectively cleansing the transaction in question and causing the transaction to be subject to review in accordance with the business judgment.

Duty of Loyalty

Each director must exercise his or her powers in the interest of the corporation and not in his or her own interest or that of another person or organization. The duty of loyalty has a number of specific applications: The director must avoid any conflicts of interest in dealings with the corporation and cannot extract personal benefits from the corporation that are not shared by all of the shareholders. The director must not personally usurp what is more appropriately an opportunity or business transaction to be offered to the corporation. For example, say an officer or director of the company was in a meeting on the company's behalf and a great opportunity to obtain the distribution rights for an exciting new technology was offered. It would be a breach of this duty to try to obtain those rights for himself and not first offer them to the corporation. Further, the director cannot act in bad faith and for a purpose other than advancing the best interests of the corporation. For example, the director cannot knowingly cause the corporation to violate the law, cannot consciously disregard his obligation to oversee the corporation's activities and thereby sanction misconduct by the corporation and its employees, and cannot waste corporate assets.

The board's duty of loyalty impacts its role in M&A in numerous ways. Essentially it means that a board member's decisions can only be driven by a desire to maximize shareholder value. A director would be violating this duty of loyalty if she supported a deal which benefited a company in which she had a stake solely because the deal would benefit her directly or indirectly. It would also be a breach of the duty of loyalty if she determined that one buyer of the company was better than another because that buyer promised her a bigger role after the sale. In short, directors cannot put their own interests before the company's.

To the extent that "interested" directors play too large of a role on a board, the board risks losing the presumption of the business judgment rule, meaning that courts will scrutinize the decisions made by a board deemed not to be impartial with respect to a particular matter. To that end, in the context of considering M&A transactions (or other situations in which one or more director could be deemed to have misaligned interests), interested directors should consider recusing themselves from discussing and voting on relevant transactions. The board could also form a special committee comprised of only outside directors to control the sale process in order to avoid any potential conflicts of interest.

Several recent Delaware cases have highlighted how the duty of loyalty impacts financial advisors in M&A transactions. The recent Del Monte, El Paso and Rural Metro decisions in the Delaware Chancery Court have shown that courts are also concerned about disloyal financial advisors. But these cases implicate boards as well. Under this recent case law, boards have a responsibility to oversee financial advisors and be on the lookout for potential conflicts of interests (e.g., a bank favoring buyers who will seek financing from that bank). In other words, the board must adhere to its Revlon duties throughout the sale process, not just at the approval stage and the disloyalty of a financial advisor can lead to board liability.

Boards need to always take their fiduciary duties seriously but this is particularly true in the context of M&A and related transactions, especially those that may be cross-border in nature. In order to do so, a diligent board may wish to hire independent counsel to advise it of its duties in the context of the particular situation the company is in. Boards should remain diligent in their oversight role and always play the role of "constructive skeptic" when political transactions and their alleged value propositions are presented for debate and appeal.

In conclusion, a board will have the best chance to avoid bad deals — and the litigation that often follows them — if they remain steadfast in their focus on core principles of stewardship and on their key fiduciary duties, develop and encourage a sound M&A process, and are diligent about keeping records of their decisions and actions.

Chapter 6

Antitakeover Measures

Dovrat Bashan
M&A, Siemens Corporation, USA

Introduction

In the wake of the global financial crisis, as stock prices declined sharply, an increasing number of public US companies adopted or renewed shareholder rights plans, also known as poison pill, after years of steady decline in the use of this notorious takeover defense mechanism.[1] As market conditions made public companies more vulnerable to hostile bids, managers prepared for takeover battles. If the beginning of the millennium signaled a trend of moving away from the poison pill, the economic crisis in 2008 brought the discussion of the poison pill and other takeover defense measures to the forefront.[2] Evidently, continuous decline in share prices of underperforming companies increases the risk of being the target of a takeover campaign by activist shareholders.[3] There is data that supports the conclusion of a

[1] Rethinking the Role of the Poison Pill? Sharkrepellent.Net (September 17, 2008), available at https://www.sharkrepellent.net/pub/rs_20080916.html, hereinafter Rethinking the Role of the Poison Pill?; Michael Klausner, *Investors' Choices: Institutional Shareholders, Private Equity, And Antitakeover Protection At The IPO Stage*, 152 U. Pa. L. Rev. 755, 757, 760 (2003), hereinafter Klausner.

[2] *Id.* Rethinking the Role of the Poison Pill?

[3] SharkRepellent study shows underperformers three times more likely to be targeted by activists than outperformers, Sharkrepellent.Net (December 16, 2013), available

negative correlation between the financial state of the market and the implementation of takeover defenses, likely as a result of increase in hostile takeovers. In 2008 for example, following the financial crisis, when the stock market reached historical low levels, unsolicited and hostile transactions constituted over 22% of all deal volume in the US by September 2008, compared with 12.1% for all of 2007.[4] From the target perspective, 2008 also saw a late-year surge in poison pill adoptions. In December 2008 alone, 28 companies adopted rights plans, and a total of 127 companies adopted rights plans over the entire year, the most in any year between 2002 and 2008. Seventy-six of the adopting companies were first-time rights plan adopters, a large increase when compared with the previous 3 years. The year before had only 42 companies adopting poison pills for the first time, the lowest number since the early 1980s.[5] In addition, the rate at which companies have allowed their existing rights plans to expire has slowed. Approximately 182 companies in 2008 allowed their rights plans to expire, as compared to a net decline of 223 during the two preceding years.[6]

In such an environment, it becomes very important for a corporation's management and board to comprehensively review their anti-takeover defenses. Arguably, an effective defense profile enables management to resist unsolicited takeover bids, protect the corporation's long-term policy, search for a better offer in the future to maximize shareholders wealth, and stand against shareholders who challenge their decisions, especially in times when market conditions do not reflect the true value of the corporation.[7]

---

at https://www.sharkrepellent.net/request?an=dt.getPage&st=undefined&pg=/pub/rs_20131216.html&rnd=975479.

[4] Reuters, *Hostile Takeovers hit Record as Market Swoons*, September 29, 2008, available at http://www.reuters.com/article/us-mergers-hostiles-idUSTRE48S2P120080929. See also Thomson Reuters, Mergers & Acquisitions Review, p. 5 (Third Quarter 2008).

[5] New Highs Set for Unsolicited M&A and Proxy Fights, Sharkrepellent.Net (January 23, 2009), available at https://www.sharkrepellent.net/pub/rs_20090122.html.

[6] See Supra Note 1, Rethinking the Role of the Poison Pill.

[7] Michael Klausner, The Empirical Revolution in Law: Fact and Fiction in Corporate Law and Governance, 65 Stan. L. Rev. 1325, 1348 (2013), hereinafter The Empirical Revolution in Law.

There is a variety of antitakeover defense measures that can assist management in achieving these goals. A corporation can either prepare in advance and adopt antitakeover defense measures against unknown threats or take action in response to a potential or actual threat, in the event that the corporation is "in play", i.e., the corporation has become a hostile takeover target.

This chapter presents an overview of the most common antitakeover defensive measures the corporation adopts in its organizational documents. As the chapter's title suggests, the reader will be introduced to concepts, methods, and uses of both proactive defense mechanisms, which can be viewed as being preventive measures adopted as part of the corporation's long-term plan that can be adopted before the corporation is "in play" or after a hostile action was taken against the corporation, and reactive defense mechanisms, which involve making the target less attractive for hostile bidders, seeking a better bidder, or even counterattacking hostile bidders. This chapter focuses mainly on the former, proactive preventive measures, by presenting the various mechanisms and the considerations in structuring a firm's optimal antitakeover defense array. Additionally, this chapter provides a brief description of economic conditions in the markets and their relation to antitakeover trends. The reader will be introduced with the concepts and methods underlying hostile takeover techniques for initiating a change of control, such as proxy contests and tender offers; the reader will learn about antitakeover defenses that help boards defend against hostile change of control activities, the latest trends in antitakeover defense formation; and the potential economic implications defense measures could have on shareholder wealth.

Although it seems that financial media covers takeover activities quite widely and frequently, hostile corporate takeovers are not as frequent as one might think in the world of publicly traded US companies.[8] Nonetheless, hostile and unsolicited takeovers draw much

---

[8] The number of hostile takeovers launched by US corporations reached 13.2% of US public mergers in 2015. M&A at a Glance, Year-End Roundup, Paul, Weiss, Rifkind, Wharton & Garrison LLP (2015), available at https://www.paulweiss.com/

attention from the financial press and academia as well as legal and financial practitioners. If the number of hostile takeovers is relatively small, why there is so much focus on antitakeover defenses? We suggest a few reasons: First, despite opposition to antitakeover defenses among academia and investors community, the vast majority of initial public offerings (IPOs) include in their charters at least one form of antitakeover defense, staggered board, described more fully below.[9] However, data shows that over the past few years, there has been a dramatic decline in the prevalence of staggered board provisions.[10] It seems that while the vast majority of public companies commence their public life with such antitakeover defense measure in place, a large number of those companies decide to eliminate this defense later on. This seemingly contradictory trend illustrates the attention and engagement that this antitakeover defense receives from management and shareholders, and their significance in the views of those who seek to repeal and maintain them under the corporation organizational documents. This leads to the second reason. Antitakeover defenses have critical influence on corporate governance. As further discussed

---

practices/transactional/mergers-acquisitions/publications/ma-at-a-glance-%E2%80%93-2015-year-end-roundup.aspx?id=21378.

[9] Steven Davidoff Solomon, The Case Against Staggered Boards, *The New York Times*, March 20, 2012, 12:43 pm, available at http://dealbook.nytimes.com/2012/03/20/the-case-against-staggered-boards/. The article provides data from SharkRepellent database according to which 86.4% of companies going public in 2012 had a staggered board. See also Corporate Governance Practices in U.S. Initial Public Offerings, Davis Polk Wardwell LLP., pp. 5, 15, June 2016, available at http://www.davispolk.com/sites/default/files/Controlled_Company_Survey_June_2016.pdf. According to one study, in 2002, 80% of IPOs made use of staggered board provisions, see Lucian Arye Bebchuk, *Investors' Choices: Why Firms Adopt Antitakeover Arrangements*, 152 U. Pa. L. Rev. 713, 725 (2003). See also The Empirical Revolution in Law, supra note 7, at 1333, for a further discussion regarding defense measures in included in charters during the IPO stage.

[10] For example, we see a significant decline in staggered boards' incidence among the S&P 500. In 2000, out of the S&P 500, 300 companies had staggered boards, but as of the end of 2013, only 60 companies had staggered boards. John C. Coffee, Jr. and Darius Palia, The Impact of Hedge Fund Activism: Evidence and Implications 14, (Working Paper No. 266, 2014), hereinafter Coffee and Palia.

below, defense measures play an important role in corporation governance and in the relations between management and shareholders. Antitakeover defenses are usually perceived as impairing shareholder power and increasing the board's governing power in the corporation. Third, while some claim that antitakeover defenses decrease shareholders' return, others suggest that takeover defenses can assist boards to increase shareholders' wealth. Therefore, it is very important for shareholders and directors to consider the impact of adopting or repealing antitakeover defenses in the corporate plan.

It should be noted that many states enacted antitakeover laws, independent from those measures adopted by the corporation itself. Antitakeover laws vary from state to state and typically affect corporations incorporated within their state. State laws will not be the focus of this chapter. However, this chapter is based on the Delaware legal framework.

Antitakeover Defense Measures — Why Do We Need Them?

Mergers and acquisitions (M&As) are often viewed as an essential element for a corporation's success and growth achievement. Planners of M&As see greater value in the merging business than in allowing independent corporations to continue operating as separate entities. Business combinations can create great economic benefits, but they might also result in harms to shareholder's interests. Different managers might have different views, and the management of the target can have plans opposed to those of the acquirer. While the acquirer sees, or believes he sees, the advantages that could come from a combination or change of control, the target might not share the same perspective. Even if the managers are interested in a deal, they might still want to reject some offers, thinking that other bidders might be a better fit[11] or that it is better to wait for a higher offer that will come in the future. As mentioned earlier, trends in takeover activities might

---

[11] For example, see Paramount Communications, Inc. v. Time, Inc., 571 A.2d 1140, 1989 Del. LEXIS 917, Fed. Sec. L. Rep. (CCH) P94, 938 (Del. 1989).

be the result of economic conditions in the market; as the financial crisis has shown, market conditions can harm the true value of the corporation, and management would want to put up shields and perhaps wait for better days. There is a variety of reasons why the board of a target may consider rejecting an offer, including ones associated with the board's fiduciary duties to the shareholders.[12]

First, defense measures can potentially enable management to reject coercive or inadequate offers from bidders, leverage bargaining power to negotiate for a higher price and secure the shareholders' most preferred transaction. Without defense measures, shareholders might elect to tender into a bidder's offer in ignorance of the true value of their shares to a bidder that did not offer them a control premium. Second, defense measures can protect incumbent management and their strategies and policy. Bidders have better chances of replacing incumbent management with little delay if the corporation has no effective defense profile, and thus of intervening with corporate policy for their own benefit, which might not necessarily be beneficial to the remaining shareholders. With the right defense measures, management has the ability to defend shareholders from abusive tender offers, choose the highest available offer, select the best partner to merge with (even if that means taking the lower bid), or wait for a bidder with the best possible offer. Later in this chapter, we will elaborate on the merits of those arguments and whether the power that defense measures provide management creates higher shareholder wealth.

The Stakeholders

The term "hostile" refers to a situation where a potential acquirer is seeking to take over control of the corporation without management

[12] With respect to the board's fiduciary duties in the sale of the corporation, see Revlon, Inc. v. Macandrews & Forbes Holdings, Inc., 506 A.2d 173, 1986 Del. LEXIS 1053, 66 A.L.R.4th 157, Fed. Sec. L. Rep. (CCH) P92,525 (Del. 1986); Unocal Corp. v. Mesa Petroleum Co., 493 A.2d 946, 1985 Del. LEXIS 482, Fed. Sec. L. Rep. (CCH) P92,077 (Del. 1985), hereinafter Unocal.

and board's support, and therefore may be confusing in this context as it is not necessarily hostile to the corporation, if one's view is that the sole purpose of the corporation is to maximize shareholders' value. For many years, shareholders and managers have been in conflict primarily over takeover defenses, including the independence of the board.[13] This conflict is associated with two approaches with respect to takeovers and antitakeover defenses. According to one view, the board of directors faces an inherent conflict of interest because antitakeover might promote management entrenchment and help directors retain their positions with the corporation, regardless of their performance. Bad management can cause share value to drop when corporations fail to perform well. In circumstances of deteriorating corporate performance, bidders who believe they can do better by replacing incumbent management seek to take control over the underperforming target. For instance, activist shareholders are more likely to target underperforming companies than outperforming companies. They see high potential in such companies as they can replace management, push their business plans, and create an opportunity for shareholders to share the higher value.[14] Antitakeover defenses arguably entrench existing management and shield them from pressure imposed by shareholders and the market, i.e., potential acquirers. From that point of view, antitakeover charters that entrench management might destroy shareholder wealth through continued poor performance, while protakeover charters allow hostile takeovers to occur and thus monitor and discipline management.[15] This ability to take control of the corporation and replace the management reduces the need for shareholder monitoring and reduce agency costs. Shareholders benefit if the corporation is susceptible to a takeover, such that when a corporation underperforms due to lack of performance by the management, a takeover can provide shareholders with

[13] See Klausner, Supra note 1.

[14] Supra note 3.

[15] Robert Daines & Michael Klausner, Do IPO Charters Maximize Firm Value? Antitakeover Provisions in IPOs, *Journal of Law Economics & Organization*, 17, pp. 83, 95, 2001.

a significant premium for their shares. If successful, the acquirer who takes over the corporation would be a majority shareholder and would be able to replace the incumbent board of directors with directors that share his views, remove the existing managers, implement his policy and eventually increase the stock value. Managers have opposing interests, they would prefer their behavior to be unconstrained and to be able to resist takeovers, which can leave them out of a job. With antitakeover defenses, management can bargain for private benefits and secure their position with the corporation at the cost of the shareholders.

A Note about Activist Shareholders

In today's corporate landscape, there is an ascension of a new subset of investors whose business plan is to make money by actively influencing corporate policy. Those shareholders are referred to as "activist shareholders" and include institutional investors or notorious raiders, such as Carl Icahn. Institutional investors, such as hedge funds, are known to be active in opposing antitakeover defense measures and seeking to maximize shareholder power.[16] For that reason, activist shareholders oppose antitakeover defenses because they impair shareholders' power and conflict with the anatomy of their business strategy in the corporations in which they invest. To achieve their goals, they seek a range of actions in relation to a corporation's management and business plan. For example, one of the most common methods used by activist shareholders is to pursue a partial slate of directors on the board to influence corporate's policy and promote their business strategy.[17] It is claimed that activists' interests may not always coincide with other shareholders' interests. According to this approach, activist shareholders seek only short-term goals and they create short term earnings at the expense of long-term value, harming long term shareholders.[18] For those

[16] Klausner, see supra note 1, at p. 757.

[17] Marcel Kahan & Edward B. Rock, Hedge Funds in Corporate Governance and Corporate Control, *University of Pennsylvania Law Review*,155, pp. 1021, 1029, 2007.

[18] Klausner, see supra note 1, at p. 762.

reasons, arguments are made to allocate power to directors rather than shareholders.[19] Antitakeover defenses, such as staggered board provisions discussed below, can achieve those goals, by giving directors the power to decide, without being pressured by shareholders claims, and by making it much more difficult and costly for short-term shareholders to control the board. Activist shareholders seek to advance "shareholder democracy" by eliminating antitakeover defenses and shareholders can use such a governance structure to influence major business decisions in the corporations they own. Shareholder power makes it easier for activist shareholders to gain substantial influence over the corporation, and arguably impair long-term value or expose the corporation to novel takeover tactics.[20]

Not every takeover creates opportunities for shareholders, and the board needs to be able to identify takeovers that could destroy wealth. In making business decisions, shareholders depend on reliable and pertinent information about the value of the corporation obtained from the board of directors, and the board is the only organ in the corporation to provide the shareholders with this information. The board and management have the relevant expertise, experience and the resources to find the true value of the corporation. The board needs to protect shareholders from the threat that shareholders will tender their shares for an inadequate tender offer. If an inadequate or coercive offer is made to the shareholders, the board must respond to it in accordance with their fiduciary duties. Antitakeover defenses empower directors' bargaining power to act as agents of shareholders. The poison pill, e.g., can help them decide the best method and timing when accepting an offer (or whether accepting an offer at all) without being pressured by the bidder or shareholders. Managers would claim that a

[19] Lucian A. Bebchuk, Alon Brav and Wei Jiang, The Long-Term Effects of Hedge Fund Activism, *Columbia Law Review*, 115, pp. 1085, 1148, 2015, hereinafter Bebchuk, Brav and Jiang.

[20] Wachtell, Lipton, Rosen & Katz, Takeover Law and Practices, March 2014, p. 81, hereinafter Takeover Law and Practices. See Bebchuk, Brav and Jiang, supra note 19, the authors argue that studies don't necessarily prove that activists damage long-term value.

Table 1: Summary — The Incentives, Duties or Rights of the Board and Shareholders.

Why the Shareholders Should Have the Power to Respond to a Takeover	Why the Board of Directors Should Have the Power to Respond to a Takeover
The board and the management are self-interested. Accepting a takeover can leave them out of a job.	The board is responsible to protect the shareholders and maximize the return for shareholders. Antitakeover defenses increase the board's bargaining power.
Shares are freely transferable and the shareholders should make the decision whether to sell their shares.	The board may think that the shares are undervalued. The true value of the corporation may be higher than the value reflected in the market.
Giving the decision to shareholders can help monitor and discipline the board and reduce agency costs.	It is a business decision and the board has the expertise and resources to make the decision.

weak corporate governance structure without antitakeover defenses exposes disaggregated and disorganized shareholders to hostile takeover against their interests. Antitakeover defensive measures give the board the power to defeat inadequate and coercive offers and protect shareholders. Arguably, giving the board the power to make the decisions will ultimately benefit the shareholders.

Certificate of Incorporation and By-laws Provisions

Many of the provisions in the corporation's certificate of incorporation or by-laws will have an effect on the corporation's "defensive profile". A corporation's defensive profile is the analysis that a hostile bidder will make when evaluating a hostile takeover and the likelihood of success of such a hostile takeover attempt as weighed against a friendly approach to the corporation's board. Provided below are the main components that will need to be reviewed in connection with any such analysis and the significance of such components to the hostile bidder's ultimate goal.

Staggered Board Provisions

Two takeover defenses are widely recognized as the most effective defenses against a hostile takeover, the poison pill and the staggered board. The trends of takeover activities in the market against staggered board corporations support this observation. For example, between the years 2007 and 2011, among S&P 1500 companies, those who were without a classified board, i.e., had directors who were elected annually, were targeted more frequently than were those who had a classified board.[21] One study shows that between 1996 and 2000, targets that had an effective staggered board had significantly better chances to stay independent following a hostile bid that was brought against the corporation. One counter method for fighting staggered boards is winning two consecutive proxy contests and replacing a majority of the board, as further discussed below. Between 1995 and 2010, not a single hostile takeover attempt was successful in winning two proxy contests, 1 year apart, as part of an attempt to gain control over the board.[22] This widely known defense measure is discussed in further detail below.

Pursuant to Delaware General Corporate Law (DGCL), the board of directors holds exclusive power to manage the corporation, unless the certificate of incorporation provides otherwise or if otherwise stated in the DGCL. The default legal framework in Delaware (and in US corporate law, in general) provides the board of directors, not shareholders, with ultimate control of the corporation's business decisions, including business decisions associated with takeover activity. Although the corporate form has a centralized management structure with broad discretion, this discretion is not

[21] Hostile M&A — Increased Use of Proxy Fights and Poison Pill Defense, SharkRepellent. Net, February 17, 2012, available at https://www.sharkrepellent.net/request?an=dt.getPage&st=undefined&pg=/pub/rs_20120217.html&Hostile_M&A_Increased_Use_of_Proxy_Fights_and_Poion_Pill_Defense&rnd=850415, hereinafter Hostile M&A — Increased Use of Proxy Fights and Poison Pill Defense.

[22] Guhan Subramanian, Delaware's Choice, 39 Del. J. Corp. L. 1, 5, 2014, hereinafter Subramanian.

entirely absolute. Shareholders rely on three basic rights as owners of the corporation that enable them to monitor managers,[23] the right to sell their shares freely to third parties, which they may use to facilitate a hostile takeover that helps monitor managers, as discussed above; the right to sue on behalf of the corporation, which can also be used as a tool to monitor managers; and the right to vote on significant corporate matters that affect the corporation's destiny, including annually voting for the election of the board of directors. Thus, managers who do not perform in line with the expectations of their shareholders will be replaced by them, either by the shareholders tendering their shares to an acquirer who will replace the management or by the shareholders replacing the management at the annual meeting.

Unless the certificate of incorporation provides otherwise, the shareholders select all members of the board of directors at the shareholders' annual meeting for a 1-year term. Under DGCL default rules, replacing the entire board of directors or a majority of the board in one annual meeting can be relatively simple. If shareholders are not satisfied with the board's performance or disagree with their decision making, they can simply replace the entire board, a majority of the board, or those directors which they wish to replace at the annual meeting.

Alternatively, the DGCL allows for a board to be classified rather than annually elected, if the corporate organizational documents permit such classification. DGCL provides that a board may be divided into one, two, or three classes by the certificate of incorporation, by the initial by-law or by a by-law adopted by a vote of the shareholders. Although there is a movement, led by activist shareholders, against staggered boards in US public companies, many corporations still implement staggered board provisions in their certificate of incorporation. As discussed in the introduction to this chapter, a vast majority of corporations undergoing IPOs include staggered board provisions

[23] Robert B. Thompson, Preemption and Federalism in Corporate Governance: Protecting Shareholder Rights to Vote, Sell and Sue, 62 LAW AND CONTEMPORARY Problems, 215, 1999.

in their certificate of incorporation at the time of the IPO.[24] Activist shareholders oppose staggered board provisions because they create a lengthy and expensive process for obtaining majority control over the board of directors. In Delaware, a staggered board may include a maximum of three classes of members of the board in which each class stands for election in consecutive years. If a corporation elects to have a three-class staggered board, one-third of the board will be elected each year and each director will serve a 3-year term. At each annual meeting held after such classification becomes effective, directors will be elected by the shareholders for a full term of 3 years to succeed those directors whose terms expire. A staggered board makes it more difficult for a shareholder to control the board because a shareholder or a group of shareholders would have to win two consecutive elections to replace a majority of the board. Winning one election allows shareholders to gain only one-third of the seats on the board at most — a minority. Only at the second elections, when another third of the board may be replaced, shareholders can potentially win a majority of the seats on the board (two-thirds of the seats), and the time between one board election to another could be as long as 13 months.[25] In order to vote in an annual meeting, the voting shareholder must be registered as a shareholder as of the record date of both elections to be entitled to vote. The record date is set by the board and could be as long as 60 days before the date of the annual meeting.[26] For those reasons, a staggered board makes the replacement of a majority of the board a longer and costly procedure that could deter dissident shareholders from influencing corporate governance through control of the board of directors. In addition, the delay factor that may result from being required to win two elections is an important factor to consider. Even if the bidder would be willing

[24] See Subramanian, supra note 22.

[25] In Delaware, if the corporation fails to hold its annual meeting, or, in lieu thereof, take action by written consent, for a period of thirteen months since its last annual meeting (or the last action by written consent), shareholders can request the Delaware Court of Chancery to order a meeting to be held upon the application of any shareholder or director.

[26] 8 Del. C. § 213.

to wait before gaining majority control over the board, by the time the bidder gains control, market conditions may change and a takeover might not be as attractive as it was initially. In addition, the bidder would have to convince shareholders to vote for his or her nominees by making an appealing firm offer to the shareholders that would have to be open for another year before the second elections take place. During a 1-year period, circumstances might change both on the target side and on the bidder's side.[27]

Consider a hypothetical. Great Startup Inc. announces its initial public offering in May 2016. Great Startup installed a staggered board provision in its certificate of incorporation, pursuant to which, the board of directors of the company would be divided into three classes so that only one-third of the directorships shall be up for election each year. The certificate of incorporation sets directorship elections pursuant to the following schedule: Class 1 shall be elected in 2016, 2019, and every 3 years thereafter. Class 2 shall be elected in 2017, 2020, and every 3 years thereafter. Class 3 shall be elected in 2018, 2021, and every 3 years thereafter.

How many seats does a hostile bidder have to win to gain majority control over the board, and how long will it take?

Effectiveness and Destaggering

A staggered board can be a very powerful antitakeover defense if structured properly. Recall that in today's US public companies, there is an increasing movement to declassify staggered boards.[28] Declassifying a staggered board enables shareholders to replace failing managers and provides a gateway to redeem other defense measures, such as a poison pill that can be redeemed only by the board of directors. However, not all staggered boards have a strong antitakeover effect. Three main tactics enable shareholders to disarm a staggered

---

[27] Lucian Arye Bebchuk, John C. Coates & Guhan Subramanian, *The Powerful Antitakeover Force of Staggered Boards: Theory, Evidence, and Policy*, 54 Stan. L. Rev. 887, 919, 2002. Hereinafter Bebchuk, Coates & Subramanian.

[28] See Subramanian, supra note 22.

Table 2: Example of a Staggered Board Provision.

Shareholders Entitled to Vote	Class	2016 Portion of the Board to be Elected	2017 Portion of the Board to be Elected	2018 Portion of the Board to be Elected	2019 Portion of the Board to be Elected	2020 Portion of the Board to be Elected	2021 Portion of the Board to be Elected
Entire shareholders vote	Class 1	Board seat 1	—	—	Board seat 1	—	—
		Board seat 2	—	—	Board seat 2	—	—
		Board seat 3	—	—	Board seat 3	—	—
	Class 2	—	Board seat 4	—	—	Board seat 4	—
		—	Board seat 5	—	—	Board seat 5	—
		—	Board seat 6	—	—	Board seat 6	—
	Class 3	—	—	Board seat 7	—	—	Board seat 7
		—	—	Board seat 8	—	—	Board seat 8
		—	—	Board seat 9	—	—	Board seat 9

board: "packing," "removing" or "converting" the board of directors, as described with further details below. Shareholders can use one of those three tactics to declassify a staggered board, either by a special meeting of the shareholders or by a written consent. Acting by written a special meeting or a written consent, shareholders can run a proxy contest to replace the board immediately and avoid the waiting to the annual meeting and the long process that it entails. To be able to act by written consent or a special meeting, the corporation organizational documents must allow shareholders to take such path. If the corporation organizational documents restrict the removal or packing of the board by shareholders, they can still act at the annual meeting to dismantle the board. However, in this case they would have to wait until the next annual meeting, which can take as long as 13 months.[29]

To declassify a staggered board, shareholders can use one of the following corporate actions[30]:

(1) Packing — By increasing the number of board seats and electing new members, shareholders can have a majority on the board. For example, if the board has seven seats and all the incumbent managers oppose taking an offer that the shareholders favor, shareholders can add eight more seats to the board, i.e., expand the board from seven seats to 15 seats, fill the seats with board members that will favor the bid, and gain majority of the board. However, some corporations limit in their certificate of incorporation or by-laws the maximum number of directors that the shareholders may elect, thereby preventing shareholders from packing the board of directors by increasing its size. If such provision is installed in the certificate of incorporation, shareholders cannot amend it without board approval, and thus will not be able to use this tactic (see discussion below).

(2) Removing — If the certificate of incorporation permits the removal of any director or all the directors without cause, a majority of shareholders who are entitled to vote can simply remove

[29] 8 Del. C. § 211.

[30] Bebchuk, Coates & Subramanian, supra note 27, at 909.

directors from the board and fill the vacancies with new members (as long as the corporation organizational documents do not restrict shareholders from filling vacancies). However, the certificate of incorporation must explicitly permit removal without cause when the board of directors of the corporation is classified. Under DGCL default rules, a board member on a classified board can be removed only for cause. Unless the certificate of incorporation provides otherwise, this requirement enhances the board's power on a classified board to retain their position for their entire term. The term "cause" was interpreted by Delaware courts to include only certain types of conducts, such as gross misconduct or neglect or false or fraudulent misrepresentation.[31]

In addition, some corporations install in their certificate of incorporation or by-laws a provision that empowers the majority of the board to fill vacancies in the board, including in the event that such vacancies result from retirement or removal of a director by shareholders. If vacancies may be filled by majority of directors rather than shareholders, removing directors might not be a helpful solution for gaining majority control of the board (see discussion below).

(3) Converting — If shareholders have the power to convert the staggered board into a unitary board, shareholders may dismantle the staggered board to elect all members of the board to a 1-year term. To be able to take this course of action, the certificate of incorporation or by-laws should empower shareholders to take resolution by special meeting or by a written consent in order to take this action with no delay, otherwise they would have to wait until the next annual meeting. However, if the staggered board provision was installed in the certificate of incorporation rather only in the by-laws, converting the board structure would have to be done with the support of the board, as further discussed below.

[31] Rohe v. Reliance Training Network, Inc., 2000 Del. Ch. LEXIS 108 (Del. Ch. July 21, 2000). It should be noted that if the shareholders vote for the election of board members under the cumulative voting method, they can remove the entire board without cause even if the board is staggered.

Adopting Staggered Board Provisions and Destaggering

A staggered board provision can be set either in the certificate of incorporation or the by-laws. The corporate document in which the staggered board was installed has critical implications for the effectiveness of the defense measure and the veto power that directors will have over takeover decisions. If a staggered board provision is installed in a corporate document and shareholders want to dismantle such provision, they would have to amend the document to repeal the provision. Initiating an amendment to the certificate of incorporation to destagger the board (or to adopt a staggered board provision) is in the sole power of the board. If the board decides to initiate an amendment to the certificate of incorporation, shareholders' approval is required to give effect to such an amendment. Shareholder voting requirement makes any amendment to the certificate of incorporation a lengthy process in US public companies. First, the board of directors must propose an amendment and call for special meeting of the shareholders or direct the shareholders to consider the proposal at the next annual meeting. Second, the board must give an advance notice of annual or special meeting with brief summary of the proposed amendment. Third, the majority of all holders of outstanding shares must vote in favor of the amendment. This process entails the risk that board will not gain an approval from the majority of shareholders in favor of the change. From the view of the shareholders, they depend on the board to initiate an amendment to the certificate of incorporation. Without obtaining the board's support, the shareholders will not be able to make any change to the certificate of incorporation, including with respect to conversion of the staggered board into a unitary board. In other words, the board would have veto power with respect to any amendment to the certificate of incorporation (and vice versa, the shareholders would have veto power on any amendment that the board initiates).[32] The veto power that the board has on amendments to the certificate of incorporation makes a certificate of

[32] 8 Del. C. § 242(b).

incorporation-staggered board provision a highly effective defense measure. On the other hand, if the staggered board provision was installed in the by-laws, changing the board structure would be a simpler task. DGCL provides that the corporation may, in its certificate of incorporation, confer the power to adopt, amend or repeal by-laws by the board of directors. Often corporations provide directors with the power to amend the by-laws.[33] While the board needs a special provision in the certificate of incorporation to permit it to make changes in the by-laws, DGCL default rules give shareholders the power to amend by-laws. Moreover, the DGCL states that the power of the shareholders to amend the by-laws cannot be taken away from them. Therefore, amending the by-laws of a corporation would require either a shareholder approval or board approval (in a corporation that allows the board to amend by-laws), and thus dismantling a by-laws-staggered board provision can be done by either the shareholders or the board. In other words, there is no veto power to one organ. If the staggered board provisions were set in the by-laws of the corporation, shareholders can always destagger the board through either a written consent or a special meeting, if they have the ability to do so, or otherwise at the annual meeting.[34]

If a three-class staggered board provision was set in the certificate of incorporation, and the corporation organizational documents do not permit shareholders to pack the board or remove directors without cause, directors can rely on a very effective antitakeover defense to maintain the independence of the corporation. Trying to take control of the board would not be a viable option and the bidder would be better off going directly to the shareholders to tender their shares. The only way to gain control over such a board would be by winning two annual board elections. Winning two elections could take as long as 13 months if the hostile takeover action was initiated immediately

---

[33] The power of the board to amend the by-laws, if such power was granted to them, is limited. Boards may reasonably amend by-laws in response to a hostile takeover, but Delaware courts have affirmed that they may review such amendments with higher level of scrutiny. See Takeover Law and Practice, supra note 20, at 129.

[34] 8 Del. C. § 109(a).

before an annual meeting and up to 25 months if such action was initiated immediately after an annual meeting of the shareholders.

For example, the board of directors of Great Startup Inc. is a three-class staggered board. The board announces that the annual meeting of the shareholders will be held on May 21, 2016. The Raider, a shareholder in Great Startup Inc., decided prior to the annual meeting that he wants to take control of the company by gaining control of the board. He initiates a proxy contest and wins one-third of the seats at the annual meeting held on May 21, 2016. Approximately a year later, the board announces that the annual meeting of the shareholders will be held on May 21, 2017. The Raider initiates a proxy contest and again wins one third of the seats on the board. Thereby, on May 21, 2017, the Raider has two-thirds of the seats on the board — he has majority control. However, if the Raider had decided to take over the company only on May 22, 2016, he would then have had to wait until May 2017 to win his first proxy contest to gain one-third of the seats, and then to wait again to May 2018 to win his second proxy contest to gain two-thirds of the seats on the board. The entire process would take 24 months before he can gain majority control and only if he is able to win two proxy contests.

Influencing the Board without Board Majority — Activist Shareholders Trends

Activist shareholders developed tactics to overcome antitakeover defenses, and some of the traditional defense measures are not as effective as they used to be. For example, activist shareholders seek the support of shareholders' allies, such as large institutional holders, to pressure boards to adopt their approach and pursue a change. One way in which activists leverage their power is by demanding a short slate on the board, i.e., a minority vote on the board of directors.[35]

[35] The *Wall Street Journal*, Ronald Barusch, Dealpolitik: Management Takes Page from Activist Playbook with 'Short Slates', July 31, 2014, 12:43 pm ET, available at http://blogs.wsj.com/moneybeat/2014/07/31/dealpolitik-management-takes-page-from-activists-playbook-with-short-slates/. Bloomberg Business, Beth Jinks Carol Hymowitz, *Activist Investors Are Finding It Easier Than Ever to Get Board Seats,*

Activists can run a short slate of directors for election at the annual meeting and gain influence and representation on the board. By running a short slate, both the corporation and the dissident shareholders avoid the risk of an expensive, drawn-out proxy battle. A study on hedge funds tactics reveals that activist shareholders favor this tactic and seek to influence the board without having to go through a proxy contest. According to this study, 48.3% of hedge fund activist events include communicating with the board or management on a regular basis, and 11.6% of hedge funds' tactics included influencing the board through board representation without a proxy contest. Only 13.2% of hedge funds' activism was done via a proxy fight in order to replace the management.[36] Another indication that both boards and activist shareholders try to avoid proxy fights is demonstrated by the number of settlements achieved by boards and activists. Although the number of proxy fights doubled between 2007 and 2011, most of these proxy fights were settled before they even got to a shareholder's vote, and the vast majority of proxy fights that were won by the acquirer were for minority vote only.[37] It seems that recently dissident shareholders don't seek majority control on the board and gain influence through minority seats or by other means. If that is the case, activist shareholders could have found a counter tactic around staggered boards to influence the corporation's policy.

The following real-life examples demonstrate how activist shareholders can gain influence on the board without launching a proxy contest. Early in 2014, Carl Icahn, a notorious activist and shareholder in eBay Inc. released a number of public letters first to the company's management and later to the shareholders of the company making demands to the board of directors of eBay. In his letters, Icahn indicated that he had nominated two of his employees to the board of directors, demanded the management to spin off eBay's

---

November 4, 2015, 12:27 PM EST available at http://www.bloomberg.com/news/articles/2015-11-04/from-icahn-to-peltz-activists-find-companies-are-caving-in-fast.

[36] Alon Brav, Wei Jiang, Frank Partnoy, and Randall Thomas, *Hedge Fund Activism, Corporate Governance, and Firm Performance*, *The Journal of Finance*, Vol. LXIII, No. 4, 1729, 1743, 2008.

[37] See Hostile M&A — Increased Use of Proxy Fights and Poison Pill Defense, supra note 21.

PayPal business, demanded an inspection of the company's books and records, criticized the sale of Skype by eBay to a group of investors that included some of eBay's executives, and claimed misconduct by the management. An exchange of letters began between the company, the shareholders and Carl Icahn that continued for months. Over the following months, a proxy contest was conducted between eBay and Icahn. The fight between the parties played out all over the media. In April 2014, eBay announced that it had reached a settlement with Icahn to end the proxy fight. Pursuant to the agreement between the parties, Icahn would withdraw his proposals to separate the company's PayPal business and to nominate his employees as directors at eBay. eBay agreed to appoint David Dorman, formerly the chief executive officer of AT&T Corp. as a 10th independent director. eBay executives eventually decided to push for a PayPal spin-off, announcing that eBay would separate PayPal into an independent publicly traded company in 2015. In January 2015, eBay and Icahn entered into an agreement to appoint Icahn's nominee, to the board of directors. On November 2015, Icahn swapped his eBay shares for an equal number of shares in PayPal. The swap completed the corporate spin-off of PayPal, a business move Icahn was able to complete by influencing the boards of directors of both companies without gaining a majority control of their boards of directors.[38]

In February 2016, American International Group (AIG) came into an agreement with Carl Icahn and John Paulson. This agreement was achieved after nearly 4 months of a loud debate between the activist investors and AIG's management. The investors were threatening to take the company to a proxy fight unless it agreed to adopt their plan to breakup the company. In the settlement achieved between the parties, Icahn got two board seats and in return he agreed to drop off his battle with the board. The parties were able to avoid an expensive and lengthy proxy fight by providing the investors with two minority seats on the board. Following the agreement, AIG's board expanded to 16 seats from 14 in order to accommodate

[38] http://www.businessinsider.com/carl-icahn-ebay-letter-2014-2; http://www.reuters.com/article/us-investments-funds-icahn-idUSKCN0T52SP20151117.

Icahn's and Paulson's representatives on the board. This move might be the beginning of the investors' campaign to split the company, pushing a change in the company's policy with his minority vote on the board.[39]

Shareholder's Rights Plan — The Poison Pill

The shareholders' rights plan, also known as the poison pill, is considered to be the most effective and notorious defense measure against a hostile takeover. The poison pill was invented in the 1980s by Martin Lipton, one of the founding partners of Wachtell, Lipton, Rosen & Katz, a distinguished Corporate and M&A law firm based in New York. In the mid-80s, poison pills were challenged at the Delaware Supreme Court and their validity was upheld. The poison pill become commonplace for public companies and since its inception, the poison pill was triggered in a very small number of occasions.[40] The strong antitakeover effect of the pill either forced bidders to negotiate a friendly deal with the board or took corporations out of the takeover market. In 2011, the poison pill was challenged again in the Delaware Supreme Court's Airgas Poison Pill case, and again, the pill was upheld by the Delaware court. In the Airgas case, the court confirmed the adoption and use of a poison pill designed to protect the corporation and its shareholders, as a legitimate exercise of the board's business judgment. The court concluded that the board of directors has the responsibility to protect the shareholders from an inadequate offer and the poison pill can be used to serve this "legitimate purpose."[41]

---

[39] Liz Moyer, AIG Will Give Board Seats to 2 Activists Who Want a Breakup, *The New York Times*, February 11, 2016, available at http://www.nytimes.com/2016/02/12/business/dealbook/aig-will-give-board-seats-to-2-activists-who-want-a-breakup.html?_r=0.

[40] The Delaware Chancery Court had first dealt with a poison pill in 2009. In Selectica, Inc. v. Versata, Inc., see Lou R. Kling and Eileen T. Nugent Negotiated Acquisitions of Companies, Subsidiaries and Divisions § 16.06, 2015, hereinafter Negotiated Acquisitions of Companies.

[41] Air Prods. & Chems., Inc., v. Airgas, Inc., C.A. No. 5249 (Del. Ch. Feb. 15, 2011).

What the poison pill does in practice is limit the power of the shareholders to sell their shares to a third party above a certain ownership threshold of such third party in the corporation. Earlier in this chapter, we discussed shareholders' three basic rights: the right to sell, sue, and vote. The right to sell enables shareholders to monitor managers and hostile bidders to takeover underperforming corporations and increase their value. Hostile bidders can go directly to the shareholders and request them to exercise their right to sell and tender their shares. The poison pill disables this possibility by excessively diluting the hostile bidder and making the takeover too expensive to be economically viable. This feature of the defense measure forces the hostile bidder to talk with the board and negotiate a "friendly" deal. That was the goal that Martin Lipton was trying to achieve when he created the defense measure, to force the bidder to negotiate a deal with the board rather than take the corporation out of the market.[42]

How Does the Poison Pill Work?

The poison pill can be structured in one of two ways: (i) the flip-in right or, (ii) the flip-over right. Here are the basic terms of the flip-in and flip-over.

The Flip-in Right

The first step is for the board to issue a dividend to the shareholders. This dividend includes a right to buy one-hundredth of a share of preferred stock on each outstanding share of common stock of the corporation. Each right holder is entitled to purchase common stock in the target at a significant discount when a hostile acquirer (or group of acquirers) crosses a certain ownership threshold. The ownership threshold is usually set between 10% and 20% ownership — the triggering event. The discount that each right holder receives results from the mechanism of the flip-in right. Once the ownership threshold is crossed, the rights flip in and each rights holder is entitled to

[42] Martin Lipton, *Corporate Governance in the Age of Finance Corporatism*, 136 U. Pa. L. Rev. 1, 30 (1987), hereinafter Lipton.

purchase common stock of twice the exercise price of the right. The price of the common stock is the market value of the stock at the time of the triggering event. Eventually, the right provides its holders with 50% discount on common stock. At a 50% discount, shareholders would most likely buy all the shares they are entitled to buy and enjoy this benefit. Following the exercise of the rights, all shareholders increase their holdings in the target, except for the hostile bidder whose rights are void. The hostile bidder is the only shareholder who doesn't participate in the rights plan. The result is substantial dilution of the hostile bidder's holdings in the corporation.[43]

Example: if the exercise price of the right under the shareholders rights plan is US$50, the holder of the right is entitled to receive shares of the target worth US$100. If the market value of the target's stock is US$5 per share at the time the hostile acquirer crossed the ownership threshold, each right holder is then entitled to purchase 20 shares of common stock for the US$50 exercise price (US$5 a share for twice the exercise price (US$50) — US$100).

The exercise price of the one-hundredth of a share of the preferred stock is determined by the board, based on the board's estimation of the corporation's stock value in the long term (usually 10 years, in many cases the term of the shareholders rights plan). Often the exercise price of the right is a multiple of three to five times the price of the stock on the date of adoption of the rights plan.[44] The flip-in right would be exercisable only upon the occurrence of a triggering event that would usually be (i) the acquisition of 10–20% of the corporation's stock by the bidder (or a group of acquirers), or (ii) after an announcement by the bidder (or a group of acquirers) of its intention to acquire stock in the corporation that will cross the level of threshold under the plan.[45] Little judicial precedent exists regarding low levels of flip-in tolerance, but commentators note that selecting too high a threshold will arguably cause the rights plan to "lose much of its effect as a deterrent against the risks created by a

[43] Martin Lipton & Erica H. Steinberger Takeovers & Freezeouts, § 6.03[2] (2015), hereinafter Takeovers & Freezeouts.

[44] Negotiated Acquisitions of Companies, supra note 39.

[45] See Takeovers & Freezeouts, supra note 42.

significant stock accumulation,"[46] whereas setting too low a level might lead "a court [...] [to] conclude that the pill is disproportionately draconian to the threat under Unocal/Unitrin principles."[47]

The flip-in right can be exchanged into common stock *in lieu* of exercising it under the mechanism described above. It is under the discretion of the board to exchange the rights to the corporation's common stock after the rights have been triggered (the crossing of the ownership threshold) but before the acquisition of 50% or more by the hostile bidder.[48]

The effectiveness of the flip-in right lies in its discriminatory feature. All shareholders of the target other than the hostile bidder are entitled to exercise the flip-in right. Excluding the hostile bidder from the shareholders rights plan results in a substantial dilution in the shareholdings of the hostile bidder. The incentive for the shareholders is clear, they can buy common stock at half price and increase their holdings in the target on the account of the hostile bidder.

Example: Great Startup Inc. has a shareholder's rights plan pursuant to which it distributes to the shareholders of the company one-hundredth of series A preferred stock for each outstanding share of common stock. Each holder has the right to purchase common stock of the company at twice the exercise price of the right under the plan. The rights are attached to Great Startup Inc.'s common stock and are not exercisable or transferable apart from the shares of the company unless and until 20% or more ownership threshold is crossed by any beneficial acquirer or group of acquirers. The rights of such acquirer or group of acquirers will be void and they will not be entitled to exercise the right.

- Great Startup Inc. has 1,000,000 shares of common stock outstanding.
- The exercise price of the flip-in right is US$100 per right.
- The term of the plan is 10 years.

---

[46] Arthur Fleischer, Jr. & Alexander R. Sussman, Takeover Defense, § 5.05 (supp. 2003).

[47] Id.

[48] Id.

- Shareholder David holds 10,000 shares, 1.0% of Great Startup Inc.'s common stock.

The Raider owns 8.0% of Great Startup Inc.'s common stock. On June 2016, the Raider decided to acquire additional stock from existing stock holders of the company. Following her recent acquisitions, she now owns 20% of Great Startup's outstanding common stock — 200,000 shares. At the time of the crossing of the 20% threshold, June 16, 2016, the stock value of Great Startup was US$25 per share.

The shareholders, other than the Raider, holders of 800,000 shares, are entitled to exercise their rights under the plan while the Raider's rights are void due to her crossing of the ownership threshold. Each holder can purchase US$200 worth of stock (twice the exercise price), which means that each right holder is entitled to receive eight shares of common stock (US$25 × 8 = US$200).

- Prior to the triggering event there were 1,000,000 outstanding shares of common stock.
- Following the triggering event there are 6,400,000 additional outstanding shares of common stock, which is the number of rights holders, 800,000 × 8 shares per right.

  The total number of outstanding stock now is 7,400,000 (the additional shares — 6,400,000 + the initial common stock outstanding: (i) shares of the raider + 200,000 + remaining shareholders — 800,000). The Raider still has only 200,000 shares, because her rights are void. Instead of having 20% value of stock, the Raiders has only 2.7% of the stock (200,000/7,400,000).
- Shareholder David now holds 90,000 shares in Great Startup Inc. (10,000 × 8 shares per right + his initial 10,000). David's 90,000 shares now represent 1.2% of Great Startup Inc.'s common stock (90,000/7,400,000).

<u>The Flip-over Right</u>

The flip-over right is intended to protect shareholders against a squeeze out that is followed by a merger. The triggering event for the exercise of the flip-over right is the acquisition of 50% or more of the corporation's assets, a merger or any other business combination with the target (e.g., in case the bidder will become a controlling shareholder in the target). Upon the triggering event, the shareholders receive a right to buy shares in the surviving corporation or the acquirer, as the case may be, for twice the exercise price of the right, i.e., half of the market price of the acquirer's stock. The mechanism would be the same as in the flip-in only that the target's shareholders are entitled to purchase their shares in the acquirer rather than the target.[49]

Example: if the acquirer's stock is traded at US$50 per share, and the exercise price of the right under the shareholders rights plan is US$100, each rights holder is entitled to receive shares of the acquirer worth US$200. Therefore, each rights holder is entitled to purchase four shares of common stock of the acquirer for the US$100 exercise price (US$50 a share for twice the exercise price (US$100) — US$200).

The flip-in and flip-over rights do not affect the corporation, its financial statements or its capital structure (unless new shares needs to be registered, see discussion below). Further, the flip-in rights are not transferable or exercisable separately from the common stock, and the rights do not include any voting rights.[50] In other words, the rights are dormant and can only be exercised upon the occurrence of a triggering event, and once exercisable they affect only the hostile bidder. The only effect that the poison pill has on the remaining shareholders is an increase in ownership of the corporation. Note that the board can adopt both the flip-in and flip-over rights in the plan and most plans include both.

The Power to Install and Redeem a Poison Pill

Which organ in the corporation can install the poison pill? Unless the corporation organizational documents provide otherwise, the board has the exclusive power to install a poison pill because it is a corporate

[49] Negotiated Acquisitions of Companies, supra note 39.
[50] Id.

Table 3: Summary — Flip-over and Flip-in.

	Flip-over	Flip-in
The basics	The target's shareholders have a right to purchase stock in the *acquirer* for half price of the stock's market price, as a dividend. The effectiveness is in the discriminatory treatment between the acquirer and the target's shareholders which dilutes the existing shareholders (prior to the flip-over) in the *acquirer*.	The target's shareholders have a right to purchase stock in the *target* for a fraction of the stock's market price, as a dividend. The effectiveness is in the discriminatory treatment between the acquirer and the target shareholders which dilutes the existing acquirer stock in the *target*.
Potential reaction by the hostile bidder	The acquirer would have to either (i) buy all or substantially all the stocks in the target or (ii) negotiate the price in order to redeem the rights.	The acquirer would have to either (i) buy all or substantially all the stocks in the target or (ii) negotiate with the board in order to redeem the rights.
Exchange	The flip-over rights cannot be exchanged, because the rights flip over to the stock of the acquirer.	The board may exchange each right for common stock of the target after the rights have been triggered and before the crossing of 50% or more ownership threshold.

action under the board's authority to issue stock and to install a stock plan. However, a board decision on a stock issuance is subject to the number of shares specified in the certificate of incorporation. The number of shares under the certificate of incorporation is the maximum number of shares that the board is authorized to issue without a shareholder approval. In the event that the contemplated plan requires issuance of additional stock, in excess of the number of stock specified in the certificate of incorporation, a shareholder approval will be required, and thus the board will have to receive the shareholders' approval for the poison pill.

The redemption of the poison pill is also under the exclusive authority of the board, as mentioned above. Only the board can redeem the pill and only if the redemption is made prior to occurrence of the triggering event (the crossing of the threshold). If the board decides to redeem the pill, the redemption is made for a nominal amount. The board's exclusive power to redeem the pill provides it with a veto power over a hostile takeover. Therefore, where the corporation has a poison pill in place, bidders must first gain the board's approval before making a bid to the shareholders.

Bidders have two viable ways around the poison pill, negotiating a friendly deal with the board or a proxy contest to replace the board with managers that will redeem the poison pill. Recall that having a proxy fight can be a lengthy and expensive process. As discussed above, the delay caused by a proxy contest can deter the bidder from taking over the corporation because of a change in market conditions or the overall costs incurred from the battle with the board (see discussion above).

A poison pill would be most effective for a corporation that has both a poison pill and a staggered board. A corporation with a poison pill and without a staggered board can prevent a hostile takeover for only as long as it takes for the hostile bidder to win one proxy battle and replace the target's board with board members who will redeem the pill. If the staggered board is not an effective measure, i.e., if the certificate of incorporation allows shareholders to remove directors without cause, pack the board and to vote by written consent or through a special meeting, shareholders can replace the board with directors that will redeem the pill with little or almost no delay. Therefore, a board that wants to retain its position in the target would seek to have both defensive measures, the poison pill and an effective staggered board.

As Table 4 shows, a poison pill can be easily adopted by the board, harder for the shareholders to dissemble, and more difficult for a bidder to overcome in comparison to a staggered board. A staggered board that was not structured effectively would not be a challenging hurdle to overcome, and more counter-tactics are available to overcome an effective staggered board than to go against a poison pill.

Table 4: Poison Pill and Staggered Board Comparison.

	Poison Pill	Staggered Board
Who has the power to adopt?	Adopting a poison pill is in the sole power of the board.	Either the board or the shareholders can adopt in the corporation's by-laws. The board must initiate the adoption and the shareholders must approve it in the corporation's charter.
Who has the power to repeal the defense measure?	Only the board can redeem a poison pill.	A by-laws-staggered board can be dismantled by either the shareholders or the board. A staggered board can be dismantled only if both the shareholders and the board approve it in the corporation's charter.
How to go around the defense measure?	Gain control over the board and redeem the pill. If the board is staggered, the acquirer must win two elections to gain majority control.	The acquirer can go directly to the shareholders and request them to tender their shares. If shareholders have the power, they can pack the board, remove directors or convert the staggered board. The acquirer must win two elections to take control over the board. Activists can sometime influence the board through minority slots or through direct communication with the board.

Recent Trends

Lately, there is a movement against the poison pill. The decrease in the number of rights plans is most likely due to rising influence from activist shareholder. Activist shareholders oppose poison pills because the pill makes a hostile takeover almost impossible, giving the board a veto power over takeover decisions. Institutional Shareholder Services (ISS), a proxy advisory firm that advises on shareholders voting matters, typically supports protakeover corporate governance. Their guidelines usually recommend either the redemption of poison pills or adoption of a short-term poison pill, the renewal of which will be subject to shareholders approval.[51] The influence of activist shareholders and ISS is evident by the market trends. In recent years, companies that decided to adopt poison pills were more likely to have done so because they felt vulnerable to hostile takeovers.[52] Recently, corporations adopt poison pills as a responsive measure designed to protect the corporation from specific threats rather than merely adopting plans as part of a routine adoption of defense measures, and when poison pills are adopted they are usually adopted for a short term.[53] In addition, some corporations adopt poison pill "on the shelf" to serve the corporation in case a quick adoption of a poison pill is required.[54] This market trend creates a ground for shareholders to be more engaged in corporation's antitakeover defense measure policy. Shareholders today have more to say on poison pill's corporate policy than what they use to be in the past, and from the corporate side, we see more corporations that give shareholders a way to input on poison pills. For example, corporations request a "say on the pill", as some corporations put the poison pill to a shareholder's vote following just a 1-year term (Martin Lipton suggests a 10-year term).[55]

A Note about Poison Pills and Recent Takeover Trends: Poison pills as well as staggered boards are not as effective against activist

---

[51] Coffee and Palia, supra note 10, at 17.

[52] See Takeovers & Freezeouts, supra note 42.

[53] A New Era in Poison Pills — Specific Purpose Poison Pills The Number of Companies with Poison Pills Falls Below 1,000 for First Time in Twenty Years, SharkRepellent.Net, April 1, 2010, available at https://www.sharkrepellent.net/request?an=dt.getPage&st=1&pg=/pub/rs_20100401.html&Specific_Purpose_Poison_Pills&rnd=42401.

[54] See Takeovers & Freezeouts, supra note 42.

[55] See Takeovers & Freezeouts, supra note 42; Shareholder Input on Poison Pills, SharkRepellent.Net, June 15, 2009, available at https://www.sharkrepellent.net/request?an=dt.getPage&st=1&pg=/pub/rs_20090615.html&Shareholder_Input_on_Poison_Pills&rnd=674362.

shareholders as they are against "traditional" hostile takeover activities. We discussed earlier in this chapter innovative methods of activists to influence the corporate business plan, win the support of other shareholders and pressure a push for change. The same untraditional methods activist shareholders use to go around staggered boards can be beneficial against poison pills and on the long term, shareholders led by activists, can pressure boards to de-stagger as well as to redeem a pill.[56]

Additional Charter and By-laws Provisions

The poison pill and staggered board, discussed in detail earlier in this chapter, are widely recognized as the most effective antitakeover defense measures, but these are not the only defense measures incorporated under the corporation organizational documents. There are other measures that a corporation can adopt as part of its defense profile. Those additional measures will not be as effective as the poison pill and staggered board, but they may affect the corporation's ability to resist a hostile takeover. The corporation's defensive profile refers to the analysis that a hostile bidder will make when evaluating a hostile takeover and the likelihood of success of such hostile takeover attempt as weighed against a friendly approach to the corporation's board. Those defense measures won't prevent a hostile takeover, they will provide additional protection against certain takeover tactics. In some circumstances, those additional defenses can enhance the effectiveness of the staggered board and poison pill and their antitakeover effect against a hostile bidder. For example, earlier in this chapter, we indicated that corporations that limit in their certificate of incorporation or by-laws the maximum number of directors that the shareholders may elect, prevent shareholders from getting majority control of the board of directors by increasing its

---

[56] For example, see *The Wall Street Journal*, Ronald Barusch, Twitter Takeover Defenses May Fly Out the Window — Dealpolitik, Feb 2, 2016, 8:03 am ET WSJ, availableathttp://blogs.wsj.com/moneybeat/2016/02/02/dealpolitik-twitter-takeover-defense-is-rare-and-endangered-bird/.

size and packing the board with directors. If shareholders have the power to increase the size of the board, they could dismantle a staggered board by increasing the number of seats on the board, filling vacancies with directors that share their views and gain majority control without being required to wait two elections. A provision in the corporation organizational documents that prevents shareholders from packing the board enhances the corporation's defensive profile, because it prevents shareholders from having the power to interfere with the governing power of the existing board of directors. In this part below, we present additional components that will need to be looked at and assessed in connection with a hostile takeover and the significance of each such measure to the hostile bidder's ultimate goal.

Elections of Directors — Cumulative Voting

Under the DGCL, the default rule is that directors are elected by plurality of the votes. Pursuant to the statutory method of the DGCL, the nominees with the largest number of votes are elected as directors up to the maximum number of directors to be chosen at the election, without regard to the votes "withheld", "against" or not cast, as each shareholder can recast all of his votes on each director.[57] As an alternative to the statutory method under the DGCL, corporations may implement the cumulative voting method. Under the cumulative voting method, each shareholder gets a total number of votes that equals the number of vacancies times the number of shares owned by him. This method enables minority shareholders to win some seats on the board.[58] The takeover effect of cumulative voting is a result of the access that minority shareholders, such as activist shareholders can gain to the board of directors. For that reason, cumulative voting is associated with vulnerability to hostile takeover

---

[57] 8 Del. C. § 215(3).
[58] 8 Del. C. § 214.

actions.[59] Through cumulative voting activist shareholders who do not own large blocks of shares can win some seats on the board and get access to internal information and influence business decisions, as discussed earlier in this chapter with more details.

For example,[60] Seed Stage Inc. a privately held company has only two shareholders. Shareholder-1 has 51 shares (majority) and Shareholder-2 has 49 shares (minority). The board of directors of the company is comprised of three board seats.

- In the statutory voting method, Shareholder-2 with 49 shares will cast all his shares — 49 on each candidate, and Shareholder-1 will cast all his shares — 51 on each candidate and therefore Shareholder-1 will always win all the seats (51 votes against 49 votes on each seat).
- In the cumulative voting method, votes can be accumulated. In this method, Shareholder-2 will have a total of 147 votes (49 votes times three seats) to cast and Shareholder-1 will have a total of 153 votes (51 votes times three seats). Each shareholder can distribute his total number of votes as he wishes among the open seats. Shareholder-2, the minority, can cast his entire 147 votes on one open seat and by doing so he might win this one seat in case that Shareholder-1, the majority, will decide to cast less than 147 votes on the same open seat.

The problem with cumulative voting is that it is uncertain and may create unpredictable results.[61] There are too many options to play when trying to form a board and the majority can distribute votes in such a way to prevent the minority from getting its representation on the board of directors (in the example above, the majority can cast

---

[59] Institutions as Relational Investors: A New Look at Cumulative Voting, 94 Colum. L. Rev. 124, 155 (1994); See also footnote 95 at The Powerful Antitakeover Force of Staggered Boards: Theory, Evidence, and Policy, *Stanford Law Review*, 54, 887. The authors show that cumulative voting can result in even more effective staggered board than with statutory voting.

[60] Just for illustration purpose, this example refers to a private corporation and not a public, although takeover activities are held in the capital markets.

[61] See footnote 95 at Bebchuk, Coates & Subramanian, supra note 27.

Table 5: Statutory and Cumulative Voting — Numerical Example.

	Director 1		**Director 2**		**Director 3**	
	Share holder-1	**Share holder-2**	**Share holder-1**	**Share holder-2**	**Share holder-1**	**Share holder-2**
Statutory vote	51 (Win)	49	51 (Win)	49	51 (Win)	49
Cumulative vote*	51	147 (Win)	51 (Win)	0	51 (Win)	0

Note: *The example above describes one potential scenario, but there could be different scenarios with different outcomes with respect to the ways shareholders would cast their votes under the cumulative voting method.

148 votes on director's one seat that the minority was voting for with his entire 147 votes and the majority shareholder will still have five votes to elect directors to the additional two open seats). In addition, it can form an uncooperative or adversarial board.

Another issue associated with takeovers is the power to remove directors in a corporation with a cumulative voting practice. Recall that some corporations restrict shareholders from removing directors without cause. If the charter or by-laws require removal for cause, the shareholders cannot gain majority control of the board simply by removing directors, because removal of any director or the entire board must be only for cause. In addition, pursuant to the DGCL, if the board of directors is classified, then directors can only be removed for cause, removal without cause in case that the board is classified would be impermissible even if the charter or by-laws allow removal without cause. If the board is not classified and the charter or by-laws authorize cumulative voting for election of directors, then shareholders can remove the entire board without cause and elect an entire new board of directors to replace incumbent directors if they have the power to fill vacancies (see further discussion below). However, if less than the entire board is to be removed, directors can be removed without cause only if the votes to remove such director/s would be sufficient to elect such director/s cumulatively voted at an election of the entire board. This provision is designed to protect minority shareholders from removing their elected directors by the majority shareholders without their approval. Minority directors that could have been nominated by activist shareholders can be protected from being removed without cause from the board in case they are not protected by any of the other practices mentioned above, such as a staggered board structure or a specific provision in the charter that prohibits removal without cause.

Removal of Directors without Cause

Removal of directors who oppose a takeover by dissident shareholders can be an important step in facilitating a takeover. Shareholders can increase their influence on the corporation's business plan by removing directors and replacing them with directors who will take actions to advance the business strategy such shareholders desire to promote. For example, shareholders can remove directors who adopt a poison pill (which is in the sole power and authority of the board, unless the charter restrict such authority) and replace them with directors who will dismantle the poison pill, as long as shareholders refill the vacancies. Pursuant to the DGCL, any director or the entire board of directors may be removed, with or without cause, by the majority of the shareholders of the corporation, unless the charter provides otherwise or in the case of a corporation whose board is classified.[62] Therefore, if the board is classified, removal without cause would not be permissible even if the charter provides otherwise. But, if the board is not classified, a corporation that wishes to restrict removal of directors can set in its charter that directors may be removed only for cause, such as fraud and criminal acts, thereby preventing dissident shareholders from causing the removal of a director without cause. If removal can only be for cause and the board is not staggered, dissident shareholders will only have to wait to the next annual meeting before they can replace any director. If the board is staggered, removal of the majority of the board would be a longer process, as discussed earlier in this chapter. Even if the shareholders can remove directors without cause,

[62] 8 Del. C. § 141(k).

filling the vacancies might not be within the power of the shareholders as further discussed below.

Remaining Directors' Right to Fill Vacancies — Newly Created Directorships and Vacancies on the Board

The DGCL provides that directors elect their nominees for vacant and new seats by a majority of the board then in office, even in the case that only one director remained, unless otherwise provided in the charter or by-laws.[63] Therefore, even if the charter, by-laws, or the DGCL give shareholders the power to remove directors or pack the board with new seats, shareholders do not elect the new board members if they were not explicitly empowered to do so under the corporation organizational documents. The new directors would be elected by the existing directors and not by the shareholders. This default rule restricts the ability of the shareholders to fill vacancies on the board with directors that share their views after they packed the board or removed directors. The rule impairs shareholders incentive to replace their board of directors and their power to elect directors. The power to fill vacancies by the board would be used by the remaining directors to nominate successor that they want to have on the board and exclude director nominees that are associated with dissident shareholders.

Supermajority Vote Required for Stockholders to Amend Certain Charter/By-laws Provisions

Pursuant to the DGCL, unless otherwise specified in the charter or by-laws, all matters other than election of directors require majority of the shares present in person or represented by proxy, at the meeting and entitled to vote on the subject matter.[64] A supermajority vote requirement, typically 75% of the shares entitled to vote, can have a defensive effect against a hostile takeover for two main reasons. First, it limits the rights of stockholders to amend certain charter and by-laws

---

[63] 8 Del. C. § 223(a)(1).

[64] 8 Del. C. § 216(2).

provisions so as to facilitate takeovers because it requires a higher portion of shareholders to approve the amendment. Second, certain business decisions that require shareholders vote, such as a sale of the corporation, would require a higher percentage of shares to approve such decision, making it more difficult for the hostile bidder to receive the approval of the shareholders and complete the takeover.

Special Meetings and Notice Considerations

When the board of a corporation has flexibility in setting annual meeting of stockholders, and such right is coupled with other restrictions on special meetings and action by consent, the board is essentially granted flexibility to determine best timing, from the board's perspective, to schedule the annual meeting of stockholders, such that any hostile takeover attempts by a hostile bidder to replace the board may be significantly delayed.

Action by Written Consent or Special Meeting

The DGCL allows shareholders to take actions they are authorized to take under law or the corporation organizational documents, without any action required from the board of directors, by either, a written consent, a written resolution by majority of the votes or any other quorum required at a shareholders meeting; or through a special meeting of the shareholders in case that the charter or by-laws provided them with such right. Unless otherwise provided in the charter or by-laws, a majority of the shares entitled to vote, in person or proxy, shall constitute a quorum for holding a special meeting, but in any event, the majority is no less than one-third of the shares entitled to vote. All matters other than election of directors may be determined by a majority of the votes present at the special meeting. The DGCL permits shareholders to act by written consent unless such power was eliminated by the charter. If the power to act by written consent was eliminated in the charter, amending the charter in order to give the shareholders this right back will require the approval of both the board and the shareholders. Recall that any amendment to the charter must always be approved by both the board of directors and the shareholders. If shareholders wish to act through a special meeting, the charter or by-laws must explicitly empower them to call a special meeting. Unlike the power to act by written consent that is given to the shareholders under the DGCL's default rules (unless the charter takes from shareholders such power), the power to act through a special meeting must be set in the corporation organizational documents.[65] If shareholders can call a special meeting or act by a written resolution, they can advance shareholders governance in the corporation by facilitating shareholders actions, without having to depend on the board's actions and they would be able to act without having to wait for the next annual meeting. For example, earlier in this chapter, we mentioned that the shareholders always have the power to amend the by-laws of the corporation. If a staggered board provision is set in the by-laws and shareholders can act by a written consent or through a special meeting, they can amend the by-laws without being required to wait for the board to call a special meeting or an annual meeting for the shareholders to dismantle the staggered board. These procedures can be a measure for shareholders to fight against undesired board's actions. In 2005, e.g., the members of the board of directors of Six Flags Inc. were replaced through a consent solicitation launched by an activist investment group. Following the replacement of three directors from the board, the chief executive officer of the company was later replaced as well. In 2014, the majority of S&P 500 corporations did not allow shareholders to act by written consent (i.e., their charters disallowed such action by written consent), but there is a new trend led by activist shareholders seeking to increase shareholders governance by providing shareholders with the ability to act by written consent or special meetings.[66]

Special Meetings and Notice Considerations

Pursuant to the DGCL, unless shareholders act by a written consent *in lieu* of a meeting, a corporation is required to hold an annual

[65] 8 Del. C. § 228.

[66] Takeover Law and Practice, supra note 20, at 13.

meeting of shareholders on a date and at a time designated by or in the manner provided in the by-laws. The purpose of the annual meeting is for the election of directors or any other proper business matter that may be transacted at the meeting.[67] The date and time of an annual meeting can be set in the by-laws, otherwise, the board is essentially granted flexibility to determine timing and place, such that any hostile takeover attempts by a hostile bidder to replace the board may be delayed. However, the board's flexibility to determine when to hold an annual meeting is limited. In Delaware, if the corporation fails to hold an annual meeting for a period of 30 days after the date designated for the annual meeting, or if no date has been designated, for a period of 13 months after the last annual meeting, the Delaware Court of Chancery can enter an order for an annual meeting upon the application of any shareholder or director of the corporation.

Although the by-laws can restrict the flexibility of the board to determine when and where to hold the annual meeting, potentially, the board can amend the by-laws to design a different time and place for an annual meeting, because corporations usually grant the board the power to amend the by-laws without requiring any action from the shareholders.[68] If shareholders cannot act by a written consent or through a special meeting, they would have to wait until the next annual meeting in order to set timing and place for the annual meeting in the by-laws.

Restrictions on Ability to Put Forward Shareholders Proposals or to Nominate Directors without Prior Notice to Company

These DGCL provisions include a nonexclusive list of procedures that may be adopted in the by-laws and that will restrict shareholders' business proposals and directors' nominees. Restrictions include: a minimum level of record or beneficial stock ownership by the

[67] 8 Del. C. § 211(b).

[68] Such amendments might be subject to higher scrutiny by the court. See Takeover Law and Practice, supra note 20, at 129.

nominating shareholder; requiring specified information about the nominating shareholder and the nominee(s); conditioning eligibility on the number or proportion of directors nominated; limiting the right of access if nominations are related to an acquisition of a significant percentage of the corporation's stock; requiring that the nominating shareholder indemnify the corporation for any loss arising from false or misleading information or statements submitted by the nominator, or any other lawful condition.[69]

In addition to the DGCL, Regulation 14a-18, shareholder proposals, under the Securities Exchange Act, also known as the town meeting provision, permits shareholders to gain access to the corporation's proxy materials and enables shareholders to promote proper shareholders resolutions. If a shareholder meets the procedure under the regulation, the corporation must include its proposal in the corporation's proxy statement. Large shareholders may still need to file a copy of their solicitation materials with the Securities Exchange Commission (SEC) and file an exempt solicitation.[70]

Blank Check Preferred

A blank check preferred stock provision authorizes the board to set the rights and privileges of any series of preferred stock at the time it is issued. Corporations that include blank check preferred provisions in their certificate of incorporation essentially grant the board a wide discretion in determining rights under any series of preferred stock the corporation may issue. Without this provision in the certificate of incorporation, the board is not authorized to issue new series of preferred stock that the corporation is not authorized to issue under the charter, unless it obtains the approval of the shareholders to amend the certificate of incorporation and to add a new series of preferred stock.[71] When the certificate of incorporation of a corporation includes a blank check preferred provision, the issuance of such stock

---

[69] 8 Del. C. § 112.

[70] 17 C.F.R. § 240.14a-8, 1997.

[71] 8 Del. C. § 161.

is a corporate action as any other corporate matter under the sole discretion of the board. The board can use its power to issue such stock as it may make any other corporate decision under its authority. The issuance of a blank check preferred stock can be used by the board to raise capital, but it can also be used as a defense tactic against hostile takeovers. The antitakeover effect of a blank check preferred results from the special rights and privileges of such series of preferred stock and from discriminating unfriendly shareholders from the issuance of the preferred stock. For example, a board that is authorized under the charter to issue a blank check preferred stock can issue a preferred stock that includes special voting rights in specific events, such as a sale of the corporation. With the issuance of a new series of preferred stock to friendly shareholders who oppose the takeover, the holders of such preferred stock can have a veto power to prevent the completion of the transaction due to their special rights and privileges as holders of such preferred stock.[72] In comparison to the poison pill discussed in detail above, a blank check preferred provision bears some similarities to the poison pill. Both measures involve the issuance of stock in a discriminatory manner to nonhostile shareholders. The issuance of the stock under the poison pill results in a massive dilution of the hostile bidder and the issuance of a blank check preferred stock provides rights to friendly shareholders that assist directors in their efforts against the hostile bidder. One important distinct feature should be noted. If the corporation organizational documents are silent with respect to the power of the board to issue a shareholders rights plan — the poison pill, as most corporations do, then the directors are authorized and empowered to issue a poison pill. However, if the certificate of incorporation is silent about directors' power to issue a blank check preferred stock, then directors must first gain shareholders' approval to include such stock in the charter before they can issue the preferred stock. In other words, the board has the power to issue a poison pill, unless such power was restricted

[72] Jennifer Arlen & Eric Talley, Precommitment and Managerial Incentives: Unregulable Defenses and The Perils of Shareholder Choice, *University of Pennsylvania Law Review*, 152, 577, p. 609, 2003.

or taken away from it by the shareholders and it has no power to issue a blank check preferred stock, unless such power was first granted to it by the shareholders.

Defense Measures — Reactions (Economic Defense)

In this chapter, we have focused on proactive defense mechanisms, which are usually perceived as preventive measures adopted as part of the corporation's long-term plan in advance and as part of the corporation's defensive profile. Another type of defense measures are reaction defenses, also known as financial defenses.[73] These measures would usually be used once an actual takeover activity is pursued against the corporation or if the corporation feels vulnerable and soon might be subject to a hostile activity. Using these practices, the management would seek to make the target less attractive for the hostile bidder in order to make him go away. Alternatively, if the corporation accepts the fact that it is "in play" and can't stay independent, then it might seek a better buyer, better in the view of the board, to eliminate the hostile activity against it. There are a variety of reactive defenses that a corporation can implement.

Disposing Free Cash Flow

One way for acquirers to finance their acquisition is by leveraging up the target's excess cash. Corporations with free cash flow are more vulnerable to takeover activity because their excess cash can be used by the hostile bidder to finance the acquisition after the takeover is completed. Additionally, corporations with free cash flow create agency problems between boards and shareholders and a conflict of interest between boards and shareholders over the payout of free cash flow. In the views of the shareholders, free cash flow should be

[73] Edward F. Greene and James J. Junewicz, A Reappraisal of Current Regulation of Mergers and Acquisitions, *University of Pennsylvania Law Review*, 132, pp. 647, 701, 1984.

distributed, but boards seek to maintain free cash flow to gain flexibility in financing resources and continue growing the corporation.[74] To defend against hostile bidders who are interested in leveraging the corporation's free cash flow, boards can dispose excess cash, and thus eliminate the acquirer's potential source of financing. This action makes the target less attractive for a takeover and might make the hostile bidder go away. There are different ways to dispose of excess cash. Distributing a dividend to shareholders is one way for boards to dispose a corporation's free cash flow. Distributing a cash dividend not only helps boards reduce excess cash but can also increase shareholders support in the board for maximizing value for their shareholders. A stock repurchase (buyback) is another effective tactic to reduce excess cash and to provide shareholders cash return on their stock. Stock repurchase programs can be executed either as a countermeasure to an actual takeover activity or in case that the market conditions and stock value of the corporation make it attractive and vulnerable for a takeover. Stock repurchase would usually be an appropriate action when the board believes that the corporation's stock is undervalued. Stock repurchase is a corporate action under the sole discretion of the board, but it is subject to some statutory restrictions and may also be subject to interorganization restriction set under the certificate of incorporation or by-laws as well as other agreements with third parties.[75] Sometimes, a stock repurchase or a cash dividend is all that a raider is seeking to achieve in its takeover campaign.[76] Corporations that lack sufficient cash to repurchase stock might incur debt to finance a stock repurchase program that would help the board gain shareholders support and fend off the hostile

[74] Jensen, Michael C., The Takeover Controversy: Analysis and Evidence, *Midland Corporate Finance Journal*, 4, 2, p. 14, 1986, available at SSRN: http://ssrn.com/abstract=173452.

[75] For example, 8 Del. C. § 160 sets restriction on stock repurchase when the repurchase "would cause any impairment of the capital of the corporation".

[76] For example, see Reuters, Sinead Carew and Malathi Nayak, *Take-Two to buy back all of Icahn shares; directors leave* Tue Nov 26, 2013 4:36pm EST, available at, http://www.reuters.com/article/us-taketwo-icahn-idUSBRE9AP0MW20131126.

bidder.[77] Taking more debt can achieve the same goals as the other tactics, it might make the corporation less attractive for a takeover.

Divestment

Selling assets of the corporation can also fend off a hostile bidder who is seeking to enhance value through synergy. Selling the corporation's most valuable assets, the crown jewel, would make the target less attractive for takeover and the board can use the consideration of the sale for distribution to the shareholders. The sale could be either to a third party or to the hostile bidder. Alternatively, a corporation can use other divestment methods to make the corporation less attractive for a takeover while increasing value for the shareholders. A spin-off, split-off and split-up[78] are three common divestment methods that a corporation can take with the objective of increasing value for the shareholders by separating valuable assets of a corporation from its remaining assets.

In today's US capital markets, takeover activities can take different forms; in some cases, divesting the corporation and selling the crown jewel might be the action which the hostile bidder is trying to achieve while the management wants to maintain such assets under their control. We discussed earlier Carl Icahn's plan to spin off PayPal from eBay. In that case, the management was against spinning off PayPal from eBay while the only purpose of activist shareholder Carl Icahn's campaign was to split the company to maximize its value in PayPal.

---

[77] For example, see Unocal, supra note 12. Unocal's response to a takeover attempt by Mesa Petroleun. In this case the board's action to take senior debt to finance the repurchase of stock were upheld by the court. Unocal Corp. v. Mesa Petroleum Co.

[78] Spin off means the transferring of underlying assets of the corporation to a new controlled subsidiary and distribute the stock of the subsidiary to the shareholders as a dividend; split off means the transferring of underlying assets of the corporation to a new controlled subsidiary and exchanging the shares of the shareholders in the parent corporation with shares of the subsidiary; split-up means the transferring of all the underlying assets of the corporation to one or more controlled subsidiaries that follows with the liquidation of the parent corporation.

Pac-Man

Pursuant to this tactic, the target becomes an acquirer. Instead of defending against a hostile takeover, a target that has enough resources may seek to acquire the hostile bidder to eliminate the takeover threat. The advantage in completing a counteroffer and acquiring the stock of the hostile bidder and not staying independent is in controlling the acquisition and combination of the two businesses.[79] The acquisition of the hostile bidder can be either by cash or stock. The basic objective of the Pac-Man, as with any other defense measure, is to maximize the value for the shareholders or stay independent. Counter tendering the hostile bidder is an attempt to make a combination transaction that as any other transaction needs to be appropriate in and of itself.[80] To launch a Pac-Man campaign, the board of directors must think that it is better for the corporations to combine the businesses rather than stay independent. Boards should realize that making a counteroffer can result in different outcomes, such as maintaining independence, higher stock value for the initial target's shareholders, acquiring the hostile bidder or bringing the attention of other players in the market to both the target and the hostile bidder.[81] Pac-Man tactics are not widely spread nowadays, although we did see recently an example of a successful Pac-Man tactic by Men's Wearhouse against Jos. A. Bank, two strong men's apparel companies. The takeover actions between the two began when Jos A. Bank launched its initial bid to acquire Men's Wearhouse. The bid was rejected by the latter and eventually Men's Wearhouse gave Jos. A. Bank's shareholders an offer that they accepted. The company that was first a target saw the opportunity in the combination transaction and became an acquirer.[82]

---

[79] See Takeovers & Freezeouts, supra note 42, at § 6.06[5].

[80] Id.

[81] Id.

[82] Steven Davidoff Solomon, Men's Wearhouse Dusts Off the Pac-Man Defense, *The New York Times*, November 26, 2013, 1:18 pm, available at http://dealbook.nytimes.com/2013/11/26/mens-wearhouse-dusts-off-the-pac-man-defense/?_r=0.

Golden Parachutes

Golden parachutes are rewards set in employment agreements of senior executives to compensate them, among other things, upon the occurrence of a change of control event. Unlike most defense measures that we have included in this part of the chapter, a golden parachute would usually be implemented in the executive's employment agreement when such executive joins the corporations which could be before any takeover activity was being taken against the corporation. Although this defense measure is a preaction defense measure and not a reaction defense measure, we have included it under this part of the chapter because of its financial feature and antitakeover effect resemblance to the remaining reactive defense measures mentioned here. The main goal of the golden parachute is to make the target less attractive to a takeover by forcing the hostile bidder to pay large amounts from the acquired corporation treasury. Golden parachutes can be as much as tens of millions of dollars once a triggering event such as a change of control occurs. For example, at one point it was reported that Marissa Mayer, Yahoo's chief executive officer, would be entitled to receive about 157 million US$ if the company is sold, and a year later, it was reported that her reward would be 37 million US$ due to a decrease in stock value. Mayer's excessive payout is comprised of cash and accelerated vesting stock.[83] Mayer is not the only executive that was reported to be entitled to receive such large rewards upon a takeover of the company. In 2015, five chief executive officers were entitled to receive a total of more than 1 billion US$ if their company was sold. While these substantial amounts might deter a hostile bidder from taking control of the corporation, it might not be an effective measure against a takeover that doesn't result in a change of control. Earlier in this chapter, we discussed activist

---

[83] Matt Krantz, Scram! 5 chief executive officer can get paid $1.3B to get lost, *USA TODAY*, December 7, 2015, 12:30 p.m., available at http://www.usatoday.com/story/money/markets/2015/12/07/cheif executive officer-severance-change-control/76910386/; David Goldman, Marissa Mayer could get up to $37 million if Yahoo gets sold, *CNN Money*, March 28, 2016, 3:30 pm., available at http://money.cnn.com/2016/03/28/technology/marissa-mayer-golden-parachute-yahoo/.

shareholders' "unconventional" tactics to influence the management and promote their business strategy. A golden parachute might not be as an effective defense measure against such tactics as it would be against a change of control event. As of 2015, 70% of fortune 500 companies offer golden parachutes in the event of a change of control to named executive officers.[84] Today, with say on pay rules in which shareholders vote on whether they approve or disapprove the company's executive compensation practices, higher scrutiny is imposed on golden parachute arrangements.[85] Corporations often add additional triggers to a change of control event before executives can cash out their rewards, such as a termination requirement following a change of control (referred to as a "double-trigger" arrangement) and other changes are being made recently by shareholders to make golden parachutes more shareholders friendly.[86]

White Knight and White Squire

Targets that face actual takeover activity by a hostile bidder can recruit a second bidder, a white knight, to acquire the corporation in a friendly deal that will be negotiated with the management instead of being taken over by the hostile bidder. If the management decides that the corporation can no longer stay independent or it is in the best interest of the shareholders to sell the corporation, seeking a friendly deal might be a better alternative (either for the shareholders, the management or for both) than being acquired by a hostile bidder. The managers can secure their positions in the corporation and maximize shareholders value in a friendly deal negotiated with a friendly acquirer. Additionally, negotiating with a white knight can be used as

---

[84] Cody Nelson, Towers Watson, The Changing Landscape of Golden Parachutes in a Say-on-Pay World, Willson Towers Watson, p. 1, May 2015, available at https://www.towerswatson.com/en-US/Insights/Newsletters/Global/executive-pay-matters/2015/Executive-Compensation-Bulletin-The-Changing-Landscape-of-Golden-Parachutes-in-a-Say-on-Pay-World, hereinafter, Nelson.

[85] Section 14A(a)(1) Dodd-Frank Wall Street Reform and Consumer Protection Act.

[86] See Nelson, supra note 82.

a pure business tactic. Talking with potential buyers enhances competition and might result with price increase for shareholders stock. If the board decides that it puts the corporation for sale that will result in a change of control, the board cannot prefer a second bidder just for being a friendly bidder, the board must go forward with the bid that would maximize value for the shareholders, whether it is friendly or hostile.[87] As discussed below, when it is clear that the corporation is up for sale, the board is subject to the Revlon duty, the duty to maximize the corporation's value at sale.[88] Therefore, for a white knight to be successful and complete the acquisition, such white knight must outbid the hostile bidder and provide the shareholders a higher value. A white squire uses the same tactic but instead of acquiring control in the target, the white squire acquires a block of shares to prevent a hostile bidder from completing its takeover. Usually the target and the white squire will enter into a standstill to restrict the white squire from getting voting power in the target.[89]

Teva-Mylan-Perrigo Takeover Actions as a Case Study

The application of some of the defense measures and countermeasures discussed above can be illustrated through the Teva-Mylan-Perrigo triangle affair. In April 2015, Teva Pharmaceutical Industries Ltd., a pharmaceutical company listed on the New York Stock Exchange, and the Tel Aviv Stock Exchange showed interest in acquiring Mylan N.V., another pharmaceutical company listed on the NASDAQ. Teva was about to make an offer to the shareholders of Mylan in an unfriendly attempt to take over the company (recall, an unfriendly bid is an action made against the board of the target corporation). Under the threat of being acquired by Teva in a hostile

---

[87] See Takeovers & Freezeouts, supra note 42, at § 6.06[5].

[88] Maximizing shareholders value doesn't necessarily mean the highest nominal value. Other factors can be taken into consideration, such as the likelihood of the highest bid to be consummated. For further details see Takeover Law and Practice, supra note 20, at 28.

[89] See Takeovers & Freezeouts, supra note 42, at § 6.06[5].

takeover, Mylan took two actions that had an antitakeover effect. First, friendly shareholders (a Dutch foundation) who had preferred shares with a call option right exercised their rights allowing the shareholders to buy half of Mylan's total outstanding shares. Exercising the call option and gaining control in Mylan will enable Mylan to block Teva's offer in the event Teva will make a hostile bid. Second, Mylan took steps to acquire Perrigo Company plc another pharmaceutical company listed on the New York Stock Exchange and Tel-Aviv Stock Exchange. The acquisition was a business decision made as part of Mylan's long-term plan to continue its growth. To complete the sale, a majority of Perrigo's shareholders had to tender their shares. Under the terms of Mylan's tender offer if less than the majority of Perrigo's shareholders tender their shares, Mylan wouldn't go forward with the sale and return the shares it bought to those shareholders who tendered their shares. The sale was not completed because only 40 of Perrigo's outstanding shares had been tendered. Eventually all three companies, Teva, Mylan, and Perrigo, remained independent, with Teva pursuing an alternative, friendly acquisition of Allergan plc, another pharmaceutical company listed on the New York Stock Exchange.[90] Below, we illustrate through these real-life events a few of the defense measures and counteractions used in this interesting triangular takeover saga.[91]

- **Mylan's First Action** — Friendly shareholders in Mylan exercised their preferred right to buy more shares of the company in order

---

[90] See further information regarding the acquisition, http://www.tevapharm.com/news/teva_to_acquire_allergan_generics_for_40_5_billion_creating_a_transformative_generics_and_specialty_company_well_positioned_to_win_in_global_healthcare_07_15.aspx.

[91] Reuters, *UPDATE 3-Mylan foundation tries to block Teva takeover bid with poison pill*, July 23, 2015, 7:08 pm EDT, available at http://www.reuters.com/article/mylan-nl-ma-teva-pharm-ind-idUSL5N1033QA20150723; Cynthia Koons, Mylan's Hostile Bid for Perrigo Fails, Bloomberg, November 13, 2015, 8:43 am EST, updated on November 13, 2015, 2:51 pm EST, available at http://www.bloomberg.com/news/articles/2015-11-13/mylan-s-hostile-bid-for-perrigo-fails-as-40-of-shares-tendered.

to gain control and block a potential hostile bid. Similar to the *blank check preferred* defense measure, Mylan used friendly shareholders to deter the hostile bidder from going forward with its actions. This defense measure was a *preaction* measure that was part of the company's policy and was only exercised once the company was under a threat.

- **Mylan's Second Action** — Following the threat by Teva, Mylan took actions to acquire Perrigo. Pursuant to Mylan, the acquisition attempt was part of the company's business strategy. Mylan's bid to Perrigo's shareholders was not only a defense measure aimed to deter the hostile bidder, it was a business decision that had an anti-takeover effect against Teva's hostile actions. The potential acquisition of Perrigo by Mylan seems to have made Teva's acquisition more difficult and less attractive. From being a target, Mylan became an acquirer (of a different target). Mylan's actions can be perceived as a *Pac-Man* defense measure. Recall, a Pac-Man defense measure must be a proper business action in and of itself.
- **Mylan's Tender Offer** — Mylan failed to acquire Perrigo because less than the majority of the shareholders tendered their shares (Mylan would have to take additional steps to takeover, but it would have been easier for Mylan once it gained majority control). Going directly to the shareholders with a *tender offer* is one avenue to bypass the board or the corporation's defense measures and takeover a company (the second one we discussed was the proxy contest). In this case, Mylan failed to gain the support of Perrigo's shareholders. This case might illustrate how difficult it is to take over a target under hostile conditions and without the blessing of the board.
- **Perrigo's Post Tender Offer Actions** — Following Mylan's unsuccessful tender offer, Perrigo's board decided to buy back shares to increase the value of the company and increase its shareholders' value. Buying back stock increases the company's share price making it less attractive to be taken over[92] and one way for the board to gain shareholders support.

---

[92] See a SharkRepellent study that shows that underperformers three times more likely to be targeted by activists than outperformers, supra note 3.

Additional Matters Relating to Antitakeover Defense Measures

Defense Measures and Shareholders Welfare

We opened this chapter by discussing what to consider before adopting a defensive profile and the benefits that effective defense measures may create, particularly the poison pill and a staggered board. We mentioned that these defense measures can create higher long-term value by good management and leverage the bargaining power of the management to maximize shareholders value. We mentioned that such defense measures can prevent shareholders from tendering their shares collectively to an inadequate offer. On the other hand, with respect to antitakeover defense measures, boards are inherently in a conflict of interest. They might adopt defense practices for their own personal benefit on the account of the shareholders. We mentioned that defense measures might cause the opposite effect to maximizing value by increasing agency costs, entrenching management and eventually reducing the firm's value. The relationship between defense measures, management performance and firm value received much attention by academia and practitioners throughout the years. Since its inception, supporters of the poison pill argued that it is a crucial factor for negotiating an acquisition and that it shows positive effect on share prices.[93] In recent years, there are studies showing that companies with certain antitakeover defenses outperformed companies without such defenses and in some cases, they have shown higher shareholder returns and stronger profitability measures.[94] Other studies have shown that even though takeover defenses increase management's bargaining power, the overall effect of a strong defense profile might negatively affect shareholders wealth. According to one study, a corporation with antitakeover defenses can receive on average a premium of as much as 6% higher on share price when compared to companies who didn't have the same antitakeover defenses. However, the study argues that overall antitakeover defenses reduce shareholders

---

[93] Dale Arthur Oesterle, The Negotiation Model of Tender Offer Defenses and The Delaware Supreme Court, Cornell Lay Review, 72, pp. 117, 120, 1986.

[94] See Takeovers & Freezeouts, supra note 42, at § 6.03[2].

wealth when taking into account takeover deterrence and the decrease in the probability of a successful sale.[95]

A study conducted by Alma Cohen and Lucian A. Bebchuk, who heads the Shareholder Rights Project at Harvard Law School, finds that staggered boards' association with shareholders wealth is statistically significant and economically meaningful. The study that focuses on the correlation between firm value and staggered boards between 1995 and 2002, suggests that staggered boards associate with low firms' value.[96] Another study from 2014 shows that shareholder activism can generate value in some circumstances. According to this study, shareholder activism receives positive reaction from the market and increases stock value of the target. More important to our discussion here is the fact that an activist campaign that results in a sale of the company or change in business strategy is also associated with an increase in stock returns.[97] However, antitakeover defense measures challenge such business actions that may increase value for shareholders. Antitakeover defenses remain a controversial issue among academia and practitioners, and the subject is often being taken from the perspective of shareholders wealth. We believe that managers should carefully review their corporation defense profile and determine on a case by case basis what is suitable for the corporation.

Limitations on the Adoption of Antitakeover Defense Measures

Courts review boards' antitakeover actions, just as they would review any other corporate action. As discussed earlier, directors can be self-interested when it comes to responding to a takeover. Nonetheless,

---

[95] D. L. Sunder, The Controversial 'Poison Pill' Takeover Defense: How valid are the Arguments in Support of it? *NMIMS Management Review*, XXIII, pp. 47, 52, 2013.

[96] Lucian A. Bebchuk & Alma Cohen, *The Costs of Entrenched Boards*, 78 J. Fin. Econ. 409, 410(2005).

[97] Posting of Matteo Tonello, The Conference Board, Harvard Law School Forum on Corporate Governance and Financial Regulation, The Activism of Carl Icahn and Bill Ackman, available at https://corpgov.law.harvard.edu/2014/05/29/the-activism-of-carl-icahn-and-bill-ackman/, May 29, 2014.

determining the adequacy of an offer is an essential element in the board's responsibility to protect shareholders from being exploited by bidders. In order to deal with this complexity, courts created a legal framework for reviewing antitakeover defenses in takeover activities. In Delaware, boards can exercise their power to defend the corporation and shareholders, subject to their fiduciary duties. A series of cases and court decisions established a framework with respect to the review and analysis of directors' fiduciary duties in defending the corporation against hostile takeovers.

- When the corporation is not facing any hostile takeover activity, and the board only seeks to be prepared in advance for the possibility of the corporation being put in play, the board can adopt antitakeover defenses as part of the corporation's plan. Courts will review such a decision as they would any other corporate decision taken by directors in the ordinary course of business. A decision to adopt antitakeover defenses will satisfy directors' duties if it is a well-informed decision, made in a good faith effort to advance shareholder and corporate interests.[98]
- When the corporation is facing an actual takeover activity and the board is seeking to respond to an alleged threat to the corporation, courts will allow the adoption of antitakeover defenses if the board has reasonable grounds for believing that (i) there is an existing threat to corporate policy, for instance, inadequacy of price; and (ii) the defense measure adopted is "reasonable in relation to the threat posed". In this regard, Delaware courts are unlikely to order a corporation's board to redeem its poison pill. Recall, poison pills are deemed to be the most effective defense against hostile takeovers, and today courts leave the decision to repeal them to the discretion of the board.[99] However, some draconian poison pills are prohibited under Delaware law.[100]

[98] Takeover Law and Practice, supra note 20, at 22.

[99] Davis, Alicia J., The Institutional Appetite for "Quack Corporate Governance", *Columbia Business Law Review* 1, p. 33, 2015.

[100] See Unocal, supra note 12.

- When a takeover bid was made and the corporation is up for sale, it will result in a change of control or sale of control, i.e., an all-cash merger transaction, a merger transaction in which a substantial part of the consideration is cash, or a controlling shareholder will take control of the corporation post merger. At the point when it is clear that a change of control will occur, the sole job of the board as an auctioneer is to sell the corporation at the highest price available for shareholders and they are not allowed to take defense actions to stay independent and fend off bidders.[101]

Summary and Notes

In this chapter, we presented different approaches to takeover activities and the views of the target's board of directors, its shareholders, and the hostile bidder. This chapter provides an overview of the opportunities and disadvantages that a hostile takeover may bring to a corporation and its shareholders. It provides a detailed overview of a variety of defense measures that can be part of a corporation's defensive profile. We focused on the main defense measures that a corporation can adopt as part of its long-term plan, such as the poison pill and staggered board, we referred to those defense measures as preaction defense measures. We presented financial or tactical defense measures that a corporation can adopt after a hostile action was taken against the corporation or is about to be taken against it, we referred to those defense measures as reaction defenses. We provided a brief analysis of the effectiveness of each defense measure in fending off a hostile bidder and we discussed the hostile bidder's traditional counteractions as well as some recent tactics of activist shareholders used against corporations with defense measures.

When considering the adequacy of a corporation's antitakeover defenses and potential implementation of new defense measures, the corporation should balance the perceived benefits of an action against the risk that such action will create conflicts with the corporation's major shareholder (and the media coverage that typically follows such

[101] Takeover Law and Practice, supra note, at 25.

conflicts). Earlier in this chapter, we reviewed corporate procedures for implementing takeover defenses. We showed that some antitakeover defenses require shareholder approval when implemented in the corporation's plan. When a corporation decides to take an action that requires shareholder approval, especially if it requires a greater than majority vote, it will be important for the corporation to assess the likelihood of obtaining the required vote. Failure to obtain required shareholder approval could signal to the market that the corporation's management (and possibly the board of directors) has lost the support of the shareholders, thereby increasing the risk to the corporation of unsolicited or hostile acquisition proposals or similar proxy contests.

In practice, acquirers are likely to consider anticipated media coverage, transaction costs, alternative targets etc., as weighted against the total benefits of a successful acquisition and that balancing exercise will dictate an acquirer's appetite for a hostile play. Such appetite or lack thereof is not always rational in the way decision-making models would view it. Nonetheless, it is critical for the decision makers to go through such balancing exercise, with the target's defensive profile being the first and a significant step in the decision-making process.

- After reading this chapter, where do you stand on control contests between shareholders and the board of directors? Which governance structure do you support? Would you favor a governance structure that increases shareholders power and influence over the corporation? When answering this question think about what kind of a decision a takeover decision is. Is it a proper business decision for the board of directors to make or an investment decision for the investors — the shareholders? Should one organ have exclusive power to decide on takeover decisions or should both organs, shareholders and boards, have mutual power on such decision?
- As discussed earlier in this chapter, throughout the years, activist shareholders came up with new tactics to influence the corporation they are vested in. Many defense measures presented in this chapter were initially designed to deal with hostile takeovers and were intended to prevent a change of control. Activist shareholders don't necessarily attempt to sell the corporation, but rather seek to

implement their investment plans to increase value. Their tactics often attempt to gain one or two seats on the board of directors instead of initiating a proxy contest for a majority control of the board. They use mass media and social media such as Twitter to engage with the board of directors and shareholders.[102] Their campaigns can take years as part of their long-term investment strategies. As activism trends and tactics change and develop, will we see managers reacting to these trends and coming up with new ways to defend their business plans against activists' influence?

- In this chapter, we did not discuss the role of the legislator in striking the balance between the shareholders and the board. While some states have legislated antitakeover defense framework, Delaware, which has an important role in the business of corporation, chose to keep the framework of antitakeover defense rules through the judicial system. What is the role of the legislator in regulating control contests? In this respect, we ask, do shareholders today have sufficient legal tools to fight back and should the legislator step in and provide shareholders more power?
- Today boards have a variety of antitakeover defense measures to use against a hostile takeover, but how aggressive can the board of directors get in protecting the corporation from a hostile takeover? Should we restrict the board's power to fend off a hostile takeover? Would you support a board of directors that caused the corporation to take substantial amount of debt to finance a stock buy-back to prevent a hostile takeover? In one case, the Supreme Court of Delaware held that such actions are a reasonable response to the threat against the corporation.[103]

[102] See Richard Levick, The Floodgates Are Open: Shareholder Activists Intensify Social Media Utilization, Forbes, April 25, 2011, 5:43 pm, available at http://www.forbes.com/sites/richardlevick/2011/04/25/the-floodgates-are-open-shareholder-activists-intensify-social-media-utilization/#1f750df350a1.

[103] See Unocal, supra note 12.

Exhibit: Summary of Antitakeover Defense Measures

Defense	Description	Effect	Additional Factors to Consider
Staggered board provisions	The corporate organizational documents may provide that the board of directors shall be classified. The board may be divided into one, two or three classes by the certificate of incorporation or by-law, such classification makes the replacement of a majority of the board of directors a longer and costly procedure.	• Enhances board entrenchment and impairs shareholders governing power. • Deters bidders who may take control and change corporate policy.	• Under the corporate organizational documents, can shareholders pack the board of directors, remove existing directors or convert the staggered board. • Where are the staggered board provisions set, in the charter or by-laws? • Can shareholders act by a written consent or special meeting? • How long would it take to win two annual elections and what are the chances to win at each election?
Shareholders' rights plan (poison pill)	A poison pill provision in the corporate organizational documents limits the power of the shareholders to sell their shares to a third party above a certain ownership threshold of such third party. The result is the elimination of a third party taking control over the corporation without the board's approval.	• Enhances board entrenchment and impairs shareholders governing power. • Deters bidders who may take control and change corporate policy. • If exercised, it dilutes controlling shareholders.	• Does the shareholders' rights plan require issuance of additional stock in excess of the authorized number of stock? • What are the chances that a proxy contest to replace the board will be successful? • Do the shareholders have right to vote on shareholders plan (either on the time of adoption/extension)? • Is there a staggered board in place or an annually elected board?

(*Continued*)

Exhibit: (*Continued*)

Defense	Description	Effect	Additional Factors to Consider
Majority voting versus cumulative voting	Cumulative voting may enable minority shareholders such as activist shareholders to win some seats on the board and gain influence on corporate policy. Majority voting impairs minority shareholders ability to gain seats on the board of directors.	Effects board entrenchment and impairs minority shareholders ability to gain access to internal information and influence the management.	Can shareholders act by a written consent or special meeting to change the corporate organizational documents?
Removal of directors without cause	Shareholders can increase their influence on the corporation's business plan by removing directors and replacing them. However, if the removal must be with cause, shareholders need to wait to the next annual meeting before they can replace any director. If the board is staggered, such replacement would be only with respect to half/third of the board.	Enhances board entrenchment and impairs shareholders governing power.	Is there a staggered board in place or an annually elected board? Where are the staggered board provisions set, in the charter or by-laws? Can shareholders act by a written consent or special meeting to change the corporate organizational documents?
Remaining directors' right to fill vacancies	Directors have the right to elect their nominees for vacant and new seats by a majority of the board then in office, unless otherwise provided in the charter or by-laws.	Enhances board entrenchment and impairs shareholders governing power.	Can shareholders act by a written consent or special meeting to change the corporate organizational documents?

Supermajority vote required for stockholders to amend certain charter/by-laws provisions	An increased threshold that affects stockholders power to amend certain charter and by-laws provisions so as to facilitate takeovers.	Impairs shareholders governing power.	Where are the staggered board provisions set, in the charter or by-laws? Can shareholders act by a written consent or special meeting to change the corporate organizational documents?
Action by written consent or special meeting	Allows shareholders to act either by a written consent or a special meeting without having to depend on the board's actions. Such provisions might be helpful in facilitating a takeover. The corporate organizational documents can interfere with such power if the board of directors choose to eliminate such shareholders rights.	Impairs shareholders governing power.	—
Restrictions on ability to put forward shareholders proposals or to nominate directors without prior notice to company	Some procedures may be adopted in the by-laws that will restrict shareholders' business proposals and directors' nominees.	Impairs shareholders governing power.	Can shareholders act by a written consent or special meeting to change the corporate organizational documents?

(*Continued*)

Exhibit: (*Continued*)

Defense	Description	Effect	Additional Factors to Consider
Blank check preferred	A blank check preferred stock provision authorizes the board to set the rights and privileges of any series of preferred stock at the time it is issued. It can also be used by the board to provide special rights to friendly shareholders who will support the board's actions.	Impairs some shareholders governing power and assists the board of directors when fighting a takeover.	Is the issuance of preferred stock in excess of the authorized number of stocks?
Disposing free cash flow/stock repurchase, cash dividend	Boards can dispose excess cash in order to eliminate the hostile bidder's potential source of financing and make the corporation less attractive for acquisition.	Deters bidders who may take control and change corporate policy.	The board have fiduciary duties. Would the board's decision constitute a valid business decision under the business judgment rule?
Divestment	Boards can sell the corporation's most valuable assets in order to eliminate the hostile bidder's potential source of financing or the assets it is going after and make the corporation less attractive for acquisition.	Deters bidders who may take control and change corporate policy.	The board have fiduciary duties. Would the board's decision constitute a valid business decision under the business judgment rule?
Pac-Man	To eliminate a takeover threat, the target's board that has enough resources may seek to acquire the hostile bidder to eliminate the takeover threat.	Eliminates a takeover.	Would the acquisition of the hostile bidder be expensive? Would it require taking additional debt? Is it a legitimate exercise of the board's business judgment?

Golden parachutes	Golden parachutes are rewards set in employment agreements of senior executives to compensate them, among other things, upon the occurrence of a change of control event. Golden parachutes make the acquisition more expensive for the acquirer to complete.	Deters bidders who may take control and change corporate policy.	Does the shareholder have a say on pay right?
White knight and white squire	The target that faces a takeover threat by a hostile bidder can recruit a second bidder to acquire the corporation in a deal that would be friendly to the board or the corporation.	The board maintains control over the process.	The board have fiduciary duties. Would the second bidder maximize shareholder's wealth or would board's decision constitute a valid business decision under the business judgment rule?

Chapter 7

Valuation Methods and Practices for M&As

Harvey Poniachek
Rutgers Business School

Introduction

This chapter discusses three major valuation approaches that are used in mergers and acquisitions (M&As), including the income approach, the market approach, and the asset approach. The primary valuation methodologies for M&As are the first two approaches. The main features of the valuation approaches, shown in Exhibit 1, are as follows:

1. The income approach could be applied in three different versions, depending on the nature of the cash flows, the capital structure of the firm or entity, and the required rate of return or discount rate. The approach derives the enterprise value (EV) or the value of a common share of a target company based on the value of the cash flows that the company expects to generate in the future. The cash flows are presently valued at the required rate of return, or the discount rate, that reflects the

Exhibit 1: Valuation Methodologies for M&A

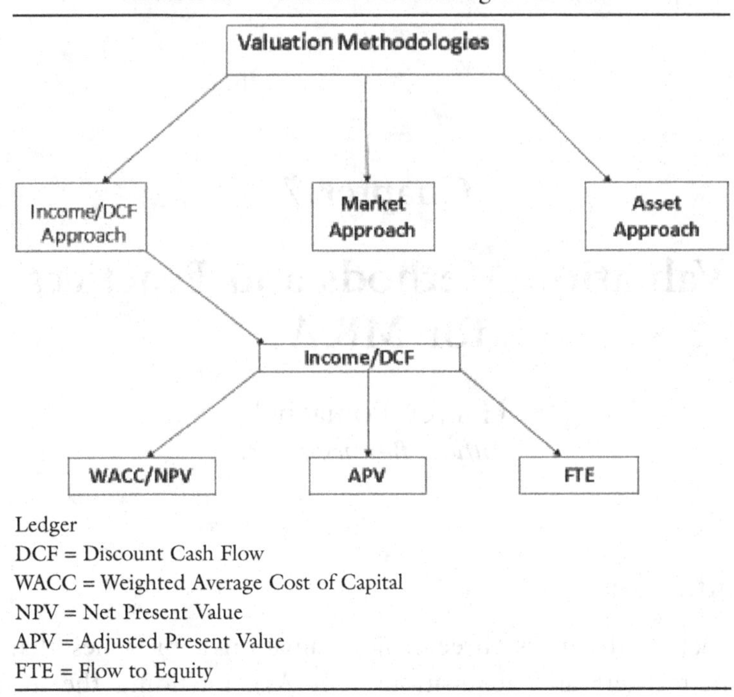

Ledger
DCF = Discount Cash Flow
WACC = Weighted Average Cost of Capital
NPV = Net Present Value
APV = Adjusted Present Value
FTE = Flow to Equity

risk associated with the cash flows. The required rate of return or the discount rate could vary and be the Weighted Average Cost of Capital (WACC), or the cost of debt, or the cost of equity for an unlevered company.

2. The market approach assesses the value of the enterprise or the value of a common share based on comparable companies and/or comparable M&A transactions, by utilizing various multiples, such as the ratio of the price per share to earnings per share (P/E), or the ratio of the enterprise value to earnings before interest and tax (EV/EBIT), and several other multiples.
3. The asset approach defines the value of common equity of a target company at book value as the difference between assets and liabilities, or by adjusting the assets and liabilities to market value and deriving their difference.

The Income Approach

The income valuation approach applies the Fair Market Value (FMV) or the investment value standard,[1] and the premise that the target company or entity is a going concern. The valuation could determine how much is the target worth, but the price paid for it would ultimately be negotiated between the buyer and seller. The purchase

---

[1] There are four standards of value, including the fair market value, fair value, intrinsic value, and investment value. The fair market value is the price, expressed in terms of cash equivalents, at which property would change hands between a hypothetical willing and able buyer and a hypothetical willing and able seller, acting at arm's length in an open and unrestricted market, when neither is under compulsion to buy or sell and when both have reasonable knowledge of the relevant facts.

The FASB ASC 820 definition of fair value is based on an exchange price concept, that is, the price to sell an asset or transfer a liability and therefore it represents an exit price, not an entry price. However, in the absence of active primary markets, fair value could be determined by reference to prices and rates from secondary markets, or by application of valuation techniques and assumptions by the concerned party company or by external valuation specialists. The ASC 820 establishes a fair value hierarchy that prioritizes the inputs used in valuation techniques into three levels (EY, p. 108): Level 1 are quoted prices (unadjusted) in active markets for identical assets and liabilities that the reporting entity can access at the measurement date; Level 2 are inputs other than quoted prices in active markets for identical assets and liabilities that are observable either directly or indirectly; and Level 3 are unobservable inputs. The fair value hierarchy is intended to increase consistency and comparability among fair value measurements. ASC 820 recognizes three valuation approaches to measure fair value: the market approach, cost approach, and income approach (EY, p. 87). See EY, Financial reporting developments, A comprehensive guide, Fair value measurement, Revised September 2016, file:///C:/Users/Harvey/Downloads/financialreportingdevelopments_bb1462_fairvaluemeasurement_15september2016%20(2).pdf; Joanne M. Flood, *GAAP 2017: Interpretation and Application of Generally Accepted Accounting Principles*, Wiley, ISBN: 978-1-119-35692-9, December 2016, Ch. 52 ASC 820 Fair Value Measurements, pp. 1043–2044; and PWC, Point of View, Fair Value: The Audit Committee's Role, June 2015.

Investment Value means the value of an asset or business to a specific prospective owner that reflects a unique situation. Intrinsic Value is the value inherent in the property itself. See Alfred M. King, *Executive's Guide to Fair Value*, Wiley, 2008, Ch. 1; Jay E. Fishman, Shannon P. Prat and William J. Morrison, *Standards of Value: Theory and Applications*, Wiley, 2007, pp. 21–26.

Exhibit 2: The Effect of Synergy and Other Influences on the Bidding Price

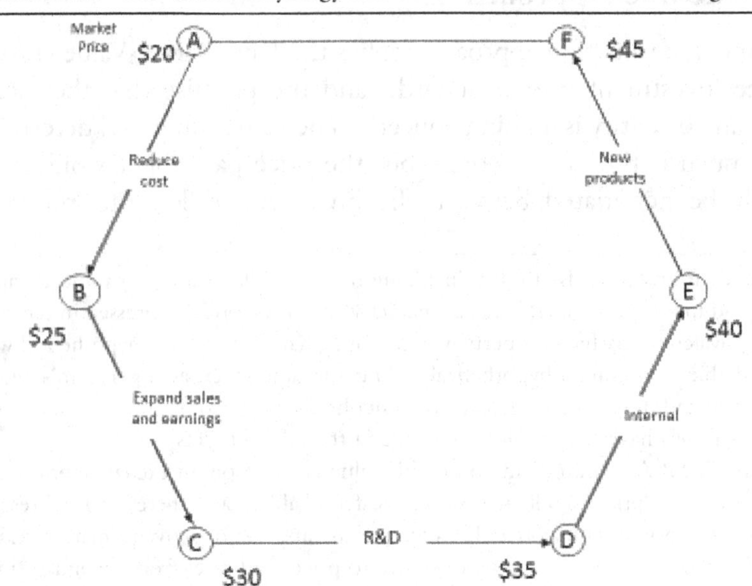

Notes

- The target's market price per share is $20, but different prospective acquirers can afford paying much higher prices for the target — depending on what they expect to do with the target following the acquisition.
- For instance, one prospective acquirer could obtain significant synergies via reduction of cost, expanding of sales and earnings, R&D, and international expansion into new markets. However, not every prospective buyer might have the same opportunities.
- Therefore, different prospective acquirers are likely to bid for the target at different prices.

price usually consists of the stand-alone value of the target company plus a fraction of the synergies expected by the buyer following the merger or acquisitions and assumption of control. Because different prospective parties expect different synergies from M&As, their offer prices could vary considerably. See Exhibit 2 on the effect of synergy and other influences on the bidding price per share.

The income approach applies the discount cash flow (DCF), where value is defined as the present value of the expected free cash flows (FCF) discounted at a required rate of return, or discount rate. The required rate of return or discount rate is based on the nature of the cash flows, the capitalization structure, and the riskiness of the target company and its cash flows.

The income application of the DCF methodology is based on solid corporate finance theories[2] and could be applied to three different circumstances as follows:

1. We can apply the net present value (NPV) methodology, which is commonly referred to as the WACC methodology, by discounting the unlevered free cash flows to the firm (FCFF) for the projected period of the first 5 years and to infinity by application of a formulary approach.[3] This approach yields the enterprise value and to obtain the equity value and price per share, interest-bearing liabilities need to be subtracted from the enterprise value and divided by the number of outstanding shares. Because the WACC was derived by using the after-tax interest rate, this approach incorporates the tax benefit of debt implicitly through the cost of capital.
2. Alternatively, we value an unlevered target company's FCF to the firm by discounting it at the unlevered cost of capital; and then estimate and add the present value of the interest tax shields, as well as other financial side effects, such as subsidies, at the cost of debt. This approach is called the adjusted present value (APV) method.
3. The third method is based on free cash flows to equity (FTE) discounted at the cost of equity for an unlevered entity, or the cost of equity for a levered company.

The valuation process starts with an analysis of the company, then reviews the industry and the macroeconomy. The first step is to prepare pro forma financial statements based on the percent of sales growth approach,[4] derive the FCF to the firm/enterprise, and derive an appropriate discount rate or the WACC. Usually three valuation scenarios are derived, including high or optimistic, average, and low

---

[2] Jonathan Berk and Peter DeMarzo, *Corporate Finance, 3rd Ed.*, Pearson, 2014, Ch. 8, pp. 233–260; Ross, Stephen A., Westerfield, Randolph W., Jafee, Jeffrey, and Jordan, Bradford D. *Corporate Finance, 11th Ed.*, McGraw-Hill Education, 2013, Ch. 4, 9.

[3] Berk, Op. Cit., p. 627.

[4] Ross, Op. Cit., p. 98.

or pessimistic, and probabilities are assigned to each[5] to obtain a probability weighted average scenario. The reasonableness of the valuations could be further examined through sensitivity analysis, including an application of a Monte Carlo simulation technique.[6] Control and liquidity discounts and premiums could be applied as necessary.[7]

The income approach of business valuation converts free cash flows to value by present valuation procedures that utilizes the time value of money, the risk profile of cash flows, and the expected growth.[8] The discount rate is determined by the capital structure of the target company, i.e., the share of debt and equity in total capitalization, the cost of debt, the tax rate, and the cost of equity that is derived through the application of the Capital Asset Pricing Method (CAPM). The risk characteristics of the anticipated cash flows is implied in the cost of debt and equity.

The valuation analysis is based on a forecast period that commonly consists of 5 years (and rarely extended beyond that horizon), and a terminal value to perpetuity that assumes that the target company will live to infinity. Based on the forecast period, FCF to the company or enterprise are derived for each year and discounted at the WACC to determine the present value. The terminal value is derived either through a formulary approach on the basis of the last year's FCF, the growth rate to perpetuity and the WACC; or through a multiple of earnings before interest and taxes (EBIT) or earnings before interest, taxes, depreciation and amortization (EBITDA). The sum of the discounted cash flow of the forecast period and the present value of the terminal value determines the enterprise value — from which debt is deducted to derive the equity value. That is, the company's equity equals the enterprise value minus debt and cash.

---

[5] Ibid., pp. 353, 357.

[6] Palisade, Monte Carlo Simulation, http://www.palisade.com/risk/monte_carlo_simulation.asp.

[7] Pratt, Shannon P., *Business Valuation Discounts and Premiums*, Wiley, 2001, Ch. 1.

[8] Ross, Op. Cit., 2013, Ch. 4, 9.

In summary, the NPV or WACC valuation approach focuses on several value drivers, including FCF to the firm, the discount rate, and the growth, which are more fully addressed below.

Free Cash Flows (FCF)

The FCF from assets or the enterprise equals to EBIT plus depreciation, which is a noncash expense, minus taxes, minus capital expenditures (CAPEX) and minus changes in net working capital (NWC). Stated algebraically, FCF is defined as follows:

$$\text{FCF} = \text{EBIT} + \text{Depreciation} - \text{Taxes} - \text{CAPEX} - \Delta\text{NWC},$$

or stated as

$$\text{FCF} = \text{EBIT}\ (1 - t) + \text{Depreciation} - \text{CAPEX} - \Delta\text{NWC}.$$

The definitions of the variables are as follows:
FCF = Free cash flows,
EBIT = Earnings before interest and taxes,
EBIT $(1 - t)$ is EBIT after taxes,
t is the marginal tax rate,
CAPEX = Capital expenditure, which equals Net Fixed Assets 2 – (Net Fixed Assets 1 + Depreciation),
ΔNWC = Change in net working capital, which equals NWC2 – NWC1, and NWC equals Current Assets (CA) – Current Liabilities (CL).

The NWC includes cash, receivables, inventory, and payables required for the operation of the business. Excess cash should be reduced to the level required for operations.

Terminal Value

A terminal value (TV) reflects the value of all cash flows from the end of the projected period to perpetuity, and it usually constitutes a significant component of the company's enterprise value, and often accounting for as much as 70% of the total value. The terminal value could be estimated in two ways: First, through a formulary approach based on the last forecasted FCF, the growth rate, and the discount rate as follows:

$$TV = FCF\ (1 + g) \div (WACC - g),$$

where

FCF $(1 + g)$ = The expected growth of free cash flow for the year after the last year of the forecasted cash flow, which is commonly year 6 and onward,

WACC = The weighted average cost of capital,

g = The expected constant annual growth rate of FCF $(1 + g)$ in perpetuity

The model assumes a sustainable growth of cash flow to perpetuity.

Second, the TV could be estimated based on a multiple of EBIT or EBITDA, where the multiple is derived from comparable companies or comparable M&A transactions. The differences between the two estimates of the TV could be attributed to too high or low discount rate; too high or low growth rate; and the use of comparable multiples that fail to match the expected risk, expected growth or macroeconomic conditions of the target company in the terminal period.

The Discount Rate

The discount rate should reflect the risk associated with the FCF. Based on the capital structure of the company being valued, we derive WACC, which serves as the discount rate for the FCF of the target company. The formula for WACC is as follows:

$$WACC = W_d\, R_d(1 - t) + W_e\, R_e,$$

where the variables are specified below:

W_d = The % share of debt in the capital structure, or $D/(D + E)$,

W_e = The % share of equity in the capital structure, or $E/(D + E)$,

D = Interest-bearing debt,

E = Equity, or the market capitalization of the firm, which equals price per share × the number of outstanding shares,

R_d = Pretax cost of debt, i.e., the yield to maturity on corporate bonds with the same credit rating and maturity of the subject company or the cost of borrowing of the subject company,

t = Marginal tax rate

If WACC is used, interest expense is eliminated and the terminal value is the market value of invested capital (MVIC). It is then necessary to reduce this value by interest-bearing debt to determine the value of equity.

R_e is the cost of equity capital. The cost of equity can be obtained from the Capital Asset Pricing Model or CAPM as follows:

$$R_e = R_f + \beta\,(R_m - R_f),$$

where

R_e = Cost of equity or the expected rate of return on the company's equity,

R_f = Risk-free rate of return on government securities over a time horizon consistent with the investment horizon. There are various risk-free rates that could be used, but the practice is to use Treasury Bills for up to 1-year maturity, Treasury Notes for up to 10-year maturity and Treasury Bonds for 30-year maturity.

β = The beta, a measure of the company's stock systematic risk or market risk or nondiversifiable risk, which reflects the company's volatility compared to the overall market index.

$(R_m - R_f)$ = Risk adjusted rate of return on the market index or the market risk premium, or equity risk premium. $(R_m - R_f)$ is usually estimated as the difference between the returns on the broad common stocks market index, such as the S&P 500, and medium or long-term government bonds, depending on the horizon of the valuation. The market-risk premium ranges between 4.5% and 5.5%.[9]

R_m = Return on the market index, usually represented by the rate of return on the S&P 500 index.

The cost of equity is an estimate of an investor's required rate of return on an investment that could be estimated based on the CAPM. However, application of the CAPM to divisions, business segments or private companies is hampered by lack of beta information. In such instances, we could derive the betas by using comparable companies through a process of unlevering and relevering (described below), or by applying the Dividend Growth Model (DGM[10]) or the Dividend Discount Model (DDM) as an alternative to CAPM.

When Beta is Unavailable: Unlevered and Relevered Betas

When firms are financed entirely by equity, the risk faced by investors reflects only business risk borne by the firm's investment and the equity beta equals the asset beta.[11] When firms are funded by debt and equity, the return is split between debtholders and shareholders. However, because debtholders have the first claim on the company's cash flows, the riskiness of the residual flows to shareholders is magnified. Thus, shareholders bear both the business risk of the company's real assets and the financial risk associated with the

---

[9] Goetzmann, William N., and Ibbotson, Roger G., *The Equity Risk Premium, Essays and Explorations*, Oxford University Press, 2006; Pablo Fernandez, Pablo, Ortiz, Alberto and Acín, Isabel Fernandez, Market Risk Premium used in 71 countries in 2016: A survey of 6,932 respondents, IESE Business School. University of Navarra, Madrid, http://www.valuewalk.com/wp-content/uploads/2016/05/SSRN-id2776636.pdf.

[10] Ross, Stephen A., Westerfield, Randolph W., Jafee, Jeffrey, and Jordan, Bradford D. *Corporate Finance, 11th Ed.*, McGraw-Hill Education, 2016, Ch. 4, 9.

[11] See for instance Shapiro, Alan C., *Modern Corporate Finance*, Macmillan, 1990, pp. 279–280.

use of debt financing. Hence, the company's equity beta exceeds its asset beta.

In the absence of debt, the unleveraged β_u is affected by the firm's operating leverage and the conditions of the industry in which the firm operates; whereas in the presence of debt, the leveraged β_l is affected by the firm's operating leverage, financial leverage and industry's conditions. Levered and unlevered betas can be defined as follows[12]:

$$\beta_l = \beta_u (1 + (1 - t)(D/E)) \quad \text{and} \quad \beta_u = \beta_l / (1 + (1 - t)(D/E)),$$

where t, D, and E are the marginal tax rate, debt, and equity, respectively.

To derive the beta for a subject company, select comparable publicly listed companies from the same industry, with similar size and cyclicality, then unlever their betas by application of the following model:

$$\beta_u = \beta_l / (1 + (1 - t)(D/E)).$$

Then relever the betas using the (D/E) ratio and marginal tax rate t of the subject firm whose levered beta (β_l) we are trying to estimate by application of the following model:

$$\beta_l = \beta_u (1 + (1 - t)(D/E)).$$

To measure the cost of capital by using comparable companies requires information on their asset beta, but instead we have the equity beta. To transform the equity beta into the asset beta we need to separate the effect of debt financing via a process known as unlevering and relevering.

---

[12] Van Horn, James C., *Financial Management and Policy, 11th Ed.*, Prentice Hall, 1988, p. 206, 2017; Koller, Tim, Goedhart, Marc and Wessels, David, McKinsey & Company, *Valuation: Measuring and Managing the Value of Companies, 5th Ed.*, Wiley, 2010, pp. 784–785.

In the absence of taxes, the beta of the combined debt and equity would equal the company's asset beta as follows:

$$\beta_{\text{assets}} = \beta_{\text{equity}}\ E/(E + D) + \beta_{\text{debt}}\ D/(E + D),$$

where the variables are as follows:

β_{equity} is the beta of the stock of the *levered* firm, or a firm that uses debt capital in its capital structure,

β_{debt} is the beta of debt, and

β_{assets} is weighted average of the equity and debt beta.

The β_{asset} is very low in practice and could be assumed at zero thus yielding

$$\beta_{\text{assets}} = \beta_{\text{equity}}\ E/(E + D).$$

Because $E/(D + E)$ must be below 1 for a levered firm, it follows that $\beta_{\text{asset}} < \beta_{\text{equity}}$. Rearranging this equation, we obtain the unlevered beta as follows:

$$\beta_{\text{equity}} = \beta_{\text{assets}} / E/(E + D) = \beta_{\text{assets}}\ (1 + D/E),$$

$$\beta_{\text{equity}} = \beta_{\text{assets}}\ (1 + (1 - t)\ D/E).$$

The equity beta of a levered firm will always be greater than the asset beta with financial leverage (assuming the asset beta is positive), and the equity beta of a levered firm will always be greater than the equity beta of an all-equity firm. By introducing corporate taxes, the relationship between the beta of the unlevered firm and the beta of the levered equity is as follows.

Because $[1 + (1 - t_C)$ Debt/Equity$]$ must be more than 1 for a levered firm, it follows that $\beta_{\text{unlevered firm}} < \beta_{\text{equity}}$.

Step 1: Unlever the beta

$$\beta_u = \beta_L / (1 + (1 - t)\ D/E),$$

where

D/E is the target's debt–equity ratio before acquisition,

β_u is the target's unlevered beta,

β_L is the target's premerger beta.

Step 2: Relever the beta

$$\beta_L = \beta_u(1 + (1 - t)\, D/E),$$

where D/E is the debt–equity ratio after relevering.

The EV (V) equals the sum of debt (D) and equity (E) as follows:

$$V = D + E.$$

Therefore, the value of equity equals the enterprise value less the value of existing debt:

$$E = V - D,$$

where debt is the market value of all interest-bearing debt outstanding at the time of the acquisition.

The valuation of a target firm raises several issues, including estimation of the potential synergies from the combination. Synergies could alter the stand-alone cash flow valuation and split the synergies between the parties in a specific negotiated manner. If the bidder pays a premium equal to the value of the synergies, all of the benefits will accrue to target shareholders and none to the acquirer. The premium paid is measured as follows:

$$\text{Premium} = ((P_{\text{paid}}/P_{\text{premerger price}}) - 1) \times 100.$$

The Dividend Discount Model: An Alternative to CAPM

In the absence of beta information, and/or data on the market risk premium or equity risk premium, we could use the Dividend Discount Model (DDM) to derive the cost of equity.[13] If the firm's dividends

[13] Ross, Op. Cit, pp. 400–401.

are expected to grow at a constant rate, g, the price of a share of stock, P, can be stated as follows:

$$P = \frac{\text{Div}}{R_s - g}.$$

The variables are as follows:
Div is the dividend per share expected next year,
R_S is the discount rate or cost of equity, and
g is the annual rate of expected growth rate of dividends.

This equation can be rearranged to yield the expected rate of return on a stock, or cost of equity as follows:

$$R_s = \frac{\text{Div}}{P} + g.$$

Hence, the annual expected return on a stock is the sum of the dividend yield (=Div/P) over the next year plus the annual rate of expected dividend growth. This formula can be used to estimate the expected return on a stock and on the market. To apply the DDM to a stock, we need to estimate both the dividend yield and the expected growth rate.

In summary, the DDM approach could be used as a second best methodology to estimate a firm's cost of capital whereas the first best approach is provided by the CAPM. Exhibit 3 provides a valuation of a US publicly listed company.

The Adjusted Present Value (APV)

The adjusted present value (APV) model is designed to value operations or assets in place.[14] The APV, like all DCF methodologies, involves projection of cash flows and values the business in a two-step

[14] Luehrman, Timothy A., Using APV: A Better Tool for Valuing Operations, *Harvard Business Review*, May–June 1997.

Exhibit 3:

BROCADE COMMUNICATIONS SYSTEMS, INC.
CONSOLIDATED STATEMENTS OF INCOME, $, 000

					Pro-Forma Income Statement				
Operations	2013	2014	2015	2016(*)	2017	2018	2019	2020	2021
Net sales	22,22,864	22,11,267	22,63,460	22,51,081	22,68,043	22,85,133	23,02,351	23,19,700	23,37,179
Cost of goods sold	8,13,985	7,45,474	7,35,387	7,89,715	7,81,921	7,87,813	7,93,749	7,99,730	8,05,756
Gross Margin	14,08,879	14,65,793	15,28,073	14,61,367	14,86,122	14,97,320	15,08,602	15,19,970	15,31,423
Selling and Administrative Expense	11,00,396	10,79,681	10,35,393	11,63,155	11,09,893	11,18,256	11,26,682	11,35,172	11,43,725
EBIT	3,08,483	3,86,112	4,92,680	2,98,212	3,76,229	3,79,064	3,81,920	3,84,798	3,87,697
Interest expences	(55,261)	(36,757)	(55,578)	(20,827)	(26,275)	(26,473)	(26,673)	(26,874)	(27,076)
Depreciation and Amortization	1,84,114	1,00,647	84,807	1,23,189	1,23,189	1,23,189	1,23,189	1,23,189	1,23,189
(*) The full year was projected by exprapolating three quarters.									
Interest charged on loan and LTD	6.98%								
Shares used in per share calculation—diluted	4,63,705	4,46,859	4,30,556	4,19,416	3,60,698	3,10,200	2,66,772	2,29,424	1,97,305

CONSOLIDATED BALANCE SHEETS, $, 000

				Pro-Forma Balance Sheet				
	2014	2015	2016	2017	2018	2019	2020	2021
Assets								
Current assets	16,58,005	18,52,199	15,99,358	16,11,409	16,23,551	16,35,785	16,48,110	16,60,529
Total assets	37,33,675	40,38,178	48,73,765	49,10,489	49,47,489	49,84,769	50,22,329	50,60,172
		21,85,979	32,74,407	32,99,080	33,23,938			
Liabilities and Stockholders' Equity								
Current liabilities	5,87,308	5,62,364	7,01,210	7,06,494	7,11,817	7,17,181	7,22,585	7,28,029
Long-term debt	5,95,450	7,95,804	15,16,761	15,28,190	15,39,705	15,51,306	15,62,996	15,74,773
Total Liabilities	13,25,614	15,04,643	24,12,962	22,34,683	22,51,522	22,68,487	22,85,580	23,02,802
Stockholders' equity	24,08,061	25,33,535	24,60,803	24,64,822	24,83,395	25,02,107	25,20,961	25,39,956
Total Liabilities and Stockholders' Equity	37,33,675	40,38,178	48,73,765	49,10,489	49,47,489	49,84,769	50,22,329	50,60,172

(Continued)

Exhibit 3: (*Continued*)

BROCADE COMMUNICATIONS SYSTEMS, INC.

FREE CASH FLOWS, $, 000

Company's FCF from Projection, $, 000										
					2016	2017	2018	2019	2020	2021
EBIT					2,98,212	3,76,229	3,79,064	3,81,920	3,84,798	3,87,697
Less Tax	34%				(1,01,392)	(1,27,918)	(1,28,882)	(1,29,853)	(1,30,831)	(1,31,817)
Plus Depreciation					1,23,189	1,40,436	1,60,097	1,82,510	2,08,062	2,37,191
CapEx					12,11,617	1,65,109	1,84,955	2,07,556	2,33,296	2,62,615
Change in NWC					6,768	6,819	6,870	6,922	6,974	7,026
Free Cash Flow (FCF)						3,44,738	3,47,335	3,49,952	3,52,589	3,55,246
Discounted CashFlow (DCF)						3,24,921	3,08,552	2,93,007	2,78,245	2,64,227

CAPM derivation	
Risk free rate (treasury bonds 30 years)	2.99%
Return on Market	10.44%
Beta	0.55
Required Return by applying the CAPM=Rf+Beta(Rm-Rf)	7.1%

Weight of Equity and Debt derivation	
Debt to Equity ratio	0.64
Weight of Equity =1-Wd	0.61
Weight of Debt = (D/E)/(1+D/E)	0.39

WACC	
Return on Equity	7.1%
Return on Debt	6.90%
Corporate Tax	34%
Weight of Equity	0.61
Weight of Debt	0.39
WACC	6.10%

Note: WACC=We*Re(levered)+Wd*Rd(1-Tax)

ENTERPRISE VALUE AND EQUITY VALUATION, ASSUMING DIFFERENT TVS, $, 000				
GROWTH RATES TO INFINITY	1.0%	1.5%	2.0%	2.5%
TERMINAL VALUE at 2021	70,36,897	78,40,597	88,40,379	101,17,968
TV discounted	52,33,937	58,31,717	65,75,339	75,25,591
NPV OF DCF+PV OF TV	67,02,887	73,00,667	80,44,290	89,94,542
EQUITY VALUATION	51,74,697	57,72,478	65,16,100	74,66,352

TV=Terminal Value

Working Notes

Sales Growth rate derivation		
Year	Value	Yearly growth
2013	22,22,864	-0.52%
2014	22,11,267	2.36%
2015	22,63,460	-0.55%
2016	22,51,081	1.72%
Average Growth rate		0.75%

(*Continued*)

Exhibit 3: (*Continued*)

Ratios of COGS to Sales		
Year	Value of COGS	Yearly Ratio
2013	8,13,985	36.62%
2014	7,45,474	33.71%
2015	7,35,387	32.49%
2016	7,89,715	35.08%
Average Growth rate		34.48%

Ratios of Sells&Admin. Ex. to Sales		
Year	Value of Sel&Admin. Ex	Yearly Ratio
2013	11,00,396	49.50%
2014	10,79,681	48.83%
2015	10,35,393	45.74%
2016	11,63,155	51.67%
Average Growth rate		48.94%

Note:Debt/Equity ratio fixed throughout the forcasting period	62%
Note:Growth on Depriciation and Amortazation was taken from average	14%

approach by first valuing the operation, and then value the financial side effects and add both values together to constitute the value of the enterprise.

Specifically, we can value an unlevered target company's FCF by discounting it at the unlevered cost of capital; and then estimate and add the present value of the interest tax shields attributed to debt as well as other financial side effects, such as subsidies, discounted at the cost of debt. Because interest payments are deductible expenses for the corporation, debt financing creates an interest tax shield for the firm that is included explicitly or implicitly in the valuation of the firm.

In applying the APV, in the first step, we derive the pro forma income statement and balance sheet for 5 years by utilizing the percent of sales approach. Based on the fifth-year FCF, we derive the expected growth rate to perpetuity, the discount rate and the terminal value. The free cash and the terminal value are present valued at the cost of equity for an unlevered company and added to form the value of the operating business.

In the second step of the APV, we value the financial side effects, which could include the debt shielding tax effect of interest, subsidies, cost of financial distress, hedges, and cost of issuing new securities.[15] For instance, the financial side effects of interest tax shields equal $D \times r \times t$, where D is the interest-bearing debt, r is the cost of debt, and t is the marginal tax rate and its terminal value that is derived through the formulary approach similar to the WACC model. The present value of the tax shielding effect for 5 years and to perpetuity provides the value of the financial side effects.

The enterprise value of the firm is the sum of the value of operation plus the value of the financial side effects, i.e., APV = NPV + NPVF, where NPV is the value of the unlevered firm and NPVF is the present value of the financial side effects.

Exhibit 4 provides an APV valuation of a US publicly traded firm that was valued via the NPV in Exhibit 3.

---

[15] Ross, Ch. 18.

Exhibit 4:

BROCADE COMMUNICATIONS SYSTEMS, INC.
CONSOLIDATED STATEMENTS OF INCOME, $, 000

					Pro-Forma Income Statement				
Operations	2013	2014	2015	2016(*)	2017	2018	2019	2020	2021
Net sales	22,22,864	22,11,267	22,63,460	22,51,081	22,68,043	22,85,133	23,02,351	23,19,700	23,37,179
Cost of goods sold	8,13,985	7,45,474	7,35,387	7,89,715	7,81,921	7,87,813	7,93,749	7,99,730	8,05,756
Gross Margin	14,08,879	14,65,793	15,28,073	14,61,367	14,86,122	14,97,320	15,08,602	15,19,970	15,31,423
Selling and Administrative Expense	11,00,396	10,79,681	10,35,393	11,63,155	11,09,893	11,18,256	11,26,682	11,35,172	11,43,725
EBIT	3,08,483	3,86,112	4,92,680	2,98,212	3,76,229	3,79,064	3,81,920	3,84,798	3,87,697
Interest expences	(55,261)	(36,757)	(55,578)	(20,827)	(26,275)	(26,473)	(26,673)	(26,874)	(27,076)
Depreciation and Amortization	1,84,114	1,00,647	84,807	1,23,189	1,23,189	1,23,189	1,23,189	1,23,189	1,23,189
(*) The full year was projected by exprapolating three quarters.									
Interest charged on loan and LTD	6.98%								
Shares used in per share calculation—diluted	4,63,705	4,46,859	4,30,556	4,19,416	3,60,698	3,10,200	2,66,772	2,29,424	1,97,305

CONSOLIDATED BALANCE SHEETS, $, 000

				Pro-Forma Balance Sheet				
	2014	2015	2016	2017	2018	2019	2020	2021
Assets								
Current assets	16,58,005	18,52,199	15,99,358	16,11,409	16,23,551	16,35,785	16,48,110	16,60,529
Total assets	37,33,675	40,38,178	48,73,765	49,10,489	49,47,489	49,84,769	50,22,329	50,60,172
Liabilities and Stockholders' Equity								
Current liabilities	5,87,308	5,62,364	7,01,210	7,06,494	7,11,817	7,17,181	7,22,585	7,28,029
Long-term debt	5,95,450	7,95,804	15,16,761	15,28,190	15,39,705	15,51,306	15,62,996	15,74,773
Total Liabilities	13,25,614	15,04,643	24,12,962	22,34,683	22,51,522	22,68,487	22,85,580	23,02,802
Stockholders' equity	24,08,061	25,33,535	24,60,803	24,64,822	24,83,395	25,02,107	25,20,961	25,39,956
Total Liabilities and Stockholders' Equity	37,33,675	40,38,178	48,73,765	49,10,489	49,47,489	49,84,769	50,22,329	50,60,172

Levered Beta	0.55
Tax rate	34%
Debt to Equity ratio	0.64
Unlevered Beta =Levered Beta/(1+(1-T)*(D/E)	0.39
CAPM with Unlevered Beta	
Risk free rate (treasury bonds 30 years)	2.99%
Return on Market	10.44%
Beta	0.39
Required Return by applying the CAPM=Rf+Beta(Rm-Rf)	5.87%

Return on Debt	6.90%

BROCADE COMMUNICATIONS SYSTEMS, INC.

FREE CASH FLOWS, $, 000

APV of Company's FCF from Projection, $, 000									
				2016	2017	2018	2019	2020	2021
EBIT				2,98,212	3,76,229	3,79,064	3,81,920	3,84,798	3,87,697
Less Tax	34%			(1,01,392)	(1,27,918)	(1,28,882)	(1,29,853)	(1,30,831)	(1,31,817)
Plus Depreciation				1,23,189	1,40,436	1,60,097	1,82,510	2,08,062	2,37,191
CapEx				12,11,617	1,77,160	1,97,097	2,19,790	2,45,622	2,75,034
Change in NWC				6,768	6,819	6,870	6,922	6,974	7,026
Free Cash Flow (FCF)					3,32,686	3,35,193	3,37,719	3,40,264	3,42,828
Discounted CashFlow (DCF)					3,14,238	2,99,050	2,84,596	2,70,840	2,57,749
Interest Tax savings (T=34%)					**8,934**	**9,001**	**9,069**	**9,137**	**9,206**
PV OF ITS (Discounted with Rd)					**8,357**	**7,876**	**7,424**	**6,997**	**6,594**

(*Continued*)

Exhibit 4: (*Continued*)

TERMINAL VALUE WITH VARIOUS GROWTH RATES, $, 000				
GROWTH RATES TO INFINITY	**1.0%**	**1.5%**	**2.0%**	**2.5%**
TERMINAL VALUE at 2021	58,68,742	64,43,887	71,36,409	79,86,323
TV discounted	42,03,940	46,15,932	51,12,004	57,20,820
NPV OF DCF+PV OF TV + PV of ITS	56,67,661	60,79,653	65,75,725	71,84,541
EQUITY VALUATION	41,39,471	45,51,463	50,47,536	56,56,352

Unlevered Beta was used to extract the effect of Debt to Return on Equity
Terminal Value =FCF from 2021*(1+g)/(CAMP(with unlevered Beta-g)
ITS =Interest *tax
PV of ITS= ITS/(1+Rd)^n
NPV =Sum of DCF+Terminal Value+PV of ITS

Sales Growth rate derivation		
Year	Value	Yearly growth
2013	22,22,864	-0.52%
2014	22,11,267	2.36%
2015	22,63,460	-0.55%
2016	22,51,081	1.72%
Average Growth rate		0.75%

Ratios of COGS to Sales		
Year	Value of COGS	Yearly Ratio
2013	$ 8,13,985	36.62%
2014	$ 7,45,474	33.71%
2015	$ 7,35,387	32.49%
2016	$ 7,89,715	35.08%
Average Growth rate		35.00%

Ra tios of Sells&Admin. Ex. to Sales		
Year	Value of Sel&Admin. Ex	Yearly Ratio
2013	11,00,396	49.50%
2014	10,79,681	48.83%
2015	10,35,393	45.74%
2016	11,63,155	51.67%
Average Growth rate		48.94%

Note:Debt/Equity ratio fixed throughout the forcasting period 62%
Note:Growth on Depriciation and Amortazation was taken from average 14%

Flow to Equity (FTE)

Discount the cash flow from the firm to the shareholders of the levered firm at the cost of levered equity capital, R_S, by the following three-step approach:

1. Calculate the levered cash flows, LCFs,
2. Calculate R_S, and
3. Value the levered cash flow at R_S.

$$R_S = R_o + (D/E)\,(1 - tc)\,(R_o - R_d)$$

Determine the free cash flow to equity (FCFE) through the following equation:

$$\text{FCFE} = \text{FCF} - (1 - t) \times (\text{Interest Payments}) + \text{Net Borrowing}.$$

1. Determine the equity cost of capital, R_e; and
2. Discount the FCF to equity using the equity cost of capital.

The Market Approach

The market approach determines the value of a company or entity by comparing it to comparable companies or comparable transactions. The method is based on the derivation of various multiples, where the most common multiples are as follows:

- The P/E ratio of the price per share to earnings per share;
- the EV/EBIT ratio of the enterprise value to operating income;
- the EV/EBITDA ratio of the enterprise value to operating profit + depreciation and amortization;
- EV/FCF the ratio of the enterprise value to operating free cash flow; and
- EV/Sales the ratio of the enterprise value to company sales.

The financial multiples are selected from a sample of comparable companies and applied to the target company to estimate its feasible range of values. Ideal comparables, also referred to as guideline companies, are in the same industry as the subject company being valued, and similar to the subject company in terms of markets, products, growth, profitability, and business risk. The market approach provides a popular valuation approach, but the reliability of the outcome depends on the goodness of the comparables.

In the application of the market approach and the use of comparable companies, several adjustments of the comparables might be necessary for the following factors:

- Company-specific risk,
- Marketability,
- Differences in the tax conditions,
- Liquidity, and
- Control and profitability.

If guideline companies are used, a decision needs to be made whether to use Market Value of Invested Capital (MVIC) or Market Value of Equity (MVE). MVIC is defined as the entire invested capital value of the firm, including equity and debt.

There are a variety of sources for guideline companies, including the SEC 10-K filings on the SEC website or through EDGAR; S&P Compustat and S&P Capital IQ, which are searchable databases of US and foreign public companies.

Comparable transactions, or comparable deals, are commonly used alongside comparable companies. The difference between comparable companies and comparable transaction multiples is that the latter will reflect a "control premium," typically 30–50%, that is not present the comparable companies. The "control premium" depends on the uniqueness of the assets and to what extent there are close substitutes for the technology, expertise, or capability in question, the distribution of financial resources between the bidder and target, or the possibility that the *ex-ante* target price was unduly inflated by market rumors.

Since publicly traded stocks are minority shares, if a controlling interest is being valued, a control premium should be considered.

Adjustments are necessary to the ratios to reflect differences of the comparable transactions.

- Degree of marketability and/or liquidity;
- Timing differences between market transactions and the valuation date;
- Strategic or investment value issues; and
- Size, depth of management, diversification of markets, products and services, and relative growth and risk.

Analysts will also look at premiums for comparable transactions by comparing the offer price to the target's price before the merger announcement at selected dates, such as 1 or 30 days, before the announcement. Because the comparables transactions might not be exact or sufficiently close to the subject company, we analyze the results by utilization of the interquartile distribution range.

Asset-Based Valuation

The asset-based approach to valuation is based on the financial accounting concept that the owners' equity is determined by subtracting the book value of a company's liabilities from the book value of its assets.[16] Under the generally accepted accounting principles (GAAP), most assets on the balance sheet are recorded at historical cost, whereas most long-term liabilities are recorded at the present value, and there is no recognition of intangibles assets. Because of the accounting approach, the "book value" of the owners' equity will normally be underestimated. However, the book value could be adjusted to FMV, by deriving the FMV of each asset and liability on the balance sheet of the subject company or entity, and then the total adjusted liabilities could be subtracted from the total adjusted assets to derive the adjusted book value. This approach increases the valuation cost and complexity, but it still

[16] NACVA, Ch. 6, Commonly Used Methods of Valuation.

ignores intangible assets if they are not listed on the balance sheet.[17] The approach sets a "floor value" of an entity. We note that this method does not address the operating earnings of the business and it would not be inappropriate to value a company or entity with intangible assets.

Liquidating value

Another asset valuation methodology is the liquidating value for firms in financial distress, or for firms whose operating prospects are very cloudy. This method is not appropriate for a going concern, but may be appropriate if there is doubt whether the company would remain in business.

Summary

The DCF method of valuation is superior for company valuation in an M&A setting. However, data used in valuation could be subject to errors for various reasons, including uncertainty about the future. Therefore, it is appropriate to use several scenarios about the future and several valuation methods to estimate the target's value.

The purpose of most valuation analysis is to support negotiators. Deriving value ranges and conducting sensitivity analysis could enhance negotiation flexibility and provide negotiators with a feasible range for a possible agreement.

---

[17] NACVA, Ch. 6, Commonly Used Methods of Valuation.

Chapter 8

Valuation of Privately Held Firms: Methodologies and Applications for M&As

Alina Niculita[1]
Shannon Pratt Valuations, Inc.

This chapter follows the general process of valuing a privately held business and it discusses five broad steps of the valuation process.

- Step 1: Defining the task or engagement
- Step 2: Perform economic, industry, and company analysis
- Step 3: Apply several valuation approaches, methods, and procedures
- Step 4: Derive the discounts and premiums
- Step 5: Reconciliation of value

The first step in the valuation is understanding the engagement and setting up a road "map" for the whole valuation process. In the first step, we discuss issues such as the subject of valuation, the purpose of valuation, and the standard of value.

Second, we discuss the economic, industry, and company analyses that are commonly performed before the application of the valuation approaches and methods.

[1] Paul Heidt, ASA of Morones Analytics contributed the sample valuation of Gourmet Burgers to this chapter.

Third, we introduce the three main valuation approaches to value a privately held business:

- Income approach,
- Market approach, and
- Asset approach.

Each of the three approaches has two or more methods that may be applied based on the specific facts and circumstances of the business to be valued.

Next, after one of more indications of value have been obtained from the application of the valuation methods, we may need to apply adjustments to the indications of value in the form of valuation discounts and premiums. There are several discounts and premiums that may be appropriate in a specific valuation engagement, but the most common are the discount for lack of marketability and the control premium.

The fifth step in the valuation process is the reconciliation of the indications of value obtained from several methods to derive a final opinion of value.

This chapter provides a broad overview of the valuation process. Throughout the chapter, we include references to several books other books and sources of information that the reader can access and learn more about the subjects presented here. At the end of the chapter, we also include a bibliography.

In order to illustrate the various theoretical concepts presented in the chapter, we use a hypothetical valuation sample that the reader can walk through as he or she reads the chapter. The subject company in our valuation sample is Gourmet Burgers ("Gourmet Burgers" or "GB" or "Subject Company"), a chain of restaurants on the West Coast that is being valued for purposes of a sale. Gourmet Burgers focuses on "better fast food" with burgers cooked to order and made of organic beef, local cheeses, and organic veggies and ketchup. The owners of Gourmet Burgers have received an offer for their business and need help in deciding whether the offer is in line with market prices. The valuation date is December 31, 2015.

Takeaways from this chapter and the learning objectives are:

- Get an overview of the broad process of valuation, from defining the engagement to delivering the valuation report,
- Become familiar with the main valuation approaches and methods used in practice to value an interest in a privately held business,
- Get an introduction to the various adjustments to value in the form of valuation discounts and premiums,
- Walk through a numerical valuation example and observe the steps involved and the application of the valuation methods, and
- Become acquainted with some of the well-known resources for valuation professionals.

Defining the Engagement

Before starting to crunch the numbers, the valuation analyst needs to have a clear answer to the following questions:

- What is the *purpose of valuation*?
- What is the *subject of valuation*?
- What is the applicable *standard of value*?
- What is the *premise of value*?
- What is the *valuation date*?

The correct answers to the above questions influence the assumptions, inputs to the valuation process.

Purpose of Valuation

One surprising aspect of the valuation process is that there is not just one single value for a business or business interest. There are several potential values for the same business or business interest, at the same time, and one determining factor of the appropriate value is the purpose of valuation. The purpose of valuation drives the whole valuation process from the standard of value to the choice of the valuation approaches or methods, and to the format of the valuation report. For instance, the same business or business interest may have a certain value for purposes of mergers and acquisitions and another value for the purposes of a buy–sell agreement or divorce settlement. There are numerous purposes of valuation, including:

- Buying or selling a business,
- Buying or selling a partial interest in a business,
- Obtaining or providing financing,
- Initial public offering,
- Leveraged buyout,
- ESOP,
- Estate, gift and income tax,
- Buy–sell agreements,
- Divorce settlements,
- Damage cases,
- Mergers and acquisitions (M&As),
- Dissenting shareholder actions, and
- Determining life insurance needs.

Subject of Valuation

The subject of valuation answers the question of ***what exactly are we valuing*** which is very important. Are we valuing a controlling or a noncontrolling interest in a business? Are we valuing a share of stock, the entire equity, or the invested capital of the business? Are we valuing the assets of the business or an interest in the corporate entity that owns the assets?

A controlling owner has control rights, i.e., the right to sell the assets of the business, to liquidate the business, to merge the business, to hire and fire management, and in general can access and use as it pleases the cash and the other assets of the company. A minority owner, on the other hand, does not have rights of control, but commonly has rights only to distributions but cannot decide when those are made. Minority owners do not have access to the assets and the cash of the business.

Additionally, a noncontrolling interest has less marketability than a controlling interest, because most buyers prefer to have control, it is easier to sell 100% control interest in a business than to sell a 10% minority interest. Because of the differences in control and marketability, a share of stock in a controlling interest is generally more valuable than a share of stock in a noncontrolling interest.

Standard of Value[2]

Standard of value addresses the definition of value or type of value. Some standards are required by law, like fair market value (FMV) for tax purposes, and some are agreed on by parties to a transaction. There are several standards of value used by valuation professionals as follows:

- FMV
- Investment value
- Fair value
- Intrinsic value

FMV is the most common valuation standard and it is defined as: "the price at which the property would change hands between a willing buyer and a willing seller, neither being under any compulsion to buy or sell, and both having reasonable knowledge of relevant facts."[3] FMV is the standard of value required by law for valuations for tax purposes. FMV usually assumes discounts for lack of control and lack of marketability.

As opposed to FMV, which is value to a hypothetical investor, *investment value* is the value to a particular investor based upon individual investment requirements. Investment value is often utilized in M&As involving strategic buyers, which is also called strategic, synergistic, or acquisition value. Investment value is also the standard of value in certain states for purposes of marital dissolution.

---

[2] See Fishman, Jay E., Shannon P. Pratt, and William Morrison, *Standards of Value: Theory and Applications, 2nd Ed.*, John Wiley & Sons, Hoboken, NJ, 2013.

[3] Treas. Reg. 20.2031-1(b). For interpretation and discussion of the standard, see also Internal Revenue Service, "IRS Revenue Ruling 59–60".

Fair value is a standard of value that is used mainly in valuations for shareholder disputes, such as dissenting shareholder cases and minority oppression cases. In such cases, fair value is a value required by state statutes or court precedents. As opposed to FMV, which usually assumes discounts for lack of control and lack of marketability, fair value usually does not assume discounts. The valuation analyst needs to get input about the interpretation of fair value from the attorney who is familiar with the law and court precedents in the specific jurisdiction. Fair value is used for financial reporting purposes and is also used in certain states for purposes of marital dissolution.

Intrinsic value is a standard of value that is commonly used for publicly traded companies and is presented in finance textbooks as the "true value" of a security. Security analysts compute intrinsic value and compare it to the stock price and make a buy, sell, or hold recommendation based on that comparison. Because intrinsic value is based on a fundamental analysis of the characteristics inherent in an investment, it is also called *fundamental value.*

Premise of Value

Premise of value refers to the assumption made about whether the business will continue to operate or liquidate. There is a going concern premise of value and a liquidation premise of value. The going concern premise of value assumes that the business will continue to operate and generate cash flows in the future. The liquidation premise of value assumes that the business will cease operations and liquidate. There are two additional types of liquidation value: orderly liquidation and forced liquidation.

Valuation Date

Another factor that impacts value is the valuation date, or the "as of date" for the valuation. The valuation date is important because the values of businesses and business interests can fluctuate drastically even over short periods of time. The values of most businesses dropped significantly during the Great Recession, when both business internal factors and the general economic conditions were negative. For a business owner looking to sell a business, it is better to value the business when the business conditions are favorable and promising, both internally and externally.

What is the ***purpose of valuation***?

The purpose of valuation is to determine whether the offer to purchase that the management received is reasonable.

What is the ***subject of valuation***?

The subject of valuation is 100% control interest in the equity of the business.

What is the applicable ***standard of value***?

The applicable standard of value is the FMV.

What is the ***premise of value***?

The premise of value is going concern value.

What is the ***valuation date***?

The valuation date is December 31, 2015.

In our sample valuation of Gourmet Burgers, the answers to the questions regarding the engagement help us understand and define the engagement.

Economic, Industry, and Company Analyses

The broad economic conditions and the state of the industry of the Subject Company can have an impact on the valuation of a privately held company. The analysis of the economy, industry, and company is a top-down approach to the financial and operating analysis of a Subject Company. Below, we briefly discuss each part of this three-prong approach to financial analysis.

Economic Analysis[4]

The current and expected economic environment has varying degrees of impact on the value of a business based on whether the Subject

[4] Business Valuation Resources *(www.bvresources.com)* publishes the *Economic Outlook Update*™, a report on the national economy on a monthly and quarterly basis.

Company is a large business with a national or international presence or a small business focused on local customers. While for a large corporation, the broad economic conditions and outlook are relevant, for a small local mom-and-pop store, the local economic conditions impacting its day-to-day customers are more important. When conducting the economic analysis, it is important to focus on those economic drivers that impact the business of the Subject Company. As a result, a good question to ask the management of the business is: *What economic factors such as inflation, interest rates, GDP growth, and commodity prices affect revenues and cash flows?* For instance, if a business uses a commodity in manufacturing its products, the current and expected price of the commodity will impact the costs, profitability, and valuation of the Subject Company, so it is important to analyze those trends as part of the economic analysis. For a small local company, the employment rates and discretionary income of its customers and the local economic environment will have more impact on its profitability and value than the national GDP trends. For a business that has cyclical operations, it is important to find out what part of the business cycle the business is currently in. The analyst needs to correlate the results of the analysis of the economic environment and outlook with assumptions made later in the valuation, such as the growth rates used in the income approach and the valuation multiples used in the market approach.

Exhibit 1, Economic Analysis and Outlook, illustrates in abbreviated terms the economic analysis section of the valuation report for Gourmet Burgers.

Industry Analysis[5]

The industry analysis and outlook influence the valuation of a privately held business because some industries are more "hot" than others. In other words, some industries are growing faster and exhibiting higher valuation multiples than others based on the life cycle of

---

[5] First Research *(www.firstresearch.com)*, a Hoover's Inc. company publishes industry reports on numerous industries organized by SIC and NAICS Code.

Exhibit 1: Economic Analysis and Outlook

To establish an understanding of a business entity or analyze future prospects for that entity, it is often beneficial to examine the economic conditions impacting the business.

National Economic Trends[6]

Despite a solid job market, the US economy slowed considerably during the fourth quarter of 2015, increasing by just 0.7%. The slowdown was largely caused by softer consumer spending, a smaller buildup of business inventories, and falling exports due to a strong dollar and tepid global demand. According to the *Fourth Quarter 2015 Survey of Professional Forecasters,* economists were forecasting that the US economy would grow by 2.5% in the first quarter and 2.6% in the second quarter of 2016, while the annual rate of GDP growth was expected at 2.6% in 2016, 2.5% in 2017, and 2.8% in 2018.

Consumer Spending

Consumer spending, which accounts for more than two-thirds of economic activity in the US, grew by 2.2% during the fourth quarter of 2015, down from increases of 3.0% in the third quarter and 3.6% in the second quarter. Spending on nondurable goods increased by 1.5% in the fourth quarter of 2015, down from 4.2% in the third quarter and 4.3% in the second quarter.

Consumer Confidence

The Conference Board reported that its consumer index, which reflects consumers' assessment of current conditions, had

(*Continued*)

[6] *National Income and Product Accounts Gross Domestic Product — Fourth Quarter 2015 (Advance Estimate)*, US Department of Commerce, Bureau of Economic Analysis, January 29, 2016.

Exhibit 1: (*Continued*)

increased in December 2015. The December 2015 reading of 96.5 was up from a reading of 92.6 in November. Based on the December 2015 index results, consumers' assessment of the current state of the economy remains positive, particularly of the job market. (*Consumer Confidence Index*, The Conference Board, December 29, 2015.)

Stock Market

At December 31, 2015, the Dow Jones Industrial Average (the "Dow") closed at 17,425, which was up 7.0% from 16,285 at the end of the third quarter of 2015. The Dow decreased by 2.2% in 2015 after increasing by 7.5% in 2014 and 26.5% in 2013.

Unemployment[7]

Since October 2014, the unemployment rate has been below 6.0% and reached its lowest level in nearly 8 years during the fourth quarter of 2015. As shown in the accompanying graph, the unemployment rate in December 2015 was 5.0%, which marked the lowest reading since April 2008.

Summary

Less consumer spending, a smaller buildup of business inventories, and falling exports slowed the US economy during the fourth quarter of 2015. Although fourth quarter GDP growth slowed, consumer confidence and the stock market improved, while the unemployment rate continued to decline during the quarter. With the expected improvement during the first quarter of 2016, the economy as of the valuation date is expected to have a positive impact on the Company.

[7] *The Employment Situation — December 2015*, Bureau of Labor Statistics, www.bls.gov.

the industry. As such, it is important to understand if the industry of the Subject Company is in a growth, maturity, or declining phase. Some industries go through periods of consolidation when there's significant M&A activity driving the valuation multiples up. The public companies in the industry of the Subject Company can be a great source of information for this step of the valuation process along with trade publications. Management interviews are particularly good opportunities for valuation analysts to find out what is going on in the industry. Here are some good questions to ask the management of the business about the industry:

Briefly describe the industry in which the Company operates
Is the industry in a period or growth or decline?
Does the industry follow the national economy?
Are there many providers of the product/service offered by the Company or a few?
Are companies acquiring one another?
List trade publications pertaining to the industry and include publisher's name and address, and
List public companies that may be considered comparable "guideline" companies.

Exhibit 2, Industry Analysis and Outlook, illustrates in abbreviated terms the industry analysis section of the valuation report for Gourmet Burgers.

Company Analysis

The company analysis starts with a review of the documents received from the business. The list of requested documents is very comprehensive, it includes financial statements, tax returns, copies of contracts, lists of property and equipment, information about the company's history, management, marketing materials, and company brochures.

Exhibit 3, Business Valuation Document Request List, represents an example of a list of requested documents for the valuation for Gourmet Burgers.

Exhibit 2: Industry Analysis and Outlook

To establish an understanding of a business entity or analyze future prospects for that entity, it is often beneficial to examine the conditions impacting the industry in which the Subject Company conducts business.

Restaurant Industry Overview[8]

Companies in this industry operate restaurants and other eating places, including full-service restaurants (FSRs), quick-service restaurants (QSRs), cafeterias and buffets, and snack bars. Industry revenue is roughly split equally between FSRs and QSRs. Among FSRs, most establishments focus on ethnic cuisine, seafood, or steak. Hamburger restaurants make up a majority of QSR locations, followed by restaurants specializing in pizza and submarine sandwiches.

The industry includes national and regional chains, franchises, and independent operators. The majority of companies are independently owned and operated, although many QSRs are franchises of large national chains. Franchises allow individual owners to leverage a well-known brand and benefit from the purchasing efficiencies and operational expertise of the franchiser. Franchise agreements generally cover a specific geographical market and outline restaurant operating requirements, such as hours of operation, menu offerings, and pricing.

Companies typically buy supplies from food distributors. Some restaurants buy directly from local farms or farmers markets. Large chains may contract with suppliers to minimize volatile commodity costs.

Competitive Landscape

Demand is driven by demographics, consumer tastes, and personal income. The profitability of individual companies can vary

(*Continued*)

[8] Restaurants, First Research Industry Profile, February 16, 2015.

Exhibit 2: (*Continued*)

with QSRs relying on efficient operations and high volume sales, while FSRs rely on high margin items and effective marketing. Large companies have advantages in purchasing, finance, and marketing, while small companies can compete by offering superior food or service.

The US restaurant industry includes about 600,000 restaurants with combined annual revenue of about $470 billion. The US industry is highly fragmented with the 50 largest companies accounting for about 20% of industry revenue.

Industry Outlook[9]

Driven by a strengthening economy, restaurant industry sales in the US were expected to hit a record high in 2015. According to the National Restaurant Association, restaurant and foodservice sales were projected to increase by 3.8% in 2015. In inflation-adjusted terms, industry sales were projected to increase 1.5% in 2015. Although 2015 will likely represent the sixth consecutive year of real growth in restaurant sales, the gains remain below what would be expected during a normal postrecession period.

The restaurant industry employs 14 million individuals and is the nation's second largest private sector employer. The restaurant industry is expected to add 1.7 million new positions in the next 10 years.

Summary

With the improving economy, restaurant industry sales are projected to increase in 2015. The economic and subsequent, industry conditions should have a positive impact on the Company.

[9] 2015 Restaurant Industry Forecast, National Restaurant Association.

Exhibit 3: Business Valuation Document Request List

- Audited, reviewed or compiled income statements and balance sheets for past 5 years if the Subject Company engages an outside CPA to perform financial statement services.
- If the above does not exist, then 5 years of internally prepared income statements and balance sheets.
- Year to date internally prepared income statement and balance sheet.
- Tax returns for the company for the past 5 years.
- Schedule showing officer and owner compensation for same periods as reported above.
- Operating Agreement or Shareholder Buy–Sell Agreement, including amendments.
- Information regarding any prior sales of ownership interests.
- Information regarding per share values reported for stock grant compensation purposes.
- Information regarding any offers to buy or sell the company.
- Copies of prior business appraisals within the past 5 years.
- Information regarding related entities: identity of entity and relationship to subject company, and description and amounts of transactions with related entity.
- Any cash flow forecasts or budgets that have been prepared for future years.
- Information regarding any nonoperating assets held by the company, such as real estate, surplus working capital, airplanes, boats. Income and expense information related to nonoperating assets.
- Information regarding any unrecorded or nonoperating liabilities, such as loan guarantees, or personal loans carried on the company's books.
- Information regarding any unusual or nonrecurring expenses, within the financial statement periods reported.
- Information regarding the nature and/or value of significant unrecorded intellectual property, such as patents, trademarks, software in development, etc.

Exhibit 3: (*Continued*)

- Prospectuses or offering memorandums used to raise capital for the company.
- Information regarding any high concentrations of business with certain suppliers or customers.
- Copies of employment contracts with top five company executives.
- Information about life insurance policies on company owners, owned by the company, including amount of premium paid by the company during the requested financial periods, coverage amount and any cash surrender value reported on the company's balance sheet.
- If the company uses a LIFO method of inventory, information showing the amount of LIFO reserve at reported balance sheet dates.
- Identification of the Standard Industrial Classification Code (SIC Code) that best fits the company's operations. See https://www.osha.gov/pls/imis/sic_manual.html for a list of SIC codes.

Financial Statements Adjustments

As part of the company analysis, adjustments to financial statements are usually considered and performed as needed. Valuation analysts usually perform adjustments to financial statements before computing common size financial statement and financial and operating ratios. Financial statements may need to be adjusted for the following types of items:

- nonrecurring revenues and expenses
- nonoperating assets and liabilities along with related revenues and expenses
- unrecorded assets and liabilities
- discretionary owner items including owner's compensation
- GAAP accounting-related adjustments and also adjustments from cash basis to accrual basis.

Exhibit 4 presents the adjustments to the financial statements of Gourmet Burgers.

Financial Statements Analysis

Part of the company analysis is an analysis of the financial statements and financial and operating ratios. Using the financial statements and the tax returns, the valuation analyst creates spreads of the historical financial statements and computes common size income statements and balance sheets and financial and operating ratios usually for the past 5 years. At this stage, a comparison financial analysis would also be performed, where the Subject Company is compared, and across various financial measures with its peers in the industry. Financial ratios include:

- Profitability ratios
- Return ratios
- Liquidity ratios
- Turnover ratios
- Debt ratios

Other items that the valuation analyst would compute and analyze include:

- an analysis of working capital and
- growth rates over the recent history

Exhibit 5 presents an analysis of historic working capital for Gourmet Burgers.

Exhibit 6 presents the profitability ratios, return on assets, and growth in EBITDA for Gourmet Burgers for 2011–2015 and a comparison with the industry median of the respective measures.

Exhibit 7 presents the historical income statements for Gourmet Burgers for the five fiscal years 2011–2015 along with common size income statements.

Exhibit 8 presents the historical balance sheets for Gourmet Burgers as of the end of the five fiscal years December 31, 2011 through 2015 along with common size balance sheets.

Exhibit 4: Earnings Analysis and Adjustments

Gourmet Burgers, Inc.
Valuation Date: December 31, 2015

	Fiscal Year Ended December 31					As a % of Sales — Fiscal Year Ended December 31				
	2011	**2012**	**2013**	**2014**	**2015**	**2011**	**2012**	**2013**	**2014**	**2015**
Total Net Sales[1]	$1,376,000	$3,791,000	$4,913,000	$5,397,000	$10,879,000	100.0%	100.0%	100.0%	100.0%	100.0%
Cost of Goods Sold[1]	968,000	2,617,000	3,385,000	3,627,000	7,495,000	70.3%	69.0%	68.9%	67.2%	68.9%
Gross Profit	408,000	1,174,000	1,528,000	1,770,000	3,384,000	29.7%	31.0%	31.1%	32.8%	31.1%
Operating Expenses:[1]										
Total Operating Expenses	317,000	889,000	1,176,000	1,460,000	2,744,000	23.0%	23.5%	23.9%	27.1%	25.2%
Reclassify: Depreciation Expense	(36,000)	(140,000)	(72,000)	(146,000)	(440,000)	(2.6%)	(3.7%)	(1.5%)	(2.7%)	(4.0%)
Less: Interest expense	(3,000)	(5,000)	(25,000)	(4,000)	(6,000)	(0.2%)	(0.1%)	(0.5%)	(0.1%)	(0.1%)
Remove: Discretionary Contributions	(2,000)	(2,000)	(2,000)	(2,000)	(2,000)	(0.1%)	(0.1%)	(0.0%)	(0.0%)	(0.0%)
Adjust: Legal and Professional Fees[2]	—	—	—	—	(36,000)	0.0%	0.0%	0.0%	0.0%	(0.3%)
Adjust: Owners' Compensation to Market[3]	—	—	—	—	116,096	0.0%	0.0%	0.0%	0.0%	1.1%
Adjusted Total Operating Expense	276,000	742,000	1,077,000	1,308,000	2,376,096	20.1%	19.6%	21.9%	24.2%	21.8%

(*Continued*)

Exhibit 4: (*Continued*)

	Fiscal Year Ended December 31					As a % of Sales — Fiscal Year Ended December 31				
	2011	**2012**	**2013**	**2014**	**2015**	**2011**	**2012**	**2013**	**2014**	**2015**
Adjusted EBITDA	132,000	432,000	451,000	462,000	1,007,904	9.6%	11.4%	9.2%	8.6%	9.3%
Less: Depreciation Expense:										
Depreciation expense reclassified from above	36,000	140,000	72,000	146,000	440,000	2.6%	3.7%	1.5%	2.7%	4.0%
Adjusted Depreciation Expense	36,000	140,000	72,000	146,000	440,000	2.6%	3.7%	1.5%	2.7%	4.0%
Adjusted EBIT	$96,000	$292,000	$379,000	$316,000	$567,904	7.0%	7.7%	7.7%	5.9%	5.2%
Other Information:										
Adjusted EBITDA	$132,000	$432,000	$451,000	$462,000	$1,007,904	9.6%	11.4%	9.2%	8.6%	9.3%
Plus: One Owner's Compensation at Market	56,000	110,000	118,000	130,000	261,096	4.1%	2.9%	2.4%	2.4%	2.4%
Equals: Seller's Discretionary Earnings ("SDE")	$188,000	$542,000	$569,000	$592,000	$1,269,000	13.7%	14.3%	11.6%	11.0%	11.7%

Notes:

(1) Per Schedule 3A.

(2) Legal and professional fees increased in 2015 due to a trademark infringement case. Decreased the legal and professional fees in 2015 by normalizing the expenses to the 2011–2014 average of 0.2% of sales.

(3) Based on our analysis, we determined the owner was compensated below market level in 2015. We set the owners' compensation equal to the median of 2.4% of sales for companies classified in NAICS 722511
(Full Service Restaurants) with sales between $5–$10 million and the median of 3.6% for all companies classified in NAICS 722511 from the Risk Management Associates (RMA) 2015-2016 Annual Statement Studies.

The adjustment is shown as follows:

	2011	2012	2013	2014	2015					
Total Actual Owners' Compensation	56,000	110,000	118,000	130,000	145,000	4.1%	2.9%	2.4%	2.4%	1.3%
Owners' Compensation at Market — 2.4%	—	—	—	—	261,096					
Owners' Compensation Adjustment	—	—	—	—	116,096					

Exhibit 5: Working Capital Analysis

Gourmet Burgers, Inc.
Valuation Date: December 31, 2015

	December 31					Industry RMA
	2011	**2012**	**2013**	**2014**	**2015**	**NAICS 722511****
Working Capital:						
Sales[(1)]	$1,376,000	$3,791,000	$4,913,000	$5,397,000	$10,879,000	NA
Current Assets[(2)]	60,000	132,000	144,000	177,500	216,000	NA
Current Liabilities[(2)]	57,000	111,000	141,000	132,000	136,000	NA
Net Working Capital (NWC)	3,000	21,000	3,000	45,500	80,000	NA
Working Capital Ratios:						
Sales/Net Working Capital	458.7	180.5	1637.7	118.6	136.0	–75.5
Net Working Capital/Sales	0.2%	0.6%	0.1%	0.8%	0.7%	–1.3%

Notes
(1) Per Schedule 3A.
(2) Per Schedule 3B.
(3) Based on 2015 sales results and industry level of working capital as a percentage of sales.
NA indicates not available or not applicable.
**Industry data based on companies classified in NAICS 722511 (Full Service Restaurants) with sales between $5–$10 million. The median is presented from the Risk Management Associates (RMA) 2015–2016 Annual Statement Studies.

Exhibit 6: Profitability, Returns, and Growth Comparative Analysis

Gourmet Burgers, Inc.

Valuation Date: December 31, 2015

	Fiscal Year Ended December 31					Average	Industry
	2011	**2012**	**2013**	**2014**	**2015**	**2011–2015**	**Median[1]**
Profitability:							
Gross Profit	$408,000	$1,174,000	$1,528,000	$1,770,000	$3,384,000	$1,653,000	na
Gross Margin	29.7%	31.0%	31.1%	32.8%	31.1%	31.1%	60.5%
Operating Income	132,000	$432,000	$451,000	$462,000	$1,007,904	497,000	na
Operating Margin	9.6%	11.4%	9.2%	8.6%	9.3%	9.6%	5.7%
Operating Ratios:							
Return on Assets	71.5%	134.1%	97.3%	71.7%	84.0%	91.7%	14.4%
Growth Rates:							
EBITDA Growth	na	nm	4.4%	2.4%	118.2%	na	na

na=not applicable; nm=not meaningful

Note: Ratios calculated using annual average asset or liability balances.

[1]Per Risk Management Association (RMA) 2015–2016 Annual Statement Studies for NAICS 722511 (Full Service Restaurants) with sales between $5–$10 million.

Net Income	$93,000	$287,000	$354,000	$312,000	$561,904
Total Assets	$130,000	$298,000	$430,000	$440,500	$897,000
Total Equity	$48,000	$7,000	$166,000	$93,500	$566,000

Exhibit 7: Historical Income Statements

Gourmet Burgers, Inc.
Valuation Date: December 31, 2015

	Fiscal Year Ended December 31					As a % of Sales — Fiscal Year Ended December 31				
	2011	**2012**	**2013**	**2014**	**2015**	**2011**	**2012**	**2013**	**2014**	**2015**
Total Net Sales	$1,376,000	$3,791,000	$4,913,000	$5,397,000	$10,879,000	100.0%	100.0%	100.0%	100.0%	100.0%
Total Cost of Goods Sold	968,000	2,617,000	3,385,000	3,627,000	7,495,000	70.3%	69.0%	68.9%	67.2%	68.9%
Gross Profit	408,000	1,174,000	1,528,000	1,770,000	3,384,000	29.7%	31.0%	31.1%	32.8%	31.1%
Operating Expenses:										
Compensation of Officers	56,000	110,000	118,000	130,000	145,000	4.1%	2.9%	2.4%	2.4%	1.3%
Repairs and Maintenance	26,000	40,000	38,000	65,000	137,000	1.9%	1.1%	0.8%	1.2%	1.3%
Rent	40,000	150,000	297,000	305,000	746,000	2.9%	4.0%	6.0%	5.7%	6.9%
Taxes and Licenses	29,000	148,000	195,000	220,000	246,000	2.1%	3.9%	4.0%	4.1%	2.3%
Depreciation	36,000	140,000	72,000	146,000	440,000	2.6%	3.7%	1.5%	2.7%	4.0%
Advertising	13,000	28,000	38,000	44,000	74,000	0.9%	0.7%	0.8%	0.8%	0.7%

Auto and Truck Expense	2,000	5,000	6,000	13,000	7,000	0.1%	0.1%	0.1%	0.2%	0.1%
Interest Expense	3,000	5,000	25,000	4,000	6,000	0.2%	0.1%	0.5%	0.1%	0.1%
Janitorial	23,000	56,000	87,000	131,000	230,000	1.7%	1.5%	1.8%	2.4%	2.1%
Charitable Contributions	2,000	2,000	2,000	2,000	2,000	0.1%	0.1%	0.0%	0.0%	0.0%
Dues and Subscriptions	2,000	2,000	4,000	3,000	7,000	0.1%	0.1%	0.1%	0.1%	0.1%
Insurance	12,000	18,000	24,000	58,000	50,000	0.9%	0.5%	0.5%	1.1%	0.5%
Legal and Professional	4,000	5,000	5,000	9,000	58,000	0.3%	0.1%	0.1%	0.2%	0.5%
Meals and Entertainment	14,000	19,000	27,000	25,000	34,000	1.0%	0.5%	0.5%	0.5%	0.3%
Merchant Fees	8,000	26,000	48,000	82,000	205,000	0.6%	0.7%	1.0%	1.5%	1.9%
Office Expense	6,000	10,000	18,000	23,000	30,000	0.4%	0.3%	0.4%	0.4%	0.3%
Travel	2,000	3,000	2,000	27,000	39,000	0.1%	0.1%	0.0%	0.5%	0.4%
Utilities	26,000	97,000	124,000	135,000	217,000	1.9%	2.6%	2.5%	2.5%	2.0%
Waste Removal	5,000	23,000	32,000	28,000	60,000	0.4%	0.6%	0.7%	0.5%	0.6%
Miscellaneous	8,000	2,000	14,000	10,000	11,000	0.6%	0.1%	0.3%	0.2%	0.1%

(*Continued*)

Exhibit 7: (*Continued*)

	Fiscal Year Ended December 31					As a % of Sales Fiscal Year Ended December 31				
	2011	2012	2013	2014	2015	2011	2012	2013	2014	2015
Total Operating Expense	317,000	889,000	1,176,000	1,460,000	2,744,000	23.0%	23.5%	23.9%	27.1%	25.2%
Net Income	$91,000	$285,000	$352,000	$310,000	$640,000	6.6%	7.5%	7.2%	5.7%	5.9%

Annual Free Cash Flow	
Net Income	$640,000
Thomas Southard Compensation	51,901
Mark McCrary Compensation	44,635
Robert Spencer Compensation	19,348
Anthony McCrary Compensation	35,297
Michael McCrary Compensation	17,830
Robin McCrary Compensation	44,147
Total Annual Free Cash Flow	$853,158
Multipled by 2	2
Company Value	1,706,316
Ownership Interest	40.5%
Mark McCrary Ownership Value	$691,058

Exhibit 8: Historical Balance Sheets

Gourmet Burgers, Inc.
Valuation Date: December 31, 2015

	December 31					As a % of Total Assets December 31				
	2011	**2012**	**2013**	**2014**	**2015**	**2011**	**2012**	**2013**	**2014**	**2015**
Current Assets:										
Cash	$52,000	$112,000	$116,000	$142,000	$163,000	40.0%	37.6%	27.0%	32.2%	18.2%
Trade Receivables, Net	2,000	6,000	8,000	10,500	14,000	1.5%	2.0%	1.9%	2.4%	1.6%
Inventory	3,000	6,000	14,000	17,000	31,000	2.3%	2.0%	3.3%	3.9%	3.5%
Prepaid Expenses	3,000	8,000	6,000	8,000	8,000	2.3%	2.7%	1.4%	1.8%	0.9%
Total Current Assets	60,000	132,000	144,000	177,500	216,000	46.2%	44.3%	33.5%	40.3%	24.1%
Fixed Assets:										
Net Fixed Assets	70,000	166,000	286,000	263,000	681,000	53.8%	55.7%	66.5%	59.7%	75.9%
Total Assets	$130,000	$298,000	$430,000	$440,500	$897,000	100.0%	100.0%	100.0%	100.0%	100.0%
Current Liabilities:										
Trade Payables	$14,000	$44,000	$59,000	$55,000	$55,000	10.8%	14.8%	13.7%	12.5%	6.1%
Other Payables	24,000	28,000	28,000	18,000	22,000	18.5%	9.4%	6.5%	4.1%	2.5%
Accrued Payroll	19,000	39,000	54,000	59,000	59,000	14.6%	13.1%	12.6%	13.4%	6.6%
Total Current Liabilities	57,000	111,000	141,000	132,000	136,000	43.8%	37.2%	32.8%	30.0%	15.2%
Long Term Liabilities:										
Long-Term Debt	25,000	180,000	123,000	215,000	195,000	19.2%	60.4%	28.6%	48.8%	21.7%
Total Long-Term Liabilities	25,000	180,000	123,000	215,000	195,000	19.2%	60.4%	28.6%	48.8%	21.7%
Total Liabilities	82,000	291,000	264,000	347,000	331,000	63.1%	97.7%	61.4%	78.8%	36.9%
Total Equity	$48,000	$7,000	$166,000	$93,500	$566,000	36.9%	2.3%	38.6%	21.2%	63.1%
Total Liabilities & Equity	$130,000	$298,000	$430,000	$440,500	$897,000	100.0%	100.0%	100.0%	100.0%	100.0%

Exhibit 9 presents the historical financial and operating ratios for Gourmet Burgers as of the end of the five fiscal years December 31, 2011 through 2015. Additionally, this exhibit includes financial and operating ratios for industry peers, other restaurants of similar size to Gourmet Burgers.

Management Interview and Site Visit

In the process of document review and financial statement analysis, questions about the business come up, and the valuation analyst may have an opportunity to interview the management of the company. Based on the purpose of the valuation, a site visit may also be part of the company analysis. The following topics are usually covered during the management interviews:

- Company background
- Products or services
- Marketing and distribution
- Competition and concentration
- Operations
- Customer base
- Supplier base
- Industry conditions
- Management and staff
- Facilities
- Contingent liabilities
- Previous transactions
- Company expectations
- Financial overview
- Risk assessment

Exhibit 10, Analysis of Normalized Financial Statements, illustrates in abbreviates terms the type of financial statement analysis that the valuation analyst would perform for Gourmet Burgers.

Exhibit 9: Financial and Operating Ratio Analysis

Gourmet Burgers, Inc.

Valuation Date: December 31, 2015

	Fiscal Year Ended December 31					**Average**	**Industry**
	2011	**2012**	**2013**	**2014**	**2015**	**2011–2015**	**Median[1]**
Liquidity Ratios:							
Current Ratio	1.1	1.2	1.0	1.3	1.6	1.2	0.9
Quick Ratio	1.0	1.1	0.9	1.2	1.4	1.1	0.6
Sales/Receivables Ratio	688.0	631.8	614.1	514.0	777.1	645.0	999.8
Days Receivables Ratio	0.5	0.6	0.6	0.7	0.5	0.6	0.4
Cost of Sales/Payables Ratio	69.1	59.5	57.4	65.9	136.3	77.6	32.1
Days Payable Ratio	5.3	6.1	6.4	5.5	2.7	5.2	11.4
Leverage Ratios:							
Fixed Worth Ratio	1.5	23.7	1.7	2.8	1.2	6.2	2.3
Debt Worth Ratio	1.7	41.6	1.6	3.7	0.6	9.8	3.6
Operating Ratios:							
Return on Assets	70.0%	133.2%	96.7%	71.2%	95.7%	93.4%	14.6%
Growth Rates:							
Revenue Growth	na	175.5%	29.6%	9.9%	101.6%	79.1%	na
Total Asset Growth	na	129.2%	44.3%	2.4%	103.6%	69.9%	na

(*Continued*)

Exhibit 9: (*Continued*)

	Fiscal Year Ended December 31					Average	Industry
	2011	2012	2013	2014	2015	2011–2015	Median[(1)]
Financial Statement Structure:							
Balance Sheet Accounts							
Cash	40.0%	37.6%	27.0%	32.2%	18.2%	31.0%	21.5%
Trade Receivables	1.5%	2.0%	1.9%	2.4%	1.6%	1.9%	1.6%
Inventory	2.3%	2.0%	3.3%	3.9%	3.5%	3.0%	7.4%
All Other Current Assets	2.3%	2.7%	1.4%	1.8%	0.9%	1.8%	2.6%
Total Current Assets	46.2%	44.3%	33.5%	40.3%	24.1%	37.7%	33.0%
Fixed Assets	53.8%	55.7%	66.5%	59.7%	75.9%	62.3%	45.1%
Intangible Assets	0.0%	0.0%	0.0%	0.0%	0.0%	0.0%	9.9%
All Other Non-Current Assets	0.0%	0.0%	0.0%	0.0%	0.0%	0.0%	11.9%
Total Assets	100.0%	100.0%	100.0%	100.0%	100.0%	100.0%	100.0%
Notes Payable-Short Term	0.0%	0.0%	0.0%	0.0%	0.0%	0.0%	6.1%
Cur. Mat.-L/T/D	0.0%	0.0%	0.0%	0.0%	0.0%	0.0%	2.9%
Trade Payables	10.8%	14.8%	13.7%	12.5%	6.1%	11.6%	12.3%
Other Payables	18.5%	9.4%	6.5%	4.1%	2.5%	8.2%	0.2%
All Other Current Liabilities	14.6%	13.1%	12.6%	13.4%	6.6%	12.0%	24.7%
Total Current Liabilities	43.8%	37.2%	32.8%	30.0%	15.2%	31.8%	46.2%
Long Term Debt	19.2%	60.4%	28.6%	48.8%	21.7%	35.8%	28.6%

Deferred Taxes	0.0%	0.0%	0.0%	0.0%	0.0%	0.0%	0.3%
All Other Non-Current Liabilities	0.0%	0.0%	0.0%	0.0%	0.0%	0.0%	15.2%
Net Worth	36.9%	2.3%	38.6%	21.2%	63.1%	32.4%	9.7%
Total Liabilities & Net Worth	100.0%	100.0%	100.0%	100.0%	100.0%	100.0%	100.0%
Income Statement Accounts							
Net Sales	100.0%	100.0%	100.0%	100.0%	100.0%	100.0%	100.0%
Gross Profit	29.7%	31.0%	31.1%	32.8%	31.1%	31.1%	60.2%
Sales & Operating Expenses	23.0%	23.5%	23.9%	27.1%	25.2%	24.5%	55.2%
Operating Profit	6.6%	7.5%	7.2%	5.7%	5.9%	6.6%	5.0%
Profit Before Taxes	6.6%	7.5%	7.2%	5.7%	5.9%	6.6%	4.2%

na = not applicable; nm=not meaningful

Note: Ratios calculated using annual average asset or liability balances.

[(1)]Per Risk Management Association (RMA) 2015–2016 Annual Statement Studies for NAICS 722511 — Full Service Restaurants with sales between $5–$10 million.

Inputs:					
Revenue	$1,376,000	$3,791,000	$4,913,000	$5,397,000	$10,879,000
COGS	968,000	2,617,000	3,385,000	3,627,000	7,495,000
Pre-Tax Profit	$91,000	$285,000	$352,000	$310,000	$640,000
Net Income	$91,000	$285,000	$352,000	$310,000	$640,000

(*Continued*)

Exhibit 9: (*Continued*)

Inputs:					
Accounts Receivable	2,000	6,000	8,000	10,500	14,000
Inventory	3,000	6,000	14,000	17,000	31,000
Current Assets	60,000	132,000	144,000	177,500	216,000
Current Assets Less Inventory	57,000	126,000	130,000	160,500	185,000
Fixed Assets, Net	70,000	166,000	286,000	263,000	681,000
Total Assets	130,000	298,000	430,000	440,500	897,000
Accounts Payable	14,000	44,000	59,000	55,000	55,000
Current Liabilities	57,000	111,000	141,000	132,000	136,000
Total Liabilities	82,000	291,000	264,000	347,000	331,000
Total Equity	$48,000	$7,000	$166,000	$93,500	$566,000

Exhibit 10: Analysis of Normalized Financial Statements[10]

This section of the report discusses the Company's financial statements after the normalizing adjustments were made. We also compared Gourmet Burgers to companies classified in NAICS 722511 (FSRs) with sales between $5 and $10 million.

Growth

Historical growth rates provide information about the Company's future growth prospects. With the increase in popularity of Gourmet Burgers, as well as the opening of new locations, the Company's sales increased from $1.38 million in 2011 to $10.88 million in 2015. From 2011 to 2015, the Company's compound annual growth rate was equal to 67.7%.

Assets and Liabilities

Gourmet Burgers' total assets increased from $130,000 at December 31, 2011 to $897,000 at December 31, 2015. The majority of the Company's total assets at the valuation date consisted of $163,000 in cash and $681,000 in fixed assets, net of accumulated depreciation.

At December 31, 2015, the Company had total liabilities equal to $331,000, down from $347,000 at the end of 2014. The Company's liabilities consisted mainly of trade and other payables in the amount of $77,000 and a notes payable with a balance of $195,000 at the valuation date.

Profitability

Profitability ratios measure the Company's return on sales. The Company's adjusted gross profit margin increased from 29.7% in 2011 to 32.8% in 2014, before decreasing slightly to 31.1% in 2015. The Company's adjusted gross profit margin averaged 31.1% from 2011 to 2015.

[10] Risk Management Associates' *2015/2016 Annual Statement Studies.*

Exhibit 10: (*Continued*)

Gourmet Burgers' adjusted operating income increased from $132,000 in 2011 to $1.0 million in 2015. The Company's adjusted operating margin fluctuated from a high of 11.4% in 2012 to a low of 8.6% in 2014. From 2011 to 2015, the Company's adjusted operating margin averaged 9.6%, which was above the industry benchmark of 5.7%.

Efficiency

Efficiency ratios are used to assess management's performance and to further analyze the Company's profitability. Gourmet Burgers' pretax return on assets (ROA) fluctuated over the review period. The Company's ROA decreased from 134.1% in 2012 to 71.1% in 2014 before increasing to 84.0% in 2015. The Company's ROA averaged 91.7% from 2011 to 2015, which was significantly higher than the industry benchmark of 14.4%.

Summary

Gourmet Burgers' sales have steadily increased from 2011 to 2015. After normalization adjustments, the Company's operating margins increased and were greater than the industry benchmark. When analyzing the Company's adjusted ROA, the Company was significantly more efficient compared to the industry at the valuation date.

Valuation Approaches, Methods, and Procedures

There is a hierarchy of terms used to describe various valuation methodologies for privately held businesses. There are three main approaches, each with two or more methods. Within each method, there are several procedures that can be applied (Table 1).

Below are the definitions of valuation approach, method, and procedure from the International Glossary of Business Valuation Terms.[11]

[11] American Society of Appraisers, *Business Valuation Standards — Glossary*, American Society of Appraisers, Herndon, VA, 2006.

Table 1: Valuation Approaches, Methods, and Procedures.

Approaches	Methods	Procedures
Income	*Discounted cash flow method* *Capitalization method*	*The equity procedure* *The invested capital procedure*
Market	*The guideline public company method* *The guideline transaction method* *Past subject company transactions* *Rules of thumb*	*The equity procedure* *The invested capital procedure*
Asset	*The adjusted net assets value method* *The excess earnings method*	

The valuation approach provides a general way of determining a value indication of a business, business ownership interest, security, or intangible asset using one or more valuation methods.

The valuation method furnishes a specific way to determine value.

The valuation procedure addresses the act, manner, and technique of performing the steps of an appraisal method.

The Income Approach

The Income approach values the business or business interest on the basis the economic income stream expected to be received from the business, hence the name of the approach. There are two methods under this approach:

- The discounted cash flow (DCF) method
- The capitalization method

DCF Method

The DCF method is based on the concept of present value, where value today, or value as of the valuation date, is the present value of the future expected cash flows discounted at a discount rate commensurate with the risk of the business. There are two steps in the DCF method:

- Step 1: Projecting the expected economic income over the life of the investment
- Step 2: Discounting each increment of that expected income back to a present value at a rate of return known as a discount rate

The formula for the DCF method is presented below.

$$PV = \frac{NCF_1}{(1+k)_1} + \frac{NCF_2}{(1+k)^2} + \cdots + \frac{NCF_n}{(1+k)^n} + \frac{T}{(1+k)^n},$$

where

PV = Present value
$NCF_{1,2\ldots n}$ = Net cash flows for the first period through the nth period
k = Cost of capital appropriate to the cash flows being discounted (e.g., the cost of equity capital if for equity, the weighted average cost of capital if for invested capital)
T = Terminal value (value beyond the end of the nth period in the discrete projection period)

Exhibit 11 presents the discounted cash flow method as applied to value Gourmet Burgers as of December 31, 2015. Projections for 2016 and 2017 are included in the cash flow forecast as well as a terminal value is estimated at the end of 2017.

The Capitalization Method

The capitalization method is based on a shortcut version of the concept of discounting. Capitalizing is dividing the next year's cash flow by a capitalization rate. There are two steps in the capitalization method:

- Step 1: Observing or estimating a single period's economic income, and
- Step 2: Dividing it by a rate of return known as a capitalization rate.

Exhibit 11: Income Approach Analysis

Gourmet Burgers, Inc.
Valuation Date: December 31, 2015

	Projected Cash Flows									
	Adjusted Actual		Adjusted Actual		Projection		Projection		Residual	
	2014		2015		2016 [1]		2017 [1]		Period [1]	
Adjusted Net Revenue	$5,397,000	100.0%	$10,879,000	100.0%	$13,598,750	100.0%	$15,638,563	100.0%	$16,107,719	100.0%
Adjusted Cost of Sales	3,627,000	67.2%	7,495,000	68.9%	9,292,135	68.3%	10,685,955	68.3%	11,006,534	68.3%
Gross Profit	1,770,000	32.8%	3,384,000	31.1%	4,306,615	31.7%	4,952,608	31.7%	5,101,186	31.7%
Adjusted Operating Expenses	1,308,000	24.2%	2,376,096	21.8%	3,078,663	22.6%	3,540,463	22.6%	3,646,677	22.6%
Adjusted EBITDA	462,000	8.6%	1,007,904	9.3%	1,227,952	9.0%	1,412,145	9.0%	1,454,509	9.0%
Less: Depreciation Expense	146,000	2.7%	440,000	4.0%	475,956	3.5%	390,964	2.5%	306,047	1.9%
Adjusted EBIT	316,000	5.9%	567,904	5.2%	751,996	5.5%	1,021,180	6.5%	1,148,462	7.1%
Proforma Income Taxes [2]					210,258	28.0%	285,523	28.0%	321,111	28.0%
Proforma Net Income					$541,737	4.0%	$735,658	4.7%	$827,352	5.1%
Plus: Depreciation					475,956		390,964		306,047	
Less: Maintenance Level Capital Expenditures					(475,956)		(390,964)		(306,047)	

(*Continued*)

Exhibit 11: (*Continued*)

	Projected Cash Flows				
	Adjusted Actual	**Adjusted Actual**	**Projection**	**Projection**	**Residual**
	2014	**2015**	**2016** [1]	**2017** [1]	**Period** [1]
Expected (Increase)/ Decrease in Working Capital[3]			260,116	27,017	6,214
Capitalization Rate[4]					14.7%
Residual Cash Flow					**$5,654,670**
Multiplied by Present Value Factor			0.920	0.778	0.778
Equals: Present Value of Annual Cash Flows			$737,412	$593,180	$4,397,988
Total Present Value of Future Cash Flows					**$5,728,580**
Less: Interest-Bearing Debt[5]					(195,000)
Total Equity Value (Non-Controlling, Fully Marketable, Rounded)					**$5,534,000**

(1) Based on discussions with management, we grew sales by 25% in projected 2016 and by 15% in projected 2017 and then by 3.5% in the residual period, which is slightly higher than the long-term rate of inflation. We set the 2016–2017 projections and residual period cost of goods sold, operating expenses, and other income equal to adjusted weighted average 2014–2015 results as a percentage of sales. We reduced depreciation as a percentage of sales over the projection period until reaching the median of 1.9% of sales for companies classified in 722511 (Full Service Restaurants) from the Risk Management Associates (RMA) 2015–2016 Annual Statement Studies.

(2) Set to a flat tax rate based on the S Corporation Economic Adjustment Model.

(3) The expected change in working capital is based on the industry benchmark of 3.5% of sales, as shown at Schedule 1A-4.

(4) Per Schedule 1A-4.

(5) The Company's interest-bearing debt consisted of long-term debt.

Assumptions					
Sales Growth		101.6%	25.0%	15.0%	3.5%
Working Capital	$45,500	$80,000	($180,116)	($207,133)	($213,347)
WC as a % of Sales	0.8%	0.7%	–1.3%	–1.3%	–1.3%
			18.2%	18.2%	18.2%
			0.500	1.500	1.500

The formula for the capitalization method is as follows:

$$PV = \frac{NCF_1}{c},$$

where
PV = Present value
NCF_1 = Net cash flow in period 1, the year ahead
c = Capitalization rate = Discount rate — long-term expected growth

Estimating Net Cash Flow

Both the DCF method and the capitalization method use some form of economic income in the numerator to estimate value. The formulas presented above use NCF as the measure of the economic income, but other measures of economic income, such as dividends or net income after taxes, may be used, with the caveat that appropriate discount rates need to be applied to each measure of economic income. NCF is the preferred measure of economic income to be used in the income approach, because it represents the money that is left over after the business funds, capital expenditures and working capital needs, as shown in the formulas below (separately for NCF to equity and NCF to invested capital[12]).

NCF to equity is the NCF available to equity holders after satisfying the business expenses and investment needs of the business as well as after paying the return to debtholders.

Net Income (after taxes)
\+ Noncash Charges
− Capital Expenditures
± Changes in interest-bearing debt
± Changes in Working Capital
= NCF to equity

[12] The formulas presented for NCF to equity and NCF to invested capital assume a capital structure formed of common equity and debt, and they do not specifically address preferred equity. If preferred equity is present, the formulas would have to be modified to reflect the correct treatment of preferred dividends, if any.

NCF to invested capital is available to all investors in the business, equity and debt, after paying for business expenses and investment needs. We show two methods to compute NCF to invested capital below, one starting from net income, and one starting from Earnings Before Interest and Taxes (EBIT).

Net Income (after taxes)
+ Noncash Charges
– Capital Expenditures
+ Interest expense, net of the tax effect (interest expense × (1 – tax rate))
± Changes in Working Capital
= NCF to invested capital

EBIT
– Income Taxes on EBIT
+ Noncash Charges
– Capital Expenditures
± Changes in Working Capital
= NCF to invested capital

The above formula that calculates NCF to invested capital starting from EBIT is applied in Exhibit 11 to calculate NCF to invested capital for Gourmet Burgers.

Equity versus Invested Capital Procedure

There are two procedures that can be used under each method of the income approach discussed above, the capitalization method and the discounting method, and they are as follows:

- The equity procedure: Under this procedure, the equity is valued directly by estimating the NCFs to equity and discounting them at the cost of the equity for the Company.
- The invested capital procedure: Under this procedure, the equity is valued indirectly by first estimating the value of the total invested capital in the Company and then subtracting the value of debt. To

value the entire invested capital, the analyst estimates the NCFs to invested capital and discounts them at the weighted average cost of capital (WACC).

The cost of equity and the WACC are discussed in the next section. In the case of Gourmet Burgers, we apply an invested capital procedure in the income approach. Exhibit 11 shows that first the value of total invested capital is estimated, and then the value of equity is arrived at after subtracting interest-bearing debt.

Developing Discount Rates[13]

To apply the DCF method, we need to estimate a discount rate, which is the rate of return available in the market on investments of comparable risk. The discount rate is a market-driven rate, representing the rate of return necessary to induce investors to commit funds to an investment given its level of risk.

The discount rate depends on whether an equity or an invested capital procedure is applied. If we are valuing equity directly by discounting net cash flows to equity, the appropriate discount rate is the cost of equity, or the rate of return required in the market by investors in equity of businesses of similar risk.

If we value the entire invested capital by discounting net cash flows to invested capital, then the appropriate discount rate would be a blended required rate of return for an investment in both the equity and debt of businesses of similar risk, or the WACC.

If we are valuing the equity directly, the appropriate discount rate would be the cost of equity.

The valuation concept that the discount rate must match the economic income measure being discounted is illustrated in Table 2.

---

[13] A full discussion of discount rates and cost of capital is beyond the scope of this chapter. See Pratt, Shannon P., and Roger Grabowski, *Cost of Capital, 5th Ed.*, John Wiley & Sons, Hoboken, NJ, 2014.

Table 2: Illustration of the Valuation Concept.

Valuation Procedure	Cash Flow in the Numerator	Discount Rate in the Denominator
Equity procedure	Net cash flow to equity	Cost of equity
Invested capital procedure	Net cash flow to invested capital	WACC

Cost of Equity

There are two main methods used by appraisers to estimate cost of equity for privately held companies:

- Adjusted Capital Asset Pricing Model (ACAPM)
- The buildup method (BUM)

A discount rate has two elements, including a "risk-free rate" and a premium for risk. A risk-free rate consists of a real rate of return for foregoing the use of money for some period of time and the expected rate of inflation over the life of the investment. A premium for risk in the context of a discount rate is needed to account for the increased risk of an investment over a risk-free investment. Both CAPM and BUM estimate cost of equity as the sum of a risk-free rate and one or more risk premiums, as shown in the formulas below.

CAPM

Rf — the risk-free rate
$+ RP_m$ — the equity risk premium (or the "market risk premium", where the market is usually either the S&P 500 index)
$\times$ Beta — the beta (as modifier to RP_m reflecting the sensitivity of the particular stock to the market)
$+ RP_s$ — Risk premium for size
$+ RP_c$ — Risk premium for the company (unsystematic risk)

BUM

Rf — the risk-free rate
$+ RP_m$ — the equity risk premium (premium for the "market," usually either the S&P 500 index or the NYSE index)

$+ RP_s$ — Risk premium for size
$\pm RP_i$ — Industry risk adjustment
$+ RP_c$ — Risk premium for the company (unsystematic risk)

Exhibit 12 shows the application of two variants of the BUM to estimate a 20% cost of equity for the Subject Company.

WACC

The WACC blends into one rate the market driven required rates of return for interest-bearing debt and equity capital. The formula for the WACC is as follows:

$$\text{WACC} = [(D/V) \times K_d \times (1 - T)] + [(E/V) \times K_e],$$

where

(D/V) = ratio of market value of interest-bearing debt to total capital
(E/V) = ratio of equity capital to total capital = $1 - (D/V)$
K_d = cost of interest-bearing debt capital
K_e = levered cost of equity capital
T = marginal tax rate

Exhibit 12 shows the application of the above formula to estimate an 18.2% WACC for the Subject Company.

Capitalization Rates

To apply the capitalization method, we need to estimate a capitalization rate as shown in the formula for the capitalization method. Once we have a discount rate, developing a capitalization rate is simple by subtracting a long-term growth rate.

c = Capitalization rate = Discount rate — long-term growth expectations

Exhibit 12 shows the application of the above formula to estimate a 14.7 % capitalization rate for the Subject Company.

Exhibit 12: Cost of Equity Capital

Gourmet Burgers, Inc.	
Valuation Date: December 31, 2015	
Weighted Average Cost of Capital (WACC)	
$WACC = (D/V \times K_d \times (1 - T)) + (E/V \times k_e)$	
where:	
D/V = ratio of interest bearing debt capital to total invested capital	10.8%[1]
E/V = ratio of equity capital to total invested capital (= 1 – D/V)	89.2%[1]
K_d = cost of interest bearing debt capital	4.7%[2]
K_e = cost of equity capital (see below for cost of equity calculation)	20.0%
T = marginal tax rate	28.0%[3]
Weighted Average Cost of Capital:	**18.2%**
Less: Expected Long-term Growth Rate:	3.5%[4]
Concluded Capitalization Rate:	**14.7%**
Concluded Cost of Equity Capital — Subject Company	
Method	**Rate**
Ibbotson Build-Up Method	20.1%
Duff & Phelps Build-Up Method	20.0%
Concluded Average Cost of Equity Capital (Discount Rate):	**20.0%**
Ibbotson Build-Up Method	
Risk-Free Rate	2.6%[5]

(*Continued*)

Exhibit 12: (*Continued*)

Weighted Average Cost of Capital (WACC)		
Equity Risk Premium		5.9%[6]
Size Premium		5.6%[6]
Company Specific Risk Premium		6.0%[7]
Company Specific Cost of Equity Capital — Ibbotson		**20.1%**
Duff & Phelps Build-Up Method		
Calculated Cost of Equity Capital		17.0%[8]
Plus: Company Specific Risk Premium		3.0%[9]
Company Specific Cost of Equity Capital — Duff & Phelps Build-Up		20.0%
Specific Company Risk Factors	**+/–Risk**	
Intense Competition	+	
Potential Acquisition Target	–	
Strong Brand Awareness	–	
Consistent Growth	–	

[1] Set equal to the median debt/total capital ratio for companies classified in SIC 5800 (Eating and Drinking Places) from the 2015 Valuation Handbook: Industry Cost of Capital.

[2] Set equal to the SIC Composite cost of debt for companies classified in SIC 5800 (Eating and Drinking Places) from the 2015 Valuation Handbook: Industry Cost of Capital.

[3] Set equal to a flat tax rate based on the S Corporation Economic Adjustment Model.

(4) We set the long-term growth rate equal to 3.5%, which is slightly higher than the long-term rate of inflation of 2.2% per *Livingston Survey*, December 2015.

(5) Long-Term (20-year) U.S. Treasury Coupon Bond Yield as of December 2015.

(6) Per the 2016 Valuation Handbook: Guide to Cost of Capital published by Duff & Phelps based on company size. The Equity Risk Premium includes a downward 1% adjustment.

(7) Based on the industry risk premium for SIC 5800 (Eating & Drinking Places) from the Duff & Phelps Risk Premium Calculator.

(8) Appraiser's subjective risk premium for specific risk characteristics of the subject company not reflected in other components of the build-up under the Ibbotson Build-Up method.

(9) Per the Duff & Phelps Risk Premium Calculator.

(10) Appraiser's subjective risk premium for specific risk characteristics of the Company under the Duff & Phelps models. Note lower specific risk under this approach given company specific attributes utilized in the Duff & Phelps Risk Premium Calculator.

Glossary of Key Inputs

R_f — Risk Free Rate: Long-term (20-year) U.S. Treasury Bond Yield (constant maturity).

ERP — Equity Risk Premium: Long-horizon expected return of large stocks over risk free securities.

ERP Adjustment — An adjustment made to reconcile a historically-derived ERP with a forward-looking ERP as of the valuation date.

b — Beta: A statistical measure of systematic risk of a stock: the sensitivity of a stock's price relative to movements of a specific market benchmark or index.

RP_{m+s} — Median Premium Over Risk Free Rate: The long-horizon expected return of stocks over risk free securities in terms of the combined effect of market risk and size risk.

RP_s — Median Premium Over CAPM: The return on small company stocks in excess of that predicted by CAPM (also known as "beta-adjusted size premium").

The Market Approach[14]

The market approach for business valuation is based on the concept of substitution, which assumes that an investor would not pay more for the subject property than for other comparable properties. In the application of the market approach, the value of a business is based upon the prices that investors are paying for similar interests in "guideline" companies or guideline transactions.[15]

The market approach includes the development of valuation multiples of market prices to various financial fundamentals of guideline companies that are then used to develop indications of value for the Subject Company. There are two commonly used methods within the market approach: (1) the guideline public company method and (2) the guideline transaction method. Additional methods include: (3) bona fide offers and past transactions in the Subject Company and (4) rules of thumb.

The Guideline Public Company Method

The guideline public company method (GPCM) is based upon a comparison of a Subject Company to guideline public companies. Market pricing multiples are developed and based upon the guideline companies' quoted trading prices and financial fundamentals.

Either an equity procedure or an invested capital may be applied under the GPCM. Under the equity method, the analyst computes equity based on the market value of equity (equity multiples) and under the invested capital procedure, the analyst computes multiples based on the market value of invested capital (MVIC) multiples. Examples of such multiples are included in Table 3.

When computing equity, or MVIC multiples, for public companies, the numerators — the equity and MVIC — are commonly

---

[14] A full discussion of market approach is beyond the scope of this chapter See Shannon P. Pratt, *The Market Approach to Valuing Businesses*, John Wiley & Sons, Hoboken, NJ, 2005.

[15] Because no two businesses are alike, or even comparable, in business valuation, the term preferred to describe "comparable" properties is "guideline" companies.

Table 3: Examples of Equity Multiples and MVIC Multiples.

Equity Multiples Divided by	MVIC Multiples Divided by
• Sales	• Sales
• Discretionary earnings (SDCF)	• Discretionary earnings (SDCF)
• EBITDA	• Gross cash flow
• EBIT	• Pretax income
• Book value of invested capital	• Dividends or withdrawals
• Adjusted book value of invested capital	• Book value of equity
	• Adjusted book value of equity

computed as of the valuation date, while for the denominators of the ratios, there are usually many options as to the possible time periods for income data as follows:

- Latest fiscal year
- Latest 12 months
- Simple average of recent years
- Weighted average of recent years
- Earnings estimates for current year or next year

After computing valuation multiples for the guideline public companies, the next step is to adjust the multiples for differences between the Subject Company and the guideline companies. Adjustments to public multiples are done based on differences in risk and growth between the public guideline companies and the Subject Company. Consideration is given to adjustments for growth prospects, size, specific company risks, as well as the quantity and quality of the market data.[16] After making the appropriate adjustments to the public pricing multiples, the adjusted multiples are then applied to the Subject Company's financial fundamentals to arrive at indications of value.

[16] A discussion of methodologies available for adjusting public multiples is beyond the scope of this chapter. See bibliography at the end of the chapter for general valuation books that address this topic as part of the market approach discussion.

GPCM Example

The GPCM was not applied to derive a value for Gourmet Burgers. The guideline public companies in the fast food/casual restaurants market were deemed to be too large and diversified to be appropriate guideline companies for Gourmet Burgers. Instead, the application of the GPCM for the valuation of a larger company is illustrated in Exhibit 13. The Subject Company is a privately held organic foods manufacturer with sales of approximately $130 million. In Exhibit E, we only show the computation and application of the MVIC/Sales valuation multiple, but other multiples can be computed and applied in a similar fashion.

A search for guideline public companies was performed, and the following companies were located and used in the analysis:

- Boulder Brands
- Dean Foods
- Lifeway Foods
- The Hain Celestial Group
- The White Wave Foods Co
- Tofutti Brands

The first table in Exhibit 13 illustrates the computation of the equity and MVIC for the guideline public companies as of the valuation date, which in this case was September 30, 2014.

The second table presents historical sales data for the public companies for the past five fiscal years as well as for the last 12 months (LTM) ended with the valuation date and illustrates the computation of the MVIC/Sales revenues using four different time frames for the revenues of the public companies as follows:

- 2009–2013 Avg. Sales
- 2011–2013 Avg. Sales
- LTM 2014 Sales
- 2013 Sales

Exhibit 13: Illustration of the Public Guideline Company Method

Company	Symbol	Stock Price 9/30/2014	Number of Shares	Maket Value of Equity	Long-term Debt	Preferred Stock	MVIC	% Long-term Debt
Boulder Brands	BDBD	$13.63	60,511,895	$825	$302	$0	$1,127	26.8%
Dean Foods	DF	$13.25	94,074,676	$1,246	$978	$0	$2,224	44.0%
Lifeway Foods	LWAY	$13.87	16,346,000	$227	$8	$0	$235	3.5%
The Hain Celestial Group	HAIN	$51.18	99,068,000	$5,070	$788	$0	$5,857	13.4%
The WhiteWave Foods Co	WWAV	$36.33	173,775,497	$6,313	$1,501	$0	$7,814	19.2%
Tofutti Brands	TOF	$4.42	5,154,000	$23	$0	$0	$23	0.1%

	Sales							5-Year Avg.	3-Year Avg.		Market Value of Invested Capital to			
Company	LTM Sep. 30, 2014	FYE 2013	FYE 2012	FYE 2011	FYE 2010	FYE 2009	2009–2013 CAGR (%)	2009–2013 Sales	2011–2013 Sales	MVIC	2009–2013 Avg. Sales	2011–2013 Avg. Sales	LTM 2014 Sales	2013 Sales
Boulder Brands	$514	$461	$370	$274	$242	$240	17.81	$317	$368	$1,127	3.6	3.1	2.2	2.4
Dean Foods	$9,404	$9,016	$9,275	$9,716	$10,820	$11,114	(5.09)	$9,988	$9,336	$2,224	0.2	0.2	0.2	0.2
Lifeway Foods	$115	$98	$81	$70	$58	$54	15.97	$72	$83	$235	3.3	2.8	2.0	2.4
The Hain Celestial Group	$2,307	$1,932	$1,542	$1,210	$995	$996	18.01	$1,335	$1,561	$5,857	4.4	3.8	2.5	3.0

(Continued)

Exhibit 13: (*Continued*)

	Sales							5-Year Avg.	3-Year Avg.		Market Value of Invested Capital to:			
Company	LTM Sep. 30, 2014	FYE 2013	FYE 2012	FYE 2011	FYE 2010	FYE 2009	2009–2013 CAGR (%)	2009–2013 Sales	2011–2013 Sales	MVIC	2009–2013 Avg. Sales	2011–2013 Avg. Sales	LTM 2014 Sales	2013 Sales
Tofutti Brands	$14	$15	$14	$16	$18	$19	(5.75)	$16	$15	$23	1.4	1.5	1.6	1.6
Mean	$2,593	$2,344	$2,262	$2,219	$2,326	$2,484	8.19	$2,316	$2,275	$2,880	2.7	2.5	1.8	2.1
Median	$1,410	$1,197	$956	$742	$618	$240	15.97	$826	$965	$1,675	3.4	2.9	2.1	2.4
Standard Deviation											1.6	1.3	0.9	1.1
Coefficent of Variation											0.6	0.5	0.5	0.5
Subject Company	$130	$120	$115	$100	$110	$120	0.00	$113	$112	na	na	na	na	na

Valution Multiple[1]	Median	Multiple Adjustment[2]	Adjusted Market Multiple	Subject Company Financial Basis	Enterprise Value	Debt	Equity value	Weight	Weighted Value
MVIC/Sales — TTM 9/30/2014	2.1	(30.0%)	1.5	$130	$193	($20)	$173	25%	$43.19
MVIC/Sales — 2013	2.4	(30.0%)	1.7	$120	$204	($20)	$184	25%	$45.95
MVIC/Sales- 3-Year Average (2011–2013)	3.4	(30.0%)	2.4	$112	$266	($20)	$246	25%	$61.48
MVIC/Sales — 5-Year Average (2009–2013)	2.9	(30.0%)	2.1	$113	$233	($20)	$213	25%	$53.26
									$204
Indicated Value from the Public Guideline Company Method								100%	$200

[1] Based on the financial data of the following publicly-traded companies: Boulder Brands, Dean Foods, Lifeway Foods, The Hain Celestial Group, WhiteWave Foods Company, and Tofutti Brands.

[2] Public multiples adjustment based on differences in risk and growth between guideline companies and the Subject Company.

Public company and subject company economic fundamentals in $ millions

MVIC = Market Value of Invested Capital

After computing the MVIC/Sales multiple for each public company and for each time frame, we compute the mean, median, standard deviation, and coefficient of variation for each multiple.

The third table in Exhibit 13 presents the adjustment of the median public multiples and the application of the adjusted multiples to the respective sales levels for the Subject Company. This table also illustrates a possible weighting of the indications of value resulting from the application of the MVIC/Sales multiples.

The Guideline Transaction Method

The guideline transaction method is similar to the GPCM in that pricing multiples are calculated and applied to the Subject Company earnings fundamentals. The guideline transaction method, however, is based upon the analysis of guideline companies (either publicly traded or closely held) that have been recently acquired in a M&A transaction, as opposed to guideline companies that are traded on an organized exchange. In addition, transaction multiples are calculated based upon the M&A transaction price rather than the companies' quoted trading prices.

Exhibits 14 and 15 illustrate in abbreviated terms the application of the guideline transaction method to derive a value for Gourmet Burgers.

Past Subject Company Transactions

Usually, the search for guideline transactions goes outside of the company subject to the valuation. But sometimes a source of "guideline transactions" is the Subject Company itself:

> "Past transactions involving the subject company may be fruitful subjects to analyze for guidance as to value."[17]

---

[17] Shannon P. Pratt with Alina V. Niculita, *Valuing a Business: The Analysis and Appraisal of Closely Held Businesses, 5th Ed.*, McGraw-Hill, 2008, p. 318.

Exhibit 14: Working Capital Analysis

Gourmet Burgers, Inc.
Valuation Date: December 31, 2015

	Number of Transactions[1]	Market Derived Valuation Ratio	Subject Company Financial Basis[2]	Indicated Value	Add Current Assets/Subtract Total Liabilities[3]	Indicated Equity Value	Weight
Asset Transactions:							
Net Sales	127	0.45 ×	$10,879,000 =	$4,949,166 +	($146,000) =	$4,803,166	33%
SDE[4]	73	3.59 ×	$1,269,000 =	$4,557,911 +	($146,000) =	$4,411,911	33%
EBITDA[5]	78	5.37 ×	$1,007,904 =	$5,414,314 +	($146,000) =	$5,268,314	33%
Acquisition Price Method Value — 100% Interest						**$4,828,000**	

[1] Based on the upper quartile of transactions of companies classified in SIC 5812 (Restaurants) with sales greater than $1 million and with a transaction date between January 1, 2013 and December 31, 2015. We selected the upper quartile of the acquired companies as the subject Company has had consistent growth since 2011.

[2] Set equal to adjusted 2015 results.

[3] In asset deals, current assets (excluding inventory) are added and total liabilities as of the calculation date are subtracted from the indication of value. This adjustment is shown as follows (Schedule 3B):

Cash	$163,000
Trade Receivables	14,000
Prepaid Expenses	8,000
Less: Total Liabilities	(331,000)
Total Interest-Bearing Debt	($146,000)

[4] SDE is equal to seller's discretionary earnings (=EBITDA + one owner's compensation).

[5] EBITDA is equal to earnings before interest, taxes, depreciation, and taxes.

Exhibit 15: Working Capital Analysis

Gourmet Burgers, Inc.
Valuation Date: December 31, 2015

	Acquisition Date	Deal Type	Description	Revenues	SDE(1)	SDE as a % of Revenue	EBITDA(2)	EBITDA as a % of Revenue	Reported Deal Price	Valuation Multiples: Deal Price to Net Sales	SDE	EBITDA
			Subject Company(3)	**$10,879,000**	**$1,269,000**	**11.7%**	**$1,007,904**	**9.3%**	**na**	**na**	**na**	**na**
Asset Transactions												
Pratts Stats:												
1	07/07/14	Asset	Italian Restaurant	$1,000,000	na	na	na	na	$350,000	0.35	na	na
2	01/23/13	Asset	Burger — Franchise	$1,000,374	na	na	$108,000	10.8%	$695,000	0.69	na	6.44
3	08/01/14	Asset	American Restaurant	$1,003,166	na	na	$163,884	16.3%	$50,000	0.05	na	0.31*
4	07/31/13	Asset	Sports Bar and Grill	$1,007,278	$69,881	6.9%	$20,981	2.1%	$175,000	0.17	2.50	8.34
5	04/24/15	Asset	Pizza Shop Franchise (3 locations)	$1,034,134	$31,970	3.1%	($28,030)	(2.7%)	$399,000	0.39	12.48*	na
6	02/03/15	Asset	All-You-Can-Eat Buffet	$1,040,000	$437,840	42.1%	$313,040	30.1%	$350,000	0.34	0.80	1.12
7	10/15/13	Asset	Pizza Shop	$1,061,196	na	na	$96,612	9.1%	$134,000	0.13	na	1.39
8	01/21/14	Asset	Wine Bar and Restaurant	$1,062,576	$161,378	15.2%	$59,072	5.6%	$400,000	0.38	2.48	6.77
9	03/13/15	Asset	Cafe Type Eatery	$1,064,099	na	na	$100,522	9.4%	$200,000	0.19	na	1.99

10	11/23/13	Asset	Mongolian Grill at a Casino	$1,066,668	$175,538	16.5%	$125,538	11.8%	$640,000	0.60	3.65	5.10
11	02/11/13	Asset	Italian Restaurant	$1,070,708	$277,451	25.9%	$229,651	21.4%	$360,000	0.34	1.30	1.57
12	11/22/13	Asset	Parisian Cafe and Bakery	$1,074,726	na	na	$323,911	30.1%	$500,000	0.47	na	1.54
13	04/01/15	Asset	Family Style Restaurant	$1,085,000	na	na	$156,051	14.4%	$250,000	0.23	na	1.60
14	06/12/15	Asset	Pizza Shop	$1,090,060	na	na	$255,977	23.5%	$550,000	0.50	na	2.15
15	08/30/13	Asset	Restaurant and Sports Bar	$1,100,000	na	na	$190,000	17.3%	$200,000	0.18	na	1.05
16	10/21/13	Asset	Pizza Restaurant	$1,100,000	na	na	$231,000	21.0%	$250,000	0.23	na	1.08
17	04/17/14	Asset	Restaurant — Franchise	$1,101,931	na	na	$43,418	3.9%	$335,000	0.30	na	7.72
18	07/31/15	Asset	Sports Bar	$1,105,690	$270,420	24.5%	$225,420	20.4%	$300,000	0.27	1.11	1.33
19	05/13/13	Asset	Restaurant	$1,117,791	$221,124	19.8%	$117,124	10.5%	$650,000	0.58	2.94	5.55
20	08/27/13	Asset	Restaurant, Bar and Grille	$1,117,990	na	na	$109,053	9.8%	$335,000	0.30	na	3.07
21	07/31/14	Asset	Tavern — Restaurant and Bar	$1,118,928	$28,200	2.5%	$0	0.0%	$229,000	0.20	8.12*	na
22	08/05/13	Asset	Italian Restaurant	$1,125,300	na	na	$225,000	20.0%	$670,000	0.60	na	2.98
23	10/09/13	Asset	Sports Bar Restaurant	$1,130,000	na	na	$100,000	8.8%	$175,000	0.15	na	1.75

(*Continued*)

Exhibit 15: (*Continued*)

	Acquisition Date	Deal Type	Description	Revenues	SDE[1]	SDE as a % of Revenue	EBITDA[2]	EBITDA as a % of Revenue	Reported Deal Price	Valuation Multiples: Deal Price to Net Sales	SDE	EBITDA
24	08/29/13	Asset	Drive In Restaurant — Franchise	$1,134,533	na	na	$225,440	19.9%	$390,278	0.34	na	1.73
25	09/03/13	Asset	Italian Restaurant	$1,147,195	na	na	$308,525	26.9%	$510,000	0.44	na	1.65
26	08/07/15	Asset	Italian Restaurant	$1,171,542	$122,016	10.4%	$27,578	2.4%	$350,000	0.30	2.87	12.69*
27	02/06/15	Asset	Restaurant	$1,180,874	na	na	na	na	$575,000	0.49	na	na
28	06/09/15	Asset	Mexican Restaurant	$1,185,290	$175,463	14.8%	$127,463	10.8%	$375,000	0.32	2.14	2.94
29	12/18/14	Asset	Restaurants|American Restaurant	$1,192,885	ma	na	($149,286)	(12.5%)	$375,000	0.31	na	na
30	08/08/13	Asset	Full Service Catering	$1,197,298	na	na	na	na	$310,000	0.26	na	na
31	03/22/13	Asset	American Restaurant	$1,199,662	na	na	$146,263	12.2%	$365,000	0.30	na	2.50
32	03/26/13	Asset	Diner	$1,200,000	na	na	$185,791	15.5%	$200,000	0.17	na	1.08
33	03/06/14	Asset	Italian Restaurant	$1,200,000	na	na	$195,000	16.3%	$305,000	0.25	na	1.56
34	08/13/14	Asset	American Restaurant	$1,200,000	na	na	$177,000	14.8%	$300,000	0.25	na	1.69
35	07/17/15	Asset	Italian Restaurant	$1,200,000	na	na	$170,000	14.2%	$335,000	0.28	na	1.97
36	12/01/14	Asset	Pizza Shop	$1,218,567	na	na	$156,604	12.9%	$600,000	0.49	na	3.83
37	11/17/14	Asset	Diner	$1,226,412	na	na	$268,374	21.9%	$445,000	0.36	na	1.66
38	10/23/13	Asset	Seafood Restaurant	$1,244,467	na	na	$119,212	9.6%	$350,000	0.28	na	2.94

39	07/15/14	Asset	Coffee Kiosk (Drive Thru)	$1,284,405	$105,158	8.2%	$65,158	5.1%	$372,000	0.29	3.54	5.71
40	06/08/14	Asset	Restaurants|American Restaurant	$1,293,348	$94,933	7.3%	$12,529	1.0%	$300,000	0.23	3.16	23.94*
41	09/30/14	Asset	Restaurants|American Restaurant	$1,295,957	na	na	$313,430	24.2%	$475,000	0.37	na	1.52
42	12/29/14	Asset	Restaurants|Fast Food Franchise	$1,317,704	$128,969	9.8%	$16,569	1.3%	$410,000	0.31	3.18	24.75*
43	03/25/13	Asset	Italian Restaurant and Pizzeria	$1,318,421	na	na	$330,993	25.1%	$590,000	0.45	na	1.78
44	08/18/14	Asset	Italian Restaurant	$1,353,988	na	na	$291,988	21.6%	$865,000	0.64	na	2.96
45	06/23/15	Asset	NY Style Bagel Deli	$1,394,894	na	na	$123,503	8.9%	$330,000	0.24	na	2.67
46	01/30/14	Asset	Italian Restaurant	$1,410,683	na	na	$97,833	6.9%	$662,000	0.47	na	6.77
47	02/20/15	Asset	Gourmet Dining Restaurant	$1,426,223	na	na	$234,067	16.4%	$500,000	0.35	na	2.14
48	03/14/14	Asset	Bar and Grill	$1,464,681	$172,811	11.8%	$87,011	5.9%	$660,000	0.45	3.82	7.59
49	03/14/14	Asset	Restaurants Brew/ Pub	$1,464,681	$259,109	17.7%	$173,309	11.8%	$660,000	0.45	2.55	3.81
50	10/31/14	Asset	Catering Company	$1,490,706	$92,437	6.2%	$14,679	1.0%	$390,000	0.26	4.22	26.57*
51	09/29/15	Asset	Fast Food Restaurant	$1,504,378	$156,703	10.4%	$56,703	3.8%	$212,500	0.14	1.36	3.75
52	09/10/13	Asset	Pizza Shop	$1,547,321	na	na	$519,443	33.6%	$725,000	0.47	na	1.40

(*Continued*)

Exhibit 15: (*Continued*)

	Acquisition Date	Deal Type	Description	Revenues	SDE[1]	SDE as a % of Revenue	EBITDA[2]	EBITDA as a % of Revenue	Reported Deal Price	Valuation Multiples — Deal Price to Net Sales	SDE	EBITDA
53	07/31/15	Asset	Bar and Restaurant	$1,600,296	$379,517	23.7%	$361,517	22.6%	$1,050,000	0.66	2.77	2.90
54	07/10/15	Asset	Quick Service Restaurant — Franchise	$1,641,896	$160,327	9.8%	$97,927	6.0%	$499,000	0.30	3.11	5.10
55	09/02/14	Asset	Bar and Restaurant	$1,666,171	na	na	na	na	$320,000	0.19	na	na
56	04/28/14	Asset	Restaurant — Franchise	$1,678,317	na	na	na	na	$395,000	0.24	na	na
57	08/25/14	Asset	Gourmet Dining	$1,699,919	na	na	$248,959	14.6%	$500,000	0.29	na	2.01
58	05/04/15	Asset	Restaurant and Bar	$1,710,757	na	na	$202,183	11.8%	$675,000	0.39	na	3.34
59	07/27/15	Asset	Full Service Restaurant	$1,745,000	$387,000	22.2%	$231,000	13.2%	$861,750	0.49	2.23	3.73
60	08/21/15	Asset	Pub and Eatery	$1,776,467	na	na	$23,578	1.3%	$100,000	0.06	na	4.24
61	10/22/14	Asset	Fine Dining Restaurant	$1,781,829	$86,959	4.9%	$11,959	0.7%	$350,000	0.20	4.02	29.27*
62	02/26/15	Asset	Family Style Restaurant	$1,800,000	na	na	$300,000	16.7%	$115,000	0.06	na	0.38*
63	04/15/13	Asset	Italian Restaurant	$1,821,070	na	na	$302,545	16.6%	$1,000,000	0.55	na	3.31
64	08/29/13	Asset	Sports Bar and Grill	$1,838,613	na	na	$112,790	6.1%	$650,000	0.35	na	5.76
65	04/17/15	Asset	Pizza Shop	$1,885,588	na	na	$709,813	37.6%	$850,000	0.45	na	1.20

66	03/29/13	Asset	Italian Restaurant	$1,970,000	$190,022	9.6%	$138,022	7.0%	$735,000	0.37	3.87	5.33
67	10/01/13	Asset	American Restaurant	$2,000,000	na	na	$500,000	25.0%	$314,500	0.16	na	0.63*
68	07/21/15	Asset	Specialty Restaurant	$2,006,650	na	na	$250,000	12.5%	$800,000	0.40	na	3.20
69	12/19/14	Asset	Seafood Restaurant	$2,070,312	na	na	$398,526	19.2%	$630,000	0.30	na	1.58
70	01/14/15	Asset	Ethnic Restaurant	$2,071,304	na	na	$307,104	14.8%	$615,000	0.30	na	2.00
71	10/22/13	Asset	Gourmet Dining	$2,085,337	$339,695	16.3%	$198,814	9.5%	$1,068,000	0.51	3.14	5.37
72	05/01/15	Asset	Family Japanese Restaurant	$2,161,561	na	na	$76,096	3.5%	$165,000	0.08	na	2.17
73	05/05/14	Asset	Cuban Restaurant	$2,190,365	na	na	$49,976	2.3%	$600,000	0.27	na	12.01*
74	08/28/15	Asset	Italian Deli and Grocery	$2,282,311	$159,466	7.0%	$34,716	1.5%	$150,000	0.07	0.94	4.32
75	03/06/15	Asset	Sports Bar	$2,363,504	$405,728	17.2%	$192,996	8.2%	$995,000	0.42	2.45	5.16
76	05/30/15	Asset	Pizza Shop	$2,430,000	na	na	$350,000	14.4%	$2,650,000	1.09	na	7.57
77	06/06/14	Asset	Restaurant	$2,733,263	$140,001	5.1%	$0	0.0%	$670,000	0.25	4.79	na
78	01/04/13	Asset	Restaurant — Franchise	$2,746,564	$361,834	13.2%	$301,834	11.0%	$600,000	0.22	1.66	1.99
79	02/19/14	Asset	Seafood Restaurant	$2,786,635	na	na	$532,526	19.1%	$1,100,000	0.39	na	2.07
80	06/30/15	Asset	Full Service Tavern-Concept Restaurant	$2,845,787	$481,554	16.9%	$395,025	13.9%	$1,580,000	0.56	3.28	4.00

(Continued)

Exhibit 15: (*Continued*)

	Acquisition Date	Deal Type	Description	Revenues	SDE[1]	SDE as a % of Revenue	EBITDA[2]	EBITDA as a % of Revenue	Reported Deal Price	Valuation Multiples: Deal Price to Net Sales	Valuation Multiples: Deal Price to SDE	Valuation Multiples: Deal Price to EBITDA
81	06/21/13	Asset	Seafood Restaurant	$2,963,609	$156,430	5.3%	$84,430	2.8%	$550,000	0.19	3.52	6.51
82	07/09/14	Asset	American Restaurant	$3,187,658	$175,761	5.5%	$50,189	1.6%	$800,000	0.25	4.55	15.94*
83	09/06/13	Asset	Catering	$3,348,266	na	na	$225,473	6.7%	$933,000	0.28	na	4.14
84	06/07/14	Asset	Restaurant Bar and Grill	$3,602,937	$531,533	14.8%	$481,533	13.4%	$2,162,500	0.60	4.07	4.49
85	05/20/15	Asset	Bar and Restaurant	$3,891,341	$713,435	18.3%	$557,743	14.3%	$1,800,000	0.46	2.52	3.23
86	03/15/15	Asset	Fast Food Hamburgers	$5,830,000	$441,516	7.6%	$258,376	4.4%	$2,200,000	0.38	4.98	8.51
87	12/09/13	Asset	54 Burger Restaurants	$71,455,000	na	na	$8,611,000	12.1%	$30,428,000	0.43	na	3.53
												Bizcomps:
1	04/22/13	Asset	Restr W/Cocktails	$1,015,000	$204,000	20.1%	na	na	$140,000	0.14	0.69	na
2	10/31/13	Asset	Restr-Family	$1,032,000	$248,000	24.0%	na	na	$425,000	0.41	1.71	na
3	08/25/14	Asset	Restr-Italian/Pizza	$1,036,000	$174,000	16.8%	na	na	$150,000	0.14	0.86	na
4	09/10/14	Asset	Restr W/Cocktails	$1,050,000	$97,000	9.2%	na	na	$110,000	0.10	1.13	na
5	08/04/14	Asset	Restr-Family	$1,078,000	$118,000	10.9%	na	na	$350,000	0.32	2.97	na
6	05/21/14	Asset	Restr-Family	$1,100,000	$148,000	13.5%	na	na	$540,000	0.49	3.65	na

7	07/07/14	Asset	Restr-Family	$1,100,000	$150,000	13.6%	na	na	$360,000	0.33	2.40	na
8	10/15/14	Asset	Fast Food Cafe	$1,134,000	$231,000	20.4%	na	na	$650,000	0.57	2.81	na
9	08/31/13	Asset	Food Catering	$1,175,000	$173,000	14.7%	na	na	$335,000	0.29	1.94	na
10	10/31/13	Asset	Fast Food Pizza	$1,200,000	$250,000	20.8%	na	na	$250,000	0.21	1.00	na
11	09/08/14	Asset	Bagel Restaurant	$1,200,000	$315,000	26.3%	na	na	$575,000	0.48	1.83	na
12	10/31/13	Asset	Restr-Family	$1,244,000	$215,000	17.3%	na	na	$350,000	0.28	1.63	na
13	03/31/13	Asset	Restr W/Cocktails	$1,318,000	$330,000	25.0%	na	na	$595,000	0.45	1.80	na
14	03/28/14	Asset	Mexican Buffett	$1,363,000	$229,000	16.8%	na	na	$239,000	0.18	1.04	na
15	09/12/13	Asset	Franchise-Pizza	$1,379,000	na	na	na	na	$199,000	0.14	na	na
16	06/30/14	Asset	Restr-Italian	$1,381,000	$219,000	15.9%	na	na	$401,000	0.29	1.83	na
17	04/17/15	Asset	Restr W/Cocktails	$1,401,000	$536,000	38.3%	na	na	$870,000	0.62	1.62	na
18	05/19/14	Asset	Restr-Family	$1,411,000	$258,000	18.3%	na	na	$336,000	0.24	1.30	na
19	08/07/13	Asset	Restr W/Health Food	$1,450,000	$172,000	11.9%	na	na	$415,000	0.29	2.41	na
20	12/05/14	Asset	Restr W/Cocktails	$1,527,000	$356,000	23.3%	na	na	$700,000	0.46	1.97	na
21	04/28/14	Asset	Restr-Family	$1,543,000	$180,000	11.7%	na	na	$250,000	0.16	1.39	na
22	09/30/13	Asset	Restr-Family	$1,547,000	$501,000	32.4%	na	na	$730,000	0.47	1.46	na
23	02/28/14	Asset	Bakery-Restaurant	$1,588,000	$247,000	15.6%	na	na	$525,000	0.33	2.13	na

(Continued)

Exhibit 15: (*Continued*)

	Acquisition Date	Deal Type	Description	Revenues	SDE[1]	SDE as a % of Revenue	EBITDA[2]	EBITDA as a % of Revenue	Reported Deal Price	Valuation Multiples: Deal Price to Net Sales	SDE	EBITDA
24	07/10/15	Asset	Franchise-Hamburgers	$1,642,000	$224,000	13.6%	na	na	$413,000	0.25	1.84	na
25	02/19/15	Asset	Restr W/Cocktails	$1,700,000	$46,000	2.7%	na	na	$78,000	0.05	1.70	na
26	07/14/14	Asset	Restr W/Cocktails	$1,702,000	$143,000	8.4%	na	na	$388,000	0.23	2.71	na
27	04/26/13	Asset	Restr-Family	$1,706,000	$284,000	16.6%	na	na	$620,000	0.36	2.18	na
28	04/22/13	Asset	Restr W/Cocktails	$1,773,000	$138,000	7.8%	na	na	$344,000	0.19	2.49	na
29	05/05/14	Asset	Restr-Ethnic	$2,190,000	$413,000	18.9%	na	na	$500,000	0.23	1.21	na
30	04/14/14	Asset	Restr-Family	$2,235,000	$342,000	15.3%	na	na	$650,000	0.29	1.90	na
31	04/15/15	Asset	Restr-Breakfast/Lunch	$2,400,000	$322,000	13.4%	na	na	$1,550,000	0.65	4.81	na
32	05/01/15	Asset	Asian Seafood Buffet	$2,451,000	$190,000	7.8%	na	na	$145,000	0.06	0.76	na
33	02/28/14	Asset	Fast Food-Burgers	$2,500,000	$505,000	20.2%	na	na	$2,215,000	0.89	4.39	na
34	03/31/14	Asset	Fast Food-Burgers	$2,550,000	$315,000	12.4%	na	na	$1,313,000	0.51	4.17	na
35	01/31/13	Asset	Restr-Italian	$2,829,000	$66,000	2.3%	na	na	$750,000	0.27	11.36*	na
36	01/09/15	Asset	Restr W/Cocktails	$3,133,000	$373,000	11.9%	na	na	$640,000	0.20	1.72	na
37	11/15/13	Asset	Restr-Family	$3,325,000	$55,000	1.7%	na	na	$115,000	0.03	2.09	na
38	03/31/13	Asset	Fast Food-Burgers	$3,710,000	$655,000	17.7%	na	na	$2,875,000	0.77	4.39	na

39	12/31/13	Asset	Fast Food-Burgers[3]	$5,851,000	$1,165,000	19.9%	na	na	$5,180,000	0.89	4.45	na
40	11/08/13	Asset	Fast Food-Hamburgers	$7,300,000	$511,000	7.0%	na	na	$1,103,000	0.15	2.16	na
			Upper Quartile:	$2,007,000	$349,000	18.6%	$292,000	17.0%	$670,000	0.45	3.59	5.37
			Mean:	$2,300,000	$263,000	14.6%	$293,000	12.1%	$854,000	0.34	2.51	3.43
			Median:	$1,411,000	$219,000	14.7%	$175,000	11.8%	$445,000	0.30	2.45	3.02
			Lower Quartile:	$1,135,000	$149,000	8.3%	$97,000	5.1%	$320,000	0.21	1.68	1.69

(1) SDE is equal to seller's discretionary earnings (=EBITDA + one owner's compensation).
(2) EBITDA is equal to earnings before interest, taxes, depreciation and amortization.
(3) Set equal to adjusted 2015 results.
(4) Based on transactions of companies classified in SIC 5812 (Restaurants) with sales greater than $1 million and transaction dates between January 1, 2013 and December 31, 2015.
*Excluded from the mean calculations.

Subject Company	1,007,904
Multiple (Median)	0.21
Concluded Value	$ 209,980

Examples of such past transactions include:

- Past subject company changes of control
- Bona fide offers
- Past acquisitions by the subject company

Because there were no past transactions in the history of Gourmet Burgers, the past transactions method was not applied.

Rules of Thumb

Rules of thumb are valuation multiples that have developed over time for certain industries, mostly because of their usage by business brokers to estimate a price for a business transaction. Rules of thumb may be used in certain situations in valuation, for instance, in industries where there are well established rules of thumb, but most likely not as a primary valuation method.[18]

Because we were able to find a high number of transactions to use in the market approach, and because of the fact that Gourmet Burgers represents a new type of "better" fast food trend versus the traditional fast food restaurants, we did not apply rules of thumb in this case.

The Asset Approach[19]

The asset approach is based on the concept that if all the assets and liabilities on the balance sheet of a business are revalued to market value, then the difference between assets and liabilities represents the market value of equity. There are two methods under the asset approach:

- The adjusted net assets value method
- The excess earnings method

[18] *Business Reference Guide* is published annually and includes rules of thumb for numerous types of businesses.

[19] An in-depth discussion of the asset approach and its methods is beyond the scope of this chapter, for more information see Shannon Pratt and Alina V. Niculita, *The Lawyer's Business Valuation Handbook: Understanding Financial Statements, Appraisal Reports, and Expert Testimony, 2nd Ed.*, 2010, American Bar Association. This section is adapted from the book.

The Adjusted Net Assets Value Method

The adjusted net asset value method uses a process of discrete revaluation, in which each asset and liability is revalued separately from historical cost to current market values. There are several steps in the application of this method:

1. Start with an accrual basis balance sheet.
2. Identify which assets and liabilities on the balance sheet require valuation.
3. Adjust historical costs for the items identified to reflect current market values.
4. Identify any off-balance-sheet assets or liabilities.
5. Estimate the value of the off-balance-sheet assets and liabilities.
6. Using the current market values of the assets and liabilities, compile the market-value-based balance sheet.
7. The difference between the market values of assets and liabilities represents the market value of the equity.

The Excess Earnings Method

The excess earnings method was originally used in 1920 and it was created to estimate the value of the goodwill that makers of alcoholic beverages lost due to prohibition. Below are the basic steps of this method:

1. Estimate a level of earnings that would be "normal" based on the subject business and its industry.
2. Estimate the net tangible asset value for the Subject Company as of the valuation date.
3. Estimate a rate of return that would be required by an investor in the tangible assets of the business.
4. Multiply the value of net tangible assets (from Step 2) by the required rate of return on net tangible assets (from Step 3).
5. Subtract the required dollar amount of return on tangible assets (from Step 4) from the estimated normalized earnings (from Step 1). This amount is called excess earnings.

Table 4: Numerical Example that Illustrates the Application of Excess Earnings Method.

Step 1	Normalized net cash flow	Estimated	\$100,000
Step 2	Net tangible asset value	Estimated	\$500,000
Step 3	Required rate of return to tangible assets	Estimated	10%
Step 4	Required return (\$) on tangible assets	(2 × 3)	\$50,000
Step 5	Excess earnings	(1 – 4)	\$50,000
Step 6	Capitalization rate for excess earnings	Estimated	25%
Step 7	Value of intangible assets	(5 × 6)	\$200,000
Step 8	Value of tangible assets	(2)	\$500,000
	Total value of entity	(7 + 8)	\$700,000

6. Select a capitalization rate that would be appropriate to capitalize excess earnings.
7. Divide the excess earnings by the excess earnings capitalization rate (from Step 6). The result is an estimate of the value of intangible assets of the subject business.
8. Add the entity's intangible value (from Step 7) to the entity's net tangible asset value (from Step 2).

The excess earnings method uses collective revaluation, because it estimates the value of the intangible assets and goodwill as a single amount. Table 4 shows a numerical example that illustrates the application of the method.

Because Gourmet Burgers is an operating company and we are valuing it on a premise of going concern, we did not apply an asset approach.

Discounts and Premiums[20]

Discounts and premiums are applied in the valuation of privately held businesses to match the indication of value resulting from the

[20] An in-depth discussion of discounts and premiums is beyond the scope of this chapter. See Pratt, Shannon P. *Business Valuation Discounts and Premiums, 2nd Ed.*,

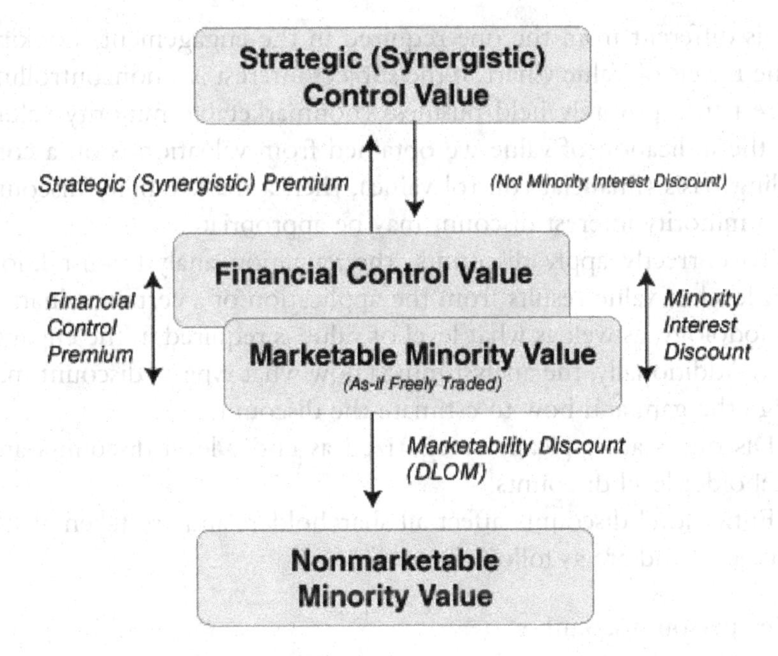

Figure 1: The Current Version of the Levels of Value Chart.

methods applied to the characteristics of the subject interest. To understand how discount and premiums fit in the context of the valuation process, a chart named Levels of Value is typically used. We include in the following the current version of the Levels of Value Chart (Figure 1).[21]

Discounts

Discounts are applied in valuation because the indication of value resulting from the valuation methodology represents a level of value

---

John Wiley & Sons, Hoboken, NJ, 2009. Mercer, Z. Christopher. *Valuing Enterprise and Shareholder Cash Flows — The Integrated Theory of Business Valuation*, Peabody Publishing, Memphis, TN, 2004.

[21] Z. Christopher Mercer, *The Integrated Theory of Business Valuation*, p. 110; "A revised and more realistic levels of value chart", http://chrismercer.net/a-revised-and-more-realistic-levels-of-value-chart.

that is different from the one required in the engagement. Looking at the Levels of Value Chart, if the subject interest is a noncontrolling interest in a privately held business (nonmarketable minority value) and the indication of value we obtained from valuation is on a controlling basis (financial control value), then a marketability discount and a minority interest discount may be appropriate.

To correctly apply discounts, the valuation analyst must know what level of value results from the application of a certain valuation methodology, as well as what level of value is required in the engagement. Additionally, the analyst must know what type of discount may bridge the gap, and how to estimate the discount.

Discounts are typically categorized as entity level discounts and shareholder level discounts.

Entity level discounts affect all shareholders and are taken at the entity level and are as follows:

- Key person discount
- Portfolio discount
- Trapped-in capital gains discount
- Discount for litigation risk
- Discount for environmental risk

Shareholder level discounts impact different shareholders differently and they are as follows:

- Discount for lack of control (DLOC) discount (or minority interest)
- Discount for lack of marketability (DLOM) (or marketability discount)
- Voting versus nonvoting shares
- Blockage discount

The most commonly applied discount in valuation is the DLOM. DLOM is applied in the valuation of interests in privately held businesses because unlike public stock that can be cashed in three business days with insignificant or no transaction costs, selling an interest in a privately held business is a much more lengthy and costly process. As a valuation text puts it, the concept of marketability is:

> "The ability to convert the business ownership interest (at whatever ownership level) to cash quickly, with the minimum transaction and administrative costs in so doing and with a high degree of certainty of realizing the expected amount of net proceeds."[22]

Premiums

Like discounts, premiums are applied in valuation because the indication of value resulting from the valuation methodology represents a level of value that is different from the one required in the engagement. For instance, looking at the levels of value chart, if the subject is a business that would likely be acquired by a strategic buyer, and the indication of value is on a financial control basis, then a strategic (synergistic) premium may be appropriate. As shown on the levels of value chart, there are two types of premiums:

- Financial control premium
- Strategic (synergistic) control premium

The valuation of Gourmet Burgers required a value on a controlling basis and a fair market standard of value. We believe that the application of the income approach and the market approach results in indications of FMV on a controlling basis. As a result, no discounts of premiums are required.

Reconciliation of Values and Conclusion

One final step in the valuation of a privately held business is the relative emphasis or weight an investor would place on the methods applied under the three valuation approaches: the income approach, the market approach, and the asset approach. As we have seen in this

---

[22] Valuing a Business, p. 417.

chapter, under each approach, we have two or more methods, and what methods are most appropriate will depend on the facts and circumstances of each individual case, such as purpose of value, standard of value, premise of value, and case law. The quality and quantity of data available under each method impact the weighting an indication of value will ultimately receive.

Guidance regarding relative weight for valuation methodologies can be found in Revenue Ruling 59-60. It suggests that the primary weight in an analysis of operating companies should be placed on measures that reflect the value of the earnings and the cash-flow generating capacity: "In general, the appraiser will accord primary consideration to earnings when valuing stocks of companies that sell products of services to the public [...]."

At the same time, Revenue Ruling 59-60 requires that the analyst consider both the (1) earnings capacity of the company and (2) the market price of stocks of corporations engaged in the same or similar line of business having their stocks actively traded in a free and open market in the valuation of a closely held company.

Finally, Revenue Ruling 59-60, recommends that the asset approach be given greater weight in comparison to the income and market approaches in the case where the company appraised is a holding company versus an operating company: "For these reasons, adjusted net worth should be accorded greater weight in valuing the stock of a closely held investment or real estate holding company, whether or not family owned, than any of the other customary yardsticks of appraisal, such as earnings and dividend paying capacity."

Conclusion Regarding Valuation of Gourmet Burgers

From the various valuation methodologies addressed in this chapter, we based the valuation of Gourmet Burgers on two methods, the discounted cash flow method and the transaction method, and we gave equal weighting to each indication of value in the determination of the final opinion of value. As shown in Exhibit 16, the fair market value of the equity in Gourmet Burgers as of December 31, 2015 is $5.2 million.

Exhibit 16: Summary of Indicated Values

Gourmet Burgers, Inc.
Valuation Date: December 31, 2015

Value Conclusion — 100% Interest		**Indicated Value**	**Weighting[1]**	**Concluded Value**
Income Approach	Schedule 1A-1	**$5,534,000**	50%	$2,767,000
Market Approach — Comparable Asset Transactions	Schedule 2A-1	**$4,828,000**	50%	$2,414,000
Fair Market Value of Equity (Controlling, Marketable Basis, Rounded)				**$5,180,000**

(1) We equally weighted the Income and Market Approaches.

Value Conclusion — 100% Interest	**Indicated Value**	**Weighting**	**Concluded Value**
Income Approach	$5,534,000	50%	$2,767,000
Market Approach — Comparable Transactions	$4,828,000	50%	$2,414,000
Fair Market Value of Equity (Controlling, Marketable Basis, Rounded)			**$5,180,000**

(1) The Asset and Market approaches were given no weighting a higher values were indicated by the income approach.

Bibliography

American Society of Appraisers. *Business Valuation Standards — Glossary.* Herndon, VA: American Society of Appraisers, 2006.

Appraisal Institute. *The Dictionary of Real Estate Appraisal, 5th Ed.* Chicago: Appraisal Institute, 2010.

Brealey, Richard A., Stewart C. Myers, and Franklin Allen. *Principles of Corporate Finance, 11th Ed.* Boston: Irwin McGraw-Hill, 2012.

Cornell, Bradford. *Corporate Valuation: Tools for Effective Appraisal and Decision Making.* New York: McGraw-Hill, 1993.

Damodaran, Aswath. *Damodaran on Valuation: Security Analysis for Investment and Corporate Finance, 3rd Ed.* Hoboken, NJ: John Wiley & Sons, 2014.

Damodaran, Aswath. *Investment Valuation: Tools and Techniques for Determining the Value of Any Asset, 3rd Ed.* Hoboken, NJ: John Wiley & Sons, 2012.

Duff & Phelps. Risk Premium Report. Chicago: Duff & Phelps, 2013 (updated annually).

Fishman, Jay E., Shannon P. Pratt, and J. Clifford Griffith. *PPC's Guide to Business Valuations, 23rd Ed.* Fort Worth, TX: Practitioners Publishing Company, 2013 (updated annually in May).

Fishman, Jay E., Shannon P. Pratt, and William Morrison. *Standards of Value: Theory and Application, 2nd Ed.* Hoboken, NJ: John Wiley & Sons, 2013.

Gary R. Trugman. *Understanding Business Valuation: A Practical Guide to Valuing Small to Medium Sized Businesses, 3rd Ed.* New York: American Institute of Certified Public Accountants, 2008.

Hitchner, James R. *Financial Valuation: Applications and Models, 3rd Ed.* Hoboken, NJ: John Wiley & Sons, 2010.

Hitchner, James R., Shannon P. Pratt, Jay E. Fishman. *A Consensus View Q&A Guide to Financial Valuation.* Ventnor City, NJ: Valuation Products and Services, 2016.

Laro, David, and Shannon P. Pratt. *Business Valuation and Federal Taxes: Procedure, Law, and Perspective, 2nd Ed.* Hoboken, NJ: John Wiley & Sons, 2011.

Mercer, Z. Christopher. *Valuing Enterprise and Shareholder Cash Flows — The Integrated Theory of Business Valuation.* Memphis, TN: Peabody Publishing, 2004.

Pratt, Shannon P. *Business Valuation Discounts and Premiums, 2nd Ed.* Hoboken, NJ: John Wiley & Sons, 2009.

Pratt, Shannon P., and Roger Grabowski. *Lawyer's Guide to Cost of Capital.* Chicago: American Bar Association, 2014.

Pratt, Shannon P., and Roger Grabowski. *Cost of Capital Applications and Examples, 5th Ed.* Hoboken, NJ: John Wiley & Sons, 2014.

Pratt, Shannon P. and Alina Niculita. *Valuing a Business: The Analysis and Appraisal of Closely Held Companies, 5th Ed.* New York: McGraw-Hill, 2008.

Pratt, Shannon P. and Alina V. Niculita, *The Lawyer's Business Valuation Handbook: Understanding Financial Statements, Appraisal Reports, and Expert Testimony, 2nd Ed.* American Bar Association, 2010.

Pratt, Shannon P., Robert F. Reilly, and Robert P. Schweihs. *Valuing Small Businesses and Professional Practices, 3rd Ed.* New York: McGraw-Hill, 1998.

Reilly, Frank K. *Investment Analysis and Portfolio Management,10th Ed.* Boston: South Western College, 2011.

Chapter 9

Accounting for M&As

Harvey Poniachek
Rutgers Business School

Introduction

A significant challenge facing accountants relates to how to account for the business combination of two or more formerly unrelated entities into a new enterprise.[1] All business combinations are required to be accounted for as acquisitions in according with the Financial Accounting Standards Board (FASB) Accounting Standard Codification (ASC) 805, Business Combinations, and ASC 820, Fair Value Measurements and Disclosure. A business combination is defined as a *transaction (or other event) in which an acquiring entity obtains control of one or more businesses on a specific date in* exchange

[1] Joanne M. Flood, Wiley GAAP 2017 [electronic resource]: *Interpretation and Application of Generally Accepted Accounting Principles*, Wiley, West Sussex, United Kingdom, 2016, Ch. 48, ASC 805 Business Combinations; and Ch. 52, ASC 820 Fair Value Measurements ("Wiley GAAP").

of consideration[2] or even without. Companies utilize various techniques for business combinations.[3]

Prior to June 2001, business combinations were accounted for under APB Opinion No. 16, Business Combinations, by using either the purchase method or the pooling of interests' method, which yielded quite different results for similar combinations.[4] On June 30,

---

[2] Consideration transferred may take many forms, including cash, tangible and intangible assets, a business or subsidiary of the acquiring entity, instruments of the acquiring entity (e.g., common stock, preferred stock, options, warrants and debt instruments) or other promised future payments of the acquiring entity, including contingent payments.

[3] Some frequently used techniques for business combinations are:

1. One or more businesses become subsidiaries of the acquirer and continue to operate as legal entities.
2. The net assets of one or more businesses are legally merged into the acquirer, and the acquiree entity ceases to exist (this is a *statutory merger* and normally the transaction is subject to approval by most of the outstanding voting shares of the acquiree).
3. The owners of the acquiree transfer their equity interests to the acquirer entity in exchange for equity interests in the acquirer.
4. All the combining entities transfer their net assets (or their owners transfer their equity interests into a new entity formed for the transaction). This is sometimes referred to as a *roll-up* or put-together transaction.
5. A former owner or group of former owners of one of the combining entities obtains control of the combined entities collectively.
6. An acquirer might hold a noncontrolling equity interest in an entity and subsequently purchase additional equity interests sufficient to give it control over the investee. These transactions are referred to as *step acquisitions* or business combinations achieved in stages.

See PWC, Business combinations and noncontrolling interests Application of the U.S. GAAP and IFRS Standards, Global Second Edition, February 2016, Ch. 2 https://www.pwc.com/us/en/cfodirect/assets/pdf/accounting-guides/pwc-guide-business-combinations-noncontrolling-interests-global-second-edition.pdf.

7. A business owner organizes a partnership, "S" corporation, or LLC to hold real estate. The real estate is the principal location of the commonly owned business and that business entity leases the real estate from the separate entity.

[4] Hemming Morse, LLP, Purchase Price Allocations Under ASC 805: A Guide to Allocating Purchase Price for Business Combination, http://www.hemming.com/wp-content/uploads/2014/08/Purchase-Price-Allocations-Under-ASC-805.pdf.

2001, the FASB released Statement of Financial Accounting Standards (SFAS) No. 141, Business Combinations, requiring that all business combinations be accounted for by the purchase method. On December 7, 2007, the FASB issued SFAS 141R, which applies to all transactions in which an acquirer obtains control of one or more businesses in exchange for consideration, or without the transfer of consideration through contract alone or through the lapse of minority veto rights. SFAS 141R is the outcome of cooperation between the FASB and the International Accounting Standard Board (IASB), thus contributing to convergence between the US and international accounting standards.[5] In July 2009, the FASB issued the ASC Topic 805, Business combinations, which became the definitive guidance on business combinations[6] and financial reporting for periods beginning on or after December 15, 2008.

The rest of this chapter reviews the principles of accounting for business combinations, including the functions and risk, as required by ASC 805; addresses issues of fair value for financial reporting; and examines issues of goodwill and its impairment testing according to ASC 350.

Accounting for Business Combinations, FASB ASC 805

Business combinations that comply with GAAP financial reporting must follow the FASB guidance set in ASC 805, Business Combinations, and ASC 820, Fair Value Measurements and Disclosure. ASC 805 requires[7] to perform a valuation process and a purchase price allocation (PPA) to the fair value of all assets acquired, liabilities assumed and contingent liabilities. The three valuation approaches are the

[5] Garth D. Stevens, Snell & Wilmer L.L.P., Get Ready for FAS 141(R), New Accounting Rules for Business Combinations August 2008.

[6] It combines the content of SFAS 141R, FASB staff positions, SEC regulations, SEC staff guidance, and other authoritative guidance on Business Combinations.

[7] *Brian Holloway,* Intangible Assets in Purchase Price Allocations, Insights, Summer 2013, www.willamette.com.

income approach,[8] the cost approach,[9] and the market approach.[10] Valuation is best addressed by an independent and experienced firm.[11] The difference between the book values of the assets (BVA) acquired and the fair values of those assets represents a step-up in the basis of the acquired assets.

If the fair value of net assets acquired is less than the total consideration paid for the acquired entity, the difference is recorded as goodwill. Goodwill is an intangible asset that has an indefinite life and it's tested annually for impairment according to ASC 350. That is, goodwill is the residual amount after allocating the purchase price to the fair value of the identifiable assets, so that the purchase price should always be equal to the fair value of identifiable assets *plus* goodwill.

The application of ASC 805 for business combinations under the acquisition method requires the following steps[12]:

- o Identify whether the acquisition is a business or an asset.
- o Determine the acquisition date.
- o Identify the assets and liabilities, and account for them in accordance with their nature and the applicable GAAP.
- o Recognize and measure the identifiable tangible and intangible assets acquired and liabilities assumed.

The buyer needs to determine whether it has acquired a business within the scope of the business combination accounting guidance,

[8] It estimates the present value of net future economic benefits (including cash earnings, cost savings, tax savings, and proceeds from sale) that accrue to the owners of an asset or a business interest.

[9] It measures the value of an asset based on the amount necessary to construct or acquire an asset of equal "utility."

[10] It determines value through the analysis of the market price of comparable assets or business interests that have been traded in arms-length transactions.

[11] Dan Daitchman, A Primer on Bargain Purchases and Negative Goodwill, http://greatamerican.com/static/pdf/industry-insights/Corporate%20Valuation%20Services/A%20Primer%20on%20Bargain%20Purchases%208-12-14.pdf.

[12] PWC, *Business Combinations and Noncontrolling Interests: Application of the U.S. GAAP and IFRS Standards, Global 2nd Ed.*, February 2016, Ch. 2 https://www.pwc.com/us/en/cfodirect/assets/pdf/accounting-guides/pwc-guide-business-combinations-noncontrolling-interests-global-second-edition.pdf.

and account for it by the fair value standard in its financial statements for the assets acquired and the liabilities assumed.[13] If the assets acquired are not a business, the reporting entity needs to account for the transaction or other event as an asset acquisition. The risks of misstating a business combination[14] arise due to

- o Incorrect determination of whether the transaction is a business combination,
- o Wrong measurement of the identifiable assets acquired, liabilities assumed and any noncontrolling interests in the acquiree, and
- o Inaccurate measurement of goodwill or a gain from a bargain purchase.

Determining whether acquired activities and assets constitute a business or just an asset would determine its accounting treatment, which differs significantly from that of an asset.[15] US GAAP requires that when an entity acquires control of another entity, the fair value of the acquired assets and liabilities be used to establish a new accounting basis by application of the acquisition method, with any excess of the consideration amount over the fair value of identifiable

---

[13] RSM, *A Guide to Accounting for Business Combinations, 2nd Ed.*, 2012.

[14] EY, Financial reporting developments, *A comprehensive guide,* Business combinations, Revised June 2016.

[15] Key differences between business combinations and asset acquisitions include:

- Transaction costs are capitalized in an asset acquisition but expensed in a business combination.
- Identifiable assets, liabilities assumed and any noncontrolling interests are generally recognized and measured as of the acquisition date at fair value in a business combination, but are measured by allocating the cost of the acquisition on a relative fair value basis in an asset acquisition.
- There is no measurement period concept for asset acquisitions. In a business combination, an acquirer has a period called the measurement period to obtain information about the facts and circumstances that existed as of the acquisition date and finalize its accounting. This cannot exceed 1 year from the acquisition date.
- Contingent consideration is recognized at its acquisition date fair value in a business combination but is generally recognized in an asset acquisition when the contingency is resolved.

net assets be attributed to goodwill.[16] An acquirer could obtain control of an acquiree in *stages*, or through a step acquisition. In a business combination achieved in stages, the acquirer needs to remeasure its previously held equity interest in the acquiree at its acquisition-date fair value and recognize the resulting gain or loss in earnings. The objective is to improve the information that a reporting entity provides about a business combination.

The objective of FASB 141R and its codification under ASC 805 are as follows:

- The acquirer needs to recognize and measure in its financial statements the identifiable assets acquired, the liabilities assumed, and any noncontrolling interest in the acquiree;
- Recognize and measure the goodwill acquired in the business combination or a gain from a bargain purchase; and
- Determine what information to disclose to enable users of the financial statements to evaluate the nature and financial effects of the business combination.

Main Features of ASC 805

(1) A transaction or event needs to satisfy the definition of a business combination and control,[17] where a business is defined as an integrated set of activities and assets. A business is defined as *an*

[16] EY, Financial reporting developments, *A comprehensive guide,* Business combinations, Revised June 2016, https://www.shinnihon.or.jp/shinnihon-library/publications/issue/us/gaap-weekly-update/pdf/GAAP-2016-07-22-03.pdf; PWC, *Business Combinations and Noncontrolling Interests: Application of the U.S. GAAP and IFRS Standards 2014, Global 2nd Ed.*, February 2016, https://www.pwc.com/us/en/cfodirect/assets/pdf/accounting-guides/pwc-guide-business-combinations-noncontrolling-interests-global-second-edition.pdf; FASB Accounting Standard Update No. 2010-29, December 2010, Business Combinations (Topic 805), http://fasb.org/jsp/FASB/Document_C/DocumentPage?cid=1176158047033&acceptedDisclaimer=true.

[17] SFAS 141R excludes joint ventures, the acquisition of an asset or a group of assets that does not constitute a business, a combination between entities or businesses under common control, and a combination between not-for-profit organizations or the acquisition of a for-profit business by a not-for-profit organization.

integrated set of activities and assets that are capable of being conducted and managed and/or that provide a return. A business consists of (1) inputs, (2) processes applied to those inputs, and (3) the ability to create outputs, the new guidance does not require outputs.[18]

- An input is a resource that creates or has the ability to create outputs when one or more processes are applied to it. Inputs include fixed assets, intellectual property or other intangible assets, and access to markets in which employees can be hired or materials can be purchased.
- A *process* is a function with the ability to create outputs when applied to one or more inputs. An organized workforce with the requisite skills and experience may apply processes necessary to create outputs by following established rules and conventions. Processes are the types of activities that an entity engages in to produce the products and/or services that it provides to the marketplace, rather than the internal activities it follows in operating its business.
- An *output* is simply the by-product resulting from applying processes to inputs. An output provides, or has the ability to provide, the desired return to investors, members, participants, or other owners.

The FASB issued on January 5, 2017 an Accounting Standards Update (ASU) 2017-011 effective after December 15, 2017 that revises the definition of a business[19] in determining whether a set of transferred assets and activities is a business.[20] To be considered a business, an acquisition would have to include an input and a substantive process[21] that together significantly contribute to the

---

[18] FASB Accounting Standard Update No. 2017-01, January 2017, Business Combinations (Topic 805), Clarifying the Definition of Business, http://www.fasb.org/jsp/FASB/Document_C/DocumentPage?cid=1176168739996&acceptedDisclaimer=true.

[19] PWC, In Brief, The Latest New in Financial Reporting, No. US2017-01, January 6, 2017.

[20] EY, No. 2017-03, 25 January 2017, Technical Line, FASB final guidance, how changes to the definition of a business will affect real estate entities.

[21] An acquired process (or a group of processes) would be considered substantive when:

ability to create outputs. Under the revised guidance, you could be a business without outputs, and it's not necessary that the acquirer retained, post combination, all the inputs or processes used by the seller in operating the business.[22]

(2) The assets acquired, the liabilities assumed, and any noncontrolling interest in the acquiree at the acquisition date, measured at their fair values as of that date, need to be recognized. A business combination achieved in stages (sometimes referred to as a *step acquisition*) needs to recognize the identifiable assets and liabilities, as well as the noncontrolling interest in the acquiree, at their fair values and remeasure its previously held equity interest in the acquiree.

(3) The buyer needs to account for the transaction using the acquisition method of accounting.

---

(1) A set is not generating outputs but includes employees that form an organized workforce with the necessary skills, knowledge or experience to perform an acquired process (or group of processes) that, when applied to an acquired input, is critical to the ability to develop or convert that input into outputs.

(2) The set has outputs (e.g., revenue is generated before and after the transaction from an in-place lease) and includes any of the following:

- Employees that form an organized workforce or an acquired contract that provides access to an organized workforce that has the necessary skills, knowledge or experience to perform an acquired process (or group of processes) that, when applied to an acquired input, is critical to the ability to continue producing outputs
- A process (or group of processes) that, when applied to an acquired input, significantly contributes to the ability to continue producing outputs and cannot be replaced without significant cost, effort, or delay in the ability to continue producing outputs.
- A process (or group of processes) that, when applied to an acquired input, significantly contributes to the ability to continue producing outputs and is considered unique or scarce.

[22] If a business is not producing outputs, the acquirer must determine whether the enterprise constitutes a business by considering whether it:

1. Has started its planned principal activities,
2. Has hired employees,
3. Has obtained intellectual property,
4. Has obtained other inputs.

Exhibit 1: Purchase Price Allocation 2015 — All Industries

	Mean	**Median**
Developed Technology	9	9
IPR&D	3	3
Trademarks & Tradenames	5	5
Customer-Related Assets	26	24
Others	3	1
Identifiable Intangibles	6	5
Total Intangibles*	37	33
Tangible Assets	31	34
Goodwill	32	33

Note: *Total intangibles = trademarks/tradenames + customer-related assets identifiable intangibles.
Source: Houlihan Lokey, 2015 Purchase Price Allocation Study, October 2016.

(4) ASC 805 requires that the purchase price be allocated to all identifiable assets acquired, including intangible assets.[23] Exhibits 1 through 3 provide survey data on US purchase price allocation for 2014–2015.

(5) Often the consideration transferred in a business combination may include a contingent consideration arrangement. Contingent consideration is an obligation of the acquirer to transfer additional assets or equity interests to the former owners of the acquired business if certain future events are met. Such an obligation should be recorded as a liability on the acquirer's books.

[23] Intangibles include marketing-related intangible assets, trademarks, trade names, noncompete agreements, and internet domain names.
Customer-related intangible assets include customer lists and existing customer relationships, whether they are contractual in nature.
Artistic-related intangible assets include works of art and literature.
Contract-based intangible assets are those that "arise from contractual arrangements," such as permits, franchise agreements, licensing and royalty agreements, and other contractual rights granted.
Technology-based intangible assets relate to "innovations or technological advances."

Exhibit 2: Purchase Price Allocation by Industry, %, Median of Purchase Consideration

	Intangibles, % of PC		Goodwill, % of PC	
	2015	2014	2015	2014
All Industries	31	28	38	39
Aerospace, Defense	33	23	43	52
Consumer, Food & Retail	32	27	38	33
Energy	21	20	27	28
Financial Institutions	2	1	6	6
Healthcare	42	43	41	41
Industrials	32	32	36	40
Infrastructure Services	26	21	32	24
Technology	36	33	52	54
Telecom	37	4	47	30

Note: PC = Purchase consideration.
Source: Houlihan Lokey, 2015 Purchase Price Allocation Study, October 2016.

Exhibit 3 A Contingent Consideration, % of Purchase Consideration, Median

	2015
All Industries	17
Aerospace, Defense	8
Consumer, Food & Retail	13
Energy	2
Financial Institutions	39
Healthcare	19
Industrials	12
Infrastructure Services	7
Technology	19
Telecom	49

(6) Acquisition and restructuring transaction costs are not part of the fair value of the acquired business, but the acquirer's acquisition-related costs are expenses in the periods in which the costs are incurred and the services are received, with one exception.

Transaction costs include finder's fees; advisory, legal, accounting, valuation, and other professional or consulting fees; general administrative costs, including the costs of maintaining an internal acquisitions department; and costs of registering and issuing debt and equity securities.

(7) Intangible assets are an increasingly important economic resource for many companies and are an increasing proportion of the assets acquired in many transactions. The intangible assets of the acquired entity must be determined through a valuation process. In an acquisition, an intangible asset must have one of two features to have allocated value: (1) it must be of a legal or contractual nature; or (2) it must be separable from the business. The separability criterion means that an acquired intangible asset is capable of being separated or divided from the acquiree and sold, transferred, licensed, rented, or exchanged, either individually or together with a related contract, identifiable asset, or liability. An intangible asset that is not individually separable from the acquiree or combined entity meets the separability criterion if it is separable in combination with a related contract, identifiable asset, or liability.

FASB Statement No. 142, Goodwill and Other Intangible Assets, addresses financial accounting and reporting for acquired goodwill and other intangible assets and supersedes APB Opinion No. 17, *Intangible Assets.* It addresses how intangible assets that are acquired should be accounted for in financial statements upon their acquisition.[24] This statement applied starting with fiscal years beginning after December 15, 2001. According to FASB 142, goodwill is no longer being amortized, but is subject to impairment testing, at least annually by comparing the fair values of those assets with their recorded amounts.

---

[24] FASB, summary of Statement No. 142, Goodwill and other Intangible Assets.

In estimating the value of an intangible asset, the appraiser must assume the economic life of that asset under the IRC Section 197 intangible assets are amortized over a 15-year period regardless of their actual life or the economic life used for amortization under GAAP.

(8) Goodwill needs to be recognized on the acquisition date, measured as a residual, as the excess of the consideration paid over the fair values of the identifiable net assets acquired. In some rare cases, an acquirer may obtain a bargain purchase where the net amount of identifiable assets acquired and liabilities assumed exceeds the sum of the consideration paid. ASC 805 requires the acquirer in a business combination resulting in a bargain purchase to recognize a gain for the amount that the values assigned to the net assets acquired exceed the consideration transferred.

Testing goodwill for impairment at least annually must follow the guidance in ASC 350 and apply a two-step process that begins with an estimation of the fair value of a reporting unit. The first step is a screen for potential impairment, and the second step measures the amount of impairment, if any. That is, the acquiree goodwill is tested for impairment at the acquiree's reporting units. Step 2 involves determining the implied fair value of goodwill and comparing it to the carrying amount of that goodwill to measure the impairment loss, if any.

(9) In-process R&D (IPR&D) will be classified as an intangible asset with an indefinite life until the project is complete or the R&D is abandoned. The recorded assets won't be written off or capitalized, but instead will be subject to impairment testing.

(10) In a reverse acquisition, some of the owners of the legal acquiree might not exchange their equity interests for equity interests of the legal parent. Those owners are treated as a noncontrolling interest in the consolidated financial statements after the reverse acquisition. Conversely, even though the legal acquirer is the acquiree for accounting purposes, the owners of the legal acquirer have an interest in the results and net assets of the combined entity.

Exhibit 4 addresses the steps and risk in application of the ASC 805.

Exhibit 4: Financial Reporting of Business Combinations: Functions and Risks

Step	Risks	Control Design Considerations
Approve the transaction	• The transaction is not presented to the Board of Directors (BOD) or others with appropriate levels of authority for approval.	• What is the approval process and who has the authority to approve acquisition transactions?
Determine whether the transaction is a business combination (see chapter 2)	• The acquisition is accounted for as a business combination, but does not meet the definition of a business combination in ASC 805.	• What is the process for determining whether the acquisition should be accounted for as a business combination (rather than as an asset acquisition, common control transaction, transaction under common ownership)?
Identify the acquirer (see section 3.2)	• The accounting acquirer is not properly identified.	• What is the process to determine the accounting acquirer under ASC 810, *Consolidation,* (voting or variable interest model) or under ASC 805 if the acquiree is a voting interest entity and the accounting acquirer is not obvious?
Determine the acquisition date (see section 3.3)	• The acquisition is not accounted for on the appropriate date.	• What is the process to determine the date in which the acquiring entity obtained control of the business?
Recognize and measure the identifiable assets acquired, liabilities assumed and any noncontrolling interests in the acquiree (see chapter 4)	• Assets acquired and liabilities assumed are not properly identified. • Assets acquired and liabilities assumed are not properly recognized and measured.	What is the process to ensure all assets acquired and liabilities assumed have been identified (e.g., intangibles, contingencies) and exist (e.g., inventory)? • What is the process to determine the fair value of assets acquired and liabilities assumed (including the

(*Continued*)

Exhibit 4: (*Continued*)

Step	Risks	Control Design Considerations
	• The valuation of assets acquired and liabilities assumed is performed by an internal or third-party valuation specialist who does not have the appropriate skills and expertise. • Key assumptions used in the valuation and development of PFI are unreasonable or not supported by the facts and circumstances. • See section F.4 for further discussion of internal control considerations for valuation analyses.	reasonableness of assumptions and estimates used in the valuation, such as PFI)? • Who performs the fair value measurement and do these individuals have the appropriate skills and expertise? • What procedures are performed to evaluate the reasonableness of the fair value measurement? Do the individuals performing the evaluation have the appropriate skills and expertise and is there segregation of incompatible duties? • When valuations are based on PFI, who develops this information and who reviews it? Who determines that the PFI is consistent with the PFI used for other purposes (e.g., board model created during due diligence procedures)? • Who evaluates the methods and assumptions used by the specialist for reasonableness and what is involved in that review? • When external specialists are used, what is the process to ensure the information provided by the specialist is accurate and complete? • See section F.4 for further discussion of internal control considerations for valuation analyses.

(*Continued*)

Exhibit 4: (*Continued*)

Step	Risks	Control Design Considerations
Identify, classify and measure the consideration transferred (see chapter 6)	• The consideration transferred by the acquirer is not properly identified. • The consideration transferred by the acquirer is not properly measured. See section F.4 for further discussion of internal control considerations for valuation analyses. • The consideration transferred by the acquirer is not properly authorized. • The value of share-based payment replacement awards is not properly attributed to consideration transferred and post combination compensation expense. • The consideration transferred includes items that should be accounted for as separate transactions (e.g., transaction costs or compensation to employees or former owners for future services).	• What is the approval process and who has the authority to approve the various forms of consideration transferred? • What is the process to identify and evaluate transactions that should be accounted for separately from the business combination (e.g., settlements of pre-existing relationships compensation to employees or former owners for future services, reimbursement to acquiree for acquisition-related costs)? • What is the process to identify and evaluate the accounting for share-based payment replacement awards including the implications of any change in control provisions either in the acquiree award or purchase agreement? • What is the process to verify that the consideration transferred (including any contingent consideration and share-based payment replacement awards) is accurately measured (including the reasonableness of assumptions and estimates used in the valuation, such as PFI) as of the acquisition date? See section F.4 for further discussion of internal control considerations for valuation analyses.

(*Continued*)

Exhibit 4: (*Continued*)

Step	Risks	Control Design Considerations
	• The contingent consideration is not properly classified as a liability or equity.	• What is the process to determine the appropriate classification of contingent consideration as either a liability or equity?
Recognize and measure goodwill or a gain from a bargain purchase (see sections 7.1 and 7.2)	• Recognized goodwill or a bargain purchase does not agree with underlying support or is not calculated correctly. • Noncontrolling interest is not properly measured and recorded. • Previously held equity interests in the acquired entity and any related gain or loss are not properly measured or recorded.	• What is the process to verify that any goodwill or a gain from a bargain purchase is properly measured and recorded? • What is the process to determine the fair value of any noncontrolling interest in the acquired entity? • What is the process to determine the fair value of any previously held equity interest in the acquired entity? • If the transaction results in a gain from a bargain purchase, is a thorough reassessment of all elements of the accounting for the acquisition performed? How is that reassessment performed? • If after the thorough reassessment a bargain purchase gain still exists, what are the reasons that would justify the bargain purchase gain?
Recognize any subsequent adjustments (see section 7.3)	• Subsequent adjustments to the provisional amounts recorded at the acquisition date are not valid measurement-period adjustments.	• What is the process to verify that subsequent adjustments to the provisional amounts recorded at the acquisition date represent valid measurement-period adjustments?

(*Continued*)

Exhibit 4: (*Continued*)

Step	Risks	Control Design Considerations
	• Subsequent adjustments to the provisional amounts recorded at the acquisition date are not properly recorded.	• What is the process to determine whether the measurement of an individual asset or liability is still provisional?

Source: EY, Financial reporting developments, *A comprehensive guide*, Business combinations, Revised June 2016.

Goodwill Impairment, FASB ASC 350, Intangibles and Others

Goodwill has an indefinite life and it's not amortized, but impaired. The implied fair value of goodwill is the excess of the fair value of the reporting unit over the fair value of the assets and liabilities purchased in a business combination.[25] Goodwill is created when the purchase price > the fair value allocation to assets acquired and liabilities assumed. Goodwill is impaired when its *implied* fair value is less than its carrying amount. The impairment test for goodwill is performed at the reporting unit, which is an operating segment or one level below an operating segment. Costs of internally developed goodwill are expensed as incurred, and goodwill acquired during acquisition of an entire entity is accounted for under ASC 805. Testing goodwill for impairment must follow the guidance in ASC 350, and must be tested at least annually at the subsidiary level.

Performing the impairment test involves a two-step process.[26] The FASB Step 0 provides the option of performing a qualitative assessment to determine whether it is more likely than not that the fair value of the reporting unit is less than the carrying amount, which implies that goodwill impairment has likely occurred and further testing is performed, and you apply Step 1. If it *is not* more likely than

[25] Op. Cit. Wiley GAAP, 25 ASC 350 Intangibles — Goodwill and Other.

[26] *PWC, In depth, A Look at current financial reporting issues, No. US2017-03, February 13, 2017.*

not that the fair value of the reporting unit is less than the carrying amount, further testing is not necessary.

Step 1 of the impairment test compares the fair value of the reporting unit to its carrying value, including goodwill.

- If the reporting unit's fair value exceeds its carrying value, goodwill is not impaired and no further computations are required.
- If it is more likely than not that a goodwill impairment exists, the entity should revalue its fair value and carrying cost.
- If the reporting unit carrying value exceeds its fair value, the second step of the impairment test is required.

Step 2. Determine whether and by how much goodwill is impaired as follows:

- Estimate the implied fair value of goodwill.
- Compare the implied fair value of goodwill to its carrying amount.
- If the carrying amount of goodwill exceeds its implied fair value, it is impaired and is written down to the implied fair value.

The fair value of a reporting unit is its market price that could be received in selling it in an orderly transaction at the measurement date. If the carrying amount of the reporting unit's goodwill exceeds the implied fair value of that goodwill, an impairment loss in the amount equal to the excess is recognized. A numerical example is addressed in Exhibit 5.

Spectral Corporation acquires FarSite Binocular Company for $5,300,000; of this amount, $3,700,000 is allocated to a variety of

Exhibit 5: Example of Goodwill Impairment

Purchase price	$5,300,000
Accounts receivable	(450,000)
Inventory	(750,000)
Production equipment	(1,000,000)
Acquired formulas and processes	(1,500,000)
= Goodwill	$1,600,000

assets, with the remaining $1,600,000 allocated to goodwill as shown below:

A few months later, Spectral's management learns that a foreign competitor has created a competing optics coating process that is superior to and less expensive than FarSite's process. Since this will likely result in a reduction in FarSite's fair value below its carrying amount, Spectral conducts another impairment test. Management assumes that the forthcoming increase in competition will reduce the expected present value of its cash flows to $3,900,000. In addition, the appraisal firm reduces its valuation of the acquired formulas and processes asset by $1,200,000. The revised impairment test follows:

FarSite division's fair value	$3,900,000
Fair value of identifiable assets	
= fair value of goodwill	(2,400,000)
	1,500,000
Carrying value of goodwill	1,600,000
Goodwill Impairment Loss	100.000

Under the revised guidance,[27] the qualitative assessment option (Step 0) and the first step of the quantitative assessment (Step 1) remain unchanged and Step 2 will be eliminated. Step 1 will be used to determine both the existence and amount of goodwill impairment. An impairment loss will be the amount by which the reporting unit's carrying amount exceeds its fair value. The revised guidance will be effective for public companies after December 15, 2019, and for all other entities after December 15, 2021.

Summary

The major accounting issues in business combinations are:

- The proper accounting basis for the assets and liabilities of the combining entities, and

[27] *PWC, In depth, A Look at current financial reporting issues, No. US2017-03, February 13, 2017.*

- The accounting for goodwill.

Business combinations that comply with GAAP financial reporting must follow the Financial Accounting Standards Board (FASB) guidance set in Accounting Standard Codification (ASC) 805,[28] Business Combinations,[29] and ASC 820. Fair Value ASC 805 requires[30] to perform a valuation process and a purchase price allocation (PPA) to the fair value of all assets acquired, liabilities assumed, and contingent liabilities. The allocation of the purchase price for business combinations under ASC 805 requires several steps, including identifying a business combination, recognizing the various assets, selecting the appropriate valuation method, and allocating the purchase prices. The valuation outcome is largely dependent on the fair values assigned to assets and liabilities on the transaction date by following ASC 820 that provides a framework for measuring fair value in business combinations.[31]

Exhibit 6 provides a summary of the various FASB accounting requirements, including the application of M&As.

---

[28] https://www.bvresources.com/docs/default-source/book-excerpts/purchase-price-allocations-special-report-excerpt.pdf?sfvrsn=4.

[29] Adam Capital, Purchase Price Allocation (ASC 805).

[30] *Brian Holloway,* Intangible Assets in Purchase Price Allocations, Insights Summer 2013 www.willamette.com.

[31] Measurements and Disclosure. ASC 805 requires to perform a valuation process and a purchase price allocation (PPA) to the fair value of all assets acquired, liabilities assumed and contingent liabilities. The allocation of the purchase price for business combinations under ASC 805 requires several steps, including identifying a business combination, recognizing the various assets, selecting the appropriate valuation method, and allocating the purchase prices. The valuation outcome is largely dependent on the fair values assigned to assets and liabilities on the transaction date by following ASC 820 that provides a framework for measuring fair value in business combinations. Valuation is best addressed by an independent and experienced firm. The difference between the book values of the assets (BVA) acquired and the fair values of those assets represents a step-up in the basis of the acquired assets. The three valuation approaches to value a business or an intangible asset are as follows: The income approach, the cost approach and the market approach.

Exhibit 6: GAAP Accounting Requirements

This exhibit references the FASB's *Accounting Standards Codification* (FASB ASC) and others

Purchase Price Allocation	
FASB ASC 805, Business Combinations	This topic provides guidance on the accounting and reporting that represent business combinations to be accounted for under the acquisition method.
FASB ASC 820, Fair Value Measurements and Disclosures	This topic defines fair value, establishes a framework for measuring fair value in generally accepted accounting principles (GAAP), and expands disclosures about fair value measurements.
FASB ASC 350, Intangibles — Goodwill and Other	This topic provides guidance on financial accounting and reporting related to goodwill and other intangibles, other than the accounting at acquisition for goodwill and other intangibles.
FASB ASC 323, Investments — Equity Method and Joint Ventures	This topic addresses application of the equity method of accounting to investments within its scope.
IFRS No. 3 — International Business Combinations	International Accounting Standards Board (IASB) issued International Financial Reporting Standard (IFRS) No. 3 with the objective to enhance the relevance, reliability and comparability of the information that an entity provides in its financial statements about a business combination and its effects. Visit www.ifrs.org to see the Standard.
IAS No. 38 — International Intangible Assets	International Accounting Standards Board (IASB) issued International Accounting Standard No. 38 with the objective to prescribe the accounting treatment for intangible assets that are not dealt with specifically in another Standard. Visit www.ifrs.org to see the Standard.
Impairment Testing	
FASB ASC 350, Intangibles — Goodwill and Other	This topic provides guidance on financial accounting and reporting related to goodwill and other intangibles, other than the accounting at acquisition for goodwill and other intangibles.

(*Continued*)

Exhibit 6: (*Continued*)

FASB ASC 360-10-40, Property, Plant and Equipment — Impairment or Disposal of Long-Lived Assets	This subtopic provides guidance on the impairment or disposal of long-lived assets.
FASB ASC 805, Business Combinations	This topic provides guidance on the accounting and reporting that represent business combinations to be accounted for under the acquisition method.
FASB ASC 820, Fair Value Measurements and Disclosures	This topic defines fair value, establishes a framework for measuring fair value in generally accepted accounting principles (GAAP), and expands disclosures about fair value measurements.
FASB ASC 350-30-35-21, Intangibles — Goodwill and Other, General Intangibles Other Than Goodwill, Subsequent Measurement, Unit of Accounting for Purposes of Testing for Impairment of Intangible Assets Not Subject to Amortization	Provides guidance on Unit of Accounting for Purposes of Testing for Impairment of Intangible Assets Not Subject to Amortization.
FASB ASC 350-20-35-61, Intangibles — Goodwill and Other, Goodwill, Subsequent Measurement, Deferred Income Taxes	Provides guidance on deferred income taxes related to goodwill.
IAS No. 36 — International — Impairment	The International Accounting Standards Board (IASB) issued International Accounting Standard No. 36 with the objective to prescribe the procedures that an entity applies to ensure that its assets are carried at no more than their recoverable amount.

(*Continued*)

Exhibit 6: (*Continued*)

Share-Based Compensation	
FASB ASC 718, Compensation — Stock Compensation	This topic provides guidance on share-based payment transactions with employees and includes the following subtopics: Awards Classified as Equity, Awards Classified as Liabilities, Employee Stock Ownership Plans, Employee Stock Purchase Plans, and Income Taxes.
SEC SAB No. 107	Securities and Exchange Commission (SEC) Staff Accounting Bulletin (SAB) No. 107 was issued in March 2005 to express views of the staff regarding the interaction between Statement of Financial Accounting Standards Statement No. 123 (revised 2004), *Share-Based Payment* ("Statement 123R" or the "Statement") and certain Securities and Exchange Commission (SEC) rules and regulations and provide the staff's views regarding the valuation of share-based payment arrangements for public companies. Please visit www.sec.gov.
FASB ASC 505-50-05, Equity, Equity-Based Payments to Nonemployees	This subtopic provides guidance surrounding equity-based payments to nonemployees.
IFRS No. 2 — International Share-Based Compensation	The International Accounting Standards Board (IASB) issued International Financial Reporting Standard (IFRS) No. 2 with the objective to specify the financial reporting by an entity when it undertakes a *share-based payment transaction.* Visit www.ifrs.org to see the Standard.
AICPA Statements on Auditing Standards	
Statement on Auditing Standards (SAS) No. 57 — Auditing Accounting Estimates	This section provides guidance to auditors on obtaining and evaluating sufficient appropriate audit evidence to support significant accounting estimates in an audit of financial statements in accordance with generally accepted auditing standards.
SAS No. 73 — Using the Work of a Specialist	This section provides guidance to the auditor who uses the work of a specialist in performing an audit in accordance with generally accepted auditing

(*Continued*)

Exhibit 6: (*Continued*)

	standards. For purposes of this section, a specialist is a person (or firm) possessing special skill or knowledge in a field other than accounting or auditing.
SAS No. 101 — Auditing Fair Value Measurements and Disclosures	This section establishes standards and provides guidance on auditing fair value measurements and disclosures contained in financial statements. In particular, this section addresses audit considerations relating to the measurement and disclosure of assets, liabilities, and specific components of equity presented or disclosed at fair value in financial statements.

Source: http://www.aicpa.org/InterestAreas/ForensicAndValuation/Resources/FairValueforFinancialReporting/Pages/FairValueRelatedAuthoritativeLiterature.aspx.

Chapter 10

Tax Aspects of M&A

Peter F. De Nicola* and Robert M. Gordon†

**Fujifilm Holdings, USA*

†*True Partners Consulting*

> In my own case the words of such an act as the Income Tax, e.g., merely dance before my eyes in a meaningless procession: cross-reference to cross-reference, exception upon exception — couched in abstract terms that offer no handle to seize hold of — leave in my mind only a confused sense of some vitally important, but successfully concealed, purport, which it is my duty to extract, but which is within my power, if at all, only after the most inordinate expenditure of time.... Much of the law is now as difficult to fathom, and more and more of it is likely to be so; for there is little doubt that we are entering a period of increasingly detailed regulation, and it will be the duty of judges to thread the path — for path there is — through these fantastic labyrinths.

Learned Hand, *Eulogy of Thomas Walter Swan*, 57 Yale L.J. 167, 169 (1947), quoted in *Welder v. United States*, 329 F. Supp. 739, 741-42 (S.D. Tex. 1971).

The Role of Tax in M&A

Suppose that a corporation ("Acquirer") approaches another corporation ("Target") to purchase the business of Target. Acquirer offers

Target $100 cash to purchase all of the business assets and liabilities of Target. Knowing that the business is only worth $60, Target eagerly accepts the offer, even though it understands that it will have to pay tax on the gain. Is this a good deal for Target and its shareholders?

The answer will depend on how the transaction is structured and what Target intends to do with the sales proceeds. For example, if Target distributes all of the proceeds to its shareholders, the shareholders could, in some cases, be subject to aggregate taxes in excess of 50–60% of the amount of the proceeds. That is probably not what the Target shareholders anticipated. On the other hand, if Target is an "S" corporation, the Target shareholders probably would only be taxed at a rate of around 40%.

This is just one simple example of how tax effects could disrupt the economic expectations of the parties. Other cases are legion: not only may one party receive a benefit at the expense of the other party, but it is even possible for both parties to end up worse off than they planned.

The federal income tax system of the US is one of the world's more opaque bodies of law: not only are there thousands of pages of statute (the Internal Revenue Code) and regulations, but there are innumerable judicial decisions, IRS rulings, and quasimetaphysical doctrines (e.g., "substance-over-form," "step transactions," etc.), all of which can be counterintuitive, arbitrary, constantly changing, and containing exceptions and exceptions to these exceptions. Then, to make it more complicated, it is necessary to layer on the effects of state, local, and foreign taxes. Applying all of these rules depends on the specific facts and circumstances of each transaction and even each step of each transaction.

One fundamental fact of the US tax system must be kept in mind at all times: corporations are treated as taxable entities separate from their shareholders (unless the corporation has elected to be treated as a subchapter "S" corporation, which results in it being treated as a flow-through entity for tax purposes). Thus, each potential M&A transaction must be analyzed to determine its tax effects on Acquirer, Target, and their respective shareholders.

This chapter can only touch briefly on the most general principles that a business person should keep in mind when planning and negotiating an M&A transaction. Because the structure of a transaction generally drives the tax result, the critical point to remember is not only to be aware of taxes when negotiating a transaction, but to consult a tax professional as early as possible (in every case, *before the structure of the transaction is agreed*) and at every subsequent step in the process.

General Tax Considerations

Seller's Considerations

Generally, gain or loss must be recognized on the sale or exchange of property. The Internal Revenue Code provides certain exceptions to this precept, including corporate reorganizations. The law does not exempt the transaction from taxation. Rather, it merely delays the gain or loss until it is realized on a subsequent sale.

Buyers and sellers often have conflicting goals in structuring an M&A. Sellers often prefer the transaction to be nontaxable so that any gain in their interest in the target corporation will be deferred to a later date. Buyers, on the other hand, may prefer an acquisition to be taxable so that they may have a higher basis in acquired assets.

In certain circumstances, a transaction may be structured as an installment sale. Rather than recognizing the gain in the year the transfer of ownership takes place, it is spread across several years as payments are received from the purchaser. This may allow the gain to be taxed at a lower rate.

Another consideration is whether the sale qualifies for capital gains treatment. The sale of stock will usually be beneficial to a noncorporate seller because it generally qualifies for a lower capital gains tax rate. The sale of assets, on the other hand, is usually beneficial to the buyer because it provides a stepped-up basis. However, the sale of depreciable assets may lead to the recapture of depreciation which will not be eligible for capital gains treatment.

Generally speaking, no gain or loss is recognized to the exchanging shareholders in a corporation that is party to a reorganization. Therefore, if the transaction is pursuant to a plan of reorganization and the stock or securities exchanged are those of a party to the reorganization, the nonrecognition provision of IRC Sec. 354(a)(1) applies. The subsequent sale of the stock received in a reorganization will be treated as a capital gain or loss computed by reference to the shareholder's basis in the stock or securities exchanged.

However, there are situations where the nonrecognition rules will not apply. For instance, if the principal amount of securities received exceeds the principal amount of the securities surrendered, or securities are received, but no securities are surrendered. In these situations, the shareholder will have to recognize gain as if he had received money in the exchange. This, if a shareholder exchanges a debt instrument with a face value of $1,000 for two instruments with a face value of $2,000, one-half of the debt security received constitutes "boot".

In many reorganizations, cash may be a component of the reorganization plan. In these cases, IRC Sec. 356 applies. Under IRC Sec 356, the exchanging shareholder must recognize gain to the extent of "boot" received in the transaction. "Boot" is cash or the fair market value (FMV) of property other than stock or securities of a party to the reorganization. Securities in corporations not party to a reorganization are considered "boot" and they are taxable to the extent of the securities' FMV. It should be noted that no loss may be recognized on the transaction.

Once it is determined under IRC Sec 356(a)(1) that a portion of the gain must be recognized, IRC Sec 356(a)(2) governs as to whether it should be treated as a capital gain or a dividend. To the extent that the distributing corporation has earnings and profits, the "boot" distributed will be treated by the shareholder as the receipt of their pro rata share of the corporation's earning and profits and taxable to them as a dividend. Any "boot" received in excess of the shareholder's pro rata earnings and profits will be taxed as a capital gain.

Buyer's Considerations

Corporate acquisitions usually are structured as a stock purchase rather than an asset purchase because it is often less cumbersome to do so. However, stock acquisitions do not allow the purchasers to recoup any portion of their investment through depreciation or amortization. The target corporation may have acquired assets years ago that are carried on its books at historical cost. The purchase price of the stock will undoubtedly reflect the current value of the underlying assets which may be significantly higher. Consequently, the purchaser may wish to step up the basis of the acquired corporation's assets. In order to achieve this result, the buyer and seller may jointly elect under Section 338(h)(10) to treat the stock sale as an asset sale for tax purposes.

A Section 338(h)(10) election, however, may be disadvantageous to the seller in situations where the tax basis of the target corporation's assets (inside basis) is lower than the seller's basis in the target corporation's stock (outside basis). This may result in the seller paying additional tax due to the disparity between the inside and outside bases. Therefore, the seller may wish to negotiate a higher selling price to compensate for the additional taxes that may be due. Any amounts paid by the purchaser to the seller for additional taxes may need to be grossed up since the compensation, itself, will be subject to tax. Consequently, a 338(h)(10) election may be viable only under very limited circumstances and after a full and thorough analysis has been completed.

Taxable and Nontaxable Transactions

Taxable transactions can take the form of a sale of either stock or assets of Target. Transactions where the only consideration is cash or a note are always taxable to Target, Target's shareholders, or both. If the consideration includes stock or securities of the Acquirer, however, the transaction may (or may not) be nontaxable.

Nontaxable transactions must generally take the form of either reorganization as defined in one of the subsections of section 368 of the Code or as the creation of a new entity, either a corporation or a partnership. Nontaxable transactions, however, do not eliminate tax: they merely defer it until some future time.

> *The basis for federal tax law is Title 26 of the United States Code, generally referred to as "The Internal Revenue Code of 1986," or the "Code." When tax professionals are overhead talking in "numbers", they are typically referring to sections or subsections of the Code or the regulations issued by the US Treasury Department to interpret the Code.*

Taxable Transactions

Forms of Taxable Transactions

Taxable M&A transactions can take the form of either stock or asset acquisitions. One of the advantages of a taxable transaction is the treatment of intangible assets. Under section 197 of the Code, intangibles such as goodwill, going concern value, workforce in place, customer and supplier based intangibles, covenants not to compete, patents, copyrights, and licenses are amortizable over 15 years for tax purposes. Typically, the purchase price is allocated to the assets acquired according to their relative FMVs with the residual being assigned to the aforementioned intangibles that are identified as part of the transaction.

Here is a form of a simple stock sale (Figure 1).

The shareholders of Target transfer the stock of Target to Acquirer in exchange for cash. After the transaction, Acquirer owns all the stock of Target and the Target shareholders have cash. This transaction has the following tax results:

1. Acquirer takes a basis in Target stock equal to the amount of cash transferred to Target shareholders in the transaction.
2. The tax basis of Target's assets remains the same and depreciation continues unchanged.

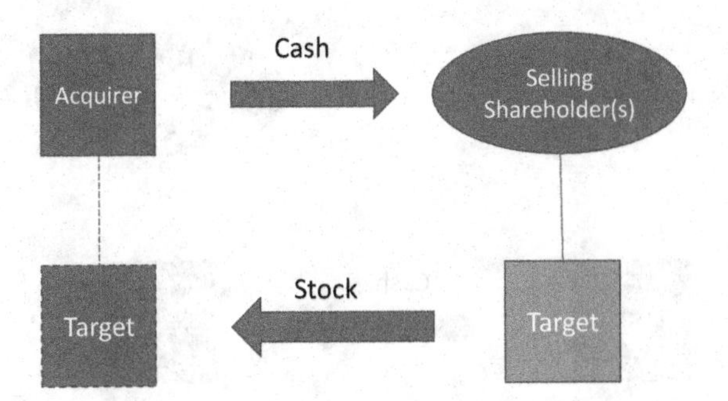

Figure 1: A Form of a Simple Stock Sale.

3. The shareholders of Target recognize taxable gain in the amount of the difference between the cash received and their tax basis in their shares of Target stock.
4. The Target shareholders' taxable gain will usually be capital gain, either long- or short-term depending on how long they owned their Target stock.

Figure 2 illustrates a simple asset sale.

In this case, Acquirer transfers cash to Target in exchange for all of Target's assets (and liabilities). After the transaction, Acquirer owns all of the assets (and liabilities) of Target and Target holds the cash. Target may liquidate at this point and transfer the cash to its shareholders. The tax results of this transaction are:

1. Acquirer takes a basis in the assets acquired from Target equal to the sum of the cash paid and the amount of any liabilities assumed. The consideration paid (cash and liabilities assumed) is allocated among the various assets according to their FMV using a residual method, which generally requires an allocation:
   a. First, to cash and cash equivalents (e.g., actively traded securities, debt instruments, etc.);
   b. Then to stock-in-trade and inventory;
   c. Then to all other tangible property;

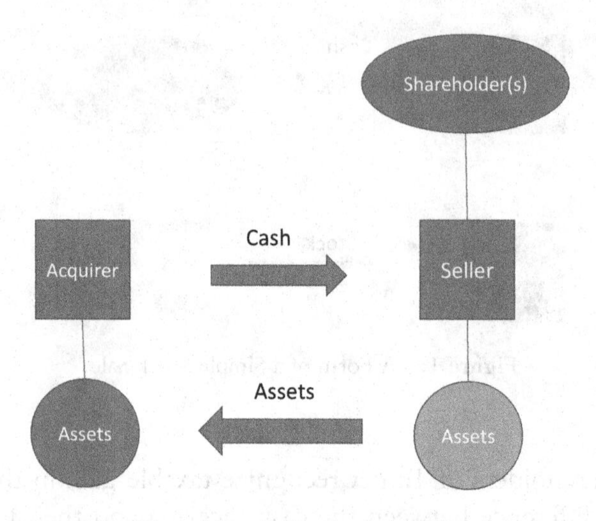

Figure 2: A Simple Asset Sale.

d. Finally, to intangibles, including goodwill and going concern value.

Acquirer will typically want to allocate as much of the purchase price as possible to depreciable assets with the shortest depreciation lives.

2. Acquirer can begin depreciating the acquired assets on the acquisition date based on their new tax basis.
3. Target must allocate the consideration received (cash plus liabilities assumed by Acquirer) using the same residual method as Acquirer (although the parties need not agree to the specific allocations).
4. Target's taxable gain will be the difference between the consideration treated as received for each asset and its adjusted tax basis as of the transaction date.
5. Target's gain will be treated as capital or ordinary depending on the classification and holding period of each asset, as well as potential recharacterization of some of the gain as ordinary that might otherwise be treated as capital.
6. If Target liquidates or distributes the cash received to its shareholders, the shareholders will also be subject to tax. The tax

treatment of this distribution depends upon a variety of factors:

- If Target liquidates and the shareholders are individuals, they will be treated as having exchanged their stock in Target for the cash received and the gain (or loss) will be capital gain (long- or short-term depending on how long they owned their Target stock);
- If Target liquidates and the shareholder is a corporation that owns at least 80% of the stock of Target, then there will be no tax to the 80% shareholder (although minority shareholders will be taxed on the difference between the cash received and their tax basis in their stock, as for individuals);
- If Target does not liquidate, any cash distribution may (or may not) be treated as a dividend, depending on a variety of factors.

Sometimes the parties will agree to an asset sale, but for a variety of nontax reasons (e.g., licenses, rights of first refusals, etc.), it may not be possible for Target to transfer some or all of its key assets. In that case, tax law allows for a special election under section 338(g) of the Code by which a stock sale can be treated as an asset sale for *tax purposes only*. The Acquirer makes the election, which can only be made if the Acquirer is a corporation that purchases at least 80% of the stock of Target over a 12-month period. This election is illustrated in Figure 3.

If the Acquirer makes a section 338(g) election, the following tax results are treated as having occurred:

1. The shareholders of Target are treated as having sold their stock and recognize taxable gain in an amount equal to the difference between their tax basis in the Target stock and the consideration received.
2. Target is treated as selling all of its assets and liabilities to a New Target (owned by Acquirer) at the close of the acquisition date for FMV (the purchase price plus the amount of any liabilities assumed).

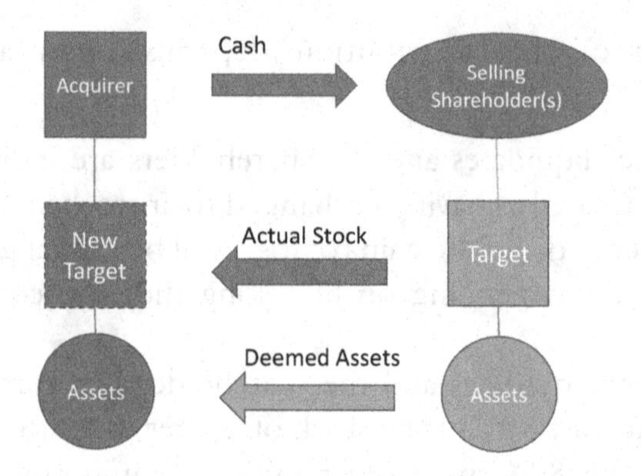

Figure 3: Election Under Section 338(G) by Which a Stock Sale Can Be Treated as an Asset Sale for *Tax Purposes Only.*

Old and New Target must allocate the consideration received on the deemed asset sale between the assets. Old Target will recognize taxable gain (capital or ordinary, depending on the nature of the asset) in an amount equal to the difference between the adjusted purchase price (consideration plus liabilities) allocated to each asset and the asset's adjusted tax basis.

The net result of a section 338(g) election, therefore, will be two levels of tax: Old Target shareholders are taxed on the gain from their sale of stock, and Old Target will recognize gain from the deemed asset sale; the tax on this second sale is typically economically borne by the Acquirer (although well-advised Acquirers will want to shift much of this burden to the Seller as part of the negotiations, typically through a lower purchase price). As a result of this double tax, section 338(g) elections only tend to be used where either the Seller or the Acquirer is not a taxpayer (e.g., a foreign corporation or if Old Target has significant amounts of net operating loss carryforwards).

Section 338 elections are one example of many situations where the tax law creates tax fictions. Other examples include where certain instruments that are nominally or legally debt are treated as stock for tax purposes and where certain partnership contributions and distributions are treated as "disguised sales."

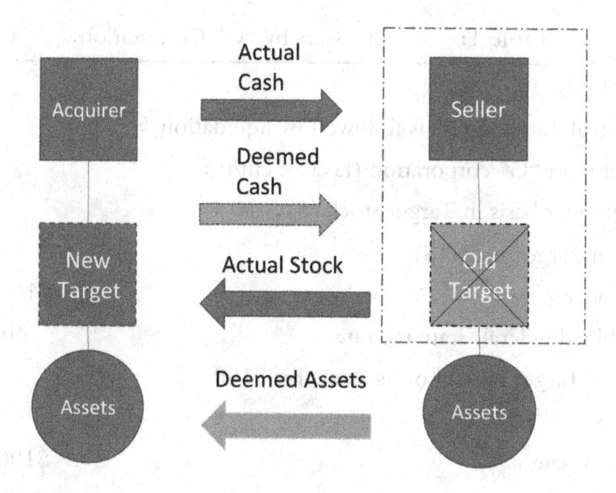

Figure 4: One Level of Tax in the Aggregate.

Section 338 elections remain useful, however, if the Target is a member of a consolidated group or is an "S" corporation. In that case, the Acquirer and the Target's owner can jointly make an election under section 338(h)(10) and recognize only one level of tax in the aggregate (Figure 4).

In a stock sale where the parties make a section 338(h)(10) election, Target is treated as if it sold its assets to a New Target for FMV and then Old Target is deemed to have liquidated. Because members of a consolidated group are generally treated as a single taxpayer, the deemed asset sale will result in the Seller group recognizing taxable gain (capital or ordinary) in an amount equal to difference between the consideration treated as received for each asset and its adjusted tax basis. The deemed liquidation of Old Target into its parent (which, to be consolidated in the first place must own at least 80% of the Target's stock) will be nontaxable. As a result, the selling group will recognize only a single level of gain.

Acquirer, while it actually purchased the stock of Target, will be treated as if it had formed a new corporation (New Target) which then acquired the assets of Old Target for FMV; in short, the stock sale is disregarded. As with an actual asset acquisition, New Target will take a tax basis in the assets equal to the sum of the consideration paid and the liabilities assumed. The consideration is allocated among

Table 1: Sale of Assets by "C" Corporation.

Assumptions	
Sale of all Target assets is followed by liquidation	
Target is an "C" corporation (taxable entity)	
Shareholder basis in Target stock ($)	—
Basis in Target assets ($)	—
Sales price	$100.00
Combined federal/state tax rate	40%
Step 1 — Target sells all of its assets for $100	
Results	
Target gain	$100.00
Target tax on gain	$40.00
Cash available after tax	$60.00
Step 2 — Target liquidates and distributes sales proceeds to shareholders	
Results	
Shareholder gain	$60.00
Shareholder tax on gain	$24.00
Cash available after tax	$36.00
Total tax paid	$64.00
Effective tax rate on sale	64.00%

the assets under the residual method according to their FMVs. The allocated amount serves as the New Target's tax basis of the assets for purposes of depreciation (Table 1).

Section 338(h)(10) elections are also available if Target is an "S" corporation because, as in the case of a consolidated Seller, the deemed liquidation of Old Target is not generally subject to a second level of tax. Thus, the Acquirer gets the benefit of an asset sale while the Seller pays tax only on the gain from the deemed sale of assets; gain from the stock sale is disregarded.

Both types of section 338 transactions require that the Acquirer must be a corporation. Regulations under section 336(e) allow for an election that permits a noncorporate Acquirer to make an election to treat a stock acquisition as an asset acquisition with a conceptual

Table 2: Sale of Assets by "S" Corporation.

Assumptions	
Sale of all Target assets is followed by liquidation	
Target is an "S" corporation (nontaxable entity)	
Shareholder basis in Target stock ($)	—
Basis in Target assets ($)	—
Sales price	$100.00
Combined federal/state tax rate	40%
Step 1 — Target sells all of its assets for $100	
Results	
Target gain	$100.00
Target tax on gain ($)	—
Cash available after tax	$100.00
Step 2 — Target liquidates and distributes sales proceeds to shareholders	
Results	
Shareholder gain	$100.00
Shareholder tax on gain	$40.00
Cash available after tax	$60.00
Total tax paid	$40.00
Effective tax rate on sale	40.00%

model similar to that under section 338(h)(10) — the sale of a consolidated subsidiary (or "S" corporation) may be treated as a taxable sale of its assets followed by a nontaxable liquidation (Table 2).

A section 336(e) election could be particularly useful where the Acquirer is a private equity firm or other business that customarily operates through a partnership form.

Asset sales may also take the form of the sale of all the ownership interests in a limited liability company (LLC). For federal income tax purposes, LLCs are generally treated as flow-through entities: that is, if there are multiple owners it is treated as a partnership but if there is only one owner, the LLC is treated as a nonentity and is disregarded. So a sale of a single member LLC is, for tax purposes, treated as the sale of assets.

Consideration in Taxable Transactions

So far, we have generally assumed that the consideration for the acquisition has been limited to cash. But the parties may, of course, agree to other types of consideration, generally limited only by the imaginations of investment bankers. The most common types of non-cash consideration in taxable transactions tend to be the assumption of liabilities, debt, and earnouts.

In the case of an asset sale, the Acquirer may assume some or all of the Target's liabilities. In general, the purchase price for a business includes the amount of liabilities assumed by the Acquirer. In many cases, there is little difficulty in determining the amount of the liabilities assumed. But sometimes — such as in connection with environmental liabilities, product liability and warranties, and pension and employment-related claims — the amount or timing of the liabilities assumed cannot be reasonably known at the time of the sale. The tax rules surrounding such contingent liabilities are particularly complex and can lead to major surprises for the parties.

First, it is important to note that the tax treatment of contingent liabilities differs significantly from financial accounting treatment. The tax rules do not allow the Acquirer to establish a "reserve"; rather, these liabilities are taken into account (either through a deduction or by adding them to the basis of the underlying acquired property) when the liabilities become "fixed and determinable" — generally, when actually paid. In some cases (e.g., pension costs for current employees), the liability can be treated as Acquirer's liability and can be deductible by the Acquirer when paid.

The Seller's treatment of contingent liabilities has been the subject of considerable controversy. There are no statutory or regulatory rules and the courts have not adopted a consistent approach. Commentators have identified three methods that taxpayers could use:

1. *Open transaction treatment.* The Seller ignores the liability and Acquirer capitalizes or deducts the cost if and when the liability becomes fixed and determinable;

2. *Netting.* The Seller includes an amount attributable to the liability as income or gain from the sale, but then takes an equal or offsetting deduction or loss; or
3. *Closed transaction treatment.* The parties agree on a value for the liability at the time of sale, the Seller recognizes gain or income, and the Acquirer receives basis for assuming that liability.

It is common for some or all of the consideration in a transaction (whether an asset or stock sale) to be in the form of debt. Debt, like other property received in connection with a sale, is subject to tax at its FMV. For debt instruments with regular, equal periodic payments of principal and market-rate interest, the FMV of the debt instrument is generally equal to its face amount. But where the terms of the debt instrument vary from this simple case, numerous special tax rules apply, including different rules for debt instruments with:

- Front-loaded payments of interest or principal;
- Back-loaded payments of interest or principal;
- Original issue discount;
- Variable rates of interest;
- Contingent payments of principal or interest; or
- Arrangements that the IRS considers abusive (typically through an uneconomic deferral of income/gain or an acceleration of deduction/loss).

In some cases, it may be possible for a Seller who receives a promissory note as full or partial consideration for a sale to defer taxable gain through the installment method of tax accounting. An installment sale occurs when the Seller receives at least one payment after the close of the tax year in which the sale occurs. By using this method, the Seller defers gain (and thus, tax) until payments are actually received. The Seller must determine a "gross profit ratio" (i.e., the ratio of profit on the sale to the total sale price) which it then multiplies by the amount of each payment received to determine the portion of that payment that is treated as taxable gain. The remaining portion of the payment is treated as nontaxable recovery of basis. Moreover, the Seller may also be required to pay interest to the IRS on the deferred tax liability.

Special rules apply to promissory notes if the payments under the instrument are contingent, either with respect to the amount due, the timing of the payment, or both. Contingent consideration is fairly common, especially when the Acquirer and the Seller cannot agree on price. These "earnouts" often provide for future payments to the Seller based on the financial performance of the business (e.g., meeting specified revenue or EBIDTA targets) or a future event (e.g., a sale of some or all of the business to a third party). The Acquirer makes this payment — if at all — in a year subsequent to the year of the initial sale if and when the contingency occurs.

Generally, the parties treat earnouts as an adjustment to the purchase price, so the Acquirer must capitalize the payments and the Seller recognizes gain or income, generally under the installment method for contingent liabilities described above.

State and Local Tax Considerations

State and local income taxes typically follow the federal income tax treatment of transactions, although there may be variations among the various states. (For example, Mississippi does not follow federal tax law regarding section 338 elections.) The location of business activities will also impact the extent to which income will be allocated and apportioned to a particular state. In addition, the Seller must consider that applicability of sales and use taxes on an asset sale (although in many states, there are exemptions for bulk sales or the sale of an entire business) and transfer taxes on real property. As a result, it is imperative for Sellers in particular to consider the impact of state and local taxes on a transaction.

Nontaxable Transactions

Any discussion of "nontaxable" transactions must begin by recognizing that these transactions are actually *not* nontaxable: rather, taxation is *deferred* until some later date. (In technical tax terminology, the gain resulting from the transaction is not *recognized* currently.) This is generally accomplished by maintaining the historical tax basis of the stock or assets that is the subject of the transaction so that the full amount of the historic gain is taxed when the stock or assets is disposed of.

Example (1)

Target has an FMV of $500. Seller owns all the shares of Target and has a tax basis of $100 in the shares. Seller exchanges all of its Target shares with Acquirer for shares of Acquirer in a transaction that qualifies as nontaxable. Seller takes a $100 tax basis in the shares of Acquirer that it receives and Acquirer takes a $100 basis in the Target shares. If Seller subsequently sells the Acquirer shares for $500, it will recognize $400 of gain just as if it had sold the shares initially for $500.

Example (2)

Target owns assets with an FMV of $500 but a tax basis of $100. Target transfers all of its assets to Acquirer in exchange for Acquirer stock and then Target liquidates, distributing all of the Acquirer shares to Target's shareholders in a transaction that qualifies as nontaxable. The Target shareholders take a $100 basis in the Acquirer stock and Acquirer takes a $100 basis in the assets that formerly belonged to Target and depreciates those assets based on that lower basis.

The rationale for this deferral is the Congress believed that the general rule of taxability can be relaxed in certain narrowly defined and specifically described situations involving more realignments of corporate structure. Nonrecognition is appropriate only for two specific types of transactions: (i) where stock or securities in a corporation is exchanged for stock and securities of another corporation that is a party to the same reorganization, and (ii) where a corporation exchanges property for stock or securities of another corporation that is a party to the same reorganization. A basic requirement for deferral, therefore, is that the transaction be characterized as a "reorganization."

> *In recent years, nontaxable transactions tend to be used primarily where the Target is a closely held corporation with one or more older shareholders. In this limited case, if the former Target shareholder holds the Acquirer's stock at his or her death, the heirs receive a fair market value basis in the shares and gain from the transaction is permanently eliminated.*

Corporate Reorganizations

Section 368(a)(1) describes the basic types of transactions that can constitute "reorganizations" and thus can be nontaxable. The relevant subsection of section 368(a)(1) gives its name to each type of transaction:

(A) a merger or consolidation of two or more corporations under a state corporate merger statute (Figure 5);
(B) the acquisition by one corporation in exchange solely for its voting stock of control (i.e., at least 80% of the voting stock and 80% of all classes of stock) of another corporation (Figure 6);
(C) the acquisition by one corporation in exchange solely for its voting stock of substantially all the assets of another corporation (Figure 7);
(D) a transfer by a corporation of all or part of its assets to another corporation if immediately after the transfer the transferor controls the transferee corporation but only if the stock or securities received from the transferee corporation are distributed to the shareholders of the transferor (Figure 8);
(E) a recapitalization;
(F) a mere change in identity, form, or place of organization of one corporation; and

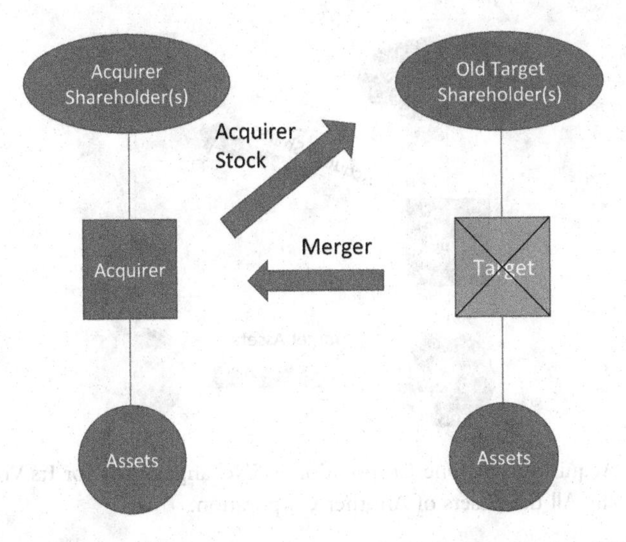

Figure 5: A Merger or Consolidation of Two or More Corporations Under a State Corporate Merger Statute.

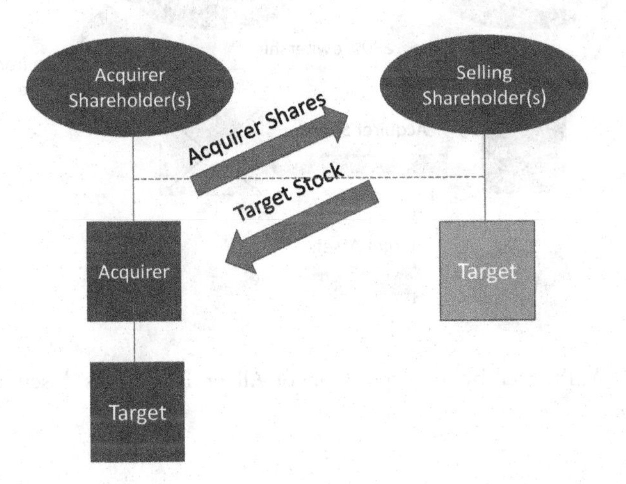

Figure 6: Acquisition by One Corporation in Exchange Solely for Its Voting Stock of Control.

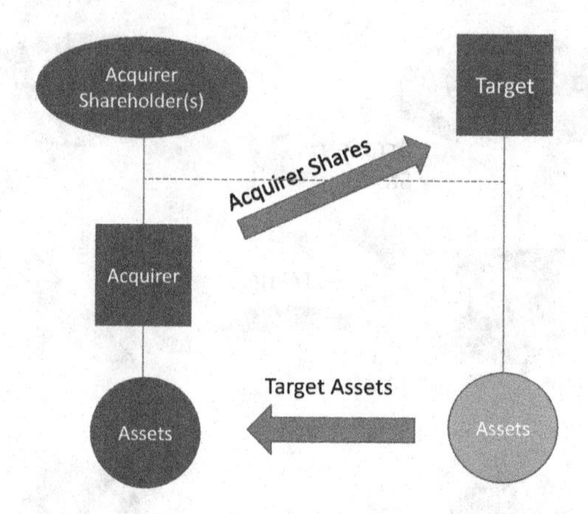

Figure 7: Acquisition by One Corporation in Exchange Solely for Its Voting Stock of Substantially All the Assets of Another Corporation.

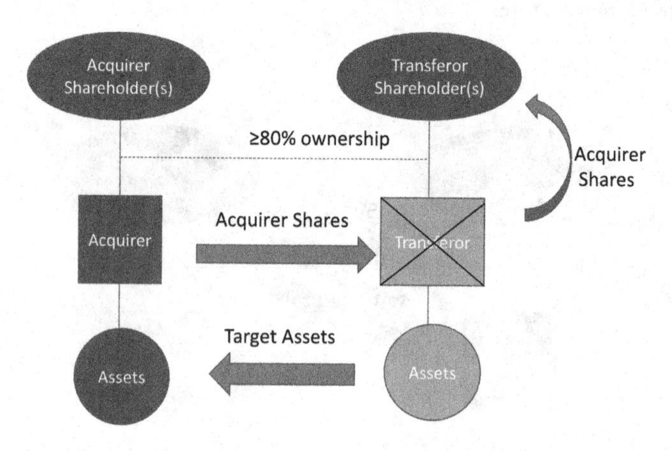

Figure 8: A Transfer by a Corporation of All or Part of Its Assets to Another Corporation.

(G) a transfer by a corporation of all or part of its assets to another corporation pursuant to a plan of bankruptcy but only if the stock or securities received from the transferee corporation are distributed to the shareholders of the transferor.

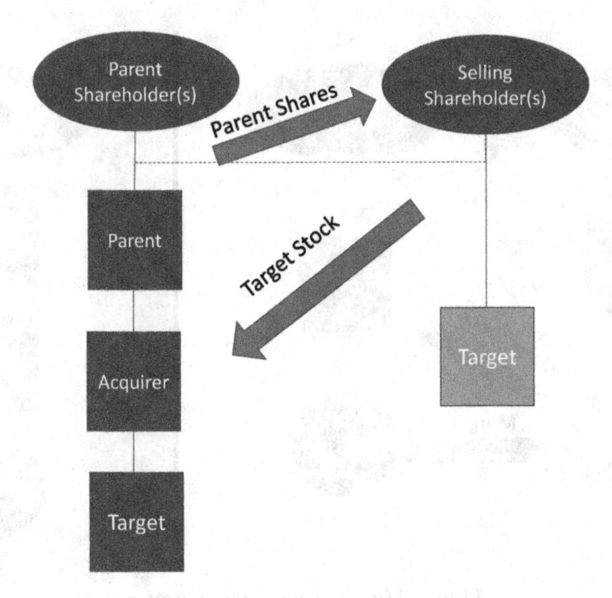

Figure 9: Stock of the Acquirer's Parent Corporation Used Instead of Stock of the Acquirer.

Some variations on these basic transactions are allowable. For example, in both (B) and (C) reorganizations, stock of the Acquirer's parent corporation may be used instead of stock of the Acquirer (Figure 9).

Another variation is a reverse transaction, in which a new corporation ("NewCo") merges with Target in exchange for the stock of NewCo's parent corporation, with Target the surviving corporation rather than NewCo (Figure 10).

The variety of reorganization forms gives a certain amount of flexibility to planning a tax-free transaction to accommodate non-tax business considerations. For example, the existence of contingent or undisclosed liabilities of Target would likely lead the Acquirer to favor a type C asset reorganization rather than a type A or B transaction, because in an asset deal, the Acquirer will not succeed to the Target's liabilities unless expressly assuming them. Similarly, if the Target has certain nontransferable rights (e.g.,

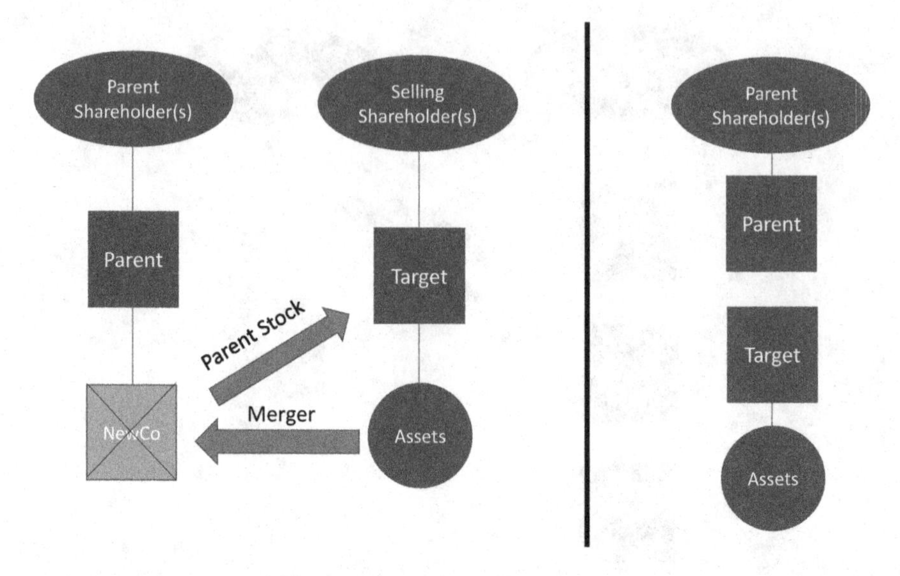

Figure 10: Reverse Transaction.

licenses or intangible property), a type B or a reverse triangular merger would be indicated. Finally, a type A merger usually requires the shareholders of both corporations to approve the transaction, so some other form should be considered where such approval may be questionable.

In addition to the detailed requirements of section 368, regulations — based on years of case law — impose additional requirements beyond those specified in the statute.

- *Continuity of interest* requires that a substantial part of the value received by the transferor must continue the transferor's equity investment. The purpose for this requirement is to ensure that transactions that resemble sales are taxed. The requirement is generally met if at least 40% of the total value of consideration received by the transferor is stock (including certain preferred stock) of the Acquirer.

> *Problems can arise if the value of either the Target or Acquirer, or both, changes between the time the amount of consideration is agreed by the parties and the closing date. For example, if the parties agree that 42% of the consideration is to be in the form of Acquirer common stock and the value of Acquirer stock declines by the time of closing, then the value of the equity consideration may be less than 40% at closing and the reorganization may fail. Many agreements handle this problem by providing for an adjustment to the amount of Acquirer stock to ensure the required continuity.*

- *Continuity of business enterprise* requires that Acquirer must continue to engage in Target's historic business. The purpose for this rule is to ensure that reorganizations are limited to readjustments of continuing interests in property under modified corporate form. If Target had more than one historic business, Acquirer need only continue one significant line of business.
- *Business purpose* requires that the corporations must have a substantial, nontax business reason for the transaction, not merely to benefit the shareholders of either Target or Acquirer. Thus, e.g., shareholder estate planning is not an acceptable business purpose for a reorganization absent some other nontax reason for undertaking the transaction.
- *Net value* requires that each corporation that is a party to the reorganization must be solvent (i.e., that the FMV of its assets must exceed its liabilities). If this were not the case, the corporation's stock would have no value; it would have no "stock" and thus the continuity of interest test would not be met.
- *A plan of reorganization* must be adopted by each corporation that is a party to the reorganization. This should be a formal action by the Board of Directors (or, if necessary, the shareholders) describing a transaction that is specifically described as a reorganization). Each corporation must also report the transaction to the IRS on its tax return.

Generally, these requirements are designed to ensure that the transaction has *economic substance* (i.e., real legal and economic rights and obligations are altered in the course of the transaction, which must reflect an intention to make a profit). In addition, the IRS can invoke the *step-transaction doctrine*, which collapses a multistep transaction into a single step to more accurately reflect the economic reality of what happened (and, perhaps not coincidentally, frustrate the taxpayer's intention to avoid tax).

Corporate Separations

Frequently, corporations with multiple lines of businesses want to divest one or more of them to focus on its core activities. Where there is no acquirer willing to pay what the corporation believes these unwanted businesses are worth, shareholder value may often be obtained by spinning off the unwanted businesses to shareholders.

Generally, a distribution by a corporation of appreciated property (which can include stock of a subsidiary) is taxable to both the corporation and the shareholder because it would otherwise subject corporate profits to only a single level of tax. As with reorganizations, however, if specific and detailed requirements can be met, no gain may be recognized on a corporate separation. Section 355 of the Code provides the detailed requirements for a nontaxable corporate separation (Figure 11):

(1) A corporation ("Distributing") distributes to its shareholders or to its security holders in exchange for its stock or securities;
(2) Solely stock or securities of a corporation ("Controlled") which it controls immediately before the distribution;
(3) The transaction is not used principally as a device for the distribution of earnings and profits of either Distributing or Controlled or both (i.e., converting ordinary income into capital gain);
(4) Either immediately after the distribution both Distributing and Controlled are engaged in and have engaged for the past 5 years in the active conduct of a trade or business, or immediately before the distribution Distributing was a holding company

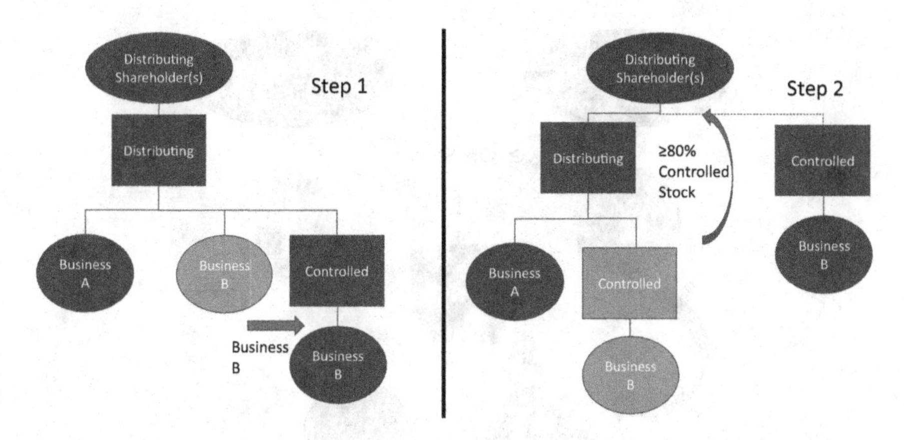

Figure 11: Detailed Requirements for a Nontaxable Corporate Separation.

whose only assets were the stock of corporations engaged in the active conduct of a trade or business;

(5) Distributing distributes control of Controlled;

(6) 50% of the distributed stock was not acquired by Distributing within the 5-year period ending on the date of the date of the distribution; and

(7) The distribution is not part of a plan or series of related transactions in which one or more persons acquire, directly or indirectly, stock representing a 50% of greater interest in Distributing or any Controlled.

If these requirements are all met, Distributing recognizes no gain on the distribution. The shareholders receiving Controlled stock or securities must allocate a portion of their pre-transaction tax basis in their Distributing stock to the Controlled stock or securities based on relative fair market values. As with reorganizations, the net effect of the transaction is that the shareholders defer — rather than eliminate — tax.

Transfers to a Corporation

Another technique to accomplish a nontaxable corporate M&A transaction is by transferring existing businesses (or stock of a corporation

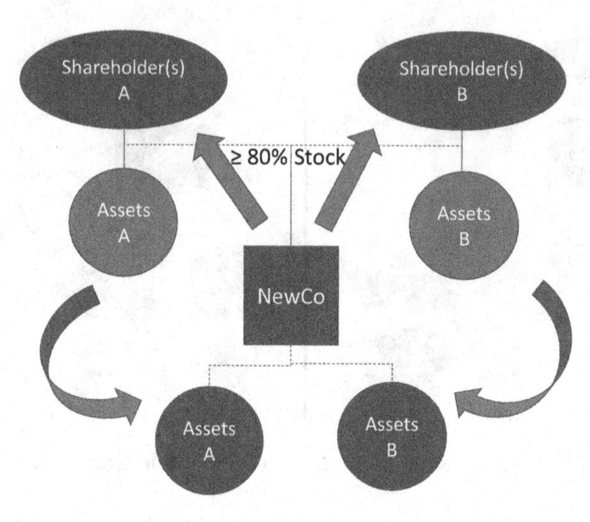

Figure 12: Accomplishment of a Nontaxable Corporate M&A Transaction.

owning such businesses) to a new corporation in exchange for stock of NewCo; the transferors as a group own sufficient stock to control NewCo immediately after the transfers. Again, this is a deferral technique: The transferors take a tax basis in the NewCo stock equal to their tax basis in the property transferred and NewCo takes a tax basis in the property equal to the property's tax basis in the hands of the transferors (Figure 12).

In this case, unlike some (but not all) of the other nontaxable transactions described above, the transferors may receive money or other property ("boot") in addition to stock or securities without disqualifying the nontaxability of the transaction. If that occurs, the shareholders will recognize gain to the extent of the FMV of the property received.

International Considerations

The opening of the European Union and economic reforms in the developing world have made most countries friendly to international M&As. Since the early 1990's, the pace of cross-border M&A activity has grown considerably. There are many benefits to companies that pursue international M&As. From a business perspective, they provide an opportunity to expand into new markets without having to build an infrastructure and customer base from scratch. From a tax perspective, many developing countries have adopted liberal tax and economic policies which provide huge benefits for companies that invest there.

International M&As, however, present many challenges as well. For instance, certain countries may require a local partner — often the government. Local labor regulations may also be quite strict thereby reducing flexibility in expanding or contracting the work force. Currency restrictions may make it difficult to repatriate profits and exchange rates can be challenging when currencies weaken or strengthen relative to the dollar. Furthermore, structuring a tax-advantaged deal may prove difficult when the buyer and seller are subject to the tax laws of different countries and the transaction may be treated differently in each.

One of the most controversial areas of international M&As is corporate inversions. In its simplest form, a foreign company acquires the stock or assets of a US company. The shareholders of the US company become the shareholders of the foreign company. The result is that the legal location of the combined entity transfers from the US to a foreign jurisdiction. Typically, the physical location or the business operation of the company remains the same.

Tax-motivated corporate inversions are the result of a significant disparity in the corporate tax rates of the US versus most of the world. The top Federal statutory rate in the US is 35%. In Ireland, for example, it is 12.5%. Under US tax law, a domestic corporation is taxed on its worldwide income. Most foreign jurisdictions take a territorial approach. That is, the income is taxed only where it is earned.

Domestic corporations benefit from a corporate inversion by potentially reducing taxes on its domestically earned income. Under the most common scheme, the US company issues debt to its new foreign parent. The domestic company can then deduct the interest and the foreign parent recognizes the interest income in a lower tax jurisdiction. Another popular strategy is to transfer ownership of intangible assets such as patents and trademarks to the foreign parent.

The income generated by these intangibles is then attributed to the foreign parent.

For several years now, lawmakers have attempted to halt corporate inversions. However, the members of both political parties favor different approaches and no consensus has been reached on how to thwart the practice through legislation. In the interim, the Treasury Department has used its regulation-making ability to make inversions more difficult. In 2014, it issued a rule that restricts the ownership of the inverted entity to less than 80% by the owners of the former US company. In 2016, Treasury attacked the practice of using intercompany loans, commonly referred to as "earnings stripping". It introduced new regulations under Section 385 to curb this practice by treating certain debt as equity thereby eliminating the interest deduction in the US.

Practical Issues

Partnerships

In a situation where there may be multiple acquirers, a joint venture may be used to purchase a target corporation or its assets. A joint venture may be structured as either a corporation or a flow-through entity such as a partnership or LLC. A flow-through entity is generally not subject to taxation at the Federal level. Rather, the partners are taxed directly on their proportionate share of the flow-through entity's income. Some states, however, do tax such entities.

Purchasing the assets of a business may be beneficial when there are two or more corporate partners neither of which owns at least 80% of the voting stock and 80% of the value of all classes of stock. Under such an arrangement, the corporate partners would be precluded from filing a consolidated tax return with the target operation. With a partnership structure, however, the income and losses of the partnership will flow through to the corporate partners in effect providing many of the same benefits of a consolidated tax return.

A noncorporate entity such as a partnership or LLC may elect to be taxed as a corporation. If the entity makes such an election, it generally is treated as a corporation under any Internal Revenue Code section relating to corporations. Consequently, a partnership or LLC that has elected to be taxed as a corporation may engage in a tax-free reorganization with another corporation.

Due Diligence

One of the most important steps in any acquisition is the tax due diligence process. In a stock acquisition, the liabilities of the target corporation will carry over to the new owners. Tax liabilities, in particular, may not be recorded on the company's books. Therefore, a purchaser must exercise caution in order to avoid surprises down the road. In negotiating the acquisition, the purchaser may wish to include a tax indemnity clause in the purchase agreement which would make the sellers contractually liable for any preclosing tax liabilities which may surface during a specified period of time after the acquisition. However, this may be neither possible nor practical in the acquisition of a publicly traded company with hundreds or thousands of shareowners.

The first step in any tax due diligence is to review the target corporation's financial statements. Accounting Standards Codification Topic 740 (ASC 740) requires any uncertain tax positions that the target may have taken be reserved as a potential liability. The purchaser must become familiar with the underlying tax issues and their potential impact on the target's operations.

The purchaser should also review the deferred taxes and liabilities recorded on the balance sheet and the components of both. Deferred tax assets (DTAs) and deferred tax liabilities (DTLs) provide the purchaser with an understanding of the timing of certain items of income and expense where there is a difference between the book and tax treatment. In particular, the buyer should understand the nature of any DTLs. If the target corporation has a DTL, it may indicate that the purchaser is paying for income that was earned during a preacquisition period. Conversely, DTAs such as net operating loss carryforwards may impact the purchase price and the purchaser should verify that they will be able to utilize the tax assets for which they are paying.

From a state perspective, the purchaser should examine the target's "tax footprint." That is, the states and localities in which the company conducts business. In the past, it was relatively straightforward to determine whether a taxpayer had nexus in a particular jurisdiction. Generally, the taxpayer had to have a physical presence there whether it took the form of an office or employees who regularly conducted business within its geographic boundaries. With internet commerce becoming more prevalent, states have rewritten the rules on nexus. Many states now have adopted the concept of "economic nexus" and have extended their reach to tax businesses whose only connection is that they make sales into their jurisdiction. As a consequence of the lack of uniformity across all states, it is imperative that the buyer have a thorough understanding of the target's business operations in order to determine if there are any noncompliance issues.

In addition to state income tax issues, sales and use taxes and unclaimed property must also be examined. The purchaser must assess whether the target company has the proper systems and procedures in place to properly collect sales tax. This is especially important for businesses where some sales may be exempt from sales tax. In these cases, the target should maintain a file of resale and exemption certificates from its customers. To the extent that the business has not properly collected sales tax from its customers, the business may be held liable.

States have become increasingly aggressive in pursuing businesses that do not properly account for unclaimed property. The funds represented by uncashed checks and unused gift cards, e.g., do not revert back to the issuer. They are required to be turned over to the state for safe keeping after a dormancy period. The purchaser should review the target's process for identifying unclaimed property and insure that any unclaimed funds have been remitted to the appropriate state.

To the extent that the purchaser has identified any potential tax issues, an indemnification may be sought from the seller. Alternatively, the purchaser may adjust the offering price as compensation for any tax risks that may be assumed with the acquisition.

Bibliography

B. Bittker & J. Eustace, *Federal Income Taxation of Corporations and Shareholders, 7th Ed.*, 2000 & Supp., Warren Gorham & Lamont, Valhalla, NY.

M. Ginsburg, J. Levin, & D. Rocap, *Mergers, Acquisitions and Buyouts*, 2016, Wolters Kluwer Legal & Regulatory U.S., New York.

D. K. Dolan, P. Jackman, P. Tretiak, & R. Dabrowski, *U.S. Taxation of International Mergers, Acquisitions and Joint Ventures*, 2010 & Supp., Warren Gorham & Lamont, Valhalla, NY.

Chapter 11

Leveraged Buyouts (LBOs): The Financial Engineering of Transactions and Evolution of LBOs

Chris Droussiotis*,†
*Leveraged & Structured Finance, SMBC
†FDU

Introduction

Definition & Terms

Since the start of recorded history, investors have been borrowing money to achieve their dreams. More than 3,000 years ago, people were borrowing money in Mesopotamia and paying interest. Christopher Columbus borrowed from the Queen of Spain, Isabella, most of the funds required for his transatlantic voyage that discovered America. At the start of the 20th century, J. P. Morgan raised through debt much of the funding required for the acquisition of Carnegie Steel, which was then combined with other steel companies to form US Steel. With a capitalization of $1.4 billion,[1] US Steel was the world's most valuable corporation.

[1] Encyclopedia.com, copyright 2006, Thomson Gate.

A Leveraged Buyout (LBO) is what occurs when an investor, typically a private equity investor (sometimes referred to as a financial sponsor), acquires an entity (which we will call "the Target Company"), using mainly borrowed funds. The Target Company can be a company, a division of a company, a business, or a collection of assets. The investor is typically not personally responsible for paying the debt incurred for the acquisition, nor is he required to add any other capital to support his or her investment; the acquisition debt is therefore described as being "nonrecourse" to the investor. The acquisition debt is obtained by issuing bonds or securing a loan, and relies on the acquired company for its repayment. The acquisition debt is repaid either from the company's operating cash flows, or from the sale of all or a portion of the company, or from the refinancing of the acquisition debt with new debt that is similarly reliant on the company for its repayment.

The amount of debt used to finance an LBO as a percentage of the purchase price, varies per the financial condition and history of the Target Company's performance, market conditions and the willingness of creditors to extend credit. Typically, the debt portion of a LBO ranges from 50% to 80% of the purchase price, but in some cases, debt may be as high as 95% of the purchase price. Companies with stable and predictable cash flows that can reliably service debt obligations represent the most attractive LBO candidates. To finance LBOs private-equity firms, issue a combination of syndicated loans and high-yield bonds which are supported by the credit strength of the Target Company. The mechanism is described later in this chapter.

History of LBOs

The LBO boom of the 1980s was spearheaded by several financial sponsors, most notably: KKR, which was founded by Jerome Kohlberg Jr., Henry Kravis, and George Roberts; The Carlyle Group, which was founded by David Rubenstein, William Conway, and Dan D'Aniello; Blackstone, which was founded by Stephan Schwartzman and Peter Peterson; and Apollo, which was founded by Leon Black.[2]

---

[2] Private Equity and M&A Database.

The acquisition of Target Companies via LBOs required equity funding in addition to debt funding. Financial sponsors would create Limited Partnership (LP) vehicles that were sponsor controlled, which would raise funding from large pension funds, insurance companies, financial institutions, and high net worth individuals, to finance the equity portion of the acquisitions. The LP vehicles were large enough to provide equity financing for numerous acquisitions, so that the financial sponsor did not need to go into fund raising mode every time they undertook an acquisition. In turn, the LP structure benefitted investors by providing them with diversification across several Target Companies. Today there are more than 6,000 private equity firms (financial sponsors) that undertake LBOs.[3]

In the 1980s, the investment bank Drexel Burnham Lambert and the head of its high-yield bond business, Michael Milken, played a leading role in establishing the high-yield bond market.[4] High-yield bonds were an important source of funds for LBOs, and provided higher leverage than banks could offer. Bank loans were another cheaper complimentary source of funds for LBOs. Bank loans would typically be underwritten by lead arranger banks, which would then reduce their risk exposure by selling the loan down to other banks. This organized process for attracting other banks to the loan financing was called a loan syndication, and LBOs were important in expanding the loan syndication market.

The signature LBO of the 1980s and 1990s was the 1989 $31.1 billion acquisition of RJR Nabisco by KKR, which was the largest LBO to that time. The LBO was described in the book (and later the movie) "Barbarians at the Gate: The Fall of RJR Nabisco" written by investigative journalists Bryan Burrough and John Helyar.[5]

---

[3] *The Economist*, Article: "The Barbarian Establishment", Print Edition, October 22, 2016, New York.

[4] *The Business Insider*, Article: "Michael Milken invented the modern junk bond, went to prison, and then became one of the most respected people on Wall Street", William D. Cohan, May 2, 2017.

[5] *Barbarians at the Gate, The Fall of RJR Nabisco*, Brian Burrough & John Helyar, Harper & Row, Publishers, 1988.

The Mega Deals of 2005–2007:

2000s: The Decade of Mega Deals and the Birth of CLOs (2003-2007)

In the mid-2000s, a combination of factors set the stage for a second LBO boom. This combination included decreasing interest rates, loosening lending standards, creation of loan funds known as Collateral Loan Obligations (CLOs) — which provided an aggressive complement to commercial bank loans, and regulatory changes for publicly traded companies (specifically the Sarbanes–Oxley Act). Mega deals included the $49 billion acquisition of the utility company TXU — the largest ever LBO — which was bought by a consortium of investors including KKR, and large LBOs for companies such as HCA, Harrahs and Sungard. Figure 1 below shows the amount of debt raised to finance these mega deals.[6]

Types of LBO Transactions

Public to Private Transactions

For a successful LBO execution, you need the cooperation of multiple parties including the investor (typically a Private Equity firm), a loan

---

[6] LoanConnector.

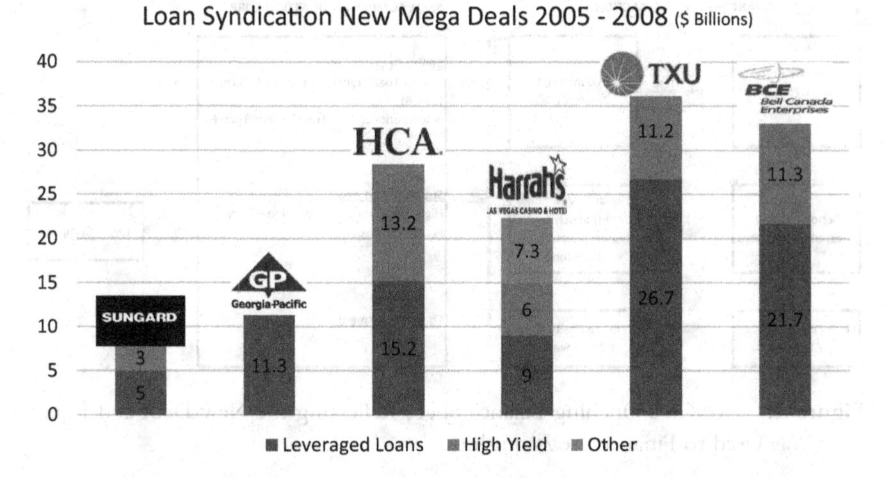

Figure 1: Amount of Debt Raised to Finance Mega Deals.

arranger (typically a commercial or investment bank) that arranges the acquisition loans, and an investment bank that underwrites the bond debt. These parties are each required to underwrite their portion of the funding at the time that the acquisition bid is made.

A shell company (let's name it Acquisition Corp.) is typically created to serve as the vehicle for the acquisition financing. Acquisition Corp. then tenders for all the shares of the public company, and if it is successful in acquiring a pre-established majority of the shares, it merges with the target company to create the surviving entity ("NewCo"), which will be responsible for paying back the acquisition debt. NewCo's opening balance sheet reflects the new debt and equity that that was used to finance the acquisition (Figure 2), and any old debt and equity that remained after the acquisition.

Private to Private Transactions

Private to private company sales are also referred to as secondary LBOs, and in such sales, a private equity firm sells the Target Company to another private equity firm. Like the public to private

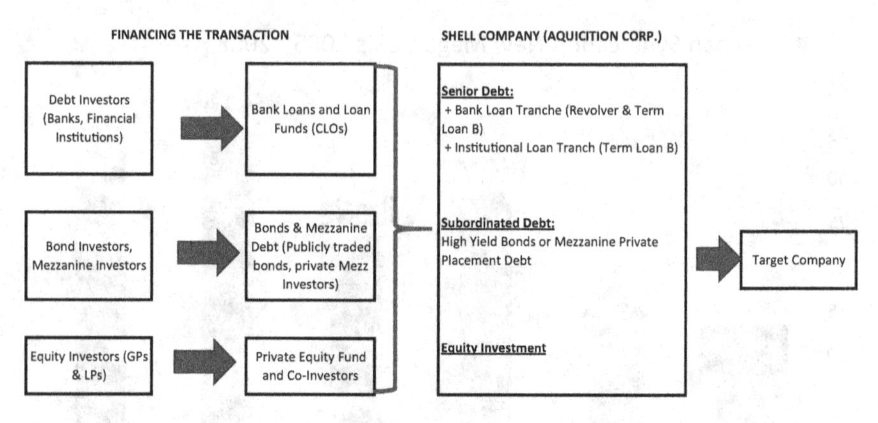

Figure 2: NewCo's Opening Balance Sheet Reflecting the New Debt and Equity That Was Used to Finance the Acquisition.

transaction described above, in private to private transactions, the new debt and equity financing is reflected in the opening balance sheet of the surviving entity (let's call it NewCo) going forward.

Typically, the Target Company's pre-existing debt is refinanced with new acquisition debt at the time of the company's change of ownership. This is required because it is normally stipulated in the Loan Agreement governing the pre-existing loan that upon a "change of control" of the borrower, the loan will become due and payable. This feature forces the refinancing of the pre-existing loan, and serves to prevent the equity investors from being repaid prior to the lenders. There have however been instances where the governing Loan Agreement permitted a change of control without forcing a refinancing of the pre-existing debt. Such Loan Agreements would still however have other controls to safeguard the lenders' and loan investors' interests. These safeguards would typically restrict the incurrence of additional debt by the loan obligor, restrict additional liens benefitting other obligors, prohibit certain types of payments (e.g., dividends to the equity) and there may also be loan acceleration triggers if the performance of the obligor materially deteriorates from its projected levels (these triggers are called financial covenants, of which the most common is based on the borrower's Total Debt/EBITDA ratio — sometimes known as the Leverage Ratio).

Management Buyouts Transactions

When an LBO is led by the existing management, it is called a Management Buyout or MBO. (Nonmanagement employees sometimes also participate in MBOs.) MBOs are more common in Europe and Asia than the US. In an MBO, management contributes its pre-existing company ownership to the buyout and raises the rest of the financing from other equity coinvestors and from bank lenders and bond investors. MBOs can serve as a defensive mechanism that allows existing management to continue running the Target Company, rather than having the company being acquired by external parties which typically bring their own management to the LBO.

A study called "Management Buyouts as a Response to Market Pressure", written by Andrei Shleifer and Robert W. Vishny suggested that the hostile takeover environment of the 1980s put pressure on existing management to take defensive measurements to keep their jobs.[7] One consequence of these measures is that companies becomes more efficient. In response to these market pressures, management of large publicly traded companies, like RJR Nabisco in the late 1980s, were proactively raising funds to defend against these raiders — basically adding debt to the existing operation by buying back the company's stock and make it almost impossible for takeover raiders to acquire the company. In the RJR Nabisco LBO, Ross Johnson, the company's CEO at the time, was trying to convince his board of directors to buy back some of RJR's shares by using funds from third-party friendly investors — called White Knights. Had Ross Johnson been successful, existing management would have continued running RJR Nabisco.[8]

---

[7] M&As, Study: "Management Buyouts as a Response to Market Pressures", Andrei Shleifer & Robert W. Vishny, University of Chicago Press, 1987.

[8] M&As, Study: "Management Buyouts as a Response to Market Pressures", Andrei Shleifer & Robert W. Vishny, University of Chicago Press, 1987.

Tax Advantages of LBOs

An equity investor that uses leverage to buy a company via an LBO can benefit from the tax deductibility of interest expense from the acquisition debt. The example below (Figure 3) shows that adding debt significantly improves the investor's ROA thus making the investment more attractive. This could motivate investors to pay more for the company than they otherwise would.

As an example, let us consider a company that has no debt, a $10 million book value for its assets and a $10 million net worth, which generates $1.5 million p.a. of EBIT. The company's After-tax Income (Net Income) assuming a 33% tax rate, would be $1 million p.a. Using this Income and Balance Sheet information, we can calculate that both the company's Return on Assets (ROA) and that it's Return on Equity (ROE) are both 10% p.a.:

LEVERAGED BUYOUTS: ENHANCING EQUITY RETURNS

Your Business

Income Statement		Balance Sheet Statement		Liabilities		
EBIT	$ 1.5 million	Assets				
Interest Exp.	0.0	Fixed Assets	$10.0 million	Debt	$ 0.0 million	ROA= 10%
Pretax Income	1.5			Equity	10.0	ROE= 10%
Taxes (33%)	0.5					
Net Income	**1.0**	**Total Assets**	**10.0**	**Total Eq. & Liab.**	**10.0**	

The Offer to Purchase at $10mm Book Value financed by 90% Debt @ 10% Rate and 10% Equity

LBO: NewCo

Income Statement		Balance Sheet Statement		Liabilities		
EBIT	$ 1.5 million	Assets				
Interest Exp.	0.9	Fixed Assets	$10.0 million	Debt	$ 9.0 million	ROA= 4%
Pretax Income	0.6			Equity	1.0	ROE= 40%
Taxes (33%)	0.2					
Net Income	**0.4**	**Total Assets**	**10.0**	**Total Eq. & Liab.**	**10.0**	

Figure 3: Example Showing That Adding Debt Significantly Improves the Investor's ROA Thus Making the Investment More Attractive.

$$\text{ROA} = \frac{\text{Net Income}}{\text{Average Total Assets}} \Rightarrow \text{ROA}\frac{\$1{,}000{,}000}{\$10{,}000{,}000} = 0.1 \text{ or } 10\%,$$

$$\text{ROE} = \frac{\text{Return on Income}}{\text{Shareholders' Equity}} \Rightarrow \text{ROE}\frac{\$1{,}000{,}000}{\$10{,}000{,}000} = 0.1 \text{ or } 10\%.$$

Now let us assume, as shown in Figure 4, that an acquirer initiates an offer to acquire the company at its book value of $10 million, which is also equal to 10 times the company's Net Income. Let us assume that this transaction will be funded with 90% debt at the cost of 10% p.a. and with 10% equity.

$$\text{Interest Expense} = \$9{,}000{,}000 \times 10\% = \$900{,}000 \text{ p.a.}$$

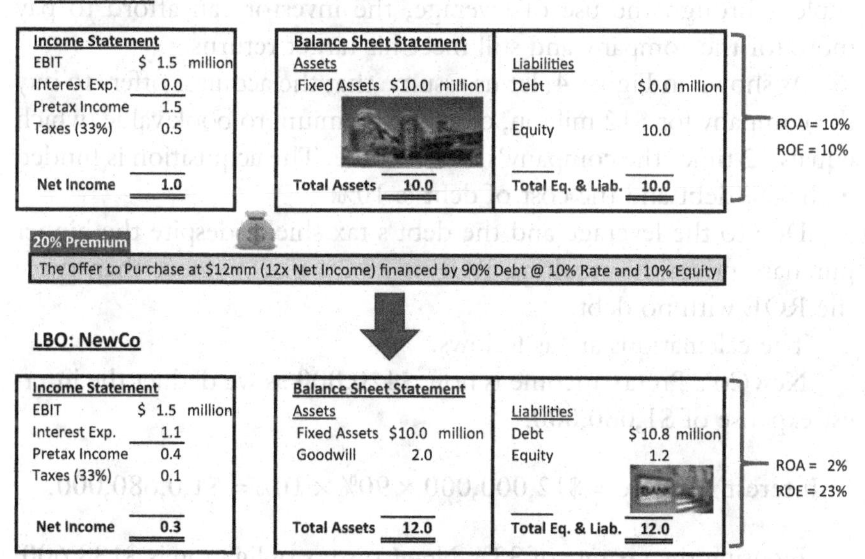

Figure 4: Acquirer Initiating an Offer to Acquire the Company at Its Book Value of $10 Million, Which Is Also Equal to 10 Times the Company's Net Income.

In this case, NewCo's Income Statement would have EBIT of $1.5 million p.a. and $900,000 p.a. of interest expense, which would yield Pretax Income of $600,000 p.a. and (After-tax) Net Income of $400,000 p.a.

Part of the additional interest expense created by the debt is offset (and in a sense subsidized by the tax payers) through a reduction in Income Taxes — this is refered to as a tax shield. In our first example, the company had a tax obligation of $500,000, while in the second example, NewCo would only have a tax obligation of approximately $200,000. Using this new Income and Balance Sheet information, we can recalculate ROE as shown below.

$$\text{ROE} = \frac{\text{Return on Income}}{\text{Shareholders' Equity}} \Rightarrow \text{ROE}\frac{\$400{,}000}{\$1{,}000{,}000} = 0.400 \text{ or } 40.00\%.$$

This example shows that the incurrence of debt creates a tax advantage for the owners of the company which can increase shareholders' returns dramatically. Since the equity return has been quatrupled through the use of leverage, the investor can afford to pay more for the company and still meet his target returns.

As shown in Figure 4, let us assume that the acquirer offers to buy the company for $12 million, or a 20% premium to book value, which equals 12 times the company's Net Income. The acquisition is funded with 90% debt and the cost of debt is 10%.

Due to the leverage and the debt's tax shield, despite the higher purchase price, the resulting ROE is 23.3% p.a. or more than twice the ROE with no debt.

The calculations are as follows.

NewCo's Pretax Income is now $420,000 as we deduct the interest expense of $1,080,000:

$$\text{Interest Expense} = \$12{,}000{,}000 \times 90\% \times 10\% = \$1{,}0{,}680{,}000.$$

By using the tax rate of 33%, NewCo's tax obligation is $138,600. After deducting taxes from NewCo's pretax income, we obtain Net Income of $281,400.

With this new Balance Sheet and Income Statement we can calculate NewCo's ROE at 23% as shown below:

$$\text{ROE} = \frac{\text{Return on Income}}{\text{Shareholders' Equity}} \Rightarrow \text{ROE}\frac{\$281,400}{\$1,200,000} = 0.23 \text{ or } 23\%.$$

Other Tax Advantages from LBOs — Historical Perspective

In earlier LBOs, various financiers were motivated by tax breaks and loopholes to enhance their return. A few examples from high profile transactions are highlighted below.

Singer Company LBO

In 1987, the Florida financier Paul A. Bilzerian, set out for LBO of the Singer Company (known for its sewing machines) which had branched out and purchased several defense and electronics companies. Each of Singer's operations were held in separate subsidiaries. Believing that the sum of the parts was worth more than the value ascribed to the overall company by the market, Mr. Bilzerian wished to break up the company and to sell each of its subsidiaries separately to avoid capital gains tax on the sale of each subsidiary, Mr. Bilzerian separated his financing vehicle (Acquisition Corp.) into a series of subsidiaries (called "mirror subsidiaries") that mirrored Singer's existing subsidiaries, and allocated the acquisition debt to each of the mirror subsidiaries according to the value attributed to each of the existing subsidiaries. Upon the acquisition of Singer, each of the mirror subsidiaries was then merged with the corresponding Singer subsidiary and the mirror debt was assumed by the Singer subsidiary. When the subsidiary's shares were sold by the parent company, the purchaser would need to pay off the assumed debt at the subsidiary, thereby depressing the value of the subsidiary's shares. This reduced the taxable income on the sale, with the effect being the same as if the tax basis of the shares had been written up by the value of the assumed debt. The mirror strategy permitted the subsidiaries to be sold with minimal taxable gains accruing to the parent company. (Despite the success of the tax structure, Bilzerian ended up miscalculating the value of the individual subsidiaries, and the common equity in the acquisition had negative returns.[9])

Congoleum MBO

Another example of an acquisition creating tax advantages for the buyer was the 1979 MBO of Congoleum Inc., a diversified firm in shipbuilding, flooring, and automotive accessories. The postacquisition Congoleum was able to write up its assets by $400MM to reflect the acquisition price. This resulted in a significant incremental tax shield for postacquisition Congoleum, which materially enhanced the attractiveness of the LBO. In recent years however, the tax code regarding asset step-ups has changed and is less favorable to LBOs.[10]

Fairfield Gear Manufacturing — Private LBO

Another example from the earlier LBOs is the 1989 acquisition of Fairfield Gear Manufacturing, an Indiana based company. Peter Joseph, Angus Littlejohn and Paul Levy founded a private equity firm called JLL which aimed to take advantage of a $29MM Net Operating Loss Tax Carryforward (NOL) that they inherited from Rexene Corporation. JLL intended to use the $29MM NOL by buying profitable companies such as Fairfield Gear Manufacturing Company (MGC), and sheltering its income by combining its tax returns with those of the company with the NOLs. JLL additionally arranged for the acquired company to sign a tax sharing agreement with JLL, which reflected in the tax benefits from the NOLs being paid by

---

[9] *The New York Times*, Article: "How Bilzerian Scored at Singer", Alison Leigh Cowan, published August 24, 1988.

[10] M&As, Study: "Management Buyouts as a Response to Market Pressures", Andrei Shleifer & Robert W. Vishny, University of Chicago Press, 1987.

postacquisition to JLL — basically instead of sending a check to the IRS, MGC would send the check to JLL.[11]

Despite new, tighter rules in calculating taxes, including restrictions on capital gain tax shields, NOL carryovers and the goodwill tax deduction, new LBOs continue to benefit from elements of the tax code, the most important of which is the tax deductibility of interest expense.

Capital Markets

Bank Debt and Institutional Floating Rate Loans

Bank Debt is the primary source of capital for an LBO transaction and provides a lower cost of capital than other debt tranches used to finance a transaction. Bank Debt, also mentioned as Senior Debt, typically consists of a revolving credit facility (a type of loan that can be paid and reborrowed multiple times until its maturity — whose main purpose is to finance the company's working capital), and one or more term loans which are only borrowed at the time of acquisition and cannot be reborrowed after repayment. The revolving credit facility can be structured as an asset-based lending facility or as a cash flow revolver. The bank debt's interest rate is usually based on a floating benchmark (usually LIBOR) plus a spread that reflects the borrower's credit quality and market receptivity.

A. Revolving Credit Facility or Working Capital Facility (RC). This is the typical "Revolver" that we come across on a company's Balance Sheet. It works similarly to the credit cards we use every day. It is a line of credit that is provided by a bank or a group of banks (aka "syndicate") to the borrowing company and has a specific withdrawal limit as well as a specified maturity date. Most companies use revolvers as an immediate injection of liquidity to support increasing capital expenditures and working

[11] *The New York Times*, Article: Company News: Neoax Unit Sales, Reuters, July 11, 1989.

capital needs. In an LBO, the revolver is usually priced at the same level as the term loan. In a typical LBO transaction, the maturity of the revolver (often referred to as its "tenor") is approximately 5 years or 1–2 years shorter than the term loan. A typical Revolver includes financial covenants (performance based financial ratios) such as the Leverage Test described above. To minimize the risk that the borrower is unable to fulfill its future interest and principal payment obligations to its banks, covenants can also be established to restrict the borrower's ability to engage in further acquisitions, to raise debt, to make dividend payments to the equity holders and to control how the borrower applies its fund. For example, a covenant may require the borrower to apply the net proceeds of an asset sale to pay down debt.

B. **Asset-Based Lending Facility (ABL).** This is type of revolver is used by companies that have a strong and liquid asset base. The lender is given priority over the borrower's current assets, and additionally the lender may obtain a second priority lien (after the Term Loan lenders) over the borrower's other collateral. The amount that can be drawn under an ABL facility is governed by advance rates against the pledged assets. For example, Accounts Receivable, which are a particularly liquid current asset, are sometimes given an advance rate of 85%. Because ABLs are supported by liquid collateral, they are lower risk loans and they command a lower interest rate than traditional revolvers (which rely upon the company's future cash flows for debt repayment).

C. **Term or Leveraged Loans (TL).** Term loans are typical secured bank loans. They have a principal amortization schedule stipulating when debt repayments have to be made, and a stated final maturity date for the loan. In contrast to Revolvers, once a term loan's principal is repaid, it cannot be reborrowed. Because term loans, like revolving loans, typically have priority security over the company's assets (other than those pledged to support the ABL facility), term loans are less expensive than other forms of debt that have lower seniority. There are two types of term loans as explained below.

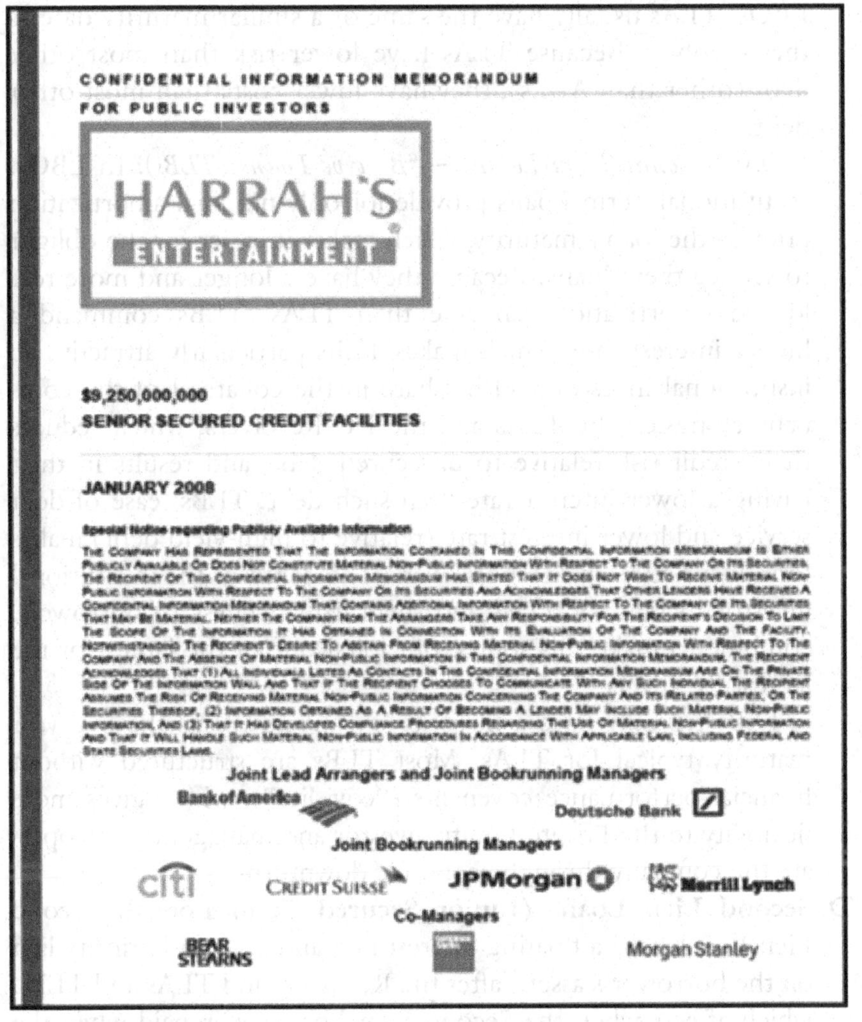

CONFIDENTIAL INFORMATION MEMORANDUM
FOR PUBLIC INVESTORS

HARRAH'S
ENTERTAINMENT

$9,250,000,000
SENIOR SECURED CREDIT FACILITIES

JANUARY 2008

Special Notice regarding Publicly Available Information

THE COMPANY HAS REPRESENTED THAT THE INFORMATION CONTAINED IN THIS CONFIDENTIAL INFORMATION MEMORANDUM IS EITHER PUBLICLY AVAILABLE OR DOES NOT CONSTITUTE MATERIAL NON-PUBLIC INFORMATION WITH RESPECT TO THE COMPANY OR ITS SECURITIES. THE RECIPIENT OF THIS CONFIDENTIAL INFORMATION MEMORANDUM HAS STATED THAT IT DOES NOT WISH TO RECEIVE MATERIAL NON-PUBLIC INFORMATION WITH RESPECT TO THE COMPANY OR ITS SECURITIES AND ACKNOWLEDGES THAT OTHER LENDERS HAVE RECEIVED A CONFIDENTIAL INFORMATION MEMORANDUM THAT CONTAINS ADDITIONAL INFORMATION WITH RESPECT TO THE COMPANY OR ITS SECURITIES THAT MAY BE MATERIAL. NEITHER THE COMPANY NOR THE ARRANGERS TAKE ANY RESPONSIBILITY FOR THE RECIPIENT'S DECISION TO LIMIT THE SCOPE OF THE INFORMATION IT HAS OBTAINED IN CONNECTION WITH ITS EVALUATION OF THE COMPANY AND THE FACILITY. NOTWITHSTANDING THE RECIPIENT'S DESIRE TO ABSTAIN FROM RECEIVING MATERIAL NON-PUBLIC INFORMATION WITH RESPECT TO THE COMPANY AND THE ABSENCE OF MATERIAL NON-PUBLIC INFORMATION IN THIS CONFIDENTIAL INFORMATION MEMORANDUM, THE RECIPIENT ACKNOWLEDGES THAT (1) ALL INDIVIDUALS LISTED AS CONTACTS IN THIS CONFIDENTIAL INFORMATION MEMORANDUM ARE ON THE PRIVATE SIDE OF THE INFORMATION WALL AND THAT IF THE RECIPIENT CHOOSES TO COMMUNICATE WITH ANY SUCH INDIVIDUAL THE RECIPIENT ASSUMES THE RISK OF RECEIVING MATERIAL NON-PUBLIC INFORMATION CONCERNING THE COMPANY AND ITS RELATED PARTIES, OR THE SECURITIES THEREOF, (2) INFORMATION OBTAINED AS A RESULT OF BECOMING A LENDER MAY INCLUDE SUCH MATERIAL NON-PUBLIC INFORMATION, AND (3) THAT IT HAS DEVELOPED COMPLIANCE PROCEDURES REGARDING THE USE OF MATERIAL NON-PUBLIC INFORMATION AND THAT IT WILL HANDLE SUCH MATERIAL NON-PUBLIC INFORMATION IN ACCORDANCE WITH APPLICABLE LAW, INCLUDING FEDERAL AND STATE SECURITIES LAWS.

Joint Lead Arrangers and Joint Bookrunning Managers

Bank of America Deutsche Bank

Joint Bookrunning Managers

citi CREDIT SUISSE JPMorgan Merrill Lynch

Co-Managers

BEAR STEARNS Morgan Stanley

Source: Intralinks.

Amortizing Term Loans — "A" type Loans (TLAs): The amortizing term loans have a specific principal repayment schedule. This type of debt is usually considered less risky because in the ordinary course of business its scheduled repayments ensure that it gets repaid first (usually from the borrower's cash flows), and it is therefore outstanding for shorter periods of time and subject to less company risk than most other types of debt. In

LBOs, TLAs usually have the same or a similar maturity date as the Revolver. Because TLAs have lower risk than most other debt (other than ABLs), they have lower costs than most other debt.

Institutional Term Loans — "B" type Loans (TLBs): In LBOs, Institutional Term Loans provide for only nominal amortization prior to the loan's maturity, which makes it easier for the obligor to service these loans. Because they have a longer and more rear loaded amortization schedule than TLAs, TLBs command a higher interest rate, which makes TLBs particularly attractive to institutional investors. TLBs share in the collateral of the company alongside the TLAs and the RC Revolvers, which reduces their credit risk relative to unsecured debt, and results in their having a lower interest rate than such debt. TLBs' ease of debt service and lower interest rate (relative to high-yield debt) makes term loans attractive to borrowers. The depth of the institutional investor market for TLBs and their attractiveness to borrowers, combine to make this source of capital one of the largest or the largest for LBOs.

TLBs typically have a maturity of 7 years versus the 5–6-year maturity typical for TLAs. Most TLBs are structured without financial performance covenants ("covi-lite"), which gives more flexibility to the Private Equity investor and management to operate the company through economic downturns.

D. **Second Lien Loans (Junior Secured Term Loans).** Second Lien Loans have a floating interest rate and a second priority lien on the borrower's assets, after the Revolvers and TLAs and TLBs, which affects when the Second Lien Loans get repaid when the borrower sells assets or if goes into bankruptcy. If a company liquidates its assets or goes into bankruptcy, it must first repay the aforementioned senior secured loans and then repay its junior secured loans — this sequence of repayments is also referred to as "waterfall" (Figure 5). The Second Lien Term Loans provide more flexibility and involve greater risk than the Senior Secured debt instruments and thus, they require a higher interest rate. Junior secured loans became particularly popular as an LBO

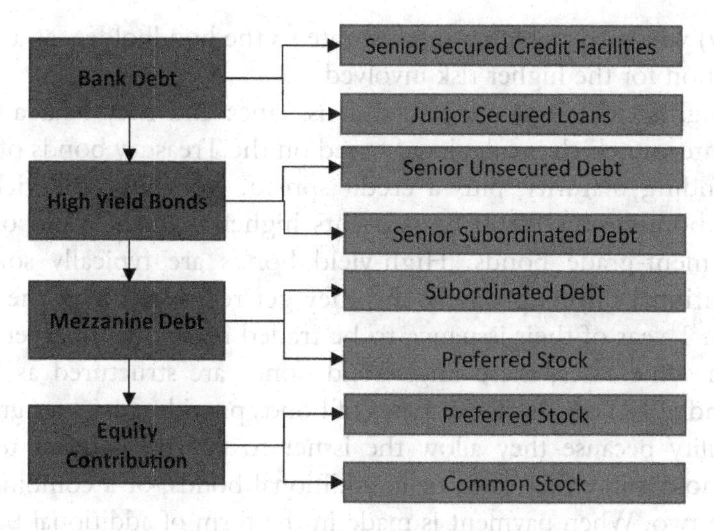

Figure 5: The Debt Hierarchy — "Waterfall".

financing option during the mid-2000s credit buildup in the US. Junior secured loans are often used in smaller LBOs that are too small and illiquid to support the issuance of High-Yield or Subordinated Debt (which is described below).

High-Yield or Subordinated Debt

High-yield bonds, also known as Subordinated Notes or "Junk" bonds, have lower credit ratings than the typical Corporate, Municipal and Treasury bonds. High-yield bonds are typically unsecured, and they offer capital for the LBO that is junior to the senior secured lenders. This capital is typically used to increase leverage beyond the levels that banks and other senior secured institutional investors are willing to offer.

Like every bond, these notes obligate the issuer to make semiannual interest payments to the bondholders and to repay the principal, in full, at the bond's maturity date (usually 8–10 years from issuance). High-yield bonds do not require principal amortization prior to their maturity date and are thereby said to have a "bullet repayment". High-yield bonds are noninvestment grade securities (BB+ and below) which pay a higher interest rate to the bondholders as a compensation for the higher risk involved.

High-yield bonds are priced at issuance and they bear a fixed rate interest which is calculated based on the Treasury bonds of corresponding maturity, plus a credit spread. Generally, the yield of these bonds is 150–300 basis points higher than the yield of the investment-grade bonds. High-yield bonds are typically sold to institutional buyers privately and they get registered with the SEC within 1 year of their issuance to be traded in an open market.

In some cases, these High-Yield bonds are structured as Paid-in-Kind (PIK) bonds. These types of bonds provide the issuer greater flexibility because they allow the issuer to pay the interest to the bondholder in either cash, or in additional bonds, or a combination of the two. When payment is made in the form of additional bonds, this can trigger an increase in the bonds' applicable interest rate.

Mezzanine Debt

Mezzanine debt refers to the financing layer between senior debt and equity. As previously shown, this type of debt ranks last in the hierarchy of debt available for financing. Like subordinated debt, mezzanine debt can be used to achieve a higher level of leverage than was attainable using senior debt and equity alone. This type of debt bears much more risk than typical bank debt and is often issued under unique terms to meet the issuer's financing needs as well as to compensate the investors for providing this capital. Mezzanine debtholders are typically insurance companies, Special Purpose Vehicles (SPVs) that invest in Mezzanine loans and hedge funds. Mezzanine debt interest payments are often structured to provide additional flexibility to the issuer and to compensate the lenders accordingly, with payments sometimes including PIK like notes or warrants which can be converted into the issuer's common stock.

Equity Contribution

The balance of the financing will come from equity, primarily in the form of cash from the sponsor. In cases where existing management participates in the LBO, they would be expected to roll over their preacquisition equity into the new financing. In the years of the mega deals (early to mid-2000s), due to the size of the large LBOs, a consortium of private equity sponsors was required for the largest acquisitions. Since the Equity is at the bottom of the "waterfall", it provides a cushion for bank loan lenders and bondholders in the event the company's enterprise value (EV) declines. In other words, if the equity contribution is 30%, in the event of a company bankruptcy and sale, the EV would need to decline by more 30% before the bondholders and then the banks would be forced to incur a loss.

The amount of debt or equity in each transaction depends on the company's debt capacity which is described later in this chapter. Figure 6 shows that the average leverage ratio of Debt/EBITDA at the time of acquisition has varied over time, depending on market sentiment regarding economic prospects and comfort levels with leverage.

As discussed later in the chapter, the amount and type of debt that an LBO can incur is primarily based on the reliability of the borrower's cash flows and its ability to repay debt. A common formula for describing leverage is Total Debt to Earnings Before Interest Taxes Depreciation and Amortization (EBITDA) — which is referred to as the Total Leverage Ratio. Figure 6 shows the historical average levels accepted by the debt investors or banks who structured these LBOs. These levels

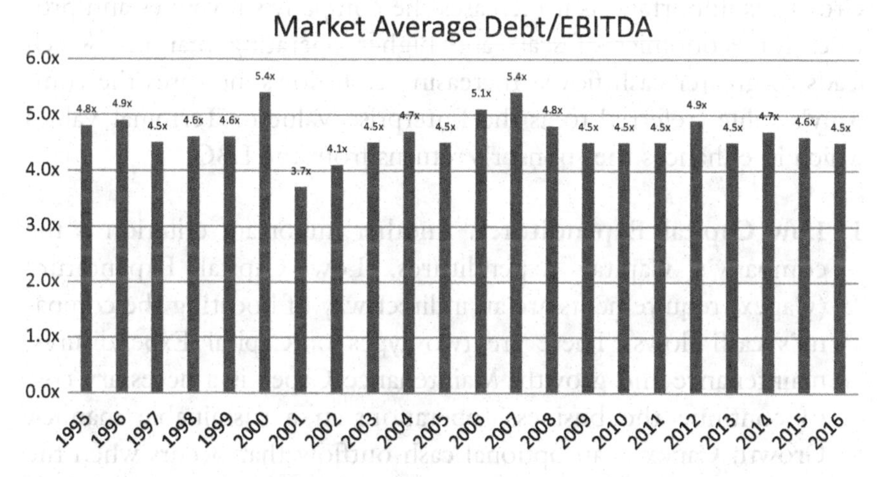

Figure 6: Determination of Debt Capacity Driven by Capital Markets.

Source: LCD Standard & Poors.

are also set by demand in the capital markets. As discussed below, Debt Capacity is the company's ability to repay debt as scheduled.

What Makes a Good LBO Candidate

The key criteria in determining whether a company is a good for sponsor acquisition via an LBO candidate are as follows.

Strong and Stable Cash Flows

Maybe the most important criteria to be met is that the LBO candidate should generate strong and stable cash flows in the future to support the great burden of leverage in its capital structure. The acquired company should demonstrate that throughout the life of the buyout, it can support the scheduled interest and principal debt repayments. For example, if a company has a stable business model and predictable positive cash flows, it is both easier and safer to forecast and stress test its cash flow results under various market scenarios.

Growth Potential

Most successful LBO candidates have the potential for future growth, to be achieved either organically or through add-on acquisitions. Growth is important as it increases the company's revenues and provides for economies of scale and higher operating margins, which leads to greater cash flows. Increasing cash flows increases the company's value (referred to as the Enterprise Value or Terminal Value) which in enhances the sponsor's returns from the LBO.

1. **Low Capital Expenditures.** Another important criterion is the company's Capital Expenditures. Low Capital Expenditure (Capex) requirements are an indirect way of boosting the company's cash flows. There are two types of Capital Expenditures, maintenance and growth. Maintenance Capex is a necessary cost to continue the business' operations in a sustainable manner. Growth Capex is an optional cash outflow that occurs when the company acquires additional assets to enhance its growth and

efficiency. Higher Capital Expenditure companies tend to be structured with lower initial leverage or Debt/EBITDA, as Capex is an item that will reduce the company's cash flow. In many LBOs, Debt/(EBITDA-Capex) is the metric used to structure the appropriate level of debt in the initial LBO structure.

2. **Strong Asset Base.** In most LBOs, a high level of leverage is used because debt is the cheapest source of capital. To provide additional safety and certainty of repayment to the lenders, the sponsor uses the Acquisition Target's assets as collateral for the loans, and a strong asset base can enhance the amount of debt that a company can incur. While company cash flows are the primary source of debt repayment (for at least for the TLAs), asset liquidation proceeds represent a fall-back source of proceeds for debt repayment and is a form of insurance for the secured lenders.
3. **Strong Management Team.** An LBO involves a lot of risk because of the leverage incurred. A strong management team is required to ensure that the company can operate efficiently under the pressure of its high leverage, and that operating miss-steps are kept to a minimum. Strong management can help increase the company's cash inflows and reduce its expenses, and in many cases private equity firms replace the company's existing management with new management that they are familiar and comfortable with, that is given big incentives to make the company perform. Private Equity firms have been known to use the same management team at different companies over time, if they have strong track record.

The Concept of Leverage and Its Advantages for Enhancing Equity Returns

Return Expectation

The main goal of every business is to maximize its shareholders' wealth. The expected ROE is mostly captured by the firm's ability to generate profits through revenue growth and cost reduction. Additional value, and thus higher returns, in an LBO is created through a combination of enterprise value growth and debt repayment. The acquirer should ensure that the Target Company can payback all the debt borrowed plus interest payments on a timely manner, which makes positive and relatively stable future cash flows one of the most important criteria for a desirable LBO. A strong asset base to provide a secondary source of repayment to the lenders is another desirable characteristic for the Target Company.

The goal for a LBO transaction is to provide its sponsors and equity investors with high equity returns to compensate them for their risk. A traditional LBO transaction lasts 3–5 years, where the last year is the exit year (the year of the company's sale). A typical equity return expectation by the LBO investors is 20–25% Internal Rate of Return (IRR).[12] This is calculated based on the investment's holding period and the entry and exit values for the equity. (Note that cash flows during the LBO are typically dedicated to the repayment of debt and that they do not go to the equity. These cash flows do however reduce the company's indebtedness, and thereby increase the value allocable to the equity upon the company's sale).

Returns Generated from Enterprise Value growth

A Financial Sponsor can generate returns by growing the Enterprise Value of the acquired business. During the investment horizon cash flow that is not used to service debt or for maintenance, capex can be reinvested to enhance the company's EBITDA. EBITDA growth which can be achieved organically (growth from within the existing business), or by acquisitions. The value of the business can also be increased if due to improved prospects, or due to a market environment where business valuations are increased, the company is rewarded by being valued at a higher multiple of its EBITDA.

Case 1. Company X is bought for $1 billion and is sold for $1.5 billion 6 years later. Company debt stays flat during the LBO.

---

[12] KWF, Study: "Minimum Expected Return of Private Equity Companies: Claims Become More Modest", June 2011.

Assumptions - Enterprise Value Growth		
Purchase Price		$1,000.0
Equity Contribution %		**25.0%**
Equity Contribution $		$250.0
Debt Contribution %		**75.0%**
Debt Contribution $		$750.0
Debt Repayment		$0.0
Remaining Debt		$750.0
Exit Price Year	6	$1,500.0

Return Calculation	
Equity Contribution	$250.0
Incremental Enterprise Value	500.0
Plus Debt Repayment	0.0
Equity Value at Exit Year	**$750.0**
IRR	**20.1%**
Cash Return	**3.0x**

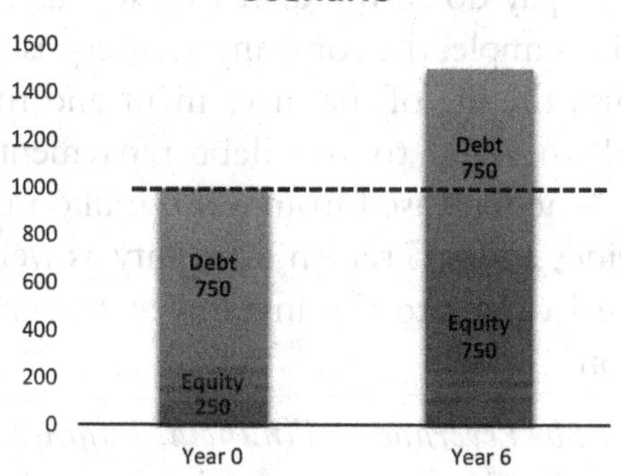

We assume that the company, after fulfilling its debt interest obligations, instead of using its remaining cash flow to pay down debt, reinvests the excess cash flow in the business to generate additional EBITDA. At the exit year, the acquirer realizes a 50% growth in the company's Enterprise Value as the company is now sold for $1.5 billion. Although the company carries the same level of debt that it incurred upon its acquisition, the company achieved EBITDA growth which was reflected in the company's Enterprise Value. This growth translates to an equity return of 20.1% p.a. over the 6-year investment period, which corresponds to a cash return of 3.0 times the initial invested capital (referred to as 3× MOIC — where MOIC means Multiple of Initial Capital).

- *Returns generated from Debt Repayment*: A Financial Sponsor can also generate returns by using the company's cash flow to pay down debt during the investment horizon. Debt repayment causes the debt to represent a smaller portion of the company's enterprise value, and for the equity value to increase by a corresponding amount.

Case 2. Company Y is bought for $1 billion, and 6 years later, it is sold at the same price. During the intervening period the acquired pursued a strategy of increasing the company's equity value by decreasing its debt.

Under this scenario, the acquired company generates a cumulative cash flow (after interest payments) of $500 million dollars. The excess cash flow is used to pay down the debt that was used to finance this acquisition. In this example, the company's Enterprise Value remained unchanged through the life of the investment and the company was resold for $1 billion. Due to the debt repayment, the Financial Sponsor's equity value increased from $250 million to $750 million, which again provides a 20.1% return on equity as well as a 3.0× multiple of the original capital to the investor at the end of the 6-year investment horizon.

- *Return Realized by Leverage — Financial Engineering*: A Financial Sponsor (Private Equity firm) can employ leverage in order to realize higher returns. The use of leverage in an LBO is beneficial for two major reasons. The use of debt creates a tax shield for the company's earnings due to the tax deductibility of interest expense (as previously discussed). Additionally, because debt is senior to equity, its holders take on less risk and require less compensation than equity investors. As a result debt is cheaper than equity, and the use of debt increases the equity's IRR provided that the LBO is successful.

Below are two cases of an LBO Transaction. In the first scenario (case 3), the transaction is financed with 25% debt and 75% equity

Assumptions - Debt Repayment		
Purchase Price		$1,000.0
Equity Contribution %		**25.0%**
Equity Contribution $		$250.0
Debt Contribution %		**75.0%**
Debt Contribution $		$750.0
Debt Repayment		$500.0
Remaining Debt		$250.0
Exit Price Year	6	$1,000.0

Return Calculation	
Equity Contribution	$250.0
Incremental Enterprise Value	0.0
Plus Debt Repayment	500.0
Equity Value at Exit Year	$750.0
IRR	**20.1%**
Cash Return	**3.0x**

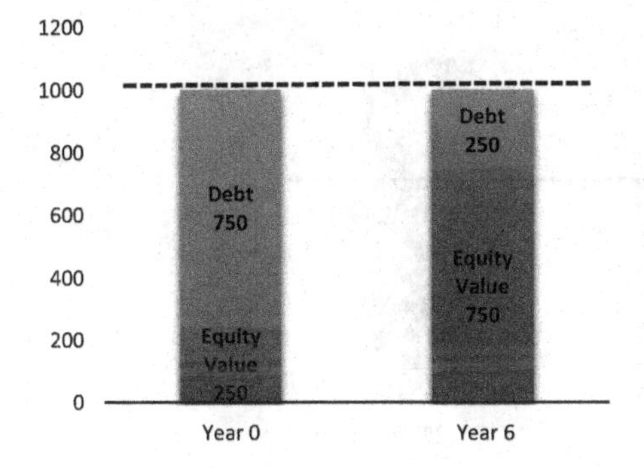

while in the second scenario (case 4), the transaction is financed with 75% debt and 25% equity.

Case 3. In case 3, the Target Company will be purchased for $1.5 billion with low leverage. We assume that the transaction will be financed with 75% equity and only 25% debt ($375 million) contributions. From the 5-year analysis, we can see that the acquisition will generate a positive steady $100 million each year and these cash flows were used to pay down principal and interest throughout the life of

Return on Equity Case 3

Case Assumptions	
Purchase Price	$1,500.0
Equity Contribution %	**75.0%**
Debt Contribution %	**25.0%**
Cost of Debt	8.0%
Cash Flow Generation	$75.0
Exit Sale Year 5	$2,300.0

	Year 0	Year 1	Year 2	Year 3	Year 4	Year 5
Equity Contribution	**($1,125.0)**					
Beginning Balance of Debt	$375.0	$375.0	$300.0	$225.0	$150.0	$75.0
Free Cash Flow	0.0	75.0	75.0	75.0	75.0	75.0
Total Debt, Ending Balance	**$375.0**	**$300.0**	**$225.0**	**$150.0**	**$75.0**	**$0.0**
Sale Price						$2,300.0
Less: Total Debt						(375.0)
Plus: Cummulative Cash Flow						375.0
Total Equity Value at Exit						**$2,300.0**
IRR						**15.4%**
Cash Return						**2.0x**

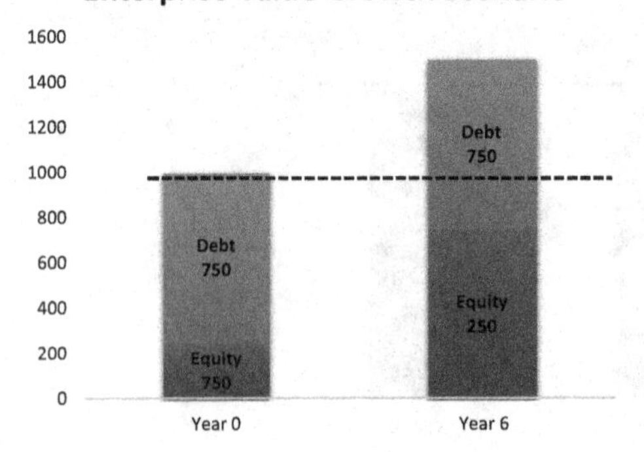

the investment (assuming no repayment of debt). At the exit year (year 5), we assume that the company will be sold for $2.0 billion. As the 75% debt contribution, issued at the time of the acquisition, will be paid down throughout the 5-year investment period, the target's equity value will be doubled by the exit year. This financing structure provides a return of 24.5% p.a. to the equity investors (Financial Sponsor) and the initial equity contribution (1.8× MOIC).

Case 4. In this scenario (case 4), we assume that the same transaction is financed with 75% debt and 25% equity contributions. The cost of

Return on Equity Case 4

Case Assumptions		
Purchase Price		$1,500.0
Equity Contribution %		**25.0%**
Debt Contribution %		**75.0%**
Cost of Debt		8.0%
Cash Flow Generation		$75.0
Exit Price Year	5	$2,300.0
Tax Rate		40.0%

	Year 0	Year 1	Year 2	Year 3	Year 4	Year 5
Equity Contribution	**($375.0)**					
Beginning Balance of Debt	0.0	$1,125.0	$1,086.0	$1,048.7	$1,013.3	$979.7
Beginning Free Cash Flow	0.0	75.0	75.0	75.0	75.0	75.0
Incremental Interest Expense	0.0	(60.0)	(62.9)	(65.9)	(69.1)	(72.4)
Interest Tax Savings	0.0	24.0	25.2	26.4	27.6	29.0
Ending Free Cash Flow	0.0	39.0	37.3	35.5	33.6	31.6
Total Debt, Ending Balance	**$1,125.0**	**$1,086.0**	**$1,048.7**	**$1,013.3**	**$979.7**	**$948.1**
Sale Price						$2,300.0
Less: Total Debt						(1,125.0)
Plus: Cumulative Cash Flow						176.9
Total Equity Value at Exit						**$1,351.9**
IRR						**29.2%**
Cash Return						**3.6x**

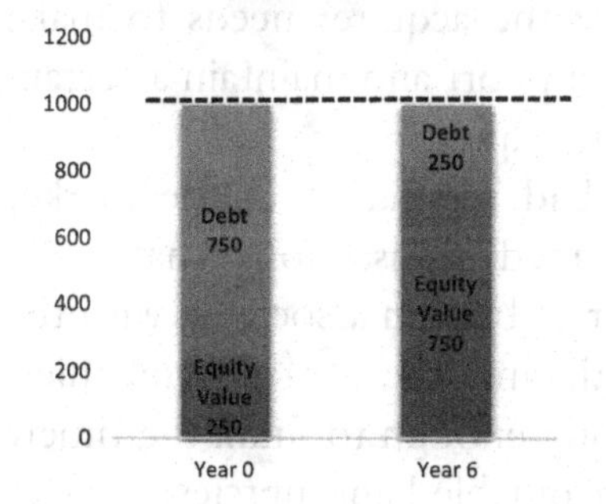

debt is 8% and is reflected on the debt's interest expense every year. Throughout the life of the investment, we assume that the target will generate a stream of positive steady cash flows of $75 million which will be used to cover the interest payment. As we previously mentioned, interest expense is tax deductible and for the purpose of this example we assume a tax rate of 40%. The company's earnings are lowered due to the interest payment which leads to lower tax expenses. At the exit year, the target will be sold for $2.0 billion with an equity value of $1.3 million. In this case, the equity contribution is much lower than the equity contribution in case 3 which provides the Financial Sponsor with a higher equity value at the exit year. The continuous reduction of debt is converted in equity value which leads to the increase of the equity return for the company's shareholders. Consequently, the calculated IRR is 24.6% and MOIC of 3.0 ×. As you can see, the equity return in this example is much higher than the one presented on the case 3 because the cost of leverage is lower than the cost of equity due to the tax deductibility of the interest expense.

Debt Capacity

Debt Capacity is the amount of financial leverage that the acquired company can support with its future cash flows. Usually, the Purchase and Exit prices are expressed as EBITDA multiples and so is debt capacity. The debt capacity of an acquisition can be determined after taking into consideration market, industry, company and structural risks associated with the specific target company. In every transaction, the debt capacity is important because the acquirer needs to make sure that the company in question can support and maintain a certain amount of debt without the risk of bankruptcy.

Around the 1980s, LBOs had a bad reputation in the market mainly because of several overleveraged transactions that were financed with over 90% debt. The interest burden associated with the debt contribution was extremely high and the target companies' annual cash flow streams were not strong enough to fulfill the timely payment obligations, which led to unavoidable bankruptcies.

In the late 1990s and until 2008, the typical financing structure of an LBO transaction consisted of 60–70% debt and 30–40% equity. At that time, the levels of leverage and especially the multiples of different debt sources in the transactions varied significantly from today. During the first decade of the 2000s, the changes in the fundamental market conditions that encouraged the flourishing of private investment vehicles such as Collateralized Loan Obligations

(CLOs), Loan Funds, and Hedge Funds, caused the leverage multiples to increase due to the high investment demand. After 2007, the turmoil in the credit market caused by the subprime mortgage crisis pushed the leverage level down from a multiple of 6.1× to a multiple less than 5.0 ×. Therefore, the equity contribution increased from approximately 30–40%.[13]

The level of debt available for a financing is largely based on the Target Company's predicted annual cash flow. Companies with steady and positive cash flows and substantial assets were attractive LBO candidates because they could support higher debt levels and could potentially support a higher debt leverage multiple.

There are three main sources that comprise the debt financing of an LBO transaction. Below are listed all three primary sources of financing. In the financing hierarchy, the instrument on the top is associated with the lowest risk possible and thus with the lowest cost of debt.

Structuring an LBO

They are various steps to structuring an LBO. Investment banks that advise the private equity investors typically consider the following:

1. Measuring debt capacity — What is the maximum debt banks and bondholders or mezzanine investors are willing to lend?
2. Building a financial model that demonstrates how the debt will be serviced and how the private equity investor will meet his or hers expected return. The financial model will build top line revenue growth for the acquisition target, cost and income margin assumptions, capital expenditure that support the projected growth level, and interest rate assumptions for each type of debt.
3. Build the equity cash flows including a measurable terminal value and appropriate discount rates.

[13] Leveraged Commentary & Data, Standards & Poors Global.

Private Company Case Study — Alexandria Hotel

To illustrate the above steps in structuring an LBO, we assume that a hotel company — Alexandria Hotel — is for sale for $120 million or 6.0× first year's EBITDA of $20 MM. Additionally the acquirer will fees (to its M&A advisor, debt underwriters and the associated lawyers) equal to 3% of the transaction costs — $3.6 million — for a total acquisition cost of $123.6 million. This is shown in Transaction Sources & Uses in Figure 8.

The commercial banks will be invited by the sponsor's investment bank advisor to underwrite the senior secured debt for the acquisition. Banks providing these loans are usually the most conservative stakeholders for the LBO transaction. In general, among other parameters, the banks approve loans based on two criteria: (1) Maximum Leverage Ratio and (2) loan to value. In the case of the Alexandria Hotel company, the banks approved (1) a $50 million loan based on 2.5× First Year EBITDA (2.5× $20mm) and (2) loan to value of approximately of 40% ($50 million/$123 million). In this case, the bank is charging floating rate LIBOR + 4.0%. Based on the forward-looking LIBOR, the average interest rate is around 5.34% p.a. (shown in Figure 9).

The next step for the equity holder is to seek Mezzanine or subordinated bond financing. Given the smaller size of the transaction ($120mm), the Mezzanine market is more suitable, as raising high-yield debt from the public markets typically requires a minimum issuance of $100 million. The Mezzanine facility will also be structured based on the leverage ratio of Debt/EBITDA. In this case, the mezzanine approved a note for up to 4.0× leverage including the bank debt portion. That is translated to a $30mm Mezzanine tranche — assuming maximum debt of $80mm based on 4.0× EBITDA leverage (4× $20mm EBITDA) minus $50mm of the bank debt. Since the Mezzanine investors are taking a second position to the banks in rights to payment, the typical Mezzanine interest rate is much higher than the bank loan (4–6% p.a. higher). In the case of Alexandria Hotel, they charged a 9.0% fixed rate for 10 years.

With the debt component of the financing determined at $80mm, the equity required to provide the remaining balance of the capital was in this case, \$43.6 million (\$123.6mm – \$80mm). At this point, the equity ran its projections to determine if the acquisition met its return expectations. One approach for calculating required equity returns is to use the Capital Asset Pricing Model (CAPM). The beta coefficient in the CAPM calculation is affected by the industry of the obligor. In this case, since the company is privately held, the beta that is used is taken from other comparable publicly traded companies in the hotel sector. Assuming the risk-free interest rate (6-year Treasury) of 1.95%, equity premium of 11.05% and a beta of 1.633×, the required equity return for the acquisition would be 20% p.a. ($Rfr + (\beta \times \text{Premium})$) or $0.0165 + (1.633 \times 0.1105) = 20$ or 20% (Figure 7).

Since we have all the cost of capital components, we can calculate the after tax Weighted Average Cost of Capital (WACC) for the acquisition at 9.84% p.a. as shown in Figure 8. The WACC will be used later to determine the value of the firm at exit or Terminal Value.

COST OF EQUITY CALCULATION E (re) = rf - β . Pe + e	
6-year Treasury Note [rf]	1.95%
Beta for Publicly Traded Hotel [β]	1.633x
Equity Premium [Pe]	11.05%
Firm Specific Risk Premium [e]	0.0%
Cost of Equity	**20.00%**

Figure 7: Cost of Equity.

TRANSACTION SOURCES & USES							
Sources:	**Debt Capacity (EBITDA x)**	**Amount**	**% Capital**	**Expected Return**	**Expected Return (After Tax)**	**WACC (After Tax)**	**EBITDA Multiple**
Bank Loan	2.5x	50,000,000	40.5%	5.364%	3.433%	1.39%	2.5x
Mezzanine Note		30,000,000	24.3%	9.000%	5.760%	1.40%	1.5x
Total Debt	4.0x	80,000,000	64.7%			2.79%	**4.0x**
Equity		43,600,000	35.3%	**20.00%**	**20.00%**	7.05%	2.2x
Total Sources		123,600,000	100.0%			9.84%	**6.2x**
Uses:	**1st Year's EBITDA Multiple**	**Amount**	**% of Total Uses**				
Purchase Price (EV - including Debt)	6.0x	**120,000,000**	97.1%				
Transaction Fees & Expenses	3.0%	3,600,000	2.9%				
Total Uses		123,600,000	100.0%				

WACD = 4.305%

Tax Rate=	36.0%

Figure 8: Transaction Sources and Uses.

The after tax Weighted Average of Cost of Debt is also calculated at 4.305% as illustrated below.

A major part of the equity analysis is to first determine the target company's debt service obligations. The bank that is financing the senior debt portion of the transaction will provide the company (obligor) the following four terms (often called the Money Terms): (1) The Amount ($50 million); (2) The Interest (LIBOR + 4.0%); (3) the Tenor (7 years) or Maturity of the loan (2016); and (4) the scheduled principal payments (Yr1: $3 million, Yr2: $5million, Yr3: $5 million, Yr4: $6 million, Yr5: $7 million, Yr6: $9 million, Yr7: $15 million). The Mezzanine loan is also structured with set loan amount ($30 million), interest rate (9.0% fixed), tenor (10 years) and scheduled principal payments (one payment at maturity) — see Figure 9. Adding both the interest and principal payments will provide the total ongoing debt obligations that the target company is projected to service. For the floating interest payment, the model (Figure 9) assumes that LIBOR will increase by 0.05% or 50 basis points per year for the next 3 years and then by 1.0% in the 4th year. Calculating the average senior bank debt interest rate the target will pay by using the IRR approach, the rate is 5.384% p.a.

Using various assumptions to predict the revenue and revenue growth, cost of revenue, and operating expenses as percentage of revenue one, can project the EBITDA levels of the company for the next 6 years. Also, calculating the depreciation, capital expenditures, and working capital as percentage of revenues, as well as taxes shown on Figure 10, one could calculate the Cash Flow Before Financing (CFBF). Please note that depreciation expense and amortization of fees (calculated $3,600,000 transaction fees found on the Transaction Sources & Uses divided by 7 years representing the bank loan tenor) are subtracted from EBITDA and then added back again — this is to calculate the projected tax expense.

The annual debt or financing obligations shown in Figure 9 are subtracted from the Cash Flow Before Financing to give the stream of cash flows the equity expect to earn — a very important line to calculate the expected equity return.

Once the stream of ongoing equity cash flows is projected, the equity analyst needs to determine the terminal value at an assume exit

DEBT ASSUMPTIONS & RETURN ANALYSIS														
Bank Loan Information	*Debt IRR*	Terms	2010	2011	2012	2013	2014	2015	2016	2017	2018	2019	2020	2021
Amount Outstanding (End of Year)		**50,000,000**	47,000,000	42,000,000	37,000,000	31,000,000	24,000,000	15,000,000	-	-	-	-	-	-
Schedule Principal Payments		**7 years**	3,000,000	5,000,000	5,000,000	6,000,000	7,000,000	9,000,000	15,000,000	-	-	-	-	-
Interest Payment (Calc based on last Year's Outs)		**5.36%**	2,150,000	2,256,000	2,226,000	2,331,000	1,953,000	1,512,000	945,000	-	-	-	-	-
Total Financing Payment	5.364%	(50,000,000)	5,150,000	7,256,000	7,226,000	8,331,000	8,953,000	10,512,000	15,945,000	-	-	-	-	-
LIBOR RATE		*0.30%*	*0.30%*	*0.80%*	*1.30%*	*2.30%*	*2.30%*	*2.30%*	*2.30%*	*2.30%*	*2.30%*	*2.30%*	*2.30%*	*2.30%*
LIBOR Rate Increase Assumptions			*0.00%*	*0.50%*	*0.50%*	*1.00%*	*0.00%*	*0.00%*	*0.00%*	*0.00%*	*0.00%*	*0.00%*	*0.00%*	*0.00%*
Corporate Bond Information														
Amount Outstanding		**30,000,000**	30,000,000	30,000,000	30,000,000	30,000,000	30,000,000	30,000,000	30,000,000	30,000,000	30,000,000	-		
Schedule Principal Payments		**10 Years**	-	-	-	-	-	-	-	-	-	30,000,000		
Interest Payment (Calc based on last Year's Outs)		**9.00%**	2,700,000	2,700,000	2,700,000	2,700,000	2,700,000	2,700,000	2,700,000	2,700,000	2,700,000	2,700,000	-	-
Total Financing Payment	9.000%	(30,000,000)	2,700,000	2,700,000	2,700,000	2,700,000	2,700,000	2,700,000	2,700,000	2,700,000	2,700,000	32,700,000	-	-
Total Financing			7,850,000	9,956,000	9,926,000	11,031,000	11,653,000	13,212,000	18,645,000	2,700,000	2,700,000	32,700,000	-	-
Total Debt Outstanding			77,000,000	72,000,000	67,000,000	61,000,000	54,000,000	**45,000,000**	30,000,000	30,000,000	30,000,000	-	-	-

Figure 9: Debt Assumptions and Return Analysis.

CASH FLOW & EQUITY RETURN ANALYSIS

Company Projections	Operating Assump.	Entry Year 2009	Year 1 2010	Year 2 2011	Year 3 2012	Year 4 2013	Year 5 2014	Exit Year 2015	2016	2017	2018	2019	2020	2021
Revenues	5.00%	growth	40,000,000	42,000,000	44,100,000	46,305,000	48,620,250	51,051,263	53,603,826	56,284,017	59,098,218	62,053,129	65,155,785	68,413,574
Cost of Revenues	35.0%	% of Revenue	(14,000,000)	(14,700,000)	(15,435,000)	(16,206,750)	(17,017,088)	(17,867,942)	(18,761,339)	(19,699,406)	(20,684,376)	(21,718,595)	(22,804,525)	(23,944,751)
Operating Costs	15.0%	% of Revenue	(6,000,000)	(6,300,000)	(6,615,000)	(6,945,750)	(7,293,038)	(7,657,689)	(8,040,574)	(8,442,603)	(8,864,733)	(9,307,969)	(9,773,368)	(10,262,036)
EBITDA	50.0%		**20,000,000**	**21,000,000**	**22,050,000**	**23,152,500**	**24,310,125**	**25,525,631**	**26,801,913**	**28,142,008**	**29,549,109**	**31,026,564**	**32,577,893**	**34,206,787**
Less Depreciation	3.00%	% of Revenue	(1,200,000)	(1,260,000)	(1,323,000)	(1,389,150)	(1,458,608)	(1,531,538)	(1,608,115)	(1,688,521)	(1,772,947)	(1,861,594)	(1,954,674)	(2,052,407)
Less Amortization of Fees	7	years	(514,286)	(514,286)	(514,286)	(514,286)	(514,286)	(514,286)						
EBIT			18,285,714	19,225,714	20,212,714	21,249,064	22,337,232	23,479,808	25,193,798	26,453,488	27,776,162	29,164,970	30,623,219	32,154,380
Less Interest (Unlevered for DCF Analysis)			-	-	-	-	-	-	-	-	-	-	-	-
EBT			18,285,714	19,225,714	20,212,714	21,249,064	22,337,232	23,479,808	25,193,798	26,453,488	27,776,162	29,164,970	30,623,219	32,154,380
Less Taxes (adj out Interest Exp)	36.0%	% of EBT	(6,582,857)	(6,921,257)	(7,276,577)	(7,649,663)	(8,041,403)	(8,452,731)	(9,069,767)	(9,523,256)	(9,999,418)	(10,499,389)	(11,024,359)	(11,575,577)
Plus Depreciation & Amortization			1,714,286	1,774,286	1,837,286	1,903,436	1,972,893	2,045,824	1,608,115	1,688,521	1,772,947	1,861,594	1,954,674	2,052,407
Less Working Capital	1.00%	% of Revenue	(400,000)	(420,000)	(441,000)	(463,050)	(486,203)	(510,513)	(536,038)	(562,840)	(590,982)	(620,531)	(651,558)	(684,136)
Less Capex	3.00%	% of Revenue	(1,200,000)	(1,260,000)	(1,323,000)	(1,389,150)	(1,458,608)	(1,531,538)	(1,608,115)	(1,688,521)	(1,772,947)	(1,861,594)	(1,954,674)	(2,052,407)
Cash Flow Before Financing (CFBF)			**11,817,143**	**12,398,743**	**13,009,423**	**13,650,637**	**14,323,912**	**15,030,850**	**15,587,992**	**16,367,392**	**17,185,762**	**18,045,050**	**18,947,302**	**19,894,667**
Less Financing (P + I)			(7,850,000)	(9,956,000)	(9,926,000)	(11,031,000)	(11,653,000)	(13,212,000)	(18,645,000)	(2,700,000)	(2,700,000)	(32,700,000)	-	-
Equity Cash Flows			3,967,143	2,442,743	3,083,423	2,619,637	2,670,912	1,818,850	(3,057,008)	13,667,392	14,485,762	(14,654,950)	18,947,302	19,894,667
Terminal Value														
EBITDA Multiple Method (initial purchase multiple)	Growth	6.0x						153,153,788						
Perpetuity Method (using WACC + growth)	3.50%	9.84%						245,812,934						
Average Terminal Value								**199,483,361**						
Debt Outstanding								45,000,000						
Equity Value (TV - Debt)								154,483,361						
Equity Cash Flows		(43,600,000)	**3,967,143**	**2,442,743**	**3,083,423**	**2,619,637**	**2,670,912**	**156,302,211**						
			x	x	x	x	x	x						
$ 1 PV Table (Expected Equity Rate)		20.00%	*0.8333398*	*0.6944552*	*0.5787172*	*0.4822680*	*0.4018931*	*0.3349135*						
PV Table (Expected Equity Rate)		61,471,300	3,305,978	1,696,376	1,784,430	1,263,367	1,073,421	52,347,728						
Initial Investment		(43,600,000)												
NPV=		17,871,300												
IRR=		27.9%												

Based on Next Year's CF

Equity Return Scenarios Given Different EBITDA Multiples

5.5x	6.0x	6.5x	7.0x
36.4%	27.9%	22.1%	17.9%

SCENARIO TABLE

		EBITDA Purchase Multiples			
	IRR= 27.9%	5.5x	6.0x	6.5x	7.0x
Revenue Growth Rates	5.00%	36.37%	27.86%	22.07%	17.85%
	5.50%	37.26%	28.71%	22.87%	18.63%
	6.00%	39.02%	30.37%	24.46%	20.16%
	6.50%	41.60%	32.81%	26.80%	22.40%
	7.00%	44.95%	35.98%	29.82%	25.30%
	7.50%	49.02%	39.81%	33.47%	28.82%
	8.00%	53.75%	44.26%	37.71%	32.89%
	8.50%	59.10%	49.29%	42.50%	37.49%
	9.00%	65.03%	54.85%	47.79%	42.57%
	9.50%	60.08%	52.03%	46.24%	41.83%

Figure 10. Cash Flow and Equity Return Analysis.

year. In the case of Alexandria, the exit year is 6 years. The Terminal Value (TV) or Enterprise Value at the exit year is calculated by using two and the average is taken from these methods. The first method used is the EBITDA Multiple method. This method assumes that the Enterprise Value in 2015 will be approximately \$153.5 million (6 × \$25.5 million 2015 EBITDA). The assumed six times multiple used, in this case, is the same multiple used to buy the company in 2010 (\$120mm acquisition price/\$20mm first year EBITDA) — the same multiple at which the company was bought. Expansion of the EBITDA multiple will always enhance the equity return as was illustrated earlier in the chapter. The second method used for calculating the Terminal Value is the perpetuity method or the Gordon growth approach. This method calculates the projected Enterprise Value by taking the Cash Flow Before Financing divided by a discount rate adjusted for growth. The discount rate used is the WACC adjusted for 3.5% growth. The formula (\$16,687,992 / (0.0984 - 0.035) results to a terminal value of approximately \$245.8 million. The large gap between the two values (\$153.1 and \$245.8mm) is due to low EBITDA multiple used. Given the high growth that is assumed in this model, typically, a higher multiple of EBITDA should be used for a more normal valuation. Ignoring the large gap in valuations by calculating the average of the two values the terminal value is projected at \$199 million. Of course, the stream of cash flows is for the corporate entity, so the terminal value needs to subtract the exit year debt to make the stream all equity. The debt outstanding (\$45 million) is taken from Figure 9, year 2016.

Once the stream of equity cash flows is set up including the value of the equity after exiting the investment in year 6, the present value of these cash flows assuming the expected equity return of 20% is \$61,471,300 which is higher the initial equity investment of \$48,800,000 calculating a positive Net Present Value of \$17,871,300, and an IRR of 27.9%. At this level the equity investor would go ahead with the purchase since it meets the minimum expected return of 20% p.a. In an auction process, the equity investor could afford to pay a little more for this company — let's say 6.5× multiple — calculated at 22.0% IRR.

Publicly Traded Company Case: RJR Nabisco

The RJR Nabisco transaction completed in 1988 was the largest LBO at the time in the history of LBOs and involved not only a great number of sophisticated players but also a complex valuation process.[14]

Historical Prospective

RJR was considered a pioneer in many aspects. For example, in 1913, the company introduced and marketed four new brands in the same period, which was considered risky but the strategy that the company followed proved to be successful. Additionally, although RJR was facing difficulties during the great depression due to the high competition of cheaper brands, it managed to keep up with the market by improving the packaging and wrapping of its products. Finally, although RJR was facing increasing competitive threats, it managed to survive by applying several strategies such as, diversifying into

RJR Nabisco/KKR Transaction Sources & Uses ($000's)

Sources	Amount	% Cap	EBITDA x	Pricing
Revolving Credit & Term Loans	-	0%		L+2.50%
Revolving Credit & Term Loans	13,600	43%		L+2.50%
Total Band Debt	13,600	43%	3.7x	
Bridge Financing	5,000	16%		Base Rate + 6% (increasing to BR+10%)
Increasing Rate Notes	5,000	16%		L+
Partnership Dent Securities	500	2%		T + 4.0%
Senior Convertibel Debentures	1,800	6%		(between 12.675% - 16.675% Fixed)
Total Subordinated Debt	12,300	39%	3.3x	
Total Debt	25,900	82%	7.0x	
Cumulative Exch. PIK Preferred Stock	4,059	13%	1.1x	
Cash Equity	1,500	5%		
Total Equity	5,559	18%		
Total Sources	31,459	100%	8.5x	
Bank Debt Provided:		Up Front Fees paid		
Dai-Ichi Kangyo Bank	600	3.25%		
Fuji Bank	600	3.25%		
Sanwa Bank	600	3.25%		
LongpTerm Crddit Bank of Japan	600	3.25%		
Miutsubishi Bank Ltd	500	3.00%		
Sumitomo Bank Ltd	500	3.00%		
Nippopn Credit Bank	500	3.00%		
Tokai Bank Ltd	400	2.75%		
Mitsui Trust & Banking	350	2.50%		
Other Japanese Regional Banks	450	2.00%		
Total provided by Japanese Banks	5,100			
Subordinated Debr Provided				
Drexel Burnham Lambert				
Merrill Lynch				
Proforma EBITDA (1989 Est)	**3,681**			
3m LIBOR (Jan 1989)	9.380%			

Uses		
Purchase Stock		25,506
Debt Refinancing		5,142
Fees:		
Drexel:		
Fees as adviser	25	
Commtiment Fee	52.5	
Funding Fee (Sub Debt)	95	
Financing Fee (Sub Debt)	54.4	
Total Drexel Fees		226.9
Merril;l Lynch		
Fees as adviser	25	
Commtiment Fee	22.5	
Funding Fee (Sub Debt)	7.5	
Financing Fee (Sub Debt)	54.4	
Total Merrill Lynch		109.4
Morgan Stanley Fees as dealer		25
Wassersteinb Parella Fees as a dealer		25
Total Investment Banking Fees		386.3
Banking Fees (200 institutions)		325
Other Transaction Expenses		100
Total Transaction Fees & Expenses		811.3
		31,459

[14] *Financial Analysts Journal*, Analysis: "RJR Nabisco: A Case Study of a Complex Leveraged Buyout", Allen Michel and Israel Shaked, September/October 1991.

non-cigarette products, increasing its presence in other continents where cigarette growth was still trending upwards, differentiating its products, and addressing increasing health concerns at home.

Why RJR was a Good LBO Candidate

As we previously discussed, a company should meet specific criteria to be considered as a good LBO candidate. RJR met all the criteria to an outstanding extent and it was considered a very attractive LBO candidate.

First, the company presented a steady growth over the years which was unaffected by business cycles. Additionally, the company had a great survival rate against market turmoil as its unlevered beta, which measures the company's business risk, was at that time 0.69. This was proof that the company was insensitive to market-wide fluctuations and that its products were noncyclical.

Secondly, the firm had low debt obligations. As we previously discussed, in an LBO, the new management uses the debt capacity of the target firm's assets and for that reason, good LBO candidates are ones that have low levels of debt. RJR at that time had a debt to assets ratio of 0.3 or 30%. Thus, the low debt provided greater opportunities for debt acquisitions and further expansions, especially since RJR involved very low systematic risk.

Finally, all the problems that RJR appeared to be facing at that time appeared to be easily dealt with and the firm's profile portrayed a high potential for additional value creation. For all the above reasons, RJR was considered an excellent LBO candidate that would create opportunities for high returns.

The RJR Valuation Process

There are three major steps that need to be considered in a company's valuation. First, in a discounted cash flow analysis, in order to determine the company's value, the future free cash flows over a number of years must be determined and discounted to the present using a risk factor — the WACC. The WACC formula is able to capture the risk of the company's future cash flows while also reflecting the company's cost of equity and debt levels.

Second, after we calculate the WACC, we need to project the company's unlevered free cash flow, which is essentially the cash remaining after capital expenditures and working capital requirements. This cash is what would be available to the capital holders before the debtholders are paid.

Finally, a terminal value must be calculated. The terminal value is the value of the cash flows after the end of the forecasting period. The terminal value can be calculated either by using the Perpetuity Growth Model which is based on the assumption that the company's future cash flows will continue to grow at a moderate and constant rate through infinity, or by using the Terminal Multiple Method which assumes that the company's worth can be approximated by a multiple of an operating metric, such as a multiple of EBITDA.

The above methodology was used to value RJR. A discount rate (WACC) of 12.06% was used to discount the projected cash flows for a period of 10 years. This calculation presented a value of $15.6 billion. Additionally, in order for the free cash flows to be projected, certain assumptions were taken into consideration including a steady growth rate of 3%. Finally, by adding all the discounted cash flows of RJR the total calculated firm value was $32.6 billion. After deducting the pre-existing long-term debt of RJR ($5.4 billion), the equity value was calculated at $27.2 billion, which divided by the company's total common shares (223.52 million) yielded a value of $121.66 per share.

Balancing Maximum Leverage to Meet Equity Expectations

The higher the leverage, the greater the risk, and the bigger the equity returns at the exit year of the LBO. However, one has to balance the risk against the expected returns, as overleveraging a company can result in disaster (bankruptcy) if the company is unable to meet its interest and debt obligations. For this reason, banks analyze companies and determine a viable amount of leverage that a specific company can take on. Additionally, after the big crisis of 2008, new capital restrictions were applied to banks which limited banks' own leverage and affected their ability to provide financing in general. Additionally, through moral suasion, the Federal Reserve made lending to very highly levered companies exceptionally unattractive to banks. These measures have served to contain the use of leverage in LBO acquisitions.

LBO Model — Building the Model and Testing the Debt Repayment & Equity Return on Excel

Building the Historical Analysis

The first step is to collect all the company's historical financial information (10K and 10Q reports if the target is a publicly traded company). The sell-side advisor is required to provide this information to interested buyers which might also include industry reports, transaction specifics, and financial projections. This information is usually contained in a Confidential Information Memorandum (CIM) with additional information provided by the management through their presentations and data room.

	SUMMARY								
		HISTORICAL							
		12 mos Dec-07	12 mos Dec-08	12 mos Dec-09	12 mos Dec-10	12 mos Dec-11	12 mos Dec-12	12 mos Dec-13	12 mos Dec-14
30	Revenues	6,153,000	5,907,000	4,696,000	5,071,000	5,624,000	6,321,000	6,115,000	5,983,000
31	Revenue Growth		4.2%	25.8%	-7.4%	-9.8%	-11.0%	3.4%	2.2%
32									
33	EBITDA	1,044,000	943,000	293,000	839,000	841,000	1,104,000	1,135,000	1,084,000
34	EBITDA Margin	17.0%	16.0%	6.2%	16.5%	15.0%	17.5%	18.6%	18.1%
35									
36	Interest Expenses	168,000	210,000	296,000	296,000	296,000	296,000	236,000	216,000
37	Capex	276,000.0	471,000.0	168,000.0	209,000.0	392,000.0	360,000.0	358,000.0	323,000.0
38	Working capital	55,000.0	(177,000.0)	43,000.0	129,000.0	(226,000.0)	396,000.0	257,000.0	64,000.0
39	Cash Taxes	189,000.0	76,000.0	(293,000.0)	27,000.0	(75,000.0)	148,000.0	263,000.0	139,000.0
40									
41	Cash & Short-term Investments	358,000	485,000	134,000	806,000	686,000	463,000	750,000	1,019,000
42	Bank Debt	3,595,000	4,008,000	2,960,000	3,351,000	2,729,000	1,808,000	1,622,000	2,944,000
43	Total Debt	3,595,000	4,008,000	2,960,000	3,351,000	2,729,000	1,808,000	1,622,000	2,944,000
44	Equity	2,076,000	1,621,000	1,824,000	2,471,000	2,954,000	3,137,000	3,360,000	1,525,000
45									
46	Senior Debt / EBITDA	3.4x	4.3x	10.1x	4.0x	3.2x	1.6x	1.4x	2.7x
47	Total Debt / EBITDA	3.4x	4.3x	10.1x	4.0x	3.2x	1.6x	1.4x	2.7x
48									
49	Net Senior Debt / EBITDA	3.1x	3.7x	9.6x	3.0x	2.4x	1.2x	0.8x	1.8x
50	Net Total Debt / EBITDA	3.1x	3.7x	9.6x	3.0x	2.4x	1.2x	0.8x	1.8x
51									
52	EBITDA / Interest	6.2x	4.5x	1.0x	2.8x	2.8x	3.7x	4.8x	5.0x
53	EBITDA - Capex / Interest	4.6x	2.2x	0.4x	2.1x	1.5x	2.5x	3.3x	3.5x
54	Debt / Capitalization	63.4%	71.2%	61.9%	57.6%	48.0%	36.6%	32.6%	65.9%

Setting Up the Transactions Sources & Uses

Assumption of Purchase Price — Use of Capital

The private equity firm might hire an advisor (buy-side advisor) to assist them with the purchase price. In general, an experienced private equity firm will use basic assumption first to run the numbers, such as EBITDA purchase multiples. The purchase price is one number that the private equity will need to adjust as negotiations and/or competitive bidding proceeds. In addition to financing the purchase price, in most LBOs, the existing debt is repaid at the time of acquisition, so this debt repayment also has to be financed. These uses of cash, and transaction fees and expenses, are all incorporated in preparing the Transaction Uses for the LBO.

Uses	Stock Price	Shares Outstanding (000s)	Amount	Enteprise Value	Multiple of EBITDA
Cash			(519,000.0)		
Stock Purchase	$ 35.00	177,000	6,195,000		
Refinance Existing Debt			2,944,000		
Assumption of Debt			-	9,139,000	8.4x
Transaction Fees & Expenses	3.00%		274,170		
Total Uses			**8,894,170**		

Assumption of Financing & Debt Repayment — Source of Capital

The Sources of Capital are determined by the Target Company's debt capacity. Debt can include bank loans and second lien loans (Secured Debt Facilities), mezzanine notes and public senior or subordinated bonds (High-Yield debt). The exact debt mix is affected by the size of the transaction and the credit appetite of the debt markets.

One of the debt capacity methods for determining the amounts of debt is to assume a senior debt leverage and total debt leverage ratio of Senior Debt/EBITDA and Total Debt/EBITDA, respectively. For

TRANSACTION SOURCES & USES							
Sources ($000s)	**Debt Capacity EBITDA x**	**Calculated Debt based on DC**	**New Commit. (Rounded)**	**Funded**	**% Cap**	**EBITDA x**	**Spread (bps) / Fixed**
Cash			519,000	519,000			
Revolver			1,000,000	-	0.0%		400.0
Term Loan A			-	-	0.0%		
Term Loan B	3.50x	3,794,000	3,800,000	3,800,000	42.7%	3.5x	400.0
New Term Loan			-		0.0%		
Other Bank Debt / Exisiting			-	-	0.0%		
Total Bank Debt			4,800,000	3,800,000	42.7%	3.5x	
Senior Secured Notes			-	-	0.0%		0.0%
Total Secured Debt			4,800,000	3,800,000	42.7%	3.5x	
Senior Unsecured / Subordinated Notes	2.00x	2,168,000	2,200,000	2,200,000	24.7%	2.0x	8.0%
Junior Subordinated Notes			-	-	0.0%		0.0%
Total Subordinated Debt			2,200,000	2,200,000	24.7%	2.0x	
Total Debt	5.50x		7,000,000	6,000,000	67.5%	5.5x	
Equity				2,894,170	32.5%	2.7x	
Total Sources			**7,000,000**	**8,894,170**	100.0%	8.2x	

argument sake, let's assume the debt markets can take 3.5× and 5.5× Senior and Total Leverage, respectively. After the debt facilities are determined, the balance of the financing should come from private equity. Sometimes, all or some of the Target's existing cash can be used as source of capital.

The Transaction Sources & Uses will also include terms of the debt facilities including interest rate and tenor. The interest rates are reflecting the market's appetite for that company's credit risk. The secured debt facilities are usually priced with a floating rate component such as LIBOR and a spread. The High-Yield debt facilities usually have a fixed interest rate.

Setting Up the Opening Pro Forma Balance Sheet by Linking the Transaction Sources & Uses

The Transaction Sources & Uses will be affect the opening pro forma balance sheet. One starts with the Target's last reported Balance Sheet, and then inserts the new debt and equity in place of the pre-existing debt and equity. Assets are written up or down as applicable, with Goodwill often being a major new entry in the Balance Sheet.

Most of the items that were used to build the Transaction Sources & Uses will be carry over as adjustments (Debt or Credit) to the existing balance sheet in the following steps:

1. The entire sources of capital including the debt and equity will be on the Credit column contributing to the starting Liabilities and Net Worth of the opening pro forma balance sheet.
2. The existing debt and the entire new worth will be zeroed out by debiting in the column.
3. Most of the transaction fees & expenses used in the Transaction Sources & Uses table will be debited in the Asset side as Capitalized Expenses which later will be amortized down to zero based on the length of time of the debt that will be repaid.
4. Cash that is used in the Transaction Sources & Uses could be either debited or credited depending on whether the private equity used the Target's existing cash as to help purchase the Target, or whether cash was added to the Balance Sheet (in order

BALANCE SHEET									Transaction Adjustm.		
	Dec-08	Dec-09	Dec-10	Dec-11	Dec-12	Dec-13	Dec-14	Dec-14E	Debit	Credit	Dec-14
ASSETS											
Cash	485,000	134,000	806,000	686,000	463,000	750,000	1,019,000	1,019,000	(519,000)		500,000
Short-Term Investments	-	-	-	-	-	-	-	-			-
Accounts Receivable	552,000	445,000	887,000	911,000	941,000	908,000	907,000	907,000			907,000
Inventory	986,000	783,000	802,000	812,000	361,000	217,000	236,000	236,000			236,000
Other Current Assets	143,000	127,000	126,000	125,000	124,000	121,000	159,000	159,000			159,000
Total Current Assets	2,166,000	1,489,000	2,621,000	2,534,000	1,889,000	1,996,000	2,321,000	2,321,000			1,802,000
Gross Fixed Assets	3,609,000	3,421,000	3,323,000	3,274,000	3,198,000	3,034,000	2,634,000	2,634,000			2,634,000
(Accum. Depreciation)											
Total Fixed Assets	3,609,000	3,421,000	3,323,000	3,274,000	3,198,000	3,034,000	2,634,000	2,634,000			2,634,000
Capitalized Exp.									274,170		274,170
Purchase Goodwill	1,639,000	-	-	-	-	-	-	-	4,670,000		4,670,000
Other Intagibles	596,000	2,063,000	2,067,000	2,053,000	2,025,000	2,032,000	1,956,000	1,956,000			1,956,000
Other Investm's & Assets	1,693,000	1,788,000	1,765,000	1,699,000	1,743,000	1,700,000	1,748,000	1,748,000			1,748,000
Total Assets	9,703,000	8,761,000	9,776,000	9,560,000	8,855,000	8,762,000	8,659,000	8,659,000			13,084,170
LIABILITIES & SHAREHOLDER EQUITY											
Accounts Payable	2,182,000	2,022,000	2,029,000	1,859,000	1,864,000	1,825,000	2,080,000	2,080,000			2,080,000
Acccrued Expenses											-
Other Current Liabilities											-
Total Current Liabilities	2,182,000	2,022,000	2,029,000	1,859,000	1,864,000	1,825,000	2,080,000	2,080,000			2,080,000
Revolver											-
Term Loan A											-
Term Loan B										3,800,000	3,800,000
New Term Loan										-	-
Other Bank Debt / Exisiting	4,008,000	2,960,000	3,351,000	2,729,000	1,808,000	1,622,000	2,944,000	2,944,000	2,944,000	-	-
Senior Secured Notes										-	-
Senior Unsecured / Subordinated Notes										2,200,000	2,200,000
Junior Subordinated Notes										-	-
Total Debt	4,008,000	2,960,000	3,351,000	2,729,000	1,808,000	1,622,000	2,944,000	2,944,000			6,000,000
Deferred Taxes	1,150,000	31,000	24,000	46,000	85,000	48,000	38,000	38,000			38,000
Other Liabilities & OPEB	719,000	1,903,000	1,886,000	1,971,000	1,956,000	1,904,000	2,069,000	2,069,000			2,069,000
Minority Interest	23,000	21,000	15,000	1,000	5,000	3,000	3,000	3,000			3,000
Total Liabilities	8,082,000	6,937,000	7,305,000	6,606,000	5,718,000	5,402,000	7,134,000	7,134,000			10,190,000
OWNER'S EQUITY											
Treasury Stock											-
Preferred Stock											-
Common Stock	2,000	2,000	2,000	2,000	2,000	2,000	2,000	2,000	2,000	2,894,170	2,894,170
Add'l Paid-in-Capital	493,000	552,000	805,000	963,000	816,000	661,000	47,000	47,000	47,000		-
Other	(391,000)	(283,000)	(283,000)	(348,000)	(338,000)	(335,000)	(508,000)	(508,000)	(508,000)		-
Retained Earnings	1,517,000	1,553,000	1,947,000	2,337,000	2,657,000	3,032,000	1,984,000	1,984,000	1,984,000		-
Total Equity	1,621,000	1,824,000	2,471,000	2,954,000	3,137,000	3,360,000	1,525,000	1,525,000			2,894,170
Total Liabilities & Equity	9,703,000	8,761,000	9,776,000	9,560,000	8,855,000	8,762,000	8,659,000	8,659,000	8,894,170	8,894,170	13,084,170

to enhance the company's financial flexibility going forward) as part of the financing.

5. Once all the above items are determined, the difference in the credit column will be Goodwill which is basically the premium paid for the company over the value of the company's identifiable assets.
6. All other balance sheet items such as Current Assets, Fixed Assets, Current Liabilities and other Long-Term Liabilities (except for debt) will carried over to the new opening pro forma balance sheet.

The Pro Forma Balance Sheet represents the target company's opening balance sheet. It is for modeling purposes the year "Zero" balance sheet.

Building the Projections

All lines of the income, cash flow and balance sheet statements need to be addressed in projecting them out. Each item is determined by certain assumptions, but in general, most items projected will grow at the same pace as the revenue will grow. Of course, each item from these statements is reviewed closely and the final projection represents the seller's and buyer's best of future expectations.

SUMMARY								
		PROJECTED						
	12 mos Dec-14	12 mos Dec-15	12 mos Dec-16	12 mos Dec-17	12 mos Dec-18	12 mos Dec-19	12 mos Dec-20	12 mos Dec-21
Revenues	5,983,000	6,098,920	6,344,146	6,650,695	6,967,341	7,256,107	7,559,378	7,877,958
Revenue Growth	-2.2%	1.9%	4.0%	4.8%	4.8%	4.1%	4.2%	4.2%
EBITDA	1,084,000	1,126,665	1,176,124	1,228,501	1,284,464	1,339,508	1,396,925	1,456,828
EBITDA Margin	18.1%	18.5%	18.5%	18.5%	18.4%	18.5%	18.5%	18.5%
Interest Expenses		366,000	361,871	373,176	380,573	396,316	383,314	369,172
Capex		333,336	346,738	363,493	380,799	396,581	413,157	430,569
Working capital		(11,434)	25,734	43,733	42,896	34,216	36,412	38,756
Cash Taxes		154,981	168,586	177,818	189,196	198,076	216,146	235,148
Cash & Short-term Investments	500,000	722,915	1,009,578	1,329,326	1,668,118	2,012,868	2,395,588	2,284,283
Bank Debt	3,800,000	3,762,000	3,724,000	3,686,000	3,648,000	3,610,000	3,572,000	3,000,000
Total Debt	6,000,000	5,962,000	5,924,000	5,886,000	5,848,000	5,810,000	5,772,000	5,200,000
Equity	2,894,170	3,255,793	3,649,160	4,064,069	4,505,527	4,967,705	5,472,045	6,020,724
Senior Debt / EBITDA	3.5x	3.3x	3.2x	3.0x	2.8x	2.7x	2.6x	2.1x
Total Debt / EBITDA	5.5x	5.3x	5.0x	4.8x	4.6x	4.3x	4.1x	3.6x
Net Senior Debt / EBITDA	3.0x	2.7x	2.3x	1.9x	1.5x	1.2x	0.8x	0.5x
Net Total Debt / EBITDA	5.1x	4.7x	4.2x	3.7x	3.3x	2.8x	2.4x	2.0x
EBITDA / Interest		3.1x	3.3x	3.3x	3.4x	3.4x	3.6x	3.9x
EBITDA - Capex / Interest		2.2x	2.3x	2.3x	2.4x	2.4x	2.6x	2.8x
Debt / Capitalization		64.7%	61.9%	59.2%	56.5%	53.9%	51.3%	46.3%

Setting Up the Operating Assumptions — Setting Up Income Statement

Revenue is the first item that is projected. The Revenue growth assumption is very important because it affects the rest of the Income Statement's items. Revenue growth depends on the target company's business. For example, for a manufacturing company, revenue growth could be based on volume and price increases/decreases. For a service company, such as a hotel company, the drivers for revenue growth would be Occupancy Rate and Average Daily Rate, and for a cable company, it could be based on subscriber growth for each product and pricing for that product.

INCOME STATEMENT								
		PROJECTED						
	12 mos Dec-14	12 mos Dec-15	12 mos Dec-16	12 mos Dec-17	12 mos Dec-18	12 mos Dec-19	12 mos Dec-20	12 mos Dec-21
REVENUE	5,983,000	6,098,920	6,344,146	6,650,695	6,967,341	7,256,107	7,559,378	7,877,958
Sales Growth	-2.2%	1.9%	4.0%	4.8%	4.8%	4.1%	4.2%	4.2%
COST OF SALES (excl. Deprec.)	1,507,000	1,514,535	1,571,274	1,651,651	1,732,814	1,802,825	1,876,741	1,954,803
Gross Profit	4,476,000	4,584,385	4,772,872	4,999,044	5,234,526	5,453,282	5,682,636	5,923,155
Gross Margin	74.8%	75.2%	75.2%	75.2%	75.1%	75.2%	75.2%	75.2%
OPERATING EXPENSES	3,392,000	3,457,720	3,596,748	3,770,543	3,950,062	4,113,775	4,285,711	4,466,327
EBITDA BEF. OTHER	1,084,000	1,126,665	1,176,124	1,228,501	1,284,464	1,339,508	1,396,925	1,456,828
% Sales	18.1%	18.5%	18.5%	18.5%	18.4%	18.5%	18.5%	18.5%
Other Expense	-	-	-	-	-	-	-	-
Other (Income)	-	-	-	-	-	-	-	-
EBITDA (Op. Cash Flow)	1,084,000	1,126,665	1,176,124	1,228,501	1,284,464	1,339,508	1,396,925	1,456,828
EBITDA Margin	18.1%	18.5%	18.5%	18.5%	18.4%	18.5%	18.5%	18.5%
Depreciation	201,000	204,894	213,133	223,431	234,069	243,770	253,959	264,661
EBIT from cont. oper.	883,000	921,771	962,992	1,005,070	1,050,395	1,095,737	1,142,967	1,192,167
Operating Margin	14.8%	15.1%	15.2%	15.1%	15.1%	15.1%	15.1%	15.1%
Amort. of Goodwill / Intagibles	-	-	-	-	-	-	-	-
Amort. of Fees	-	39,167	39,167	39,167	39,167	39,167	39,167	39,167
Other Non-Oper. Cash Expense	-	-	-	-	-	-	-	-
Other Non-Oper. Cash (Income)	-	-	-	-	-	-	-	-
EBIT	883,000	882,604	923,824	965,903	1,011,228	1,056,570	1,103,799	1,153,000
INTEREST EXPENSE (INCOME):								
Short Term Investment (Income)		-	(2,229)	(7,644)	(16,587)	(35,044)	(45,386)	(56,868)
Revolver		-	-	-	-	-	-	-
Term Loan A		-	-	-	-	-	-	-
Term Loan B		190,000	188,100	204,820	221,160	255,360	252,700	250,040
New Term Loan		-	-	-	-	-	-	-
Other Bank Debt / Exisiting		-	-	-	-	-	-	-
Senior Secured Notes		-	-	-	-	-	-	-
Senior Unsecured / Subordinated Notes		176,000	176,000	176,000	176,000	176,000	176,000	176,000
Junior Subordinated Notes		-	-	-	-	-	-	-
Total Interest Expense		366,000	361,871	373,176	380,573	396,316	383,314	369,172
EBT and Gain on Asset Sales		516,604	561,954	592,727	630,655	660,254	720,485	783,828
Gain on Asset Sales		-	-	-	-	-	-	-
Income Before Taxes		516,604	561,954	592,727	630,655	660,254	720,485	783,828
Tax Rate		30.0%	30.0%	30.0%	30.0%	30.0%	30.0%	30.0%
Tax Expense		154,981	168,586	177,818	189,196	198,076	216,146	235,148
Net Income bef. Extraordinary		361,623	393,367	414,909	441,458	462,178	504,340	548,679
Extraord. Chrge (after tax)		-	-	-	-	-	-	-
NET INCOME (LOSS)		361,623	393,367	414,909	441,458	462,178	504,340	548,679

Cost of Revenues and Operating Expenses could be calculated based on a percentage of revenue or each item within those expense categories could be driven by detailed expense analysis. The analysis could include hourly wages, number of workers and daily shifts — all annualized. Other expense drivers could be based on fixed or variable components. Operating expenses such as selling, general and administrative expenses are usually driven as a percentage of revenue unless they are specific expenses that the private equity firm identifies. In many cases, the private equity will include cost savings and cost rationalization. These cost savings could include one-time reduction of personnel, plant closures or ongoing expense controls that will improve operating margins going forward.

Setting Up Other Assumptions in the Income Statement

After the EBITDA, there are some other expenses that need to be addressed in the income statement. These items are as follows:

1. *Depreciation*: Depreciation expense is either calculated as % of Revenue or based upon depreciation schedules that are built off the actual assets. These depreciation expenses are based on fixed assets' useful life.
2. *Amortization Expenses*: These expenses are calculated based on amortization schedules. For example, Capitalized Expense reflects the fees and expenses charged in the LBO (which are then capitalized), and the amortization of this asset is based on the life of the underlying benefit. In the case of bank loan fees and loan legal expenses, the expense would be amortized over the life of the loan — usually 7 years.
3. *Interest Payments*: These payments are carried over from the debt schedule page.
4. *Taxes*: The tax rate used for calculating annual tax expenses is either given or is based on the specific tax situation of the borrower. The conservative assumption for this tax rate is usually 40%.

The annual tax expense is calculated by multiplying the tax rate times the Earnings before tax (after interest payments).

5. *Other nonoperating expense items*: In many cases, the projections include other nonoperating expenses such as one-time expense related to the LBO or predetermined expenses such as private equity management fees. These expenses are based on set schedules or as a percent of income or revenue.

OPERATING ASSUMPTIONS (INCOME, CASH FLOW AND BALANCE SHEET STATEMENTS)				PROJECTED				
	Dec-14	Dec-15	Dec-16	Dec-17	Dec-18	Dec-19	Dec-20	Dec-21
Revenue Growth								
Owned, Leased and Consolidated Joint Venture Hotels	-4.4%	-2.0%	0.0%	2.0%	3.0%	3.0%	3.0%	3.0%
Management Fees, Franchise Fees and Other Income	9.5%	10.0%	14.0%	12.0%	10.0%	7.0%	7.0%	7.0%
Vacation Ownership and Residential	-27.1%	-10.0%	-5.0%	0.0%	0.0%	0.0%	0.0%	0.0%
Other Revenues from Managed and Franchised Properties	3.7%	4.0%	4.0%	4.0%	4.0%	4.0%	4.0%	4.0%
Cost of Good as % of Sales								
Owned, Leased and Consolidated Joint Venture Hotels	24.4%	24.4%	24.4%	24.4%	24.4%	24.4%	24.4%	24.4%
Management Fees, Franchise Fees and Other Income	35.6%	35.6%	35.6%	35.6%	35.6%	35.6%	35.6%	35.6%
Vacation Ownership and Residential	55.9%	55.9%	55.9%	55.9%	55.9%	55.9%	55.9%	55.9%
Other Revenues from Managed and Franchised Properties	13.9%	13.9%	13.9%	13.9%	13.9%	13.9%	13.9%	13.9%
Operating Expense as % of Total Revenue	56.7%	56.7%	56.7%	56.7%	56.7%	56.7%	56.7%	56.7%
Depreciation % of Revenue	3.4%	3.4%	3.4%	3.4%	3.4%	3.4%	3.4%	3.4%
Other Expenses % of Revenue		0.0%	0.0%	0.0%	0.0%	0.0%	0.0%	0.0%
Other Income % of Revenue		0.0%	0.0%	0.0%	0.0%	0.0%	0.0%	0.0%
Other Non-Oper. Expenses % of Revenue		0.0%	0.0%	0.0%	0.0%	0.0%	0.0%	0.0%
Other Non-Operating Income % of Revenue		0.0%	0.0%	0.0%	0.0%	0.0%	0.0%	0.0%
Amort. of Goodwill / Intagibles		-	-	-	-	-	-	-
Amort. of Fees		-	-	-	-	-	-	-
Capex % of Revenue	5.5%	5.5%	5.5%	5.5%	5.5%	5.5%	5.5%	5.5%
Other Investments % of Revenue	-0.1%	0.0%	0.0%	0.0%	0.0%	0.0%	0.0%	0.0%
Accounts Receivable Days		55.3	55.3	55.3	55.3	55.3	55.3	55.3
Inventory Turns		6.39	6.39	6.39	6.39	6.39	6.39	6.39
Other Current Assets % of Revenue		2.7%	2.7%	2.7%	2.7%	2.7%	2.7%	2.7%
Accounts Payable Days		503.8	503.8	503.8	503.8	503.8	503.8	503.8
Acccrued Expenses % of Revenue		0.0%	0.0%	0.0%	0.0%	0.0%	0.0%	0.0%
Other Current Liabilities % of Revenues		0.0%	0.0%	0.0%	0.0%	0.0%	0.0%	0.0%

Debt Schedule — Principal & Interest Payments — Building the Balance Sheet

Setting up the projected debt schedule involves the calculation of interest and principal payments. The principal payments are usually negotiated with the bank that leads the bank financing. Normally bank loan facilities have scheduled principal payments set for every year from 1–10% of the initial loan.[15] The junior debt such as Mezzanine notes or corporate bonds do not normally have scheduled amortization, and the only principal payment is paid at the end of term. In many cases, the private equity runs a "cash sweep" approach that uses excess cash to prepay the bank debt. This in turn affects bank

[15] Leveraged Commentary & Data, Standards & Poors Global.

debt outstandings, interest expense, the interest expense tax shield, and taxes. These items affect the balance sheet, income statement, and cash flow statement of the borrower.

The bank loan is based on a floating reference rate such as LIBOR plus a spread. The model could assume that LIBOR will be based on the LIBOR futures curve, or it could simply assume an increase every year up to a particular level. For a fixed debt facility, such as corporate bonds, the bond is not payable until maturity and the projected interest payment should be the same every year.

DEBT SCHEDULES / ANALYSIS								
				PROJECTED				
	Dec-14	Dec-15	Dec-16	Dec-17	Dec-18	Dec-19	Dec-20	Dec-21
Interest Rate Assumptions								
LIBOR Rate	1.00%	1.00%	1.00%	1.50%	2.00%	3.00%	3.00%	3.00%
LIBOR lincrease / Decrease		0.0%	0.0%	0.5%	0.5%	1.0%	0.0%	0.0%
Short-Term Investments								
Outstanding	-	222,915	509,578	829,326	1,168,118	1,512,868	1,895,588	1,784,283
Increase / (Decrease)		222,915	286,663	319,748	338,792	344,750	382,721	(111,305)
Interest		-	2,229	7,644	16,587	35,044	45,386	56,868
Interest rate		1.00%	1.00%	1.50%	2.00%	3.00%	3.00%	3.00%
Revolver								
Outstanding	-	-	-	-	-	-	-	-
Increase / (Decrease)		-	-	-	-	-	-	-
Scheduled Amortization		-	-	-	-	-	-	-
Cash Sweep if any		-	-	-	-	-	-	-
Interest		-	-	-	-	-	-	-
Interest rate		5.00%	5.00%	5.50%	6.00%	7.00%	7.00%	7.00%
Term Loan A								
Outstanding	-	-	-	-	-	-	-	-
Increase / (Decrease)		-	-	-	-	-	-	-
Scheduled Amortization		-	-	-	-	-	-	-
Cash Sweep if any		-	-	-	-	-	-	-
Interest		-	-	-	-	-	-	-
Interest rate		1.00%	1.00%	1.50%	2.00%	3.00%	3.00%	3.00%
Term Loan B								
Outstanding	3,800,000	3,762,000	3,724,000	3,686,000	3,648,000	3,610,000	3,572,000	-
Increase / (Decrease)		(38,000)	(38,000)	(38,000)	(38,000)	(38,000)	(38,000)	(3,572,000)
Scheduled Amortization		(38,000)	(38,000)	(38,000)	(38,000)	(38,000)	(38,000)	(3,572,000)
Cash Sweep if any		(260,915)	(324,663)	(357,748)	(376,792)	(382,750)	(420,721)	(460,695)
Interest		190,000	188,100	204,820	221,160	255,360	252,700	250,040
Interest rate		5.00%	5.00%	5.50%	6.00%	7.00%	7.00%	7.00%
Senior Unsecured / Subordinated Notes								
Outstanding	2,200,000	2,200,000	2,200,000	2,200,000	2,200,000	2,200,000	2,200,000	2,200,000
Increase / (Decrease)		-	-	-	-	-	-	-
Interest		176,000	176,000	176,000	176,000	176,000	176,000	176,000
Interest rate		8.0%	8.0%	8.0%	8.0%	8.0%	8.0%	8.0%

Setting Up Working Capital, Capital Expenditure and Other Cash Flow Items — Linking the Changes of the Balance Sheet.

The Cash Flow Statement items such as changes in working capital and capital expenditures are to an extent driven from revenue growth. The working capital line in the Cash Flow Statement includes changes in accounts receivable, inventory, payables and accrued expenses.

These changes are the difference between this year's and last year's Balance Sheet levels for these to entries. If the asset increases from one year to the next, the difference is recorded as a negative cash item in the cash flow statement. If the asset decreases from one year to the next, that difference is recorded as a positive cash item in the cash flow statement. Any liability or net worth changes in the balance sheet are recorded in the cash flow statement as positive cash if these changes increase from year to year and negative if these changes decrease from year to year.

CASH FLOW STATEMENT							
	PROJECTED						
	12 mos	12 mos	12 mos	12 mos	12 mos	12 mos	12 mos
	Dec-15	Dec-16	Dec-17	Dec-18	Dec-19	Dec-20	Dec-21
OPERATING ACTIVITIES:							
Net Income (Loss)	361,623	393,367	414,909	441,458	462,178	504,340	548,679
Depreciation	204,894	213,133	223,431	234,069	243,770	253,959	264,661
Amort. Goodwill & Fees	39,167	39,167	39,167	39,167	39,167	39,167	39,167
Non-Oper. Expense (Income)	-	-	-	-	-	-	-
Gain on Sale of Assets	-	-	-	-	-	-	-
Interest Expense	366,000	361,871	373,176	380,573	396,316	383,314	369,172
Tax Expense	154,981	168,586	177,818	189,196	198,076	216,146	235,148
Adjusted EBITDA (Op. Cash Flow)	1,126,665	1,176,124	1,228,501	1,284,464	1,339,508	1,396,925	1,456,828
Cash Taxes	(154,981)	(168,586)	(177,818)	(189,196)	(198,076)	(216,146)	(235,148)
Change in Working Capital	(11,434)	25,734	43,733	42,896	34,216	36,412	38,756
Non-Oper. Income (Expense)							
Change in Other Assets	-	-	-	-	-	-	-
Change in Other Liabilities	-	-	-	-	-	-	-
Subtotal	960,251	1,033,273	1,094,417	1,138,164	1,175,648	1,217,192	1,260,436
INVESTMENT ACTIVITIES:							
Capital Expenditures	(333,336)	(346,738)	(363,493)	(380,799)	(396,581)	(413,157)	(430,569)
Other Investments	-	-	-	-	-	-	-
Acquistions	-	-	-	-	-	-	-
Total Capex / Acquisitions	(333,336)	(346,738)	(363,493)	(380,799)	(396,581)	(413,157)	(430,569)
Divestitures	-	-	-	-	-	-	-
Other Investments	-	-	-	-	-	-	-
Subtotal	(333,336)	(346,738)	(363,493)	(380,799)	(396,581)	(413,157)	(430,569)
AVAILABLE CASH FLOW (FACF)	626,915	686,534	730,924	757,365	779,066	804,035	829,867
FINANCING ACTIVITIES:							
Cash Interest Expense	(366,000)	(361,871)	(373,176)	(380,573)	(396,316)	(383,314)	(369,172)
Cash Common Stock Dividends (-)	-	-	-	-	-	-	-
Cash Preferred Stock Dividends (-)	-	-	-	-	-	-	-
Preferred Stock Issued (Purchased)	-	-	-	-	-	-	-
Common Equity Issued (Purchased)	-	-	-	-	-	-	-
Cash Available for Debt Amortization	260,915	324,663	357,748	376,792	382,750	420,721	460,695
Revolver	-	-	-	-	-	-	-
Term Loan A	-	-	-	-	-	-	-
Term Loan B	(38,000)	(38,000)	(38,000)	(38,000)	(38,000)	(38,000)	(3,572,000)
New Term Loan	-	-	-	-	-	-	3,000,000
Other Bank Debt / Exisiting	-	-	-	-	-	-	-
Senior Secured Notes	-	-	-	-	-	-	-
Senior Unsecured / Subordinated Notes	-	-	-	-	-	-	-
Junior Subordinated Notes	-	-	-	-	-	-	-
Total Debt Payments	(38,000)	(38,000)	(38,000)	(38,000)	(38,000)	(38,000)	(572,000)
FX Effect							
Free Cash Flow	222,915	286,663	319,748	338,792	344,750	382,721	(111,305)
Beginning Cash Balance	-	222,915	509,578	829,326	1,168,118	1,512,868	1,895,588
Required Operating Cash	-	-	-	-	-	-	-
CASH SURPLUS/(NEEDS)	222,915	509,578	829,326	1,168,118	1,512,868	1,895,588	1,784,283

The Capital Expenditures are usually broken down into two categories: maintenance and growth capital expenditures. Both capital expenditures are typically presented as a percentage of revenue, unless the private equity runs a specific schedule for capital expenditures.

Setting Up the Projected Balance Sheet

After the time zero Balance Sheet is set, some Balance Sheet items are driven from last year's Balance Sheet and this year's Income Statement and possibly the Cash Flow Statement. For example,

BALANCE SHEET								
				PROJECTED				
	Dec-14	Dec-15	Dec-16	Dec-17	Dec-18	Dec-19	Dec-20	Dec-21
ASSETS								
Cash	500,000	500,000	500,000	500,000	500,000	500,000	500,000	500,000
Short-Term Investments	-	222,915	509,578	829,326	1,168,118	1,512,868	1,895,588	1,784,283
Accounts Receivable	907,000	924,573	961,748	1,008,220	1,056,222	1,099,998	1,145,973	1,194,268
Inventory	236,000	237,180	246,065	258,653	271,363	282,327	293,902	306,127
Other Current Assets	159,000	162,081	168,598	176,744	185,159	192,833	200,893	209,359
Total Current Assets	1,802,000	2,046,749	2,385,990	2,772,943	3,180,862	3,588,026	4,036,356	3,994,038
Gross Fixed Assets	2,634,000	2,967,336	3,314,074	3,677,567	4,058,366	4,454,947	4,868,104	5,298,673
(Accum. Depreciation)		(204,894)	(418,027)	(641,458)	(875,528)	(1,119,298)	(1,373,257)	(1,637,918)
Total Fixed Assets	2,634,000	2,762,441	2,896,047	3,036,108	3,182,838	3,335,649	3,494,847	3,660,755
Capitalized Exp.	274,170	235,003	195,836	156,669	117,501	78,334	39,167	0
Purchase Goodwill	4,670,000	4,670,000	4,670,000	4,670,000	4,670,000	4,670,000	4,670,000	4,670,000
Other Intagibles	1,956,000	1,956,000	1,956,000	1,956,000	1,956,000	1,956,000	1,956,000	1,956,000
Other Investm's & Assets	1,748,000	1,748,000	1,748,000	1,748,000	1,748,000	1,748,000	1,748,000	1,748,000
Total Assets	13,084,170	13,418,193	13,851,872	14,339,720	14,855,202	15,376,009	15,944,371	16,028,792
LIABILITIES & SHAREHOLDER EQUITY								
Accounts Payable	2,080,000	2,090,400	2,168,712	2,279,651	2,391,675	2,488,305	2,590,326	2,698,069
Acccrued Expenses	-	-	-	-	-	-	-	-
Other Current Liabilities	-	-	-	-	-	-	-	-
Total Current Liabilities	2,080,000	2,090,400	2,168,712	2,279,651	2,391,675	2,488,305	2,590,326	2,698,069
Revolver	-	-	-	-	-	-	-	-
Term Loan A	-	-	-	-	-	-	-	-
Term Loan B	3,800,000	3,762,000	3,724,000	3,686,000	3,648,000	3,610,000	3,572,000	-
New Term Loan	-	-	-	-	-	-	-	3,000,000
Other Bank Debt / Exisiting	-	-	-	-	-	-	-	-
Senior Secured Notes	-	-	-	-	-	-	-	-
Senior Unsecured / Subordinated Notes	2,200,000	2,200,000	2,200,000	2,200,000	2,200,000	2,200,000	2,200,000	2,200,000
Junior Subordinated Notes	-	-	-	-	-	-	-	-
Total Debt	6,000,000	5,962,000	5,924,000	5,886,000	5,848,000	5,810,000	5,772,000	5,200,000
Deferred Taxes	38,000	38,000	38,000	38,000	38,000	38,000	38,000	38,000
Other Liabilities & OPEB	2,069,000	2,069,000	2,069,000	2,069,000	2,069,000	2,069,000	2,069,000	2,069,000
Minority Interest	3,000	3,000	3,000	3,000	3,000	3,000	3,000	3,000
Total Liabilities	10,190,000	10,162,400	10,202,712	10,275,651	10,349,675	10,408,305	10,472,326	10,008,069
OWNER'S EQUITY								
Treasury Stock	-	-	-	-	-	-	-	-
Preferred Stock	-	-	-	-	-	-	-	-
Common Stock	2,894,170	2,894,170	2,894,170	2,894,170	2,894,170	2,894,170	2,894,170	2,894,170
Add'l Paid-in-Capital	-	-	-	-	-	-	-	-
Other	-	-	-	-	-	-	-	-
Retained Earnings	-	361,623	754,990	1,169,899	1,611,357	2,073,535	2,577,875	3,126,554
Total Equity	2,894,170	3,255,793	3,649,160	4,064,069	4,505,527	4,967,705	5,472,045	6,020,724
Total Liabilities & Equity	13,084,170	13,418,193	13,851,872	14,339,720	14,855,202	15,376,009	15,944,371	16,028,792

Capitalized Expenses reflect last year's Balance Sheet level minus this year's Capitalized Expense Amortization, and Retained Earnings reflect last year's level plus Net Income (because there are no dividends in most LBOs). Property, Plant and Equipment reflects last years' level, less this year's depreciation, plus this year's Capital Expenditures.

On the other hand, some Balance Sheet items, such as Accounts Receivable and Accounts Payable are not affected by the previous year's Balance Sheet and are instead a function of Revenues or Expenses. If however one wishes to more closely project these entries and wants to project them based on a particular turnover ratio, one can project them as follows:

1. Accounts Receivables (A/R): A function of Revenues divided by annual A/R turnover.
2. Inventory: A function of Revenues divided by annual Inventory turnover.
3. Accounts Payable (A/P): A function of Supplier Expenses divided by A/P turnover.

Tying it all Together

For the model to work correctly, so that future projected Assets are equal to future projected Liabilities, all model entries must tie in to other entries, as follows:

a. All the entries in the Income Statement must tie back to the Cash Flow Statement.
b. All entries in the Cash Flow Statement that are not dependent on Balance Sheet entries (e.g., Capital Expenditures) must tie back to the Balance Sheet.
c. All entries in the Balance Sheet Statement that are not dependent on the Cash Flow Statement (e.g., Accounts Payable) must tie back to the Balance Sheet.

Securities Exchange Commission & Bank Regulations

Securities Exchange Commission (SEC)[16]

The SEC's Office of Investor Education and Advocacy issued an Investor Bulletin to educate individual investors about high-yield corporate bonds, also called "junk bonds." These bonds are primarily used for LBOs. While they generally offer a higher yield than investment-grade bonds, high-yield bonds also carry a higher risk of default.

The SEC states the following regarding High-Yield Bonds:

"Some investors with a greater risk tolerance may find high-yield corporate bonds attractive, particularly in low interest rate environments. If you are considering buying a high-yield bond, it is important that you understand the risks involved. These are as follows:

> "Default risk. Also, referred to as credit risk, this is the risk that a company will fail to make timely interest or principal payments and default on its bond. Defaults also can occur if the company fails to meet certain terms of its debt agreement. Because high-yield bonds are typically issued by companies with higher risks of default, this risk is particularly important to consider when investing in high-yield bonds.
>
> "Interest rate risk. Market interest rates have a major impact on bond investments. The price of a bond moves in the opposite direction than market interest rates — like opposing ends of a seesaw. This presents investors with interest rate risk, which is common to all bonds. In addition, the longer the bond's maturity, the more time there is for rates to change and, as a result, affect the price of the bond. Therefore, bonds with longer maturities generally present greater interest rate risk than bonds of similar credit quality that have shorter maturities.

[16] Securities & Exchange Commission Commentary.

"Economic risk. If the economy falters, some investors are likely to try to sell their bonds. In what is known as a "flight to quality," several investors may decide to replace their riskier high-yield bonds with safer ones, such as U.S. treasury bonds. If there are more sellers than buyers for high-yield bonds, the supply will exceed demand and prices of the bonds will fall. In addition, some companies that issue high-yield bonds may be less able to weather challenging economic circumstances, increasing the risk of default.

"Liquidity risk. Liquidity is the ability to sell an asset, such as a bond, for cash when the owner chooses. Bonds that are traded frequently and at high volumes may have stronger liquidity than bonds that trade less frequently. Liquidity risk is the risk that investors seeking to sell their bonds may not receive a price that reflects the true value of the bonds (based on the bond's interest rate and creditworthiness of the company). High-yield bonds may be subject to more liquidity risk than, for example, investment-grade bonds."

Leveraged Lending Guidelines[17]

Following the financial crisis of 2008, the Office of the Comptroller of the Currency (OCC), the Board of Governors of the Federal Reserve System (Board), and the Federal Deposit Insurance Corporation (FDIC) issued lending guidance for financing LBOs. Accordingly, these government agencies, in a letter issued on October 2013, stated that "given the high-risk profile of leveraged transactions, financial institutions engaged in leveraged lending need to adopt a risk management framework that has an intensive and frequent review and monitoring process. The framework should have as its foundation written risk objectives, risk acceptance criteria, and risk controls. A lack of robust risk management processes and controls at a financial institution with significant leveraged lending activities could contribute to supervisory findings that the financial institution is engaged in unsafe-and-unsound banking practices". This letter had

[17] Comptroller of Currency, the Board of Federal Reserve System and the Federal Deposit Insurance Corporation, Letter: March 2013.

a significant impact of how banks lend money to finance LBOs. For one, in order to avoid criticism, the initial Leveraged Ratio of Total Debt/EBITDA needs to be at 6.0× or less, or the transaction model needs to show (to the Regulators' satisfaction) that 50% of the transaction's total debt will be repaid in less than 7 years.

Summary of Key Points

- An LBO is the acquisition by an investor of a company with mostly borrowed money. The Debt for the acquisition is scheduled to be repaid by the operating cash flows of the company and/or proceeds from selling the company or refinancing the acquisition debt with new debt. The investor is not personally responsible for paying the debt nor is he required to add any other capital to support his or her investment.
- LBOs have been around for 100 years but became more organized in the late 1980s with the creation of the syndicated loan market and the organization by the financial sponsors of mega private equity funds to be used for LBOs.
- There are three types of LBOs: Public to Private Transactions, Private to Private Transactions and Management Buyouts.
- LBOs typically reduce a company's tax payments (and hence increase the returns available to its equity investors), primarily due to the tax shield from interest expense, and also on occasion due to the tax shield from increased depreciation and amortization expense following the write-up of a company's assets upon its LBO.
- Over the years, some LBO tax benefits and strategies have however been eliminated.
- The debt financing of an LBO is provided by the traditional commercial banks, by Collateralized Loan Obligation funds, insurance companies, hedge funds and other types of funds, and in the case of public High-Yield Bonds, by more varied public investors.
- There are many types of debt facilities used in the financing of an LBO including Bank Debt, High-Yield Debt and Mezzanine Notes.

- A good LBO needs to have strong cash flows, good growth prospects, low capital expenditures, a strong asset base, and strong management.
- The concept of leverage enhances the equity returns because of the low cost of debt. The equity return can be enhanced by Enterprise Value growth, debt repayment, and by acquisition multiple expansion.
- In structuring an LBO, the first measurement is debt capacity. Basically, what is the maximum level of debt that a company can support.
- LBO financial modeling starts with complete historical information, a considered projection of future operating performance, and a modelling of the acquisition debt and the projected equity returns.
- The SEC regulates High-Yield issuance, while the OCC, the Board of the Federal Reserve System ("the Fed"), and the FDIC regulate banks' lending for LBOs.

Recommended Reading

Investment Banking, Valuation, Leveraged Buyouts, and Mergers & Acquisitions, Joshua Rosenbaum and Joshua Pearl, John Wiley & Sons Publishing, New York, 2009.

ProfessorDrou.com spreadsheets and analysis material on Debt Capacity, LBO financing and Capital Markets.

Chapter 12
Restructuring & Divestitures

Christophe van Gampelaere
Global PMI Partners

Introduction

"About 35% to 45% of merger and acquisition activities involve a divestiture".[1]

The chapter learning objectives

In this chapter, you will learn about:

- various types of divestiture,
- what triggers a divestment,
- the elements of a divestment process, and
- Transition Service Agreements (TSAs) & stranded costs.

The main issues addressed in this chapter

This chapter starts with a description of the various types of divestiture. It presents a framework wherein these occur. The framework covers the process from end to end. It starts with the rationale and triggers for divesting; it goes on to assess the impact on the parent company, the target and the acquirer; it describes associated risks and issues and the parties involved in a divestiture. It touches on how to

[1] Capron, Mitchell, & Swaminathan, 2001.

prepare for an exit and how to become either independent or integrated into the buyer.

We address the theoretical elements of a divestment process, covering the phases in a divestiture process, and we provide the reader with some useful templates and leading practices. We end with an overview of lessons learned.

Examples, data and charts are peppered throughout the chapter, and the reader is provided with some useful tables, tools, and templates.

Highlights of the literature

- The Business Model Canvas™[2] as a divestment decision-making tool
- Global PMI Partner's Acquisition Carve-out Framework™ (GPMIP Acquisition Carve-out Framework)[3]

The takeaways from this chapter

- Divestment typologies by divestment complexity, by deal characteristic and by target owners
- TSA template
- Divestiture program structure
- TSA governance structure

Types of Divestiture

What Is a Divestiture?

A divestiture is a term covering a broad spectrum of activities where a parent company divests itself of part of its business. Divestitures range from simple, stand-alone events to complex undertakings with far-reaching ramifications. We call the divested entity the "Target" (reflecting the Acquirer's point of view). The term 'target' is generally accepted and understood in the investment community.

---

[2] Osterwalder A. & Peigneur Y. *Business Model Generation.* Wiley, New York, 2013.
[3] Scola, A & Whitaker S. *Cross-border Mergers & Acquisitions.* Wiley, New York, 2016, chapter 17.

Divestiture Typologies

Typology by Divestment Complexity

Any divestment requires an upfront strategic analysis by the Parent on the rationale behind the divestment.

If and when a decision is taken, there are nine distinct types of divestiture targets, depending on the complexity to divest the business, as shown in Figure 1.

We identify nine target types:

1. Group
2. Single stand-alone entity
3. Single legal entity connected to the Parent
4. Multiple legal entities connected to Seller
5. Legal entities + certain assets or people
6. Business unit with history of BU reporting
7. Business unit without BU numbers
8. Loosely defined operational unit
9. Various assets "put in a box"

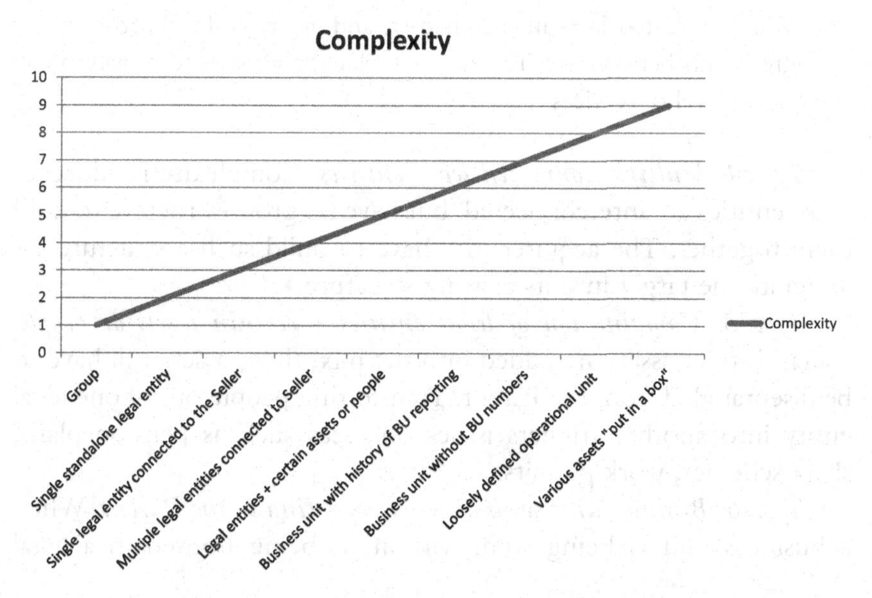

Figure 1: Increasing Level of Deal Complexity.

Type 1: *Group of companies.* The complexity from a divestiture point of view is relatively straightforward. None of the above factors adding complexity to the deal apply. There is still significant work to be done however. GPMIP's Acquisition and Carve-Out Framework™, described further down this chapter notes the need to prepare the target to be put on the market and facilitate the acquirer's due diligence (DD) process.

Type 2: *Single stand-alone legal entity.* The additional complexity of selling one stand-alone legal entity versus a group of companies is related to the ease in finding the right acquirer. The smaller the entity, the more diseconomies of scale play a role in preparing the target for a sale.

Commissioning a Vendor Due Diligence (VDD) report is relatively more expensive as is setting up a data room and hiring advisors to prepare.

Type 3: *Single connected legal entity.* If the target is a distinct legal entity, but is connected to the parent, the issue of TSAs comes into play. Being connected to the parent means that certain group functions are provided by other companies in the group. These functions can be anything, but IT, Finance, HR and Legal are often at least partially provided by related group companies.

> TSAs are treated later in the chapter, and are typically short-term agreements between the Target and a related company, to provide a certain level of services.

Type 4: *Multiple connected legal entities.* Complexity is added as these entities are interconnected, but have no group structure to hold them together. The acquirer may have to build such a structure, or integrate the target into its existing structure.

Type 5: *Combination of legal entities + certain assets or people.* When distinct assets are added into the mix, those assets will have to be disentangled from the Parent. Transferring people out of one legal entity into another triggers issues on areas such as pension plans, share schemes, work permits.

Type 6: *Business unit with distinct reporting to the Parent.* When a business unit is being sold, without it being housed in a legal entity, we enter a completely new realm. Assets, people, systems, policies, procedures, and contracts will all be affected. The acquirer can still obtain some clarity on the business performance, since there are management reports. The question is how those reports can at all be tied in to the Parent's reported figures, and how much of costs and revenues can really be allocated to the Target.

Type 7: *Business unit without distinct reporting to the Parent.* The lack of distinct reporting adds another layer of risk for the buyer. That risk will be discounted in the acquisition price. On a positive side, there is still an organizational unit, and members of that unit will be able to provide some clarity on business practices. They will often be very much performing part of their functions for the Parent company, and dividing up the organization may not be a straightforward exercise.

Type 8: *Loosely defined operational unit.* This type of target lacks the organizational clarity of the previous type, and makes all divestiture and integration activities that much more difficult.

Type 9: *Collection of "bits & pieces in a box"*. The most complex divestiture, both for buyer and for seller, is the "bits & pieces in a box" deal. Anything can go in, like:

- fixed, tangible or financial assets, licenses, intellectual property, client lists
- liabilities such as payable loans, payroll liabilities; some are difficult to transfer, like tax liabilities, potential claims, off-balance-sheet obligations
- some assets are hard not to transfer, like land, a factory, people, inventory, contracts.

Deal complexity is related to the ability of the seller to describe, value, and separate assets, liabilities, and interdependencies, including regulatory compliance with local transfer of business laws, and costs incurred by the Parent to separate the business. Based on the above, Table 1 shows a list of elements that remove complexity from a divestiture. Conversely, the absence of any of these elements will add complexity.

Table 1: Factors Removing Complexity in a Divestiture.

The Target is incorporated in a separate legal entity
The Target's customers and suppliers are distinct and not linked to the Parent's other business activities
The Target's offer is distinct and not linked to the Parent's other business activities
The Target's infrastructure is distinct and not linked to the Parent's other business activities
The Target's financial viability is distinct and not linked to the Parent's other business activities
The Target has regular management reports on its business activities
The Target has its own management team
Low level of integration with the parent company: no shared applications, no joint backbones, no shared IT and accounting departments. Wherever there is an integration, there is a clear and objective cost allocation and recharge
Seller has a professional firm assisting the divestiture process
The deal is a share deal, as opposed to an asset deal
There are no legal contracts binding the Parent and Target to third parties, i.e., no shared contracts, no bulk contracts, no change of control clauses, no joint purchase agreements
All employees working for the Target are employed by the Target
Logistics are not interlinked
There are no shared sites, a change of ownership will not trigger any procedures such as environmental audits
The Target's processes are independent of the Parent's processes
R&D is strictly separated: no joint development, no shared IP, know-how is clearly documented, no joint projects

Typology by Divestment Complexity

The deal characteristics summarized in Table 2 are not mutually exclusive. The issues and risks in each get multiplied as more types of divestiture deals are combined.

Share deal versus asset deal: An asset deal is not necessarily "bits and pieces thrown in a box". In fact, it can encompass a complete business unit, or all people, assets and activities from a legal entity, and the only thing missing would be the original legal entity vehicle. There are numerous reasons for doing an asset deal. The Acquirer

Table 2: Typology by Deal Characteristic.

No.	Characteristic	Simple	Complex
1	Transaction type	Share deal	Asset deal
2	Future cooperation	None	Intensive
3	Geographic spread	National	Global
4	Distressed sale	None	Multiple
5	Time	No pressure	Pressure

may push for one, as it allows him to choose from an "à la carte" menu, or it may protect him from potential liabilities residing in the legal entity. On the other hand, the Seller may push for an asset deal, when the legal entity holds recoverable tax losses.

High versus low level of future cooperation with Target: If the Parent, Target, and Acquirer need to align or partially tie in their business models, they can achieve this in a number of ways. Future cooperation can be cemented through long-term service level agreements (LTSAs) or by creating a joint venture (JV) between Parent and Acquirer.

Multinational target: Multinational targets are identified by their presence in multiple countries or continents. Language and culture barriers need to be overcome by the acquirer.

Even though the M&A world is aware of the importance of culture, the practical implications have yet to make it into a practical on-the-ground application.

Culture does not need to be abstract and intangible. It is a surprisingly easy topic to quantify and handle. The most important hurdles to clear are psychological ones — on the one hand not to overdramatize how difficult it is to handle and on the other hand not to brush it aside as something that will get solved automatically in due time.

A divestiture in a distressed environment: When the Parent, Target or Buyer are going through a period of distress, there is increased risk for costly mistakes and omissions. Any internal company upheaval like a restructuring, a change in strategy, or the implementation of a strategic project requires management's attention. Add to that the workload of a divestiture of integration, and something will have to give an ideal environment for competitors to steal your customers, for employees to leave the firm, for quality issues to find their way into the value chain. All of these risks are added to "business as usual" at a time where stakeholders are extra watchful of the company.

A divestiture deal is announced, the deadline is set: As long as the deal is not announced, management and employees have time to prepare. There is time to map many of the risks described earlier, and to take mitigating actions. Once the divestment is made public, outside pressure from the market, investors, potential acquirers and advisers will rise. They will expect a deadline, and internally, top management may push for an even earlier exit.

Form of Divestments by Target Owner

Divestments take the form of carve-outs, spin-offs, split-offs, split-ups, or JVs. The terms *divestiture* and carve-out are often used intermittently. However, from a parent shareholder point of view, there is a difference.

Carve-out: The parent sells shares of the target. Share ownership can be open to the public like in an IPO, or closed, when a trade buyer or a private equity firm acquire ownership. The shareholder of the parent company continues to hold shares in the parent company. He will not hold shares of the divested unit.

> About carve-out deadlines
>
> When Philips carved out its semiconductors unit in 2006, the initial deadline was end of October.
>
> Workstream leaders complained there was not enough time to get ready, and more months were needed. Despite this, the CEO told the carve-out team in June that the deadline would be brought forward by 2 months to early September.
>
> The carve-out was successful and raised €2 bn more than expected.

Spin-off: The parent creates an ownership vehicle that holds the activities of the divested entity, and distributes the shares of the target to its existing shareholders. The shareholder of the parent company continues to own parent shares, in addition to the target shares. The parent shareholder ends up with shares of the parent as well as the target. A Bloomberg index of spin-off stocks has outpaced the S&P 500 by five percentage points annually over the10 years period to 2014.

Split-off: The parent offers its shareholders shares of the target in exchange for their parents' shares. The parent shareholder ends up with shares of either the parent, or the target.

Split-up: The parent splits its activities, with clearly defined business ownership of the separated business units. There is no external buyer (yet), and the shares remain with the existing shareholders. When Hewlett-Packard split up its personal computers and printer business, it did so "to gain independence, focus, financial resources, and flexibility." The smaller of the two often has the advantage of a small stock company, outperforming its bigger sibling.

Joint Venture ("JV"): The parent shareholder maintains partial (minority or majority) ownership in the target. The other shares are sold to private equity or a trade buyer. Some studies[4] show an advantage of a JV over an independent company in that JVs are more cost efficient, management is more likely to combine production factors, and benefits are derived from positive efficiency effects and the combination of skills and know-how from the two partners.

Typology of Buyer and Parties Involved

Types of Buyer

The target's financials will look different to each category of buyer. We recommend that the seller consider the financials from the buyer's point of view, in order to enhance his position in the negotiation process.

Buyers fall into a number of categories:

---

[4] Bancassurance efficiency gains in the insurance industry: the Italian case
Franco Fiordelisi a, b,; Ornella Riccia,
(a) University of Rome III, Italy.
(b) Bangor Business School, Bangor University, UK.

1. *trade buyer*
2. *private equity*
3. *public*
4. *existing management (Management Buy Out — MBO)*
5. *new management (Management Buy In — MBI)*
6. *existing parent shareholders (spin-off and split-off)*

Parties involved

Throughout the divestment process, a host of internal and external parties will be involved: the Board of directors, strategy advisers, management, unions, the community; regulators, consultants, legal councils, tax advisors, accountants, the Securities and Exchange Commission, and other watchdogs ...

Each with their interests and challenges, both from buyer and seller.

Triggers of a Divestment

Divestitures are part of a corporate process, they don't happen in a vacuum. We see divestments happening following a strategic review, to comply with anticompetition rules, to satisfy shareholder demands and to raise cash.

Divesting Following a Strategic Review

A divestment may be triggered as it becomes clear that a business activity is no longer strategic to the parent company.

The starting point for a good discussion on what is strategic, and what is not, is a shared understanding of what a business model actually is.

The Business Model Canvas

The Business Model Canvas (Figure 2) provides a useful framework to describe a company's business model. It is a model that facilitates

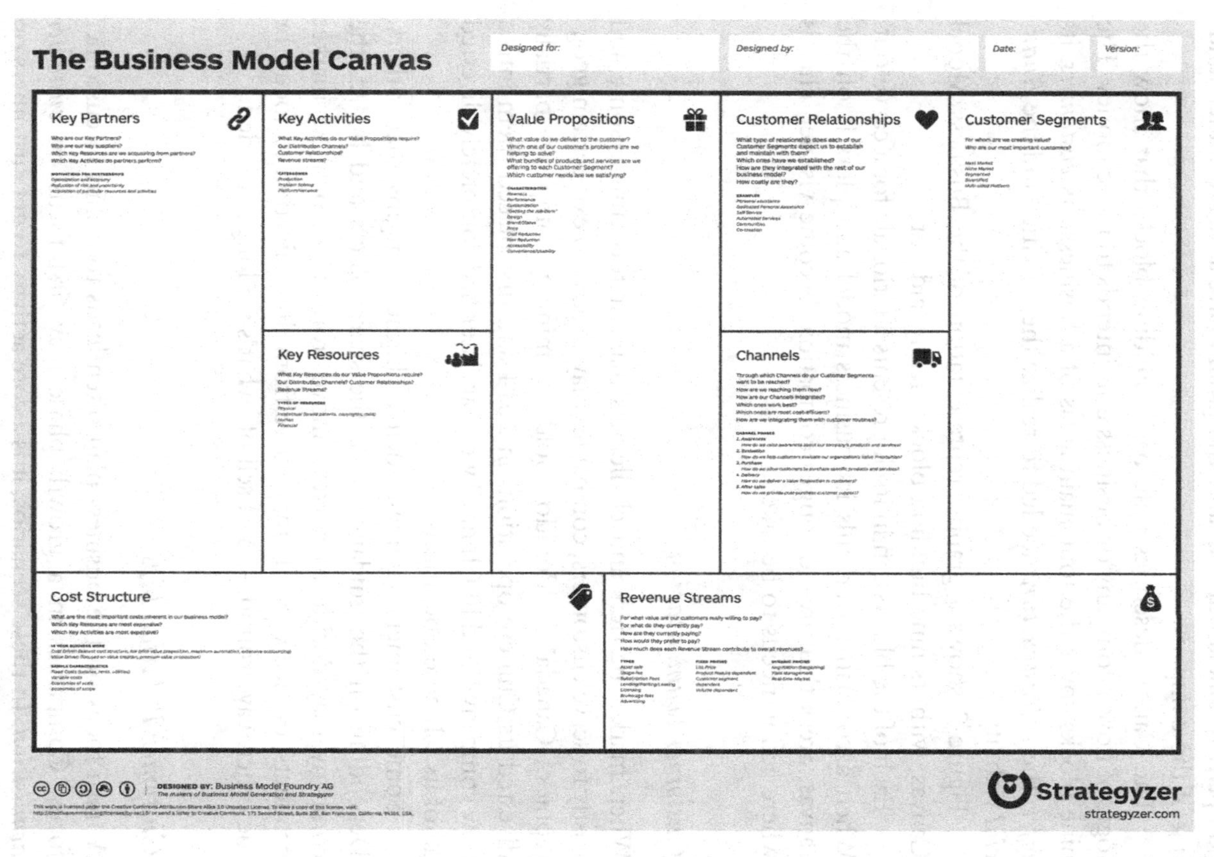

Figure 2: The Business Model Canvas.

description and discussions. It allows all individuals involved in the company to talk about the same things and have a shared understanding of the company.

The Canvas describes nine basic building blocks that show the logic of how a company or business unit intends to make money. The nine blocks cover the four main areas of a business: its *customers*, its *offer*, the *infrastructure* needed to realize the activities and the *financial* viability.

Figure 2 shows a graphic representation of the Business Model Canvas, with its nine building blocks clearly laid out.

Each of the blocks can in itself presents a rationale for a carve-out. When a company overhauls its business model and plots it on the canvas, areas that are no longer compatible become visible. That is where action needs to be taken.

Customer Segmentation

When market barriers and challenges make it too cumbersome and costly to serve customers, companies may choose to exit certain geographies. Canada's Eldorado Gold, a mining company, partially divested its Chinese operations in 2014 and first placed them into a new company listed in China. Two years later had completely divested all of its Chinese operations.

Some customers segments deliver higher margins than others. Depending on the guidance from the shareholders and board, the company may decide to make a move from mass to niche market products, or vice-versa. It may move from diversification to focus, or the other way around — and sell off what's no longer needed.

Customer Relationships

A fresh focus on the business plan often leads to a shift in customer focus. Companies in a growth phase may first focus on *customer acquisition*. In these scenarios, it is a core activity to get customers on the network (telecoms), to establish a broad customer base (acquiring "eyeballs" for internet companies). In a later stage, *customer retention* may become more important. By then, customer acquisition may have become so routine that it can be spun off. Ricoh, the Japanese printer manufacturer, has done just that, and now offers its expertise to the wide world.

Upselling to the existing customer base is the next rung on the customer relationship ladder. However, as a consequence of focusing on the upselling customer relationship model, certain BU's may no longer adequately served by the parent company. Left as an orphan, the unit may linger, not get the management attention needed, and overall drag the parent's results down. When the Belgian chemical giant UCB sold its amino acid arm in 2000, it was to get rid of a marginal activity, generating low margins to customers to whom UCB thought you could no up-sell. Fifteen years later, the company had increased revenue and EBITDA tenfold.

Customer Channels

Sometimes, the mother company is not able to make its customers aware of some products and services; channels through which customers want to be reached may not be cost effective, or cannot be integrated with the parent's others channels. Sometimes the after-sales effort of the target is not effective. If these problems cannot be solved within the parent, a carve-out of certain business activities may be the best way forward.

Value Propositions

When the Target's core business offering is no longer a strategic value proposition for the Parent, such as in the UCB case mentioned above, the Parent may decide to sell the unit. The same is applicable if the bundling of the Parent's services or products no longer include the Target's, or if the product or service moved along on the BCG matrix from "cash cow" to "dog". After the carve, the Parent improved flexibility will allow it to pursue its goals.

Key Activities and Resources

The key activities and assets form a company's central infrastructure to make its business model work. These assets can be physical, intellectual, financial, and human. For a microchip manufacturer, a capital-intensive production facility is a key asset. A microchip designer focuses on human resources.

Reasons for Selling Off Key Activities and Assets

a. *Changing business model*: As a company's business model evolves over time, certain activities may no longer be regarded "key". Firms may choose to reduce dependency on in-house teams, to spread risks, or reduce uncertainty. This can result in outsourcing of production, or technological platforms, or complete IT departments. Where Apple first made its own computers, it now outsources production to others. Its key activity no longer lies in the production of hardware.
b. *Lack of high-quality management*: Sometimes there's just not enough high-quality management around to manage all business units effectively, such as in the example where UCB sold of its amino acid activities.
c. *Failure of integrating a previous acquisition*: As half to 75% of all acquisitions fail to reach their stated objectives, there is no lack of examples of Parents selling failed acquisitions, i.e., if they are lucky enough to find someone to buy the Target. Daimler was still able to sell Chrysler to Cerberus, but Hewlett-Packard had to write off \$8.8 billion of its \$10.2 billion acquisition of Autonomy.[5] Since its \$25 billion Compaq merger, where HP lost half of its market value, the company has endured numerous problems with failed acquisitions (3COM, EDS, Palm, Autonomy).

Many reasons for selling key activities have a financial aspect. They may improve return on capital employed, maximize value, clean up nonoperating assets, or improve working capital.

---

[5] Lim, P.J. Who to Follow After a Split-Up. Money. Com.

Divesting to Comply with Anticompetition Rules

Such divestments usually coincide with a major cross-border acquisition and merger. In some territories covered by a merger, the combined company may have a monopolistic or oligopolistic market position, and the anticompetition authorities may only clear a merger upon certain conditions.

In 2016, the European Commission has cleared under the European Union merger regulation the proposed acquisition of SABMiller, the world's second largest brewer, by AB InBev, the world's largest brewer. The clearance is conditional on AB InBev selling practically the entire SABMiller beer business in Europe.

Divesting to Satisfy Shareholders

The performance of certain business units can have a disproportionate effect on a company's share price. Philips sold its semiconductor activities in 2006 to a private equity consortium as semiconductors are typically sensitive to the mood swings of economic booms and bust cycles. Philips timed its exit well, selling the business at the top of the market. The buyers heavily leveraged the deal, and pushed the debt down into the target company, as of then called NXP Semiconductors.

Divesting to Raise Cash

Sometimes, companies sell their crown jewels in order to remain able to honor their debt repayment obligations to banks. This happened in 2012, when RCS Media Group sold its very well performing book publishing business Flammarion to Editions Gallimard.

As to the example of NXP Semiconductors, even though continued growth was projected in the company's business plan, the economic cycle turned downwards again. Two years later in 2008, the company had to sell off two major business units in order to raise cash, honor the bank covenants, and stay independent.

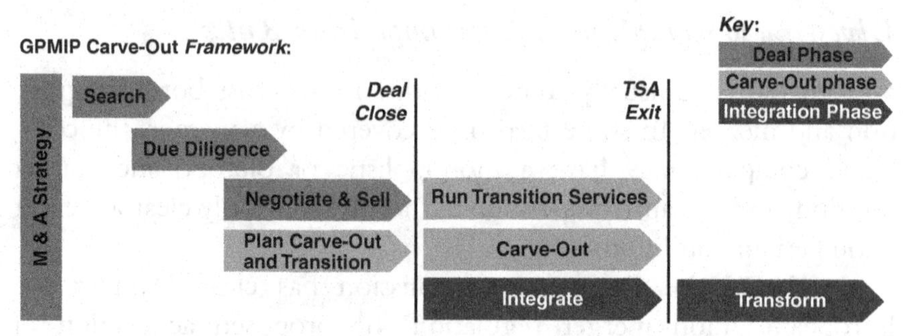

Figure 3: GPMIP Acquisition Carve-Out Framework™.[6]

Elements of a Divestment Process

Any carve-out, be it a simple one or a highly complex undertaking, is an end-to-end process. GPMIP Acquisition Carve-Out Framework™ illustrates this as follows (Figure 3).

M&A Strategy Phase

The start of any divestment process is the M&A strategy phase. For the Seller, this means a thorough assessment by the Board of Directors and management of the rationale for divestment. This is often done with the help of strategy consultants. Ideally, management has the luxury of preparing the target for sale: the so-called "exit readiness" process, which sets the deal up for success. As the Parent puts the Target on the market because it no longer fits in its business model, equally, potential buyers may have identified gaps in their own business model, gaps that can be plugged by acquiring the Target. Both buyer and seller go through this "M&A Strategy" phase.

Search Phase

We view the "search phase" from the seller's point of view: the search for a buyer. Depending on the drivers for the divestiture, a seller may

[6] Scola, A & Whitaker S. *Cross-border Mergers & Acquisitions.* Wiley, New York, 2016, chapter 17.

Table 3: Exit Priorities for the Seller.

Exit priority	Driver	Negative impact for seller
Speed	A sense of urgency, e.g., — to stop cash bleed — to generate money to enable the parent to honor debt covenants	— Lower selling price — Potentially lower quality of TSAs — Less visibility on stranded costs
High selling price	— Selling the business at the top of the market — To generate money for use elsewhere in the business — Opportunistic	— Investing time and effort in multiple and parallel sales scenarios such as IPO, MBO, MBI, PE buyer, industry buyer — Longer sales process — Going through a bidding process
Confidentiality	— Finding the right buyer — Protection of image — Avoidance of uncertainty with suppliers, customers, strategic partners, and personnel	— No bidding process — Fewer parallel sale tracks — Generally lower price

have different priorities in the sale process, summarized in Table 3. Depending on the priority, the search process will be different.

We recommend any seller to invest in finding the right advisor to help with the search for the appropriate acquirer. The usual intermediaries are the big investment banks, some Big Four, and local small boutiques, specialized in an approach tailored to the seller's industry or specifically suited to his exit priority.

Prevent the sale from dragging on too long. Extended sales processes lead to value erosion, uncertainty, competitors taking advantage of uncertain times, and key personnel leaving.

DD Phase

Data Room

A classic Due Diligence ("DD") process is undertaken by the acquirer. The seller's responsibility is to prepare a physical or a virtual data room. If he has time to prepare the sale, the quality of the data room will be enhanced, more potential buyers may be retained, and the selling price is likely to be higher. The seller may be assisted by legal, tax and financial advisers in the preparation of the data room.

TSAs

Specific for a divestiture is that in addition to the classic data room, a seller can prepare a very detailed menu of TSAs. Indeed, when the target is very much integrated into the parent company group, any buyer will significantly discount his offer price if he has no visibility on the "black box" of how entwined the business is with the parent. A seller will obtain a higher price if he can provide clarity on each of the services delivered to, or by the target.

Vendor Due Diligence ("VDD")

Not specific to a divestiture, but in vogue, is the VDD report. It is a DD report commissioned by the seller to a Big 4 advisor and made available to certain interested parties. The advantage of a VDD report in a divestiture situation is the objective opinion provided by the advisory firm. In addition to the traditional Financial Due Diligence chapters on quality of earning, on- and off-balance-sheet items, working capital and net debt, a VDD for a carve-out answers specific questions like "does the carved out entity contain only leftovers?"; "can the management structure hold the company afloat?"; "where does the intellectual property reside?".

Plan Carve-out and Transition

The approach to planning a carve-out will depend very much on both the exit priority and the complexity of the target, (see the section "Typology by Divestment Complexity"). To a higher or lesser degree, exit readiness requires certain elements we see returning in the planning for the carveout.

Asset Preparation

Assets will be taxed and valued by the buyer, so it makes sense to clean up the fixed asset register, write off and remove any obsolete inventory, and comb through the accounts receivable aging balance.

Tying In Customers, Suppliers, Management and Key Personnel

If no formal contracts exist with customers and suppliers, now is the time to formalize such relations, preferably covering the target for potentially adverse "change of ownership" clauses.

Involving key target management and personnel early on is important to avoid value leakage, and gain insights from the experts on how to conduct the carveout.

Normalization and Optimization of Earnings

Any activities not belonging to the target are taken out of it, so as to present as clean as possible a business case. At the same time, management may want to present an optimum EBITDA, since deals are often at least partly valued in multiples of EBITDA.

Working Capital Optimization

As for EBITDA, any improvement in working capital has a disproportionately positive impact on the selling price. The longer in advance this can be prepared, the better, as working capital is often measured over a historical period of 12–36 months.

Process Description and Preparation of TSAs

Process descriptions provide visibility to a buyer. Such transparency typically keeps more bidders in the process, resulting in a higher sales price.

Preparation of the Carve-out Management Office

The elements of a carve-out management office are: the overall governance structure; defining the workstreams, the carve-out master plan; the team charters, the action list: the risks and issues log; the meeting cadence; the communications office; the reporting dashboards.

The building blocks of the overall governance structure are the Steering Committee, the Carve-out Management Office (CMO), and the functional workstreams, as depicted in Figure 4.

The Steering Committee typically consists of the Seller's CEO, a major representative of the Target, and an independent outside advisor. It provides the major guidelines on how to separate the business, the timeline to deadline, internal and external resources dedicated to the task, and it provides endorsement of the carve-out. Steering Committee members spend 5–10% of the their time on the separation.

The Carve-out Management Office (CMO) is responsible for the planning and implementing the carve-out. It does this by giving direction, coordinating interdependencies between workstreams, reporting progress and resolving issues. The CMO provide knowledge, insights and support while ensuring overall project compliance, risk management, and Day One readiness.

The leader in the CMO can be someone with an important future role in the Target or is sometimes a retired management team

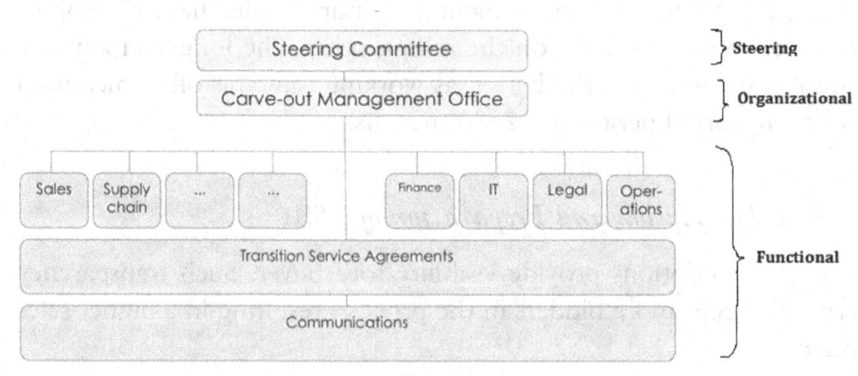

Figure 4. The Carve-out Governance Structure.

member being brought back in because of his knowledge of the business and stakeholders. The carve-out leader is supported by internal or external project managers. Leading and supporting a CMO is a full-time job, right up to Day One.

The workstreams are the functional areas where the carve-out needs to be attained. These areas cover all of the Target's business, such as IT, finance, human resources, sales and marketing, etc. The workstreams are often tailored to match the way the company is organized. TSA and communications workstreams are added or embedded in other workstreams.

The nominal workstream lead is usually the internal head of the function. While the lead spends between 20% and 40% of his time on the project, he will often delegation to a full-time internal or external expert to lead the effort on the ground.

A workstream has the responsibility of executing activity steps and attaining milestones, while minimizing business disruption. The workstream needs to communicate up to CMO and down to active team members.

People, processes, systems, assets, legal, financial: these are areas of focus that return in each workstream. We advise workstream leads to go through checklists and work with their advisors, focusing on these areas.

Postclose Phase

The postclose phase consists of three major parts: one where the Target is dependent on its parent, formalized through the TSAs; a second where the Target either needs to be integrated in the acquirer, or needs to become a completely stand-alone entity; and third where in both cases it needs to wean itself off of the TSAs.

TSAs and Stranded Costs

A TSA is a contract between buyer and seller that covers postclosing support for the target so that it can continue operating until such time as it can be set up independently, or integrated into the acquirer.

Without such a contract, there is no incentive whatsoever for the seller to continue providing services. Creating TSAs as a hind-thought is extremely difficult, as the seller's management needs to focus on its own business, and is not incentivized to work on distracting business.

A solid TSA consists of two parts: (1) A TSA master agreement setting out the governance structure of the individual TSAs, and (2) individual TSA schedules setting out the details of the specific service.

The TSA master agreement as well as the individual schedules are part of the Sale and Purchase Agreement (SPA). However, since many of the details of the agreement can only be worked out after Signing, or sometimes even after Closing, the SPA will provide a window for both parties to complete any unfinished details as soon as possible.

The TSA Master Agreement

The TSA master agreement contains the following elements: frequency of invoicing; currencies used; invoicing entities; procedures for extensions, modifications, early terminations, and adding TSAs; TSA management structure.

Figure 7 shows a typical TSA Management structure, with a single point of contact for the buyer and the seller, each supported by one person responsible for each workstream.

The duration of regular TSAs ranges from a few weeks to a maximum of 18 months. Anything exceeding that has the nature of a LTSA.

Table 4: TSA Types.

TSA type	Nature	Comment
Regular TSA	Service provided by the Parent to the Target	Short duration
Reverse TSA	Service provided by the Target to the Parent	Short duration
LTSA	Between Parent and Target	Multiple year duration

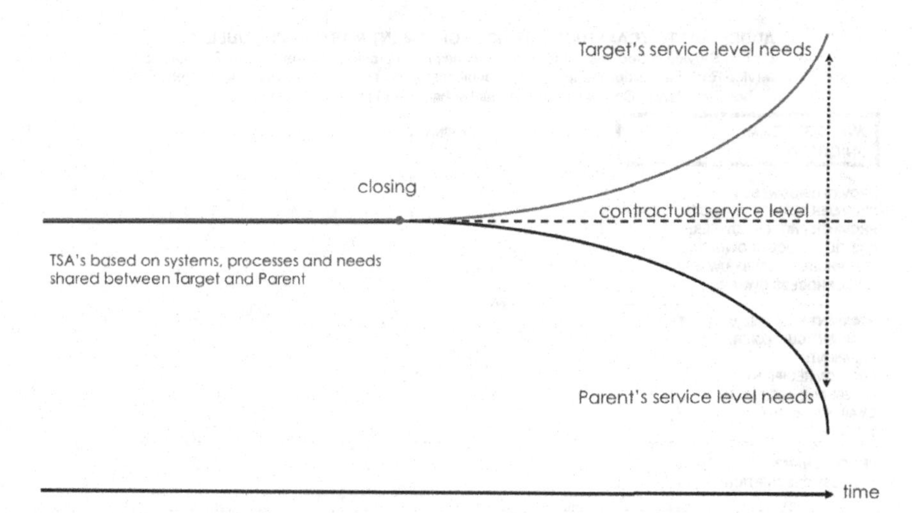

Figure 5. Increasing Tension Between TSA Contractual Service Level, Recipient's Needs, and Provider's Ability to Deliver.

A note on the duration: a TSA is drafted at a certain moment in time. It is a picture of the service provider's ability, tools, needs, and processes to provide the service. Likewise, the service recipient receives a service level more or less suited at that same moment in time. Then, as both businesses continue to develop, their needs and abilities change, adding even more stress to delivering and receiving a certain service that no longer suits either of them.

Figure 5 illustrates this, where the parent is service provider, and the target is service recipient.

Figure 5 shows the need for both service provider and service recipient to quickly get off the TSAs.

Individual TSA Schedules

The individual TSA schedules contain the following elements (Figure 6):

- reference to the TSA master schedule
- unique identifier
- start date and termination date

ADDENDUM TO TRANSITION SERVICE AGREEMENT MASTER SCHEDULES

The Transition Service schedules set forth the services to be provided by the Service Provider to the Service Recipient under the terms and conditions of the Transition Services Agreement between Parent Company (and its legal subsidiaries) and Target Company.

WORK STREAM:	**TERMINATION DATE:**
UNIQUE ID:	**TSA TYPE:**

PROVIDER BUSINESS UNIT:
PROVIDER SERVICE PROVIDER:
PROVIDER PROCESS OWNER:
POSITION PROCESS OWNER:
TELEPHONE PROCESS OWNER:
EMAIL PROCESS OWNER:

RECIPIENT BUSINESS UNIT:
RECIPIENT CUSTOMER:
RECIPIENT:
POSITION RECIPIENT:
TELEPHONE RECIPIENT:
EMAIL RECIPIENT:

PROCESS NAME:
PROCESS DESCRIPTION:

COST DRIVER:
HISTORICAL QUARTERLY COST:

MONTHLY FEES (€):

APRIL 20XX:	JULY 20XX:	OCTOBER 20XX:
MAY 20XX:	AUGUST 20XX:	NOVEMBER 20XX:
JUNE 20XX:	SEPTEMBER 20XX:	DECEMBER 20XX:
Q2 20XX:	Q3 20XX:	Q2 20XX:

PERFORMANCE METRICS:
THIRD PARTY RELATIONSHIPS:
INTERNAL INTERDEPENDENCIES:
SYSTEMS:
IT-SEPARATION:
LICENSES:
TSA COMMENTS:
FEE VALIDATION COMMENTS:

Figure 6: Sample of an Individual TSA Schedule.

- TSA type (regular, reverse, long term)
- service provider details: business unit, function, service owner, name, telephone, email
- service recipient details: business unit, function, service owner, name, telephone, email
- process name and functional area
- process description
- detailed service deliverables
- interdependencies with other internal functional areas

- systems and licenses needed
- required third-party services and tools
- cost drivers
- service fee

Calculating the Service Fee

The service fee can be difficult to calculate. Usually parties agree to apply a cost mark-up on the cost drivers. The mark-up can be set to increase over time, in order to ween the service recipient off the TSA. We typically see an initial mark-up of 5–7%, moving on to 15–25% over time.

The list below provides a comprehensive overview of the elements driving the cost:

(1) personnel costs
- fully loaded salary, including pension costs, bonus, holiday pay
- cost of allocated office space and overhead

(2) cost of third party services
- allocation of a percentage of license fees
- allocation of a percentage of monthly maintenance costs
- ad hoc costs

(3) cost of internal interdependent services
- e.g. IT support

Restrictions are usually imposed by third-party service providers, specifically on the use of software to service others than the Parent company. The license agreements for ERP or HR tools do now allow the user to provide services to users outside of the company. Some software providers will allow for a grace period, but then require the Target to buy its own license.

Stranded Costs

Stranded costs are costs that were previously allocated to the Target, but now need to be borne by the remaining group companies. A typical stranded cost is the cost of head office, such as the cost of being listed on a public exchange, the head office building, top management. These costs remain the same after the divestment, and will need to be borne by fewer group entities.

Other examples of stranded costs are: increased supplier costs as a result of decreased negotiation power, subsidies received in the past that may have to be reimbursed, and increased insurance costs.

The TSA Governance

A TSA governance structure (Figure 7) resembles the CMO structure: it has the same workstreams, and the workstream leads are also responsible for their TSA, although they may delegate the tasks of detailing the TSAs under their remit to others.

The difference with the CMO set-up is that there are two sets of workstream representatives (one per separated unit) with one single point of contact (SPOC) each and neutral facilitators. This system avoids misalignments between workstreams.

This TSA governance structure prevents workstream leaders from Target and Parent to have direct negotiations on services. The SPOC's of both sides centralize the knowledge and input from their teams, and then talk to each other. The intervention of an intermediary is needed if a buyer has been identified, but the deal has either not been signed, or is in the period between signing and closing. The intermediary can act as a "clean team", ensuring that no sensitive information crosses from one side to the other.

We recommend that each TSA is eventually signed off by four parties: the two workstream representatives, and the two SPOCs.

Getting off the TSAs

Given the importance of not stretching the duration of the TSAs, Target and Parent can bake in some mechanism to discourage dependency on them. They can do the following:

- continue the TSA governance until the last TSA has run out
- limit duration of each TSA, by providing a start and ending date

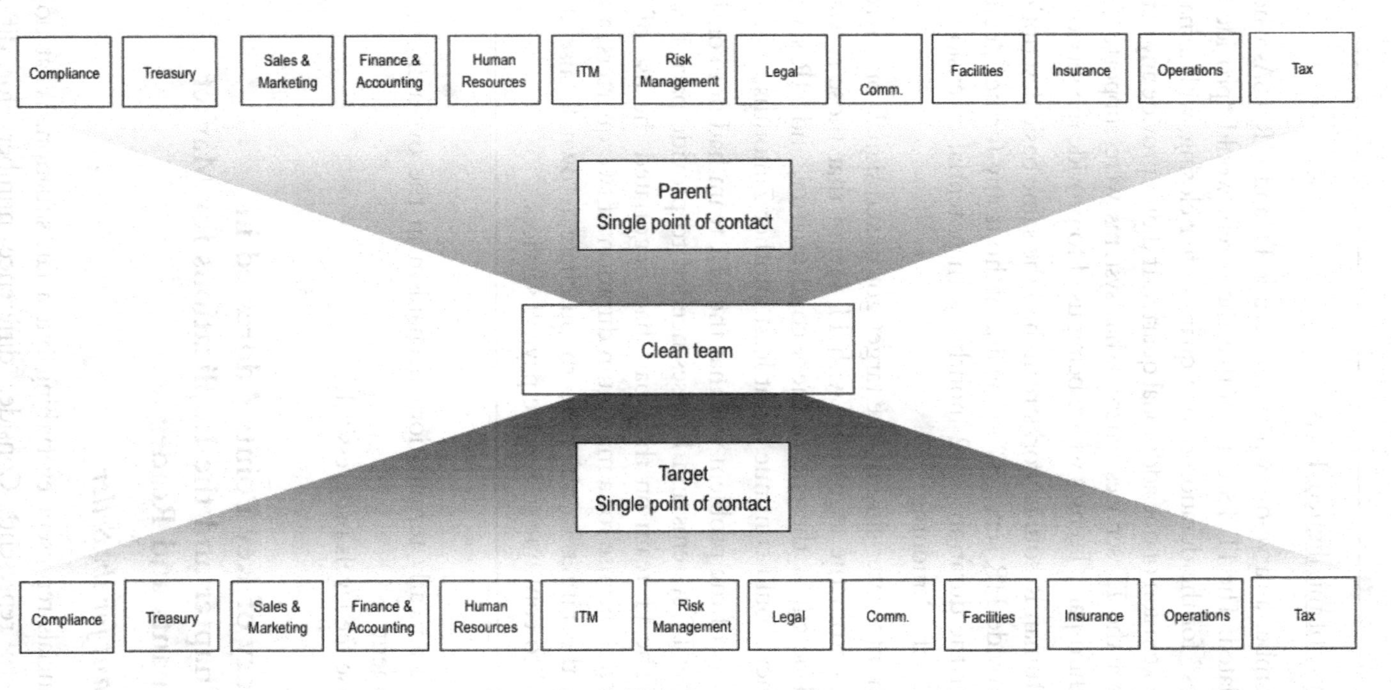

Figure 7: A TSA Governance Structure.

Example of misaligned TSAs

I remember a carve-out where very crude IT and HR TSAs where negotiated. The IT TSA stated that the parent would "provide IT services" for the duration of one quarter after closing, with a maximum extension of one additional quarter. It didn't provide any detail on what the IT services where, what systems were supported, or what third-party licenses where being used to provide the services.

The Human Resource workstream had the same basic description to "provide HR services" — again, without any further details, but for the duration of 12 months, with potential extensions of periods of 12 months.

Five months after closing, the target got mixed signals on payroll services from the ex-parent, with IT saying that those services would be cut at the end of the second quarter, and HR saying that they would continue for at least another 7 months.

The crux of the problem was that the HR team had not considered the IT systems and licenses needed to provide payroll services. The IT team on their part had negotiated the use of its PeopleSoft license for a maximum duration of two quarters, after which the target would have to purchase is own license if it wanted to continue to receive payroll services.

- include an early termination mechanism in the overarching TSA agreement
- increase fee levels progressively

Summary of Key Points Addressed in This Chapter and the Implications for Market Participants and Reader

Important for the Seller

The financials represent everything but a fair situation. What do you want it to represent? Consider difference numbers for different audiences. Consider what the numbers mean for the different categories of buyers.

Important for the Buyers

- TSA costs and description
- To get an independent opinion on the assets being transferred (do you get the leftovers?)
- Locked box mechanism requires caution

Lessons Learned

- Early preparation
- Identification of key risk areas
- Parallel alternative exit strategies
- Strong project management and control of the divestment process
- Strict time restricted exit window
- Perform internal exit readiness audit
- Diffuse or tackle head-on internal political factors (to whom are key assets, people, processes, rights, IP & licenses allocated, who gets the leftovers?)
- Identify the impact of stand-alone costs for the Seller (e.g., shared service center, overhead cost, shared supplier agreements
- Use of TSAs, Reverse TSA, LTSAs

○ Suggested end of chapter questions

Terminology Used

- Acquirer
- Big 5 advisory firm
- Business Model Canvas
- Buyer
- Carve-out
- Closing
- Divestiture

- Due Diligence (DD)
- Exit Readiness
- Joint Venture (JV)
- Long-Term Service Level Agreements (LTSA)
- Post-closing
- Reverse Transition Service Agreements (RTSAs)
- Sale and Purchase Agreement (SPA)
- Signing
- Spin-off
- Split-off
- Split-up
- Stranded costs
- Strategy
- Target
- Transition Service Agreement (TSA)
- Vendor Due Diligence (VDD)
- Workstream

Reference

Langer, R. New Methods of Drug Delivery. Science 1990, 249, 1527–1533.
Starbursting. The Economist, March 24, 2011.

Chapter 13

Cross-Border M&As

Harvey Poniachek
Rutgers Business School

Introduction

Foreign Direct Investment (FDI) flows consist of equity capital, retained earnings, and intercompany debt,[1] and the entry modes into foreign countries include

- Greenfield investment,
- Cross-border mergers and acquisitions (M&As) of existing foreign firms, and
- Joint ventures (JVs) (i.e., strategic alliances) with foreign or local firms.[2]

A Greenfield investment in a foreign market is an investment from scratch, it is relatively slow and requires substantial resources. Cross-border M&As face high risks and complexities that arise from

---

[1] OECD, FDI in Figures, April 2016.

[2] Jamie D. Collins, Tim R. Holcomb, S. Trevis Certo, Michael A. Hitt, Richard H. Lester, Learning by doing: Cross-border mergers and acquisitions, *Journal of Business Research*, 62, pp. 1329–1334 (2009).

differences in political and economic environment, culture, national laws, tax and accounting rules that could impede these investments.[3] Despite the complexities and high risk, cross-borders M&As afford attractive growth opportunities. The postmerger integration of the acquired company might be hindered by cultural differences, communication and coordination problems. JVs are the least costly entry mode because risks and benefits are shared.

The rest of this chapter addresses cross-border M&As, data, and trends; theory and factors affecting cross-border M&As; the mergers process; performance and risk; valuation; and cross-border investment in the US.

Cross-Border M&As

In today's global economy, multinational companies (MNCs) increasingly utilize cross-border M&As to avail themselves of significant opportunities to grow and enhance corporate competitiveness, diversify geographically, support their customers abroad, and gain access to natural resources. Yet, cross-border M&As present major challenges to integrate and manage, involve lower performance than in domestic transactions and a high failure rate,[4] and do not necessarily create shareholders value.

An Economist Intelligence Unit survey suggests that large companies view cross-border M&A as the main vehicle for future growth.[5] Many companies with strong financial conditions pursue M&A opportunities to strengthen and expand their core business, particularly in high growth markets. In pursuing M&A targets, about two-thirds are strategic buyers and about one-third financial buyers.[6] Of the financial

---

[3] Caleb Stroup, International deal experience and cross border acquisitions, *Economic Inquiry*, 55(1), pp. 73–97 (2017).

[4] Daniel Rottig, Successfully managing international mergers and acquisitions: A descriptive framework, international business: Research, teaching and practice, *The Journal of the AIB-SE* 2(1) (2007).

[5] The Economist Intelligence Unit on behalf of Clifford Chance, Cross-Border M&A: Perspective on a Changing World, May 3, 2012.

[6] Marsh Merer Kroll in Cooperation with the Economist Intelligence Unit, M&A Beyond Borders: Opportunities and Risks, 2008, http://graphics.eiu.com/upload/eb/marsh_cross_border_report.pdf.

buyers, private equity is by far the most frequently cited source of M&A deals and is second to home market strategic buyers.

Private equity investments are usually more likely to be involved in a cross-border transaction than firms without private equity backing,[7] and private firms' holdings are more likely to become a target in a cross-border M&A transaction than other firms. Private equity firms that participate in international deals have a wide international network of contacts and connections, including international accounting firms, law firms, consultancy firms, and other private equity firms. Such networks reduce information asymmetries in potential M&A transactions, and help identify and assess prospective cross-border targets and raise financing. Buyers capitalize on low cost of funding, with cash deals accounted for 62% of transactions in 2016, compared with 54% in 2015.

Cross-border M&As have long been an important strategy to expand abroad, and the European Union and the US were the largest acquirer and target countries accounting for 85%. China's cross-border M&A expanded from $1.7 billion in 2000 to $43 billion in 2011[8] and mainly attributed to purchases of natural resource related companies primarily by government entities.[9]

The 2000s witnessed an explosion in cross-border M&A that reflected a shift in the composition of foreign direct investment away from Greenfield investment.[10] See Exhibit 1 for FDI composition in various geographic areas around the world, and the M&A and Greenfield investments in 2015 and 2016. Global M&A activity totaled $4.2 trillion in 2010 and 4.9 trillion in 2016.

---

[7] Mark Humphery-Jenner, Zacharias Sautner, and Jo-Ann Suchard, Cross-border mergers and acquisitions: The role of private equity firms, *Strategic Management Journal*, 38(8), pp. 1567–1752 (2017).

[8] Nan Hu, Yun (Ivy) Zhang and Songtao Tany, Determinants of Chinese cross-border M&As, *Annals of Economics and Finance*, 17(1), pp. 209–233 (2016).

[9] Ibid.

[10] Julian di Giovanni, What Drives Capital Flows? The Case of Cross-Border M&A Activity and Financial Deepening, Department of Economics, University of California Berkeley, November 24, 2003.

Exhibit 1: FDI Inflows, Cross-Border M&As, 2015–2016, Billions of $

	FDI Inflows		**Cross-Border M&As**		**Greenfield Projects**	
	2015	**2016**	**2015**	**2016**	**2015**	**2016**
World	1750	1525	735	831	769	810
Developed Economies	963	972	642	779	276	243
European Union	475	389	268	359	161	139
North America	391	414	318	365	85	68
Developing Countries	749	600	83	47	455	540
Africa	54	51	20	10	68	103
Latin America & Carib.	166	135	11	3	73	75
Developing Asia	527	413	50	34	314	361
Transitional Economies	38	52	10	5	38	28

Source: UNCTAD, Global Investment Trend Monitor, No. 25, February 1, 2017.

The past three decades have witnessed a dramatic expansion in cross-border acquisitions, with the volume expanding from 23% of total merger volume in 1998 to 33% in 2015.[11] As the world's economy becomes increasingly integrated, cross-border mergers are likely to become more important. In recent years, there has been a rapid growth of cross-border M&As flows to emerging countries, including China, India and Russia, that now account for approximately one-third of overall activities.[12] Based on the data cited in Exhibit 1, in 2016, cross-border M&As surged to 54% of total FDI, up from 42% in the prior year, whereas greenfield investments were 15% of FDI in 2016, down from 44% in the prior year. Cross-border takeovers have become increasingly important and

[11] Isil Erel, Rose C. Liao and Michael S. Weisbach, Determinants of cross-border mergers and acquisitions, *Journal of Finance*, LXVII (3), 2012.

[12] Olivier Bertrand and Marie-Ann Betschinger, Performance of domestic and cross-border acquisitions: empirical evidence from Russian acquirers, European Bank for Reconstruction and Development, Working Paper No. 129, June 2011.

Exhibit 2: M&As Worldwide

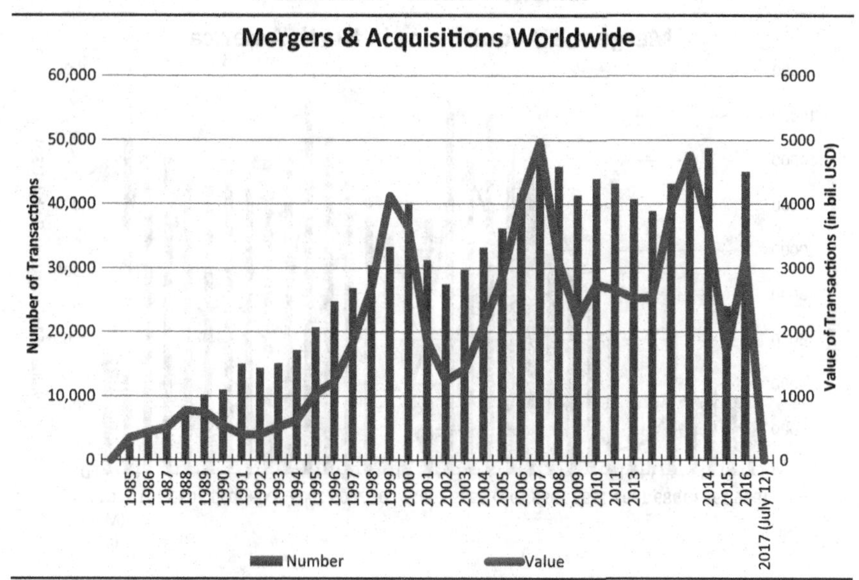

Source: https://imaa-institute.org/mergers-and-acquisitions-statistics/.

the outlook is for continuous growth in the future.[13,14] Exhibits 2, 3 and 4 show M&As worldwide, in North America and in Europe, since the mid-1980s.

Theory: Factors Affecting Cross-Border Deals

The motivation and process of cross-border M&As are in the main similar to those of domestic M&A, but due to their international nature they involve unique challenges associated with different economic, institutional (i.e., regulatory), and cultural structures. Compared to domestic transactions, cross-border deals pose increased information asymmetries as acquirers need to navigate different legal

[13] Mark Humphery-Jenner, Zacharias Sautner, and Jo-Ann Suchard, Cross-Border Mergers and Acquisitions: The Role of Private Equity Firms, Duisenberg school of finance — Tinbergen Institute Discussion Paper, March 06, 2012.
[14] J.P. Morgan, 2017 M&A Global Outlook: Finding Opportunities in a Dynamic Market.

Exhibit 3: M&As North America

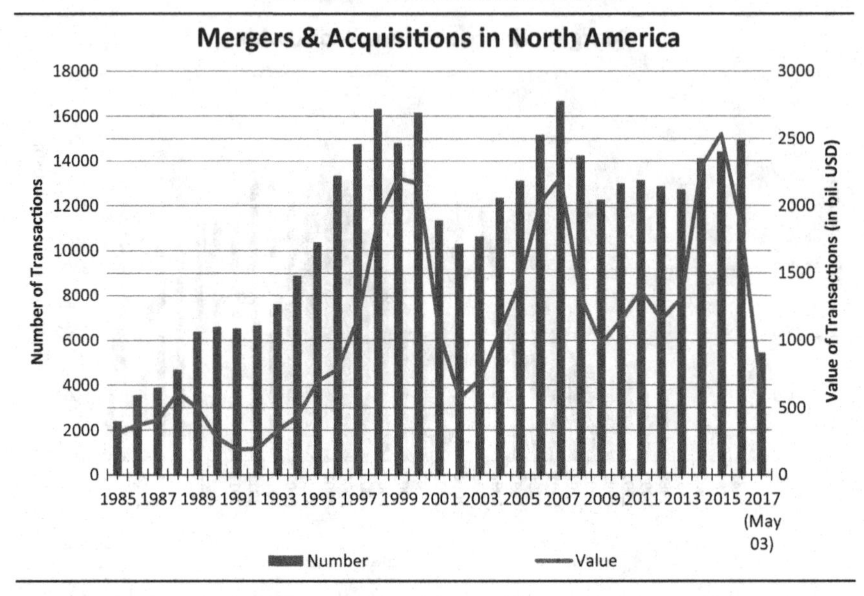

Source: https://imaa-institute.org/mergers-and-acquisitions-statistics/.

Exhibit 4: M&As Europe

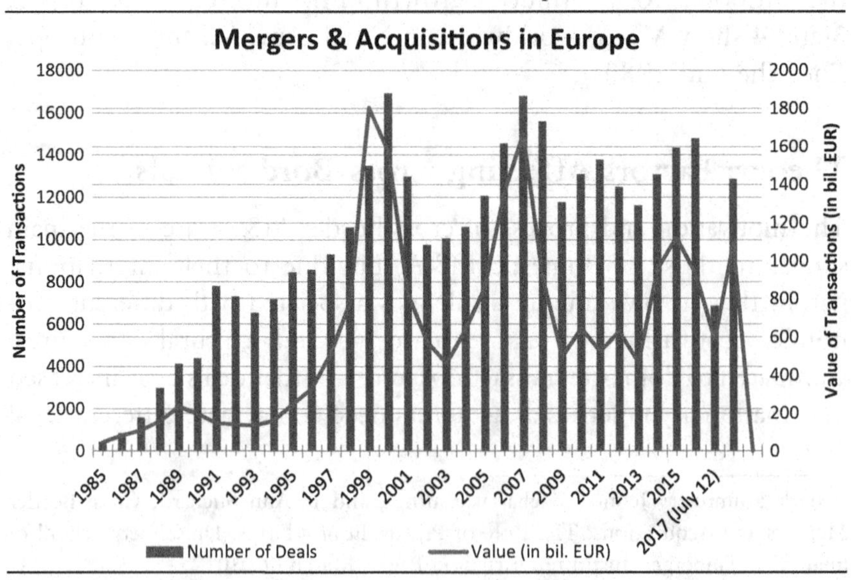

Source: https://imaa-institute.org/mergers-and-acquisitions-statistics/.

regimes, languages, accounting standards, or corporate cultures, all with the hindrance of geographic distance. These factors might make it difficult for acquirers to effectively assess the value and risks of targets in cross-border transactions. The legal and regulatory environment is an important determinant of M&As around the world, where greater legal protection for investors is likely to generate more deals at higher premium.[15]

A sample study of 56,978 cross-border mergers during 1990–2007 found that essentially cross-border mergers occur for the same reasons as domestic ones. However, international markets add additional complexities and risk that can impede mergers. Factors that affected cross-border M&As include geography proximity, bilateral trade, the quality of corporate governance, accounting disclosure, tax effects differences, valuation implication of exchange rate fluctuations and stock market movements, and macroeconomic changes.[16]

Cross-border acquisitions, as opposed to greenfield investment, have several advantages, including being a quicker, a more cost-effective way of gaining competitive advantage, and being able to benefit from under valuation of foreign targets.[17] Cross-border M&As can be used to access new and lucrative markets, as well as expand the market for a firm's current goods. Thus, international M&As may be motivated to take advantage of a new opportunity or to avoid future threat.[18] Yet, cross-border acquisitions are subject to considerable risks of failure and unsuccessful performance.

Although some of the determinants of M&As are common to both US and cross-border deals, there are many important country-level differences that are observed in cross-border deals. A sample of

---

[15] Stefano Rossi and Paolo Volpin, Cross-Country Determinants of Mergers and Acquisitions, London Business School, December 2002.

[16] Isil Erel, Rose C. Liao and Michael S. Weisbach, Determinants of cross-border mergers and acquisitions, *Journal of Finance*, LXVII(3) (2012).

[17] Ibid., Ch. 17, Foreign Direct Investment and Political Risk.

[18] Katsuhiko Shimizu, Michael A. Hitt, Deepa Vaidyanath and Vincenzo Pisano, Theoretical foundations of cross-border mergers and acquisitions: A review of current research and recommendations for the future, *Journal of International Management*, 10(3), pp. 307–353, DOI: 10.1016.2004.05.005.

12,131 cross-border mergers for the period 1996–2012 found that cross-border transactions led by acquiring firms with an appreciating currency generated higher abnormal announcement returns.[19] A strongly appreciated currency allows an acquirer to acquire targets in countries with weaker currencies, yielding profitable investment for the acquiring firm. Appreciation-motived acquisitions creates wealth for the shareholders of the acquiring firm if the acquirer locked in the currency advantage.

Currency movements enable cross-border acquisitions to create value either through higher expected earnings or lower cost of capital. However,[20] the lack of effective shareholder protection seems to offset any benefit from appreciation-driven cross-border deals, which is exactly what agency theory predicts. Firms in countries whose stock market increased in value and their currency appreciated tend to be acquirers, while firms from countries with depreciating currencies and poorly performing stock markets tend to be targets.

Firms with experience operating in a foreign country are more likely to acquire a target in that country. Thus, while prior domestic and international M&As appear to influence subsequent international M&As, learning from prior international M&As is especially important. An extensive empirical study of 30,000 corporate directors over a 28-year period shows that experienced directors have an important influence on a company's propensity to globalize its acquisition investments.[21] The learning associated with a firm's prior acquisition experience increases the likelihood that the firm will engage in subsequent international acquisitions.[22]

Various theories explain cross-border M&As. According to industrial organization literature, the motives for cross-border M&As include

[19] Chen Lin, Micah S. Officer, and Beibei Shen, Currency appreciation shocks and shareholder wealth creation in cross-border mergers and acquisitions, December 2013.

[20] *Ibid.*

[21] Caleb Stroup, Op. Cit.

[22] Jamie D. Collins, Tim R. Holcomb, S. Trevis Certo, Michael A. Hitt, Richard H. Lester, Learning by doing: Cross-border mergers and acquisitions, *Journal of Business Research*, 62, pp. 1329–1334 (2009).

efficiency and strategic.[23] Efficiency gains arise from increased economies of scale or scope, whereas strategic gains arise if M&As contributes to changes in the market structure and firms' competitive position and profit level. The literature provides additional motives to merge, including

- High-Tobin's *q*-ratio firms are those with the best technology and seek to expand their capital stock,
- Building empires allow to diversify and hedge against sectoral shocks,
- Managers might be motivated by managerial compensation or pure ego, and
- Attractive corporate taxation.

An alternative interpretation of M&A classified theories into seven categories which include efficiency, monopoly, raider, valuation, empire-building, process and disturbance theory, to which we could add several more.

Multinational capital budgeting[24] for investment in foreign countries applies the same theoretical framework as domestic capital budgeting with very few differences. The multinational capital budgeting process is as follows:

- Determine the initial capital investment,
- Estimate the expected cash flows from the project's life and the terminal or salvage value,
- Calculate the appropriate discount rate, and
- Apply the NPV or IRR to determine the feasibility of the project.

In international investment, the issue is how to adjust for the various risks, including foreign exchange, interest, country, and market risk. One can adjust for risk either via the discount rate or the cash

---

[23] Nicolas Coeurdacier, Roberto A. De Santis and Antonin Aviat, Cross-Border Mergers and acquisitions Financial and Institutional Forces, European Central Bank, Working Paper, Series No. 1018/March 2009.

[24] Eiteman, David K, Stonehill, Arthur I. and Moffett, Michael H, *Multinational Business Finance, 14th Ed.*, Pearson, London, 2016, Ch. 18, Multinational capital budgeting and cross-border acquisitions.

flows, but not for both at the same time. Although adjusting the discount rate might be easier, adjustment of the cash flow is probably more appropriate.

The profitability of the acquiring firm has a stronger impact on cross-border deals than in domestic deals.[25] Countries with large "national champions", that is, large and successful domestic corporations, are capable of coping with the high fixed costs of internationalization and have a strong incentive to acquire abroad. Deregulations and increased competition have induced a substantial increase in cross-border M&As in the banking sector. Cultural distance constitutes a barrier to international expansion and the main reason for the failure of international acquisitions.[26]

Process

The cross-border M&A process involves similar functions that involve a domestic M&A and were discussed in Chapter 2. Acquiring a company involves a multistep process[27] that starts with strategic evaluation, preliminary analysis, and feasibility study and ends with due diligence and completion of the deal. A typical process might take 8–10 months from initial strategic evaluation of multiple acquisition targets to completion.

A typical M&A process includes the following functions[28]:

- Strategy,
- Fundraising/Sourcing of Capital,

[25] Stefano Caiazza, Alberto Franco Pozzolo and Giovanni Trovanto, Do domestic and cross-border M&As differ? Cross-country evidence from the banking sector, Economics and Statistics Discussion Paper, No. 061/11, SSRN-id1443919.

[26] Daniel Rottig, Successfully managing international mergers and acquisitions: A descriptive framework, international business: Research, teaching and practice, *The Journal of the AIB-SE*, 2(1) (2007).

[27] Starting a Business, Mergers and Acquisitions — Opportunities and Process, Swedish Trade & Invest Council, August 2015.

[28] Jan Vild and Claudia Zeisberger, Strategic Buyers vs. Private Equity Buyers in an Investment Process, Faculty & Research Working Paper, March 2014, 2014/39/DSC/EFE, INSEAD.

- Screening and Identification of the Target,
- Valuation and Deal Financing,
- Negotiation,
- Due Diligence,
- Execution of the Deal, and
- Postmerger Integration. [29]

An alternative formulation of the M&A process commonly follows the following steps[30]:

- Strategic Planning,
- Identify and Evaluate of Potential Targets,[31]
- Initial Contact,[32]

---

[29] Jens Koerner, The M&A Process Revisited — Identifying a Suitable Phase Model, Faculty of Business and Economics, Mendel University in Brno, 613 00 Brno, Czech Republic.

[30] Jim Downey and Technical Information Service, December 2008, Mergers and acquisitions, Topic Gateway Series No. 54, December 2008.

[31] This step includes:

1. Develop a list of companies,
2. Size screen (i.e., revenues),
3. Profitability screen (i.e., margins),
4. Customer screen,
5. Distribution channel screen,
6. Manufacturing/delivery screen,
7. Technology screen,
8. Corporate culture screen,
9. Investigation of remaining targets, and
10. Recommended shortlist.

[32] This step includes:

- confidentiality agreements,
- preliminary disclosure information (help to ascertain strategic fit, business performance and potential synergies),
- memorandum (timetable, rules of engagement, bid procedure),
- financial results and projections, and
- initial indication of interest (non-binding bid, initial due diligence, availability of funds, conditions to closing).

- Valuation of the Target Company,[33]
- Due Diligence is an In-Depth,[34]
- Deal Execution Includes the Negotiation of the Deal,[35] and
- Integration — after Closing is Complete, the Acquiring Company Must Start the Process of Integrating the Acquired Company into their Business.[36]

---

[33] The most commonly used valuation methods include the discounted cash flow (DCF), and the market approach that uses comparable companies in terms of industry, size, capital structure or growth rates where a market value can be obtained to establish a value for the target company.

[34] Investigation and analysis of every aspect of a company, its management and its operations. The primary objectives of due diligence include:

- identifying potential deal breakers,
- obtaining information for the valuation,
- gathering information that could be useful for the negotiation team,
- identifying areas that need immediate management attention post acquisition
- identifying synergies and possible costs,
- developing a basis for postmerger integration plans, and
- verifying the sellers' representations.

[35] The acquiring business will need to bring together a mix of experiences and backgrounds into the deal team, when a definitive agreement has been negotiated to the satisfaction of the buyer and seller, a formal "closing" is normally held. Several preclosing activities will need to be performed:

- communication plan — internal, local community, investors,
- antitrust and/or government filings,
- interim management of operations,
- preclosing due diligence, and
- transfer of funds.

[36] Typically, the goals of integration are to:

- integrate the business quickly into one organization which is the right size for the future
- integrate and retain the best people from both organizations into one high performing team
- build support for the new organization with employees, customers, and suppliers
- achieve valuation commitments.

Performance & Risk

M&As are complex transactions with many potential problems, a high failure rate and poor performance due to poor management during the merger process.[37] M&As involve extremely complex procedures and deals are categorized into those that failed to create value, those that neither created nor destroyed value, and those that exceeded their industry trend.

Assessing whether an M&A deal is successful or a failure depends on the frame of reference.[38] A common benchmark for measuring performance is investors' required rate of return, with three possible outcomes:

- Value is created when the rate of return is higher than the required rate of return.
- Value is destroyed when the investment rate of return is below the required rate of return.

Most acquiring businesses will prepare a 100-day plan to cover the initial period of integration. The purpose of the plan is to:

- identify key events and activities that should take place in the first 100 days to achieve the above integration goals
- identify the required resources to integrate the new businesses
- develop a plan for each functional area including sales, marketing, finance, IT, HR and operations
- ensure open communication
- drive synergy realization
- achieve transition from integration to business team.

The objective is to ascertain whether the expected results of the M&A have materialized.

[37] Jens Koerner, The M&A Process Revisited — Identifying a Suitable Phase Model, Faculty of Business and Economics, Mendel University in Brno, 613 00 Brno, Czech Republic.

[38] Robert F. Bruner, *Deals from Hell,* Wiley, New York, 2005, Ch. 2, Where M&A strays and where it pays.

- Value is conserved when the investment just earns its required rate of return.

Bruner reviewed the evidence from some 115 M&A studies from 1971 to 2001[39] and observed that the conventional view that failure is the average outcome of all M&A is false. Empirical studies show that shareholders of the selling firms earn large abnormal returns from M&A, while the shareholders of buyers generally earn about the required rate of return on investment and the shareholders of the buyers and sellers *combined* earn significant positive returns.[40] Synergies, efficiency and value creating seem hard to obtain and the advice is to be realistic about the expected benefits, and avoid over-payment. A company is *more likely* to fail in its M&A under the following circumstances[41]:

- It enters a fundamentally unprofitable industry.
- It lacks the necessary industry know-how.
- The expected economic benefits (synergy) of the deal are improbable or not incremental to the deal.
- It lacks a competition advantage in the business.
- It is not very creative in deal structuring.
- Poor postmerger integration.

---

[39] Robert F. Bruner, Does M&A pay? A survey of evidence for the decision-maker, *Journal of Applied Finance*, 12(1), pp. 48–68 (2002).

[40] There are four approaches to measure M&A profitability according to Robert F. Bruner, Does M&A pay? A survey of evidence for the decision-maker, *Journal of Applied Finance*, 12(1), pp. 48–68 (2002):

- Event studies measure the abnormal returns to shareholders in the period surrounding the announcement of a transaction. The abnormal return is the return on the transaction less a benchmark return that is reflected by the capital asset pricing model (CAPM),
- Accounting studies examine the financial results before and after the transaction,
- Surveys of executives whether an acquisition or merger created value, and
- Clinical studies of transaction samples and application of econometric methods.

[41] Bruner, Op. Cit., *Deals from Hell*, Wiley, New York, 2005.

A KPMG survey[42] of 107 executives from companies with 700 largest international deals from 1996 to 1998 found that 83% of corporate M&As failed to enhance shareholder value. KPMG identified six "keys" or variables — three hard keys and three soft keys — that were necessary for a deal to succeed. Successful companies achieved long-term success by prioritizing three hard key activities in the predeal, which had an impact on ability to deliver financial benefits from the deal. The keys are:

- Synergy evaluation,
- Integration project planning, and
- Due diligence.

The three soft keys that affect performance are:

- Selecting the management team,
- Resolving cultural issues, and
- Communications.

These results highlight the importance of giving early emphasis to management team selection, cultural assessments, and communications plans.

A sample of 4,430 acquisitions showed that international acquisitions by US firms are characterized by significantly lower performance (based on stock returns and operating performance) than US-domestic transactions.[43] However, an empirical study of US cross-border M&As during the period 1990–1999 found no evidence of a significant decrease in excess values of the US acquiring firms in the 2-year period surrounding the acquisition.[44] The results suggest that

---

[42] KPMG, Unlocking Shareholders Value: The Keys to Success, M&A, A Global Research Report, 1999.

[43] Daniel Rottig, Successfully managing international mergers and acquisitions: A descriptive framework, international business: research, teaching and practice, *The Journal of the AIB-SE*, 2(1), 2007.

[44] Marcelo B. Dos Santos, Vihang Errunza and Darius Miller, Does Corporate International, Diversification Destroy Value? Evidence from Cross-Border Mergers

cross-border acquisition does not lead to any value destruction in the acquisitions of "fairly valued" foreign firms, and does not lead to an international diversification discount. However, cross-border M&As that occur in unrelated industries lead to value destruction, which is consistent with the existence of an industrial diversification discount. US firms with operations already abroad do not experience any significant change in excess value.

The net effects of M&A activity remain unclear and a subject of ongoing debate among academic researchers. Some argue that M&As create synergies that benefit both the acquiring company and the consumers, whereas others argue that M&A activities create agency problems, resulting in less than optimal returns. Analysis of M&As of the US pharmaceutical industry during 1981–2004 found short- and long-term abnormal returns for acquisitions but not for mergers, and differences exist between acquisitions of foreign-based, as opposed to US-based targets.[45] US acquisitions of foreign companies are less likely to be successful than deals with US companies, and acquisitions are more likely than mergers to accomplish the firms' goals.

Valuation

To value foreign companies for acquisition, we could apply the same methodologies that are used in valuation of domestic firms, but several international complexities need to be recognized that might affect the outcome.[46] These complexities include the following:

- International accounting differences,
- International taxation,
- Translation of foreign-currency financial statements,

---

and Acquisitions, July 30, 2003.

[45] Mahmud Hassan, Mahmud Hassan, Dilip K. Patro, Howard P. Tuckman, and Xiaoli Wang, Do mergers and acquisitions create shareholder wealth in the pharmaceutical industry? *International Journal of Pharmaceutical and Healthcare Marketing*, 1(1), pp. 58–78 (2007).

[46] Tim Koller, Marc Goedhart and David Wessels, *Valuation: Measuring and Managing the Value of Companies, 5th Ed.*, McKinsey & Company, Wiley, New York, 2010.

- Forecasting cash flows in foreign and domestic currency,
- Estimating the cost of capital in foreign currency, and
- Incorporating foreign-currency risk in valuations.

International accounting differences are rapidly becoming less of an issue, as the major differences between the International Financial Reporting Standards (IFRS) and the US GAAP have disappeared, and most major countries have harmonized their accounting practices by adopting the IFRS.[47] Taxation of corporate income and profit distributions differs across countries, and could have significant implications for valuation.[48]

To value a company's international operations, the following steps need to be pursued:

- First forecast the foreign entity's cash flow in their functional currency.
- Second, derive the cost of capital.
- Third, calculate the net present value to derive the entity's enterprise value, and
- Fourth, deduct the interest-bearing debt and excess cash to obtain the value of equity.

Estimating the WACC for a foreign entity follows the same methodology as used for a domestic firm. If cash flows are derived in foreign currency, they should be discounted at a foreign-currency discount rate. The cost of equity estimation uses the market risk premium and beta measured in terms of a global market portfolio, which is based on the MSCI World Index. However, in the absence of this index, the S&P 500 Index is a good substitute. A beta measured relative to a local market index does not necessarily represent the risk contribution of that stock to a diversified global portfolio.

---

[47] *Ibid.*

[48] Issues of concern could be as follows: What are the relevant tax rate and taxable income? Can fiscal grouping be applied to offset profits and losses of different entities? What are the relevant cross-border taxation issues? How does taxation affect shareholders in different countries?

Exhibit 4: M&A Valuation Multiples

	Value/EBITDA		**% Premium**	
	2013	**2014**	**2013**	**2014**
Average Industry Total				
World	14.8	15.2	28.2	27.5
Americas	13.3	15.0	36.6	35.5
USA	14.5	16.3	35.9	35.4
Canada	11.8	10.5	42.2	40.1
EMEA	13.1	13.0	26.4	25.6
Europe	13.3	13.1	27.1	26.1
UK	12.3	13.7	39.2	33.8
Asia, excluding Japan	17.4	18.0	23.8	23.5
Japan	11.3	18.0	30.8	26.2

Source: Thomson Reuters, Mergers & Acquisitions Review, Financial Advisors, 2016.

Note: Premium over a 4-week stock price prior to announcement.

Practitioners often make ad hoc adjustments to the discount rate to reflect political risk, foreign-investment risk, or foreign-currency risk, but these risks are best addressed by adjusting expected cash flows. Note that foreign-currency risk and foreign-investment risk are already reflected in the spot and forward exchange rates. The most important aspect of estimating costs of capital for foreign entities is to ensure consistency between the currency denomination of the cash flow and the currency of the discount rate.

Data on pricing cross-border deals is cited in Exhibit 4. The global value/EBITDA and the % premium in 2014 and 2013 were 15% and 27.5%, with the US and Canada reporting the highest pricing; whereas Asia and Europe, Middle East and Africa (EMEA) were quite lower.

Emerging Markets

Valuation of businesses in emerging markets is more challenging than in developed countries because of higher risks, illiquid capital markets, controls on the flow of capital, less-rigorous accounting standards, and disclosure levels. There is no consensus among academics, investment bankers, and industry practitioners on how to address these complexities, promoting ad hoc adjustments.[49] A conference on valuation in emerging markets[50] that constitute some 30 countries concluded that, first, there is currently no clear single "best practice" for the valuation of assets and securities in emerging markets; second, emerging markets differ from developed markets in areas such as accounting transparency, liquidity, corruption, volatility, governance, taxes, and transaction costs — that are likely to affect firm valuation.

McKinsey recommends a triangulation valuation approach based on three methods.

- First, discount cash flows and derive probability-weighted scenarios that explicitly model the risks that the business faces,
- Second, compare the value obtained from a DCF approach with a country risk premium built into the cost of capital, and
- Third, conduct a valuation based on comparable multiples.

The basics of estimating a DCF value are the same in emerging markets as elsewhere, but some complexities need addressing, including

- Foreign exchange rates and interest rate,
- Factoring inflation into historical financial analysis and cash flow projections,
- Incorporating special emerging-market risks consistently in the valuation,
- Estimating the cost of capital in emerging markets, and
- Using market-based references such as trading multiples and transaction multiples when interpreting and calibrating valuation results.

---

[49] Tim Koller, Marc Goedhart and David Wessels, *Valuation Measuring and Managing the Value of Companies, 5th Ed.*, McKinsey & Company, Ch. 33, Wiley, New York, 2010.

[50] Robert F. Bruner, Robert M. Conroy, Javier Estrada, Mark Kritzman and Wei Li, Introduction to Valuation in Emerging Markets, Darden Graduate Business School, University of Virginia, May 2002.

To value companies in emerging markets, we use concepts like the ones applied to developed markets, but unique circumstances need addressing. Inflation, which is often high in emerging markets, should be factored into the cash flow projections by combining insights from both real and nominal financial analyses. Emerging market risks can be incorporated through DCF scenarios by developing alternative scenarios for future cash flows and discounting rates and then weighting the values by the scenario probabilities. The cost of equity for emerging markets is estimated by utilizing the Capital Assets Pricing Model (CAPM), a global risk-free rate, market risk premium, and beta. The cost of debt is reflected by the local yield on corporate bonds to which we add a country risk premium. The Weighted Average Cost of Capital (WACC) is then derived for the subject company based on the relative shares of equity and debt. Since the value of companies in emerging markets is often more volatile than in developed markets, the DCF results should incorporate a country risk premium and utilize multiple valuation scenarios.

Cross-Border Investment in the US

More than 30% of global M&As involves cross-border transactions, and 15% percent of the foreign acquisitions in the US were made by companies from emerging economies. The US is hospitable to foreign acquirers, but thorough advance preparation is necessary. Yet most deals are likely to fail because of poor planning and execution.[51]

US global FDI reached $6.4 trillion (at market value) at the end of 2016, experiencing a CAGR of 9.1% from 2000 to end of 2016 (on cost basis); and FDI into the US reached a market value of $6.6 trillion at the end of 2016, experiencing a CAGR of 7% since 2000 (on a cost basis).

[51] Wachtell, Lipton, Rosen & Katz, Cross-Border M&A — Checklist for Successful Acquisitions in the U.S., January 28, 2014; Wachtel, Lipton, Rosen, & Katz, and King & Wood Mallesons, Checklist for successful acquisitions in the U.S., 2016.

Appendix of this chapter is a survey by the US Department of Commerce, Survey of Current Business, Direct Investment Positions for 2016, July 2017. The Appendix provides data on US investment abroad and foreign investment into the US by country and industry.

Summary Note

Cross-border investments through M&As have become very popular and in many instances have emerged as a two-way street. For instance, the US outbound M&As are virtually of the same magnitude as the inbound transactions. Cross-border deals are more complex due to international risk and peculiarities; however, in essence, domestic and cross-border transactions are quite similar in terms of the process and analytical requirements. The risk involved in cross-border M&As is quite higher than in domestic transactions and risk hedging applications are observed for currencies and country risks.

Appendix

Direct Investment Positions for 2016 Country and Industry Detail

By Derrick T. Jenniges and Sarah A. Stutzman

OUTWARD AND INWARD U.S. foreign direct investment continued to grow in 2016 both in level and as a share of total U.S. corporate assets and liabilities. The U.S. direct investment position abroad valued at historical cost grew 5.6 percent to $5,332.2 billion, compared with an average annual growth rate of 8.2 percent in 2006–2015 (Table A and Chart 1). The foreign direct investment position in the United States valued at historical cost grew 12.8 percent to $3,725.4 billion, compared with an average annual growth rate of 6.7 percent in 2006–2015. In the context of total U.S. corporate assets and liabilities, the share of total assets accounted for by the outward position edged up less than 0.1 percentage point at 4.8 percent in 2015 and 2016, while the share of liabilities accounted for by the inward position increased 0.3 percentage point from 3.3 percent to 3.6 percent.[1]

This article presents details on the U.S. direct investment positions on a directional basis by country and by industry. On a directional basis, direct investment claims and liabilities are classified

[1] The data on U.S. nonfinancial and financial corporate assets and liabilities are from table L.103 and table L.108, respectively, of the U.S. Federal Reserve's Financial Accounts of the United States.

Table A. Direct Investment Positions on a Historical-Cost Basis, 1982–2016

	Billions of dollars		Percent change from preceding year	
Yearend	**Outward position**[1]	**Inward position**[2]	**Outward position**[1]	**Inward position**[2]
1982	207.8	124.7	—	—
1983	212.2	137.1	2.1	9.9
1984	218.1	164.6	2.8	20.1
1985	238.4	184.6	9.3	12.2
1986	270.5	220.4	13.5	19.4
1987	326.3	263.4	20.6	19.5
1988	347.2	314.8	6.4	19.5
1989	381.8	368.9	10.0	17.2
1990	430.5	394.9	12.8	7.0
1991	467.8	419.1	8.7	6.1
1992	502.1	423.1	7.3	1.0
1993	564.3	467.4	12.4	10.5
1994	612.9	480.7	([3])	([3])
1995	699.0	535.6	14.1	11.4
1996	795.2	598.0	13.8	11.7
1997	871.3	681.8	9.6	14.0
1998	1,000.7	778.4	14.8	14.2
1999	1,216.0	955.7	21.5	22.8
2000	1,316.2	1,256.9	8.2	31.5
2001	1,460.4	1,344.0	10.9	6.9
2002	1,616.5	1,327.2	10.7	-1.3
2003	1,769.6	1,395.2	9.5	5.1
2004	2,160.8	1,520.3	22.1	9.0
2005	2,241.7	1,634.1	3.7	7.5
2006	2,477.3	1,840.5	10.5	12.6
2007	2,994.0	1,993.2	([4])	([4])
2008	3,232.5	2,046.7	8.0	2.7
2009	3,565.0	2,069.4	10.3	1.1
2010	3,741.9	2,280.0	5.0	10.2
2011	4,050.0	2,433.8	8.2	6.7
2012	4,410.0	2,584.7	8.9	6.2

(*Continued*)

Table A. (*Continued*)

	Billions of dollars		Percent change from preceding year	
Yearend	Outward position[1]	Inward position[2]	Outward position[1]	Inward position[2]
2013	4,579.7	2,727.8	3.8	5.5
2014	4,910.1[r]	2,945.8[r]	7.2	8.0
2015	5,048.8[r]	3,303.6[r]	2.8	12.1
2016	5,332.2[p]	3,725.4[p]	5.6	12.8

p Preliminary r Revised

[1] U.S. direct investment position abroad.

[2] Foreign direct investment position in the United States.

[3] The direct investment positions reflect a discontinuity between 1993 and 1994 because of the reclassification of debt instruments between parent companies and affiliates that are non-depository financial intermediaries from direct investment to other investment accounts.

[4] The direct investment positions reflect a discontinuity between 2006 and 2007 because of the reclassification of permanent debt between affiliated depository institutions from direct investment to other investment accounts.

according to whether the direct investor is a U.S. resident or a foreign resident. Outward investment occurs between a U.S. parent and its foreign affiliates, and inward direct investment occurs between a foreign parent and its U.S. affiliates. In each case, the position measures the parent's net financial claims on its affiliates.[2]

The positions presented in this article are valued on a historical-cost basis rather than on a market-value or current-cost basis, because detailed

[2] Aggregate estimates are also available on an asset/liability basis. Assets include U.S. parent and U.S. affiliate claims, and liabilities include U.S. parent and U.S. affiliate liabilities. For estimates on both a directional basis and an asset/liability basis, see "Table 2.1 U.S. Direct Investment Positions at the End of the Period" of the U.S. international investment position accounts. For more details on the difference between the directional basis and the asset/liability basis, see the box **"Comprehensive Restructuring of the U.S. International Economic Accounts"** in Marilyn Ibarra-Caton and Raymond J. Mataloni Jr., "Direct Investment Positions for 2013: Country and Industry Detail," Survey of Current Business 94 (July 2014): 2.

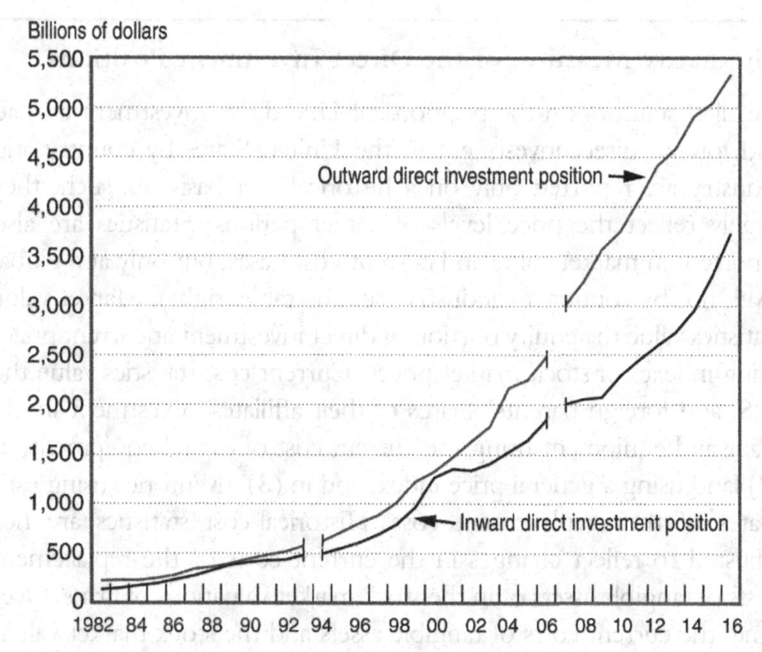

Chart 1. Direct Investment Positions on a Historical-Cost Basis, 1982–2016

Note: There are discontinuities between 1993 and 1994 and between 2006 and 2007. See footnotes 3 and 4 in table A.

U.S. Bureau of Economic Analysis

statistics by country and industry are available only on a historical-cost basis. (See the box "Alternative Measures of the Direct Investment Positions.") On a historical-cost basis, positions generally reflect prices at the time of the investment rather than current prices. This valuation is derived principally from the accounting records of affiliates, which are primarily compiled under U.S. Generally Accepted Accounting Principles (GAAP) or International Financial Reporting Standards (IFRS).[3]

[3] For a discussion of the U.S. GAAP or IFRS and the implications for the measurement of the direct investment positions at historical cost, see the box **"Accounting Standards and the Direct Investment Positions"** in Kevin B. Barefoot and Marilyn Ibarra-Caton, "Direct Investment Positions for 2010: Country and Industry Detail," SURVEY 91 (July 2011): 127.

Alternative Measures of the Direct Investment Positions

Detailed statistics on the positions of U.S. direct investment abroad and foreign direct investment in the United States by country and industry are reported only on a historical-cost basis. As such, they largely reflect the price levels of earlier periods. Statistics are also reported on market-value and current-cost bases, but only at a global level, not by country or industry (see the table, right). Market-value statistics value the equity portion of direct investment at current prices using indexes of stock market prices. Current-cost statistics value the U.S. and foreign parents' shares of their affiliates' investment in (1) plant and equipment using the current cost of capital equipment, in (2) land using a general price index, and in (3) inventories using estimates of their replacement cost. Historical-cost statistics are not adjusted to reflect changes in the current costs or the replacement costs of tangible assets or in the stock market valuations of firms. Over time, the current costs of tangible assets and the stock market valuations of firms tend to increase. As a result, historical-cost statistics tend to be lower than the current-cost and market-value statistics for the same positions. Market-value statistics are discussed in **"The U.S. Net International Investment Position at the End of the First Quarter of 2017, Year 2016, and Annual Update"** in this issue.

Alternative Direct Investment Position Estimates, 2015 and 2016
[Millions of dollars]

Valuation method	Position at yearend 2015[r]	Changes in 2016			Position at yearend Total Financial 2016[p]
		Total	Financial transactions	Other changes in position	
Outward:					
Historical cost	5,048,773	283,452	280,681	2,771	5,332,225
Current cost	5,783,737	304,985	318,267	−13,282	6,088,721
Market value	6,007,773	353,646	318,267	35,379	6,361,419
Inward:					
Historical cost	3,303,586	421,832	457,125	−35,293	3,725,418
Current cost	3,929,734	461,897	395,996	65,901	4,391,632
Market value	5,709,658	845,963	395,996	449,967	6,555,622

p Preliminary   r Revised

The year-to-year changes in the positions reflect financial transactions — investment in equity and debt instruments — and other changes in the position, such as capital gains and losses and currency-translation adjustments. The directional measure of direct investment financial transactions presented in this article differs from the measure of direct investment financial transactions featured in the U.S. international transactions accounts (ITAs) because the reinvestment of earnings component of financial transactions discussed in this article excludes a current-cost adjustment that is included in the ITA financial transactions and because the measure in the ITAs is on an asset/liability basis.[4] "Financial transactions" is used throughout this article for "financial transactions without current-cost adjustment," "reinvestment of earnings" is used for "reinvestment of earnings without current-cost adjustment," and "earnings" is used for "earnings without current-cost adjustment." In addition, "outward direct investment" and "outward" are shorthand for "U.S. direct investment abroad," and "inward direct investment" and "inward" are shorthand for "foreign direct investment in the United States."

This article presents details about the change in the direct investment positions by type of direct investment transaction, such as equity or debt. It also presents direct investment positions by primary industry of the affiliate and by country. The outward statistics are classified by country of the foreign affiliate with which the U.S. parent has direct transactions and positions. The inward statistics are classified by (1) country of the foreign parent or of other members of the foreign parent group that have direct transactions and positions with the U.S. affiliate and by (2) country of ultimate beneficial owner (UBO). Updates to previously released statistics are also discussed.

U.S. Direct Investment Abroad (Outward)

The U.S. direct investment position abroad valued at historical cost — the book value of U.S. direct investors' equity in, and net

[4] For an explanation of the current-cost adjustment, see the direct investment section in **"Chapter 11: International Investment Position Accounts"** in *U.S. International Economic Accounts: Concepts and Methods.*

Table B. Change in the Outward Direct Investment Position on a Historical-Cost Basis by Component
[Billions of dollars]

	2015	2016
Total change in position during period	138.7	283.5
Financial transactions without current-cost adjustment	262.6	280.7
Equity	277.4	309.9
Reinvestment of earnings without current-cost adjustment	271.8	278.8
Equity other than reinvestment of earnings	5.6	31.1
Increases	70.2	91.8
Decreases	64.6	60.7
Debt instruments	–14.8	–29.2
Other changes in position	–123.9	2.8
Capital gains and losses of affiliates	–16.1	10.9
Translation adjustments	–84.3	–20.1
Other changes in volume and valuation	–23.5	11.9

outstanding loans to, their foreign affiliates — was $5,332.2 billion at the end of 2016. The position grew $283.5 billion, or 5.6 percent, in 2016 after growing 2.8 percent in 2015. For 2006–2015, the average annual growth rate was 8.2 percent. The growth in 2016 reflected direct investment financial transactions outflows of $280.7 billion, primarily reinvestment of earnings in equity investment, and other changes in position of $2.8 billion, (Table B).

The equity component of the position grew 6.5 percent to $5,143.1 billion; the debt component of the position decreased 14.0 percent to $189.1 billion (Table C). The equity position grew in all major industries except mining. The decrease in the debt position was concentrated in finance and insurance and holding companies.

Five host countries — the Netherlands, the United Kingdom, Luxembourg, Ireland, and Canada — accounted for more than half

Table C. Outward Direct Investment Position on a Historical-Cost Basis by Account for Selected Countries, 2016

[Billions of dollars]

	Total	Equity[1]	Debt instruments: Net	Debt instruments: U.S. parents' receivables	Debt instruments: U.S. parents' payable
All countries	**5,332.2**	**5,143.1**	**189.1**	**797.2**	**608.1**
Canada	**363.9**	**345.0**	**18.9**	**49.1**	**30.2**
Europe	**3,174.9**	**3,031.3**	**143.6**	**469.0**	**325.5**
Of which:					
Netherlands	847.4	810.4	37.0	69.2	32.2
United Kingdom	682.4	612.7	69.7	131.2	61.6
Luxembourg	607.8	568.3	39.6	92.9	53.3
Ireland	387.1	373.1	14.0	83.2	69.3
Switzerland	172.6	190.4	-17.8	21.3	39.0
Germany	107.7	108.6	-0.9	19.6	20.5
Latin America and Other Western Hemisphere	**843.4**	**880.2**	**-36.9**	**85.4**	**122.3**
Of which:					
Bermuda	288.8	353.6	-64.7	18.0	82.7
United Kingdom Islands, Caribbean[2]	265.5	257.6	7.9	15.4	7.5
Mexico	87.6	83.2	4.5	14.1	9.6
Africa	**57.5**	**50.2**	**7.2**	**11.8**	**4.5**
Of which:					
Egypt	22.2	21.9	0.3	0.4	0.2
Middle East	**45.9**	**60.5**	**-14.6**	**16.8**	**31.4**
Of which:					
United Arab Emirates	13.4	10.8	2.5	6.9	4.3
Asia and Pacific	**846.7**	**775.9**	**70.8**	**165.1**	**94.3**
Of which:					
Singapore	258.9	250.0	8.9	20.5	11.6
Australia	165.3	102.4	63.0	81.5	18.6

(*Continued*)

Table C. (*Continued*)

			Debt instruments		
	Total	Equity[1]	Net	U.S. parents' receivables	U.S. parents' payable
Japan	114.6	129.1	-14.5	9.4	23.9
China	92.5	86.0	6.5	15.3	8.8
Hong Kong	65.6	62.3	3.3	13.9	10.6
Korea, Republic of	39.1	36.1	3.0	5.0	2.0
India	32.9	31.7	1.2	6.2	5.0

[1] Includes capital stock, additional paid-in capital, retained earnings, and cumulative translation adjustments.

[2] The "United Kingdom Islands, Caribbean" consists of the British Virgin Islands, the Cayman Islands, Montserrat, and the Turks and Caicos Islands.

of the total position at the end of 2016 (tables C and 1.2 and charts 2 and 3). For the eighth consecutive year, the position in the Netherlands was the largest — at $847.4 billion, or 15.9 percent of the total. Four-fifths of the position in the Netherlands was accounted for by holding companies that likely invested funds in other countries (see the section "Indirect ownership"). The position in the United Kingdom was $682.4 billion, or 12.8 percent of the total position; nearly three-fourths of the position was accounted for by holding companies and finance and insurance. In Luxembourg, the position was $607.8 billion, or 11.4 percent of the total; holding companies accounted for most of the position. The position in Ireland was $387.1 billion, or 7.3 percent of the total, and in Canada, it was $363.9 billion, or 6.8 percent of the total.

Changes by component

The $283.5 billion increase in the outward direct investment position reflected financial transactions outflows and other changes in position (Table B and Chart 4).

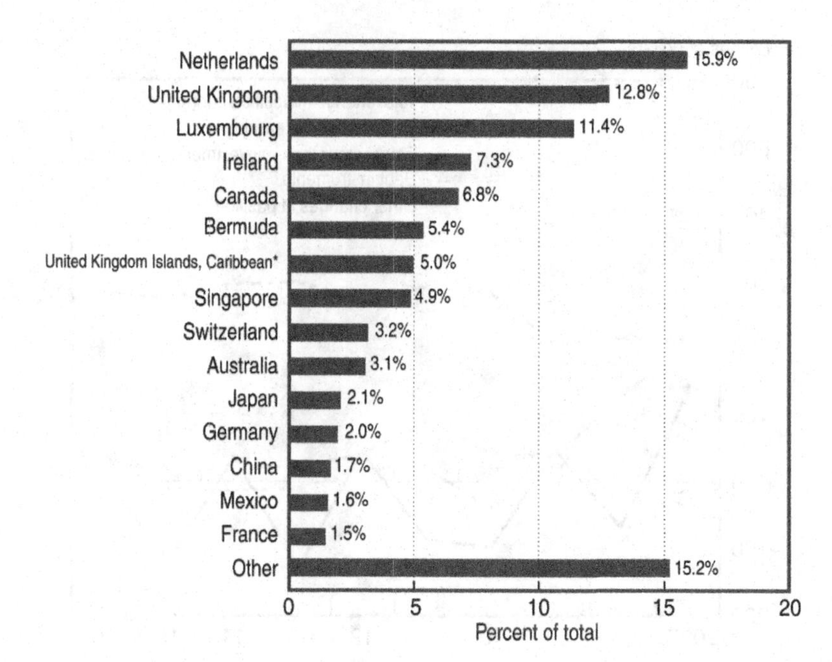

Chart 2. Outward Direct Investment Position by Country of Foreign Affiliate at Yearend 2016

*British Virgin Islands, Cayman Islands, Montserrat, and Turks and Caicos Islands. U.S. Bureau of Economic Analysis

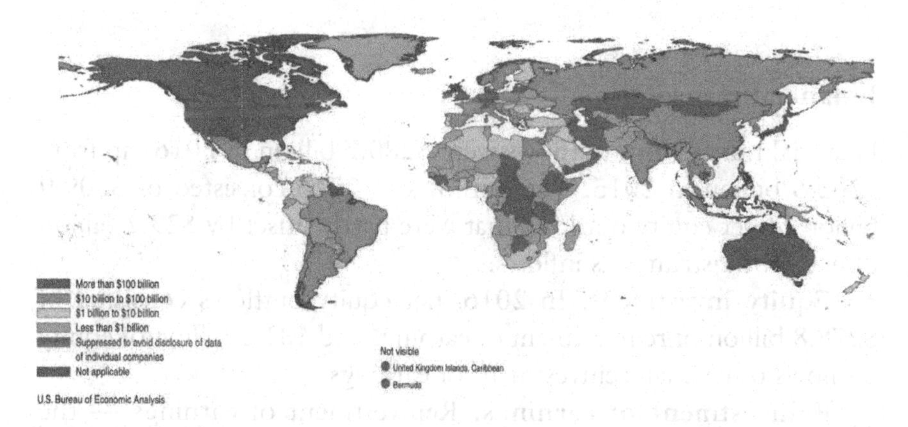

Chart 3. Outward Direct Investment Position on a Historical-Cost Basis at Yearend 2016

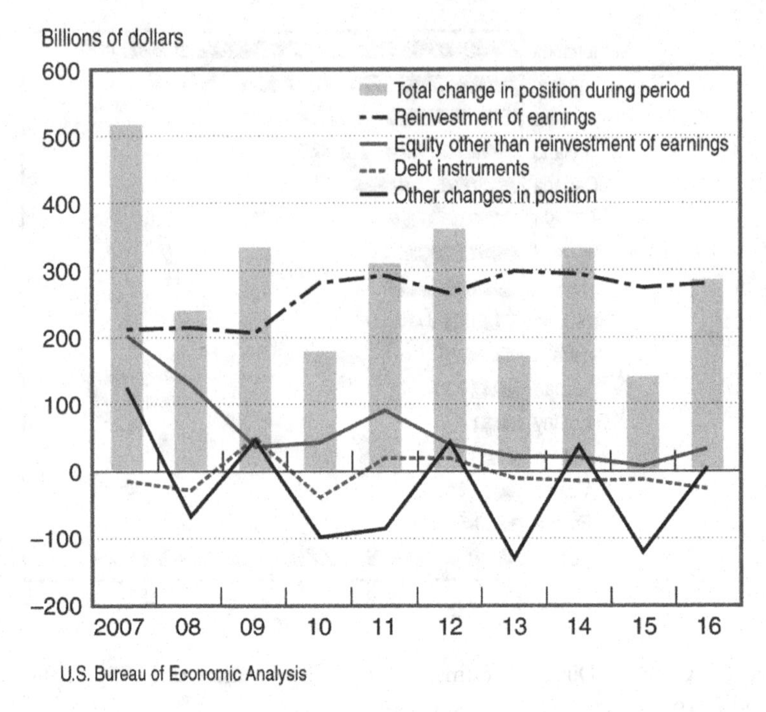

Chart 4. Change in the Outward Direct Investment Position by Component, 2007–2016

Financial transactions

Financial transactions outflows were $280.7 billion in 2016, up from $262.6 billion in 2015. The outflows in 2016 consisted of $309.9 billion of net equity outflows that were partly offset by $29.2 billion of net debt instruments inflows.

Equity investment. In 2016, net equity outflows consisted of $278.8 billion of reinvestment of earnings and $31.1 billion of equity outflows other than reinvestment of earnings.

Reinvestment of earnings. Reinvestment of earnings — the difference between the U.S. parents' share of their foreign affiliates' current-period earnings and any dividends paid to their parents — increased $7.0 billion, or 2.6 percent, to $278.8 billion in 2016.[5] The increase was the result of a $2.3 billion increase in foreign affiliate earnings and a $4.6 billion decrease in distributed earnings. The share of current-year earnings that was reinvested (the reinvestment ratio) rose to 69.8 percent in 2016 from 68.4 percent in 2015.

Equity other than reinvestment of earnings. U.S. parent net equity outflows other than reinvestment of earnings were $31.1 billion in 2016, up from $5.6 billion in 2015. The net outflows in 2016 resulted from increases in equity totaling $91.8 billion that were partly offset by decreases totaling $60.7 billion. The $91.8 billion increase in equity reflected $44.5 billion in equity for the acquisition or establishment of new foreign affiliates and $47.3 billion in equity contributions to existing foreign affiliates. Equity increases were up 30.8 percent in 2016 despite a 15.5 percent decrease in the value of global merger and acquisition activity for non-U.S. target companies.[6] The $60.7 billion decrease in equity reflected $13.2 billion in liquidations or sales of affiliates and $47.5 billion in repatriations of capital from foreign affiliates to their U.S. parents.

Debt instruments investment. In 2016, U.S. parents' borrowing and lending transactions with their foreign affiliates decreased their net debt instruments position in these affiliates by $29.2 billion, compared with a decrease of $14.8 billion in 2015. The decrease in 2016 resulted from an $11.1 billion decrease in U.S. parent debt

---

[5] These estimates for 2016 are the second in a series of four estimates for 2016. Recent experience has shown that subsequent estimates of reinvestment of earnings could be revised downward; for example, the third estimate of reinvestment of earnings for 2015 was 4.6 percent lower than the second estimate, and the third estimate for 2014 was 3.9 percent lower than the second estimate. Revisions from the second estimates to the third estimates largely result from reconciling dividends reported on BEA's quarterly direct investment surveys with those reported on BEAs annual surveys, in which affiliates generally report data based on their audited financial statements.

[6] Andrew Kelly, *Mergers and Acquisitions Review: Financial Advisors, Full Year 2016* (Thomson Reuters, 2017).

claims on their foreign affiliates and an $18.1 billion increase in U.S. parent debt obligations to their foreign affiliates.

Other changes in position

Other changes in position totaled $2.8 billion in 2016, compared with –$123.9 billion in 2015. Other changes in position in 2016 consisted of capital gains and losses of $10.9 billion, currency-translation adjustments of –$20.1 billion, and other changes in volume and valuation of $11.9 billion. The largest capital gains resulted from sales of financial assets by finance and insurance affiliates. Translation adjustments reflected the decrease in the U.S. dollar value of investments in foreign affiliates caused by a 4.6 percent appreciation of the U.S. dollar's direct investment-weighted exchange value at yearend. The largest dollar appreciations occurred against the British pound and the Mexican peso. Other changes in volume and valuation mainly resulted from differences between affiliates' current sale or purchase price and their book value. Other changes in position of –$123.9 billion in 2015 was mainly driven by translation adjustments.

Changes by area and by country

In 2016, the outward direct investment position increased in three of the six major geographic areas (Table D). U.S. parents' investment in their European affiliates had the largest dollar increase. The remainder of the increase by major area occurred in Asia and Pacific and in Canada. Decreases in the outward position occurred in Latin America and Other Western Hemisphere, Africa, and the Middle East.

Europe. The U.S. direct investment position in Europe increased $255.4 billion in 2016. The largest increases occurred in the Netherlands, the United Kingdom, Luxembourg, and Ireland. In the Netherlands, Luxembourg, and Ireland, the increases were driven by reinvestment of earnings in holding companies. In the United Kingdom, the increase was concentrated in reinvestment of earnings

Table D. Change in the Outward Direct Investment Position on a Historical-Cost Basis by Country of Foreign Affiliate, 2016

	Change	
	Billions of dollars	**Percent**
All countries	**283.5**	**5.6**
Canada	**17.2**	**5.0**
Europe	**255.4**	**8.7**
Of which:		
Netherlands	64.1	8.2
United Kingdom	57.2	9.2
Luxembourg	54.8	9.9
Ireland	52.8	15.8
Switzerland	16.9	10.9
Belgium	9.7	21.0
Germany	5.6	5.5
Austria	4.1	34.5
Latin America and Other Western Hemisphere	**–30.0**	**–3.4**
Of which:		
United Kingdom Islands, Caribbean[1]	–21.1	–7.4
Bermuda	–16.0	–5.2
Mexico	0.8	1.0
Brazil	6.9	11.9
Africa	**–1.8**	**–3.0**
Of which:		
Egypt	–1.0	–4.4
Middle East	**–0.7**	**–1.4**
Of which:		
United Arab Emirates	–2.3	–14.5
Asia and Pacific	**43.4**	**5.4**
Of which:		
Japan	10.5	10.1
Singapore	8.1	3.2

(*Continued*)

Table D. (*Continued*)

	Change	
	Billions of dollars	**Percent**
China	8.0	9.4
Australia	6.6	4.2
India	3.0	10.0
Korea, Republic of	2.1	5.8
Hong Kong	1.5	2.4

[1] The "United Kingdom Islands, Caribbean" consists of the British Virgin Islands, the Cayman Islands, Montserrat, and the Turks and Caicos Islands.

and in other equity; reinvestment of earnings was concentrated in holding companies and finance and insurance.

Asia and Pacific. The U.S. direct investment position in Asia and Pacific increased $43.4 billion in 2016. The largest increase occurred in Japan, driven by capital gains, reinvestment of earnings, and translation adjustments. Capital gains resulted from sales of financial assets, and reinvestment of earnings was concentrated in finance and insurance and in manufacturing. The next largest increases occurred in Singapore and China, where increases in both countries were driven by reinvestment of earnings. In Singapore, reinvestment of earnings was concentrated in wholesale trade, manufacturing, and finance and insurance, whereas in China, it was concentrated in manufacturing.

Canada. The U.S. direct investment position in Canada increased $17.2 billion in 2016. Nearly three-fourths of the increase occurred in reinvestment of earnings, which was concentrated in manufacturing, holding companies, and wholesale trade. Most of the remaining increase occurred as a result of equity increases in other industries.

Latin America and Other Western Hemisphere. The U.S. direct investment position in Latin America and Other Western Hemisphere decreased $30.0 billion in 2016. The largest two decreases occurred in the "United Kingdom Islands, Caribbean" (which consists of the British Virgin Islands, the Cayman Islands, Montserrat, and the Turks and Caicos Islands) and in Bermuda. The decreases in both territories

> **Data Availability**
>
> Detailed statistics on the outward direct investment position and related financial transactions and income for 1982–2016, along with statistics on the inward direct investment position and related financial transactions and income for 1980–2016, are available on BEA's **Web site**.
>
> More detailed statistics on positions, financial transactions, and related income for both outward and inward direct investment will be available by the end of July 2017 on BEA's Web site and will be published in the September 2017 SURVEY OF CURRENT BUSINESS.

of the United Kingdom were concentrated in other changes in volume and valuation and reflect ownership changes as affiliates became indirectly owned by European affiliates.

Africa. The U.S. direct investment position in Africa decreased $1.8 billion in 2016. The largest decrease occurred in Egypt, where the decrease was the result of capital losses, translation adjustments, and decreases in U.S. parent receivables associated with debt instruments. Translation adjustments reflected a 132.1 percent appreciation of the U.S. dollar against the Egyptian pound based on yearend exchange rates.

Middle East. The U.S. direct investment position in the Middle East decreased $0.7 billion in 2016. The largest decrease ($2.3 billion) occurred in the United Arab Emirates. The decrease was driven by decreases in U.S. parent receivables associated with debt instruments.

Indirect ownership

The share of foreign affiliates that are indirectly owned by their U.S. parent through another foreign affiliate has been increasing for the past three decades. For example, in 2014 (the latest year for which statistics are available), equity investment in other foreign affiliates

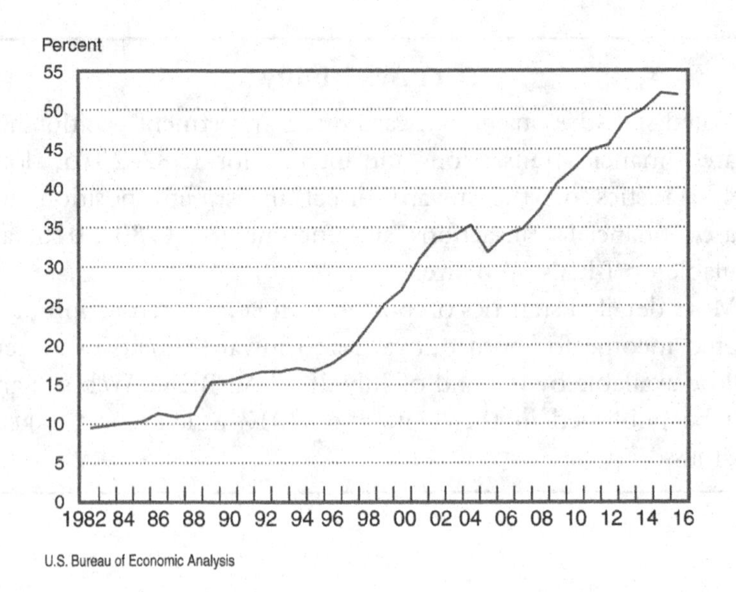

Chart 5. Holding Companies' Share of the Outward Direct Investment Position, 1982–2016

accounted for 30 percent of the total assets of majority-owned foreign affiliates, compared with 7 percent in 1982. Affiliates in any industry can own other foreign affiliates, but much of this investment is funneled through holding company affiliates. (A holding company's primary activity is holding the securities or financial assets of other companies.) In 2016, foreign affiliates classified as holding companies accounted for 51.8 percent of the outward direct investment position, compared with 9.4 percent in 1982 (Chart 5).

One result of the rising prevalence of holding companies is that outward investment statistics on positions and related flows indicate industry and country patterns that may not reflect where foreign affiliates produce and sell goods and services.[7] Statistics on the outward

[7] For more information about the effects of holding companies on the outward investment series, see the "Technical Note" in Maria Borga and Raymond J. Mataloni Jr., "Direct Investment Positions for 2000: Country and Industry Detail," Survey 81 (July 2001): 23–25.

position and related transactions are allocated to the industries and countries of the affiliates with which the U.S. parent companies have direct transactions and positions, but these industries and countries do not represent the full range and distribution of the industries and countries of the affiliates whose operations the parents ultimately own or control.[8]

Data from BEA's surveys of the activities of multinational enterprises (AMNEs) suggest the degree to which indirect ownership structures may affect the country and industry distributions of the outward position data. The statistics on the activities of foreign affiliates are classified in the country where the affiliate's physical assets are located or where its primary activity is carried out and in the industry that reflects the affiliate's primary activity. Thus, the AMNE statistics more closely reflect the countries and industries in which the goods and services are produced by the foreign affiliates than the statistics classified by the country and industry of the affiliate with which the parent company has a direct position or transaction. For example, while foreign affiliates in Luxembourg represent 11.0 percent of the outward position in 2014 (the latest year for which detailed AMNE statistics are available), they account for less than 1 percent of value added of foreign affiliates (Table E).

Another reason for the differences between the position statistics and the AMNE statistics is that the AMNE statistics, unlike the position statistics, are not adjusted for the percentage of U.S. ownership; therefore, the countries and industries in which a relatively large share of minority-owned affiliates operate will appear more important in the AMNE statistics than in the position statistics. The AMNE statistics are also not adjusted for duplication in some measures of affiliate operations — such as assets and earnings. For example, if a U.S. parent company owns two foreign affiliates, a directly held affiliate A and an affiliate B that is indirectly held through affiliate A, the position will capture only the parent's share of affiliate A's assets (which will include affiliate A's investment in affiliate B). However, the AMNE statistics

[8]This convention follows international statistical guidelines in the *Balance of Payments and International Investment Position Manual, Sixth Edition* (Washington, DC: International Monetary Fund, 2009).

Table E. Outward Direct Investment Position on a Historical-Cost Basis and Value Added by Country of Foreign Affiliate, 2014

	Share	
	Outward position	**Value added**
All countries	**100.0**	**100.0**
Canada	**7.3**	**10.2**
Europe	**57.0**	**48.2**
Of which:		
United Kingdom	12.7	11.6
Ireland	5.6	5.4
Switzerland	2.9	3.7
Netherlands	15.0	2.3
Luxembourg	11.0	0.3
Latin America and Other Western Hemisphere	**17.8**	**11.5**
Of which:		
Mexico	1.8	3.4
Bermuda	6.0	0.7
United Kingdom Islands, Caribbean[1]	5.8	0.1
Africa	1.4	3.5
Middle East	1.0	2.2
Asia and Pacific	15.6	24.4

[1] The "United Kingdom Islands, Caribbean" consists of the British Virgin Islands, the Cayman Islands, Montserrat, and the Turks and Caicos Islands.

will include the total assets of affiliate A (including the portion of affiliate A's assets that represents its investment in affiliate B) and affiliate B's assets. A's a result, affiliate A's investment in affiliate B is essentially double-counted in the total assets measure of the AMNE statistics.

Foreign Direct Investment in the United States (Inward)

The foreign direct investment position in the United States valued at historical cost — the book value of foreign direct investors' equity in, and net outstanding loans to, their U.S. affiliates — was $3,725.4 billion at the end of 2016. The position grew $421.8 billion, or 12.8 percent, in 2016 after growing 12.1 percent in 2015. For 2006–2015, the average annual growth rate was 6.7 percent. The growth in 2016 reflected $457.1 billion of direct investment financial transactions inflows, primarily equity investment other than reinvestment of earnings, that were partly offset by other changes in position of –$35.3 billion.

The equity component of the position increased 10.6 percent to $2,953.3 billion; the debt component of the position grew 20.8 percent to $772.1 billion. The equity position in U.S. affiliates in six major industry groups — manufacturing, mining, wholesale trade, retail trade, information, and professional and technical services — grew an average of 9.3

Acknowledgments

Jessica M. Hanson, Chief of the Direct Transactions and Positions Branch, provided overall supervision for the preparation of the direct investment statistics. Barbara K. Hubbard provided overall supervision of the computer programming for data estimation and tabulation.

The statistics on the U.S. direct investment position abroad are based largely on data from BEA's quarterly surveys of transactions between U.S. parent companies and their foreign affiliates. The surveys were conducted under the supervision of Leila C. Morrison, working with Iris Branscome, Maryam Fatima, Jared M. Felice, Louis C. Luu, James Y. Shin, and Jacob P. Simmons. Computer programming for data estimation and tabulation was provided by Kevin R. Smith and Karen E. Minor.

The statistics on the foreign direct investment position in the United States are based largely on data from BEA's quarterly surveys of transactions between U.S. affiliates and their foreign parents. The surveys were conducted under the supervision of Peter J. Fox, working with Akeeia P. Griffin, Susan M. LaPorte, Gazala I. Merchant, and Helen P. Yiu. Computer programming for data estimation and tabulation was provided by Karen E. Minor and Paula D. Brown.

percent, compared with a 3.8 percent increase in total owners' equity in all U.S. businesses in those same industry groups, based on data from the Census Bureau's *Quarterly Financial Report.*[9] The total increase in the foreign equity position, which represents U.S. business equity controlled by foreign direct investors, was larger than the growth in total U.S. business equity in manufacturing and mining, reflecting a greater level of foreign ownership for U.S. businesses within these sectors.

The top five investing countries accounted for more than half of the overall foreign direct investment position in the United States. The United Kingdom was the largest investing country with a position of $555.7 billion, or 14.9 percent of the total (Tables F and 2.2 and Charts 6 and 7). Japan was the second-largest investing country with a position of $421.1 billion, or 11.3 percent of the total. Luxembourg was the third largest with a position of $417.4 billion, Canada was the fourth largest with a position of $371.5 billion, and the Netherlands was the fifth largest with a position of $355.2 billion. These investments are classified by the country of the first owner outside the United States with a direct claim on the U.S. affiliate. For a classification of the inward position by country of the ultimate owner, see the section "Indirect ownership."

Changes by component

The $421.8 billion increase in the inward direct investment position resulted from financial transactions of $457.1 billion that were partly offset by other changes in position of –$35.3 billion (Table G and Chart 8).

Financial transactions

Financial transactions inflows were $457.1 billion in 2016, down from $465.8 billion in 2015. The transactions consisted of $340.6 billion of net equity inflows and $116.6 billion of net debt instruments inflows.

---

[9] At yearend 2016, these six industry group accounted for 63.1 percent of the equity position on foreign direct investment in the United States. The *Quarterly Financial Report* presents balance sheet and income statement data for all U.S. businesses in these sex groups.

Table F. Inward Direct Investment Position on a Historical-Cost Basis by Account for Selected Countries, 2016

[Billions of dollars]

			Debt instruments		
	Total	**Equity**[1]	**Net**	**U.S. affiliates' payables**	**U.S. affiliates' receivables**
All countries	**3,725.4**	**2,953.3**	**772.1**	**1,177.7**	**405.5**
Canada	**371.5**	**347.8**	**23.7**	**51.2**	**27.5**
Europe	**2,605.6**	**1,926.2**	**679.4**	**965.2**	**285.9**
Of which:					
United Kingdom	555.7	434.9	120.8	176.8	56.0
Luxembourg	417.4	220.8	196.6	215.3	18.7
Netherlands	355.2	264.7	90.6	112.1	21.6
Switzerland	310.8	144.3	166.5	205.7	39.2
Germany	291.7	262.0	29.7	52.1	22.5
France	252.9	224.3	28.6	45.8	17.2
Latin America and Other Western Hemisphere	**124.8**	**146.0**	**-21.2**	**38.7**	**59.9**
Of which:					
United Kingdom Islands, Caribbean[2]	86.1	76.7	9.4	20.3	11.0
Africa	**4.4**	**5.3**	**–0.9**	**1.2**	**2.1**
Middle East	**19.8**	**14.4**	**5.4**	**8.8**	**3.4**
Of which:					
Israel	8.1	6.1 5	2.0	4.6	2.6
Asia and Pacific	**599.4**	**513.6**	**85.8**	**112.5**	**26.7**
Of which:					
Japan	421.1	377.3	43.8	53.5	9.7
Australia	46.9	45.6	1.3	5.7	4.3
Korea, Republic of	40.9	29.3	11.7	13.5	1.9

[1] Includes capital stock, additional paid-in capital, retained earnings, and cumulative translation adjustments.

[2] The "United Kingdom Islands, Caribbean" consists of the British Virgin Islands, the Cayman Islands, Montserrat, and the Turks and Caicos Islands.

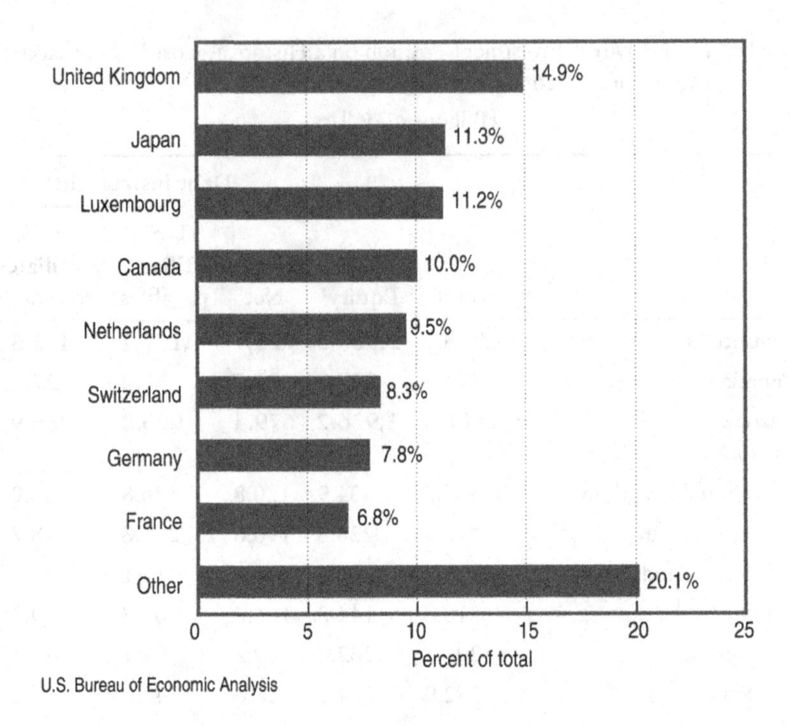

Chart 6. Inward Direct Investment Position by Country of Each Member of the Foreign Parent Group at Yearend 2016

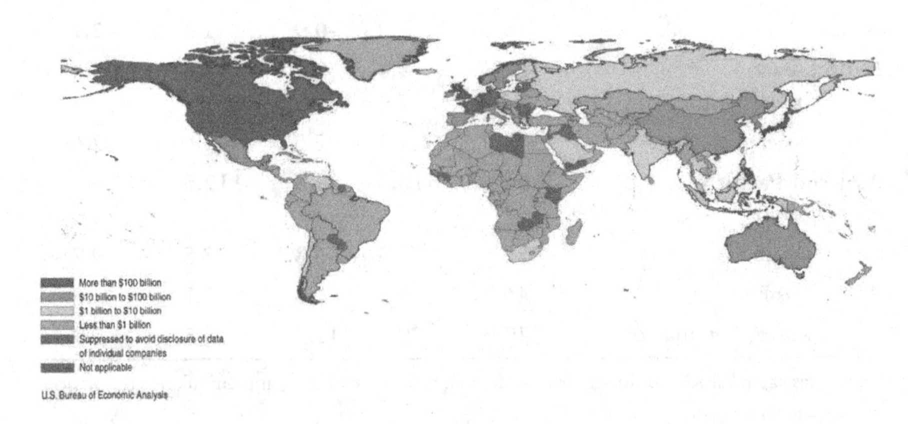

Chart 7. Inward Direct Investment Position on a Historical-Cost Basis at Yearend 2016

Table G. Change in the Inward Direct Investment Position on a Historical-Cost Basis by Component

[Billions of dollars]

	2010	2016
Total change in position during period	357.8	421.8
Financial transactions without current-cost adjustment	465.8	457.1
Equity	379.2	340.6
Reinvestment of earnings without current-cost adjustment	69.8	86.5
Equity other than reinvestment of earnings	309.4	254.1
Increases	354.5	274.4
Decreases	-45.0	-20.3
Debt instruments	86.5	116.6
Other changes in position	-108.0	-35.3
Capital gains and losses of affiliates	-36.9	-19.7
Translation adjustments	-5.5	-2.1
Other changes in volume and valuation	-65.5	-13.5

Equity investment. In 2016, net equity investment inflows of $340.6 billion consisted of $254.1 billion of inflows of equity other than reinvestment of earnings and $86.5 billion of reinvestment of earnings.

Reinvestment of earnings. Reinvestment of earnings — the difference between the foreign parent's share of their U.S. affiliates' current-period earnings and any dividends paid to their parents — added $86.5 billion to the inward direct investment position in 2016, compared with $69.8 billion in 2015.[10] Total earnings increased 5.5

[10]These estimates for 2016 are the second in a series of four estimates for 2016. Recent experience has shown that subsequent estimates of reinvestment of earnings could be revised downward; for example, the third estimate of reinvestment of earnings in 2015 was 10.3 percent lower than the second estimate, and the third estimate in 2014 was 1.3 percent lower than the second estimate. Revisions from the second estimates to the third estimates largely result from reconciling dividends reported on

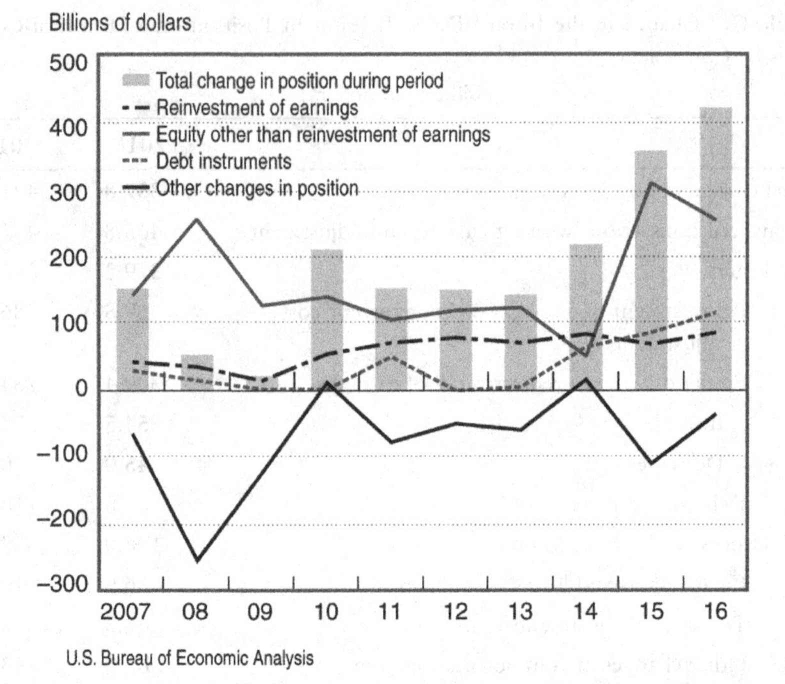

Chart 8. Change in the Inward Direct Investment Position by Component, 2007–2016

percent, and the share of current-year earnings that was reinvested (the reinvestment ratio) increased from 58.0 percent in 2015 to 68.1 percent in 2016.

Equity other than reinvestment of earnings. Net equity inflows other than reinvestment of earnings were $254.1 billion in 2016, compared with inflows of $309.4 billion in 2015. The net inflows in 2016 reflected increases totaling $274.4 billion that were partly offset by decreases totaling $20.3 billion. The $274.4 billion increase in equity reflected $202.5 billion in equity for the acquisition or establishment of new affiliates and $71.9 billion in equity contributions to existing affiliates. About 44 percent of the equity investments for new

BEA's quarterly direct investment surveys with those reported on BEA's annual surveys, in which affiliates generally report data based on their audited financial statements.

affiliates occurred in manufacturing, about half of which were in chemicals. A significant portion of these transactions were described in the press as corporate inversions. The $20.3 billion decrease in equity reflected $7.3 billion in equity for the sale or liquidation of affiliates and $12.9 billion for the return of capital to the foreign parent.

Debt instruments investment. U.S. affiliates' borrowing and lending transactions with their foreign parent groups increased the inward direct investment position $116.6 billion in 2016 after increasing it $86.5 billion in 2015. The increase in 2016 resulted from a $109.5 billion increase in U.S. affiliate debt obligations to members of their foreign parent groups and a $7.0 billion decrease in U.S. affiliate debt claims on members of their foreign parent groups.

Other changes in position

Other changes in position decreased the inward position $35.3 billion in 2016 after decreasing it $108.0 billion in 2015. The position decreased $13.5 billion as a result of differences between the purchase price and book value of acquired U.S. businesses. For consistent historical-cost valuation, when a U.S. affiliate is acquired, the equity position increases by the amount of the foreign parent's share of the U.S. affiliate's book value. In cases where the purchase price (included in financial transactions) exceeds the book value of the U.S. business, negative adjustments to volume and valuation are used to reconcile the financial transactions and the direct investment position.

Capital gains and losses decreased the position $19.7 billion. Currency-translation adjustments decreased the position $2.1 billion. These translation adjustments tend to be smaller for inward investment than for outward investment because most U.S. affiliates maintain their accounting records in U.S. dollars.

Changes by area and by country

In 2016, the inward direct investment position increased for all major geographic areas (Table H). The position increased the most for investors from Europe, followed by investors from Canada and from Asia and Pacific.

Table H. Change in the Inward Direct Investment Position on a Historical-Cost Basis by Country of Each Member of the Foreign Parent Group, 2016

	Change	
	Billions of dollars	**Percent**
All countries	**421.8**	**12.8**
Canada	**49.4**	**15.3**
Europe	**328.9**	**14.4**
Of which:		
Luxembourg	69.5	20.0
Switzerland	61.5	24.7
Netherlands	55.5	18.5
Ireland	49.6	138.6
United Kingdom	43.5	8.5
France	20.4	8.8
Germany	12.0	4.3
Norway	4.8	23.4
Denmark	3.8	26.3
Austria	3.5	49.7
Sweden	3.5	8.1
Belgium	–9.4	–10.5
Latin America and Other Western Hemisphere	**7.5**	**6.4**
Of which:		
Bermuda	16.8	(*)
Mexico	1.5	10.2
Brazil	–2.4	(*)
United Kingdom Islands, Caribbean[1]	–8.7	–9.2
Africa	**0.1**	**1.5**
Middle East	**1.7**	**9.1**
Of which:		
Saudi Arabia	0.7	14.0
Israel	0.7	9.3
Asia and Pacific	**34.4**	**6.1**
Of which:		

(*Continued*)

Table H. (*Continued*)

	Change	
	Billions of dollars	**Percent**
Japan	18.9	4.7
China	10.7	63.8
Singapore	2.3	10.5
Hong Kong	0.7	6.0
Korea, Republic of	0.4	0.9
Taiwan	0.3	4.4
Australia	–0.3	–0.7

*Undefined.

[1] The "United Kingdom Islands, Caribbean" consists of the British Virgin Islands, the Cayman Islands, Montserrat, and the Turks and Caicos Islands.

Europe. The inward direct investment position increased $328.9 billion in 2016. The three largest increases were from Luxembourg, Switzerland, and the Netherlands. For Luxembourg, the increase mainly reflected inflows of debt instruments and equity inflows to acquire or establish new affiliates. For the Netherlands, the increase reflected equity inflows to acquire or establish new affiliates. For Switzerland, the increase reflected inflows of debt instruments and equity contributions.

Canada. The inward direct investment position increased $49.4 billion in 2016. The increase in the position reflected equity inflows for the acquisition or establishment of new affiliates and was concentrated in other industries.

Asia and Pacific. The inward direct investment position increased $34.4 billion in 2016. Most of the increase was accounted for by increases from Japan and China. For Japan, increases reflected equity inflows to acquire or establish new affiliates and reinvestment of earnings in existing affiliates that were partly offset by capital losses. For China, the change was largely due to equity inflows for the acquisition or establishment of new affiliates and was concentrated in manufacturing.

Latin America and Other Western Hemisphere. The inward direct investment position increased $7.5 billion in 2016. The increase was mainly due to financial flows from Bermuda and concentrated in finance and insurance and wholesale trade.

Middle East. The inward direct investment position from the Middle East increased $1.7 billion. The increase was mainly due to equity inflows from Israel as well as reinvestment of earnings by Saudi Arabia.

Africa. The inward direct investment position from Africa increased $0.1 billion, mainly from reinvestment of earnings in existing affiliates.

Indirect ownership

Foreign multinational enterprises (MNEs) may own their U.S. affiliates indirectly through ownership chains that extend across multiple foreign countries. The statistics on inward direct investment positions that are presented in this article are classified by the country of the foreign parent or by the member of the foreign parent group with a positive or negative net debt investment in the U.S. affiliate.[11] The position is classified by the first country of the entity outside the United States with a direct claim on the U.S. affiliate. In addition to the data collected by the country of foreign parent, BEA collects data on the country of the ultimate beneficial owner (UBO) of the U.S. affiliate.[12] BEA also presents the inward position classified by country of UBO.[13]

For most affiliates, the country of the UBO is also the country of the foreign parent. According to U.S. affiliate responses on the 2012 Benchmark Survey of Foreign Direct Investment in the United States, the country of the UBO and that of its foreign parent was the same for 87 percent of the affiliates. Together, these affiliates accounted for

---

[11] This convention follows guidelines in the *International Monetary Fund's Balance of Payments and International Investment Position Manual.*

[12] The UBO is defined as the entity that ultimately owns or controls an affiliate and thus ultimately derives the benefits and assumes the risks from owning or controlling an affiliate.

[13] The statistics classified by country of UBO for both the direct investment position and direct investment income will be available in late July on BEA's Web site.

more than 80 percent of the total assets, sales, and employment of all affiliates. However, for some countries, especially financial centers through which MNEs may channel their investments, the position classified by country of UBO can differ significantly from that classified by country of foreign parent (Table I).

For some countries — most notably, Luxembourg, the Netherlands, Switzerland, and the "United Kingdom Islands, Caribbean" — the positions classified by country of foreign parent were higher than those classified by country of UBO. For other countries — most notably, Ireland, Bermuda, and several countries in the Middle East — positions classified by country of UBO were higher than those classified by country of foreign parent.

Ireland is an example of a country with a tax and regulatory environment that attracts the corporate headquarters of multinational firms.[14] For Ireland, the higher position by country of UBO represents investments by MNEs that are organized with entities in Ireland at the top tier of the corporate group, including U.S. corporations that have reorganized their ownership structure. In such reorganizations, sometimes referred to as "corporate inversions," the U.S. corporation forms a new corporation (or acquires an existing corporation) in a foreign country of convenience and simultaneously inverts its ownership structure so that the U.S. corporation is now a U.S. affiliate of the foreign corporation.[15] An affiliate in a third country, such as the Netherlands, is often created between the Irish UBO and the U.S. affiliate that may allow the company to reduce its tax liability further.

For countries in the Middle East, positions by country of UBO are higher than those classified by country of foreign parent because investments from the Middle East are often routed through affiliates in other countries. Possible reasons for Middle Eastern UBOs to hold their U.S.

---

[14] For a summary of research on the effects of taxation on multinational firms, see Mihir A. Desai, C. Fritz Foley, and James R. Hines Jr., "Taxation and Multinational Activity: New Evidence, New Interpretations," Survey 86 (February 2006): 16–22.

[15] See Jessica M. Hanson, Howard I. Krakower, Raymond J. Mataloni Jr., and Kate L.S. Pinard, "The Effects of Corporate Inversions on the International and National Economic Accounts," Survey 95 (February 2015).

Table I. Inward Direct Investment Position on a Historical-Cost Basis by Country of Each Member of the Foreign Parent Group and by Country of the Ultimate Beneficial Owner (UBO), 2016[1]

[Billions of dollars]

	By country of foreign parent group member	By country of UBO
All countries	**3,725.4**	**3,725.4**
Canada	**371.5**	**453.6**
Europe	**2,605.6**	**2,237.6**
Of which:		
France	252.9	267.6
Germany	291.7	372.8
Ireland	85.5	279.6
Luxembourg	417.4	31.1
Netherlands	355.2	191.9
Switzerland	310.8	196.6
United Kingdom	555.7	598.3
Latin America and Other Western Hemisphere	**124.8**	**162.7**
Of which:		
Bermuda	9.4	33.5
Mexico	16.8	34.4
Africa	**4.4**	**4.6**
Middle East	**19.8**	**98.6**
Of which:		
Israel	8.1	55.4
Asia and Pacific	**599.4**	**693.7**
Of which:		
Australia	46.9	54.3
China	27.5	58.2
Hong Kong	11.6	15.2
Japan	421.1	424.3
Korea, Republic of	40.9	38.8
Singapore	23.9	73.7
United States		74.4

[1] The UBO is that person, proceeding up a U.S. affiliate's ownership chain, beginning with and including the foreign parent, that is not owned more than 50 percent by another person. The country of UBO is often the same as that of the foreign parent, but it may be a different foreign country or the United States.

investments indirectly through intermediate subsidiaries in other countries include tax and regulatory policies and privacy protection.

Updates to the Statistics

The statistics on direct investment positions by country and by industry for 2016 presented in this article are preliminary. Updated statistics on positions and related financial transactions for 2014–2015 incorporate newly available data collected on (1) BEA's quarterly surveys of transactions between parents and their affiliates and (2) BEA's annual and benchmark surveys of the activities of multinational enterprises. Updated positions for 2014 reflect revisions to financial transactions and other changes in position for 2014 (Table J). Updated positions for 2015 reflect revisions to financial transactions and other changes in position for 2015 and to positions for 2014.

BEA has processed the 2014 Benchmark Survey of U.S. Direct Investment Abroad and has begun to incorporate the benchmark data into the direct investment position and financial transactions statistics, starting with the annual updates that were released in June 2017. In June 2018, BEA will release rebench-marked direct investment series that fully incorporate the 2014 benchmark survey for statistics covering 2014 through 2017.

Table J. Updates to the 2014 and 2015 Positions by Component
[Billions of dollars]

	Outward position		**Inward position**	
	2014	**2015**	**2014**	**2015**
Total revision	80.6	8.1	32.5	169.4
Financial transactions without current-cost adjustment	2.5	-40.6	30.1	117.4
Other changes in position	78.2	–31.9	2.4	19.5
Revision to the prior year's position		80.6		32.5

Table 1.1: U.S. Direct investment Position Abroad on a Historical-Cost Basis, 2015

[Millions of dollars]

	All industries	Mining	Manufacturing									Wholesale trade	Information	Depository institutions	Finance (except depository institutions) and insurance	Professional, scientific, and technical services	Holding companies (nonbank)	Other industries
			Total	Food	Chemicals	Primary and fabricated metals	Machinery	Computers and electronic products	Electrical equipment, appliances, and components	Transportation equipment	Other manufacturing							
All countries	**5,048,773**	**198,800**	**620,746**	**61,197**	**142,820**	**26,949**	**40,848**	**90,293**	**13,353**	**60,771**	**184,516**	**227,815**	**181,688**	**123,194**	**657,685**	**111,160**	**2,622,873**	**304,812**
Canada	**346,746**	**21,196**	**99,779**	**12,656**	**9,123**	**7,065**	**3,574**	**7,632**	**2,834**	**6,978**	**49,918**	**22,053**	**8,122**	**3,425**	**51,194**	**7,394**	**93,879**	**39,705**
Europe[1]	**2,919,510**	**25,724**	**284,787**	**28,597**	**86,031**	**12,874**	**24,042**	**28,323**	**5,369**	**20,226**	**79,326**	**76,811**	**118,216**	**61,650**	**295,343**	**67,493**	**1,800,433**	**189,053**
Austria	11,814	4	1,896	(D)	–423	(D)	282	1,182	(D)	89	299	931	55	42	1,123	93	(D)	(D)
Belgium	46,120	(D)	28,308	1,218	16,750	136	846	4,056	3	677	4,621	9,190	489	(D)	3,991	1,719	557	(D)
Czech Republic	5,847	0	3,643	(D)	207	132	106	191	(D)	1,565	651	178	189	(D)	60	166	(D)	190
Denmark	12,969	235	3,203	(D)	122	(D)	564	1,475	5	3	814	1,348	785	(D)	773	–8	6,445	(D)
Finland	1,239	0	–589	(D)	52	4	(D)	(D)	10	(*)	258	119	969	(D)	–5	565	62	(D)
France	77,860	(D)	21,361	4,307	3,276	3,056	1,478	1,279	507	674	6,784	4,690	3,124	2,395	16,111	3,913	16,233	(D)
Germany	102,068	290	27,021	347	4,564	1,239	4,671	3,371	559	4,359	7,910	11,905	5,827	1,657	11,975	4,251	40,155	–1,013
Greece	605	0	1,235	76	146	0	10	14	0	0	989	46	47	(D)	–331	28	0	(D)
Hungary	6,302	(D)	1,363	3	59	1	131	184	(D)	956	(D)	731	614	(D)	1,943	(D)	(D)	299
Ireland	334,325	(D)	17,097	424	14,980	183	70	–3,135	175	241	4,160	1,560	38,712	(D)	15,053	12,505	177,550	(D)
Italy	26,300	254	8,789	812	1,207	601	845	1,214	147	734	3,230	4,118	3,407	2,213	3,016	181	287	4,035
Luxembourg	553,066	(D)	14,100	(D)	–101	(D)	(D)	(D)	(D)	(D)	9,436	375	(D)	(D)	29,439	747	486,535	7,539
Netherlands	783,309	1,185	53,234	4,860	14,527	673	3,319	4,445	1,191	520	23,699	10,649	20,555	627	42,969	6,358	639,147	8,586
Norway	34,736	5,863	1,122	(D)	286	(D)	252	105	(D)	–3	52	258	1,752	(D)	582	139	23,257	(D)
Poland	11,239	(D)	4,308	(D)	388	127	81	164	(D)	2,014	3	2,112	235	(D)	361	143	10	(D)
Portugal	2,240	(*)	445	(D)	108	–36	(D)	101	(*)	166	71	732	67	–1	349	–27	10	664
Russia	8,543	(D)	3,786	(D)	462	(D)	297	152	(D)	(D)	106	519	608	(D)	24	209	268	(D)
Spain	36,280	(D)	13,860	1,521	5,432	–41	28	2,295	257	3,518	851	2,693	1,594	(D)	3,147	548	10,182	2,870
Sweden	30,497	–1	3,211	1,204	4	–32	861	302	(D)	524	(D)	2,213	1,206	(D)	5,810	656	14,721	(D)
Switzerland	155,710	151	32,081	72	15,371	95	1,871	3,396	1,221	(D)	(D)	10,725	7,227	(D)	19,389	2,692	44,085	(D)
Turkey	3,058	6	2,050	(D)	440	0	(D)	(D)	0	357	483	685	–33	(D)	(D)	22	–2	147
United Kingdom	625,124	5,987	40,724	7,432	8,069	3,502	5,987	7,903	630	2,220	4,982	10,062	27,872	21,077	137,057	31,479	296,916	53,951
Other	50,257	2,486	2,540	728	106	130	78	86	10	1,069	333	970	(D)	(D)	(D)	(D)	36,917	1,972
Latin America and Other Western Hemisphere	**873,398**	**53,590**	**57,215**	**6,729**	**8,473**	**2,246**	**3,459**	**–1,238**	**2,173**	**13,894**	**21,480**	**32,256**	**21,199**	**22,329**	**195,818**	**3,572**	**463,298**	**24,121**
South America	124,523	29,129	31,303	2,709	11,615	(D)	2,447	1,342	710	2,023	(D)	6,726	10,373	(D)	19,873	1,917	14,870	(D)
Argentina	13,600	933	3,492	373	1,343	(D)	226	–322	7	690	(D)	1,046	1,408	(D)	934	–25	(D)	165
Brazil	57,579	7,351	17,388	1,360	6,161	607	2,099	1,203	166	695	5,096	2,572	6,784	(D)	9,106	608	7,649	(D)
Chile	28,543	12,768	4,287	13	1,759	1	34	242	(D)	(D)	1,918	1,511	528	(D)	7,351	440	393	(D)
Colombia	6,522	2,876	1,203	67	574	(D)	–1	137	(D)	165	363	459	–86	(D)	809	400	122	(D)
Ecuador	491	521	212	65	29	(*)	(*)	4	0	32	83	178	5	(D)	154	(D)	6	–44
Peru	5,743	3,562	605	(D)	125	(*)	50	40	1	0	(D)	335	57	(D)	(D)	(D)	(D)	141
Venezuela	9,568	612	3,476	(D)	1,565	13	(D)	23	(D)	(D)	471	461	(D)	0	(D)	912	1,456	272
Other	2,478	506	641	(D)	59	(*)	(D)	15	2	3	(D)	164	(D)	(D)	369	79	17	281
Central America	97,020	10,001	32,742	3,892	(D)	1,205	(D)	–3,126	1,463	11,875	10,853	3,769	2,872	(D)	11,852	157	22,749	(D)
Costa Rica	1,423	0	1,602	73	272	8	0	243	(D)	0	(D)	–310	57	(D)	(D)	87	19	–509

Honduras	1,147	0	810	(D)	−15	0	0	(D)	0	(D)	(D)	−6	3	(D)	(D)	(*)	11	50
Mexico	86,795	9,998	29,291	3,600	5,272	1,196	852	−3,422	1,349	(D)	(D)	3,766	2,766	884	8,998	18	20,363	10,710
Panama	3,751	(D)	134	(D)	119	0	1	6	(D)	0	(D)	333	29	(D)	527	36	2,330	310
Other	3,903	(D)	904	55	(D)	0	(D)	(D)	(D)	0	(D)	−13	17	(D)	(D)	16	26	(D)
Other Western Hemisphere	651,855	14,460	−6,830	128	(D)	(D)	(D)	546	0	−5	(D)	21,761	7,953	14,157	164,094	1,498	425,678	9,085
Barbados	15,548	25	(D)	(D)	(*)	0	0	0	0	(D)	0	8,739	12	0	4,338	4	1,828	(D)
Bermuda	304,812	(D)	(D)	0	(D)	0	(D)	(D)	0	(D)	(D)	(D)	3,783	(D)	29,713	(D)	264,359	3,902
Dominican Republic	1,299	0	751	4	14	(D)	(*)	(*)	0	0	(D)	65	57	(D)	(*)	5	3	(D)
United Kingdom Islands, Caribbean[2]	286,679	9,386	54	(D)	(D)	0	(D)	(D)	0	0	−257	642	3,206	12,613	114,210	212	142,872	3,484
Other	43,518	(D)	(D)	35	−26	(D)	5	0	0	0	(D)	(D)	894	(D)	15,832	(D)	16,616	934
Africa	**59,266**	**35,632**	**4,344**	**757**	**1,439**	**(D)**	**547**	**−262**	**−72**	**(D)**	**915**	**2,206**	**963**	**(D)**	**3,402**	**1,423**	**7,206**	**(D)**
Egypt	23,236	(D)	525	(D)	134	−1	101	(D)	(D)	42	79	(D)	(D)	(D)	(D)	(D)	(D)	(D)
Nigeria	4,558	2,147	208	(D)	30	0	150	(D)	(*)	0	−5	(D)	(D)	(D)	(*)	1	(D)	(D)
South Africa	5,336	−93	2,524	188	971	59	195	61	(D)	780	(D)	628	112	(D)	230	482	313	(D)
Other	26,136	(D)	1,086	(D)	304	(D)	100	(D)	1	(D)	(D)	(D)	(D)	(D)	(D)	(D)	(D)	1,130
Middle East	**46,583**	**14,652**	**9,610**	**785**	**2,445**	**(D)**	**947**	**3,374**	**11**	**(D)**	**1,631**	**2,185**	**1,408**	**(D)**	**1,171**	**1,805**	**12,300**	**(D)**
Israel	9,119	−1	6,186	(D)	253	0	452	3,330	7	(D)	1,697	498	734	(D)	147	654	(D)	575
Saudi Arabia	9,669	1,066	255	(D)	421	(D)	122	(D)	(*)	(D)	(D)	341	(D)	−3	27	183	(D)	243
United Arab Emirates	15,625	8,336	1,749	(D)	(D)	(D)	401	(D)	4	0	315	1,340	(D)	(D)	698	591	(D)	1,334
Other	12,171	5,252	1,420	(D)	(D)	(D)	−28	1	0	0	(D)	5	70	(D)	299	377	(D)	(D)
Asia and Pacific	**803,269**	**48,006**	**165,011**	**11,673**	**35,309**	**4,453**	**8,277**	**52,464**	**3,039**	**18,548**	**31,247**	**92,306**	**31,780**	**32,267**	**110,756**	**29,472**	**245,757**	**47,914**
Australia	158,726	30,597	15,042	2,970	2,261	297	1,493	1,571	111	1,471	4,869	5,813	5,607	455	9,095	8,890	75,696	7,531
China	84,525	2,973	41,466	4,110	8,974	1,911	3,404	6,604	477	9,856	6,130	12,422	2,478	4,256	3,174	1,363	7,409	8,984
Hong Kong	64,105	4	4,190	79	1,290	(D)	−97	1,818	305	(D)	742	17,977	8,086	1,760	6,979	2,048	18,095	4,966
India	29,939	528	7,255	624	1,283	38	946	1,107	820	1,259	1,178	3,504	−625	(D)	2,590	10,577	487	(D)
Indonesia	13,352	10,096	363	(D)	413	2	10	−12	(D)	−62	−23	187	76	(D)	463	−14	1,371	(D)
Japan	104,128	6	21,143	115	2,214	288	362	7,591	(D)	675	(D)	5,938	7,938	(D)	51,574	2,700	3,387	(D)
Korea, Republic of	36,931	(D)	13,326	1,008	2,918	253	158	3,058	(D)	2,705	(D)	1,759	202	(D)	9,463	385	(D)	1,977
Malaysia	14,968	716	4,257	(D)	641	51	596	1,478	−78	(D)	862	446	4	(D)	2,660	525	(D)	891
New Zealand	7,929	141	1,454	(D)	160	7	96	214	3	12	(D)	599	180	(D)	2,763	402	1,414	(D)
Philippines	5,390	(D)	1,848	(D)	323	(D)	45	539	(D)	−148	367	537	−30	(D)	184	504	644	563
Singapore	250,748	1,111	42,231	406	11,818	662	950	25,952	194	1,554	694	39,026	7,493	792	19,862	1,363	130,529	8,340
Taiwan	15,307	1	5,538	(D)	980	(D)	209	3,363	150	101	571	3,164	323	(D)	1,195	207	861	(D)
Thailand	10,594	1,459	6,098	887	1,877	(D)	97	−690	(D)	768	(D)	684	22	723	255	473	186	694
Other	6,627	677	800	110	159	(D)	9	−129	1	66	(D)	249	25	(D)	498	49	79	(D)
Addenda:																		
European Union (28)[3]	2,674,409	16,188	245,315	25,300	69,429	12,320	21,428	24,400	4,070	19,115	69,252	64,362	108,597	51,038	272,967	64,338	1,696,775	154,827
OPEC[4]	56,051	20,280	7,082	865	3,988	157	706	83	(D)	280	(D)	2,632	2,666	(D)	1,833	1,391	16,600	(D)

* A nonzero value between −$500,000 and $500,000.

D Data are suppressed to avoid the disclosure of the data of individual companies.

1. In 2015, the euro area included Austria, Belgium, Cyprus, Estonia, Finland, France, Germany, Greece, Ireland, Italy, Latvia, Lithuania, Luxembourg, Malta, the Netherlands, Portugal, Slovakia, Slovenia and Spain. In 2015, the U.S. direct investment position in the euro area was $1,979,349 million.

2. The "United Kingdom Islands, Caribbean" consists of the British Virgin Islands, the Cayman Islands, Montserrat, and the Turks and Caicos Islands.

3. The European Union (28) comprises Austria, Belgium, Bulgaria, Croatia, Cyprus, the Czech Republic, Denmark, Estonia, Finland, France, Germany, Greece, Hungary, Ireland, Italy, Latvia, Lithuania, Luxembourg, Malta, the Netherlands, Poland, Portugal, Romania, Slovakia, Slovenia, Spain, Sweden, and the United Kingdom.

4. OPEC is the Organization of Petroleum Exporting Countries. In 2015, its members were Algeria, Angola, Ecuador, Iran, Iraq, Kuwait, Libya, Nigeria, Qatar, Saudi Arabia, the United Arab Emirates, and Venezuela.

NOTE. The estimates for 2015 are revised.

Table 1.2: U.S. Direct investment Position Abroad on a Historical-Cost Basis, 2016

[Millions of dollars]

	All industries	Mining	Manufacturing									Whole-sale trade	Infor-mation	Deposi-tory institu-tions	Finance (except depository institutions) and insurance	Pro-fessional, scientific, and technical services	Holding companies (nonbank)	Other indus-tries
			Total	Food	Chemi-cals	Primary and fabri-cated metals	Machin-ery	Com-puters and electronic products	Electrical equipment, appliances, and components	Trans-portation equip-ment	Other manu-facturing							
All countries	**5,332,225**	**198,742**	**666,580**	**60,602**	**147,836**	**25,512**	**46,404**	**97,015**	**12,893**	**71,362**	**204,956**	**244,296**	**195,187**	**129,319**	**674,664**	**120,159**	**2,761,524**	**341,754**
Canada	**363,914**	**19,351**	**103,460**	**13,142**	**8,912**	**6,643**	**3,310**	**8,103**	**3,063**	**10,445**	**49,843**	**23,715**	**8,122**	**4,311**	**52,437**	**8,197**	**98,099**	**46,220**
Europe[1]	**3,174,885**	**24,425**	**319,216**	**27,662**	**94,122**	**11,586**	**28,504**	**33,254**	**4,419**	**23,044**	**96,624**	**84,529**	**129,065**	**65,082**	**321,990**	**69,856**	**1,944,300**	**216,421**
Austria	15,891	–19	2,881	(D)	89	(D)	279	1,155	(D)	109	772	984	85	(D)	1,263	87	(D)	(D)
Belgium	55,822	(D)	37,353	1,646	17,715	261	853	4,106	(D)	710	(D)	9,110	550	(D)	4,250	1,667	252	(D)
Czech Republic	5,524	0	3,838	(D)	207	133	138	180	(D)	1,783	(D)	170	198	(D)	52	183	(D)	288
Denmark	13,643	255	3,836	(D)	100	(D)	594	1,495	5	3	1,532	1,420	801	(D)	592	12	6,603	(D)
Finland	3,395	0	1,109	(D)	61	3	(D)	165	11	(*)	357	154	944	(D)	–4	571	173	(D)
France	78,062	276	20,954	4,037	3,388	2,657	1,492	1,077	610	989	6,705	5,444	2,025	2,373	16,181	4,358	16,526	9,924
Germany	107,711	302	30,430	356	4,927	1,309	5,094	4,853	520	4,887	8,483	12,029	5,567	1,268	11,901	5,013	40,686	516
Greece	628	0	1,307	77	157	(*)	10	(D)	0	0	(D)	69	47	(D)	–391	31	(*)	(D)
Hungary	6,552	(D)	1,268	(D)	51	(*)	11	276	(D)	1,124	–193	808	630	–3	2,039	37	110	(D)
Ireland	387,092	(D)	21,000	484	17,756	199	82	–2,071	81	267	4,202	1,754	44,724	(D)	13,590	10,944	209,454	(D)
Italy	24,686	258	8,968	818	1,324	681	1,103	1,156	–365	848	3,403	3,746	2,233	2,705	2,275	–19	293	4,227
Luxembourg	607,849	(D)	10,430	(D)	–94	(D)	(D)	(D)	(D)	(D)	5,472	185	3,693	(D)	23,358	1,210	546,860	10,052
Netherlands	847,391	1,013	53,738	4,927	14,848	725	4,326	4,309	457	412	23,733	17,612	24,486	176	58,391	5,293	672,951	13,731
Norway	32,318	5,463	1,851	–13	335	(D)	(D)	219	(D)	–3	63	288	1,844	(D)	655	123	(D)	(D)
Poland	11,621	13	4,800	1,372	326	135	84	169	(D)	2,482	(D)	2,043	230	(D)	333	141	5	(D)
Portugal	2,273	(*)	392	(D)	107	–41	(D)	85	–2	169	53	826	85	–3	348	–21	10	635
Russia	10,574	(D)	4,129	2,485	629	30	193	292	(D)	(D)	334	739	889	(D)	74	241	553	(D)
Spain	37,388	(D)	14,885	1,758	5,795	57	119	2,138	239	3,747	1,032	2,537	1,141	(D)	3,226	536	11,265	2,383
Sweden	27,145	–1	2,744	1,133	–235	–64	684	262	(D)	538	(D)	2,439	1,234	(D)	3,330	697	13,773	(D)
Switzerland	172,608	(D)	37,087	–316	17,992	(D)	2,732	4,110	1,376	(D)	10,286	10,295	8,337	(D)	19,539	3,105	52,092	32,806
Turkey	3,109	3	2,057	(D)	441	(*)	206	157	0	342	(D)	799	–115	(D)	(D)	45	–2	168
United Kingdom	682,361	4,662	51,933	6,732	8,112	2,812	7,521	8,222	754	2,340	15,440	10,088	29,025	21,308	158,354	34,467	314,931	57,594
Other	41,242	2,395	2,224	700	91	–157	74	(D)	11	1,138	(D)	991	412	(D)	(D)	1,134	28,479	(D)
Latin America and Other Western Hemisphere	**843,357**	**55,345**	**54,905**	**7,862**	**3,773**	**2,263**	**3,208**	**–563**	**2,153**	**14,850**	**21,359**	**32,238**	**20,017**	**22,663**	**179,452**	**4,533**	**448,542**	**25,662**
South America	131,629	30,437	31,554	3,700	11,651	(D)	2,285	1,279	848	1,752	(D)	6,360	9,522	(D)	22,984	2,839	16,340	(D)
Argentina	13,721	1,018	2,988	324	1,562	(D)	256	–392	7	350	(D)	500	1,706	(D)	976	–25	(D)	142
Brazil	64,438	7,608	18,578	2,316	6,475	627	1,890	1,236	345	572	5,117	2,838	5,513	4,442	12,713	1,580	8,849	2,318
Chile	29,428	13,165	4,743	26	1,964	1	46	194	(D)	(D)	(D)	1,595	531	(D)	7,022	442	527	(D)
Colombia	6,217	2,302	1,164	50	693	(D)	–13	148	(D)	243	238	455	–141	(D)	970	474	153	(D)
Ecuador	509	541	189	76	–3	(*)	(*)	5	0	(D)	(D)	153	5	(D)	157	(D)	5	(D)
Peru	6,187	4,054	540	41	121	(*)	49	40	1	0	288	252	57	(D)	108	(D)	(D)	296
Venezuela	7,984	611	2,681	(D)	776	6	36	33	(D)	138	475	381	(D)	0	(D)	782	1,012	263
Other	3,145	1,137	671	(D)	63	1	22	15	2	3	(D)	187	(D)	(D)	(D)	82	17	295
Central America	98,557	11,106	33,249	4,034	(D)	1,281	(D)	–3,161	1,305	13,100	10,551	3,992	1,618	(D)	12,279	–239	24,168	(D)
Costa Rica	1,565	0	1,610	72	278	9	0	232	137	0	882	–194	59	(D)	(D)	50	19	–468

Honduras	1,140	0	804	(D)	–28	0	0	(D)	0	(D)	(D)	(D)	3	(D)	(D)	(*)	12	44
Mexico	87,635	10,925	29,617	3,707	4,890	1,272	822	–3,372	1,166	(D)	(D)	3,794	1,451	(D)	9,659	–304	21,397	(D)
Panama	4,377	(D)	204	(D)	111	0	1	10	(D)	0	(D)	462	(D)	(D)	516	–1	2,719	159
Other	3,841	(D)	1,014	75	(D)	(*)	(D)	(D)	(D)	0	(D)	(D)	(D)	(D)	(D)	16	21	338
Other Western Hemisphere	613,171	13,802	–9,898	128	(D)	(D)	(D)	1,319	0	–2	(D)	21,886	8,877	13,872	144,189	1,933	408,034	10,476
Barbados	18,990	27	(D)	(D)	(*)	0	(D)	0	0	0	0	(D)	12	0	10,304	4	1,958	(D)
Bermuda	288,822	253	(D)	0	(D)	0	(D)	625	0	–2	(D)	(D)	4,568	202	29,831	409	250,409	3,683
Dominican Republic	1,401	0	(D)	–21	17	(D)	(*)	(*)	0	0	703	145	12	(D)	(*)	(D)	2	240
United Kingdom Islands, Caribbean [2]	265,548	9,413	1,299	(D)	95	(D)	(D)	694	0	0	461	666	3,308	12,431	92,054	634	140,523	5,220
Other	38,411	4,109	483	(D)	–52	(D)	5	0	0	0	(D)	3,023	977	(D)	12,000	(D)	15,142	(D)
Africa	**57,465**	**34,717**	**4,054**	**438**	**1,311**	**(D)**	**526**	**–329**	**–67**	**(D)**	**1,148**	**1,895**	**926**	**(D)**	**3,243**	**1,451**	**6,958**	**(D)**
Egypt	22,202	(D)	–9	(D)	–24	(*)	70	(D)	(D)	–20	99	(D)	(D)	(D)	(D)	(D)	(D)	(D)
Nigeria	3,819	1,996	120	(D)	17	(*)	141	(D)	(*)	0	(D)	(D)	(D)	(D)	(*)	1	(D)	31
South Africa	5,061	–321	2,605	147	1,076	49	201	40	(D)	829	(D)	451	135	(D)	312	525	187	(D)
Other	26,382	(D)	1,338	(D)	241	(D)	115	(D)	1	(D)	(D)	(D)	(D)	(D)	(D)	(D)	(D)	1,251
Middle East	**45,925**	**14,119**	**10,379**	**898**	**2,768**	**(D)**	**993**	**3,548**	**11**	**(D)**	**1,707**	**2,149**	**1,350**	**(D)**	**1,836**	**2,112**	**12,699**	**(D)**
Israel	9,669	(D)	6,706	(D)	336	3	502	3,476	7	(D)	1,903	430	622	(D)	143	781	(D)	633
Saudi Arabia	9,825	1,131	325	(D)	484	(D)	126	(D)	(*)	(D)	(D)	322	(D)	(*)	36	252	7,824	(D)
United Arab Emirates	13,355	7,579	2,020	(D)	(D)	(D)	402	(D)	4	(D)	331	1,394	(D)	(D)	645	620	(D)	–756
Other	13,075	(D)	1,329	(D)	(D)	(D)	–38	1	0	0	(D)	2	32	(D)	1,011	459	(D)	282
Asia and Pacific	**846,680**	**50,784**	**174,565**	**10,599**	**36,950**	**4,694**	**9,863**	**53,003**	**3,315**	**21,866**	**34,275**	**99,770**	**35,706**	**33,481**	**115,705**	**34,010**	**250,924**	**51,733**
Australia	165,347	32,346	15,516	2,975	2,100	207	1,703	1,861	96	1,307	5,267	5,514	5,990	530	6,577	9,801	81,331	7,742
China	92,481	2,688	47,040	3,944	10,210	1,867	3,751	7,611	700	12,747	6,210	12,978	2,603	4,386	2,857	1,512	8,304	10,114
Hong Kong	65,625	2	4,023	79	1,144	186	16	1,836	336	–377	802	19,869	8,152	2,079	7,005	2,357	17,145	4,994
India	32,939	720	7,383	100	1,606	33	1,230	1,240	807	1,105	1,262	4,233	–253	(D)	2,196	12,168	501	(D)
Indonesia	14,563	10,840	446	(D)	440	2	13	–15	(D)	–61	34	206	65	(D)	303	20	1,761	(D)
Japan	114,637	4	20,058	130	2,658	310	990	4,173	(D)	821	(D)	6,822	8,947	3,635	58,754	3,460	3,949	9,008
Korea, Republic of	39,068	(D)	15,257	1,089	2,241	257	193	4,852	(D)	3,191	(D)	1,843	512	(D)	8,936	577	(D)	2,023
Malaysia	13,897	807	4,023	(D)	669	52	705	915	–48	(D)	985	427	126	(D)	2,519	687	(D)	1,013
New Zealand	8,430	129	1,795	(D)	192	7	122	247	6	12	(D)	664	197	(D)	2,805	423	1,423	(D)
Philippines	5,896	52	1,761	(D)	357	(D)	46	350	(D)	–138	389	623	99	(D)	211	566	692	(D)
Singapore	258,864	987	42,529	64	11,730	789	750	26,264	160	1,907	865	42,435	8,800	1,312	21,551	1,613	130,096	9,541
Taiwan	16,187	1	6,034	(D)	1,056	(D)	226	3,655	154	35	618	3,281	413	3,560	1,165	232	991	510
Thailand	11,774	1,424	7,654	974	2,381	(D)	107	–7	(D)	779	(D)	617	28	295	265	518	244	729
Other	6,972	(D)	1,047	102	167	(D)	9	19	1	(D)	380	258	26	(D)	562	76	127	3,688
Addenda:																		
European Union (28) [3]	2,921,744	14,789	273,764	24,989	74,709	11,079	24,568	28,469	2,965	21,744	85,240	72,126	118,040	54,098	299,205	66,213	1,843,833	179,676
OPEC [4]	67,090	29,958	7,013	934	3,812	192	714	108	(D)	223	(D)	2,612	3,001	(D)	2,492	1,500	18,156	(D)

* A nonzero value between –$500,000 and $500,000

D Data are suppressed to avoid the disclosure of the data of individual companies.

1. In 2016, the euro area included Austria, Belgium, Cyprus, Estonia, Finland, France, Germany, Greece, Ireland, Italy, Latvia, Lithuania, Luxembourg, Malta, the Netherlands, Portugal, Slovakia, Slovenia and Spain. In 2016, the U.S. direct investment position in the euro area was $2,171,797 million.

2. The "United Kingdom Islands, Caribbean" consists of the British Virgin Islands, the Cayman Islands, Montserrat, and the Turks and Caicos Islands.

3. The European Union (28) comprises Austria, Belgium, Bulgaria, Croatia, Cyprus, the Czech Republic, Denmark, Estonia, Finland, France, Germany, Greece, Hungary, Ireland, Italy, Latvia, Lithuania, Luxembourg, Malta, the Netherlands, Poland, Portugal, Romania, Slovakia, Slovenia, Spain, Sweden, and the United Kingdom.

4. OPEC is the Organization of Petroleum Exporting Countries. In 2016, its members were Algeria, Angola, Ecuador, Gabon, Iran, Iraq, Kuwait, Libya, Nigeria, Qatar, Saudi Arabia, the United Arab Emirates, and Venezuela.

NOTE. The estimates for 2016 are preliminary

Table 2.1: Foreign Direct investment Position in the United States on a Historical-Cost Basis, 2015

[Millions of dollars]

	All industries	Manufacturing									Whole-sale trade	Retail trade	Infor-mation	Deposi-tory institu-tions	Finance (except depository institutions) and insurance	Real estate and rental and leasing	Pro-fessional, scientific, and technical services	Other indus-tries
		Total	Food	Chemi-cals	Primary and fabri-cated metals	Machin-ery	Com-puters and electronic products	Electrical equipment, appliances, and components	Trans-portation equip-ment	Other manuf-acturing								
All countries	**3,303,586**	**1,362,109**	**89,217**	**566,595**	**67,171**	**90,721**	**58,069**	**38,901**	**134,623**	**316,812**	**362,747**	**63,245**	**169,861**	**193,436**	**407,227**	**74,759**	**154,272**	**515,930**
Canada	**322,118**	**114,373**	**4,507**	**80,514**	**5,708**	**514**	**943**	**–89**	**8,237**	**14,040**	**20,259**	**7,727**	**6,326**	**46,901**	**55,008**	**10,378**	**7,844**	**53,301**
Europe [1]	**2,276,695**	**1,036,344**	**65,419**	**447,370**	**47,897**	**64,659**	**37,366**	**36,787**	**79,266**	**257,580**	**179,099**	**46,613**	**134,494**	**105,188**	**265,829**	**36,364**	**121,578**	**351,186**
Austria	7,088	3,133	(D)	(D)	553	523	(D)	1	22	1,861	(D)	(D)	6	(D)	3	(D)	(D)	45
Belgium	89,231	53,672	(D)	16,083	558	1,568	–65	(D)	(D)	(D)	18,219	(D)	(D)	(D)	(D)	119	307	7,331
Denmark	14,432	4,614	(D)	642	(D)	2,115	(D)	3	9	511	6,041	–1	9	0	1	37	34	3,697
Finland	6,482	2,053	(D)	(D)	(D)	1,435	15	(D)	(D)	217	2,458	(*)	(D)	(D)	(*)	2	(D)	(D)
France	232,431	107,965	2,004	60,300	2,548	356	4,273	(D)	9,765	(D)	16,648	4,122	18,289	20,336	32,898	1,017	9,806	21,349
Germany	279,735	103,382	334	27,227	7,827	14,040	604	1,006	39,798	12,547	25,538	(D)	(D)	19,604	39,791	9,722	(D)	28,560
Ireland	35,814	–12,611	(D)	7,825	271	–334	(D)	(D)	0	(D)	–2,913	(D)	(D)	7	5,782	(D)	35,919	3,167
Italy	27,690	7,278	472	992	450	1,624	(D)	(D)	(D)	(D)	2,172	4,199	138	(D)	(D)	(D)	(D)	2,972
Luxembourg	347,864	233,055	(D)	162,098	4,016	(D)	(D)	(D)	902	36,146	18,312	2,883	21,112	0	16,964	1,923	6,322	47,294
Netherlands	299,780	137,343	(D)	20,555	434	(D)	14,220	(D)	2,440	46,639	24,159	4,886	8,841	(D)	34,121	1,709	31,182	(D)
Norway	20,706	2,180	1	(D)	(D)	(D)	–5	(D)	8	(D)	15,209	(*)	(D)	(D)	(D)	1,712	265	(D)
Spain	66,985	9,726	(D)	(D)	(D)	(D)	(D)	(D)	(D)	1,496	102	(D)	135	16,350	(D)	1,486	499	(D)
Sweden	43,416	38,303	3	(D)	7,367	3,316	(D)	(D)	(D)	5,385	–4,352	(D)	(D)	(D)	122	(D)	(D)	4,203
Switzerland	249,225	110,526	(D)	30,964	1,453	3,570	416	(D)	186	(D)	21,244	(D)	15,791	(D)	55,990	(D)	1,327	34,568
United Kingdom	512,139	214,693	6,567	92,730	14,007	3,331	4,747	–55	19,798	73,568	34,677	3,719	30,499	(D)	56,028	8,672	10,793	(D)
Other	43,678	21,032	3,164	6,616	4,969	12	65	94	1,064	5,049	(D)	(D)	432	807	(D)	4,702	93	(D)
Latin America and Other Western Hemisphere	**117,301**	**36,079**	**14,853**	**(D)**	**2,470**	**(D)**	**–338**	**–78**	**256**	**8,515**	**1,748**	**(D)**	**1,412**	**6,944**	**9,055**	**10,147**	**4,563**	**(D)**
South and Central America	25,755	9,252	3,184	–221	2,026	(D)	–105	(D)	40	4,655	–726	(D)	–72	6,199	1,104	1,284	12	(D)
Brazil	551	530	(D)	–427	(D)	–139	–6	(D)	743	(D)	–2,104	–1	–39	1,299	724	(D)	–48	(D)
Mexico	15,209	3,911	(D)	102	888	–64	–77	–9	–696	(D)	1,214	124	(D)	1,038	270	(D)	82	8,141
Panama	2,592	(D)	0	(D)	(D)	(D)	(*)	(*)	5	(D)	(D)	21	2	(D)	110	636	–2	705
Venezuela	4,187	(D)	–9	(D)	(D)	2	–1	(D)	–3	(D)	23	(D)	4	(D)	(D)	(D)	–15	(D)
Other	3,216	797	(D)	–27	(D)	(D)	–21	(D)	–9	51	(D)	42	(D)	(D)	(D)	(D)	–6	(D)
Other Western Hemisphere	91,546	26,828	11,669	(D)	444	(D)	–233	(D)	216	3,860	2,474	910	1,484	745	7,952	8,863	4,551	37,741
Bahamas	805	(D)	(D)	0	(D)	0	(*)	0	(D)	(*)	(D)	0	(*)	(D)	121	(D)	(D)	403
Bermuda	–7,411	5,519	(D)	(D)	(D)	(D)	(D)	0	0	707	(D)	7	(D)	0	–14,811	1,360	3,490	(D)
Curacao	1,630	170	–3	(D)	0	(D)	1	0	0	(D)	(D)	(D)	(D)	(D)	17	558	(D)	462

United Kingdom Islands, Caribbean [2]	94,773	20,990	(D)	(D)	(D)	(D)	(D)	(D)	(D)	2,957	9,492	889	1,193	(D)	22,580	6,257	534	(D)
Other	1,749	(D)	−3	(D)	(*)	0	(D)	0	0	(D)	551	(D)	(D)	8	45	(D)	(D)	63
Africa	**4,330**	**(D)**	**(D)**	**(D)**	**(D)**	**−6**	**(D)**	**(D)**	**(D)**	**−48**	**(D)**	**(D)**	**(D)**	**(D)**	**10**	**518**	**110**	**(D)**
South Africa	2,942	(D)	(D)	(D)	(D)	(D)	−2	(*)	(D)	(D)	(D)	(D)	(D)	0	(D)	2	(D)	437
Other	1,388	29	(D)	−32	(D)	(D)	(D)	(D)	(D)	(D)	(D)	0	(D)	(D)	(D)	516	(D)	(D)
Middle East	**18,169**	**(D)**	**(D)**	**3,746**	**(D)**	**49**	**(D)**	**(D)**	**(D)**	**−113**	**(D)**	**(D)**	**(D)**	**(D)**	**2,166**	**1,707**	**−43**	**2,021**
Israel	7,442	4,091	(D)	3,697	(D)	(D)	198	(*)	(D)	−69	422	(D)	(D)	1,891	(D)	580	−19	−693
Kuwait	1,113	3	0	0	0	0	(D)	(D)	(D)	(D)	0	0	(*)	(D)	(D)	1,140	0	−50
Lebanon	−14	1	0	0	0	0	0	0	1	0	(*)	0	0	0	2	(D)	(D)	(D)
Saudi Arabia	(D)	−91	0	(D)	(D)	−3	−1	(D)	0	−5	(D)	0	2	(D)	0	30	(D)	(D)
United Arab Emirates	2,755	(D)	0	(D)	(D)	(D)	1	−9	−1	−32	(D)	(*)	(D)	(D)	(D)	(D)	−25	838
Other	(D)	−67	0	(D)	0	(D)	(D)	0	0	(D)	−67	2	(D)	(D)	(D)	(D)	(D)	1,928
Asia and Pacific	**564,974**	**169,058**	**4,368**	**31,724**	**11,185**	**(D)**	**19,803**	**(D)**	**46,814**	**36,838**	**155,770**	**7,739**	**26,826**	**32,374**	**75,158**	**15,646**	**20,220**	**62,182**
Australia	47,270	15,281	1,102	(D)	1,613	−74	−22	−5	−16	(D)	3,711	(D)	−1	1,484	4,635	32	(D)	(D)
China	16,769	4,235	−21	182	(D)	19	439	58	641	(D)	1,077	(D)	46	2,863	450	2,659	−230	(D)
Hong Kong	10,991	1,892	(D)	(D)	−2	(D)	756	(D)	(D)	−48	2,705	10	(D)	724	−23	931	225	(D)
India	9,629	801	(D)	244	7	−22	130	−2	4	(D)	405	0	(D)	1,500	(D)	(*)	3,460	(D)
Japan	402,164	128,535	3,298	22,543	7,830	14,271	9,055	2,006	44,285	25,247	116,572	7,101	24,983	21,942	61,429	11,706	9,367	20,529
Korea, Republic of	40,585	6,128	(D)	(D)	553	(D)	25	−4	1,316	1,324	26,698	1	−10	1,085	550	(D)	66	(D)
Malaysia	1,278	298	(D)	−3	(D)	(D)	(D)	(*)	(*)	(D)	472	0	(D)	(D)	(D)	(D)	2	(D)
New Zealand	439	−393	(D)	1	(D)	(D)	−1	(D)	(D)	1	694	(*)	1	0	2	73	5	57
Singapore	21,654	8,753	(D)	−22	14	−33	(D)	(D)	(D)	81	2,642	(D)	−172	456	(D)	(D)	(D)	1,483
Taiwan	6,890	2,856	(*)	(D)	1	(D)	104	(D)	18	(D)	449	(D)	120	1,936	(D)	19	8	(D)
Other	7,306	672	(D)	−39	(D)	(D)	(D)	21	231	74	344	−4	2	(D)	(D)	63	17	(D)
Addenda:																		
European Union (28) [3]	1,981,879	914,607	40,735	409,933	42,648	61,072	36,958	(D)	79,045	(D)	141,820	36,373	118,661	102,479	209,759	32,789	119,988	305,404
OPEC [4]	15,461	2,788	(D)	(*)	(D)	(D)	(D)	(D)	(D)	(D)	(D)	(D)	(D)	1,454	2,048	1,131	−46	(D)

* A nonzero value between −$500,000 and $500,000.

D Data are suppressed to avoid the disclosure of the data of individual companies.

1. In 2015, the euro area included Austria, Belgium, Cyprus, Estonia, Finland, France, Germany, Greece, Ireland, Italy, Latvia, Lithuania, Luxembourg, Malta, the Netherlands, Portugal, Slovakia, Slovenia, and Spain. In 2015, the direct investment position of the euro area in the United States was $1,398,037 million.

2. The "United Kingdom Islands, Caribbean" consists of the British Virgin Islands, the Cayman Islands, Montserrat, and the Turks and Caicos Islands.

3. The European Union (28) comprises Austria, Belgium, Bulgaria, Croatia, Cyprus, the Czech Republic, Denmark, Estonia, Finland, France, Germany, Greece, Hungary, Ireland, Italy, Latvia, Lithuania, Luxembourg, Malta, the Netherlands, Poland, Portugal, Romania, Slovakia, Slovenia, Spain, Sweden, and the United Kingdom.

4. OPEC is the Organization of Petroleum Exporting Countries. In 2015, Its members were Algeria, Angola, Ecuador, Iran, Iraq, Kuwait, Libya, Nigeria, Qatar, Saudi Arabia, the United Arab Emirates, and Venezuela.

NOTE. The estimates for 2015 are revised.

Table 2.2: Foreign Direct investment Position in the United States on a Historical-Cost Basis, 2016

[Millions of dollars]

		Manufacturing															
	All industries	Total	Food	Chemicals	Primary and fabricated metals	Machinery	Computers and electronic products	Electrical equipment, appliances, and components	Transportation equipment	Other manufacturing	Wholesale trade	Retail trade	Information	Depository institutions	Finance (except depository institutions) and insurance	Real estate and rental and leasing	Professional, scientific, and technical services	Other industries
All countries	**3,725,418**	**1,532,365**	**95,606**	**653,594**	**65,627**	**94,026**	**76,899**	**43,297**	**143,834**	**359,482**	**367,596**	**72,403**	**185,806**	**190,665**	**504,780**	**82,261**	**197,948**	**591,595**
Canada	**371,468**	**114,760**	**4,946**	**(D)**	**4,838**	**317**	**1,224**	**–128**	**8,831**	**(D)**	**21,677**	**7,942**	**7,667**	**(D)**	**62,441**	**11,449**	**8,738**	**(D)**
Europe [1]	**2,605,559**	**1,195,643**	**73,276**	**534,813**	**45,915**	**76,038**	**47,329**	**40,874**	**83,135**	**294,263**	**187,257**	**54,761**	**148,651**	**94,526**	**333,427**	**39,275**	**163,701**	**388,319**
Austria	10,611	3,264	(D)	(D)	542	713	(D)	1	26	1,813	(D)	(D)	6	(D)	4	28	–14	42
Belgium	79,854	55,799	(D)	17,669	374	(D)	–66	(D)	10	(D)	8,394	(D)	(D)	(D)	(D)	(D)	315	7,418
Denmark	18,233	5,146	(D)	701	(D)	2,329	(D)	7	(D)	680	6,380	(D)	(D)	0	2	35	42	6,007
Finland	5,874	1,906	(D)	(D)	(D)	1,367	–2	(D)	(D)	218	2,486	(*)	(D)	0	(D)	3	(D)	(D)
France	252,864	118,351	2,149	74,275	2,290	366	3,208	(D)	10,282	(D)	17,242	4,650	17,788	8,944	48,099	(D)	13,624	(D)
Germany	291,697	104,161	349	21,007	7,476	14,029	808	954	43,498	16,041	28,177	(D)	(D)	22,996	41,643	11,247	(D)	29,907
Ireland	85,460	21,727	875	42,921	(D)	(D)	(D)	(D)	(*)	–20,037	–2,119	(D)	(D)	(D)	5,410	(D)	(D)	20,315
Italy	30,010	8,285	552	1,268	519	1,659	(D)	17	(D)	2,436	2,193	4,311	136	(D)	(D)	136	(D)	4,165
Luxembourg	417,386	251,828	16,241	158,613	4,673	(D)	(D)	(D)	632	44,560	25,659	2,992	20,767	0	11,544	1,985	(D)	(D)
Netherlands	355,242	160,767	(D)	29,259	495	(D)	19,194	(D)	2,299	51,715	27,972	8,646	21,900	(D)	40,142	966	32,209	(D)
Norway	25,548	1,432	1	(D)	(D)	(D)	–5	(D)	(D)	(D)	(D)	(*)	(D)	(D)	(D)	369	(D)	160
Spain	68,169	9,638	(D)	(D)	(D)	488	(D)	(D)	707	1,558	215	(D)	930	14,979	(D)	1,734	529	(D)
Sweden	46,933	40,177	4	16,806	7,830	3,154	(D)	(D)	(D)	6,113	–4,223	(D)	(D)	(D)	117	(D)	(D)	5,223
Switzerland	310,759	149,994	(D)	57,909	2,275	(D)	3,705	(D)	(D)	50,794	22,770	(D)	15,652	(D)	81,790	1,265	2,834	28,719
United Kingdom	555,687	235,364	6,581	100,332	13,240	6,081	4,853	–248	18,968	85,556	28,382	4,789	30,563	(D)	78,491	10,688	14,311	(D)
Other	51,231	27,805	7,918	9,744	4,926	(D)	74	66	1,059	(D)	(D)	(D)	63	878	42	4,618	92	(D)
Latin America and Other Western Hemisphere	**124,798**	**21,982**	**11,201**	**560**	**2,469**	**–197**	**–75**	**–26**	**197**	**7,854**	**5,160**	**1,218**	**2,175**	**6,665**	**(D)**	**10,454**	**4,363**	**(D)**
South and Central America	25,805	9,984	2,945	319	(D)	–309	–337	(D)	197	5,195	–1,056	205	364	6,067	(D)	1,300	10	(D)
Brazil	–1,831	–67	–212	–421	(D)	–137	–19	–15	(D)	–77	–2,929	–2	–33	1,389	710	87	–43	–942
Mexico	16,757	4,713	3,157	457	954	–87	–315	5	–391	934	1,556	127	357	798	212	434	77	8,482
Panama	2,922	(D)	0	(D)	(D)	(D)	(*)	(*)	5	(D)	(*)	(D)	1	(D)	106	653	–2	702
Venezuela	4,457	(D)	–9	(D)	–5	(D)	0	0	(D)	(D)	19	(D)	4	(D)	(*)	18	(D)	–21
Other	3,500	742	9	84	(D)	–74	–3	(D)	(D)	–76	297	(D)	35	2,611	(D)	108	(D)	(D)
Other Western Hemisphere	98,993	11,997	8,256	242	(D)	112	262	(D)	(*)	2,659	6,216	1,013	1,812	598	19,959	9,154	4,353	43,890
Bahamas	484	5	3	0	(D)	0	(D)	0	1	(D)	(D)	–1	(*)	0	123	57	(D)	375
Bermuda	9,361	–2,871	(D)	–368	(D)	33	–2,047	0	0	(D)	–3,359	7	492	0	(D)	802	3,269	(D)

Curacao	1,660	(D)	−2	(D)	0	(D)	1	0	0	(D)	(D)	(D)	(D)	(D)	17	570	(D)	444
United Kingdom Islands, Caribbean [2]	86,054	14,625	(D)	592	(D)	82	2,297	(D)	−1	(D)	9,277	1,014	1,186	(D)	22,188	7,360	592	(D)
Other	1,434	(D)	−1	(D)	0	(D)	(D)	0	0	(D)	496	(D)	(D)	8	(D)	365	(D)	47
Africa	**4,394**	**2,320**	**(D)**	**(D)**	**(D)**	**(D)**	**(D)**	**(D)**	**(D)**	**(D)**	**(D)**	**(D)**	**9**	**(D)**	**7**	**520**	**112**	**1,137**
South Africa	3,114	(D)	−4	(D)	1	−26	(D)	(*)	−3	(D)	185	(D)	7	0	(D)	2	−33	(D)
Other	1,280	(D)	(D)	(D)	(D)	(D)	0	(D)	(D)	(D)	(D)	0	2	(D)	(D)	518	145	(D)
Middle East	**19,826**	**3,731**	**(D)**	**2,952**	**(D)**	**(D)**	**(D)**	**(D)**	**(D)**	**−134**	**(D)**	**(D)**	**851**	**(D)**	**(D)**	**2,963**	**853**	**2,058**
Israel	8,136	3,900	(D)	2,894	(D)	(D)	531	0	(D)	−108	472	(D)	(D)	1,970	(D)	574	(D)	−740
Kuwait	1,122	4	0	0	0	0	(D)	(D)	3	0	(*)	0	(*)	(D)	(D)	(D)	0	(D)
Lebanon	−13	2	0	0	0	0	0	0	1	(*)	(*)	0	0	0	3	(D)	(D)	(D)
Saudi Arabia	(D)	−119	0	(D)	(D)	(*)	(*)	(D)	0	(D)	(D)	0	2	(D)	0	30	−15	43
United Arab Emirates	2,843	(D)	0	(D)	(D)	−5	(D)	(D)	−1	(D)	(D)	(D)	(D)	(D)	(D)	(D)	(D)	878
Other	(D)	(D)	0	−1	0	(D)	(D)	0	0	(D)	(D)	(D)	(D)	−34	(D)	15	2	1,978
Asia and Pacific	**599,373**	**193,928**	**6,045**	**33,321**	**12,508**	**17,588**	**27,904**	**2,606**	**51,621**	**42,336**	**146,923**	**8,431**	**26,452**	**36,312**	**87,047**	**17,601**	**20,181**	**62,498**
Australia	46,926	16,010	1,151	(D)	2,392	−69	−8	−4	−6	(D)	3,509	(D)	−9	1,579	3,921	−252	(D)	(D)
China	27,475	14,038	−39	197	(D)	29	7,926	118	2,106	(D)	1,142	−16	(D)	3,076	425	3,627	−172	(D)
Hong Kong	11,649	1,680	(D)	(D)	−2	21	397	(D)	(D)	23	2,772	(D)	(D)	790	−7	986	240	3,473
India	9,852	978	(D)	420	9	(*)	6	3	−29	(D)	345	(D)	241	1,467	(D)	(*)	3,635	2,357
Japan	421,103	139,638	3,351	23,696	8,234	(D)	9,895	2,046	47,494	(D)	107,167	7,899	24,565	25,464	73,277	12,822	8,852	21,418
Korea, Republic of	40,937	7,194	(D)	(D)	634	(D)	31	−3	1,553	1,314	27,180	1	−38	1,177	489	89	53	4,791
Malaysia	1,136	91	34	−3	4	−11	40	(*)	(*)	27	480	0	1	(D)	(D)	(D)	4	114
New Zealand	176	−475	(D)	(D)	(D)	(*)	(*)	(D)	(D)	(D)	(D)	(*)	1	0	2	73	(D)	59
Singapore	23,933	9,743	−38	92	20	−30	(D)	102	(D)	3	2,812	(D)	−169	490	(D)	87	(D)	1,791
Taiwan	7,196	3,133	(*)	(D)	3	17	82	(D)	20	(D)	413	61	125	1,860	4	20	9	1,572
Other	8,991	1,898	(D)	−25	(D)	−21	(D)	96	200	69	(D)	−2	7	(D)	(D)	(D)	34	(D)
Addenda:																		
European Union (28) [3]	2,241,063	1,032,496	47,768	466,812	40,581	72,591	43,632	(D)	82,912	(D)	141,596	44,335	132,947	92,690	251,561	36,957	160,608	347,874
OPEC [4]	18,311	3,129	−16	(D)	−130	−30	−4	(D)	5	(D)	(D)	(D)	−18	1,518	(D)	2,405	−53	4,426

* A nonzero value between −$500,000 and $500,000

D Data are suppressed to avoid the disclosure of the data of individual companies.

1. In 2016, the euro area included Austria, Belgium, Cyprus, Estonia, Finland, France, Germany, Greece, Ireland, Italy, Latvia, Lithuania, Luxembourg, Malta, the Netherlands, Portugal, Slovakia, Slovenia, and Spain. In 2016, the direct investment position of the euro area in the United States was $1,602,354 million.

2. The "United Kingdom Islands, Caribbean" consists of the British Virgin Islands, the Cayman Islands, Montserrat, and the Turks and Caicos Islands.

3. The European Union (28) comprises Austria, Belgium, Bulgaria, Croatia, Cyprus, the Czech Republic, Denmark, Estonia, Finland, France, Germany, Greece, Hungary, Ireland, Italy, Latvia, Lithuania, Luxembourg, Malta, the Netherlands, Poland, Portugal, Romania, Slovakia, Slovenia, Spain, Sweden, and the United Kingdom.

4. OPEC is the Organization of Petroleum Exporting Countries. In 2016, Its members were Algeria, Angola, Ecuador, Gabon, Iran, Iraq, Kuwait, Libya, Nigeria, Qatar, Saudi Arabia, the United Arab Emirates, and Venezuela.

NOTE. The estimates for 2016 are preliminary.

Chapter 14

M&As in Bankruptcy and Reorganization: The Implications on M&A

Frank A. Oswald, Kyle J. Ortiz, and Katherine A. Crispi
Togut, Segal & Segal LLP, Manhattan, NY

If an acquisition target has been experiencing financial distress or is insolvent, the transaction parties may want to effectuate an M&A transaction in the context of a bankruptcy proceeding under Chapter 11 of title 11 of the US Code (the "Bankruptcy Code"). There are a number of advantages to effectuating an M&A transaction inside a Chapter 11 proceeding, but there are also certain risks to attempting such a transaction.

One of the reasons an acquisition in a Chapter 11 proceeding may be attractive to an acquirer is that the entity in Chapter 11 (referred to herein as the "Debtor") can use the reorganization process to address certain cost and operational issues (that would otherwise make an acquisition target less attractive) prior to consummation of an M&A deal. For instance, a Debtor in Chapter 11 has the ability to reject or renegotiate less favorable leases, certain types of contracts, and, in certain instances, even labor agreements otherwise protected by collective bargaining agreements. Additionally, through the operation of the automatic stay (which is explained in greater detail below) the filing of a Chapter 11 case puts a freeze on all collections activities and outstanding litigations pending against a Debtor. This automatic stay can provide the critical breathing room needed to finalize an M&A transaction. There are many additional advantages to effectuating a transaction pursuant to a Chapter 11 proceeding, including obtaining financing on a senior secured basis where a lender would not otherwise provide financing and the possibility of obtaining third-party releases in connection with pretransaction activities for key parties.

Although Chapter 11 provides many benefits to a potential acquirer, Chapter 11 is not without its costs, risks, and uncertainties. Chapter 11 is a court supervised process and the Debtor will need to ask for court authority to take nearly all actions during the Chapter 11 that fall outside the ordinary course of business. Further, any sale that occurs during Chapter 11 will generally be subject to higher and better offers and all actions will be scrutinized and subject to potential objection by a Debtor's creditors and other parties in interest. The bankruptcy court also has an independent duty to review relief requested and even if no other party objects may ultimately either reject a proposed transaction in its entirety or strike certain key provisions that could make a potential acquirer decide to forego a proposed transaction.

There is also a risk in any Chapter 11 that the prepetition management will be replaced or that another party will propose an alternative Chapter 11 Plan. Although a Debtor has the exclusive right to propose a Chapter 11 Plan for a period of time at the beginning of a Chapter 11 case, once that "exclusivity period" expires, any party in interest may propose a competing Chapter 11 Plan.[1] Finally, in light of all of the above, a Chapter 11 proceeding can often be both expensive and time consuming.

If the deal parties determine that the potential benefits of pursing a transaction in a Chapter 11 outweigh the risks, there are a number of ways to effectuate an M&A transaction in Chapter 11. Parties may

---

[1]The time given is 120 days according to section 11 U.S.C.A. §1121, and up to 18 months depending on cause.

reach an agreement outside of Chapter 11 and then file a Chapter 11 petition to effectuate the proposed transaction within a Chapter 11 proceeding. When creditors' votes for such a transaction are solicited prior to filing the bankruptcy petition, this is referred to as a prepackaged Chapter 11. Where the debtor and a purchaser have agreed to a Plan and/or a restructuring support agreement, but the larger creditor body has not yet been solicited, this is called a prearranged Chapter 11. A potential purchaser or acquirer may also seek to acquire a Debtor that is already in Chapter 11 either pursuant to a section 363 sale or a Chapter 11 Plan.[2]

This chapter provides an overview of some key provisions of the Bankruptcy Code to understand M&A in the Chapter 11 context and then discusses in greater detail various strategies for, and the advantages and disadvantages of, attempting an M&A transaction in the Chapter 11 context. This chapter will also provide a few examples of acquisitions that were accomplished in the Chapter 11 context.

Bankruptcy Overview

Article I of the US Constitution authorizes Congress to establish "uniform laws on the subject of Bankruptcies throughout the United States."[3] The Bankruptcy Code was enacted in 1978 and, as amended, continues to be the federal law on the subject of Bankruptcies.

Although filing for Chapter 11 entitles a Debtor to numerous protections, the general rule is that nonbankruptcy law continues to apply within a Chapter 11 case, and in any other bankruptcy proceeding, except where the Bankruptcy Code specifically provides otherwise. This concept is sometimes referred to as the "*Butner* Principle" in light of the Supreme Court's succinct encapsulation of this concept in *Butner v. United States*:

> Congress has generally left the determination of property rights in the assets of a bankrupt's estate to state law. Property interests are

---

[2] 11 U.S.C. §363.

[3] U.S. Const. art. I, §8, cl. 4.

> created and defined by state law. Unless some federal interest requires a different result, there is no reason why such interests should be analyzed differently simply because an interested party is involved in a bankruptcy proceeding.
>
> *Butner v. United States*, 440 U.S. 48, 55 (1979).

Chapter 11: Reorganization

Chapter 11 of the Bankruptcy Code provides a mechanism by which businesses can restructure their capital structure and make certain operational fixes all while protected from creditors pre-Chapter 11 claims by the automatic stay in section 363. It is applicable in virtually all industries and has been used by corporations in a wide range of fields from brokerage firms to airlines to retailers to energy companies. Chapter 11 provides for *reorganization*, a process by which the Debtor resolves its financial difficulties through a combination of, among other actions, reducing or eliminating certain debts and obligations, improving efficiency, and selling or otherwise disposing of underperforming assets.[4] Chapter 11 can also provide for the going concern sale or the orderly wind down of the Debtor.

The filing of a Chapter 11 proceeding does not necessarily indicate a business failure. Otherwise solvent companies may find themselves in need of bankruptcy protection due to a mass tort liability, a significant adverse judgment, the loss of a key supplier or customer, unfavorable legacy contracts, commodity price fluctuations, and a whole host of other causes. Chapter 11 provides companies with a forum to address short-term insolvency and restructure their obligations in a way that hopefully allows them to emerge as a going concern

---

[4] There are several other chapters of the Bankruptcy Code, including Chapter 7 concerning liquidations, Chapter 9 governing the adjustment of debts of a municipality, Chapter 12 governing the adjustment of debts of a family farmer or fisherman, Chapter 13 governing the adjustment of debts of an individual with regular income, and Chapter 15 governing ancillary and other cross-border cases, but the vast majority of M&A transactions that are effectuated in a bankruptcy proceeding are effectuated pursuant to a Chapter 11 reorganization proceeding.

entity that continues to do business, provide jobs and services, and contribute to the economy.

Key Players in Chapter 11

Debtor in Possession

Unless circumstances such as fraud or other issues amount to "good cause," the prepetition management of a Debtor will generally retain control of the operating business during a Chapter 11 proceeding as the so-called "debtor in possession," or "DIP." Section 1107 of the Bankruptcy Code empowers a debtor in possession with, subject to certain limitations, all the rights and powers of a bankruptcy trustee.[5] Thus the debtor in possession generally is able to continue to operate its business in the ordinary course.

Secured Creditors

Creditors who have valid prepetition liens or security interests in assets of the Debtor are well protected during a Chapter 11 case. In order for a Debtor to use any assets encumbered by such liens or security interests during its Chapter 11 case, it must provide "adequate protection" to the secured creditor to ensure there is no diminution in the value of their security interest.[6]

A secured creditor may have a security interest in more than just hard assets. For instance, a secured creditor may have a security interest in "cash collateral" which refers to cash and cash equivalents in which a creditor has a secured interest.[7] This cash collateral may only be used with the permission of the secured party or by an order of the bankruptcy court.

---

[5] 11 U.S.C. §1107.

[6] 11 U.S.C. §361.

[7] This may include, e.g., accounts receivable in which a creditor has a secured interest. When the receivables are paid off, this cash payment becomes cash collateral. 11 U.S.C. §363, 364.

Secured creditors often play a somewhat minimal role if they are oversecured (meaning the value of their collateral exceeds the value of their claim) and there is no concern about diminution in the value of their collateral. However, secured creditors will take a very active role if they are concerned with the Debtor plans to use their collateral or otherwise act in a manner that may diminish the value of such collateral. Section 361 of the Bankruptcy Code provides protections to secured creditors to ensure that they are "adequately protected" in the event the Debtor intends to use their collateral, including cash collateral.

Secured creditors looking to acquire a Debtor or certain of its assets have the advantage of being able to "credit bid," whereby they can credit money owed to them toward the purchase price of acquiring a Debtor.[8] Credit bidding may be attractive to a secured creditor if it believes it can get better return on its collateral as the owner than what the Debtor's prepetition management has been able to provide.

Unsecured Creditors and the Creditors' Committee

A Debtor's secured creditors are not the only interested parties that will have a say in the Debtor's restructuring. An often more vocal group (because they aren't secured) is the unsecured creditors' committee (the "Creditors' Committee"). The Creditors' Committee is appointed by a representative of the US Department of Justice and is typically composed of the seven largest unsecured creditors, although an effort will be made to ensure that the Creditors' Committee is made up of a diverse group of creditor interests.[9] The Creditors' Committee is a fiduciary to the entire unsecured creditor body (not just the creditors on the Creditors' Committee) and generally will monitor the Debtor and the Chapter 11 case to ensure that unsecured creditors are treated fairly and receive the maximum possible recovery from the reorganization.

---

[8] 11 U.S.C. §363.

[9] Equity holders, tort victims, or other similar interests may, but do not always, form their own committees. 11 U.S.C. §1102(a)(2). Typically they will have to demonstrate a reasonable likelihood of recovery to be able to receive recognition.

DIP Lender

Even with the benefit of the Automatic Stay, Chapter 11 Debtors often require financing during the pendency of their Chapter 11 case to ensure that they are able to continue to operate their business until a Chapter 11 Plan, or some other resolution, is reached and finalized. However, not surprisingly, a Chapter 11 Debtor will often find that lenders are not willing to extend financing to a Debtor in bankruptcy without special protections, particularly if the Debtor's assets are encumbered by prepetition liens and security interests.

Thus, a Debtor will typically have to provide a postpetition DIP lender a "priming lien" which is a secured claim that has "super priority" over existing debt (including secured debt), equity and other claims. In addition to offering a priming lien, a Debtor may entice a lender with security interests in unencumbered property and subordinate liens. DIP financing must be approved by the bankruptcy court. Additionally when a priming lien is to be granted, the Debtor will be required to demonstrate that secured lenders primed by the priming lien are otherwise "adequately protected."[10] Additionally, the Debtor will have to demonstrate that it was "unable to obtain unsecured credit allowable under section 503(b)(1) of [the Bankruptcy Code] as an administrative expense" before seeking secured DIP financing.[11]

In addition to a priming lien, DIP loans often come with numerous strings attached that give DIP lenders the ability to determine or limit how the Debtor uses the proceeds of the DIP loan. A typical DIP financing agreement will involve a budget that sets out the types of expenses a Debtor may incur and the amount of collateral they may use for each category of expense. Additionally, a DIP facility will often require that certain case milestones (such as selling assets, and filing and confirming a Chapter 11 Plan) are achieved by certain predetermined dates or the Debtor will be in default under the DIP loan. Thus, a DIP lender is typically afforded a significant level of control over the Chapter 11 case and the Debtors' use of DIP loan proceeds.

[10] 11 U.S.C. §364(c).

[11] 11 U.S.C §364(c), (d).

In many instances, a potential acquirer may provide the DIP loan and provide specific milestones to ensure that the proposed transaction closes within a certain time frame. Providing the DIP loan is one means through which a potential acquirer can drive a deal. It may also provide them with the ability to credit bid.

Key Provisions of the Bankruptcy Code

The Automatic Stay

Perhaps the most important protection afforded to a Chapter 11 Debtor is section 362 of the Bankruptcy Code, which provides for an automatic stay (the "Automatic Stay") of, among other things, all prepetition collection activities, enforcement actions, litigations, and the commencement of any actions against a Debtor that could have been brought pre petition. The Automatic Stay springs into place upon the filing of a Chapter 11 petition (or other petition for relief) under the Bankruptcy Code and, as its name suggests, is automatic.[12]

The Automatic Stay is meant to provide a Debtor with a "breathing spell" after the commencement of its Chapter 11 cases, shielding it from creditor harassment and from a multitude of litigations in a variety of forums at a time when the Debtor's personnel should be focused on the Chapter 11 cases.[13]

Under the Automatic Stay, once a Debtor files for bankruptcy, any and all collection efforts by creditors must cease completely.[14] This includes liquidation of any collateral a creditor may have a right to.[15] It is because of the Automatic Stay that bankruptcy is often referred to as "bankruptcy protection."[16]

---

[12] See 11 U.S.C. §362(a).

[13] See, e.g., *E. Refactories Co. v. Forty Eight Insulations*, 157 F.3d 169 (2d Cir. 1998).

[14] 11 U.S.C. §362(a)(3).

[15] 11 U.S.C. §362(a)(6).

[16] See e.g., *In re Deliland Foods Corp.*, CIV. A. 04-851-KAJ, 2005 WL 751929, at *1 (D Del Mar. 31, 2005) (using the term "bankruptcy protection").

Use, Sale, or Lease of Property

Section 363(b) of the Bankruptcy Code allows a Debtor, after notice and a hearing, to use, sell, or lease property of the estate outside the ordinary course of business.[17] A Debtor may use this provision to sell assets, entire business units, or even substantially all of its assets. Additionally, section 363(f) allows a Debtor to sell property "free and clear" of any third-party interest in such property in certain circumstances. This provision makes a sale of substantially all of a Debtor's assets pursuant to section 363 especially attractive to a prospective acquirer.

Taxes

A Chapter 11 debtor will often have net operating loss carryforwards (NOLs), tax credits, and certain other tax attributes for federal income tax purposes that in certain circumstances can be passed on to a reorganized debtor and may have significant value to an acquirer that can use those NOLs to offset future tax liabilities.

Contracts

Section 365 of the Bankruptcy Code allows a debtor to "assume," "assume and assign" or "reject" leases and certain types of contracts that have not been fully performed on both sides, also known as "executory contracts." The term "executory contract" is not defined in the Bankruptcy Code, but the most widely accepted definition is the one created by Professor Vern Countryman, which states that an executory contract is "a contract under which the obligation of both the debtor and the counterparty to the contract are so far underperformed that the failure of either to complete performance would constitute a material breach excusing the performance of the other."[18]

---

[17] See 11 U.S.C. §363.

[18] Vern Countryman, Executory Contracts in Bankruptcy (Part I), 57 Minn L. Rev. 439 (1973).

If an executory contract is rejected, the rejection terminates the Debtor's obligation to perform and gives the counterparty a prepetition claim for breach of contract. If a Debtor assumes a contract or lease, this binds the Debtor to the prepetition obligation. A Debtor may also assume an executory contract and assign it to a third party even if the contract does not permit assignments.[19,20] However, to do so, the Debtor will first have to cure any defaults.

This power under section 365 of the Bankruptcy Code to assume or reject unperformed leases and contracts allows a Debtor to pick and choose the contracts and leases it believes are most critical to its future operations and relieve it of burdensome contracts. Additionally, the Bankruptcy Code provides that contract counterparties must continue to perform under the lease or contract until the debtor makes a determination whether it will assume or reject each contract. Furthermore, bankruptcy courts have held that so called "*Ipso Facto* Provisions" that automatically cancel or terminate contracts and leases upon the filing of a bankruptcy petition are void and unenforceable.

Consequently, from the perspective of a potential acquirer of a Chapter 11 Debtor, this power is one of the more attractive features of Chapter 11 as the Debtor can reject its most unfavorable contracts and leases pursuant to section 365 of the Bankruptcy Code before the M&A transaction takes place pursuant to a section 363 sale, a Chapter 11 Plan, or otherwise.

The Chapter 11 Plan Process

The goal of Chapter 11 is for a Debtor to propose and confirm a Chapter 11 Plan that restructures the Debtor's debts allowing it to emerge from Chapter 11 with a fresh start. A Chapter 11 Plan is essentially a contract between the Debtor and its creditor constituency to restructure its prepetition debts and govern the relationship between the parties post confirmation of the Plan and the Debtor's

[19] With certain limited exceptions, such as with a contract to make a lien or extend debt financing. Section 365(c)(1)(a).

[20] With an exception for certain types of contracts, i.e., IP.

emergence from bankruptcy. According to 11 U.S.C. §1123 of the Bankruptcy Code, the Chapter 11 Plan sets forth how the Debtor plans to address creditor claims and to reorganize itself to continue as a viable entity. The Chapter 11 Plan is proposed,[21] voted on by creditors, and, if successful, will be confirmed by the bankruptcy court. Then, once any conditions precedents are achieved, the Chapter 11 Plan will become effective. Upon this "effective date," the Debtor emerges from Chapter 11 as a reorganized entity free of most of its prepetition obligations and with its relationship to creditors dictated by the Chapter 11 Plan. A creditor or other entity looking to acquire a Debtor or a portion of a Debtor through a Chapter 11 Plan should recognize that the Chapter 11 Plan process is complex and can be time consuming. Some of the key requirements and hurdles to Chapter 11 Plan confirmation are outlined below.

Disclosure Statement

As previously noted, Chapter 11 is an open and public process, and, thus, any transaction accomplished in Chapter 11 will have to be publicly disclosed and vetted. Indeed, Section 1125 of the Bankruptcy Code requires (except in certain small business cases) a Debtor to file and have the bankruptcy court approve a written "disclosure statement" to accompany any proposed Chapter 11 Plan. The disclosure statement must contain *adequate information* so that a reasonable creditor can make an informed decision on whether to vote in favor of or against a particular Chapter 11 Plan. "Adequate information" is defined in the Bankruptcy Code and includes such information as the nature and history of the Debtor and condition of the Debtor's book and records, discussion of potential material tax consequences of the Plan to the Debtor and a hypothetical investor. Upon notice to creditors and other parties in interest, a hearing is held to determine the adequacy of the information contained in the disclosure statement. Once the bankruptcy court has approved a Debtor's disclosure statement, the Debtor will send the disclosure statement and Chapter 11

[21] As discussed above, the Debtor has a 120-day exclusivity period to propose the Plan.

Plan to all creditors entitled to vote on the Chapter 11 Plan to solicit their vote in a process referred to as solicitation.

Solicitation

In order for a Chapter 11 Plan to be confirmed, each class of creditors and equity holders whose interests would be "impaired" by the proposed Chapter 11 Plan must vote in favor of the Chapter 11 Plan. Creditors are ***impaired*** where they would receive less than the stated value of their debts. Under section 1126 of the Bankruptcy Code, a plan is accepted by creditors where: (1) a majority of class members voted in favor of it; and (2) those voting in favor held at least two-thirds of the total value of the class's claims.

However, a plan can be "crammed down" even if an impaired class does not vote in favor of the Plan where the Plan does not discriminate unfairly and the dissenting class will receive at least the same amount of value under the Plan that it would be entitled to in a liquidation.

Thus, an acquirer seeking to acquire a Debtor pursuant to a Chapter 11 Plan will want to ensure that the transaction and accompanying Chapter 11 Plan will be approved by the requisite number of creditors. The parties may be required to give extra value to certain classes of creditors (colloquially referred to as a "Tip") to ensure the Chapter 11 Plan is approved. This can be more economical than a prolonged battle to confirm the Plan. However, it must be remembered that although parties are permitted to agree to deals with parties in interest to ensure the Chapter 11 Plan gets the required votes, the Plan must always comply with the absolute priority rule. The absolute priority rule essentially states that a Chapter 11 Plan cannot provide a return to a junior class of creditors unless all more senior classes have been paid in full or have agreed to a lesser treatment. For instance, the Second Circuit overturned a bankruptcy court's approval of *DBSD*'s Chapter 11 Plan over the objection of unsecured creditors because it found that the debtors had violated the absolute priority rule.[22] Pursuant to DBSD's plan, holders of second lien debt, who

[22] See *In re DBSD N. Am., Inc.*, 634 F.3d 79, 93 (2d Cir. 2011).

were senior to other unsecured creditors, agreed to transfer part of their distribution under the plan to DBSD's existing shareholder. Such transfers are generally called "gifting" and are often used to obtain the support of a stakeholder considered important to confirmation and consummation of the plan.

Because unsecured creditors were not paid in full under DBSD's plan, the plan could only be confirmed over their objection if the shareholder did not receive any property under the plan on account of its interest that was junior to the unsecured creditors. Some courts have approved plans that contained "gifting" on the theory that the senior creditors were voluntarily offering a portion of *their* recovered property to the stakeholders receiving the "gift." In those cases, courts held that the junior stakeholders were not receiving property on account of their claims or interests but, rather, merely that the senior creditors were "gifting" them a portion of the senior creditors' property, which such creditors could distributing however they saw fit. The Second Circuit held, however, that DBSD's existing shareholder nonetheless received property under the plan on account of its interest, rendering the plan unconfirmable.

Feasibility

Another important aspect of Plan confirmation is that the bankruptcy court must make a determination that the Plan is "feasible." This determination is very fact intensive, and is generally a case-by-case analysis. In support of a Chapter 11 Plan, Debtors and/or creditors' committees may provide evidence of feasibility including the adequacy of the new entity's capital structure, analysis of creditor recovery, and potential valuation. Valuations and projected valuations will generally be performed under one, or some combination of, three methodologies: (1) comparable companies analysis, (2) comparable transactions analysis, and (3) discounted cash flow.

Thus, even if the requisite votes are obtained, an acquirer will need to ensure that the Chapter 11 Plan through which they will acquire the Debtor is feasible. In practice, establishing feasibility is a relatively low bar, but a bankruptcy court has an independent duty to review a Chapter 11 Plan for feasibility and will reject plans that are based on little more than a pipe dream. For example, in *In re American Capital Equipment*, the bankruptcy court found that where the plan's success was overwhelmingly contingent on "wholly speculative litigation proceeds, the feasibility issue rendered the plan 'patently unconfirmable.'"[23]

Mergers & Acquisitions (M&As) in Bankruptcy

There are multiple options for acquiring a company or part of a company in bankruptcy at different stages in the Chapter 11 case. Generally any acquisition in the Chapter 11 context will be effectuated pursuant to either a Chapter 11 Plan or a sale pursuant to section 363 of the Bankruptcy Code, which can be done more quickly than a Plan. One of, if not the most, attractive features of acquiring an entity in Chapter 11 is the ability to pick and choose which assets and/or business lines an acquirer wishes to acquire.

M&As Pursuant to a Chapter 11 Plan

There are a number of ways that an entity can acquire a Debtor or key assets of a Debtor pursuant to a Chapter 11 Plan.

Merger Effectuated Pursuant to a Plan

The most straightforward way to effectuate a merger or acquisition pursuant to a Chapter 11 Plan is for the Debtor and their merger partner to propose a Chapter 11 Plan that contemplates a merger. If the Plan is approved and goes effective, the merger will be finalized (so long as it does not violate any applicable nonbankruptcy law such as the antitrust laws — remember the *Butner* principle). The merger parties may also want to separately obtain approval of the merger agreement under section 363 of the Bankruptcy Code and then file the Chapter 11 Plan to effectuate and consummate the merger.

---

[23] *In re Am. Capital Equip., LLC*, 688 F.3d 145, 156 (3d Cir. 2012).

One notable recent example of a merger effectuated pursuant to a Chapter 11 Plan was the merger of AMR Corporation (the parent of American Airlines) and US Airways to form American Airlines Group. In that case, the parties first sought approval of the merge agreement pursuant to section 363 of the Bankruptcy Code and then effectuated the merger through a Chapter 11 Plan.

Debt for Equity Swap

A significant creditor may also be able to acquire a Debtor through a debt for equity swap pursuant to a Chapter 11 Plan. A creditor may agree pursuant to a Chapter 11 Plan to have its prepetition debt paid in the form of equity in the reorganized Debtor. In certain instances, a large creditor may be able to acquire enough equity to obtain controlling ownership of the Debtor once the Chapter 11 Plan becomes effective. For a creditor who either believes in the Debtor's business or needs the Debtor to continue its own business (such as a vendor for which the Debtor is its main customer or supplier), a debt for equity swap may be attractive. Additionally, such Chapter 11 Plans are often easier to confirm because by agreeing to have its claim paid with equity in the reorganized Debtor, the acquiring creditor may free up cash and assets that can be used to satisfy other claims, making a Chapter 11 Plan more likely to garner the votes of other creditors necessary to confirm a Chapter 11 Plan.[24]

For instance, in *Jennifer Convertibles, Inc.*, the Debtors agreed to convert debt owned by a supplier into a controlling stake in the reorganized Jennifer Convertibles in accordance with an agreement effectuated immediately before the petition was filed.[25] This allowed

---

[24] See, e.g., *In re Trump Entertainment Resorts, Inc.*, 526 BR 116, 120 (Bankr. D. Del. 2015) ("The Debtors proposed but not yet confirmed chapter 11 plan of reorganization (the "Plan") does not contemplate any sort of significant asset transfer. Instead, the Plan contemplates cancellation of pre-existing equity, a nominal distribution to unsecured creditors, and a debt-for-equity swap of substantially all amounts owing under the Pre–Petition Credit Agreement").

[25] *In re Jennifer Convertibles, Inc.*, 447 B.R. 713, 725 (Bankr. S.D.N.Y. 2011).

the supplier to not only ensure the continued existence of a critical customer, but to become a more vertically integrated enterprise.

It is not just a Debtor's pre-existing creditors that can acquire a company through a debt for equity swap. Creditors' claims against a Debtor are freely tradable and hedge funds and claims traders may be able to buy up sufficient amounts of claims to take control of a bankruptcy process by accumulating a sufficient number of claims that they acquire blocking vote and a Debtor won't be able to confirm a Plan without their consent.

As one example, in 2003, a Wilbur Ross controlled parity, acquired Burlington Industries, Inc. in a bankruptcy auction after having purchased a significant portion of the company's unsecured bonds and bank debt. Ross acquired Burlington for $614 million in 2003, outbidding Berkshire Hathaway in the process.[26] In another example from 2003, Eddie Lampert's ESL Investments acquired Kmart through the purchase of bonds and bank debt during the pendency of Kmart's Chapter 11 case.[27] Lampert helped steer Kmart through the bankruptcy reorganization and became chairman when Kmart emerged from Chapter 11. Within less than 2 years after Kmart's exit from Chapter 11, the stock price soared from $15 per share to $109 per share. Clearly, acquiring bankruptcy debt and converting it to equity can be profitable.

Lampert's success notwithstanding, this debt for equity strategy can be risky because the amount paid to purchase the claims is committed before the "control" effect is certain. Further there are restrictions on the purchase of claims by fiduciaries. Some bankruptcy courts have held that a fiduciary may only recover the amount paid for the claim, as opposed to its face value.

Timing of Transaction

There are several different stages in the bankruptcy process an acquirer may seek to acquire a distressed company through a Chapter

---

[26] WL Ross & Co. LLC Completes Acquisition of Burlington Industries, BUSINESSWIRE (November 11, 2003) http://www.businesswire.com/news/home/20031111005491/en/WL-Ross-LLC-Completes-Acquisition-Burlington-Industries.

[27] See generally *Campo v. Sears Holdings Corp.*, 635 F.Supp.2d 323, 325 (S.D.N.Y. 2009), *aff'd*, 371 Fed App'x 212 (2d Cir. 2010).

11 Plan, including, as is often the case, before the Debtor files for Chapter 11.

A "*Prepackaged* Plan" or "Prepack bankruptcy" is one where a deal has been negotiated with creditors and financers before the bankruptcy petition has been filed. Generally bargaining for postpetition financing, contract rejection and assumption, and debt forgiveness will have taken place before the Debtor files for Chapter 11. The Debtor will enter bankruptcy with a business plan for postreorganization recovery, and a first draft of a Chapter 11 Plan for which it has already solicited votes. While most local bankruptcy court rules alleviate the need for a disclosure statement hearing, a prepack involves most of the same aspects as a traditional Chapter 11 Plan — except that solicitation and negotiation occur pre petition.

The ability to conduct negotiations without court oversight is one of the attractive features of a prepack. Still, the bankruptcy court will review these prepetition activities to determine whether solicitation complied with applicable disclosure laws and regulations, such as securities laws. If solicitations begin prepetition and continue after the petition is filed, the Debtor will be required to propose a disclosure statement. Thus, it is in the interest of creditors to conclude solicitations in advance of filing the petition. Section 341(e) of the Code provides that the bankruptcy court may waive the mandatory meeting of creditors and equity holders where the debtor has solicited votes on the plan before the case was filed.[28]

Obviously, where parties are motivated and amenable to reaching an agreement, a prepack is more desirable and convenient as the time spent "in bankruptcy" is reduced as are the transactional costs. Additionally, there is more certainty and the parties are only briefly subject to the court's calendar, procedures, and oversight. Yet, while the average amount of postpetition time is usually between 45 and 60 days, the *overall* time savings may be little to nonexistent. A purchaser may still end up spending time, maybe even more, negotiating, conducting due diligence etc., prepetition as it does not have the protection of the Bankruptcy Code to keep creditors at bay. Further, where there are many diverse creditors, the process may be prohibitively

---

[28] 11 U.S.C. 341.

cumbersome as a Debtor attempts to negotiate with all these creditors without the powers and protections of the Bankruptcy Code.

"Prearranged Plan" and Restructuring Support Agreements

As Debtors and interested parties continue to innovate around the potential constraints of a traditional Chapter 11 case, a distinction has arisen between "prepackaged" and "prearranged" bankruptcies. A prearranged case is similar to a prepack, except voting on the plan does not occur until filing of the petition. As in a prepack, however, the Debtor has negotiated the terms of the restructuring with each of its key creditor constituencies (aside from trade creditors) prior to filing the petition. A prenegotiated bankruptcy does require that a disclosure statement still be filed and approved by the bankruptcy court — this typically happens very soon after the petition is filed if not on the first day. Similarly to a prepack, if the debtor begins solicitation of acceptances of the plan pre petition and continues after the Chapter 11 case is commenced, court approval of the disclosure statement is required before the solicitation can continue. Prenegotiated plans are not subject to the same SEC proxy rules as prepacks.

The primary risk with a prenegotiated plan is that the plan may not garner the necessary votes after the petition is filed, at which point the Debtor would have to resort to the traditional Chapter 11 process. Additionally, a prearranged plan generally will take longer. The Debtor will often file and quickly thereafter seek approval of a restructuring support agreement. The Debtor will then propose a plan and disclosure statement. Having not solicited prepetition, the debtor may find certain parties in interest, such as a Creditors' Committee, unsupportive. Additionally, market conditions may make the prearranged plan unfeasible. For instance, in *Endeavour Operating Company*, the Debtors filed for Chapter 11 in October 2014 after reaching a restructuring support agreement with certain key bondholders that was premised on oil prices north of $90 a barrel, but by the time the Debtors had filed their Chapter 11 plan and were preparing to solicit votes, the price of oil had dropped below $50 a barrel. The Debtors were forced to abandon the restructuring support agreement and the plan they had proposed and the case was eventually dismissed pursuant to a structured dismissal.

Outside Acquirer Steps In During Chapter 11 Case

Another way a transaction may occur pursuant to Chapter 11 is when a competitor or other acquirer seeks to acquire a Debtor already in Chapter 11. Even if such Debtor would prefer to propose a stand-alone restructuring, if a merge partner offers superior economics, the Debtor may be forced to accept such a merger or risk creditors voting against their stand-alone plan.

Acquisition through a "363 Sale"

A Debtor in a Chapter 11 proceeding may sell all or some of its assets outside a Chapter 11 Plan context pursuant to section 363 of the Bankruptcy Code, which provides that a Debtor "after notice and a hearing, may use, sell, or lease, other than in the ordinary course of business, property of the [Debtor]."[29]

Where a Debtor is looking to sell substantially all of its assets, or its most valuable ones, the bankruptcy court must approve it under section 363 of the Bankruptcy Code. Section 363 can be used to sell even "substantially all" of a Debtor's assets. An acquirer will find section 363 attractive because it allows them to pick and choose the assets they want and, in most instances, to acquire such assets "free and clear" of liens and claims. Additionally, a section 363 sale can often be accomplished faster than a Chapter 11 Plan because it does not require a disclosure statement or a creditor vote. For instance, substantially all of the assets of *GM* and *Chrysler* were sold pursuant to 363 sales just a few months after the two automakers filed their respective Chapter 11 petitions.

Still, under section 363, a potential acquirer's proposed transaction will be subject to court and creditor scrutiny and in most cases, the proposed transaction will be subjected to higher and better offers

---

[29] 11 U.S.C. 363(b)(1).

pursuant to a court supervised auction process to ensure the Debtor receives maximum returns. Most often, to demonstrate to a bankruptcy court that a Debtor obtained the highest and best offer for its assets (especially if it is selling substantially all of its assets), the debtor will be required to conduct an auction process. A sale pursuant to an auction generally unfolds in two stages. In the first stage, the debtor obtains court approval of solicitation and bidding and auction procedures for the sale. In the second stage, the debtor obtains court approval of the sale that ultimately results from the auction. Between these two stages, the Debtor the carries out the auction and sale.

First Stage

In approving sale procedures, bankruptcy courts place high importance on keeping these auctions competitive. Section 363(n) of the Bankruptcy Code provides for both compensatory and punitive damages if collusive bidding is found. Collusive bidding in the bankruptcy context is where bidders attempt to control the sale price by agreement.

An important part of these procedures involves "credit bidding." As noted above, credit bidding is where secured creditors bidding in the auction are allowed to bid up to the amount of the debt they are owed by the Debtor as opposed to new cash. Section 363(k) of the Code provides that a secured creditor is allowed to credit bid unless the court, for cause, orders otherwise.[30] Several bankruptcy courts have grappled with what constitutes "cause," thus it serves creditor-purchasers to remember that credit bidding is a right subject to court approval rather than an entitlement.[31]

Generally, to ensure competitive bidding, a Debtor will use a "stalking horse" bidder. A stalking horse bidder is a potential buyer

---

[30] 11 U.S.C.A. §363(k).

[31] *In re Fisker Automotive Holdings, Inc.*, 510 B.R. 55 (Bankr. D. Del. 2014) (limiting, for cause, bidder's credit bid to $25 million to avoid freeze bidding where the proposed sale purchaser insisted on an unfair process, i.e., a hurried process, and the validity of its secured status has not been determined).

who submits a bid that sets a price floor at auction to encourage competitive bidding. The stalking horse negotiates the bid with the Debtor ahead of time and generally negotiates a break-up fee and reimbursements if the Debtor sells the assets to another buyer as compensation for its efforts in setting a floor. The overall value of these negotiated amounts is usually 3% or less of the sale price.

In addition, the Debtor must comply with all bidding and auction procedures approved by the bankruptcy court and provide notice to all parties with an interest in the assets to be sold.

The Auction

The auction is then carried out wherein the potential purchasers conduct due diligence, negotiate a purchase agreement, arrange financing, and ensure compliance with applicable antitrust and other regulations. Through this process, the Debtor typically consults with the Creditors' Committee and other parties in interest (such as lenders) in accepting a winning bid.

The purchase agreement between the winning bidder (now the purchaser) and the Debtor will likely contain a mechanism through which the Debtor will assign contracts it has assumed to the purchaser. However, just as a counterparty to a contract may object on various grounds where a Debtor moves to assume a contract, they may also object to a Debtor's assignment of the contract. Where a contract is nonexecutory or has some restrictions on its assignment, a purchaser may negotiate directly with the counterparty.

The negotiated purchase agreement will usually include deadlines by which the Debtor must seek bankruptcy court approval of the sale, as well as deadlines for the court to enter an order approving the sale. While such deadlines will not prevent the court from having jurisdiction after a certain date, they may serve to terminate the purchase agreement.

Second Stage

After a winning bidder is identified and a purchase agreement entered into, the Debtor must obtain a sale approval order from the court.

The standard for a bankruptcy court's approval of a 363 sale is the *business justification standard.*[32] This means that a Debtor must provide a sound business reason for the sale. In addition to applying the business justification standard, bankruptcy courts will also look at whether interested parties were provided adequate and reasonable notice, whether the sale price is fair, and whether the parties acted in good faith. Creditors may object to a proposed sale if they believe the Debtor is not receiving sufficient value or if the sale will leave the reorganized Debtor less valuable. Additionally, in the case of a sale of substantially all of a Debtor's assets, creditors often argue that the sale is so significant it is essentially an attempt by the Debtor's and the purchaser to effectuate a *Sub Rosa* Chapter 11 Plan without the disclosure and voting procedures required for plan approval.

Once the Sale Approval Order has been entered, it is extremely hard to overturn it when the parties to the transaction have acted in good faith.

Hybrid

Although recently parties have often used section 363 as an avenue to sell substantially all of a Debtor's assets, it is more traditionally used to purchase any number of assets, and, as such, allows an acquirer to potentially choose only those assets most attractive to it. An acquirer does not have to acquire an entire enterprise through a 363 sale and can purchase only a portion of the Debtor's business. For example, in the recent Chapter 11 proceedings of *Relativity Fashion, et al.*, In re Relativity Fashion, LLC, No. 15-11989 (MEW), 2016 WL 675544 (Bankr. S.D.N.Y. Feb. 18, 2016), Relativity had two main business lines, their television business and their film business. Relativity filed their Chapter 11 case in August 2015, sold their television film business pursuant to a section 363 sale in October 2015, and then confirmed a Chapter 11 Plan to restructure their business around the film

[32] *See In re MF Glob. Inc.*, 535 BR 596, 605 (Bankr. S.D.N.Y. 2015) (according the business judgment of a trustee is entitled to "great deference").

business pursuant to a Chapter 11 Plan in February 2016. Relativity is a prime example of the flexibility and optionality that Chapter 11 provides both Debtors and potential acquirers.

Conclusion

Although typically only available when the acquisition target is insolvent, acquisition in a Chapter 11 proceeding provides numerous benefits to an acquirer and a transaction in Chapter 11 may be preferable. At the same time, Chapter 11 is an open, public, and sometimes competitive and costly process. As such, a potential acquirer will have to contend with numerous additional parties in interest and the oversight of a bankruptcy court.

Chapter 15

Bankruptcy Reorganization and its Implications on M&As in the European Union

Heike Luecke
Department of Law, Kingston University, UK

Introduction

This chapter provides an overview of the bankruptcy[1] reorganisation landscape in the European Union (EU)[2] and its implications on Mergers & Acquisitions (M&As). The EU is a political and economic union comprising 28 countries called Member States.[3] Originally

[1] In the UK the term "bankruptcy" is used for individual persons, whereas the term "insolvency" is used for companies Are you looking at the UK or just England & Wales?

[2] In the following "EU".

[3] The BREXIT will potentially have an impact on the English insolvency landscape. However, at this point in time, the question of what will be the future terms of the relationship between the EU and the United Kingdom cannot be answered determinately. Once Article 50 of the Treaty of the Functioning of the EU (TFEU) is invoked, the leaving the EU process will start and it is expected that this process can take at least two years to complete. One of the most likely scenario is a bilateral agreement between the UK and the EU, which might include the recognition of the EIR in the UK. The challenge is that these agreements negotiated after the BREXIT will

founded on the basis of an economic union, the EU now covers various policy areas, such as climate, environment, justice, and migration. The Union is founded on fundamental values *inter alia*, liberty, the rule of law and democracy,[4] and competences and functioning of the EU are based on Treaties which have been agreed in consensus by the Member States. The aims outlined in the EU Treaties are implemented by different types of legal acts namely, regulations, directives, decisions, recommendations, and opinions.[5] Whereas regulations become directly applicable in all Member States, directives only set a legal goal for all EU countries to achieve, requiring further implementation in the Member States. Decisions are only binding to whom they are addressed, e.g., for one particular Member State and is directly applicable for the addressees. Recommendations are not legally binding, but serving to express a certain view and suggesting specified practices. With an opinion, the institutions are able to make a nonbinding statement.[6]

Insolvency Law does not fall under the competency of the EU, excepting the case of cross-border insolvencies where the European Council Regulation on Insolvency Proceedings[7] applies. On principle, each Member State has its own national insolvency regime. Hence, in contrast to the United States of America (US), there is no uniformed insolvency reorganization procedure within the EU as yet. At the end of 2015, however, an Expert Group[8] was set up to support the Commission to prepare a legislative Proposal suggesting that the EU minimum standards for a harmonized restructuring and insolvency

---

have to be ratified by all Member States, which will make the negotiations very difficult. (more, see Leader, J. *UK Corporate Restructuring after Brexit: an uncertain future* (2016); http://www.eversheds.com/global/en/what/articles/index.page?ArticleID=en/restructuring_insolvency/UK_Corporate_Restructuring_After_Brexit, last accessed 04.12.2016.

[4] Article 2 of the Treaty of the EU.

[5] Article 288 of the TFEU, https://europa.eu/european-union/eu-law/legal-acts_en

[6] https://europa.eu/european-union/law/legal-acts_en.

[7] Council Regulation (EC) no 1346/2000 on Insolvency Proceedings, [2000] OJ L 160/1; in the following "EIR".

[8] Consisting of 22 independent experts (legal professionals and academics).

law across the EU.[9] The Member States have so far partly and selectively implemented the features suggested and the Commission conducted consultations coming up with the result that the stakeholders supported the objective for early restructuring frameworks to be harmonized. However, due to the complexity of links with other areas of law such as company law, the Member States reiterate that the harmonization should be maintained on the level of principles.[10]

As a result, the European Commission published a proposal for a new directive on the 22nd of November 2016, the proposal of a "Directive on preventive restructuring frameworks, second chance and measures to increase the efficiency of restructuring, insolvency and discharge procedures and amending Directive 2012/30/EU".[11]

The Proposal aims at reducing the obstacles to the free flow of capital originated in the Member States' divergence in their insolvency and restructuring frameworks. All Member States should have "key principles on effective and preventive restructuring and second chance frameworks".[12] The focus of the Proposal is not on harmonizing core aspects of insolvency law, as for example a harmonized definition of insolvency or the ranking of claims, but on adapting insolvency procedures to enable the debtor in distress to have the possibility of an early restructuring.[13] The overarching aim of the Proposals is to foster the rescue culture in the EU by setting common objectives, mainly in form of principles or in parts in more detailed rules.[14]

So far, however, the regulations and frameworks in place at EU level do not regulate substantial law in the sense of procedures, but facilitate cross-border insolvencies and harmonize insolvency and restructuring laws. There is no single uniform reorganization procedure for all EU Member States regulated under the EIR comparable

---

[9] http://ec.europa.eu/justice/civil/commercial/insolvency/index_en.htm.

[10] Proposal of a "Directive on preventive restructuring frameworks, second chance and measures to increase the efficiency of restructuring, insolvency and discharge procedures and amending Directive 2012/30/EU p. 17.

[11] 2016/0359 (COD), hereafter "Proposal".

[12] Proposal, p. 5.

[13] Proposal, p. 6.

[14] Proposal pp. 6, 7.

to the Chapter 11 procedure in the US as yet. It would go beyond the scope of this chapter to look at all available reorganization procedures.

The aim of this chapter is not to offer a comprehensive comparative study,[15] but to discuss the common features of reorganization procedures within the EU and their implications for M&As. The common features are oriented toward the minimum standards suggested by the Recommendation on a new approach to business failure and insolvency".[16] The Recommendation constitutes the current situation on EU level and is therefore is taken as a benchmark. An EU recommendation is a nonbinding act[17] and the Member States are not obliged to implement any of these suggestions.

The new Proposal, however, is a proposal for a new EU directive which, once agreed upon, the Member States would have to implement within a given time frame, in this case 2 years,[18] into their national laws. In other words, unlike the Recommendation, the proposed directive obliges the Member States to change their existing insolvency procedures in line with the directive. It is important therefore, to consider the minimum standards for preventive restructuring proceedings included in the new Proposal.

Part A

M&As with Insolvent Companies

Introduction

The following paragraphs outline the implications of reorganizations within the EU on M&As.

---

[15] See, e.g., Clifford Chance "A Guide to European Restructuring and Insolvency Procedures" (2015) https://financialmarketstoolkit.cliffordchance.com/en/financial-markets-resources/resources-by-type/guides/a-guide-to-european-restructuring-and-insolvency-procedures.html, last accessed December 4, 2016.

[16] Commission Recommendation of March 12, 2014 on a new approach to business failure and insolvency (2014/135/EU), in the following "Recommendation".

[17] See Article 288 Treaty of the Functioning of the European Union (TFEU).

[18] See Proposal, Article 34.

A merger for a company in financial difficulties with a healthy competitor is one way to improve the financial situation and supporting the rescue of the business instead of its potentially disappearance from the market. A merger with an insolvent or imminently insolvent company could also be seen as attractive from the perspective that the aim of modern insolvency regimes is focused more on rescuing companies rather than on their liquidation. Instead of disappearing from the market, a merger with a healthy company means is a quick way of rescue.

Reorganization is understood in a broad sense, including rescuing the business, a merger with another company or an acquisition by another company is included in this definition because at least the business itself will be rescued.

The EC Merger Regulation[19] governs EU mergers and passing the jurisdiction on to the Commission where a concentration of businesses has "Community dimension".[20] On the other hand, the Cross-Border Mergers Directive aims at facilitating these kind of complex and difficult mergers as part of the EU's competition policy for the Single Market.[21]

Mergers on national level are governed by a variety of different national M&A regulations which differ from Member State to Member State. However, the focus here is not on explaining on how EU merger control operates within the EU, but on general challenges with M&A's involving companies in financial difficulties and the use of certain reorganization procedures for such transactions.

[19] Council Regulation (EC) No 139/2004 of 20 January 2004 on the control of concentrations between undertakings (the EC Merger Regulation). *Official Journal L*, 24, pp. 1–22 (2004).

[20] Ibid, further details on EU mergers see Dave Anderson and Sarah Ward *EU Merger Control* Practical Law Global Guide. Community dimension refers to both intra-community trade between EU Member States and to trade with third countries which has implications for the EU's Single (Common) Market.

[21] Directive 2005/56/EC of the European Parliament and of the Council of October 26, 2005 on cross-border mergers of limited liability companies.

EC Merger Regulation/Horizontal Merger Guideline

A failing company in the market would could have a detrimental effect on competition due to the loss of one or more market players.[22] The merger involving a company in financial difficulties should therefore be evaluated differently for which premerger competitive conditions should not be the yardstick.

The so-called "failing firm" defence offers opportunities for companies, one being in financial difficulties, to merge although under normal circumstances the merger would be seen as anticompetitive.

The failing firm defence in the EU was developed through case law, first mentioned in the *Aerospatiale* case.[23] In this case, the parties referred to the concept of "rescue merger"; the relevance of this concept was, however, left open in the decision.[24]

The concept was recognized for the first time in 1993 in the *Kali and Salz* case,[25] amended by the Commission in the *BASF* case.[26] The Horizontal Merger Guidelines now set the criteria for the application of the failing firm defence.[27] A normally problematic merger could be seen compatible with the regulations of the common market, provided one of the companies is a so-called "failing firm".[28] The Guidelines set three criteria which have to be met:

(a) First, the allegedly failing firm would in the near future be forced out of the market because of financial difficulties if not taken over

[22] Jurgita Malinauskaite, The failing firm defence in EU merger control: the story of Sisyphus? *International Company and Commercial Law Review*, p. 308 (2012).

[23] Case No. IV/M053 — *Aerospatiale-Alenia/de Havilland.*

[24] See more details in Jurgita Malinauskaite, The failing firm defence in EU merger control: the story of Sisyphus? *International Company and Commercial Law Review* p. 308 (2012).

[25] *Kali-Salz/MdK/Treuhand (IV/M.308) EUVL L186, 21/07/1993* (*Kali & Salz 1993*) and *France v Commission (C-68/94 & C-30/95) [1998] E.C.R. I-1375* (*Kali & Salz 1998*).

[26] *BASF/Eurodiol/Pantochim (COMP/M.2314), Commission decision of July 11, 2001.*

[27] Guidelines on the assessment of horizontal mergers under the Council Regulation on the control of concentrations between undertakings, *Official Journal C*, 031, February 5, 2004, pp. 0005–0018.

[28] Ibid, VIII. Failing Firm, 89.

by another undertaking. Second, there is no less anticompetitive alternative purchase than the notified merger. Third, in the absence of a merger, the assets of the failing firm would inevitably exit the market."[29] For the first criterion, there needs to be evidence that the acquired firm is unlikely to meet its financial obligations in the near future. This does not mean that insolvency proceedings must have been initiated, but it has to be demonstrated that the opening of insolvency proceedings is quite likely without the merger.[30] There is not a set formula for this criterion and the Commission would evaluate the situation from case to case.[31]

(b) The assessment of the second criterion is based on the question whether there is a less anticompetitive purchase alternative to the merger, looking at whether there are alternative market options, which would result in less harmful effects to the competition.[32] In practice, this can be demonstrated by showing that alternative investors were given an opportunity to enter into negotiations.

(c) To fulfil the third criterion, it has to be substantiated that all assets of the failing firm would exit the market without the merger. This criterion is the most difficult to prove in practice.[33] In the US, the defence is based on an "absolute" assumption that the loss of all assets is sufficient to conclude that the merger is a "lesser devil", whereas in the EU, it is part of a general causality analysis. In other words, the loss of the assets helps to justify the exception, but does not give absolute justification for the approval.[34]

In summary, it can be concluded that the failing firm defence facilitates M&As and can be seen as an incentive for companies in financial distress to use a merger or acquisition to avoid liquidation.

---

[29] Ibid, p. 90.

[30] Jurgita Malinauskaite, The failing firm defence in EU merger control: the story of Sisyphus? *International Company and Commercial Law Review* pp. 308, 310 (2012).

[31] Jurgita Malinauskaite, The failing firm defence in EU merger control: the story of Sisyphus? *International Company and Commercial Law Review* pp. 308, 310 (2012).

[32] Mika Oinonen, Mergers with a financially distressed company in the US and EU: alike, but not the same, *European Competition Law Review* pp. 538, 542 (2013).

[33] Ibid.

[34] Ibid, p. 545.

Part B

Merger-Friendly Features

In addition to the question whether the merger or acquisition is in conformity with the Merger Regulations, the question of whether the failing firm defence is applicable at all, is the question of which insolvency procedures might facilitate M&As and help to conduct them.

The challenge of this exposition is as yet the lack of a harmonized insolvency procedure on EU level comparable to the Chapter 11 procedure in the US. Instead of looking at each available reorganization procedure and its implications within the EU, the focus here is to look more abstractly at certain features of reorganization procedures in general, inspired by the minimal standards suggested by the Recommendation. The new Proposal is paving the way for more harmonized preventive restructuring proceedings on EU level and is therefore considered as well.

As emphasized above, although there is a great variety of different reorganization procedures amongst the Member States, there is a clear tendency away from liquidation toward corporate rescue. Certain features can be seen as particularly rescue friendly. The minimum standards set out by the "Recommendation on a new approach to business failure and insolvency"[35] as published by the European Commission in March 2014 are all designed to prevent insolvency and to rescue the company in financial difficulties. In the following sections, these features are looked at from the perspective of "merger-friendliness".

The Proposal is analyzed in this chapter; however, the Recommendation does represent the *status quo* at the moment and is therefore taken as the benchmark. The Proposal still has to go through certain legislative stages and will possibly be amended. Once the directive is in force, the Member States will have 2 years for implementing it nationally. Therefore, the *status quo* of nonharmonized procedures within the EU will remain unaltered for the next 2–3 years. Even once

---

[35] Commission Recommendation of March 12, 2014 on a new approach to business failure and insolvency (2014/135/EU).

implemented, the directive just gives a framework for minimum standards and does not provide one uniform insolvency procedure for all Member States.

The attempt to harmonize restructuring proceedings on EU level must be regarded positively, as the lack of harmonization of the Member States' legal systems has a negative effect on the coordination of insolvency systems. Investors shy away from investing or entering into new business relationships in other EU countries due to the uncertainty over insolvency regulations and the risks involved.[36] It is therefore important that uniformity and alignment of insolvency regulations are promoted and developed at both regional and international levels.[37] International harmonization of insolvency laws will finally facilitate a functioning and effective marketplace.[38]

The Minimum Standards of the Recommendation

The aim of the Recommendation is to "ensure that viable enterprises in financial difficulties, wherever they are located in the Union, have access to national insolvency frameworks which enable them to restructure at an early stage with a view to preventing their insolvency, and therefore maximize the total value to creditors, employees, owners and the economy as a whole".[39] This should be attained by asking all Member States to have a preventive restructuring framework; in other words, having procedures in place which enable businesses

---

[36] Proposal, p. 2.

[37] Ian Flechter, Spreading the gospel: the mission of insolvency law, and the insolvency practitioner, in the early 21st century, *Journal of Business Law*, pp. 523, 530, 531 (2014); Action Plan on Building a Capital Market Union — Communication from the Commission to the European Parliament, the Council, the European Economic and Social Committee and the Committee of the Regions. COM, p. 468 (2015).

[38] See in more detail on harmonization to strengthen Europe's economy: Action Plan on Building a Capital Market Union — Communication from the Commission to the European Parliament, the Council, the European Economic and Social Committee and the Committee of the Regions, COM, p. 468 (2015).

[39] Recommendation, Recital 1.

"to restructure at an early stage with a view to preventing their insolvency."[40] In addition, the Recommendation aims to give "honest bankrupt entrepreneurs a second chance."[41] Different to the situation in the US, insolvency in the EU is still afflicted with the stigma of failure. Six minimum standards are set out to achieve the aim and encourages all Member States to implement these into their insolvency regime. These principles are early recourse, minimized court involvement, debtor in possession, court-order stay, the ability to bind dissenting creditors to a restructuring plan, and the protection for new finance.[42]

The Commission recommended that all Member States to implement these six minimum standards into their reorganization procedures, thereby setting a guideline of those features considered desirable for an ideal reorganization proceeding. These features are therefore taken here and analyzed in the light of their "merger-friendliness".

Debtor in Possession

Leaving the debtor in possession is seen as facilitative for restructurings, which could also be regarded a positive aspect in assisting the progress of M&As. Having existing management in charge of negotiations might speed up the merger process as a way for them to rescue the business, maintaining employment rather than liquidating the assets involving the loss of jobs. In case the existing management is against a merger, leaving the debtor in charge might not be the optimal solution. However, in practice, the existing management is regularly replaced by a restructuring expert, often suggested by the main creditors. In this case, leaving the debtor in charge could be seen as a positive driver for an M&A, as the restructuring expert provides the expertise and knowledge with an interest in implementing a merger or acquisition in order to rescue the business.

---

[40] Ibid.

[41] Ibid.

[42] For more details, see Recommendation.

Ability to Bind Dissenting Creditors

The Commission suggests in the Recommendation that a restructuring plan, negotiated between debtor and creditors, obtained approval by the required majority and sanctioned by a court, should have the effect that these decisions would as well bind all dissenting creditors.[43] The ability to bind dissenting creditors can be seen as an important characteristic of a "merger-friendly" reorganization. A restructuring plan approved by the required majority in affected classes and approved by a court should bind dissenting creditors and shareholders. Procedures with such a "cram-down" nature allow the majority to outvote and bind dissenting creditors and shareholders, promoting the success of a potential merger. A procedure needing the approval of all or nearly all parties bears the risk of "hold-out creditors" pursuing their individual interest while blocking a viable restructuring attempt. It is important to have the possibility to bind dissenting creditors, as in practice, creditors may often simply want to create a disruptive factor, trying to pressure creditors with greater claims to pay their claims off in full or at least at a premium.[44] A cram-down like effect, would forestall any misuse of this bargain power and enable an otherwise mutually agreed M&A.

Court-Order Stay

The Recommendation suggests that the debtor should be protected from enforcement actions of individual creditors, enabling the assets of the business to stay together.[45] A court-order stay in a restructuring procedure could be regarded "merger-friendly" as it avoids the piecemeal dismemberment by creditors and helps the assets of the business kept together.[46] It gives the company in financial distress "breathing

[43] Recommendation, Recital 16–20.

[44] Pilkington C. *Schemes of Arrangement in Corporate Restructuring* (Sweet&Maxwell, London, 2013), p. 12.

[45] Ibid.

[46] Kristin van Zwieten, *Restructuring Law: Recommendations from the European Commission* EBRD, Law in transition online, http://www.ebrd.com/downloads/research/law/lit114e.pdf.

space" to negotiate a merger without the fear of individual creditors enforcing their rights.

A court-order stay might, however, in practice, not be necessary and even prove cumbersome.[47] It could be argued that the lack of a court-order stay could encourage the creditors to work for a consensual approach. This in turn could promote a more open discussion and the willingness to find an amicable solution amongst the parties. A moratorium needs approval by the court as well implying higher costs and delay in the procedure. The lack of a moratorium stands for more time efficiency and lower costs.[48] It is therefore recommended that consideration is given to how the attitudes and perceptions of the involved parties could be changed, rather than to impose more formal rules, such as a moratorium, bringing with it a certain aftertaste of a forced consent.[49] Leaving the creditors more room in taking part in the decision-making process might have the psychological effect of producing agreement to a consensual solution. Showing the creditors the benefits of such an approach would anyhow be the best way forward.[50] In the special situation of a restructuring via a merger or acquisition, the arguments of trying to achieve a consensual approach instead of relying on a court-order stay could be seen as the better solution as well. For an M&A with complex issues, an open discussion to find an amicable solution for all parties involved is in practice the most likely workable way for a successful result.

Minimized Court Involvement

The Commission furthermore recommends to have restructuring procedures in place which do not require the opening of formal court

---

[47] John Tribe, Company voluntary arrangements and rescue: A new hope and a Tudor orthodoxy, *Journal of Business Law*, pp. 454, 458 (2009).

[48] Ibid.

[49] Also see Vanessa Finch, Re-invigorating corporate rescue, *Journal of Business Law*, p. 527 (2003).

[50] Tribe J, The extension of small company voluntary arrangements: A response to the conservative party's corporate restructuring proposal. In: Paul Omar (ed.) *International Insolvency Law Reforms and Challenges* (Ashgate Publishing Limited, Farnham, 2013), p. 221.

proceedings, suggesting limiting court involvement only where necessary to safeguard the rights of creditors and other affected parties.[51] Overall the recommendation aims at reducing court involvement to the minimum.

Minimizing the court involvement facilitates restructurings as the participation of a court is always accompanied with delays and costs.

Insolvency Law has an economic mandate; the creditors and shareholders bear the risk of potential failure and should therefore be the main actors in an insolvency proceeding. The court should only interfere if needed to safeguard the rights of the involved parties. Opening of court proceedings should not be mandatory, but a supervision of the proceedings by a third party should be encouraged. Court involvement is time consuming and costly, and should therefore only be encouraged where necessary to protect the interests of the involved parties.[52]

Minimized court involvement is a positive aspect of a restructuring procedure. The opening of formal court proceedings could hinder or at least complicate a potential merger or acquisition.

Early Recourse

The insolvency regimes in many Member States require the debtor to be insolvent in order to commence restructuring proceedings.[53] The Recommendation pleads for restructuring regimes offering access at an early stage, without the need of the company factually being insolvent.[54] To prevent the misuse of insolvency procedures by solvent companies, it is recommended to restrict access to restructuring proceedings to debtors being in "financial difficulties" or with the "likelihood of

[51] Recommendation, Recital 8, Kristin van Zwieten, *Restructuring Law: Recommendations from the European Commission* EBRD, Law in transition online, http://www.ebrd.com/downloads/research/law/lit114e.pdf.

[52] Also see Recommendation, Recital 17.

[53] Kristin van Zwieten, *Restructuring Law: Recommendations from the European Commission* EBRD, Law in transition online, http://www.ebrd.com/downloads/research/law/lit114e.pdf, p. 5.

[54] Recommendation, Recital 6a.

insolvency".[55] An early recourse to insolvency proceedings enhances the chances for a restructuring and offers an incentive for the directors to seek for help at an early stage.

An early intervention is beneficial for a merger or an acquisition. The earlier the company in financial distress is involved in the M&A process, the more assets are left and the better are the chances for a success. A procedure accessible at an early stage can therefore be regarded as M&A friendly.

The Proposal on Preventive Frameworks, Second Chance and Measures to Increase the Efficiency of Restructuring, Insolvency, and Discharge Procedures

The Proposal's aim to preserve value in insolvency by setting a framework for more harmonized restructuring proceedings. Insolvency concerns have a substantial Union dimension.[56]

A material divergence between the restructuring proceedings in the different Member States still exists and several jurisdictions' insolvency frameworks continue to focus on liquidation rather than restructuring. Approximately 25% of all insolvencies in the EU are cross-border insolvencies.[57] Subsequently, a more harmonized legal framework is necessary for a well-functioning single market.

The Proposal aims at carrying forward the attempt to align the insolvency and restructuring proceedings amongst the Member States. It builds on the Recommendation which, however, will not trigger any legal obligations, whereas the proposed directive, once into force, has to be implemented into the national laws of the Member States. The Proposal reinforces the Recommendation, going beyond it by "establishing targeted rules on increasing the efficiency of all types of procedures..."[58] In other words, the Proposal is in parts similar to the Recommendation, in parts more extensive. The

---

[55] Ibid.

[56] Proposal p. 2.

[57] Proposal p. 2.

[58] Proposal p. 9.

proposed features involved are looked at and analyzed with regard to their "M&A-friendliness".

Whereas the main aim of the Proposal is to strengthen the rescue culture in the EU, the set common objective and rules of the Proposal will be looked at from the perspective of a restructuring via an M&A.

The most important part of the Proposal here is Title II "preventive restructuring frameworks". It sets a framework with core elements for preventive restructuring, aiming at giving a debtor in financial difficulties access to procedures facilitating restructurings.[59] The Proposal keeps the option open on whether a Member State may offer one or more procedures.[60]

Debtor in Possession

The Proposal stipulates in Article 5 that "Members States shall ensure that debtors accessing preventive restructuring procedures remain totally or at least partially in control of their assets and the day-to-day operation of the business."[61] Practitioners may have a role, but do not need to be appointed in every case, see Article 5(2), (3).

In other words, all Member States have to introduce a debtor-in-possession procedure, which conform with the framework of the Proposal. It is still up to the Member States to decide, subject to their respective national laws, how to implement this into their procedure. However, if this directive comes into force, no Member States will have to have a debtor-in-possession procedure in the one or other form.

The advantages leaving the debtor in possession to implement an M&A procedure are discussed above.[62]

Ability to Bind Dissenting Creditors

The Proposal provides for having a framework in place which offer the possibility to bind dissenting creditors if the majority of the

---

[59] Title II of the Proposal.

[60] Article 4 of the Proposal.

[61] Article 5 of the Proposal.

[62] See p. 7.

affected parties approved the plan. Article 9 explains in more detail the situations in which a "cram down of dissenting creditors"[63] should be allowed; the affected parties have to be treated in separate classes[64]; the class formation has to be examined by the judicial or administrative authority[65] and sets minimum standards for the defining "majority".[66] Article 11 sets out the framework for the so-called "cross-class cram down", defined as "the confirmation by a judicial or administrative authority of a restructuring plan over the dissent of one or several affected classes of creditors."[67] Parties not affected by the restructuring should have no voting rights in relation to the restructuring plan at all.[68] The Proposal is very detailed in this respect and goes further than the Recommendation. This reflects that the Commission is of the opinion that a "cram down" is one essential feature of a well-functioning restructuring procedure.

This detailed Proposal is also beneficial for M&As as eliminating the possibility of individual creditors to block an otherwise mutually agreed M&A, increasing the chance of a successful M&A procedure.

Court-Order Stay

Articles 6 and 7 are designed to regulate the possibility of a debtor's access to a stay of individual enforcement actions. In line with the recommendation, the Proposal aims at preventing the piecemeal dismemberment of the business by creditors. Article 6 provides that a stay should be accessible for the debtor "if and to the extent such a

---

[63] Defined in Article 2, 7 as "the confirmation by judicial or administrative authority of a restructuring plan that has the support of a majority in value of creditors or a majority in value in each class of creditors over the dissent of a minority of creditors or the dissent of a minority of creditors within each class".

[64] Article 9, 2.

[65] Article 9, 3.

[66] Article 9, 4.

[67] Article 2, 8.

[68] See Article 9 of the Proposal.

stay is necessary to support the negotiations of a restructuring plan".[69] The wording does not suggest that a court-order stay has to be implemented as a Member State could argue that it is not necessary for the procedure they suggest. However, following the argument above,[70] a court-order stay cannot always be seen positively. Therefore, to leave it up to the Member State and possibly even to the individual situation to apply for a court-order stay where, e.g., a mutual agreement is unlikely and therefore making a stay necessary, is seen as positive. The same does apply for restructuring via an M&A, where a stay might be needed in some cases, but not ultimately for every case.

Minimized Court Involvement

With regards to the court involvement, the Proposal just regulates that "Member States shall put provisions limiting the involvement of a judicial or administrative authority to where it is necessary and proportionate so that rights of any affected parties are safeguarded."[71] To make it mandatory for the national legislator to eliminate the necessity to always involve the courts for carrying out a restructuring proceeding is seen positively for implementing an M&A as well on the basis of the considerations discussed above.[72]

Early Recourse

Article 4 requires Member States to have proceedings available not only for debtor's being insolvent, but for debtor's in financial difficulties and also in case of the likelihood of insolvency.[73] This reflects the approach of the Recommendation which is seen as a positive feature

---

[69] Article 6, 1; article 6, 4–7 deals in more detail with the duration of such a stay, which is again more detailed than the Recommendation.

[70] See p. 8.

[71] Article 4, 3 of the Proposal.

[72] See p. 9.

[73] See article 4, 1 of the Proposal.

for a potential M&A process as an early recourse increases the changes of remaining assets.[74]

Summary Proposal

A Directive coming into force, the Member States have to transpose all the features and rules into their national laws, contrasting to the current situation, where the Member States are able to design their own procedures not being bound by the current Recommendation to follow. The implementation of the Directive will bring minimum common standards into the market with regard to M&As, while under the current differences in the material insolvency laws, M&As face varying challenges and legal hurdles, making it obvious that a better harmonized EU insolvency landscape will have a positive effect on the accomplishments of M&As.

Schemes of Arrangement in England & Wales

After looking at certain common features of reorganization procedures within the EU, the English schemes of arrangement (SoA) procedure, section 895 Companies Act 2006, is used as an example of one procedure frequently used for M&As in England in the current insolvency landscape in England.[75] This procedure is further taken as valid example, coming very close to the intended harmonized preventive restructuring frameworks of the Proposal, and could be seen as a benchmark for the intended new framework procedure of the Proposal.

Strictly speaking, an SoA is not an insolvency procedure as such, but it authorizes a company, whether insolvent or not, to come to a compromise agreement with its creditors with the aim of restructuring the company to help it out of its financial distress. The SoA

---

[74] See p. 9.

[75] Despite the Brexit, it is still worth looking at England and Wales as an example as England is known as the "rescue-friendliest" insolvency regime in the EU, due to its flexibility and variety of procedures. This is reflected in EU companies trying to get into the benefit of these procedures, see forum shopping.

procedure is in its nature closest to the Chapter 11 procedure in the US, aiming at restructuring the debtor and available before the actual state of insolvency.[76] The trend goes toward "*ex ante* solutions" rather than "*ex poste*" reactions to financial difficulties.[77]

The popularity of the SoA procedure is supported by the trend of foreign companies in financial difficulties using the SoA procedure in England due to its attractiveness and flexibility. This "restructuring migration"[78] or "the new forum shopping" is a way of getting into the benefit of the English SoA procedure without the necessity of moving the COMI to the favourable country.[79] This avenue was used in a number of cases, *inter alia Rodenstock*,[80] *Primacom, Wind Hellas, La Seda*, and *Marconi*.[81]

The SoA procedure offers a more efficient and user-friendly procedure than the local alternative procedures,[82] considering the minimal formal requirements, the flexibility with regard to the content, and the binding nature once approved.

The SoA is attractive to implement M&As as it offers the majority of the merger-friendly features discussed above.

---

[76] Tribe Companies Act schemes of arrangement (n 750) 390; see chapter 3.3.5.

[77] Vanessa Finch, The recasting of insolvency law, MLR, 68, p. 713 (2005).

[78] For example, Robert Hickmott, Forum shopping is dead: long live migration!, JIBFL, p. 272 (2007).

[79] The English courts can under section 895 (2) (b) CA 06 sanction an SoA with regard to any company "liable to be wound up under the Insolvency Act", which includes foreign companies. However, case law defines three preconditions restricting an English Court granting such an order with regard to an overseas company. The first condition is a sufficient connection with England; the second is that there has to be a reasonable possibility for the persons applying for the winding-up order to benefit from the order. The third condition is that there has to be at least one person interested in the distribution of the debtor's assets under jurisdiction of the court, over whom the court has jurisdiction.

[80] *Re Rodenstock GmbH* [2011] 1104.

[81] See further with pre and post restructuring debt figures: Pilkington C., *Schemes of Arrangement in Corporate Restructuring* (Sweet&Maxwell, London, 2013), table cases, pp. 2, 3.

[82] Pilkington C., *Schemes of Arrangement in Corporate Restructuring* (Sweet&Maxwell, London, 2013), p. 1; see table cases, pp. 2, 3, with over £20 billion of debts which were restructured through these procedures for companies registered outside the UK.

Debtor in Possession

The nature of the SoA procedure implies the management staying in possession, with the procedure being used to find a compromise between debtors and creditors and not representing an official insolvency procedure. It could be argued that the procedure could be handled more "efficiently, expertly, accountably, and fairly than procedures involving external practitioners", always on the *proviso* that the company is managed by a qualified director fully capable of initiating turnarounds.[83]

Ability to Bind Dissenting Creditors

The agreement in an SoA procedure, once approved, binds all creditors, including the secured creditors; in other words, it is not possible for dissenting creditors to block the scheme. The SoA procedure can be seen as the only procedure in England and Wales with a cram-down nature as it is a forced inclusion of the dissenting creditors and shareholders are protected by the formation of the classes during the procedure. This feature cannot be found in any restructuring procedure among EU Member States. This makes the SoA procedure, owing to this certainty once approved, a very attractive tool for restructurings as well as for M&As.

Court-Order Stay

The SoA procedure does not offer a court order stay, involving the risk that individual creditors enforcing their claims. However, as highlighted above, it could be argued that a court-order stay is not necessary or could even be seen as burdensome. In practice, an informal stand-still agreement is frequently arranged and the parties are encouraged to find a mutual solution without an imposed court-order stay. Therefore, the lack of an automatic court-order stay in this

---

[83] Pilkington C., *Schemes of Arrangement in Corporate Restructuring* (Sweet&Maxwell, London, 2013).

procedure is not considered as merger-unfriendly. The flexibility of this procedure offers the involved parties the possibility to find an amicable solution with regard to the conditions of the M&A.

Minimised Court Involvement

Within the SoA procedure, the court is only involved to sanction the scheme. The court will normally sanction the scheme if the majority of the creditors or group of creditors representing 75% in value of the company's debts agree on the compromise solution laid down in the scheme.[84] The court maintains a discretion under section 899 CA 2006, putting no obligation of the court and there is no provision for entitlement to such a sanction.[85]

Early Recourse

The SoA is a company law procedure, used for insolvent companies, not requiring the actual insolvency of the debtor. Due to its nature, it is not even necessary that the debtor is in financial difficulties or imminently insolvent. It can therefore be commenced without the need of proof of any stage of insolvency, in this going beyond the Recommendation and the Proposal.

SoA as an M&A Tool in Practice

Overall, the SoA procedure combines most of the analyzed merger-friendly features. Except for an automatic stay, it embraces all the suggested features of the Recommendation and of the Proposal. It can be seen as a "consensual takeover technique for acquiring a profitable target company."[86]

---

[84] See section 899 (1) CA 2006.

[85] Milman, SoA and other restructuring regimes (n 758) 1; *Scottish Lion Insurance Co Ltd v (First) Goodrich Corp* (2009) CSIH 6; [2010] BCC 650.

[86] William Charnely, David Milman, Restructuring tools available to the UK corporate law practitioner: established devices and new models, *Company Law Newsletter* (2013).

The Takeover Code in the UK contains special provisions for takeovers implemented by SoAs. The general provisions apply, with appendix 7, however, setting out more customised provisions for a takeover implemented via an SoA procedure. [87]

Conclusion

Since there is no uniform reorganization regime within the EU and each Member State has its own insolvency and restructuring regime, the impact on M&As cannot be analyzed and answered one-dimensionally. There are certain attempts to harmonize insolvency and restructuring laws on EU level with a number of features of insolvency procedures to be seen as restructuring-friendly. These aspects, inspired by the Recommendation and the Proposal have been looked at from the perspective of a merger or acquisition attempt as one way of rescuing the business of a debtor in financial difficulties.

M&As on EU level are regulated under the EC Merger Regulations. With regard to companies in financial difficulties, the failing firm defence offers an exception to merge with or acquire a company in financial distress, despite the fact that the merger or acquisition would normally be regarded as anticompetitive.

There are a variety of features of the different insolvency procedures which could facilitate mergers or acquisitions of failing companies. The advantage of such a diversity is that a debtor can cherry pick a procedure to suit his needs and forum-shop within the EU and move the COMI in line with the implications of the EIR. M&As with a cross-border mandate have to negotiate applicable laws regulating the M&A process. A choice of different procedures could be seen as positive as it allows for the most appropriate procedure pertaining to the individual case. However, a more harmonized insolvency and restructuring landscape would offer a greater benefit for M&As. In M&A processes with a cross-border dimension, the involved parties need to additionally negotiate the appropriate national procedure, whereas harmonized procedures for all Member

[87] Appendix 7 of the Takeover Code.

States would be less time consuming, allowing to put a better focus on the actual implementation of the M&A.

The current state in the EU restructuring landscape is that all Member States have their own restructuring procedures, more or less reflecting the features of the Recommendation. Once the proposed Directive comes into force, the Member States will be obliged to implement the restructuring, and as analyzed, also M&A-friendly features into their national insolvency and restructuring regimes.

Interestingly enough, most of the features proposed seemed to be inspired by the English SoA procedure. In practice, this procedure is considered as a favorable restructuring tool, not only by English companies, but also by companies from different Member States in a position to use the possibility of forum shopping.

The use of the SoA procedure for implementing M&A's in the UK demonstrates that the features of these procedure are M&A-friendly. This is an indicator that the new Proposal will change the EU insolvency landscape positively with regards to their M&A-friendliness.

Chapter 16

Postmerger Integration: Lessons from Experience and Research in Successful Corporations

Stefan Hofmeyer
PMI Partners

Introduction

Postmerger integration (PMI) is not the most exciting topic for the majority of executives — but a critical one. Multibillion dollar investment success or failure is decided in part by actions during the PMI stage of a deal.

When leading, participating in, or being impacted by an acquisition, the material in this chapter will help you understand the PMI process and provide leading practices to build corporate value, and your personal value, during a merger or acquisition.

To support this understanding, we reference studies that have real-world application, review examples of mergers and acquisitions (M&As) and their related challenge, and provide a framework to execute PMI.

Purpose of PMI

Companies acquire to take advantage of synergies, to diversify, to vertically integrate, and to gain market share. To realize goals of a merger or acquisition, integration between the acquiring and target companies needs to occur at some level. This simply can be interface points between operational areas for reporting and compliance purposes, or it can be a complex global effort, integrating people, process, technology, and information.

What is often misunderstood about M&As is that overall company value is often lost immediately after a merger or acquisition announcement. Employee stability is disrupted causing higher levels of attrition, efficiencies are decreased, sales drop off as sales teams are uncertain of their compensation, and clients look to renegotiate. PMI is work framed to gain business value, overcoming the value lost due to the merger or acquisition event and then realizing synergistic gains.

It is common knowledge that a majority of M&As fail to meet pro forma expectations. In a literature review of M&As Performance Evaluation, 50–80% of M&As never produce anticipated benefits.[1] In my own 2013 survey of 50 executives with M&A integration experience,[2] 38% of executives found that their transactions met board level expectations, while 52% of executives felt their transactions were only somewhat successful.

The good news is that this suboptimal level of success does not have to be the case if M&A integration is planned and executed correctly.

Planning for PMI — Intensive and Short Timelines

In a merger or acquisition, it can be difficult to focus on the planning and execution of postclose activities for a variety of reasons, such as the uncertainty of the deal, deal team members not expected to be involved post close or incentivized by postclose results, and/or integration team members not participating due to confidentiality concerns and bandwidth issues. Even significantly sized companies can fail to plan sufficiently for postacquisition or PMI.

---

[1] Nitin Vazirani, Mergers and acquisitions performance evaluation — A literature review, *SIES Journal of Management*, 8(2) (2012).

[2] Stefan Hofmeyer and ModalMinds, 2013 M&A Integration Survey, published by Stefan Hofmeyer, San Francisco.

Deal team members are focused on turning corporate strategy into a successful close by evaluating targets and negotiating the deal. Time is of the essence and anything too operational (i.e., not strategic or not contributing to deal close) often is seen as secondary. When a deal progresses and the merger or acquisition is likely, integration team members can then engage to start planning in a very intensive way, but under short timelines.

After deal close, timing and speed of integration execution is critical. Employees will read initial signs to determine if they should look elsewhere for employment. The market/customers will determine what the new company will look like. As a specific example, marketing-related integration research by Homburg Bucerius suggests[3]:

> *"In general, managers should strive for speed in integrating their marketing operations after a merger or acquisition. Our research provides managers with information about the circumstances in which speed is particularly beneficial. For example, the effect of integration speed on market-related performance is particularly strong when the relatedness of the merging firms' market positioning is low, the relative size of the acquired firm is high, and the firms are service firms."*

Resource Allocation and Engagement — Stretched Internal Teams or Consultants

Unless companies involved in the acquisition or merger are serial acquirers, there is not a standing integration team available to plan and execute the integration. Responsible parties tasked with integration planning are typically operational teams pulled together to support the effort, in addition to any outside consultants required. This team is comprised of operations staff balancing their regular work, executives who have completed integrations before, or

[3] Christian Homburg and Matthias Bucerius, A marketing perspective on mergers and acquisitions: How marketing integration affects postmerger performance, *Journal of Marketing*, 69, pp. 95–113 (2005).

consultants that have PMI expertise, but who do not necessarily know the day-to-day workings of the companies involved.

Consultant teams help by providing integration planning structure and speed of execution. A common mistake is to outsource risk of the integration to a consulting firm. In short, consultants need to be managed, with ultimate responsibility of the integration on internal teams, as the internal teams know the business intimately and take long-term ownership.

The challenge for internal resources is they have their daily activities to deal with and are more apt to hold a longer-term operational mindset, versus a project mindset where delivery speed is more of emphasis. Additionally, internal integration team member compensation is often tied only to their operational activities instead of their integration activities, resulting in pressure to address operational tasks before integration tasks.

Who to engage on the integration should be a thoughtful choice. This is not only for executing the integration, but also to allow employees to internalize their future organization. As an example of research, Lupina-Wegener, Drzensky, Ullrich, and van Dick argue[4]:

> *"Employees may internalize the future of their organization if they have the possibility to have a part in shaping it. We therefore suggest that the participation of lower and midlevel management is important. Furthermore, participation of frontline employees may help upper management to identify best practices from both e-merger organizations. Even if participation may require increased efforts for coordination, we would stress the importance of participative decision-making."*

Culture Differences

Acquiring and target companies may differ in a variety of ways impacting a deal. Looking past the financials and strategy of a deal, a significant

[4] Anna Lupina-Wegener, Frank Drzensky, Johannes Ullrich, and Rolf van Dick, Focusing on the bright tomorrow? A longitudinal study of organizational identification and projected continuity in a corporate merger, *British Journal of Social Psychology*, 53, pp. 752–772 (2014).

consideration is the culture of the companies being integrated. Companies may differ in that one may be more entrepreneurial where employees may not initially like working for a larger firm. Companies may also have been competitors and may take time to attain a feeling of belonging and take pride in the new company or brand. Regional or country culture differences have an impact as well — will an integrated US team work smoothly with a Chinese or Indian based team? This is an important question.

Well-known examples of deals that have been considered failures due to culture include the following.

Sprint Nextel Merger

An example of culture challenges includes the Sprint Nextel merger in 2005 where the management style played a role, as Kim Hart writes in her 2007 Washington Post article[5]:

> *"Two sharply different corporate cultures have resulted in clashes in everything from advertising strategy to cellphone technologies, preventing Sprint Nextel from becoming the merger of equals envisioned. The discord was on display almost immediately. At a Nextel managers meeting held just after the merger was announced in December 2004, chief executive Tim Donahue revved up the crowd with a pep-rally-style speech. Donahue, dressed in a sweater vest and khakis, drew cheers by chanting, 'Let's go stick it to Verizon!' He then introduced a special guest — Gary Forsee, Sprint's chief executive and the architect of the merger, who had flown in from Sprint's Kansas City headquarters. Forsee walked onto the stage wearing a suit and proceeded to outline his expectations for the combined company in a PowerPoint presentation. The room fell silent."*

In 2009, Sprint Nextel took a $29.45 billion fourth-quarter loss because of a write-down related in part due to its merger with Nextel Communications.[6]

---

[5] Kim Hart, No cultural merger at Sprint Nextel, *Washington Post*, November 24, 2007.
[6] Laura M. Holson, Sprint Nextel posts $29.5 billion loss, *The New York Times*, February 29, 2008.

AOL Time Warner Merger

When the economy and the industry you are in are good, success may come easy. However, when the economy turns and cultural risks exist, dramatic failures happen, as Rita Gunther McGrath published in 2015 related to the AOL Time Warner merger[7]:

> *"Merging the cultures of the combined companies was problematic from the get go. Certainly the lawyers and professionals involved with the merger did the conventional due diligence on the numbers. What also needed to happen, and evidently didn't, was due diligence on the culture. The aggressive and, many said, arrogant AOL people "horrified" the more staid and corporate Time Warner side. Cooperation and promised synergies failed to materialize as mutual disrespect came to color their relationships."*

In 2002, during the dot com crash, AOL Time Warner reported a net loss of $98.7 billion after taking a fourth-quarter charge of $45.5 billion, mostly due to writing down the value of its troubled America Online unit.[8]

Ways of Working Alignment

Companies work differently. This includes management style where one company may be managed in a more top down manner versus a more democratic bottom up approach. Compensation models, and for that matter, organizational models may be completely different. There will be varying levels of internal process maturity — the acquiring company may be quite lean and results driven, while the target company may be more formal with well-defined processes, and greater bureaucracy to meet the needs of their business. Ways of

[7] Rita Gunther McGrath, *15 years later, lessons from the failed AOL-Time Warner merger*, January 10, 2015.

[8] Martin Peers and Julia Angwin, AOL posts a $98.7 billion loss on new goodwill write-down, *The Wall Street Journal*, January 30, 2003.

working alignment in the new company can in large part lead to the success or failure of an acquisition.

P&G's Acquisition of Gillette

As an example of ways of working sensitivity, after the 2005 acquisition of Gillette, P&G used a transitional approach to ensure new process was best-of-bread and accepted within the integrated company.[9]

> *"When P&G bought Gillette, it focused on mapping the two companies' processes to get the best of both. It formed nearly a hundred global integration teams, consisting where possible of matched pairs of executives from the same functions in each company. Initially many Gillette employees stayed with their legacy brands and previous staff-support structures. People from Gillette were allowed (and in China, encouraged) to use their own processes until they learned P&G's methods. For the first year, P&G refrained from rating Gillette people on 'building the business,' to give them learning time before their bonuses would be tied to that goal."*

Although P&G performance was sluggish after the acquisition of Gillette, the ways-of-working integration was seen as a success in contributing to the integration.

Business Continuity

An often-overlooked challenge is business continuity during integration. The biggest area to address immediately is in sales to ensure the sales teams keep selling and meeting their targets, while the longer-term sales strategy is being developed. Customer support may be inundated with questions once the announcement is made — consistency in answering these questions is of utmost importance. Product development also has no time to pause. Internal activities must be

[9] Rosabeth Moss Kanter, Mergers that stick, *Harvard Business Review*, October 2009.

addressed, such as how to pay employees in the new company, how to acquire goods and services, how to pay vendors, and the list goes on.

United Airline's Acquisition of Continental Airlines

In the multiyear acquisition integration of Continental Airlines starting in 2010, United Airlines experienced many bumps in the road as exemplified in a 2012 New York Times article[10]:

> *"The list of United's troubles this year has been long. Its reservation system failed twice, shutting its Web site, and stranding disabling airport kiosks passengers as flights were delayed or canceled."*

Unfortunately, systems failures are quite common during system cutover, directly impacting sales and the reputation of a newly combined organization.

Synergy Realization

To round out issues and challenges, it is critically important to consider synergies and how they will be realized. As discussed earlier, the deal team that established deal drivers may not be hands-on with PMI activities. Without a proper handover from the deal team, operations teams will fall into doing work that they've done in the past as a standalone company, versus changing to address synergies.

DaimlerChrysler Merger

As noted by authors Krug, Wright, and Kroll,[11] in addition to culture differences and poor communication, synergy realization can be

[10] Jad Mouawad, *For United, big problems at biggest airline, The New York Times*, November 28, 2012.

[11] Jeffrey A. Krug, Peter Wright, and Mark J. Kroll, Top management turnover following mergers and acquisitions: solid research to date but still much to be learned. *The Academy of Management Perspectives*, 3015(1), pp. 30–46 (2015).

fundamentally flawed. Relating to synergy expectations set by CEO Juergen Schrempp in the DaimlerChrysler merger:

> *"The creation of a single organization created opportunities to drive cost savings through purchasing economies, consolidation of facilities, exchange of components and technology, and shared distribution. Schrempp promised annual savings of $3 billion. The merger agreement, however, required a clear separation between brands and prohibited shared platforms and combined dealerships."*

From the merger of Daimler and Chrysler in 1998 to the selling to Cerberus in 2007, $36.7 Billion in value was lost.

Legal and Regulatory Considerations

Legal and regulatory challenges exist, especially in the case of publicly listed companies. This includes uncertainties of government antitrust related approvals, which can postpone or halt integration planning activities and the ability to engage internal team members pre-deal. Also a consideration is announcement timing, especially for global companies where markets are open 24 × 7, and post close employment considerations and impact of country specific regulations. Although not all ramifications can be addressed in this chapter, it is important to be cognizant of legal and regulatory implications when addressing PMI activities.

Complexities are significant as shown in web of interdependencies in the diagram below developed by PMI Expert Andrew Scola[12]:

Analytical Approaches, Models, Practices

Primary deal types include an asset deal, where the seller maintains their legal entity (and potential liabilities), and a stock deal, where the

[12] Scott Whitaker, *Cross-Border Mergers and Acquisitions* (Hoboken, NJ: John Wiley & Sons, 2016).

Exhibit 1: Web of Key Legal, Financial, Political and Social Interdependencies Related to Cross-Border Integration

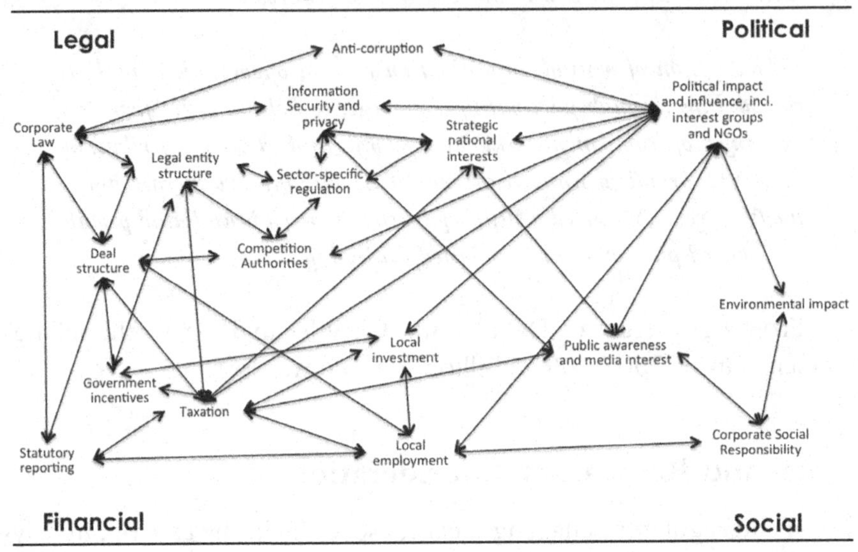

acquirer acquires the company as whole. These deal types may guide the type of integration best suited for the acquisition. Additionally, deal drivers provide a significant basis for integration approach and level of integration required. Is the deal only to acquire intellectual property or talent where little or no integration is needed? Are business functions being combined in a hybrid fashion that includes a best of breed merging of people, process and technology of both companies?

Integration Approaches

Haspeslagh and Jemison identify three main acquisition approaches as Preservation, Absorption and Stand-alone.[13] Below we describe ramifications of each related to integration.

[13] Philippe C. Haspeslagh and David B. Jemison, *Managing Acquisitions: Creating Value Through Corporate Renewal*, The Free Press (1991).

Absorption

In the absorption model, the acquirer incorporates, or absorbs, the acquired company into their current business using the acquirer's tools and process. Activity here involves transitioning people, process, technology, and data into the acquirer's ways of working. Benefits are typically economies of scale related to the sharing of the acquiring company's business processes, and cost cutting synergies related to rationalizing the target company's redundant supporting services. The main challenge for such an approach is the need to have the acquired company's resources adapt to the acquiring company's systems and processes.

Preservation

Preservation, or leaving a company as stand-alone, has limited integration needs except in the interface points between the acquired and parent company. Although an acquired company may be considered as stand-alone, this is rarely a pure case. If integration is planned to be minimal, integration can still be underestimated for such activities as changing financial reporting requirements for the parent company, and policies, procedures, and agreements the acquired company may need to follow, such as policies to complete vendor rationalization.

Symbiosis

Symbiosis, or best of breed integration, allows for selecting the best of both the target and acquired companies to take advantage of complementary strengths. Although this approach has the greatest potential to achieve synergies over time, these types of integrations require significant change management and increase the level of risk during the acquisition. One area of significant work relates to IT integration, such as combining ERP systems, reservation or sales systems, vendor systems, HR systems, and so on. This type of integration can take 6 months to a year or longer to complete and has significant impact to the day-to-day operation of the business.

As part of strategic assessment of a target, a variation of these approaches can be considered. During integration planning, approaches can be further defined and variations with business units and functions can be discussed. For instance, one business unit may be preserved while the other is absorbed, or in the case of business functions, finance may be kept stand-alone while sales may become best of breed.

Integration Process

M&A integration consulting firms and internal integration teams of acquiring organizations each have their own flavor of a PMI approach and methodology. In my own company, Global PMI Partners, we came together initially as nine different companies practicing PMI, and as a whole, we developed the standard GPMIP Acquisition Integration Framework™ (AIF). Although the names and grouping of activities may be unique to our firm, the tasks are applicable across any organization.

Early in the M&A process, deal teams focus on defining their acquisition strategy, searching for targets based on defined deal drivers, and completing *Due Diligence.* In *Due Diligence*, when the target company starts to look very promising and work transitions from assessment to negotiating, this is the time to start ramping up integration planning efforts. Global PMI Partners calls this the *Relate* phase — the phase where integration planning and stand-up

Exhibit 2: GPMIP Acquisition Integration Framework™ (AIF)

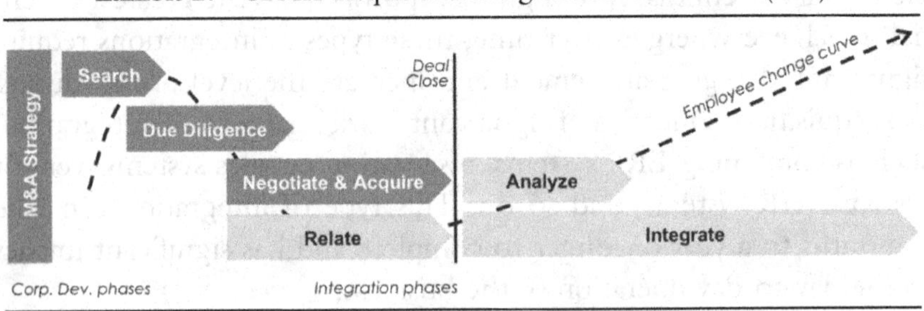

efforts occur prior to close. After deal close, more information is available, including access to target company employees and data. During the *Analyze* phase, we check assumptions made in initial *Relate* phase planning, and update plans accordingly. Since the integration execution activities (what we call the *Integrate* phase) must be immediate starting at deal close, these activities run in parallel.

Preclose Planning

It is a very intense time during preclose while deal team negotiations are ongoing. As the deal team is negotiating, there is little time for integration team collaboration. This environment changes quickly once the deal is signed and full attention is placed on integration next steps. Next steps that must be planned as far in advance as possible include communicating the deal to governing bodies, investors, the public, employees, vendors, and customers. For employees, integration timing, expediency, consistent messaging, establishing a vision for the new company, and communicating purpose and tasks is of greatest value.

Integration Charter

Integration planning must be methodical and efficient. A charter is created for this purpose and establishes the scope of effort, key participants, goals and objectives, and key milestones to set a baseline for planning. A charter should be concise, setting integration expectations to both the executive team and integration participants.

The Integration Team and IMO Structure

Resources established in the charter are part of an integration organization that is called the Integration Management Office (IMO). The Integration Management Office can govern one-to-many integrations with functional integration leads, otherwise known as workstream leads, who report up into the IMO. These leads represent HR, Operations, IT, Sales, Legal, Finance, and other functions of the

Exhibit 3: Typical IMO Organization[14]

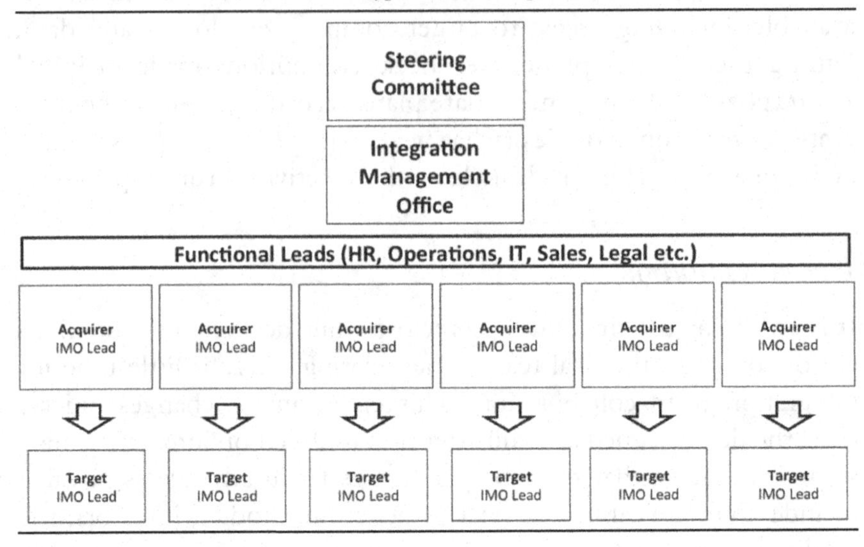

organization. In addition to workstream management, the IMO also is responsible for Transition Services Agreement (TSA) management in carveout situations and integration methodology management, technical and process support, and integration postmortem analysis.

Note the many of the named participants in the IMO are not engaged until after close. Prior to close, these resources are engaged on a need to know basis, as confidentiality allows, and in line with antitrust laws. In some cases, a clean team can be established to assess sensitive competitive data that is stored in a virtual or physical data room (or clean room). The team can be comprised of third parties, former employees, and active employees. However, if the deal falls through, due to antitrust regulations, participants may be barred to returning to either the target or acquiring company given the sensitive competitive information that they have been made aware of.

[14] Scott Whitaker, *Cross-Border Mergers and Acquisitions* (Hoboken, NJ: John Wiley & Sons, 2016).

Integration 100-Day Planning and Integration Playbook Development

Clear and swift execution of an integration plan is vital to the success of any acquisition or merger. The 100-day plan is critical as it is the primary window for operationalizing newco (newco is an integration practitioners name for the combined company). Plans are

Exhibit 4: Playbook Artifacts

Playbook Section	Typical Section Components	
Purpose and Scope	Integration Strategy & Objectives Playbook Scope/Usage Guiding Principles Preclose Legal Guidelines	IMO & Team Charters IMO Kick Off Agendas/Decks Strategic Frameworks
Integration Management Plan	Governance Model(s) & Process IMO Roles & Responsibilities IMO Infrastructure Functional Org Models Phasing Constructs Integration Leader Requirements	Integration Resourcing Model(s) Functional Workplans Day 1 Framework Planning Communication Plan/Matrixes Cross Functional Dependency Mapping Input from All Other Developed Plans
Integration Planning Processes	Discovery Process & Checklists DD to Integration Process Flows Data Harvesting Process/ Templates Talent Assessment Worksheets Cultural & Change Assessments On Boarding process/materials Talent Assessment Process First 30/90 Templates Retention Planning Worksheets	Transaction Scenario Matrix Training & Orientation Tool Evaluation Criteria Tool Usage Guidelines Escalation Protocols Employee Communication Plans Divestiture/TSA Planning Templates Workstream Prioritization Matrices
Executing and Monitoring Processes	IMO Weekly Meeting Structure/ Agendas Integration Dashboard Functional Status Reporting Templates IMO Calendar Synergy Identification & Tracking IMO Budgeting Scorecards & Measurements	End State Process Tracking Issues/Risk Logs Day 1 /Week 1 Planners Day 1 Checklists After Action Reviews (Lessons Learned) Employee Surveys Scope Change Requests Risk Assessment

developed and aligned with the standard *Project Management Body of Knowledge*.[15] They include approaches to address overall integration management, scope, time, cost, quality, human resources, communications, risk management, procurement management, and stakeholder management.

Plan information is reflected in a playbook, which is a comprehensive set of activities and tools that an integration team uses to drive their work and that can be used as a standard across multiple acquisitions or mergers. Depending on the complexity of the integration, the playbook can drive tasks directly for the integration or be placed in Gantt chart to manage complexities of the integration related to dependencies, resource leveling, and completion tracking.

As mentioned in my previous book contribution for *Cross-Border Mergers and Acquisitions*, the following are typical playbook artifacts.[16]

Initial Execution of Activities

Till preclose of the deal and after initial planning, the engaged IMO team prepares for announcement of the deal and establishes the functioning IMO, including setting up supporting technology tools, holding recurring IMO meetings, and preparing for day one activities. This is also the time to engage deal team members, validate integration plans, confirm deal drivers and expectations, and prepare the integration team members for their immediate tasking. The integration team will look to obtain as much information as possible from the data room (a room where all documents are stored for due diligence purposes) to guide the integration and updates plans accordingly. Once these initial activities are complete, the integration team is ready for close and day one of the new organization.

---

[15] Project Management Institute, *Project Management Body of Knowledge*, 5th *Ed.*, (Newtown Square, PA: Project Management Institute, 2012).

[16] Scott Whitaker, *Cross-Border Mergers and Acquisitions* (Hoboken, NJ: John Wiley & Sons, 2016).

Take special note that corporate values and expectations should be set to a clear and realistic level. Based on research, Harrison, Hoskisson, and Jonsen argue[17]:

> *"Employees will reciprocate positively through additional effort if they feel that the newly formed firm's behavior during the post-merger integration period is consistent with the implicit contracts they have formed through expectations based on espoused firm values. We refer to this concept as organizational authenticity. A violation of implicit contracts — through either over-promising or significant under-promising — will lead to negative reciprocity."*

Postclose Execution

Day One

First impressions are important. Day One sets the example for the rest of the integration. During Day One, the integration team can openly work with their entire team both at the acquiring company and target, and information can be freely shared as one company. This is also a time when employees, customers, vendors, and investors are paying close attention to determine how the integration progresses. Communication starts to be executed with consistent talking points across all communication channels (presentations, calls, letters, etc.) and mission critical integration execution activities start.

Integration Execution

We are now in what my firm Global PMI Partners calls the "Integrate" phase where the bulk of integration activity occurs. A kickoff presentation typically is executed on Day One or soon after to

---

[17] Jeffrey S. Harrison, Robert E. Hoskisson, Karsten Jonsen, Walking the talk: A multistakeholder exploration of organizational authenticity, employee productivity, and post-merger performance, *The Academy of Management Perspectives*, 28(1), pp. 38–56 (2014).

onboard the full integration team. Mission critical tasks are also started for treasury, legal, intellectual property, tax and legal filings, technology support, etc. to keep the newco running in the near term. Tasks for the first 30, 60, 90 days are then started according to a 100-day plan. The following are examples of tasks to be completed post Day One:

- Identifying and implementing "Quick Wins" between the two companies, such as near-term operational improvement and establishing a longer-term operational improvement roadmap.
- Addressing the newco organization structure and communicating with employees, addressing any at risk employees and interviewing key management. This includes ensuring the onboarding of new employees runs smoothly.
- Reaching out to customers and vendors to confirm ongoing relationships. Internally this also includes setting expectations of how the combined sales and marketing teams will work together.
- Addressing near-term finance, treasury, tax, legal, and risk functions and deliverables. This includes making sure general banking, payroll, insurance, and all regulatory requirements are addressed.
- Addressing immediate technology changes (email, phones, websites, etc.) and longer-term system conversions or upgrade plans.
- Developing and transitioning as needed HR policies and procedures to harmonize policies for all employees.

These and many other items will be considered as part of integration activities that the IMO will manage. As part of this management, the IMO will keep in mind key rationale for the deal and tying this rationale to quantifiable synergies.

Further Detailed Planning

As integration starts Day One, there is much more information available to the integration team. What we call the *Analyze* phase is the time period post close that is dedicated to confirming preclose assumptions and building out detail plans driven by each workstream lead. Activities are then realized in Gantt charts for tracking and integrated in a coordinated fashion as part of the IMO integration governance.

Integration Transition and Assessment Summary

Operationalization

Although M&A integrations can take as little as a month for uncomplicated acquisitions, complex integrations such as symbiotic or best-of-breed integrations can take years. At a point defined by the integration management with use of exit criteria, the integration efforts can transition to a fully operationalized environment and general internal project and program management offices can take over.

Integration and Overall M&A Assessment

I have found that executive level assessment of success or failure tends to be anecdotal. To ensure M&A assessment is taken seriously and quantified, assessment tasks are best identified during initial planning and used as exit criteria to wrap-up integration activities — lessons learned output can then be used as entrance criteria for new integration planning activities. Where possible, quantifiable synergies can be tracked through the integration that were developed initially as part of the deal thesis. This data cannot only be used to rate success, but more importantly, it can be used to analyze progress of the integration and be used as input to integration decision making in the future.

Index

O

S

Printed in the United States
By Bookmasters